Microcomputer Applications for Business Series

AN INTRODUCTION TO

Lotus® 1-2-3®

RELEASE 2.3/2.4

Microcomputer Applications for Business Series

AN INTRODUCTION TO
Lotus® 1-2-3®

RELEASE 2.3/2.4

with
WYSIWYG
and
SmartIcons

■   ■   ■

Roy Ageloff
University of Rhode Island

Course Technology, Inc. *One Main Street, Cambridge, MA 02142*

An Introduction to Lotus 1-2-3 Release 2.3/2.4 is published by Course Technology, Inc.

Editorial Director	Joseph B. Dougherty
Product Managers	Susan Solomon Communications
	Katherine T. Pinard
Production Manager	Josh Bernoff
Production Editor	Robin M. Geller
Editorial Assistant	Erin Bridgeford
Desktop Publishers	Debbie Masi
	Kim Munsell
Copyeditor	Nancy Wirtes
Proofreader	Darlene Bordwell
Quality Assurance Supervisor	Rob Spadoni
Student Testers	Jeff Goding
	John Mihnos
	Mark Vodnik
Manufacturing and Package Designer	Mark Dec
Cover Designer	Darci Mehall

An Introduction to Lotus 1-2-3 Release 2.3/2.4 © 1993 by Course Technology, Inc.

Portions © 1989, 1991 by Lotus Development Corporation, used by permission.

Trademarks

Course Technology and the open book logo are registered trademarks of Course Technology, Inc.
Lotus and 1-2-3 are registered trademarks of Lotus Development Corporation.
Some of the product names used in this book have been used for identification purposes only and may be trademarks or registered trademarks of their respective manufacturers and sellers.

Disclaimer

Course Technology, Inc. reserves the right to revise this publication and from time to time make changes in its content without notice.

ISBN 1-56527-058-4
ISBN 1-56527-059-2 (text and 3½-inch Lotus 1-2-3 Release 2.4)

Printed in the United States of America
10 9

From Lotus Development Corporation

Today's global businesses require a workforce that knows how to use personal computers and other information technology for communication, analysis, and decision making. Thus, today's business professionals must be adept at using software tools, such as 1-2-3, to communicate, analyze, and solve complex problems.

Lotus is assisting students and instructors with tools that help them accomplish this goal. We are delighted to be working again with Course Technology to bring you *An Introduction to Lotus 1-2-3 Release 2.3/2.4*, a high-quality text and software combination now updated for Release 2.4 of Lotus 1-2-3. We hope this text and accompanying full-function, full-capacity software help prepare students for challenging careers in the business world.

■   ■   ■

From the Publisher

At Course Technology, Inc., we believe that technology will transform the way that people teach and learn. We are very excited about bringing you, college professors and students, the most practical and affordable technology-related products available.

The Course Technology Development Process

Our development process is unparalleled in the higher education publishing industry. Every product we create goes through an exacting process of design, development, review, and testing.

Reviewers give us direction and insight that shape our manuscripts and bring them up to the latest standards. Every manuscript is quality tested. Students whose background matches the intended audience work through every keystroke, carefully checking for clarity, and pointing out errors in logic and sequence. Together with our own technical reviewers, these testers help us ensure that everything that carries our name is error-free and easy to use.

Course Technology Products

We show both *how* and *why* technology is critical to solving problems in college and in whatever field you choose to teach or pursue. Our time-tested, step-by-step instructions provide unparalleled clarity. Examples and applications are chosen and crafted to motivate students.

The Course Technology Team

This book will suit your needs because it was delivered quickly, efficiently, and affordably. In every aspect of our business, we rely on a commitment to quality and the use of technology. Every employee contributes to this process. The names of all of our employees, each equity holders in the company, are listed below:

Stephen M. Bayle, Josh Bernoff, Susan Bothwell, Irene Brennan, Erin Bridgeford, Marcia Cole, Susan Collins, John M. Connolly, David Crocco, Lisa D'Alessandro, Tracy Day, Mark Dec, Howard S. Diamond, Katie Donovan, Joseph B. Dougherty, Don Fabricant, Kevin Flanagan, Robin M. Geller, Suzanne Goguen, David Haar, Deanne Hart, Nicole Jones, Matt Kenslea, Suzanne Licht, Paddy Marcotte, Debbie Masi, Kathleen McCann, Laurie Michelangelo, Kim Munsell, Diana Murphy, Paul Murphy, Amy Oliver, Debbie Parlee, Darren Perl, George J. Pilla, Katherine T. Pinard, Rob Spadoni, Kathy Sutherland, David Upton, Kristin Usher, Mark Valentine, Jacqueline Winspear

Preface

An Introduction to Lotus 1-2-3 Release 2.3/2.4 continues in the tradition of Course Technology, Inc.'s new approach to microcomputer applications education by combining a carefully developed text with fully functional software. It is designed for any first course on how spreadsheets are used in business and assumes students have no previous knowledge of computers.

The Textbook

This textbook presents a unique approach to teaching how to use Lotus 1-2-3. Students learn to plan before they press keys. They learn to analyze the business problem and design the worksheet. Then they solve the problem by following a distinctive step-by-step methodology, frequently referring back to their original plan. From this process students learn that a spreadsheet is not meant just to record data and perform calculations, but that it is a valuable tool to help them make informed business decisions.

The Lotus 1-2-3 tutorials begin with "Using Spreadsheets in Business," which presents an overview of business and of how spreadsheets are used in business, as well as real examples of how recent business graduates use spreadsheets as decision-making tools. Eight hands-on tutorials contain step-by-step instructions on how to use 1-2-3 to solve business problems.

Approach

An Introduction to Lotus 1-2-3 employs a problem-solving approach to teach students how to use 1-2-3. This approach is achieved by including the following features in each tutorial:

Objectives A list of objectives orients students to the goals of each tutorial.

Tutorial Case This case presents a business problem that the student will solve in the tutorial. The business problem is geared to what the typical student taking this course is likely to know or is able to intuit about business. Thus, the process of solving the problem using 1-2-3 will be meaningful to the student. All of the key business areas — accounting, finance, marketing, production, and management — are represented.

This textbook includes modules that cover WYSIWYG (What-You-See-Is-What-You-Get) and SmartIcons. 1-2-3's WYSIWYG feature allows students to enhance their spreadsheets for more sophisticated presentations. SmartIcons, available only in 1-2-3 Release 2.4, provide short-cuts for the most commonly used 1-2-3 tasks.

Planning the Worksheet   Each tutorial's case also includes discussion about planning the worksheet. Students learn to analyze the business problem and then set clear goals for the solution before they press keys. Planning sheets and worksheet sketches are introduced as basic tools.

Step-by-Step Methodology   This unique methodology integrates concepts and key-strokes. Students are asked to press keys always within the context of solving the problem. The text constantly guides students, letting them know where they are in the problem-solving process and referring them back to the planning sheet and sketch.

Page Design   Each page is designed to help students easily differentiate between what they are to *do* and what they are to *read*. In addition, the numerous screen shots include labels that direct students' attention to what they should look at on the screen.

Exercises   Each tutorial concludes with meaningful, conceptual questions that test students' understanding of what they learned in the tutorial.

Tutorial Assignments   These assignments provide students with additional practice on the individual 1-2-3 skills that they learned in the tutorial. Students practice by modifying the business problem that they solved in the tutorial.

Case Problems   Each tutorial concludes with several additional business problems that have approximately the same scope as the Tutorial Case. Students are asked to use the 1-2-3 skills they learned in the tutorial to solve the case. Optional **WYSIWYG Assignments** are included.

The Lotus 1-2-3 Software

An Introduction to Lotus 1-2-3 is available with a full-sized (256 columns by 8,192 rows) and fully functional version of the Lotus 1-2-3 spreadsheet software, including the WYSIWYG and SmartIcons add-ins. All 1-2-3 features are included with the exception of the Translate, Access, Viewer, Backsolver and Auditor add-ins.

The Lotus 1-2-3 software is available on 3½-inch diskettes. (If you need 5¼-inch diskettes, see your instructor.) Installation instructions accompany the software.

Coupon

Students who buy this textbook packaged without Lotus 1-2-3 software can purchase their own copy of the software for a nominal price. Look for the valuable upgrade coupon included with this textbook.

The Supplements

Data Disk

The Data Disk includes all of the worksheets needed to complete all of the Tutorial Cases, Exercises, Tutorial Assignments, and Case Problems. It is available in 3½-inch format. (If you need a 5¼-inch diskette, see your instructor.)

Instructor's Manual

This supplement includes:

- Answers and solutions to the all of the text's Exercises, Tutorial Assignments, and Case Problems
- A 3½-inch diskette containing solutions to all of the text's Tutorial Assignments and Case Problems
- Transparency masters of key illustrations in the text selected by the author

Test Bank

This supplement contains approximately 50 questions per tutorial in true/false, multiple choice, matching, and short answer formats. Each question has been quality-assurance tested by students for accuracy and clarity.

Electronic Test Bank

This Electronic Test Bank allows professors to edit individual test questions, select questions individually or at random, and print out scrambled versions of the same test to any supported printer. In addition, technical support is available from Publishing Innovations at (508) 741-8010.

Acknowledgments

Many people provided their special contributions to the successful completion of this book. While "thank you" never seems enough, these are my thanks to each of them.

I want to thank the many reviewers of this text, in particular: Joyce Capen, Central Michigan University; Judy Foster, Diablo Valley College; Sue Higgins, Community College of Rhode Island; Jon E. Juarez, New Mexico State University, Dona Ana Branch Community College; Charles Lake, Faulkner State College; Bob Love, Ocean County College; Mel Martin, ETON Technical Institute; June A. Parsons, Northern Michigan University; John Ross, Indiana University at Kokomo; Clive Sanford, University of North Texas; and David Stephan, Baruch College, CUNY.

Thanks to my colleagues and friends, Marco Urbano, Stu Westin, Richard Mojena, and Hilda Allred, for their case and tutorial suggestions. Thanks also to Lo-Ping Esther Ling for her thorough reading of the entire manuscript and her sound suggestions for improvement.

My appreciation goes to the Course Technology staff for producing a quality, professional product. I especially thank Paddy Marcotte and Robin Geller for managing production; Kim Munsell and Debbie Masi for the desktop publishing; Rob Spadoni for quality assurance; and Darlene Bordwell for her attention to proofreading.

Thanks to Lotus Development Corporation, in particular, Alan Minard.

To John Connolly goes my admiration and thanks for creating an exciting, innovative company that will have a significant impact on education of college students for years to come.

Last, but certainly not least, I give special thanks to editor Susan Solomon for her advice, counsel, and suggestions that have significantly shaped and improved this text. Thank you also to Kitty Pinard for her assistance preparing this text.

To my wife, Hilda, and daughter, Shana, a special thanks for their encouragement and support during this project. Without their efforts I'd never have completed this project "on-time."

Roy Ageloff

■   ■   ■

Brief Contents

Table of Contents

Copying the Data Disk for the Lotus 1-2-3 Tutorials

Diskettes can be damaged. To avoid losing data, one of the first things you should do when you get a diskette with data or programs on it is copy the original diskette onto another diskette or onto your hard drive, and store the original diskette in a safe place. That way, if the working copies are ever lost or damaged, you can always make new working copies from the stored originals.

In this section, you will copy the Data Disk that comes with this text. Find the description of your computer system below and follow the appropriate instructions.

- If your computer system has a hard disk and you are permitted to save files on the hard disk, turn to the section "Copying the Data Disk to a Hard Disk" on the next page.
- If you plan to load and save your files to a floppy diskette, continue reading the section "Copying the Data Disk to a Blank Diskette" below.

Copying the Data Disk to a Blank Diskette

Before you begin, make sure you have the Data Disk labeled *An Introduction to Lotus 1-2-3 R2.3/2.4* that came with this book and one blank, formatted diskette of the same size. Using a felt-tip pen, write the words "Lotus 1-2-3 data diskette" on the label of the blank, formatted diskette. Before putting the original Data Diskette in the diskette drive, make sure that it is write-protected.

To make a working copy of the Data Disk:

❶ If your computer does not have a hard drive, insert your computer's Systems Disk into a disk drive and make that drive current. For example, if your Systems Disk is in drive A, type **A:** to make A the current drive. If your computer has a hard drive, go to the next step.

② If the size of your Data Disk matches drive A, type **diskcopy a: a:** and press **[Enter]**.
If the size of your Data Disk matches drive B, type **diskcopy b: b:** and press **[Enter]**.

③ Your computer prompts you to insert the Source diskette in the drive you specified. If your Systems Disk is in that drive, remove it. Insert the Data Disk in the specified drive and press **[Enter]**.

After a few moments, your computer will prompt you for the Target diskette.

④ Replace the original Data Disk with the blank formatted diskette and press **[Enter]**.

⑤ Continue swapping Source and Target diskettes as instructed until you see a message that asks if you want to copy another disk. Type **n** to answer no.

⑥ Remove the working copy from the diskette drive. Store your original Data Disk in a safe place and use your working copy from now on.

Continue with "Using Spreadsheets in Business" on page L 3.

Copying the Data Disk to a Hard Disk

Before you begin, make sure you have the Data Disk labeled *An Introduction to Lotus 1-2-3 R2.3/2.4* that came with this book. Before putting the original Data Disk into the diskette drive, make sure that it is write-protected.

To create a directory on your hard disk for the Data Disk:

① At the C:\123 prompt, type **md data** and press **[Enter]** to create a directory.

② Type **cd data** and press **[Enter]** to make \123\DATA the current directory.

Now you are ready to copy the Data Disk to the hard disk.

③ If the size of the Data Disk matches drive A insert the Data Disk in drive A.
If the size of the Data Disk matches drive B, insert the Data Disk in drive B.

④ Be sure C:\123\DATA is the current directory.
If the Data Disk is in drive A, type **copy a:*.*** and press **[Enter]** to copy the Data Disk to your hard disk.
If the Data Disk is in drive B, type **copy b:*.*** and press **[Enter]** to copy the Data Disk to your hard disk.

⑤ After copying is complete, remove the Data Disk from the diskette drive.

⑥ Store the original 1-2-3 Data Disk in a safe place.

Continue with "Using Spreadsheets in Business" on page L 3.

Lotus 1-2-3 Tutorials

- **Using Spreadsheets in Business**

Using Spreadsheets in Business

Generations of frustrated people who worked with numbers using only pencils and erasers would envy you. They added long columns of numbers, and if a figure changed, they had to erase and recalculate. Or they multiplied to determine percentages and erased and multiplied again if a mistake crept in. The arrival of the calculator saved time, but until computers became available, people remained subject to the tyranny of pencil and eraser.

With Lotus 1-2-3, the computer automatically erases and re-calculates for you, saving countless hours. Projects whose complexity could eat up pencils and erasers can now be accomplished in minutes. When you learn how to use 1-2-3, imagine how much easier it will be to create a budget, prepare an invoice, or calculate interest on a loan. Instead of one option, you can evaluate several, for example, "What if advertising costs average $2,000 instead of $1,500 per month?" "What if this year's bonus is 4 percent, 6 percent, or 8 percent?"

Not surprisingly, businesses are enthusiastic users of spreadsheet software. That's because in almost any department of a company, spreadsheets can help people do their jobs more quickly and more effectively.

TOPICS

This chapter covers the following topics:

- What Is a Business?

- Computers in Business

- What Is a Spreadsheet?

- How Are Spreadsheets Used in Business?

  Using Spreadsheets in Accounting

  Using Spreadsheets in Marketing

  Using Spreadsheets in Finance

  Using Spreadsheets in Human Resource Management

- What You Will Learn About Spreadsheets in Business

What Is a Business?

Your local drugstore is a business, as are the neighborhood cleaner, florist, market, and restaurants. So are Sears, General Motors, and Kodak. All of these businesses provide products and services people need; in return, they earn money to compensate employees and owners for their hard work and money invested. Thus, we can say that a *business* is an organization that seeks profit by providing goods or services.

You may be planning a business career as, for example, a store owner, stockbroker, accountant, or manager. Even if you are not a business major, you engage in business activities. If you earn money, you have to decide how to spend it, how to save it, and what taxes to pay. If you become a lawyer or a doctor, you will have to pay rent for your office and compensate your employees; you may have to market your skills to prospective clients or patients. If you become an artist, you will have to acquire materials and sell your works. So even if you don't decide on a traditional business career, you can still use a spreadsheet program to help you make wise business decisions.

Computers in Business

People — employees — are an important resource in any business. To be effective employees, people need information. Information is sometimes described as a company's most valuable resource. It enables employees to review past business decisions and activities, and learn from their mistakes. It provides an accurate picture of the company's present position and a basis for forecasting the future. Decisions made throughout a company reflect the quality of information available to its employees.

In every department of a company, data accumulate — on sales volume and promotion costs, for example, on customers, and on expenses for furniture, supplies, and entertainment. The challenge faced by all businesspeople is to transform data into meaningful information, to process data by creating structured reports. When this is done well, employees can rely on accurate information and thus provide better products and services for customers.

Pencils and erasers, even calculators and filing cabinets, are of little help in managing and organizing large quantities of data. Fortunately, computers have dramatically improved companies' ability to process data, to pull information together, and to provide reports on all aspects of their operations.

Spreadsheets are one of the most valuable computer tools for producing usable information. The availability of spreadsheet software made businesses recognize the speed and flexibility of the microcomputer. With 1-2-3 on microcomputers throughout a company, decision makers at every level can analyze past experience, forecast the future, and, even more importantly, test assumptions by posing "what if?" questions and studying the results. Let's define spreadsheets and then see how they can be used in various business settings.

What Is Spreadsheet Software?

To understand what a spreadsheet is, we must first look at the language of accounting. If you have ever seen a budget, listing months across the top of a page and income and expense items vertically along the left, you have seen a type of accounting worksheet, or ledger (Figure 1). A **worksheet** is a grid of intersecting vertical **columns** and horizontal **rows** that organizes data in an easily understandable way. With this grid organization, data are entered

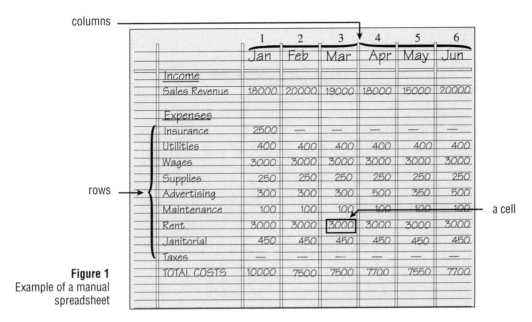

Figure 1
Example of a manual spreadsheet

into the appropriate **cells**, the intersections of rows and columns. Until recently, you would have to use a calculator and a pencil to calculate totals and place them in the proper cells.

With the advent of the microcomputer came the *electronic* worksheet. This computer software, called **spreadsheet software**, creates a similar grid or worksheet on your computer screen (Figure 2) and instructs the computer to perform the calculations for you.

Figure 2
Example of an electronic worksheet

You don't have to be a computer expert to use a spreadsheet. You simply tell the software what result you want in certain cells, and the software adds the numbers in rows or columns, multiplies the contents of one cell by another, or applies formulas.

What if you want to see what happens if sales, salaries, or supplies vary? What if you simply change your mind or make a mistake? To consider another option or to correct an error, you enter the appropriate numbers and instructions. The computer recalculates and changes all relevant cells for you. You can print various versions of a worksheet, store them, and study their meanings at your convenience before you make a decision. You can even display the results in graphic form, for example, as a pie chart or a bar graph (Figure 3).

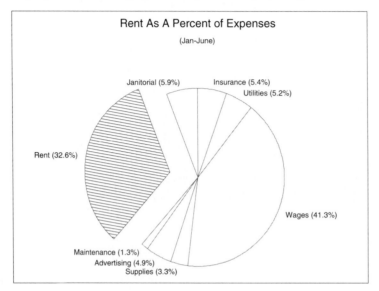

Figure 3
Example of a pie chart generated by Lotus 1-2-3

You can use 1-2-3 not only to produce a visual aid to clarify information, but also to produce reports that search for and extract specific data. With its data management function, for example, you can instruct 1-2-3 to list all employees at a certain salary level or to prepare a report showing all invoices that are 30 days overdue. The graphing and data management functions of 1-2-3 provide additional tools for interpreting, displaying, and reporting data.

How Are Spreadsheets Used in Business?

Although businesses depend on spreadsheets to summarize numerical data and to keep records, spreadsheets are most powerful as a decision-making tool. The spreadsheet's ability to answer the question "What if?" helps businesspeople make sound decisions. For example, suppose you are planning to start your own business. The "what if" feature of 1-2-3 enables you to measure the effects on profit of paying one employee or two, of renting a more or a less expensive space, and of obtaining loans at different interest rates. What if sales the first six months are 100 units? 250 units? What if you pay employees a straight salary? Salary plus commission? 1-2-3 helps you see the whole picture and eliminates much of the guesswork.

This "what if" ability makes spreadsheets essential throughout an organization — in accounting, marketing, finance, and human resources management. Let's first define these basic business functions and then use a real example to demonstrate the use of spreadsheets in each. The people who contributed examples to this book are enthusiastic about their spreadsheet projects. Spreadsheets have enabled them to organize and display information and to make instant calculations. For entry-level employees all the way to top management, spreadsheets are an invaluable tool.

Using Spreadsheets in Accounting

Called "the language of business," accounting communicates information about the financial well-being of a company. Accountants classify transactions — for example, as purchases, sales, or entertainment costs — then record and summarize the financial data and help interpret the data for decision makers. They help managers find answers to questions like, "Will the company have enough cash to pay the bills next quarter?" "Which of our products is least profitable?" People outside the firm, such as potential investors or bankers, look to the financial statements prepared by accountants to learn about a company's debt or cash surplus.

As organizations expand and grow more complex, the practice of accounting becomes more sophisticated. Thus, accounting is becoming increasingly dependent on computers to measure, analyze, and report information that is so essential in business today. For example, Veronica Villarreal's project at Mesilla Valley Mall illustrates the power of spreadsheets to record accounting information and produce reports. After Veronica earned an associate's degree in business, she began working in the business office of the mall. When she arrived, gift certificates good for merchandise in mall stores were recorded and totaled by hand (Figure 4). This was a time-consuming job because it was done twice — once when a certificate was issued and again when it was redeemed.

Figure 4
A sample gift certificate

Veronica's manager asked her to use 1-2-3 to design a worksheet for tracking gift certificates, which were sold to customers, issued as special promotions, and presented as employee-of-the-month awards. The manager wanted to keep track of how many certificates in each category were issued each month. Furthermore, he wanted his staff to have a reliable way of recording which certificates were redeemed and which were still outstanding.

Veronica designed a worksheet that made keeping track of the gift certificates quicker and easier. A simplified version of her worksheet appears in Figure 5 on the following page.

```
A1: [W2]                                                    READY

    A   B       C       D        E        F        G        H
1                     Mesilla Valley Mall Gift Certificate
2
3
4
5       Cert #             Customer                  Cert    Cert Not
6                  Amt       Sale    Promo    EOM    Cleared  Cleared
7                --------  --------  -------- -------- -------- --------
8       668        50                           50      50
9       669        10        10                                  10
10      670        25        25                          25
11      671        25        25                                  25
12      672        50                 50                         50
13      673        50                 50                 50
14      674        15        15                          15
15      675        50        50                                  50
16               --------  --------  -------- -------- -------- --------
17      Subtotal  275       125       100      50      140      135
18
19
20
CERTIF.WK1                    UNDO
```

Figure 5
A simplified version of
Veronica Villarreal's
worksheet

By eliminating tedious repetitive calculations, spreadsheets provide time for creative problem solving. They are essential for recording, summarizing, and analyzing data and producing accounting information such as monthly income statements, cash flow reports, budgets, and, as we've seen, even gift certificates.

Using Spreadsheets in Marketing

Building a better mousetrap won't earn profits for a company unless people need and want a better mousetrap. *Marketing* involves ensuring that a company's products or services satisfy customers' needs. When people find what they want and need, they will pay the company for its products or services, thus generating profits for that company.

To provide this important link between the company and its customers, market research identifies target customers by their age, income, lifestyle, and so on; it then attempts to determine the wants and needs of these target customers. Through advertising, the company strives to inform consumers about what it has to offer them. A systematic marketing effort depends on accurate information for planning a successful strategy and measuring sales results.

At Rauh Good Darlo & Barnes Advertising Agency, Kelly Seelig uses a spreadsheet for planning and scheduling advertising campaigns for her clients. She develops a budget for ads in newspapers and magazines, and for radio and television commercials. Then she schedules these ads over a period of months for maximum effectiveness. Kelly finds a spreadsheet ideal for creating her media plan.

A portion of her media schedule worksheet for magazine advertising shows expenditures for each publication by month and calculates totals by month and by publication (Figure 6). The printed worksheet helps Kelly and her client, in this case a hotel, to see when and where the dollars will be spent. What if they schedule more or fewer ads? The impact on the budget is immediately clear.

```
                              Media Schedule

     Publication      Jan      Feb      Mar      Apr      May      Jun    Subtotal

     HOTEL & TRAV             $6,094                     $6,094           $12,188
     Calif Sect.             Spr Is                      Sum Is
     Circ:   63,795          4-color                     4-color

     CALIF MAG               $3,600   $3,330                              $6,930
     Trav. Planner           1/4 pg   1/4 pg
     Circ:  356,438

     LOS ANGELES                                         $6,525           $6,525
     Issued annually                                     1/2 pg
     Circ:  222,629                                      4-color

     SUNSET         $2,695                               $1,348           $4,043
     Entire circ.   1/4 pg                               1/4 pg
     Circ:1,400,000 w/copy                               w/copy
                    ------   ------   ------   ------   ------   ------ -------
     SUBTOTALS      $2,695   $9,694   $3,330      $0   $13,967      $0 $29,686
```

Figure 6
A portion of the printout for Kelly Seelig's media schedule worksheet

Spreadsheets have many applications in marketing, not only in advertising but also in market research, product management, and sales. Marketing personnel rely on spreadsheets to analyze past experience, forecast future results, and test various assumptions. Spreadsheets help marketing personnel collect and interpret data about customers and measure the company's effectiveness in communicating with its customers. 1-2-3 can be the vital ingredient in a successful marketing effort.

Using Spreadsheets in Finance

In any business, you must consider not only your customers and what products they need and want, but also where to obtain funds for materials, manufacturing, and employee compensation. Sales of your product can vary from month to month, so you must be certain that you have cash on hand to pay the bills, including taxes, and that you can control expenses.

Finance is the business function of planning how to obtain funds and how to use them to achieve the company's goals. In addition to sales dollars, companies can obtain funds by selling shares in ownership (stocks and bonds), attracting venture capital, and borrowing money. Accountants collect, organize, and present data that the specialists in finance interpret to ensure the financial health of the company. Since forecasting, budgeting, and tax management are among their duties, finance specialists process volumes of numerical data. They rely on computers to transform these data quickly into useful information.

Spreadsheets enable people with a finance background to find creative solutions to problems. At Ungermann-Bass, a computer communications company, Wendy Ray studied this high-tech company's method of paying its bills. She knew that many of the company's suppliers offered discounts for prompt payment of their invoices, but the accounting department at Ungermann-Bass wasn't paying early enough to take advantage of these savings. Wendy decided to use a 1-2-3 worksheet to determine how many discounts were taken and how many were lost. With the data on 1-2-3, Wendy presented well-documented information to a company vice president and recommended a change in payment policy.

Figure 7 is a summary worksheet showing discounts taken for two quarters, the first before Wendy's recommendations were adopted and the second after. Notice that her worksheet analysis enabled the company to increase the number of discounts taken in those quarters from 91.14 percent to 97.95 percent. In a year, the company saved over $100,000, thanks to Wendy's recommendations.

<figure>

A1: [W14]   READY

	A	B	C	D	E	F
1			Discounts Taken Summary			
2						
3	Date	Discounts	Discounts	% Taken	Discounts	% Lost
4		Available	Taken		Lost	
5						
6	October	23,576	19,052	80.81%	4,524	19.19%
7	November	32,149	28,911	89.93%	3,238	10.07%
8	December	36,647	36,225	98.85%	422	1.15%
9	Quarter Total	92,372	84,188	91.14%	8,184	8.86%
10						
11						
12	January	34,607	33,964	98.14%	643	1.86%
13	February	23,577	23,326	98.94%	251	1.06%
14	March	20,238	19,525	96.48%	713	3.52%
15	Quarter Total	78,422	76,815	97.95%	1,607	2.05%
16						
17						
18						
19						
20						

DISCOUNT.WK1   UNDO

</figure>

Figure 7
A portion of Wendy Ray's summary worksheet

Besides helping to control expenses, finance specialists respond to requests for information coming from different departments of the company. The manufacturing department may ask for monthly reports of actual spending compared to its expense budget. Marketing may want to keep abreast of how its sales results to date compare with forecasts. 1-2-3 can generate these reports and provide comparisons with last year's results.

Without spreadsheets, these analyses and projections would require laborious calculations, subject at every step to errors. The spreadsheet user's ability to ask, "What if?" and have 1-2-3 recalculate all the numbers has significantly improved financial planning and control.

Using Spreadsheets in Human Resource Management

A marketable product and the funds to manufacture it aren't enough. Businesses need people to get the job done. *Human resources management* is the process of determining a company's needs for employees and finding, training, and motivating those employees.

Each unit of a company must concern itself with managing the human resource; many companies also have a human resources or personnel department. Among such a department's tasks is providing job enrichment and compensation incentives to promote employee satisfaction and productivity and to reduce turnover. Human resource specialists are often charged with administering payroll and benefits, keeping salary records, and evaluating various forms of compensation such as profit sharing and bonuses. By facilitating the record-keeping functions, computers free human resource specialists to invest more time in training and motivating employees.

For example, human resource administrator Thalia Ohara of *PC World* magazine uses 1-2-3 to track profit sharing earned by employees. Profit sharing is a system that rewards employees for their role in producing profits by paying them a percentage of those profits.

At *PC World*, the amount of profit-sharing funds each employee earns is a percentage of the employee's gross salary. The profit-sharing worksheet that Thalia created shows each employee's profit sharing earned for the year, which is deposited in the employee's account (Figure 8). When an employee earns a raise in salary, Thalia enters the new salary, and 1-2-3 recalculates the amount of profit sharing and revises the totals. Profit sharing encourages employees to stay with the company for at least seven years. If they leave before seven years, they can withdraw only a percentage of the contribution, called the vesting percentage, based on their years of service.

```
A1: [W1]                                                      READY
┌─────────────────────────────────────────────────────────────────┐
│     A      B        C       D      E       F       G       H      │
│1                                                                  │
│2                        Profit Sharing Plan                       │
│3                                                                  │
│4    Participant  Vesting    Date  Contrib  Annual  Amount  Pay out│
│5                   %       Hired    %      Salary  Contrib  Amount │
│6                                                                  │
│7    V. Barnerd    10%   4/10/89    12% $50,000  $6,000    $600    │
│8    D. Bridges     0%   6/18/90    12%  28,000   3,360       0    │
│9    W. Callaway   20%   8/24/88    12%  35,000   4,200     840    │
│10   G. Chico     100% 11/26/82    12%  42,000   5,040   5,040    │
│11   T. Elia       40%   1/05/87    12%  38,000   4,560   1,824    │
│12   J. Hull        0%   4/02/90    12%  24,000   2,880       0    │
│13   G. Liu        10%   5/22/89    12%  40,000   4,800     480    │
│14                                                                  │
│15                                                                  │
│16                                                                  │
│17                                                                  │
│18                                                                  │
│19                                                                  │
│20                                                                  │
│PROFSHAR.WK1            UNDO                                        │
└─────────────────────────────────────────────────────────────────┘
```

Figure 8
A portion of Thalia
Ohara's profit sharing
worksheet

As shown in this example, Thalia has streamlined and simplified salary and benefits administration, thanks to her worksheet. From tracking parking passes to calculating salaries, profit sharing, and bonuses, 1-2-3 makes human resources management more flexible and efficient.

What You Will Learn About Spreadsheets in Business

Spreadsheets have transformed the business of business by giving people quick access to information vital for doing their jobs. *Lotus 1-2-3 for Business* places this essential software tool in your hands right from the beginning. Through step-by-step tutorials, you will have the opportunity to apply spreadsheet principles to real business problems. As you learn about spreadsheets in business, you will develop business problem-solving skills that you can use in other courses and that you can take with you to whatever career you choose.

Lotus 1-2-3 is recognized as the spreadsheet standard. If you can list 1-2-3 skills on your resume, it will catch an employer's eye. Employers know that 1-2-3 enables employees to perform their jobs more efficiently and effectively. Because 1-2-3 improves your productivity, it increases your chances to get a job, to advance in your job, and to be successful.

In the tutorials and the cases that follow, you will look at 1-2-3 in a business context. *Lotus 1-2-3 for Business* will help you see that business problem solving is more than just collecting and recording data, and that learning to use spreadsheets is more than simply pressing the right keys on your computer. *Lotus 1-2-3 for Business* emphasizes transforming data into information useful for understanding business relationships and for making sound business decisions.

Tutorial 1

An Overview of Lotus 1-2-3

This tutorial introduces you to terms you will use to describe a 1-2-3 worksheet. You will also learn to navigate a worksheet using a keyboard and a mouse. Finally, you will tour 1-2-3 and see some demonstrations of its worksheet, graphics, database, and macro capabilities.

Before you begin, be sure you have initialized 1-2-3 and installed it on your computer, as described in the installation instructions.

OBJECTIVES

In this tutorial you will learn to:

- Follow the numbered steps in *Lotus 1-2-3 for Business*

- Start 1-2-3

- Use worksheet terminology

- Move the cell pointer

- Select commands

- Enter data in a worksheet

- View a 1-2-3 graphics demonstration

- Use a 1-2-3 database demonstration

- Run a 1-2-3 macro

- Use Help

- Quit 1-2-3

How to Follow the Numbered Steps in the Lotus 1-2-3 Tutorials

In the Lotus 1-2-3 tutorials, you will follow step-by-step instructions. These instructions are displayed as numbered lists on a shaded background, as shown in Figure 1-1. Notice in this figure:

- Boldface indicates keys that you should press.
- Function keys, such as **[F2]**, are followed by the 1-2-3 key name in parentheses.
- Key combinations, such as **[Alt][F4]**, mean that you press and hold down the first key, and then while holding the first key, you press the second key. You then release both keys.

To use the UNDO command:

① Press **[F2]** (EDIT).

② Press **[Backspace]** three times to erase PAY, the incorrect label.

③ Type **SALARY**, the correct label, and then press **[Enter]**. The new correct label is now in cell C7. See Figure 1-30.

④ Press **[Alt][F4]** to view the incorrect label once more. Press **[Alt][F4]** again to restore the correct label.

Figure 1-1
Example of
step-by-step
instructions

Starting 1-2-3

Start your computer. Be certain that the DOS prompt appears. If you are using 1-2-3 in a lab, you might need to ask your instructor or technical support person for instructions.

To start 1-2-3:

① If your worksheet files are stored on a hard disk, go to Step 2.

   If your worksheet files are on your data diskette, place the diskette in drive A.

② Be sure that the current drive is the drive where you installed 1-2-3. On most systems this is drive C. If 1-2-3 is installed on drive C and if your current drive is not C, then type **C:** and press **[Enter]**.

③ Now change to the subdirectory where 1-2-3 has been copied. For example, if the name of the subdirectory is "123r23," you would type **cd\123r23** and press **[Enter]** to switch to the directory where 1-2-3 is stored. Check with your instructor or technical support person for the name of the subdirectory.

④ At the DOS prompt type **123** and press **[Enter]**. The 1-2-3 program is loaded into computer memory. Figure 1-2 shows the usage of computer memory after 1-2-3 has been loaded.

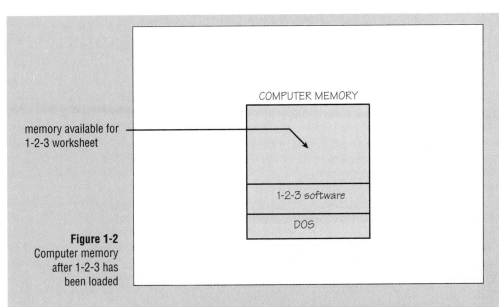

memory available for
1-2-3 worksheet

Figure 1-2
Computer memory
after 1-2-3 has
been loaded

An introductory screen appears, followed by a blank 1-2-3 worksheet. See Figure 1-3. If the blank worksheet does not appear, your copy of 1-2-3 may not be installed correctly. See the instructions in the installation guide or check with your instructor or technical support person.

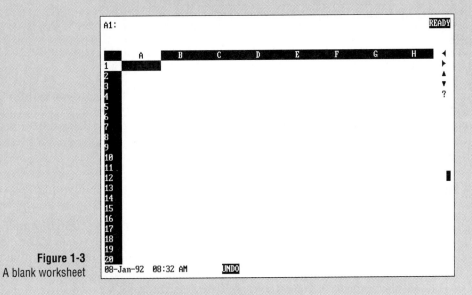

Figure 1-3
A blank worksheet

The Worksheet

The **worksheet** is the basic structure for storing and organizing data when you are using spreadsheet software such as Lotus 1-2-3. In Lotus 1-2-3 the worksheet is a grid made up of columns and rows. The worksheet contains 8,192 rows and 256 columns.

A **row number** in the left border of the worksheet identifies each row (Figure 1-4). Rows are numbered consecutively from 1 to 8192. A **column letter** in the top border of the worksheet identifies each column. Columns are lettered A-Z, then AA-AZ, then BA-BZ, and so on to column IV. A **cell** is a unit of the worksheet that stores data. It is formed by the intersection of a column and a row and is identified by its column letter and row number. For example, the intersection of column B and row 8 is cell B8. B8 is called the **cell address**; whenever you specify a cell address, be sure to name the column letter first and then the row number.

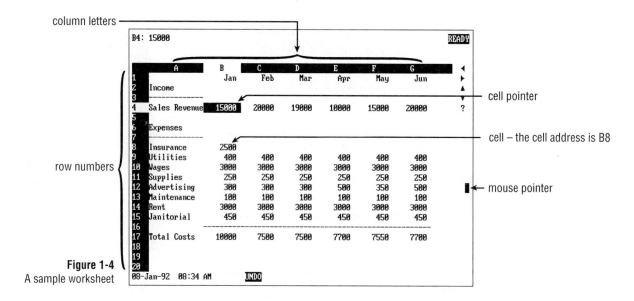

Figure 1-4
A sample worksheet

Notice the highlighted rectangle in cell B4 in Figure 1-4. This is called the **cell pointer**. The cell pointer appears in only one cell of the worksheet, but you can move the cell pointer to any cell of the worksheet. The **current cell** is the cell in which the cell pointer rests and in which you enter data.

The 1-2-3 Screen

The 1-2-3 screen is made up of three areas: the **worksheet area**, the **control panel**, and the **status line** (Figure 1-5). The 1-2-3 screen cannot display all 8,192 rows and 256 columns of a worksheet at one time. Typically a 1-2-3 screen displays 20 rows and eight columns at a time (the number of columns might vary if the width of a column has changed). The rows and columns that appear on your screen are a window into your worksheet and represent the **worksheet area**.

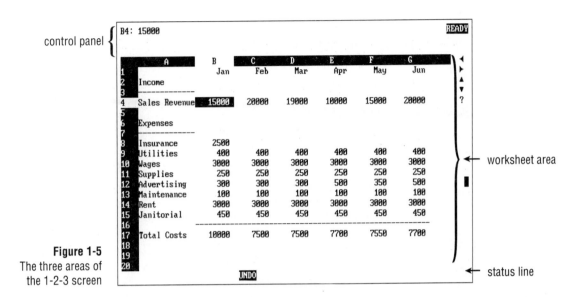

Figure 1-5
The three areas of
the 1-2-3 screen

The top three lines of the 1-2-3 screen contain the control panel. The **control panel** displays information about the current cell and about commands (Figure 1-6).

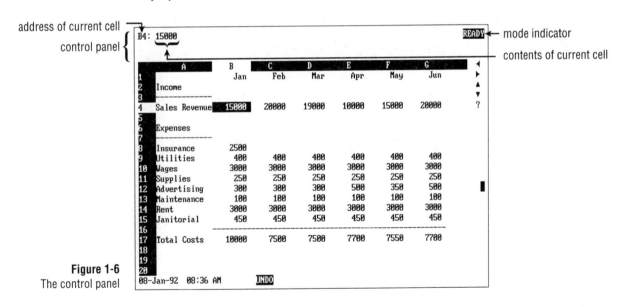

Figure 1-6
The control panel

The *first line* of the control panel displays information about the current cell and the mode, or state, of 1-2-3. At the far left of the first line, 1-2-3 displays the **address**, or location, of the current cell and its contents.

At the far right of the first line of the control panel, 1-2-3 displays the **mode indicator**, which tells you what **mode**, or state, 1-2-3 is currently in. For example, when 1-2-3 is ready for you to type or select a command, 1-2-3 is in READY mode. When you are performing a task in 1-2-3, the mode indicator changes to show the current status of the task. Figure 1-7 on the following page lists some of the mode indicator messages.

Mode Indicator	Meaning
EDIT	You pressed (F2) [EDIT] to edit an entry or entered a formula incorrectly.
ERROR	1-2-3 is displaying an error message. Press (F1) [HELP] to display a Help screen that describes the error or press [Esc] or [enter] to clear the error message.
FILES	1-2-3 is displaying a menu of filenames in the control panel. Press (F3) [NAME] to display a full-screen menu of filenames.
FIND	You selected /Data Query Find or pressed (F7) [QUERY] to repeat the last /Data Query Find you specified, and 1-2-3 is highlighting a database record that matches your criteria.
FRMT	You selected /Data Parse Format-Line Edit to edit a format line.
HELP	You pressed (F1) [HELP], and 1-2-3 is displaying a Help screen.
LABEL	You are entering a label.
MENU	You pressed / (Slash) or < (Less-than symbol), and 1-2-3 is displaying a menu of commands.
NAMES	1-2-3 is displaying a menu of range names, graph names, or attached add-in names.
POINT	1-2-3 is prompting you to specify a range, or you are creating a formula by highlighting a range.
READY	1-2-3 is ready for you to enter data or select a command.
STAT	You selected /Worksheet Status or /Worksheet Global Default Status, and 1-2-3 is displaying the corresponding status screen.

Figure 1-7
Mode indicator
messages

The *second line* of the control panel displays the current entry when you are creating or editing the entry. It can also display the **main menu**, which is a list of commands, and the submenus that appear after you make a selection from the main menu. The rectangular highlight that appears on a command in the menu is called the **menu pointer**.

The *third line* of the control panel displays information about the command highlighted by the menu pointer. 1-2-3 lists either the submenu commands for the highlighted command or a description of the highlighted command.

The **status line** (Figure 1-8) is the bottom line of the screen. It displays the date-and-time indicator and the status indicators.

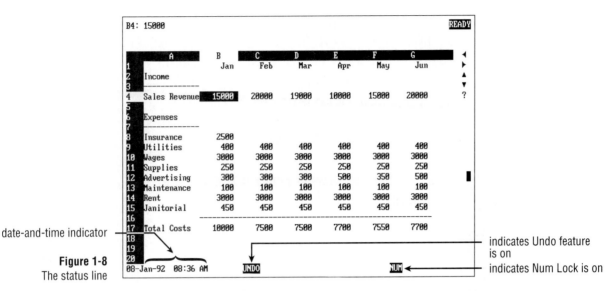

date-and-time indicator

Figure 1-8
The status line

indicates Undo feature
is on

indicates Num Lock is on

The **date-and-time indicator** appears in the left corner of the status line. It usually displays the current date and time.

A **status indicator** appears when you use certain 1-2-3 keys and when a particular program condition exists. For example, UNDO indicates you can press the key combination [Alt][F4] (UNDO) to undo your last action, and NUM indicates the [NUM LOCK] key is on.

Moving the Cell Pointer Using the Keyboard

To be able to enter or view data in your worksheet, you need to learn how to move the cell pointer. **Pointer-movement keys** enable you to move the cell pointer from cell to cell within your worksheet. You move the cell pointer up, down, left, and right with the pointer-movement keys on your keyboard. Figure 1-9 lists the most commonly used pointer-movement keys. Let's try moving the cell pointer one cell at a time. As you move it within the worksheet, notice how the location of the cell pointer changes in the status line of the control panel.

Key	Moves cell pointer
[→]	Right one cell
[←]	Left one cell
[↓]	Down one cell
[↑]	Up one cell
[Tab]	Right one screen
[Shift][Tab]	Left one screen
[Ctrl][→]	Right one screen
[Ctrl][←]	Left one screen
[Home]	To cell A1
[PgDn]	Down one screen
[PgUp]	Up one screen

Figure 1-9
Commonly used pointer-movement keys

To move the cell pointer in the worksheet:

① Press **[Home]** once to move the cell pointer to cell A1, if it is not currently in cell A1.

② Press **[→]** once to move the cell pointer to cell B1.

③ Press **[↓]** once to move the cell pointer to cell B2.

④ Press **[PgDn]** once to move the cell pointer down one screen. The cell pointer now appears in cell B22, and rows 21 to 40 appear on the screen. See Figure 1-10.

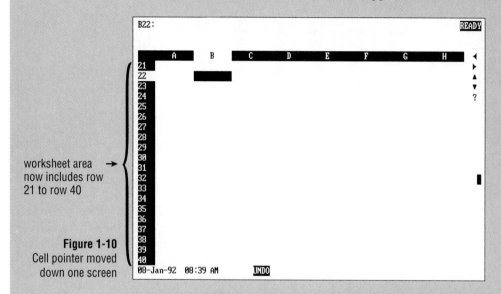

worksheet area → now includes row 21 to row 40

Figure 1-10
Cell pointer moved
down one screen

Then press **[PgUp]** to move the cell pointer back up one screen. When a pointer-movement keystroke moves the cell pointer into a cell not currently in the worksheet area, 1-2-3 shifts the worksheet area to display a different part of the worksheet.

⑤ Press **[Tab]** once to move the cell pointer right one screen. Press **[Shift][Tab]** to move left one screen. Remember that to use the key combinations, such as [Shift][Tab], you press and hold the first key. Then while holding the first key, you press the second key. Then release both.

Moving the Cell Pointer Using the [End] Key

The [End] key allows you to move around the worksheet quickly. If you press a pointer-movement key after pressing [End], the cell pointer jumps to another cell according to the following rules:

- If the cell pointer is currently in an empty cell, the cell pointer moves in the direction of the arrow key pressed to the first *nonblank* cell or the end of the worksheet.

- If the cell pointer is currently in a nonblank cell, the cell pointer moves in the direction of the arrow key pressed to the first *nonblank* cell at the intersection of a blank and a nonblank cell.

• If you press [Home] after pressing [End], the cell pointer moves to the last cell in the worksheet.

To move the cell pointer using the [End] key:

① Press **[Home]** to return to cell A1.

② Press **[End]**. Notice the indicator END in the status line.

③ Press [↓]. The worksheet scrolls to the last row in the worksheet. The cell pointer should be in cell A8192. See Figure 1-11.

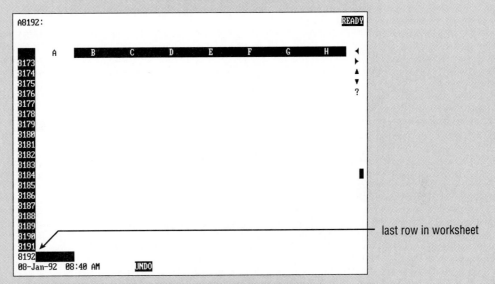

Figure 1-11
Using the [End] key

last row in worksheet

④ Press **[End]** and then press **[→]** to move to the last column of the worksheet. The cell pointer should be in cell IV8192. See Figure 1-12.

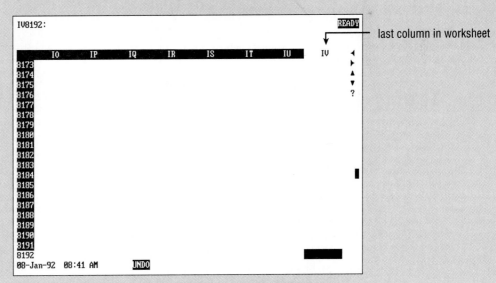

last column in worksheet

Figure 1-12
Using [End] to move
to the last column in
the worksheet

The [Home] key provides a quick way for you to return to the beginning of the worksheet.

⑤ Press **[Home]** to return to cell A1.

Moving the Cell Pointer Using the GoTo Key

The GoTo key, [F5], gives you a way to jump directly to any cell in the worksheet. When you press [F5], 1-2-3 prompts you for the new cell address. You enter a cell address, and 1-2-3 immediately moves the cell pointer to that location. Let's try it.

To move the cell pointer to cell D55 using the GoTo key:

❶ With the cell pointer in cell A1, press **[F5]**. You are prompted for the cell location you want to move to. See Figure 1-13.

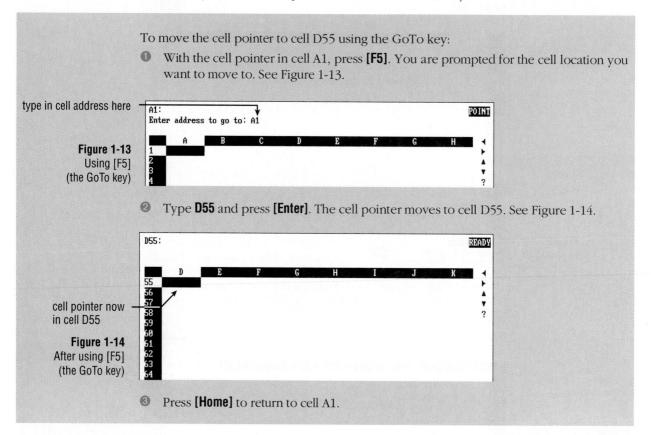

type in cell address here

Figure 1-13
Using [F5]
(the GoTo key)

❷ Type **D55** and press **[Enter]**. The cell pointer moves to cell D55. See Figure 1-14.

cell pointer now
in cell D55

Figure 1-14
After using [F5]
(the GoTo key)

❸ Press **[Home]** to return to cell A1.

Moving the Cell Pointer Using a Mouse

In 1-2-3 you can also use a mouse for many tasks, including moving the cell pointer. If your computer doesn't have a mouse, go to the next section.

You can tell that your mouse software is loaded if you see a small square block in the middle of your screen when you start 1-2-3 (Figure 1-15). This symbol is called the **mouse pointer**. If you don't see this block and you have a mouse, check with your instructor or technical support person. The mouse pointer moves on the screen exactly as you move the mouse around your desktop. For example, if you move the mouse to the right, the mouse pointer moves to the right.

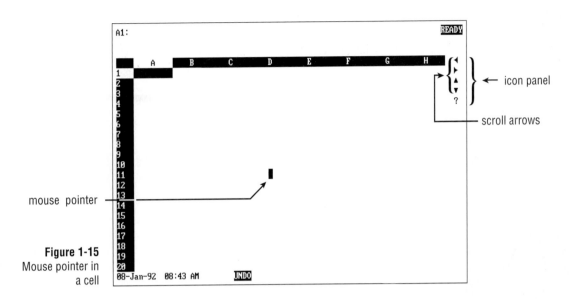

Figure 1-15
Mouse pointer in
a cell

Before you use a mouse, you should be familiar with the following terms: point, click, drag, icon, and icon panel.

Point means to position the mouse pointer on a specific object or area on the screen. You move the mouse in the direction you want the pointer to move.

Click means to press and immediately release the mouse button. Typically you select an object by pointing to that object on the screen and then clicking the mouse button. In most cases you click the left mouse button to select something and click the right mouse button to cancel your selection.

Drag means to press and hold down the left mouse button *while you move* the mouse pointer to another location and then to release the mouse button.

An **icon** is a symbol that represents an action. If a mouse is installed on your computer, five icons — four scroll arrows, facing up, down, left, and right, and a ? — appear on the right side of the screen in an **icon panel** (Figure 1-15). Clicking on one of the scroll arrows has the same effect as pressing one of the arrow keys on the keyboard. The cell pointer moves in the direction indicated by the scroll arrow. Clicking on the ? brings up the Help screen.

There are several ways you can use the mouse to move the cell pointer to another cell when 1-2-3 is in READY mode. The simplest way is to point to a cell on the screen and then click the left mouse button.

To move the cell pointer to cells on the screen:

❶ Move the mouse pointer to cell B5 and click the left mouse button. The cell pointer moves to cell B5.

❷ Move the mouse pointer to cell D10 and click the left mouse button. The cell pointer moves to cell D10.

Another way to use the mouse to move the cell pointer is to use the icons in the icon panel. Pointing to one of the triangles in the icon panel and clicking the left mouse button moves the cell pointer one cell in the direction the triangle points.

To move the cell pointer using the icon panel:

❶ With the cell pointer in cell D10, place the mouse pointer on the down scroll arrow. See Figure 1-16.

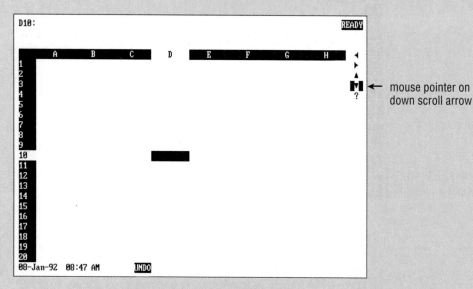

D10:   READY

← mouse pointer on down scroll arrow

Figure 1-16
Using the icon panel to move the cell pointer

08-Jan-92 08:47 AM   UNDO

❷ Click the left mouse button. The cell pointer moves to cell D11.

❸ With the mouse pointer pointing to the down scroll arrow in the icon panel, click the left button again. The cell pointer moves to cell D12.

You can also move the cell pointer to a cell not currently displayed on the screen. As you have already learned, 1-2-3 has over two million cells, not all of which appear on the screen at the same time. If a cell does not appear on the screen, you cannot point to it. To move the cell pointer to a cell off the screen using a mouse, you use the icon panel.

To move the cell pointer to a cell off the screen:

❶ Place the mouse pointer on the down scroll arrow and hold down the left mouse button until the cell pointer is in cell D50. When the cell pointer reaches cell D50, release the left mouse button.

Most worksheets have initial instructions on the first screen. To get there quickly, you return to cell A1.

To move the cell pointer to cell A1:

❶ Place the mouse pointer in the small blank area above the first visible row and to the left of the first visible column. See Figure 1-17.

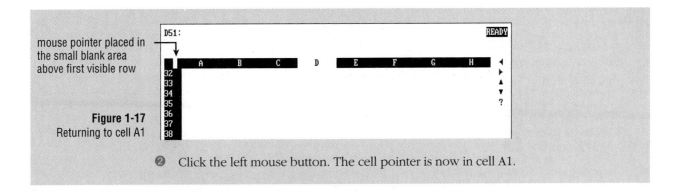

mouse pointer placed in the small blank area above first visible row

Figure 1-17
Returning to cell A1

❷   Click the left mouse button. The cell pointer is now in cell A1.

In this book we assume that you are using a keyboard to work with 1-2-3, but you should feel free to use a mouse if you have one.

Selecting Commands

To perform operations on the data in a worksheet, you issue commands. These **commands** enable you to accomplish various tasks such as copying, moving, printing, graphing, and saving a worksheet. The commands are displayed as a list of options, called a **menu**, from which you select the command you want to execute.

In 1-2-3 you access the main menu by pressing the slash key (/). Take a second now to locate the slash key in the lower right corner of your keyboard. Whenever you press the slash key, the 1-2-3 main menu appears in the control panel. When a menu is displayed in the control panel, the mode indicator changes to MENU, and the third line of the control panel describes the options for the highlighted command. Then you select a command from the menu to perform the task you desire.

There are two ways to select a command. You can type the first letter or character of the command, or you can press [→], [←], [Spacebar], [Home], or [End] to move the **menu pointer**, the rectangular highlight, to the command and then press [Enter] to select it. Selecting commands by highlighting takes a little more time, but it allows you to view more information about each highlighted command in the menu line. This is especially useful if you are unfamiliar with 1-2-3.

Let's practice using each of these methods for selecting commands by issuing a very common command in 1-2-3 — the command to retrieve a file. To retrieve a data file, you first specify which drive or directory contains the file. As you work through the next steps, remember that you can press [Esc] to back up one step if you make a mistake.

To specify the current data directory:
❶   Press [/] (Slash) to display the main menu. See Figure 1-18 on the following page. The Worksheet command is highlighted.

menu pointer→

options for
Worksheet
command

Figure 1-18
The 1-2-3 main menu

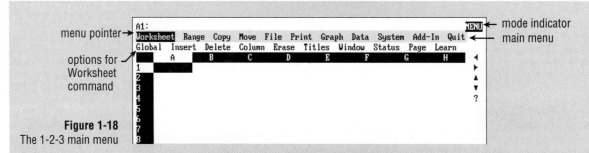

If you have a mouse, you can also display the main menu by moving the mouse pointer into the control panel.

② Press [→] four times to highlight File. As you do, notice how the menu line in the control panel changes.

③ Press **[Enter]** to select File and display the File menu. See Figure 1-19. The Retrieve command is highlighted.

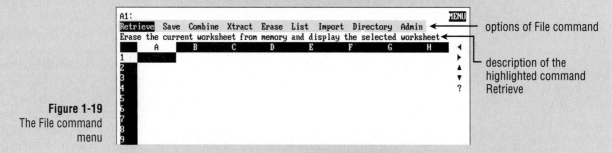

Figure 1-19
The File command menu

④ Notice on the menu that the next to last command is Directory. Type **d**, the first letter of Directory, to select it. A prompt then appears on the input line of the control panel asking you to provide specific information. See Figure 1-20.

If you have a mouse, you can also select menu commands and menu options by moving the mouse pointer to the command and clicking the left mouse button.

prompt to indicate
where data diskette is
located

Figure 1-20
Entering the
location of your
data diskette

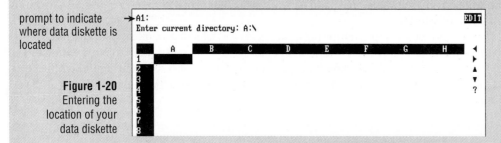

⑤ If your data diskette is in drive A, type **A:** and press **[Enter]**. If the drive or directory name where you copied your data diskettes is different, type that drive and the directory name.

The prompt and the menu disappear, and the READY mode indicator appears in the upper right corner of your screen.

You are now ready to issue the File Retrieve command. This command lets you bring onto the screen worksheet files that are stored on your data diskette or on your hard disk so you can view and work with them.

To retrieve a file:

❶ Press [/] to display the main menu.

❷ Select File either by using the pointer-movement keys to highlight File and then pressing **[Enter]** or by pressing **F**.

❸ Select Retrieve (**R**).

A menu of worksheet filenames from the drive or directory you specified appears on the menu line of the control panel.

❹ The highlight is on the first file, C1TOUR1.WK1. To select it, press **[Enter]**.

The worksheet file C1TOUR1.WK1 appears on the screen (Figure 1-21). This worksheet contains a company's quarterly and year-to-date sales in five international cities. Let's now take a tour of this worksheet and view its data.

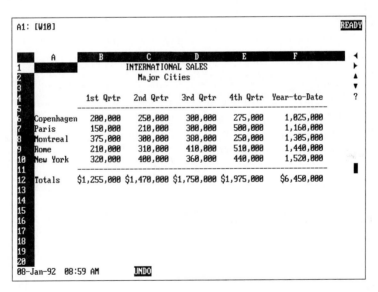

Figure 1-21
Worksheet for C1TOUR1

To view data in the worksheet:

❶ Press [→] and [↓] as needed to move the cell pointer to B6. Notice that the control panel displays the value contained in B6.

❷ Press [↓] until the cell pointer is in B12.

Notice that the control panel shows @SUM(B6..B10) as the contents of the current cell. @SUM is a special 1-2-3 function, or built-in formula, that performs calculations. In this case, @SUM adds the contents of cells B6 through B10 and displays the total in cell B12.

❸ Press **[Home]** to return to cell A1.

Entering Data in a Worksheet

You enter data in a worksheet by moving the cell pointer to a cell, typing the data, and pressing [Enter]. As you type, the mode indicator changes to LABEL or VALUE, depending on how 1-2-3 interprets what you type. In 1-2-3 words are called **labels**. Numbers and formulas are called **values**.

Let's practice entering some data. You will change the data of cell C10 from $400,000 to $350,000. You will then see how 1-2-3 updates the totals automatically. If you make any typing errors and have not yet pressed [Enter], use [Backspace] to erase characters to the left of the cursor. If you have already pressed [Enter], move the cell pointer to the cell with the error. Then retype the entry and press [Enter].

To enter data:

❶ Before you enter any new data, notice that the value in cell C12 is $1,470,000 and that the year-to-date total in cell F12 is $6,450,000.

❷ Move the cell pointer to cell C10.

❸ Type **350000** (four zeros but no comma).

Notice that 1-2-3 displays what you type in the control panel.

❹ Press **[Enter]** and watch how 1-2-3 recalculates all totals that depend on the new value, as shown in Figure 1-22.

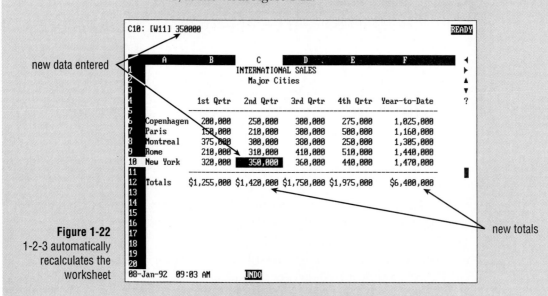

new data entered

new totals

Figure 1-22
1-2-3 automatically
recalculates the
worksheet

1-2-3 adjusts the first-quarter total in C12 to $1,420,000 and the year-to-date total in F12 to $6,400,000. If 1-2-3 does not adjust the totals on your worksheet, try pressing [F9] (CALC) to recalculate the totals.

1-2-3 Graphics

Whenever you use graphs or charts to present information, you are using **graphics**. Graphing or charting data in a worksheet helps you understand the relationships among the data and helps you analyze your results. Let's tour a few of the types of 1-2-3 graphics that you will learn how to create in the tutorials. To view these graphics, your computer system must have a graphics adapter, so check with your technical support person.

To view a graph of this worksheet's data:

❶ Select /Graph (**/G**) to view the Graph menu and a form called the **Graph Settings dialog box**. See Figure 1-23.

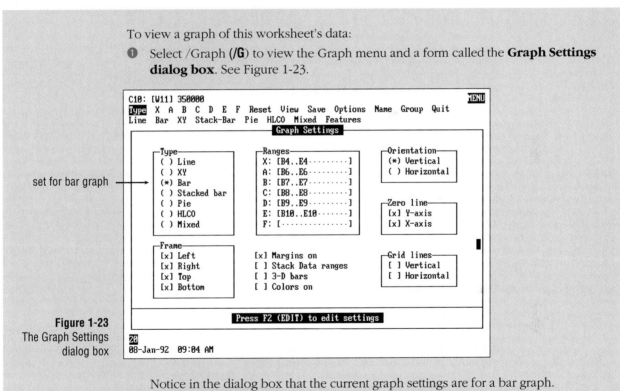

Figure 1-23
The Graph Settings
dialog box

Notice in the dialog box that the current graph settings are for a bar graph.

❷ Select View (**V**) to display the graph. See Figure 1-24 on the following page.

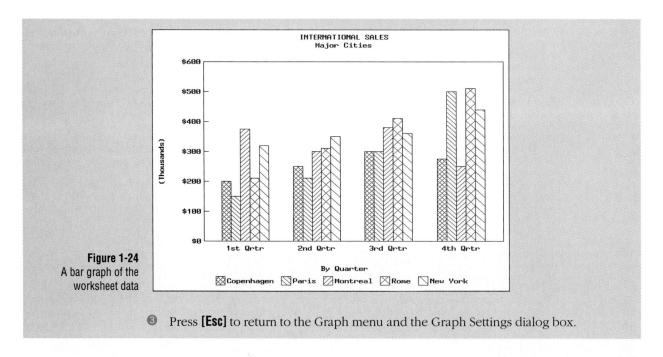

Figure 1-24
A bar graph of the
worksheet data

❸   Press **[Esc]** to return to the Graph menu and the Graph Settings dialog box.

Now let's see how easy it is to create a different type of graph using the same worksheet data.

To view a stacked bar graph of this worksheet's data:
❶   Select Type and then select Stack-Bar (**TS**).
❷   Select View (**V**) to display the new graph.
❸   When you are ready, press **[Esc]** to return to the Graph menu.
❹   Select Quit (**Q**) to quit the graph menu and return to the worksheet.

With 1-2-3 you can create several types of graphs, including bar graphs, pie charts, stacked bar graphs, and line graphs. You can add titles and legends to enhance the appearance and the readability of your graphs.

Using a 1-2-3 Database

A **database** is an organized collection of data. Examples of business databases are a list of customers and the status of their accounts; employee information, such as social security number, salary, and job title; and inventory information, such as stock numbers, quantity in stock, color, and so on. In a list of customers, for example, all the data about each customer are called a **record**, and each individual fact about each customer — name, account status, invoice number, and so on — is called a **field**. In 1-2-3 the columns correspond to the fields and the rows correspond to the records.

Suppose you wanted to create a list of customers who owe your company money, and you wanted to arrange them in order from those owing the most to those owing the least. 1-2-3 can perform several database tasks, such as sorting, to help you organize your data.

To sort a database:

❶ Select /File Retrieve (**/FR**).

When you attempt to retrieve another worksheet without first saving a worksheet that you have modified, the control panel displays the warning "WORKSHEET CHANGES NOT SAVED! Retrieve file anyway?" In this case we do not want to save the worksheet changes, so select Yes (**Y**). A list of worksheet filenames appears on the control panel.

❷ Highlight the filename C1TOUR2.WK1 and press **[Enter]**. Notice that this file contains a database of accounts receivable with paid and unpaid invoice amounts. See Figure 1-25.

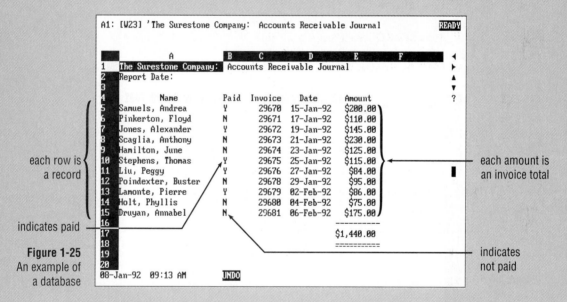

Figure 1-25
An example of a database

each row is a record

indicates paid

each amount is an invoice total

indicates not paid

Each record in this database (from row 5 through row 15) has a number in the Amount field (column E) that represents an invoice total. 1-2-3 can sort these records based on amounts to determine who owes the most money.

❸ Select /Data Sort (**/DS**).

1-2-3 displays a Sort Settings dialog box in which the sort instructions appear. In the Sort Settings dialog box, the primary key is the field 1-2-3 should use to sort the database. In our example, we want the primary-key field to be the Amount field, or column E, and the sort-order setting to be Descending, which instructs 1-2-3 to sort the amounts from the largest to the smallest value. See Figure 1-26 on the following page.

identifies Amount as
column to be sorted

indicates from
largest to smallest

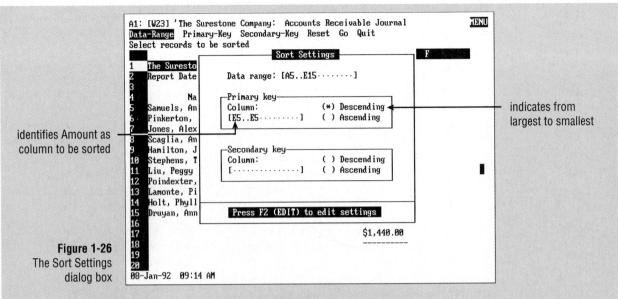

Figure 1-26
The Sort Settings
dialog box

④ Select Go (**G**). See Figure 1-27.

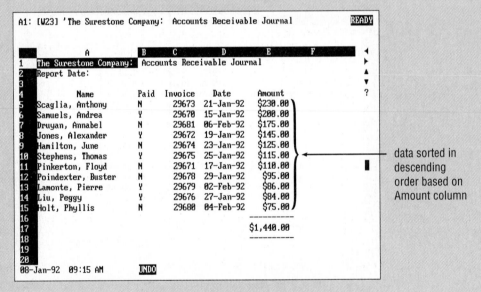

data sorted in
descending
order based on
Amount column

Figure 1-27
Worksheet
after data are
sorted

Watch how quickly 1-2-3 sorts the database according to the invoice amounts in descending order, from largest to smallest. It saves you time and energy and can be a valuable decision-making tool.

Running a 1-2-3 Macro

With 1-2-3 you can create and store *sets* of commands and key strokes called **macro instructions** or **macros**. Macros automate repetitive 1-2-3 tasks, such as entering a date in your worksheet. Suppose, for example, that you must create a weekly report of all customers who have not paid invoices over $100. Once you have created a macro for this task, you can generate the report automatically each week by running the macro.

To run a macro:

1. Press **[Alt][F3]** (RUN) to begin.

   The names of several macros in this worksheet appear. See Figure 1-28.

names of macros →

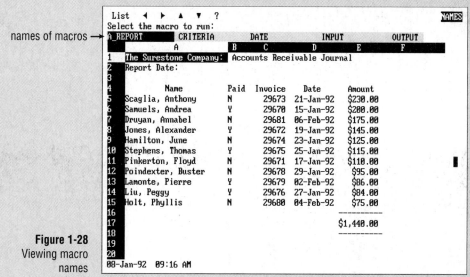

Figure 1-28
Viewing macro
names

2. Press **[→]** twice to move the menu pointer to DATE, then press **[Enter]**.

   The DATE macro runs, automatically entering the date in cell D2 of your worksheet. Next let's generate the report.

3. Press **[Alt][F3]** (RUN).

4. Since A_REPORT is already highlighted, press **[Enter]** to run this macro.

   The A_REPORT macro compares the amount of each unpaid invoice to a specified amount, in this case, $100. 1-2-3 then creates a list of the customers who owe more than $100. See Figure 1-29 on the following page.

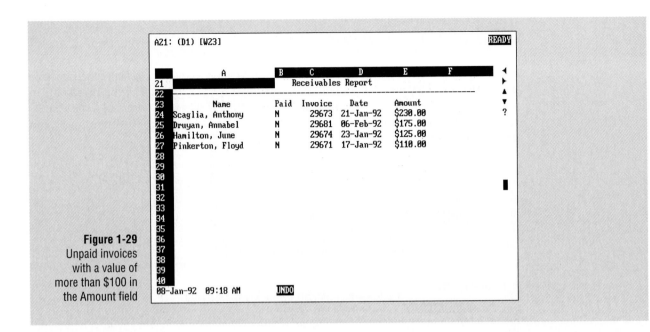

Figure 1-29
Unpaid invoices
with a value of
more than $100 in
the Amount field

Using On-line Help

If you have difficulty using a 1-2-3 command, you can press [F1] (HELP) at any time while you are using 1-2-3 to get helpful information on many topics. When a Help screen appears, the worksheet on which you are working temporarily disappears.

To use Help:

● Press **[F1]** (HELP).

1-2-3 displays the 1-2-3 Main Help Index. See Figure 1-30.

If you have a mouse, you can also display the 1-2-3 Main Help Index by clicking the left mouse button on the (?) (the Help icon) located in the top-right portion of your screen.

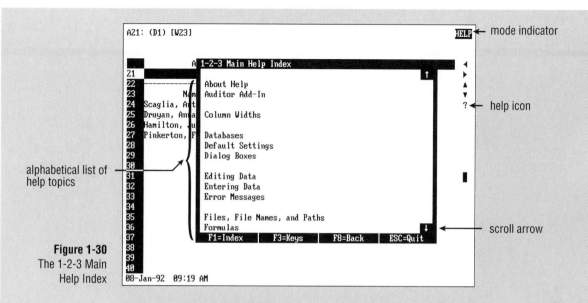

Figure 1-30
The 1-2-3 Main
Help Index

The Help index lists topics you might need help with. If you wanted to see additional help topics, you'd press [PgDn]. If you have a mouse, you can also click the left mouse button on the scroll arrow located in the bottom right corner of the Help window. To select any topic in the Help index, you'd highlight the topic in the index and press [Enter]. Let's try that now.

❷ Highlight the topic Error Messages and press **[Enter]**.

If you have a mouse, you can also click the left mouse button on the topic.

1-2-3 displays a Help screen about error messages. See Figure 1-31. You can use the pointer-movement keys to scroll through the information on error messages.

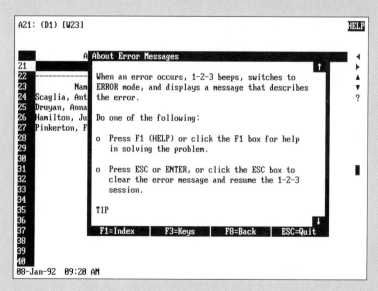

Figure 1-31
Help screen about
error messages

❸ When you are ready to return to the worksheet, press **[Esc]** to return to READY mode.

Quitting 1-2-3

You have completed the tour of 1-2-3. Now it's time to learn how to end, or quit, a 1-2-3 session.

> **To quit 1-2-3:**
> ❶ Select /Quit Yes (**/QY**).
>
> If you have entered data into the worksheet or changed the data, a prompt appears asking if you want to quit without saving your changes. If this happens, select Yes (**Y**) to quit without saving.

Exercises

1. How many rows are in a 1-2-3 worksheet? How many columns?

2. What keys move the cell pointer one key at a time?

3. How do you move the cell pointer to cell A1 from any other cell in the worksheet?

4. What key do you press to get Help?

5. How do you display the 1-2-3 main menu?

6. How do you exit 1-2-3 and return to DOS?

7. The cell pointer is in cell A1. If you press [PgDn], in what cell will the cell pointer be found?

8. How would you move the cell pointer one full screen to the right?

9. What is the difference between a cell and a cell pointer?

10. What is the cell address of a cell in column C and row 24?

11. Follow the steps on page L 27 to retrieve the file C1TOUR1.WK1. Do the following:
    a. Use the GoTo key to jump immediately to cell C10.
    b. Move to the last cell in the worksheet using the keystrokes that go immediately to that cell. What cell is the last cell in the worksheet?
    c. Return to cell A1 using the fewest number of keystrokes.
    d. Press **[End][↓]**. Where is the cell pointer located now?
    e. Press **[End][↓]** again. Where is the cell pointer located now?
    f. Press **[End][→]**. Where is the cell pointer located now?
    g. Press **[End][↑]**. Where is the cell pointer located now?
    h. Press **[End][←]**. Where is the cell pointer located now?

Setting Up Your Copy of 1-2-3

Default Directories

When you first install 1-2-3, Lotus 1-2-3 automatically stores and retrieves worksheet files from the same directory where the Lotus 1-2-3 programs are stored. This directory is called the **default directory**. Typically your 1-2-3 worksheet files are stored on a different directory or drive than the Lotus 1-2-3 software, so you should change the default drive to the drive/directory where you plan to save your worksheets.

To permanently change the default drive and directory:

❶ Select /Worksheet Global Default Directory (**/WGDD**). The Default Settings dialog box appears. Figure 1 shows that the current default directory is c:\123r24.

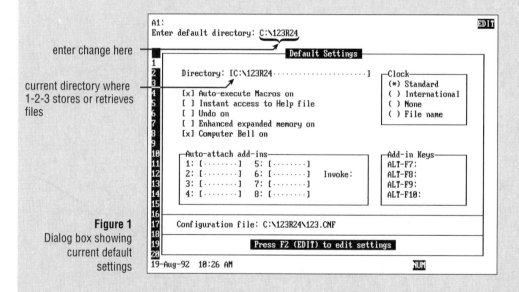

enter change here →

current directory where 1-2-3 stores or retrieves files

Figure 1
Dialog box showing current default settings

1-2-3 prompts you to enter the letter of the drive or the drive and directory from which you will load and save your worksheet files.

❷ Press **[Esc]** to erase the current directory setting.

Type the drive/directory where you will store your worksheets. Most likely this will be drive A if your worksheet files are stored on a diskette or a directory such as C:\123r23\data if your worksheet files are stored on your hard disk.

❸ If you will be storing your worksheet files on a diskette, place a diskette in drive A before you type **A:** and press **[Enter]**. See Figure 2 on the following page.

If you will be storing your worksheet files on a hard disk, type **C:\123r24\data** and press **[Enter]** or check with your technical support person for the name of the directory in which you will store your data files.

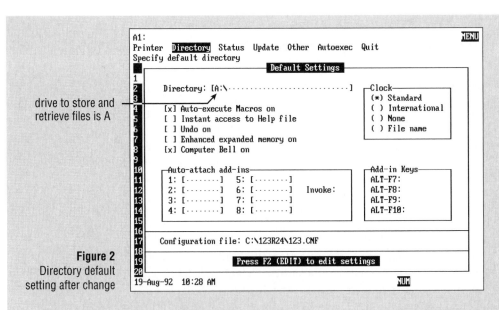

drive to store and
retrieve files is A

Figure 2
Directory default
setting after change

To change the default directory permanently, so each time you load Lotus 1-2-3, it looks to this new drive or directory:

④ Select Update (**U**).

⑤ To return to the worksheet, select Quit (**Q**).

Displaying Worksheet Filenames on the Worksheet Screen

The name of the worksheet file will appear in the lower left corner of each worksheet displayed beginning in Tutorial 2. If you want to set up your copy of Lotus 1-2-3 so that the name of the worksheet file appears in the lower left corner of your screen, then you need to change the default standard clock setting (date and time) to File name. If you don't change this setting, 1-2-3 displays the date and time in the lower left corner of your worksheet instead of the filename. You can work the tutorials with either the date and time or the filename displayed. It is a matter of personal preference.

To change the default setting so filenames are displayed on the screen:

① Select /Worksheet Global Default Other (**/WGDO**). See Figure 3. The dialog box indicates that the Standard clock setting (date and time) is the current setting.

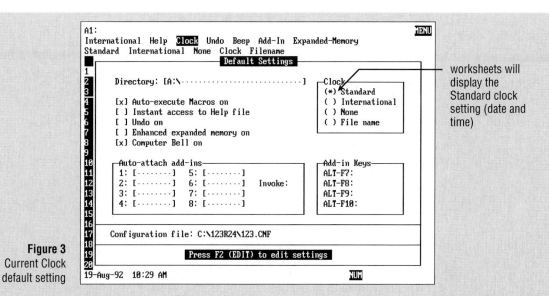

Figure 3
Current Clock
default setting

worksheets will
display the
Standard clock
setting (date and
time)

② Select Clock File name (**CF**) to change the settings to display the filename instead of the date and time. See Figure 4.

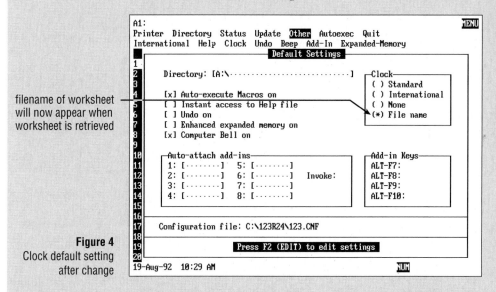

filename of worksheet
will now appear when
worksheet is retrieved

Figure 4
Clock default setting
after change

To save these settings permanently:

③ Select Update (**U**).

④ To return to the worksheet, select Quit (**Q**).

Enabling and Disabling Undo

The Undo feature is an important safeguard against time-consuming mistakes. You can use it whenever the UNDO indicator is displayed on the status line at the bottom of the worksheet screen.

Initially when Lotus 1-2-3 Release 2.4 is installed, the Undo feature is disabled. This means that pressing [Alt][F4] (UNDO) has no effect. To use the Undo feature, you must first turn it on, that is, *enable* it. You should use the following steps to enable Undo when you have no worksheet loaded, for example, immediately after you start 1-2-3.

To enable the Undo feature:

①   Select /Worksheet Global Default Other (**/WGDO**).

②   Select Undo Enable (**UE**). See Figure 5. The dialog box indicates Undo is on.

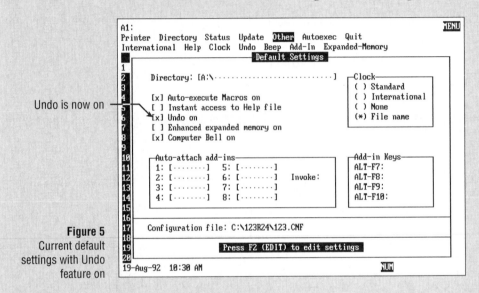

Figure 5
Current default
settings with Undo
feature on

Undo is now on →

You may want to save these settings permanently, in which case the Undo feature will automatically be enabled whenever you load 1-2-3.

③   Select Update (**U**).

④   To return to the worksheet, select Quit (**Q**).

The Undo feature requires that a portion of memory be reserved to store the previous version of the worksheet. Because of limited computer memory, there may be times when you will have to disable the Undo feature in order to perform other 1-2-3 functions. For example, this situation may occur when you are using a feature of Lotus 1-2-3 called WYSIWYG. If you see the message "out of memory" on your screen, disable the Undo feature.

To disable Undo:

①   Select /Worksheet Global Default Other (**/WGDO**).

②   Select Undo Disable (**UD**).

③   To return to the worksheet, select Quit (**Q**).

Tutorial 2

Creating a Worksheet

Preparing a Simple Payroll

Case: Krier Marine Services

Vince Diorio is an Information Systems major at the University of Rhode Island. To help pay for his tuition, he works part-time three days a week at a nearby marina, Krier Marine Services. Vince works in the Krier business office, and his responsibilities range from making coffee to keeping the company's books.

Recently Jim and Marcia Krier, the owners of the marina, asked Vince if he could help them computerize the payroll for their four part-time employees. They explained to Vince that the employees work a different number of hours each week for different rates of pay. Marcia does the payroll manually and finds it time consuming. Moreover, whenever she makes errors, she is embarrassed and annoyed at having to take additional time to correct them. Jim and Marcia hope that Vince can help them.

Vince immediately agrees to help. He tells the Kriers that he knows how to use Lotus 1-2-3 and that he can build a spreadsheet that will save Marcia time and reduce errors.

Vince does not begin working with the 1-2-3 software immediately. He knows that effective worksheets are well planned and carefully designed. So he sits down and follows a process he learned in his courses at school.

OBJECTIVES

In this tutorial you will learn to:

- Retrieve and save files

- Enter numbers, labels, and formulas

- Correct mistakes and erase entries

- Edit entries and use the UNDO key

- Define a range

- Print a worksheet

- Erase a worksheet

Planning the Worksheet

Planning the worksheet first is a good habit to establish. If you plan first, your worksheet will be clear, accurate, and useful. Your plan will guide you as you try to solve business problems using 1-2-3.

You can divide your planning into four phases:

- defining the problem
- designing the worksheet
- building the worksheet
- testing the worksheet

Defining the Problem

Begin by outlining what you want to accomplish. Take a piece of paper and a pencil and do the following:

1. List your goal(s).

2. Identify and list the results you want to see in the worksheet. This information is often called *output*.

3. Identify and write down the information you want to put into the worksheet. This information is often called *input*.

4. Determine and list the calculations that will produce the results you desire. These calculations become the *formulas* you will use in the worksheet.

When you finish, you will have completed the first phase of planning. You will have defined the problem and be ready to design the worksheet. Figure 2-1a shows how Vince defined the Krier payroll problem.

My Goal(s):
    Develop a worksheet that calculates the
    Krier Marine Services payroll.

What results do I want to see?
    Weekly Payroll Report

What information do I need?
    Employee name
    Number of hours each employee worked
     during the week
    Employee's rate of pay per hour

What calculations will I perform?
    Gross pay for each employee

Figure 2-1a
Vince's planning
sheet

Designing the Worksheet

Next, on a piece of paper sketch what you think the worksheet should look like. Include titles, row and column headings, totals, and other items of the worksheet. Figure 2-1b shows Vince's sketch.

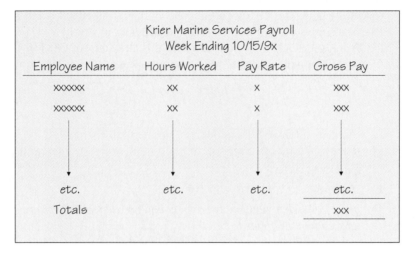

Figure 2-1b
Vince's sketch

Building the Worksheet

After you have defined the problem and sketched the worksheet, you are ready to type your worksheet design into 1-2-3. You enter titles, labels, formulas, input, and other items you listed and sketched when you defined your goal(s) and designed the worksheet.

Testing the Worksheet

After you have built a new worksheet, you should test it before you start to use it. If possible, develop some sample data, also known as test data, and manually calculate the results. Then put the same test data into your 1-2-3 worksheet. Are the results the same? If you discover any differences, you should find the reason(s) and correct any errors in the worksheet.

After completing this fourth phase, you are ready to begin using the worksheet.

■   ■   ■

In Tutorial 2 you will use Vince's problem definition and sketch (Figures 2-1a and 2-1b) as a guide when you build the worksheet for the Krier Marine Services payroll. You will create the worksheet that Vince developed for the Kriers. First you will retrieve a partially completed worksheet, which will serve as your starting point. Next you will enter the payroll data, employee names, hours worked, and rates of pay. Then you will enter formulas to calculate total gross pay for each employee. Finally you will calculate the gross pay for all employees. When the worksheet is complete, you will learn how to print and save it.

Retrieving the Worksheet

Vince Diorio has started working on the spreadsheet for Krier Marine Services. His worksheet is stored as a file on the Lotus 1-2-3 Data Disk. This file is named C2KRIER1. To use this file, you will retrieve it, that is, read the file into computer memory. Let's retrieve C2KRIER1 now. The file from which you work will either be on a diskette copy of the Sample Files Disk or be a copy of C2KRIER1 that you put on your hard disk. If you want to start over for any reason, such as to recover from a mistake, retrieve C2KRIER1.WK1 again and repeat the steps. You will learn how to correct mistakes as you work through this tutorial.

To retrieve a 1-2-3 worksheet file:

❶ If your data are on a diskette, insert the diskette into drive A. If your data are on the hard disk, go to Step 2.

❷ Start 1-2-3 as you learned in Tutorial 1.

❸ Press / (Slash) to activate the 1-2-3 main menu, which shows a list of commands you may choose. See Figure 2-2.

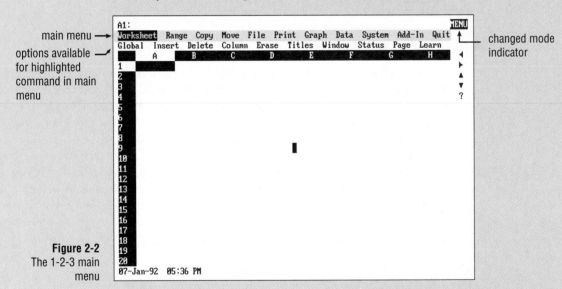

main menu →
options available →
for highlighted
command in main
menu

changed mode
indicator

Figure 2-2
The 1-2-3 main
menu

The mode indicator in the upper right corner has changed from READY to MENU, and the 1-2-3 main menu appears on the second line of the control panel. This line lists the main actions or commands from which you may select. The third line of the control panel lists the commands available if you select the command currently highlighted in the second line. As you highlight different commands by moving the menu pointer across the menu, a new menu appears as each command is highlighted.

There are two ways to select a command from the command line:

• You can highlight a menu choice by pressing [→] or [←] to move the menu pointer to the command you want and press [Enter].

- You can type the first character of the command you wish to select. For example, to select File you type F.

④ Select File (**F**). The choices available from the 1-2-3 main menu now appear on the second line of the control panel. See Figure 2-3.

description of the Retrieve command

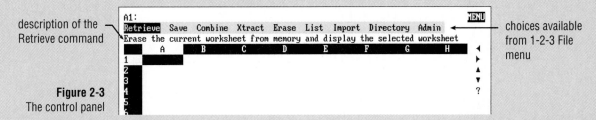

choices available from 1-2-3 File menu

Figure 2-3
The control panel

⑤ Select Retrieve (**R**) to display the names of the first five worksheet files in the control panel. The files are listed in alphabetical order. The top of your screen should look similar to Figure 2-4.

the drive where 1-2-3 is looking for files (may be different on your system)

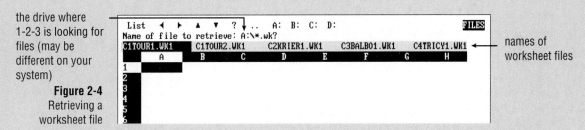

names of worksheet files

Figure 2-4
Retrieving a worksheet file

If the filenames do not appear, press [Esc] to return to READY mode. Lotus 1-2-3 may not know where your data are stored. See page L 37 of Tutorial 1 for assistance. If you accidentally press the wrong key and select the wrong command from the menu, you can return to the previous step by pressing the [Esc] key. If you continue to press [Esc], you back up a step at a time until you return to READY mode. You can also press [Ctrl] [Break] to immediately return to READY mode.

If the worksheet filename that you are looking for appears in the control panel, highlight the name and press [Enter]. However, if you don't see the filename on the control panel, you can do one of the following:

- Press [→], [Spacebar], or [←] until you highlight the worksheet filename you desire. Then press [Enter].
- Type the filename of the worksheet file you desire.
- Press [F3] (NAME). 1-2-3 displays a full-screen list of the worksheet files located on the current drive and directory. Select the desired worksheet file by highlighting it, then press [Enter].

⑥ Using the [→] or [←] key, highlight the worksheet file C2KRIER1.WK1. Then press **[Enter]**. 1-2-3 retrieves the file you selected. See Figure 2-5 on the following page.

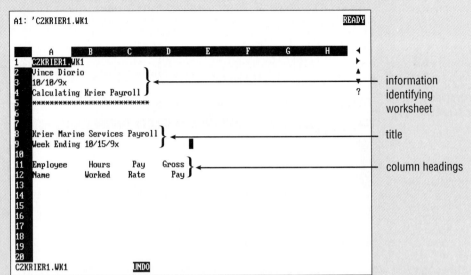

Figure 2-5
Worksheet screen
after C2KRIER1.WK1
retrieved

Your worksheet screen may display the date and time in the lower left corner of the screen instead of the current worksheet filename. You can change your Lotus 1-2-3 setup so the filename appears on the screen. See pages L 38 and L 39 of Tutorial 1 for assistance. Although the worksheet screens in this text display the worksheet filenames, displaying the date and time instead will not affect your worksheet. Whether you display filenames or the date and time is a matter of personal preference.

The worksheet file you retrieved contains the beginning of the worksheet that Vince plans to use in developing the payroll worksheet. Currently the worksheet consists of a title and descriptive column headings. These headings represent the data he will enter or calculate.

You no doubt have noticed that beginning in cell A1 there are four lines of identifying information:

- the name of the worksheet file
- the name of the person who developed the worksheet
- the date the worksheet was created or last modified
- a description of the worksheet.

You should include such a section of identifying information in *every* worksheet you develop, to remind you about what the worksheet contains.

To help you understand what occurs when you retrieve a worksheet file, look at Figure 2-6. When you select File Retrieve and then select the worksheet file C2KRIER1.WK1, 1-2-3 copies the worksheet file from the disk to the computer's memory. C2KRIER1.WK1 is, therefore, in both the computer memory and disk storage.

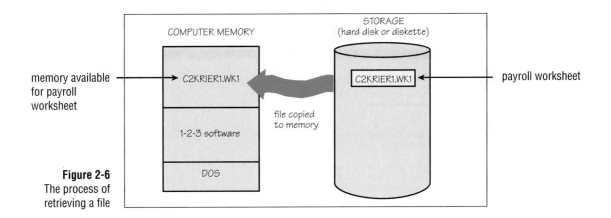

Figure 2-6
The process of
retrieving a file

Entering Labels

Most of the data you enter into a worksheet will be descriptive text, numbers, or formulas. To enter data into a worksheet, you move the cell pointer to the cell where you want the data to appear. You then type the data and press the [Enter] key. 1-2-3 stores what you typed in the cell.

1-2-3 categorizes all entries you type in a cell as either labels or values. **Labels** are descriptive text such as column headings or textual data. If the first character you type is a letter, 1-2-3 assumes you are entering a label in that cell. Also, if you begin typing with one of the four special characters ' " ^ \, called **label prefixes**, 1-2-3 will store any characters that follow as a label. As soon as you begin entering a letter or a label prefix, you'll notice that the mode indicator, in the upper right corner of your screen, changes from READY to LABEL.

If you want to enter text that begins with a number, such as the street address *100 Fairgrounds Road*, you must type a label prefix before the street address so that 1-2-3 knows you want this entry treated as a label even though it begins with a number. The most common label prefix is the apostrophe. In other words, you would type *'100 Fairgrounds Road* instead of *100 Fairgrounds Road*, and 1-2-3 would treat this entry as a label. The label prefix does not appear in the cell, but it does appear in the control panel when the cell pointer is in that cell.

If you forget to type the label prefix when entering text that begins with a number, 1-2-3 will beep. You should then press [Esc] to cancel the entry and return to READY mode.

The next step in developing Vince's worksheet is to enter the names of the Krier part-time employees. These entries are labels.

To enter an employee name:

① Press [↓] to move the cell pointer to cell A14.

② Type **Bramble**. Before you press [Enter], look at the top left of the screen. See Figure 2-7 on the following page.

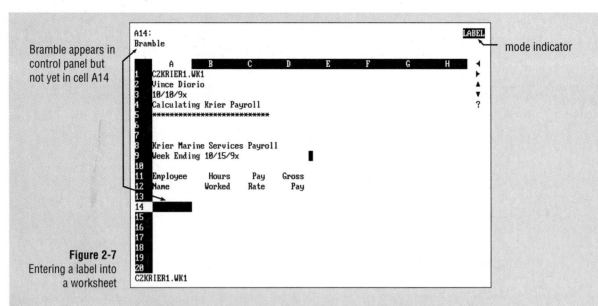

Bramble appears in control panel but not yet in cell A14

mode indicator

Figure 2-7
Entering a label into a worksheet

Notice that Bramble appears in the control panel but not in cell A14. Also notice that the mode indicator in the upper right corner of your screen has changed from READY to LABEL mode. This is because when you typed the letter B, 1-2-3 recognized it as a label.

❸   Press **[Enter]**. Bramble now appears in cell A14. See Figure 2-8.

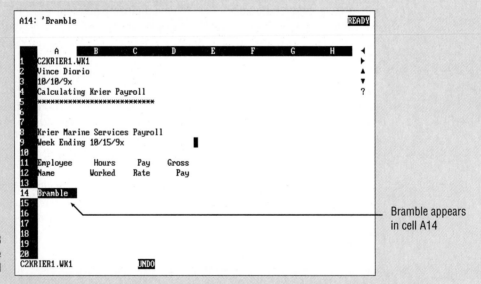

Figure 2-8
Name of employee appears in cell

Bramble appears in cell A14

When you press the [Enter] key, the cell pointer remains in cell A14.

To enter the name of the second employee:

❹   Press **[↓]** once to move the cell pointer to cell A15.

❺   Type **Juarez** and then press **[Enter]**.

To enter the third employee:

❻   Press **[↓]** once to move the cell pointer to cell A16.

❼ Type **Smith** and then press **[Enter]**.

To enter the fourth employee:

❽ Press **[↓]** once to move the cell pointer to cell A17.

❾ Type **Diorio** and then press **[Enter]**.

The names of the four employees should now appear on your worksheet. See Figure 2-9.

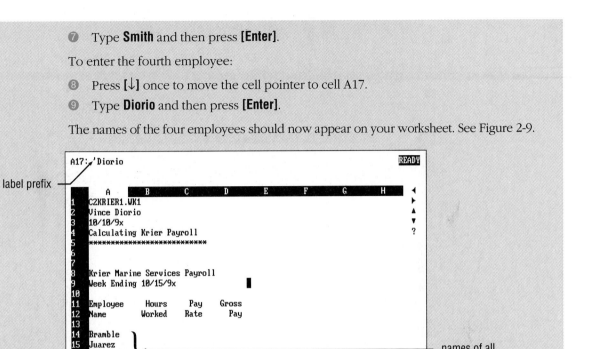

label prefix →

Figure 2-9
Names of
employees appear in
worksheet

← names of all
employees have
been entered

When the cell pointer is in a cell that contains a label, the control panel displays the cell address, an apostrophe, and the label you entered. See Figure 2-9. The apostrophe before the label is the label prefix. 1-2-3 automatically enters a label prefix whenever you enter labels in a worksheet.

Correcting Errors

The following steps show you two of the many ways to correct errors you make when you are entering text or numbers.

To correct errors as you are typing:

❶ Move the cell pointer to A16 and type **Smiht** but do not press [Enter]. Clearly this label is misspelled. Since you haven't pressed [Enter], you can use [Backspace] to correct the error. On most keyboards, this key is above the [Enter] key.

❷ Press **[Backspace]** twice to erase the last two characters you typed.

❸ Type the correct text — **th** — and press **[Enter]**.

If you notice an error *after* the text or value appears in the cell, you can correct the error by retyping the entry.

To correct errors in a cell:

1   Be sure the cell pointer is in cell A16 and type **Smiht.** Press **[Enter]**. Smiht appears in cell A16. See Figure 2-10.

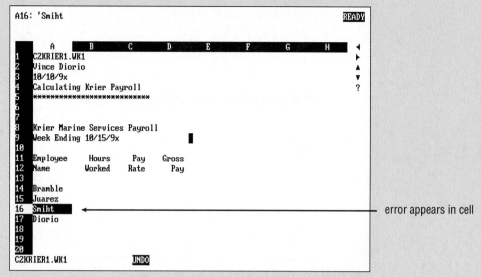

Figure 2-10
Correcting errors in a cell

error appears in cell

2   Type **Smith** in cell A16 and press **[Enter]**. As you can see, 1-2-3 enters the new text over the old. This is commonly called *typing over.*

Entering Values

A value in 1-2-3 can be a number or a formula. 1-2-3 interprets an entry in a cell as a **value** if the first character you type is a number (0 through 9) or one of the special characters + − @ . (# $. As soon as you begin entering a number or one of these special characters, you'll notice that the mode indicator changes from READY to VALUE.

When you are entering numbers, keep the following points in mind:

- Numbers cannot contain spaces or commas.
- A number cannot have more than one decimal point.
- Numbers are always right-justified when displayed in cells.
- If you type a plus sign (+) before a number or enter a number in parentheses, the + and the ( ) will not appear in the cell.
- If you enter a number with a percent sign (%), 1-2-3 will automatically divide the number preceding the sign by 100.

Next, enter the hours worked by each employee at Krier Marine Services.

To enter the hours worked:

1 Move the cell pointer to cell B14, the location of Bramble's hours worked.

Bramble worked 15 hours.

2 Type **15** and press **[Enter]**. Do not include any symbols or punctuation, such as a comma, when entering values.

3 Press **[↓]** once to move the cell pointer to cell B15, the location of Juarez's hours worked.

Juarez worked 28 hours.

4 Type **28** and press **[Enter]**.

5 Press **[↓]** once to move the cell pointer to cell B16, the location of Smith's hours worked.

Smith worked 40 hours.

6 Type **40** and press **[Enter]**.

7 Press **[↓]** to move the cell pointer to cell B17, the location of Diorio's hours worked.

Diorio worked 22 hours.

8 Type **22** and press **[Enter]**. Your screen should look like Figure 2-11.

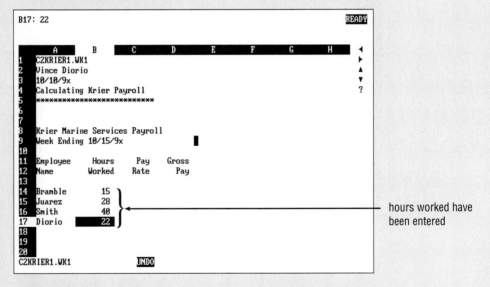

Figure 2-11
Hours worked entered into worksheet

There is another, faster way to enter data. You can enter data in a cell and move the cell pointer to a cell on any side of that cell in one step by pressing a pointer-movement key instead of [Enter]. The **pointer-movement keys** are the directional keys, such as [→], [←], [↑], [↓], [PgDn], and [PgUp], that you press to move the pointer in the worksheet. To learn how to do this, let's enter the hourly pay rates for each employee.

To enter hourly pay rates using pointer-movement keys:

❶ Move the cell pointer to C14, the location of Bramble's pay rate.

Bramble earns $7 an hour.

❷ Type **7** and press [↓] instead of the [Enter] key. Notice that you entered the value in cell C14 and moved the cell pointer to cell C15, the cell immediately below C14. C15 is the location of Juarez's pay rate.

Juarez earns $5 an hour.

❸ With the cell pointer in C15, type **5** and press [↓].

Smith earns $7 an hour.

❹ In cell C16 type **7** and press [↓].

Diorio earns $5 an hour.

❺ In cell C17 type **5** and press **[Enter]**. You have now entered all the data. Your worksheet should be similar to Figure 2-12.

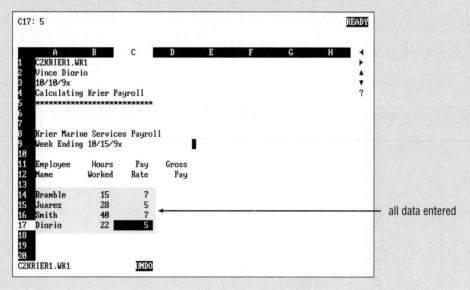

Figure 2-12
Pay rates entered
into worksheet

all data entered

Saving a Worksheet

When you create or modify a worksheet, it is only temporarily stored in the computer's memory. To store your work permanently, you must save the worksheet to your hard disk or data diskette. It is always a good idea to save frequently as you work, rather than to wait until you've finished. Suppose the power goes out or you step away from your computer and someone starts working with another file. Unless you have been saving as you go along, all of your work could be lost.

Next we'll save all the entries you have made so far to a new file named S2KRIER1.WK1. Before you save the file, you should change cell A1 to S2KRIER1.WK1 so the identifying information in the worksheet will be consistent with the new filename.

To change the filename in cell A1 and then save the file:

❶ Press **[Home]** to move the cell pointer to cell A1.

❷ Type **S2KRIER1.WK1** and press **[Enter]**.

❸ Select /File Save (**/FS**). Notice that the mode indicator in the upper right corner changes to EDIT. See Figure 2-13.

1-2-3 prompts you for a filename in the control panel. It also shows the current filename, and the drive from which you retrieved the file.

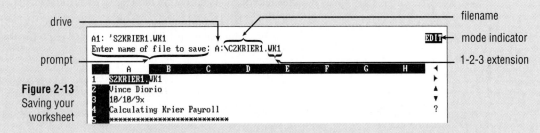

Figure 2-13
Saving your worksheet

❹ Type **S2KRIER1**. Notice that you do not have to erase the current filename.

In 1-2-3 all filenames must consist of not more than eight characters. You can use uppercase or lowercase letters, numbers, and the special characters $ & % ( ) { } – _ to create a filename. 1-2-3 converts any lowercase letters to uppercase letters once you press [Enter]. You cannot use spaces in a filename.

❺ Press **[Enter]** to save the file in the drive and the directory you specified. 1-2-3 will automatically add the file extension .WK1 to the filename.

Figure 2-14 shows the process that occurs when you select File Save and type S2KRIER1. 1-2-3 copies the worksheet file from the computer's memory to your disk storage.

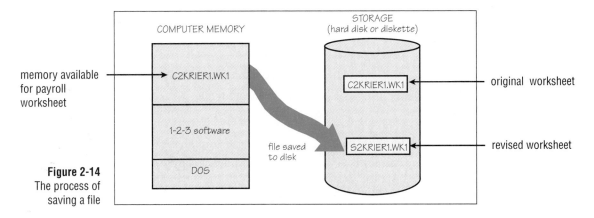

Figure 2-14
The process of saving a file

You have now saved your worksheet, including all the employee data you entered.

Worksheet Filenames in the Lotus 1-2-3 Tutorials

Besides saving frequently, another good habit to follow is to use descriptive names that will help you identify the contents of your files. Worksheet filenames can contain up to eight characters. These characters can be letters, numbers, and all symbols except for spaces, commas, colons, and asterisks. Although eight characters do not often allow you to create complete names, you can create meaningful abbreviations. For example, the Data Disk for Lotus 1-2-3 contains over 50 files. To name these files so that you can recognize their contents, we categorized them as follows:

File Category	Description
Tutorial Case	The files you use to work through each tutorial
Tutorial Assignment	The files that contain the worksheets you need to complete the Tutorial Assignments at the end of each tutorial
Case Problem	The files that contain the worksheets you need to complete the Case Problems at the end of each tutorial or the Additional Cases in Part 3
Saved Worksheet	Any worksheet that you have saved
Module Case	The files you use to work through each module
Exercise Assignments	The files you use to complete the Exercises at the end of each tutorial
Reference Assignments	The files you use to complete the Reference Assignments
WYSIWYG Solutions	All saved worksheets with WYSIWYG enhancements

We used these categories to help name the worksheet files on your data diskette. Let's take the filename C2KRIER1, for example. This name may appear to have no meaning, but it does contain meaningful abbreviations. The first character of every worksheet filename on your data diskette identifies the file as one of the eight file categories discussed above. Thus,

If the first character is:	the file category is:
C	Tutorial **C**ase
T	**T**utorial Assignment
P	Case **P**roblem
S	**S**aved Worksheet
M	**M**odule Case
E	**E**xercise Assignment
R	**R**eference Assignment
W	**W**YSIWYG Solution

Based on these categories, we know that the file C2KRIER1 is a Tutorial Case file.

The second character of every worksheet file identifies the tutorial from which the file comes. Thus, C2KRIER1 is a Tutorial Case from Tutorial 2. The remaining six characters of the filename identify the specific file. All worksheets in tutorials are assigned a name, and the number that follows the name indicates a version number. Thus, C2KRIER1 is the first Tutorial Case worksheet from Tutorial 2. T2KRIER1 is the first worksheet found in the Tutorial Assignments from Tutorial

2, while T2KRIER2 is a second version of that worksheet. As another example, P2TOYS is the filename of the Case Problem "Sales in Toyland" from Tutorial 2.

Using Formulas

In addition to labels and values, you can enter formulas in cells. A formula is an entry in a worksheet that performs a calculation. A **formula** is a mathematical expression that can include numeric constants, cell addresses, arithmetic operators, and parentheses. An **arithmetic operator** indicates the desired arithmetic operation. The arithmetic operators, used in Lotus 1-2-3 are as follows:

Arithmetic Operation	Arithmetic Operator Used in Lotus	Example	Description
Addition	+	10+A15	Add 10 to the value in cell A15 from 10.
Subtraction	−	10–A15	Subtract the value in cell A15.
Multiplication	*	10*A15	Multiply 10 by the value in cell A15.
Division	/	10/A15	Divide 10 by the value in A15.
Exponentiation	∧	10∧A15	Raise 10 to the value stored in A15.

Using formulas is one way to tap into the power of a spreadsheet like 1-2-3. Once you have entered a formula, 1-2-3 will perform the calculations and make the necessary changes to your data. You will get the new results immediately and with little effort.

Rules of Arithmetic Precedence

The computer performs arithmetic on only one operation at a time. Thus, if a formula contains two or more arithmetic operators, for example 1+.05*1000, the computer performs the operations in a particular sequence, based on the following hierarchy:

Arithmetic Hierarchy	Arithmetic Operation
Calculated first	Exponentiation
Calculated second	Multiplication and division
Calculated third	Addition and subtraction

The sequence in which arithmetic operators are performed is called the **order of precedence.** Exponentiation (raising a number to a power) is performed before all other arithmetic operations; in other words, exponentiation is given precedence over all other operations. Multiplication and division are performed before addition and subtraction.

For example, consider the expression 1+.05*1000. The calculations are performed in the following order:

- First, .05 is multiplied by 1000, since multiplication takes precedence over addition.
- Second, the result of step 1, 50, is added to 1, giving the final result, 51.

Left-to-right Rule

If a formula contains two or more arithmetic operators that have equal precedence, then operations with the same precedence are calculated in order from left to right. For example, in the expression 1+1005−1000 the calculations are performed in the following order:

- First, 1 is added to 1005, since the addition operation appears before the subtraction operation, with which it has equal precedence.
- Second, 1000 is subtracted from the result of step 1, 1006, giving the final result, 6.

Use of Parentheses

Sometimes you want the arithmetic operations to be performed in an order different from that determined by the precedence rules. In those cases you can use parentheses to change the order in which the calculations are performed. Operations inside parentheses are calculated before operations not in parentheses.

For example, suppose you want to calculate the average daily sales of two stores. The first store had sales of $1000, and the second store had sales of $2000; the average sales of the two stores is $1500. If you enter the formula 1000+2000/2, 1-2-3 will give you an incorrect answer, because this formula would be calculated as follows:

- First, 2000 is divided by 2, since division is performed before addition.
- Second, 1000 is added to the result of step 1, 1000. This gives the result of 2000, not the 1500 you expected.

But if you use parentheses in the formula, such as (1000+2000)/2, you can ensure that 1-2-3 will give you the correct result. This formula is calculated as follows:

- First, 1000 is added to 2000, since operations in parentheses are evaluated before operations outside parentheses.
- Second, the result of step 1, 3000, is divided by 2, giving the result 1500.

Entering Formulas

Now that you know how to use formulas, you are ready to calculate the gross pay for each employee. Gross pay is the number of hours worked multiplied by the rate of pay (hours worked × rate of pay). You do not need to do the multiplication yourself; you enter a formula, such as +B14*C14, that tells 1-2-3 which cells to multiply. 1-2-3 performs the calculations immediately and displays the results in the cell that contains the formula. The following steps show you one way to enter a formula.

To enter a formula to compute Bramble's gross pay:

❶ Move the cell pointer to cell D14, the location of Bramble's gross pay.

② Type **+B14*C14**. When the first element in a formula is a cell address, you must begin the formula with + or –; otherwise, 1-2-3 interprets what you type as a label and not a formula.

Notice that the formula appears in the control panel as you type and that 1-2-3 is now in VALUE mode. See Figure 2-15. Remember, if you make a mistake, you can use [Backspace] if you are still entering the formula, or you can retype the formula if you have pressed [Enter].

formula to calculate — Bramble's gross pay

mode has changed

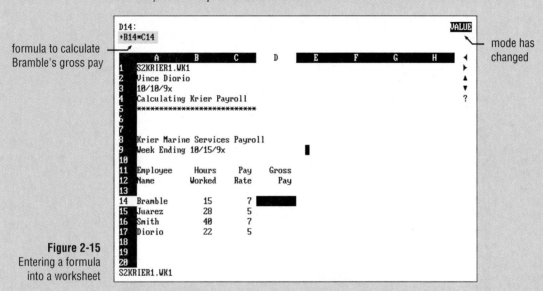

Figure 2-15
Entering a formula
into a worksheet

③ Press **[Enter]**. 1-2-3 calculates the formula's value, 105, and the result appears in cell D14. If you get a different result, check the formula or the data values in B14 and C14. Retype, if you find any errors. See Figure 2-16.

formula appears in — control panel

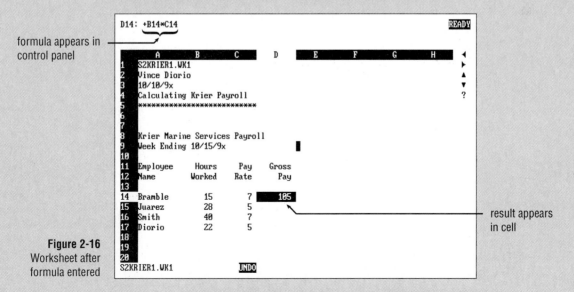

result appears
in cell

Figure 2-16
Worksheet after
formula entered

Now enter the formula in cell D15 to calculate Juarez's gross pay.

④ Move the cell pointer to cell D15. Type **+B15*C15** and press **[Enter]**. The result, 140, appears in cell D15.

Now enter the formula in cell D16 to calculate Smith's gross pay.

⑤ Move the cell pointer to cell D16, type **+B16*C16**, and press **[Enter]**. The gross pay for Smith is 280, which appears in cell D16.

Finally, enter the formula in cell D17 to calculate Diorio's gross pay.

⑥ Move the cell pointer to cell D17, type **+B17*C17**, and press **[Enter]**. Diorio's pay is 110, which appears in cell D17.

Figure 2-17 shows the gross pay calculated for all the employees.

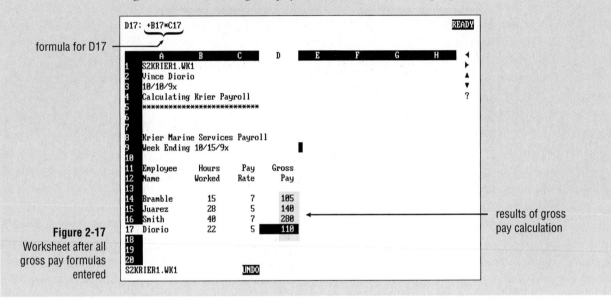

formula for D17 —

results of gross pay calculation

Figure 2-17
Worksheet after all gross pay formulas entered

Calculating a Sum

Now let's calculate the total gross pay for all employees by adding the gross pay of Bramble, Juarez, Smith, and Diorio, that is, adding the values of cells D14, D15, D16, and D17.

To calculate a sum:

❶ Move the cell pointer to cell A19. Type the label **Total** and press **[Enter]**.

❷ Move the cell pointer to cell D19. This is the cell in which we want to put the total gross pay.

The correct formula to calculate gross pay is +D14+D15+D16+D17. But for now, let's intentionally enter an incorrect formula.

❸ Type **+D14+D15+C17+D17** and press **[Enter]**. 1-2-3 calculates a total using this formula, and 360 appears in cell D19. See Figure 2-18.

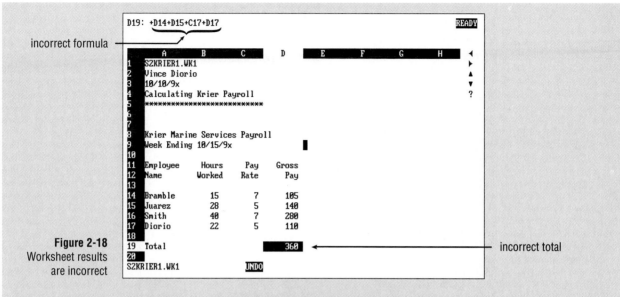

incorrect formula ———

D19: +D14+D15+C17+D17   READY

	A	B	C	D	E	F	G	H
1	S2KRIER1.WK1							
2	Vince Diorio							
3	10/10/9x							
4	Calculating Krier Payroll							
5	******************************							
6								
7								
8	Krier Marine Services Payroll							
9	Week Ending 10/15/9x							
10								
11	Employee	Hours	Pay	Gross				
12	Name	Worked	Rate	Pay				
13								
14	Bramble	15	7	105				
15	Juarez	28	5	140				
16	Smith	40	7	280				
17	Diorio	22	5	110				
18								
19	Total			360				
20								

S2KRIER1.WK1   UNDO

——— incorrect total

Figure 2-18
Worksheet results
are incorrect

Is the sum correct? If you add the gross pay of each employee (105 + 140 + 280 + 110), you get 635. Why does 360 appear in cell D19? Look at the formula in the control panel. The correct formula is +D14+D15+D16+D17, but your panel shows +D14+D15+C17+D17.

We made this error intentionally to demonstrate that you always run the risk of making errors when you create a worksheet. Be sure to check your entries and formulas. In this case, you would add the results manually and compare them to the value in the worksheet.

Editing Entries in a Cell

If you notice an error in your worksheet, you have already learned that you can move the cell pointer to the cell with the error and retype the entry that contains the error. You can also use EDIT mode to correct the problem. EDIT mode is sometimes faster and easier to use, because you change only the incorrect characters and leave the rest of the entry intact. In 1-2-3 you use [F2] (EDIT) to edit an entry. In the following steps, you'll edit cell D19, which contains the incorrect formula for total gross pay.

To edit the contents of a cell:

① Be sure the cell pointer is in cell D19.

② Press **[F2]** (EDIT). The formula +D14+D15+C17+D17 appears in the second line of the control panel. The cursor appears at the end of the entry, and you are ready for editing. See Figure 2-19 on the following page.

formula to be edited ⟶

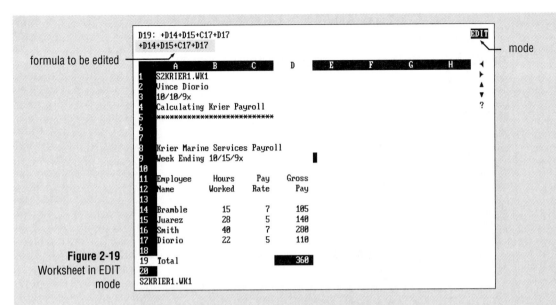

— mode

Figure 2-19
Worksheet in EDIT
mode

When you first press [F2], 1-2-3 is in EDIT mode. Any new character you enter is inserted at the cursor, and any characters to the right of the cursor are moved one position to the right. You can activate overtype mode by pressing [Ins]. In this mode any character you type replaces the character directly above the cursor. When 1-2-3 is in overtype mode, you will see the OVR indicator on the status line at the bottom of the screen. Pressing [Ins] again switches 1-2-3 back to insert mode. Figure 2-20 provides a list of keys you can use in EDIT mode.

Key	Action
[→]	Moves cursor one position to right
[←]	Moves cursor one position to left
[Home]	Moves cursor to first position in entry
[End]	Moves cursor one position to right of last character in the entry
[Backspace]	Deletes character to left of cursor
[Del]	Deletes character above cursor
[Ins]	Switches between insert mode and overtype mode
[Enter]	Completes the edit and returns to READY mode
[Esc]	Clears edit line; when pressed again leaves EDIT mode without making changes and returns to READY mode

Figure 2-20
Keys and their
actions in EDIT
mode

❸   Press [←] to position the cursor under the letter C in the formula. Press **[Del]** three times to erase C17, the incorrect portion of the formula.

❹   Type **D16**. Press **[Enter]** and, as you do, notice that the value in D19 changes to 635, the correct total gross pay. Notice also that the correct formula, +D14+D15+D16+D17, appears in the control panel. See Figure 2-21.

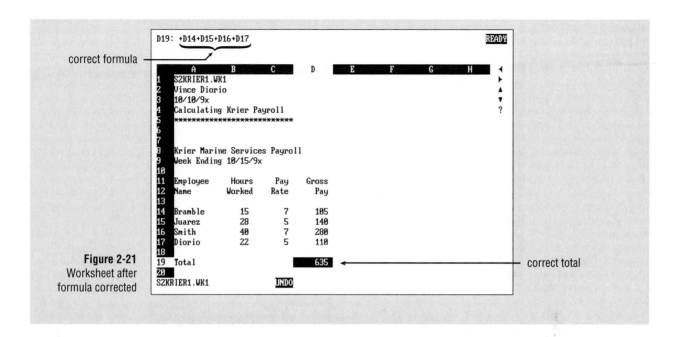

correct formula ——→

D19: +D14+D15+D16+D17   READY

	A	B	C	D	E	F	G	H
1	S2KRIER1.WK1
2	Vince Diorio
3	10/10/9x
4	Calculating Krier Payroll
5	*****************************
6	
7	
8	Krier Marine Services Payroll
9	Week Ending 10/15/9x
10	
11	Employee	Hours	Pay	Gross
12	Name	Worked	Rate	Pay
13	
14	Bramble	15	7	105
15	Juarez	28	5	140
16	Smith	40	7	280
17	Diorio	22	5	110
18	
19	Total			635
20	

S2KRIER1.WK1   UNDO

Figure 2-21
Worksheet after
formula corrected

635 ←——— correct total

Be sure to take advantage of the [F2] (EDIT) key. It is often easier and more efficient to correct mistakes by typing only what needs to be changed.

Entering Lines

Worksheets often contain a row of lines below column headings and above and below subtotals to make the worksheet more readable. In addition, double lines are often used to indicate final totals. You could enter as many minus signs (–) or equal signs (=) as you need to create lines, but 1-2-3 provides a more convenient way. You first type \ (Backslash, not the slash symbol, /) and then type the character you want to use to draw the line. The backslash is a special label prefix that instructs 1-2-3 to repeat the character that follows it until the cell is filled.

To fill a cell with characters:

① Move the cell pointer to cell A13. This is a blank cell under a column heading.

② Type \ (Backslash) followed by a – (Minus Sign) to fill the cell with minus signs.

③ Press **[Enter]**. See Figure 2-22 on the following page. Notice how minus signs fill cell A13, producing a line in this cell.

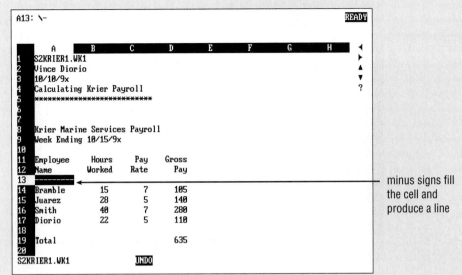

Figure 2-22
Entering lines in a worksheet

minus signs fill the cell and produce a line

④ Move the cell pointer to cell B13, type **\—**, then press **[Enter]**.

⑤ Move the cell pointer to cell C13, type **\—**, then press **[Enter]**.

⑥ Move the cell pointer to cell D13, type **\—**, then press **[Enter]**. You have now entered a line across row 13.

⑦ Move the cell pointer to cell D18, type **\—**, then press **[Enter]**. This enters a line in the gross pay column.

Your screen should be similar to Figure 2-23.

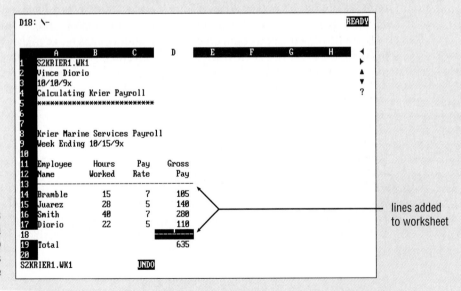

Figure 2-23
Lines added to a worksheet to improve its appearance

lines added to worksheet

Using UNDO to Correct Mistakes

What would you do if you accidentally typed over or erased a complicated formula? It would probably be a lot of work to figure out the formula again and reenter it. The UNDO feature can help. You can use it to cancel the *most recent* operation you performed on your worksheet.

To use UNDO, two indicators must appear on the screen. The word UNDO must appear in the status indicator at the bottom of your screen. Also, the word READY must appear in the mode indicator in the upper right corner of the screen. This means that your worksheet is in READY mode and can accept a keystroke. If UNDO does not appear in the status line at the bottom of your screen, you cannot do the steps in this section. To load UNDO, see pages L 43 and L 44.

Let's make an intentional mistake and use UNDO to correct it. Instead of typing the label ========= in cell D20, where it belongs, you will type it in cell D19, where it will erase the formula for total gross pay. Then you'll restore the original formula by using the UNDO feature.

To intentionally make a mistake:

1. Move the cell pointer to cell D19, the cell that contains the formula for total gross pay.
2. Type **\ =** and press **[Enter]**. See Figure 2-24.

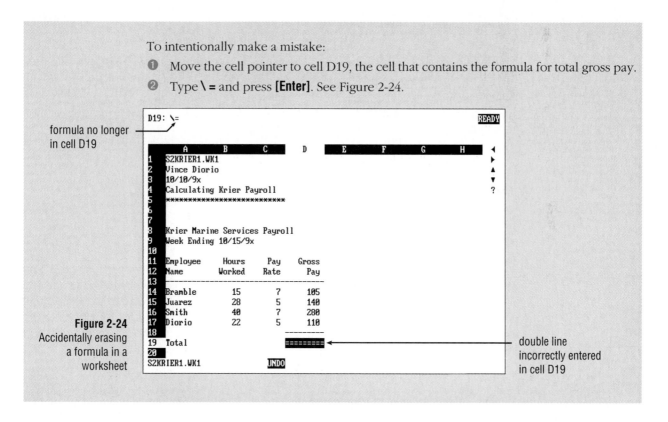

formula no longer in cell D19

Figure 2-24
Accidentally erasing a formula in a worksheet

double line incorrectly entered in cell D19

You have erased the entire formula and replaced it with =========, but don't worry. You can undo the mistake.

To use UNDO to cancel your *most recent* operation:

❶ Press the **[Alt]** key and, while holding it down, press the **[F4]** key ([Alt][F4]). Then release both keys. [Alt][F4] (UNDO) undoes your intentional mistake and restores the formula in D19. The value in D19 should again be 635.

❷ Now move the cell pointer to D20, the cell in which you should enter the double line. Type **\ =** and press **[Enter]**. See Figure 2-25.

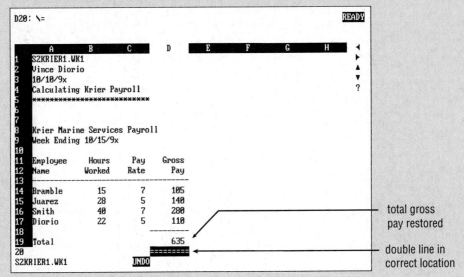

Figure 2-25
The worksheet after
UNDO returns the
formula to the cell

Saving a File Using an Existing Filename

As discussed earlier in the tutorial, 1-2-3 does not automatically save your worksheet. You must use the File Save command to make a permanent copy of your worksheet on your data diskette. You used the File Save command earlier; however, since you last issued that command you made several changes to your worksheet. These changes have not been saved. To do that you must update the worksheet file on your data diskette by saving the worksheet again.

To save the worksheet:

❶ Select /File Save (**/FS**). The name of the current worksheet appears in the control panel.

❷ S2KRIER1.WK1, the filename of the current worksheet appears in the control panel. Since you want to update this worksheet by saving the changes, press **[Enter]**.

Because the filename you are saving already exists on your data diskette, 1-2-3 presents you with three options. See Figure 2-26.

options appear in → control panel

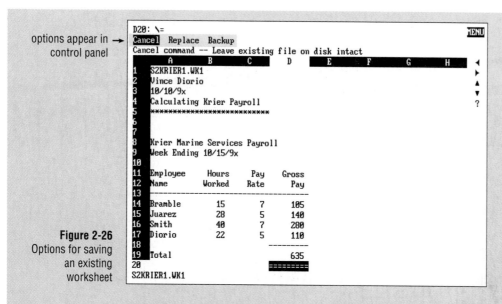

Figure 2-26
Options for saving an existing worksheet

Cancel – This option returns you to READY mode without saving the current worksheet.

Replace – This option replaces the contents of the worksheet file on your data diskette with the current worksheet in computer memory.

Backup – This option saves the current worksheet and keeps a copy of the previous version of the worksheet. 1-2-3 copies the worksheet file with the same filename but with a BAK extension. The current worksheet is saved with the existing filename and the extension WK1.

Since you want to update the file with the changes, you should use the *Replace* option.

❸ Select Replace (**R**). The updated worksheet file, S2KRIER1.WK1, now contains the current worksheet.

Understanding Ranges

Vince has completed the payroll worksheet for Krier Marine Services. Now he wants to print it. The Print command requires you to identify the range of cells that you want to print. Therefore, you need to understand the term "range" before using the Print command.

A **range** in 1-2-3 consists of one or more cells that form a rectangular shape. A range may be a single cell, a row of cells, a column of cells, or a rectangular block of cells. To define a range, you indicate the upper left corner cell of the rectangle and the lower right corner cell of the rectangle. Two periods [..] separate these entries and represent all the values between the beginning cell and the ending cell, for example, C14..C17. The notation C14..C17 is referred to as a **range address**.

Figure 2-27 illustrates several examples of ranges that you can define in a worksheet.

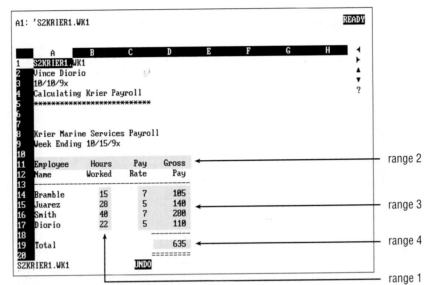

Figure 2-27
Examples of ranges

- The first example, labeled range 1, is identified as B14..B17. This range forms a column of cells located in column B, beginning in row 14 and ending in row 17.
- The second example, range 2, represents a row of cells. The range is defined as A11..D11, which means the range of cells beginning at cell A11 and ending at D11.
- The third example, range 3, represents the rectangular block of cells C14..D17. A block of cells is identified in a worksheet by specifying a pair of diagonally opposite corner cells. C14, the upper left corner, and D17, the bottom right corner, define a block of eight cells.
- The fourth example, range 4, represents the single cell D19..D19. A single cell defined as a range has the same starting and ending cell.

Using the Print Command

You have entered the data, calculated gross pay and totals, saved your worksheet, and learned about ranges. You are now ready to print the Krier payroll worksheet and learn the basics of using the Print command. In 1-2-3 you print by first specifying a range to print and then printing the worksheet. You can print all or part of your worksheet by first defining a rectangular range of cells that you want to print. Vince wants to print the payroll report using the range A8 through D20.

To specify the print range A8..D20:

❶ Select /Print Printer (**/PP**). 1-2-3 displays a menu with eight options and a Print Settings dialog box. See Figure 2-28.

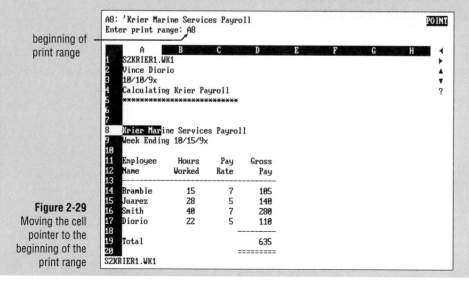

Figure 2-28
Print Settings
dialog box

As you learned in Tutorial 1, a dialog box is a box of options. Besides showing the options for saving an existing worksheet, Figure 2-28 also shows the Print Settings dialog box. This box displays the current print settings. You can select your print settings by making menu selections or by making selections directly from the dialog box. Module 1 contains more information about the use of dialog boxes.

Anytime you print, the printed output will be formatted according to the specifications indicated in the dialog box. If you want to see the worksheet instead of the Print Settings dialog box, you can press the function key [F6]. Press [F6] again, and the Print Settings dialog box reappears.

❷   Select Range (**R**). The worksheet reappears.

To define the print range, you must specify two cell addresses that are diagonally across from each other. Usually the upper left corner and the lower right corner cells define the range.

❸   Move the cell pointer to A8, the upper left corner cell in the print range. See Figure 2-29.

Figure 2-29
Moving the cell
pointer to the
beginning of the
print range

④ Type **[.]** (Period). This fixes, or **anchors**, the cell pointer in the current cell. Whenever you want to specify a range, you should move the cell pointer to the top left corner cell of a range and anchor this position by pressing [.] (Period). See Figure 2-30 and compare it to Figure 2-29. Notice how 1-2-3 indicates that the cell pointer is anchored.

.. indicates range is anchored

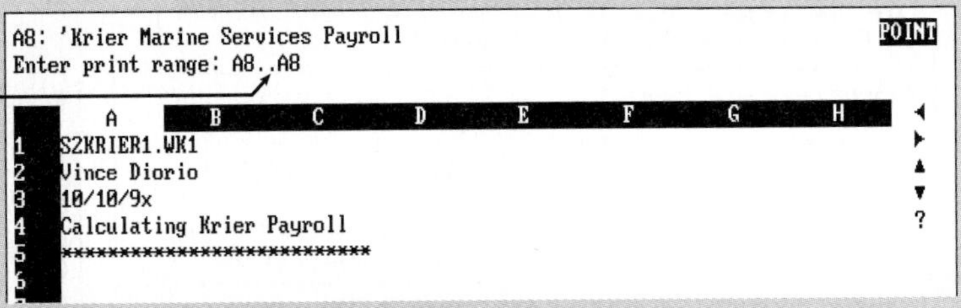

Figure 2-30
Anchoring the cell pointer

```
A8: 'Krier Marine Services Payroll                          POINT
Enter print range: A8..A8

        A       B       C       D       E       F       G       H    ◄
1 S2KRIER1.WK1                                                        ►
2 Vince Diorio                                                        ▲
3 10/10/9x                                                            ▼
4 Calculating Krier Payroll                                           ?
5 ******************************
6
```

Once the cell pointer is anchored, pressing the pointer-movement keys expands the highlighted range.

⑤ Press **[↓]** and **[→]**, as needed, to highlight the range A8..D20. The address of the highlighted range appears in the control panel. See Figure 2-31.

print range defined

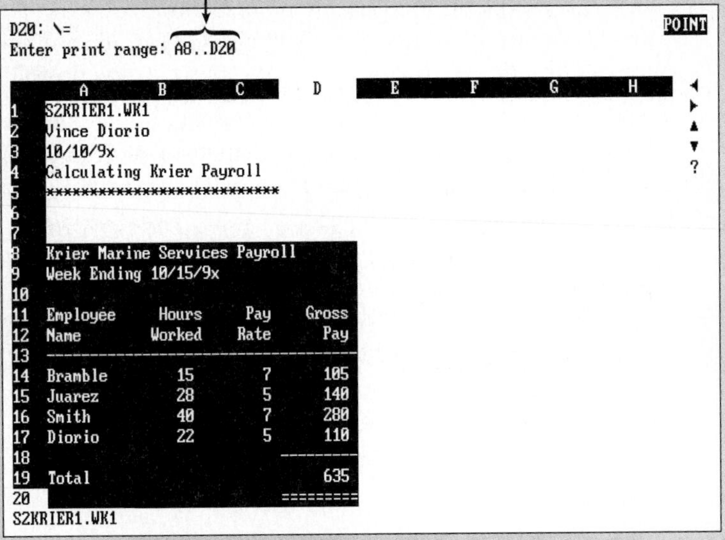

Figure 2-31
Highlighting the print range

```
D20: \=                                                    POINT
Enter print range: A8..D20

        A       B       C       D       E       F       G       H    ◄
1 S2KRIER1.WK1                                                        ►
2 Vince Diorio                                                        ▲
3 10/10/9x                                                            ▼
4 Calculating Krier Payroll                                           ?
5 ******************************
6
7
8 Krier Marine Services Payroll
9 Week Ending 10/15/9x
10
11 Employee    Hours    Pay    Gross
12 Name        Worked   Rate   Pay
13 ─────────────────────────────────
14 Bramble       15       7     105
15 Juarez        28       5     140
16 Smith         40       7     280
17 Diorio        22       5     110
18                            ──────
19 Total                        635
20                            ══════
S2KRIER1.WK1
```

⑥ Press **[Enter]**. This completes the definition of the range, which now appears in the Print Settings dialog box. See Figure 2-32.

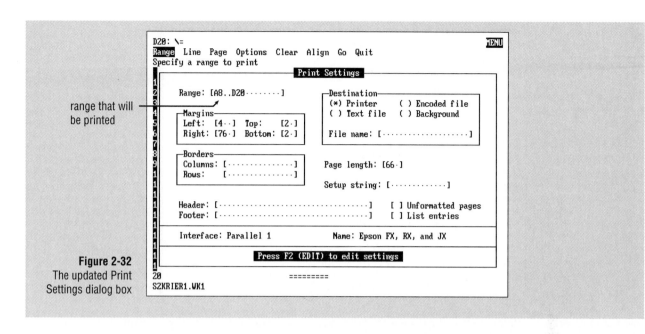

range that will
be printed

Figure 2-32
The updated Print
Settings dialog box

Now that you've instructed 1-2-3 what cells you want to print, you are ready to print the worksheet.

To print a specified range:

❶ Make sure your paper is positioned properly in your printer and the printer is on-line.

❷ Select Align (**A**) to tell 1-2-3 that the paper is correctly positioned at the top of the page and ready for printing. You should always choose Align before beginning to print.

❸ Select Go (**G**) to print the specified range. If the range does not print, your copy of 1-2-3 may not be installed correctly.

❹ Select Page (**P**). You need not wait for the printing to finish before you select Page. The Page command tells 1-2-3 to advance the paper to the top of the next page when it is finished printing. See Figure 2-33 on the following page.

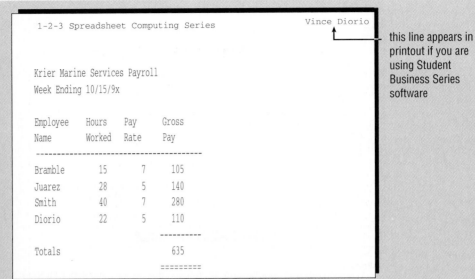

```
        1-2-3 Spreadsheet Computing Series        Vince Diorio


        Krier Marine Services Payroll
        Week Ending 10/15/9x


        Employee   Hours   Pay    Gross
        Name       Worked  Rate   Pay
        ----------------------------------------
        Bramble      15      7     105
        Juarez       28      5     140
        Smith        40      7     280
        Diorio       22      5     110
                                  ----------
        Totals                     635
                                  =========
```

this line appears in printout if you are using Student Business Series software

Figure 2-33
Printout of Krier Marine Services payroll worksheet

If you are having trouble printing, you may need to check with your technical support person for the proper printing procedures in your lab.

⑤ Select Quit (**Q**) to leave the Print menu and return to READY mode with your worksheet displayed on your screen.

⑥ Save your worksheet as S2KRIER1 one last time (**/FS**). Press **[Enter]** and select Replace (**R**). This saves the print settings with the worksheet.

Erasing the Entire Worksheet

Once you have completed a worksheet, you may wish to start a new one. You can do this easily, but always remember to save your current worksheet. Then you can clear the worksheet from memory by using the Worksheet Erase command. You can also use this command if you begin a worksheet but decide you don't want it and have to start over. Let's erase the Krier payroll worksheet.

To erase a worksheet:

① Select /Worksheet Erase (**/WE**).

1-2-3 displays a prompt to give you a chance to change your mind. If you select "No," the worksheet will *not* be erased. If you select "Yes," the worksheet will be erased from computer memory.

② Type **Y** (Yes) if you are sure you want to erase the worksheet. After you type Y, the worksheet disappears from the screen. See Figure 2-34. 1-2-3 does *not* erase the worksheet from your data diskette, only from the computer's memory.

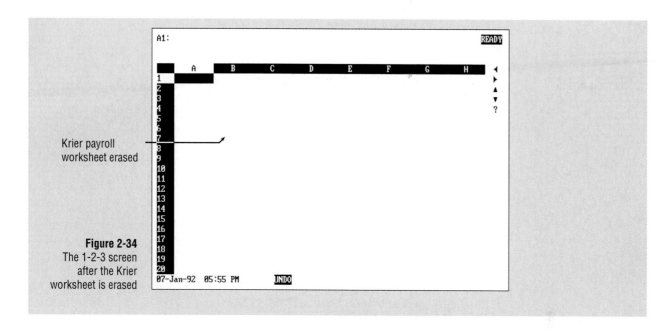

Krier payroll
worksheet erased

Figure 2-34
The 1-2-3 screen
after the Krier
worksheet is erased

If you attempt to erase a worksheet without first saving a new or modified worksheet, the control panel will display the following warning: "WORKSHEET CHANGES NOT SAVED! Erase worksheet anyway?"

If you did not want to save the worksheet, you would select "Yes" and your worksheet would be erased. However, if you did want to save your worksheet but forgot, you would type "No" and you'd return to READY mode. Then you would issue the /File Save command to save your worksheet. After saving your worksheet, you could then issue the Worksheet Erase command.

Quitting 1-2-3

When you are ready to quit 1-2-3, you choose the Quit command. You are then returned to the operating system prompt.

To quit a 1-2-3 session:

❶ Select /Quit (**Q**).

You are given the chance to change your mind. If you select "No" in response to the prompt, 1-2-3 returns to READY mode. If you select "Yes," you end the 1-2-3 session and return to DOS.

❷ Select Yes (**Y**). You are returned to the DOS prompt.

If you have changed the worksheet since the last time you saved it, 1-2-3 displays another Yes/No prompt. If you do not want to save the worksheet, select "Yes" and you leave 1-2-3. However, if you forgot to save your worksheet, type "No" and you return to READY mode. Then issue the /File Save command. After you save your worksheet, you can issue the Quit command.

■   ■   ■

Exercises

1. Would you enter the following data items as labels or values?
    a. 227-3541   (phone number)
    b. 6.45   (pay rate)
    c. 02384   (zip code)
    d. 46 Main Street   (address)
    e. 25   (units on hand)

2. Load 1-2-3 and enter the following numbers and labels in your worksheet. If you have a problem after any entry, press [Esc] to return to READY mode. For each entry, explain why you got the result you did.
    a. In cell A1 type the street address **1 Main Street**
        In cell A2 type **'1 Main Street**
    b. In cell A5 type the phone number **755-5122**
        In cell A6 type **'755-5122**
    c. In cell A10 type the zip code **02892**
        In cell A11 type **'02892**
    d. In cell A14 type **.25**
        In cell A15 type **25%**
    e. In cell A17 type **6000**
        In cell A18 type **6,000**
    f. Print the worksheet.

3. Create a new worksheet by entering the following values: 10 in cell A1, 20 in cell B1, and 3 in cell C1. For each formula, first calculate the result by hand. Then enter each formula in the specified cell and compare the results.

	Cell	Formula	Hand-calculated result	1-2-3 calculated result
a.	D3	+A1+B1-C1		
b.	D4	+A1-C1+B1		
c.	D6	+A1+B1/C1		
d.	D7	+(A1+B1)/C1		
e.	D9	+A1/B1*C1		
f.	D10	+A1/(B1*C1)		
g.	D13	+B1/A1^C1		
h.	D14	(B1/A1)^C1		

    i. Print the worksheet.

4. Which of the following ranges defines a row of cells? Which range defines a block of cells?
    a. B1..B7
    b. B1..D7
    c. B1..E1
    d. B1..B1

5. You want to display a series of plus signs, +++++++++, in a cell. How do you accomplish this task?

6. Which of the following filenames can be used to name a 1-2-3 worksheet?
   a. Q1.WK1
   b. 1991.WK1
   c. ACCTREC.WK1
   d. ACCT REC.WK1
   e. ACCT_REC.WK1
   f. ACCT.REC.WK1

7. What key(s) would you press to accomplish the following tasks?
   a. get to the Command menu
   b. back up one step in the 1-2-3 menu system
   c. move to cell A1
   d. edit a formula in a cell

Tutorial Assignments

1. Retrieve the file T2KRIER1, find the error, and correct it. (When 1-2-3 displays the list of worksheet files, press [PgDn] several times to find the worksheet file T2KRIER1.) What do you think the person who created the worksheet did when entering the gross pay formula for Bramble? Print the worksheet.

2. Retrieve the file T2KRIER2. Why isn't total gross pay adding correctly? Correct the worksheet and print it.

3. Retrieve the file T2KRIER3. Why is Bramble's gross pay zero? Hint: Think about how labels and values are stored in 1-2-3. Correct the error and print the worksheet.

Retrieve the file T2KRIER4 and do the following:

4. Juarez worked 30 hours for the week, not the 28 hours that was entered. Correct this.

5. Smith's name is actually Smythe. Change the name.

6. In cell B19, write a formula to calculate total hours worked.

7. Add a single line in cell B18 and a double line in cell B20.

Continue using the file T2KRIER4 to complete the following problems on federal withholding tax (FWT). FWT is the amount of money that an employer withholds from an employee's paycheck to pay federal taxes.

8. Assume that the amount withheld from an employee's pay check is 15 percent (.15) of gross pay. Use column E in your worksheet to display FWT. Include the column heading FWT in cell E12. Enter the formula for withholding tax for each employee (gross pay × .15) in cells E14, E15, E16, and E17.

9. Net pay is the gross pay less deductions (gross pay – FWT). Use column F to display the net pay for each employee. Enter the column label Net in cell F11 and the column label Pay in cell F12. Enter the net pay formula for each employee in cells F14, F15, F16, and F17.

10. Calculate the total FWT and the total net pay for all employees. Display these totals in cells E19 and F19, respectively.

11.   Add single and double lines where appropriate.

12.   Change cell A1 to S2KRIER4.WK1. Now save your worksheet as S2KRIER4.WK1.

13.   Print the entire worksheet, including the identifying data at the top of the worksheet. Your print range is A1..F20.

Case Problems

1.   Sales in Toyland

An article in the *Wall Street Journal* focusing on sales in the toy industry for 1990 presented the data shown in Figure 2-35.

Toy Companies Nine-month Sales 1990 (in millions)		
Company	1990	1989
Galoob	105	169
Hasbro	1027	993
Matchbox	140	156
Mattel	1042	878
Tonka	541	625
Tyco	334	269

Figure 2-35

Retrieve the worksheet P2TOYS and do the following:

1.   Calculate total sales for the toy industry for 1989 and 1990.

2.   Calculate the change in sales from 1989 to 1990. Place this result in column D. Label the column heading Change and use the following formula:

Change = 1990 sales – 1989 sales

3.   Save the worksheet as S2TOYS.

4.   Print the worksheet.

2.   Travel Agency Survey

A travel industry association conducted a study of American travel habits. Figure 2-36 shows the amount of passenger miles traveled in the United States by various modes of transportation.

U.S. Travel Habits	
Mode of Transportation	Passenger Miles (billions)
Cars	1586.3
Airlines	346.5
Buses	45.2
Railroad	18.7

Figure 2-36

Retrieve the worksheet P2TRVL and do the following:

1. Enter the formula to compute total U.S. passenger miles.

2. Enter the formula to compute the percent that each mode of transportation represents of the total U.S. passenger miles. (Divide the passenger miles for each mode of transportation by total passenger miles and then multiply by 100.)

3. Save your worksheet as S2TRVL.

4. Print your worksheet.

3. A Trend Toward More Bankruptcies

Ms. Ganni is a lawyer who administers bankruptcy filings. In the last few years she has seen a rapid increase in the number of bankruptcy cases. She states, "I know the number of bankruptcy cases I've handled has increased enormously. I don't have time for lunch anymore, much less time to analyze all the cases. We need more staff; our system is overloaded!"

As her assistant you must help Ms. Ganni make a case to her bosses for additional resources.

Retrieve the worksheet file P2BNKRPT and do the following:

1. Calculate the total number of bankruptcies in 1989 and 1990.

2. Calculate the percent change in bankruptcies this year compared to last year for each type of bankruptcy as well as the overall percent change. The formula to calculate percent change in bankruptcies for each bankruptcy type in 1990 is

$$\left(\frac{(Bankruptcies\ in\ 1990 - Bankruptcies\ in\ 1989)}{Bankruptcies\ in\ 1989} \right) \times 100$$

3. Save the worksheet as S2BNKRPT.

4. Print the worksheet.

4. Calculating Commissions at Esquire's Clothing

Esquire's Clothing pays its salesforce their commissions every three months. Commissions are based on sales for the previous three months.

Do the following:

1. Retrieve the worksheet file P2COMM.

2. Include the following calculations in your worksheet:
    a.   the quarterly sales for each salesperson
    b.   the quarterly commission for each salesperson based on the following formula:

    quarterly sales for each salesperson × *salesperson's commission rate*

    c.   the quarterly net sales (the amount remaining after commission is deducted) for each salesperson based on the following formula:

    quarterly sales for each salesperson – salesperson's commission amount

    d.   totals for each column except the Commission Rate column.

5. Save the worksheet as S2COMM.

6. Print the worksheet.

Tutorial 3

Modifying a Worksheet

Pricing a Mutual Fund

OBJECTIVES

In this tutorial you will learn to:

■ Use the @SUM function

■ Change the way numbers are displayed

■ Change column widths

■ Adjust text alignments

■ Insert rows

■ Move a group of rows or columns to another worksheet area

■ Erase a group of cells

Case: Allegiance Incorporated

Pauline Wu graduated last June with a degree in finance. Today she is beginning her new job as a portfolio accountant with Allegiance Incorporated, an investment company. Pauline is excited about getting this job, not only because Allegiance is reputed to be one of the best mutual fund companies in the United States, but also because Allegiance is known for the superior training it provides its new employees.

People who have money to invest but who do not want to manage the investment themselves invest their money with Allegiance. Allegiance employs trained professionals to manage the money in what are called mutual funds. In these funds the money is invested in stocks, bonds, and other publicly traded securities and managed by Allegiance employees, often called portfolio managers.

For example, a portfolio manager might manage a $10 million fund that was started by selling one million shares at $10 a share to people who then became the shareholders of the fund. The manager of this fund then invests the $10 million by buying shares in companies such as IBM, AT&T, and Coca-Cola. The goal of the portfolio manager and the shareholders is that the shares purchased will increase in value so the shareholders will make money.

As a portfolio accountant, Pauline will be responsible for reporting correct information to portfolio managers so they will be able to track how well a fund is performing. One of Pauline's responsibilities in her new job is each day to calculate the value of the Balboa Equity Fund and to report this information to the national newspapers so shareholders can know the value of a share in this fund. Pauline knows that is an important responsibility. Even a minor error in her calculations could cause Allegiance to lose substantial amounts of money. She is eager to begin the new employee training program because it will help her to perform these important calculations accurately.

Pauline first meets the other new portfolio accountants and her training supervisor, Rochelle Osterhaut. Rochelle begins the training by discussing their daily responsibility to calculate the value of a mutual fund share. She hands out a fact sheet (Figure 3-1) that lists details about the Balboa Equity Fund. Rochelle explains that their first assignment is to use this information to calculate the value of a share of the Balboa Fund. She also reminds them that in college they probably learned that the value per share of a fund is usually called the *net asset value*, or *NAV*.

```
Balboa Equity Fund   -   Fact Sheet

Mutual Fund Shares       2000

Net Asset Value            ?


Company Name      Shares Purchased      Current Price

IBM                    100                  91
Coca-Cola               50                  69 1/4
Texaco                 100                  58 3/4
Boeing                 150                  44 1/2
```

Figure 3-1
Balboa Equity Fund
fact sheet

Rochelle explains that to calculate the NAV they must first determine the market value of each investment owned by the fund. To do this, they multiply the current price of each company share owned by the fund by the total number of shares of this company that the fund purchased. For example, Balboa Equity Fund owns 100 shares of IBM, whose current price is $91 per share. Thus, the market value of these shares in the Balboa Fund is $9,100. After the market value of each security is determined, the accountants add together the market value of each investment and other assets owned by the fund, such as cash on hand. After calculating this total they divide it by the number of shares owned by the fund's shareholders. The result is the NAV. In other words,

$$NAV = \frac{(current\ price \times shares\ of\ company\ A\ owned\ by\ fund\,) + (current\ price \times shares\ of\ company\ B\ owned\ by\ fund\,) + ...}{number\ of\ shares\ of\ the\ mutual\ fund\ owned\ by\ fund's\ shareholders}$$

Pauline is eager to begin the assignment. She decides to use Lotus 1-2-3 to help make the calculations and to produce a professional-looking report. First, however, she thinks about the project; she outlines her thoughts on a planning sheet and sketches the worksheet (Figures 3-2a and 3-2b).

Planning Sheet
My Goal:
   Calculate Net Asset Value for Balboa Equity Fund each day

What results do I want to see?
   Net Asset Value (Price/Share) of Balboa Equity Fund
   Breakdown of company's that make up the fund along with the
   market value of company's stock

What information do I need?
    For each company stock owned by the fund
      Name of the company
      Number of shares of the company's stock owned by fund
      Current price company's stock is selling for

What calculations will I perform?
   Calculate market value of each stock in the fund
   Calculate total value for all stock in the fund
   Calculate Net Asst Value

Figure 3-2a
Pauline's planning
sheet

Mutual Fund Shares
Price per share (NAV)

Company Name	# of Shares	Current Price	Market Value
XXXX	XX	XX.XXX	XXXX.XX
XXXX	XX	XX.XXX	XXXX.XX
.			
.			
.			
Totals			XXXX.XX

Figure 3-2b
Pauline's
worksheet sketch

In this tutorial, you will create the same worksheet that Pauline creates. You will experience the power of the specialized @functions, which speed and simplify the use of formulas, learn more about entering and editing data quickly, and learn how to make changes in the appearance of the worksheet.

Retrieving the Worksheet

Let's begin by retrieving the worksheet.

To retrieve the worksheet:

① Select /File Retrieve (**/FR**) and highlight C3BALBO1.WK1. Press **[Enter]**. See Figure 3-3a.

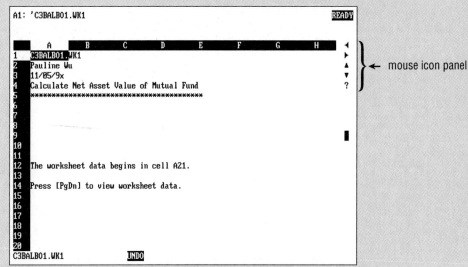

Figure 3-3a
Initial screen from
C3BALBO1.WK1

The initial screen contains documentation about the worksheet and instructions to go to cell A21 to view the worksheet data.

② Press **[PgDn]**. See Figure 3-3b.

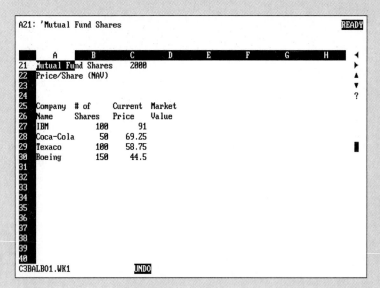

Figure 3-3b
Data on Balboa Equity
Fund

This worksheet contains the Balboa Equity Fund Portfolio data. It includes the company names and the number of shares of each company's stock that the fund purchased. It also shows the current day's stock market price for a share of each company that is part of the Balboa Fund Portfolio. In addition, the worksheet shows the number of mutual fund shares owned by people who have invested in the Balboa Fund.

Entering Formulas

Now that you have the basic data entered in the worksheet, your first step in pricing the mutual fund is to calculate the market value of each company's stock in the fund. The market value is calculated by multiplying the number of shares owned of each company's stock by the current market price of that company's stock, that is,

$$market\ value = number\ of\ shares \times current\ market\ price$$

To calculate the market value for each company:

First calculate the market value for IBM.

❶ Move the cell pointer to D27. Type **+B27*C27** and press **[↓]**.

To calculate the market value for Coca-Cola:

❷ In cell D28 type **+B28*C28** and press **[↓]**.

To calculate the market value for Texaco:

❸ In cell D29 type **+B29*C29** and press **[↓]**.

To calculate the market value for Boeing:

❹ In cell D30 type **+B30*C30** and press **[Enter]**. See Figure 3-4.

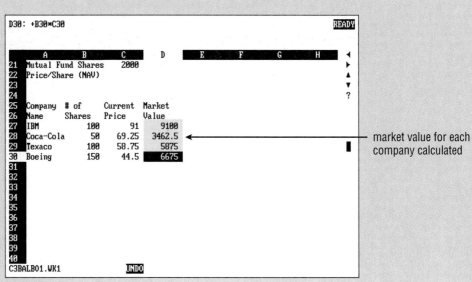

Figure 3-4
Worksheet after
market value formula
entered

market value for each
company calculated

Using the @SUM Function

Now that you have calculated the market value of each company's stock in this fund, you need to calculate the total market value of the fund. The total market value of the fund is the sum of the market values of all the companies in the fund, that is,

total market value = market value of IBM + market value of Coca-Cola + ...

Remember that in Tutorial 2 you summed the total gross pay by specifying the cell location of each employee's gross pay. Similarly you could calculate the total market value by entering the formula +D27+D28+D29+D30, but this would be tedious. It would be especially tedious if the fund had perhaps 75 different companies instead of just 4. To make the process much easier, you'll use 1-2-3's @SUM (pronounced "at sum") function. This function allows you to total the values in a range of cells.

What Is an @Function?

An **@function** is a predefined routine that performs a series of operations or calculations and then gives you a result. It can be thought of as a *predefined formula* that is built into 1-2-3. Functions save you the trouble of creating your own formulas to perform various arithmetic tasks.

Many functions are available in 1-2-3. They are divided into eight categories: mathematical, statistical, database, financial, logical, string, date/time, and special.

Each function begins with the @ (at) symbol followed by the name of the function. The name of the function suggests its purpose. In parentheses following the function name, you put any information the function needs to perform its tasks. The information in parentheses is referred to as the **arguments** of the function. Depending on the @function, the arguments may be values, references to cells or ranges, range names, formulas, and even other @functions. The general format of a function in 1-2-3 is

---

@FUNCTION(arguments)

where:

   @ is the symbol that indicates that a function follows.

   FUNCTION is the name of the function.

   arguments represents the required information that the function needs to
      do its tasks.

Example:

   @SUM(D27..D30)

Pauline is ready to calculate the total market value of the Balboa Equity Fund. To do this, she will use the @SUM function. Remember, the @SUM function adds a range of numbers. You specify the addresses of the first and the last cell of the range you want to add. In other words, @SUM(D27..D30) is equivalent to +D27+D28+D29+D30. The expression in parentheses, D27..D30, is the argument, representing the range of cells that will be added.

To use the @SUM function to calculate total market value:

① Move the cell pointer to A31 to enter the label. Type **[Spacebar] [Spacebar] Totals**. Press **[Enter]**.

② Now move the cell pointer to D31, where you will enter the formula to total the company market values.

③ Type **@sum(** to begin the formula. You may use either uppercase or lowercase when typing the function name SUM.

④ Press **[↑]** to move the cell pointer to D27, the starting point for adding the market values of all companies in this fund. See Figure 3-5.

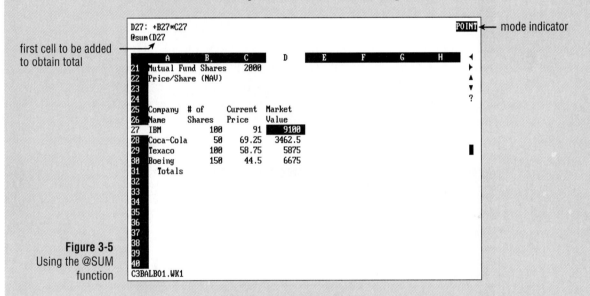

first cell to be added
to obtain total

mode indicator

Figure 3-5
Using the @SUM
function

⑤ Type **[.]** (Period) to anchor the cell. Two periods appear in the control panel to indicate that the cell is now anchored.

⑥   Press **[↓]** to highlight the range D27..D30. See Figure 3-6.

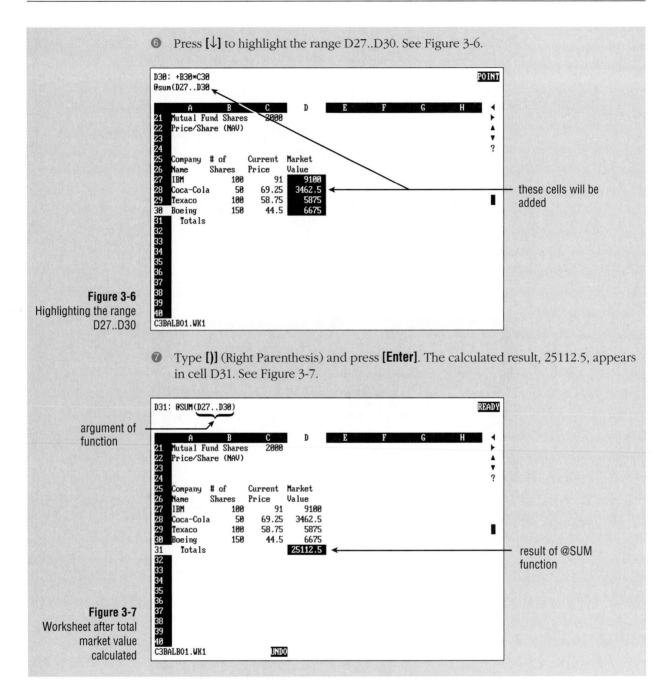

Figure 3-6
Highlighting the range
D27..D30

⑦   Type **[)]** (Right Parenthesis) and press **[Enter]**. The calculated result, 25112.5, appears in cell D31. See Figure 3-7.

Figure 3-7
Worksheet after total
market value
calculated

You have now calculated the market value for the Balboa Equity Fund.

The final calculation to determine the NAV is to divide the total market value of the fund by the number of shares of the fund that have been sold. In other words,

$$NAV = \frac{\textit{total market value of mutual fund}}{\textit{number of shares of fund owned by investors}}$$

To calculate the NAV:

❶ Move the cell pointer to C22, where the NAV will be calculated.

❷ Type **+D31/C21** and then press **[Enter]**.

The / (Slash) symbol represents division when used in a formula.

You've now completed the calculations of the NAV. Figure 3-8 shows the worksheet with the NAV calculated. Each share is worth $12.55625.

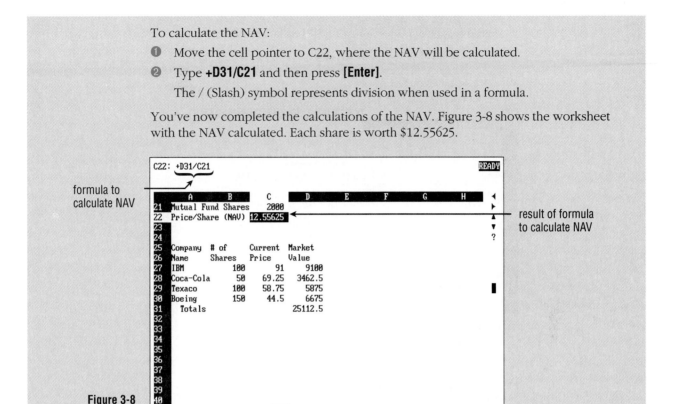

formula to calculate NAV

result of formula to calculate NAV

Figure 3-8
The NAV calculated

Improving the Appearance of the Worksheet

Although Pauline has completed the calculations for pricing the mutual fund, she is not pleased with the appearance of the worksheet. For instance, the numbers in the current price and market value columns are not aligned at the decimal point. In addition, the monetary values do not show dollar signs, and the column headings are not aligned over the numbers in the columns. Some improvements are needed to make the worksheet easier to read and use.

In the next several sections of this tutorial, you will learn to improve your worksheet's appearance. Figure 3-9 shows how the worksheet will look when you are finished.

```
A21: [W32] 'Balboa Equity Fund                                    READY

                      A              B      C       D       E     ◄
21  Balboa Equity Fund                                           ▶
22  Net Asset Value for November 5, 199x                         ▲
23                                                               ▼
24                                                               ?
25  Company                        # of  Current   Market
26  Name                          Shares  Price    Value
27  ------------------------------------------------------------
28  International Business Machines  100  $91.00  $9,100.00
29  Coca-Cola                         50   69.25   3,462.50      ■
30  Texaco                           100   58.75   5,875.00
31  Boeing                           150   44.50   6,675.00
32  ------------------------------------------------------------
33     Totals                                     $25,112.50
34
35
36  Mutual Fund Shares                      2000
37  Price/Share (NAV)                    12.55625
38
39
40
S3BALBO1.WK1                  UNDO
```

Figure 3-9
Final version of
worksheet

Formatting Numbers

You probably found the numeric values in your worksheet difficult to read, because the lists of current prices and market values are not aligned at the decimal point. Unless you instruct 1-2-3 otherwise, it displays numbers with a minus sign for negative values, no thousand separators, and no trailing zeros to the right of the decimal point. This is called the **General format**, and it is 1-2-3's default format. *Default* refers to a format or setting that 1-2-3 automatically uses unless you specifically change it. You can change how 1-2-3 displays data by using the Format command. 1-2-3 provides several alternative formats that you can use to change the way numbers appear in your worksheet.

Figure 3-10 shows some of the types of numeric formatting available in 1-2-3. These formats allow you to alter the number of decimal places displayed with a number. They may include dollar signs and commas with numbers; they can place parentheses around negative numbers; and they can add percent signs to numbers representing percentages.

Format Type	Description	Examples
General	This is the default format; 1-2-3 stores numbers in this format when you first enter them.	0.5 −125
Fixed	This displays numbers to a fixed number of decimal places that you specify.	0.50 1200.57
Currency	Numbers are preceded by dollar signs, and commas are inserted after the thousands and millions places. Negative numbers appear in parentheses.	$1,200.57 ($125.00)
, (Comma)	Commas are inserted after the thousands and millions places. Negative numbers appear in parentheses.	1,200.57 (125.00)
Percent	This multiplies the value by 100 and inserts the percent sign to the right of the value.	50% 14.1%
Scientific	Numbers are displayed as a power of 10. For example, the number 120000000 is displayed as 1.2E+08. The number 1.2E+08 is interpreted as "1.2 times 10 to the power of 8," or 1.2 times 100000000.	1.2E+08

Figure 3-10
Numeric formats

You can format all the cells in your worksheet using the Worksheet Global Format command, which treats all the cells similarly. Or you can format a block of cells, a column, a row, or a single cell using the Range Format command. In the next steps, you will change the format of the current price and market value columns. To do this, you will use the Range Format command.

Pauline decides to include dollar signs for the first value in columns that contain dollar values as well as for cells that contain totals. She will format all the other values in columns that contain dollar values using the Comma format to two decimal places. Let's first format the Current Price and Market Value columns beginning in cell C28 using the Comma format.

To format the current prices and market values in Comma format with two decimal places:

❶ Move the cell pointer to C28, the first cell of the column Current Price to be formatted with the Comma format.

➋   Select /Range Format (**/RF**). The second line of the control panel lists all the formats available in 1-2-3. See Figure 3-11.

format commands in 1-2-3

description of Fixed format

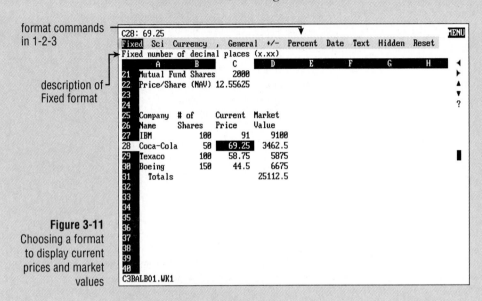

Figure 3-11
Choosing a format
to display current
prices and market
values

Select the Comma format.

➌   Select **[,]** (Comma).

At this point, 1-2-3 asks you to enter the number of decimal places.

➍   Type **2** and press **[Enter]**. Since 2 is the default, it is not necessary to type 2. If you wanted zero decimal places, you'd type 0 before pressing [Enter].

➎   At the range prompt highlight the range C28..D30. Press **[Enter]**. See Figure 3-12.

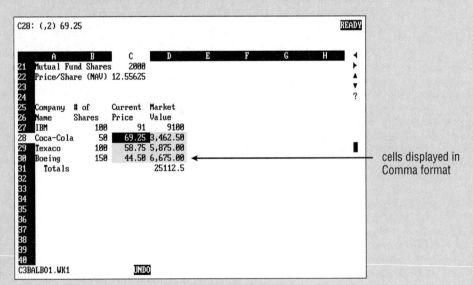

cells displayed in
Comma format

Figure 3-12
Formatting the
worksheet with the
Comma format

Notice that 1-2-3 displays (,2) in the control panel, which means this cell is for-matted with the Comma format and two decimal places. In general whenever the cell pointer is in a cell whose format has been changed with a Range Format command, the control panel displays the first character of the cell format name and the number of decimal places the cell will display.

Formatting Considerations

You should be aware of the following when you are formatting numbers:

- If you reduce the number of decimal places of a number, 1-2-3 rounds the number that appears in the cell. For example, if you type the value 25.6273 into a cell but decide to display the number with only two decimal places, the rounded number 25.63 appears in the cell. If you decide to display three decimal places, the number 25.627 appears in the cell.

- For all calculations 1-2-3 uses the value stored in the cell rather than the value that appears in the cell. Thus, for an entry stored as 25.6273 but appearing as 25.63, 1-2-3 uses 25.6273 for all calculations.

- Numeric formatting commands affect the way numbers are displayed on the screen, but they do not alter the cell's actual contents. If you want 1-2-3 to use a rounded number in a calculation, you can use the @ROUND function. The format of this function is @ROUND(*value,places*), where *value* is the number that you want to round and *places* is the number of decimal places that you want in the result. For example, @ROUND(10.131,0) rounds 10.131 to the nearest whole number, that is, 10. Thus, in the formula @ROUND(10.131,0)*2 1-2-3 uses the value 10, not 10.131, when multiplying by 2. The value displayed is 20.

Now let's format the first values in the columns Current Price and Market Value, using Currency format with two decimal places.

To change the first values in the columns Current Price and Market Value columns to Currency format:

❶ Move the cell pointer to C27, the first cell under Current Price.

❷ Select /Range Format Currency (**/RFC**).

❸ At the prompt for the number of decimal places, press **[Enter]**.

④ At the range prompt, press [→] to highlight the range C27..D27. Press **[Enter]**. See Figure 3-13.

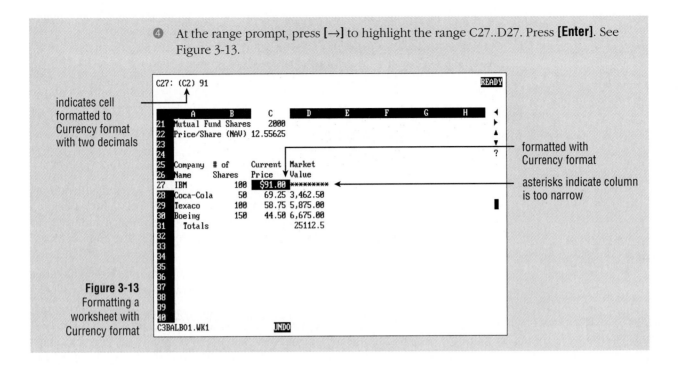

indicates cell formatted to Currency format with two decimals

formatted with Currency format

asterisks indicate column is too narrow

Figure 3-13
Formatting a worksheet with Currency format

Changing Column Widths

What happened to the first value in the column Market Value? Why do asterisks appear in cell D27? The asterisks indicate that the column is not wide enough to display the value. 1-2-3 measures column width by the number of characters displayed in a column. A single column can be up to 240 characters wide. 1-2-3 has a default width of 9 characters in a cell. In this case, therefore, the values do not fit. The asterisks indicate that the market value formatted using Currency format requires more than a 9-character-wide column. You must, therefore, increase the width of the Market Value column.

You can change the widths of all the columns in a worksheet at one time. We use the term **global** to describe a change that involves the *entire* worksheet. You can also make a single column wider or narrower. In the next steps you will widen a single column.

To change the width of column D:

❶ Make sure the cell pointer is in any cell in column D.

❷ Select /Worksheet Column Set-width (**/WCS**). See Figure 3-14.

preparing to change →
column width

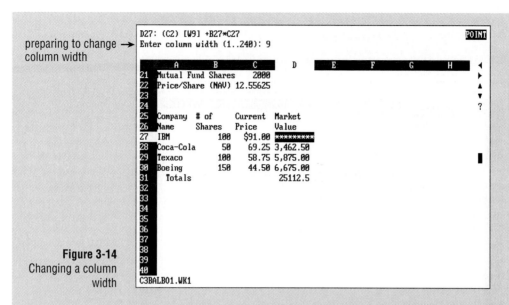

Figure 3-14
Changing a column
width

You can use two methods to enter a new column width: using the pointer-movement keys or typing a number. First, let's use the pointer-movement keys.

③ Press **[→]** until the column is wide enough to display the values.

Notice how the column width increases by one character each time you press the key. See Figure 3-15.

column width
is 10

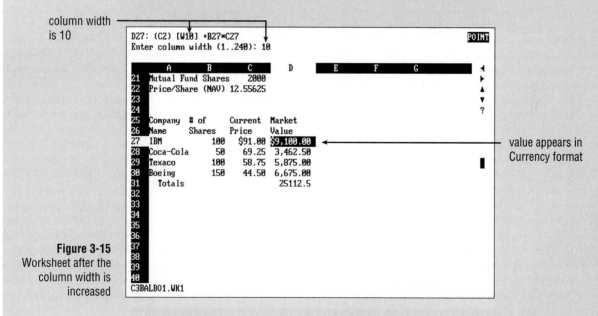

value appears in
Currency format

Figure 3-15
Worksheet after the
column width is
increased

④ Press **[Enter]**.

Now let's try the second method to widen a column: typing a number. Let's widen the column to 12 characters so it can accommodate an even larger number.

⑤ Select /Worksheet Column Set-width (**/WCS**).

⑥   Type **12** and press **[Enter]**. See Figure 3-16.

indicates cell
formatted with
Currency format
and 2 decimal
places

indicates width
of column is 12
characters

column is 12
characters wide

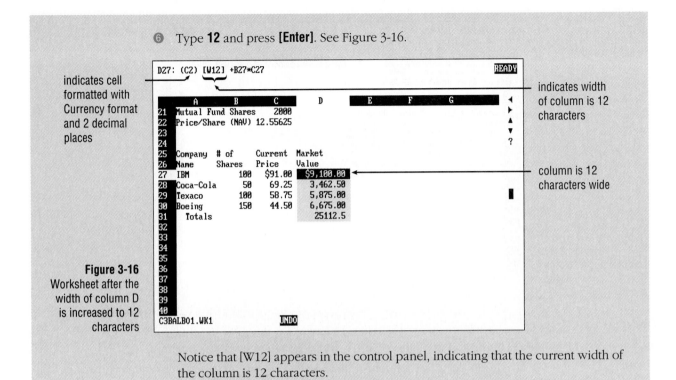

Figure 3-16
Worksheet after the
width of column D
is increased to 12
characters

Notice that [W12] appears in the control panel, indicating that the current width of
the column is 12 characters.

Remember that all columns have a default width of nine characters. You can change the
column width to accommodate labels and numbers that are longer than the column's width.
Sometimes you might find nine characters too large. In such cases, you can reduce the width
of a column by following the same steps you did to widen it. Just remember to choose a
number less than 9 or press [←] to lessen the column width.

As Pauline looks at the worksheet, she realizes she still needs to format the cell that
contains the total market value. She will format this cell using the Currency format so a dollar
sign will appear with the total.

To format the cell containing the total market value:

❶   Move the cell pointer to cell D31, the cell where the total market value is displayed.

❷   Select /Range Format Currency (**/RFC**).

❸   At the prompt for number of decimal places, press **[Enter]**.

❹   Since you are formatting only cell D31, the desired range is already highlighted.
Press **[Enter]**. See Figure 3-17.

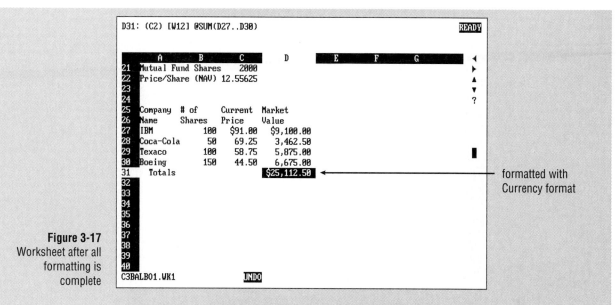

```
D31: (C2) [W12] @SUM(D27..D30)                              READY

          A         B         C         D        E      F      G     ◄
21 Mutual Fund Shares        2000                                     ►
22 Price/Share (NAV) 12.55625                                        ▲
23                                                                    ▼
24                                                                    ?
25 Company   # of     Current  Market
26 Name      Shares   Price    Value
27 IBM          100   $91.00   $9,100.00
28 Coca-Cola     50    69.25    3,462.50
29 Texaco       100    58.75    5,875.00
30 Boeing       150    44.50    6,675.00                       █
31    Totals                   $25,112.50  ◄───────────────        formatted with
32                                                                  Currency format
33
34
35
36
37
38
39
40
C3BALB01.WK1              UNDO
```

Figure 3-17
Worksheet after all formatting is complete

This time no asterisk appears in the cell because the width of the Market Value column (column D) has been expanded to display 12 characters.

Long Labels

Another reason to change the width of a column is to accommodate labels that are longer than nine characters. Often text entered into a cell is longer than the column's width. For example, the company name Hewlett-Packard requires more than nine characters. These text items are called **long labels.** If the cell to the right of the cell containing a long label is blank, the long label extends into the adjacent cell. However, if the cell to the right is not blank, then only the characters that fit into the column's current width will appear. Because the default column width is nine characters, only the first nine characters will appear in the cell unless you change the width.

Let's suppose that Pauline does not want to abbreviate the names of the companies in the fund. Let's enter the full name for IBM, International Business Machines, and observe the result.

To enter a long label:

❶ Move the cell pointer to A27.

❷ Type **International Business Machines** and press **[Enter]**. Since the default column width for column A is 9, only the first nine characters appear — Internati. Look at the control panel; notice that the entire label appears there. This indicates that 1-2-3 has stored the entire label in the cell, but since the width of the column is 9 and the cell to the right of the company name is not blank, only the first nine characters appear on your screen. See Figure 3-18 on the following page.

entire name is
stored

only 9 characters
appear in cell

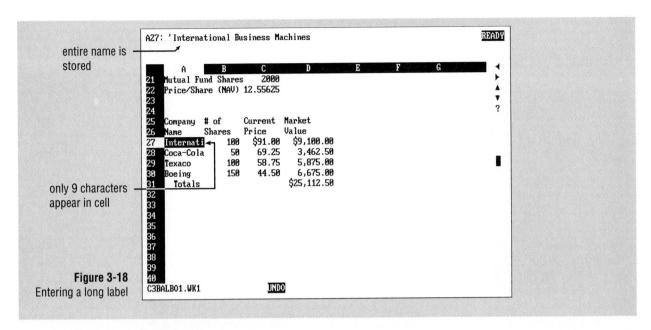

Figure 3-18
Entering a long label

Pauline wants the entire name of the company to appear, so we must increase the column width.

To increase the column width:

❶ Select /Worksheet Column Set-width (**/WCS**).

❷ Type **32** to allow enough characters for the entire name to appear on the screen.

❸ Press **[Enter]**. See Figure 3-19.

width of cell is
32 characters

entire name appears
in cell

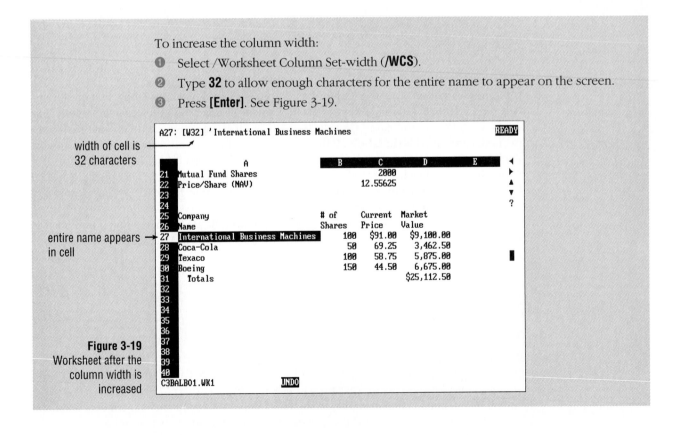

Figure 3-19
Worksheet after the
column width is
increased

Adjusting Labels within a Cell

As you have seen, when you enter a label, 1-2-3 places it by default against the left edge of the cell. Such a label is said to be **left-justified** and has an apostrophe (') label prefix. You can easily change the alignment of labels, that is, center or right-justify them, to suit your needs.

Let's learn how to right-justify the labels in Pauline's worksheet so the headings are over the data in each column.

To right-justify the column headings for the number of shares, the current price, and the market value:

❶ Move the cell pointer to B25.

❷ Select /Range Label Right (**/RLR**). See Figure 3-20. Notice that 1-2-3 automatically anchors the range at cell B25 because the prompt in the control panel indicates a range address rather than a cell address.

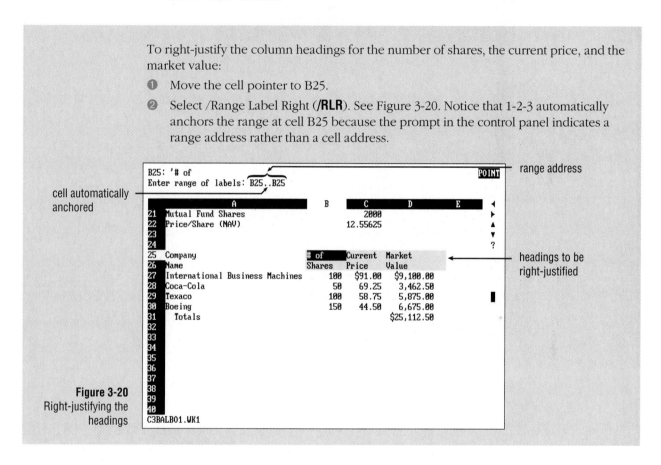

Figure 3-20
Right-justifying the headings

❸ Move the [→] and [↓] keys until the cell range B25..D26 is highlighted. Press **[Enter]**. See Figure 3-21.

" label prefix means the label is right-justified in the cell

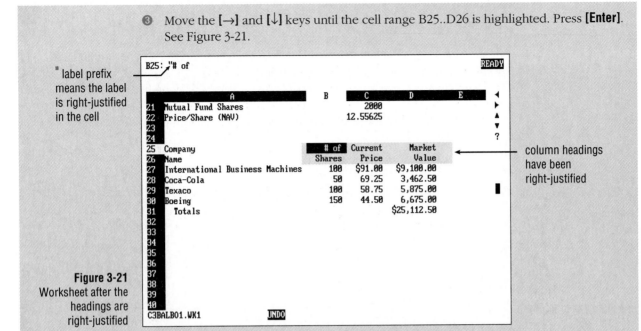

column headings have been right-justified

Figure 3-21
Worksheet after the headings are right-justified

The headings in columns B, C, and D are now right-justified.

Notice in the control panel that a " (Quote) character now precedes the label. The " character is the label prefix 1-2-3 uses to indicate a right-justified label.

To center the labels, you would select Range Label Center in Step 2.

You can also control label alignment as you type labels. For example, to center a label, type the ∧ (Caret) character (found on the [6] key) in front of any label. To right-justify a label, type a "(Quote) character in front of the label.

Before going on, let's save the worksheet.

To save the worksheet:

❶ Press **[Home]** to move the cell pointer to cell A1. Type **S3BALBO1.WK1** and press **[Enter]**. This changes the identifying information in cell A1 so it will be consistent with the new filename.

❷ Save your worksheet (**/FS**), using the name S3BALBO1.

Inserting Rows

You could improve the worksheet's appearance by inserting a line between the column heading and the first company name. In addition, it would look better with a line between the last company name and the row Totals. But there isn't any room. Running out of room often happens when you are in the process of creating a worksheet. Fortunately, with 1-2-3 you can insert or delete one or more rows between adjacent rows. You can also insert one or more columns between adjacent columns. You use the Insert command to insert new rows or columns into your worksheet.

To insert a blank row between A26 and A27 in the worksheet:

❶ Move the cell pointer to A27, the first row above which you want new rows inserted.

❷ Select /Worksheet Insert Row (**/WIR**).

The prompt "Enter row insert range: A27..A27" appears on the control panel. Since you are adding only one row, do not change the range. If you wanted to insert more rows, you would press [↓] for every row you wanted to insert.

❸ Press **[Enter]**. 1-2-3 inserts one blank row. All the other rows are pushed down below the blank row. Notice also that 1-2-3 adjusts all formula relationships. See Figure 3-22.

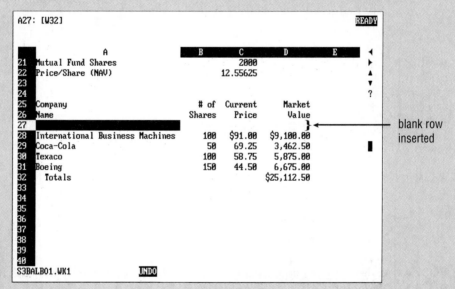

Figure 3-22
Inserting rows into the worksheet

To insert a blank row after Boeing and before the total value row:

❹ Move the cell pointer to A32.

❺ Select /Worksheet Insert Row (**/WIR**).

❻ Press **[Enter]**. A blank row is inserted between Boeing and the label Totals.

Now let's add some lines to improve the worksheet's appearance. Often in worksheets a single line is inserted between the column headings and the data to help users read the worksheet. To insert such a line you can type \ – to fill each cell with a dashed line. Let's do that now.

To underline the column headings:

❶   Move the cell pointer to A27. Type **\ –** and press **[Enter]**.

❷   Repeat Step 1 for cells B27, C27, and D27.

To add a row of lines to row 32:

❸   Move the cell pointer to A32. Type **\ –** and press **[Enter]**.

❹   Repeat Step 3 for cells B32, C32, and D32. See Figure 3-23.

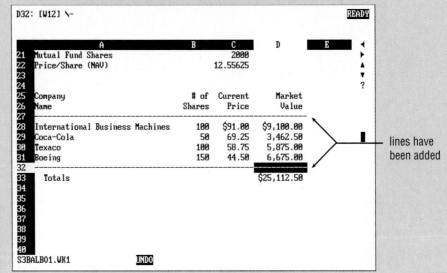

Figure 3-23
Adding dashed
lines to separate
headings and total
from the data

Moving Data

Pauline has made several changes that have improved the appearance of her worksheet. However, after reviewing the current worksheet, Pauline decides that she wants to make additional changes to improve it even more. First, she wants the summary data on mutual fund shares and net asset value to follow the company data. She feels the companies that make up the fund should be placed before the summary information on the NAV. (Report layout often is a matter of personal preference.) In addition, she realizes the report is actually incomplete because the company sells many different mutual funds. The worksheet does not indicate that these data are only for the Balboa Equity Fund. Also, she prices the fund at the end of each day, but the worksheet doesn't indicate the date of this report. Thus, Pauline decides to add the following two lines to the worksheet:

Balboa Equity Fund
Net Asset Value for November 5, 199X

She wants to place this title above the column headings, exactly where the Mutual Fund Shares label is now. How can she rearrange the worksheet without starting over?

Fortunately Lotus 1-2-3 has a Move command. Its function is to move data from one part of the worksheet to another part of the same worksheet. The data that are moved from one location to another disappear from the first location. The Move command is a powerful tool for creating and designing worksheets. Let's move the information on the number of shares owned and the NAV to begin in cell A36, so this information appears after the individual companies in the fund.

To move the range A21..C22 to a new location:

❶ Move the cell pointer to A21, the upper left corner of the range you want to move.

❷ Select /Move (**/M**). A21..A21 appears on the control panel as the "Move what?" range. The two periods mean the range is already anchored in cell A21. See Figure 3-24.

prompt for Move command
cell is anchored

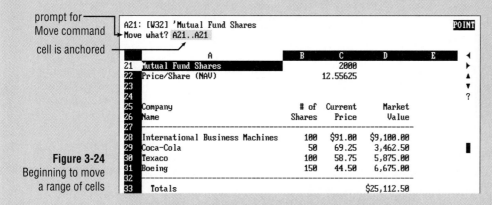

Figure 3-24
Beginning to move a range of cells

You next identify the entire range you want to move (A21 to C22):

❸ Highlight A21..C22. The highlighted area will be moved. See Figure 3-25.

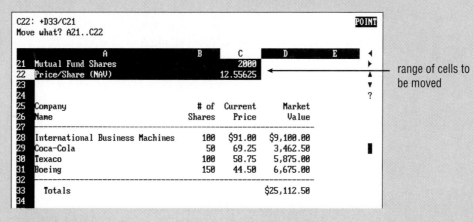

range of cells to be moved

Figure 3-25
Highlighting the range of cells to be moved

❹ Press **[Enter]**.

Now you identify where you want to move this block of cells. Specify the upper left corner of the new location for this block of cells:

❺ Move the cell pointer to A36, the first cell of the "To where?" range. This is the cell where you want the label "Mutual Fund Shares" to begin.

⑥ Press **[Enter]**. The block of cells moves to its new location. See Figure 3-26. Notice that A21..C22 is empty.

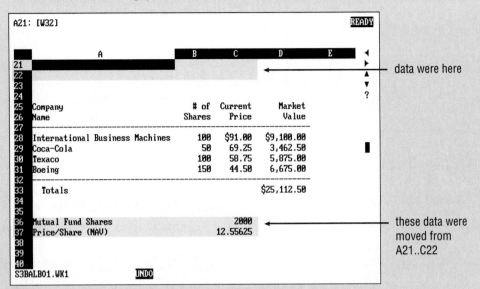

Figure 3-26
Worksheet after
range is moved

When you move part or even all of your worksheet, the worksheet retains all the functional relationships. 1-2-3 automatically adjusts all the formulas in "Move what?" range.

If the UNDO feature is enabled, you can remove the effects of a Move command by pressing [Alt][F4] before executing another command.

When you have completed moving the data, the cell pointer returns to the cell where you started the command.

⑦ Move the cell pointer to the cell that contains the NAV, C37, and examine the formula in the control panel. The formula is now +D33/C36. When the formula was in cell C22, the formula was +D33/C21. 1-2-3 automatically adjusted the formula when the data were moved.

Now you are ready to enter the two-line title: Balboa Equity Fund and Net Asset Value for November 5, 199X.

To enter the title:
① Move the cell pointer to cell A21.
② Type **Balboa Equity Fund** and press [↓].
③ In cell A22 type **Net Asset Value for November 5, 199x** and press **[Enter]**. See Figure 3-27.

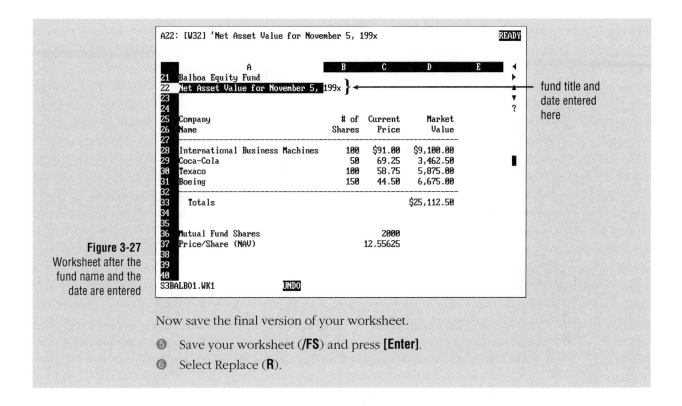

Figure 3-27
Worksheet after the
fund name and the
date are entered

Now save the final version of your worksheet.

⑤ Save your worksheet (**/FS**) and press **[Enter]**.

⑥ Select Replace (**R**).

Erasing a Range of Cells

Now that the worksheet is complete, Pauline thinks about how she will use it on a daily basis. Each day Pauline will enter the current day's price for each company's stock. To make sure that she doesn't accidentally use a price from the previous day, she wants to erase all the prices in the Current Price column before she enters the prices for each day. To erase the prices, she will use the Range Erase command.

To erase the current prices in column C:

① Move the cell pointer to C28, the first cell to be erased.

② Select /Range Erase (**/RE**). The control panel reveals the address of the current cell and prompts you to specify the range you want to erase.

③ Press [↓] to highlight the range C28..C31. See Figure 3-28 on the following page.

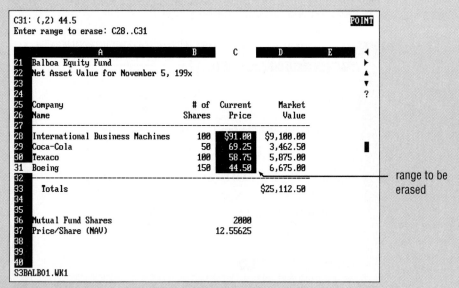

Figure 3-28
Erasing a range of
cells

④ Press **[Enter]**. 1-2-3 erases the entries in C28 to C31. The cell pointer returns to C28, the first cell in the range. See Figure 3-29.

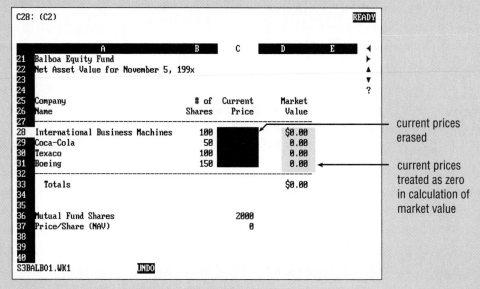

Figure 3-29
Worksheet after the
prices are erased

Notice that the market values are now zero. That is because their values are based on the daily prices, which are blank. 1-2-3 treats the blank cells as zero for any calculations that reference these cells.

Another way to clear a cell is with the [Del] key. You would place the cell pointer in the cell you want to erase and press [Del].

Do not use [Spacebar] to erase the contents of a cell. Use the Range Erase command or the [Del] key.

The worksheet is now ready for Pauline to enter the prices for the next day.

Now that you have completed Tutorial 3, you can read Module 2, *Using WYSIWYG to Enhance and Print 1-2-3 Worksheets* and Module 4, *Using SmartIcons.* Check with your instructor.

■   ■   ■

Exercises

1. Suppose that you have a worksheet in which cells F6, F7, F8, and F9 have values stored in them. Write two different formulas to calculate the total of these four cells.

2. Which formula adds six entries in row 3?
   a. +A3+A4+A5+A6+A7+A8
   b. @SUM(B3..E3)
   c. @SUM(D3..I3)
   d. +M3+N3+O3+P3

3. Suppose you type the value 1005.254 in cell A5. What format type would you select to have the following values appear in the cell?
   a. $1,005.25
   b. 1,005.3
   c. 1005

4. Figure 3-30 shows a worksheet you started typing. You typed the company name, Allied Freight, in cell A3, and the address, 227 Mill St Canton Ohio 13456, in B3. Why does the complete address appear in cell B3 but only Allied Fr in A3?

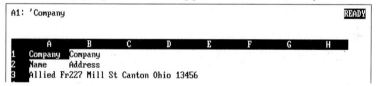

Figure 3-30

5. Figure 3-31 shows part of a worksheet. How would you improve the appearance of this worksheet?   What command(s) would you use?

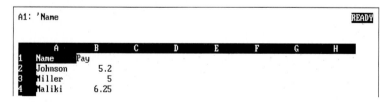

Figure 3-31

6. Retrieve the file E3FILE1.WK1. All the values are currently displayed in the General format. Use the Range Format command to answer 6a through 6d.
   a. Format the values in column C with Fixed format and two decimal places.
   b. Format the values in column D with Fixed format and zero decimal places.
   c. Format the values in column E with Comma format and one decimal place.
   d. Format the values in column F with Currency format and two decimal places.
   e. How are negative numbers displayed for each type of format?

7. Retrieve the file E3FILE2.WK1.
   a. What value was entered in cell A4? B4? C4? D4? E4?
   b. How have the values in the range A4..A6 been formatted? In B4..B6? In C4..C6? In D4..D6? In E4..E6?
   c. Multiply by hand the values displayed in A4 and A5; B4 and B5; C4 and C5; D4 and D5; and E4 and E5.
   d. Compare the results from 7c with the corresponding values in A6, B6, C6, D6, and E6. What conclusion can you draw about how 1-2-3 performs its calculations?

Tutorial Assignments

1. Retrieve the worksheet file T3BALBO1.WK1. The formula in cell C37 is not correct. Price/Share (NAV) shows "ERR" when the worksheet is retrieved.
   a. Explain why ERR is displayed as the value for NAV.
   b. Correct the error.
   c. Save the corrected worksheet as S3BALBO2.
   d. Print the corrected worksheet.

Retrieve the worksheet file T3BALBO2.WK1 and do the following:

2. Adjust two of the labels — Mutual Fund Shares and Price/Share (NAV) — so they are right-justified in their cells, A36 and A37, respectively.

3. Move the values associated with the labels in Tutorial Assignment 2 from cells C36 and C37 to B36 and B37.

4. Format NAV in cell B37 to two decimal places using the Currency format.

5. Print the revised worksheet. Use the print range A21..D37.

6. Save this worksheet as S3BALBO3.

7. Erase the entire worksheet.

8. Retrieve the worksheet file S3BALBO3.WK1.

9. Erase the current prices in the worksheet and then enter the following prices for November 6, 199X: 92, 68.50, 59, and 49. Remember to change the date in the worksheet. Save the worksheet as S3BALBO4. Print the worksheet.

The following exercises involve the worksheet developed in Tutorial 2. Retrieve the file T3KRIER1.WK1 and do the following:

10. In cell B19, use the @SUM function to calculate total hours for all employees.

11. Format the pay rate and gross pay columns to two decimal places using the Currency format.

12. A new employee, Jalecki, has been hired. Insert this name between the names Bramble and Juarez.

13. Save the revised worksheet as S3KRIER1.

14. Print the revised worksheet.

Case Problems

1. Z & Z Electronics Performance Report

Craig Keifer is the general manager of the manufacturing division of Z & Z Electronics. Each year Craig prepares estimated costs for manufacturing cabinets for computers and other electronic equipment. Manufacturing costs include wages/salaries, raw materials, utilities, supplies, and other costs. Craig also prepares a monthly performance report to measure his division's monthly performance compared to his estimate. This report compares the estimated costs with the actual costs for the month just ended and the year-to-date (YTD) cumulative costs. Craig also calculates the difference between estimated and actual costs, called the *variance*, for both the monthly and the cumulative periods. He does this by subtracting estimated costs from the actual costs, in other words,

variance = actual costs – estimated costs

Retrieve the P3PERFRM.WK1 worksheet. This worksheet contains the cost data for the month of March 1992, as well as cumulative costs since the beginning of the year.

1. Calculate the total costs for both the estimated and the actual cost columns (columns B, C, E, and F).

2. Calculate the variances for each cost for both monthly and year-to-date periods (columns D and G).

3. Improve the appearance of the worksheet. Add titles and lines under headings, format values, increase column widths, and make any other changes that will make the report more readable.

4. Save your worksheet as S3PERFRM.

5. Print your worksheet.

WYSIWYG Assignments

1. Attach WYSIWYG.

2. Add the following enhancements:
   a. Remove any dashed lines before you insert solid lines under column headings and above and below totals.
   b. Use a 14-point Swiss font for the report title line(s).
   c. Boldface the column headings.

3. Save your worksheet as W3PERFRM.

4. Print the entire worksheet on one page.

2. Ford Motor Company Car Sales

A Ford executive is preparing a presentation for a local Chamber of Commerce. The executive asks his assistant, Steve Duncan, to prepare a 1-2-3 worksheet with Ford's sales history (units sold) from 1985 to 1988. Steve starts to summarize the data for Ford's three divisions, Ford,

Mercury, and Lincoln, but he becomes ill and cannot finish the assignment. His worksheet file, P3FORD.WK1, is incomplete:

- He has not entered data for the Mercury division, which is shown in Figure 3-32. The data for the Mercury division should be placed between the Ford and the Lincoln divisions.

- Each division's sales need to be subtotaled, and then all three divisions' sales should be added to provide total sales for Ford Motor Company for each year. Only the labels for the subtotals appear in the worksheet.

- Finally, the worksheet must be more professional in appearance before the executive distributes it to the Chamber of Commerce.

Units Sold—Mercury Division				
Mercury Division	**1985**	**1986**	**1987**	**1988**
Topaz	73554	65498	63217	85936
Sable	879	91314	103399	118117
Cougar	118554	112812	110112	102415
Grand Marquis	134139	118364	119015	115141

Figure 3-32

Complete Steve's worksheet by doing the following:

1. Retrieve the worksheet file P3FORD.WK1.

2. Add the data for the Mercury division between the Ford and the Lincoln divisions.

3. Calculate subtotals for each division.

4. Calculate total sales for all the divisions.

5. Improve the appearance of the worksheet. Include a title, the date, and lines under the column headings, align the column headings, and make any other changes you feel are appropriate.

6. Save your worksheet as S3FORD.

7. Print the worksheet.

WYSIWYG Assignments

1. Attach WYSIWYG.

2. Add the following enhancements:
    a. Remove any dashed lines before you insert solid lines under column headings and above and below totals.
    b. Use a 14-point Swiss font for the report title line(s).
    c. Enclose the report title in a box.
    d. Shade the row containing the totals for Total Ford Division.

3. Save your worksheet as W3FORD.

4. Print the entire worksheet on one page.

3. Calculating the Dow Jones Industrial Average

The Dow Jones Industrial Average (DJIA) is the best-known indicator of how stock prices fluctuate on the New York Stock Exchange (NYSE). The DJIA represents the average price of 30 large, well-known industrial corporations considered leaders in their industry. All the companies are listed on the NYSE.

Each day the DJIA is calculated by summing the closing price of each of the 30 companies and dividing by a divisor. The formula for calculating the DJIA is

$$DJIA = \frac{sum\ of\ daily\ closing\ prices\ for\ 30\ companies}{divisor}$$

On December 31, 1991, the DJIA was 3168.83. The divisor was .5593.

Retrieve the file P3DOW.WK1 and do the following:

1. Finish the calculation of the DJIA (cell B43). (Your answer will be within ± .25 of 3168.83.)

2. Experts suggest that changes in higher-priced stocks have a greater impact on the DJIA than changes in lower-priced stocks. For example, if Merck, a high-priced stock, were to increase by 10% (assume no other stock prices change), the new DJIA would change more than if Bethlehem Steel, a low-priced stock, were to increase by 10%.
    a. In column C, labeled Merck's Adjmt, increase Merck's price by 10% (1.10 × current price) and calculate the new DJIA (cell C43).
    b. In column D, the Bethlehem Steel column, increase Bethlehem Steel's price by 10% and calculate the DJIA (cell D43).
    c. Compare the new averages against the original average by calculating the percent change. Use the following formulas:

    For the percent change in column C:

    $$percent\ change = \frac{(Merck\ adjusted\ DJIA\ -\ original\ DJIA)}{original\ DJIA}$$

    For the percent change in column D:

    $$percent\ change = \frac{(Bethlehem\ Steel\ adjusted\ DJIA\ -\ original\ DJIA)}{original\ DJIA}$$

    Note that the original DJIA is in cell B43. How do these new averages compare to the original average?

3. Format your worksheet so it is more readable. Consider formatting values, centering or right-justifying column headings, adding descriptive labels, and making any other changes you think will improve the appearance of your worksheet.

4. Save your worksheet as S3DOW.

5. Print your final worksheet.

WYSIWYG Assignments

1. Attach WYSIWYG.

2. Add the following enhancements:
    a. Remove any dashed lines before you insert solid lines under column headings and above and below totals.

    b.   Use a 14-point Swiss font for the two lines of the report title.
    c.   Change the font of the range A10..D60 to 12-point Dutch font.
    d.   Use a drop shadow to enhance the row containing the DJIA.

3.   Save your worksheet as W3DOW.

4.   Print the entire worksheet on one page.

4. Cash Budgeting at Foreman's Appliances

Jason Ballentine, the business manager for Foreman's Appliances, a small retail appliance store, is in the process of preparing a cash budget for January. The store has a loan that must be paid the first week in February. Jason wants to determine if the business will have enough cash to make the loan payment to the bank.

    Jason sketches the projected budget so that it will have the format shown in Figure 3-33.

Projected Cash Receipts and Disbursements	
January 199x	
Cash balance, January 1, 199x	xxxx
Projected receipts during January:	
Cash sales during month xxxx	
Collections from credit sales xxxx	
Total cash receipts	xxxx
Projected disbursements during January:	
Payments for goods purchased xxxx	
Salaries xxxx	
Rent xxxx	
Utilities xxxx	
Total cash disbursements	xxxx
Cash balance, January 31, 199x	xxxx

Figure 3-33

Next Jason determines that he must perform the calculations in Figure 3-34 to prepare the cash budget.

1.   Total cash receipts during January is sum of cash sales and collections from credit sales.
2.   Total cash disbursements during month is the sum of payments for goods purchased, salaries, rent, and utilities.
3.   Cash balance at the end of the month equals the cash balance at beginning of month plus total cash receipts less total cash disbursements.

Figure 3-34

Finally, Jason plans to use the inputs shown in Figure 3-35 to prepare the cash budget.

Cash balance at beginning of month	32000
Cash sales during month	9000
Collections from credit sales	17500
Payments for goods purchased	15000
Salaries	4800
Rent	1500
Utilities	800

Figure 3-35

Do the following:

1. Prepare a cash budget worksheet based on Jason's information. Enter labels, input values, and formulas.

2. Format the values in the worksheet using the Currency format with zero decimal places.

3. Save your worksheet as S3BUD.

4. Print the projected cash budget.

5. After printing the first budget, Jason remembers that starting this month rent will increase to $1650 a month. Modify the projected cash budget. Print the worksheet with the revised projected cash budget.

WYSIWYG Assignments

1. Attach WYSIWYG.

2. Add the following enhancements:
   a. Remove any dashed lines before you insert solid lines under column headings and above and below totals.
   b. Use a 24-point Swiss font for the first report title line. Use a 14-point Swiss font for the second line.
   c. Boldface the rows with the labels Projected Receipts and Projected Disbursements.
   d. Shade the last row, Cash Balance, January 31, 199X.

3. Save your worksheet as W3BUDGT.

4. Print the entire worksheet on one page.

Tutorial 4

Working with Larger Worksheets

Preparing a Revenue Report

Case: TriCycle Industries

Nick Theodorakis is the assistant sales manager for TriCycle Industries, a recycling center serving the tri-state area of Kentucky, Indiana, and Illinois. For the last two years, TriCycle's sales were not high enough to generate a profit. This year, however, TriCycle has been profitable and has come very close to achieving its sales goals.

As assistant sales manager, Nick services 15 customer accounts, scouts for new accounts, and provides administrative assistance to the TriCycle sales manager, Kay Schilling. At the end of each quarter, Nick assists Kay in preparing a quarterly sales report. Kay then formally presents the report to top management at TriCycle's quarterly meeting.

OBJECTIVES

In this tutorial you will learn to:

- Copy the contents of cells to other locations in the worksheet

- Copy relative cell references

- Copy absolute cell references

- Assign names to cell ranges

- Print with compressed type

Kay meets with Nick to discuss this quarter's report. She shows him the data she has compiled:

TriCycle Industries
1992 Revenue
(000 Omitted)

Recycled Material	First Quarter	Second Quarter	Third Quarter	Fourth Quarter
Plastics	2890	2942	3378	3837
Glass	2701	2862	2869	3601
Aluminum	2247	2282	2489	2602

Kay points out that these data represent the revenue for all four quarters of 1992. She wants to include totals and some additional information to help the top executives compare 1992 revenues to previous years. She asks Nick to create a worksheet using the data she's collected thus far and also showing the following items:

- total revenue by quarter
- total revenue for the year 1992 by recycled material
- total 1992 revenue
- contribution of revenue from each material as a percentage of total 1992 revenue
- average quarterly sales for each material

Nick agrees and offers to give special attention to the appearance of the worksheet, because he knows how important this report will be. Nick spends time thinking about the project and develops a planning sheet and a sketch to assist him in completing the worksheet (Figures 4-1a and 4-1b).

Planning Sheet

My Goal:
   Prepare the sales Report for TriCycle management

What results do I want to see?
   Sales Revenue Report including totals by quarter and recycled material
   Contribution of each recycled material to total revenue

What information do I need?
   Quarterly sales revenue for each recycled material

What calculations will I perform?
   Calculate total revenue for each quarter
   Calculate total revenue for each recycled material for the year
   Calculate total revenue for year
   Calculate percent contribution of each recycled material to total revenue
   Calculate average quarterly sales for each material

Figure 4-1a
Nick's planning
sheet

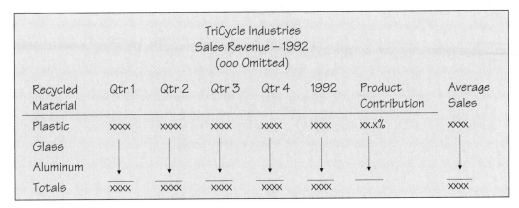

Figure 4-1b
Nick's worksheet
sketch

In this tutorial you will use Kay's data to create Nick's report. You will learn how to copy formulas, a process that saves a great deal of time in creating a worksheet. You will also put to use several valuable 1-2-3 features, such as how to name ranges. You will also learn more about printing with 1-2-3, specifically how to use compressed type to print more data on one line.

Retrieving the Worksheet

Your first step in this tutorial is to retrieve the worksheet that Nick has started based on Kay's data.

To retrieve the worksheet:

1. Retrieve the file C4TRICY1.WK1. See Figure 4-2.

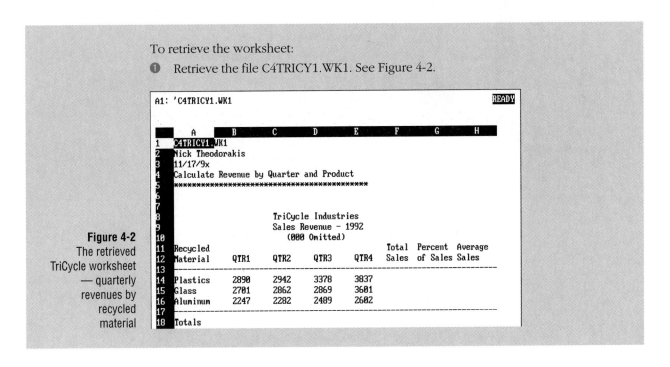

Figure 4-2
The retrieved
TriCycle worksheet
— quarterly
revenues by
recycled
material

This file contains the quarterly revenues of TriCycle Industries categorized by the material they recycle. Titles have been entered, as have revenue amounts for each material for each quarter.

How did TriCycle perform in each quarter? Let's calculate total revenues for each quarter to summarize TriCycle's revenue picture. In Tutorial 3 you used the @SUM function to calculate the total market value of a mutual fund. Now you will use the @SUM function to calculate the total revenue for each quarter.

To calculate total revenue for the first quarter:

① Move the cell pointer to B18.

② Type **@sum(** to begin the formula.

③ Move the cell pointer to B14 and then type **[.]** (Period) to anchor the cell pointer.

④ Press **[↓]** to highlight the range B14..B16. See Figure 4-3.

range of cells to sum

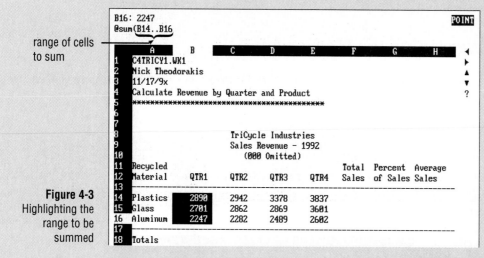

Figure 4-3
Highlighting the range to be summed

⑤ Type **[)]** (Right Parenthesis) and press **[Enter]**. The total revenue in quarter 1, 7838, appears in cell B18. See Figure 4-4.

formula to calculate total revenue in quarter 1

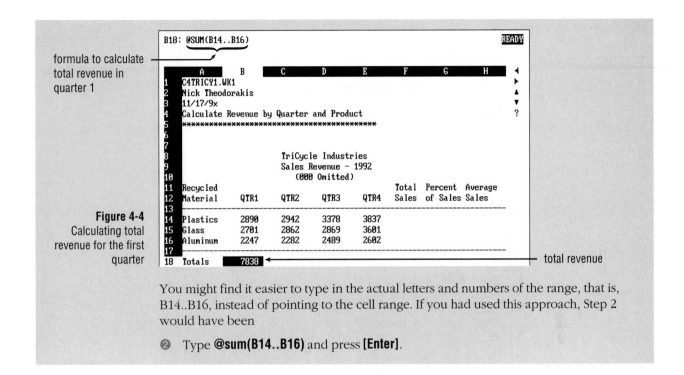

Figure 4-4
Calculating total revenue for the first quarter

total revenue

You might find it easier to type in the actual letters and numbers of the range, that is, B14..B16, instead of pointing to the cell range. If you had used this approach, Step 2 would have been

❷ Type **@sum(B14..B16)** and press **[Enter]**.

Copying Formulas

You can continue to use the @SUM function to calculate total revenues for the remaining quarters. A faster approach, however, is to use the Copy command. Experienced 1-2-3 users rely on the Copy command because it saves time and decreases the likelihood of errors. Let's calculate total revenues for quarters 2, 3, and 4 by copying the formula in cell B18 to cells C18, D18, and E18.

To copy a formula to cells C18, D18, and E18:

First specify the cell or range you want to copy.

❶ With the cell pointer in B18, the cell whose formula will be copied, select /Copy **(/C)**.

The control panel displays B18..B18 as the "Copy what?" range, meaning cell B18 is the cell you want to copy to other cells. See Figure 4-5 on the following page.

formula to
be copied

cells whose
contents you
want to copy

Figure 4-5
Copying a formula

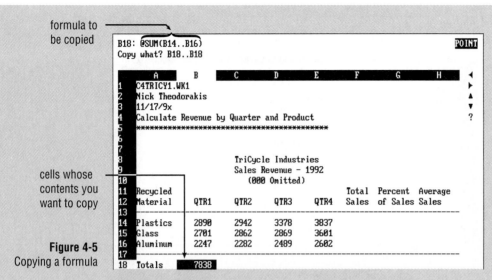

❷   Press **[Enter]**, because B18 is the only cell formula you want to copy. Notice that the control panel text changes and requests the range of cells where the formula is to be copied. See Figure 4-6.

formula to
be copied

cell not
anchored

Figure 4-6
Getting ready to
specify where the
formula will be
copied to

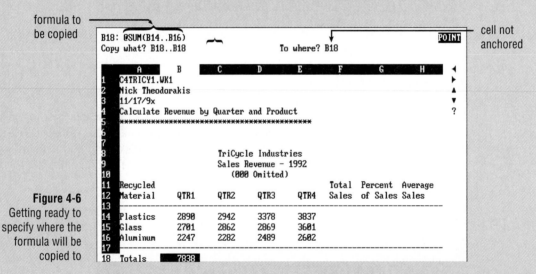

❸   Move the cell pointer to C18, the first cell in the range to which you are copying the formula.

Now anchor this cell pointer.

❹   Press **[.]** (Period) to anchor the cell pointer. This designates C18 as the first cell in the "To where?" range. See Figure 4-7.

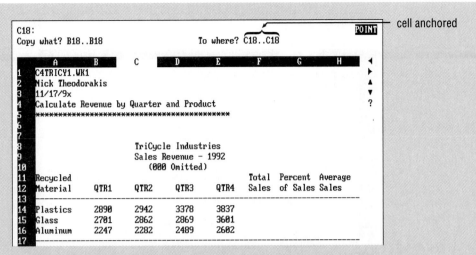

Figure 4-7
Anchoring the cell
pointer

⑤ Press [→] as needed to highlight the range C18 to E18. This is the entire "To where?"
range. See Figure 4-8.

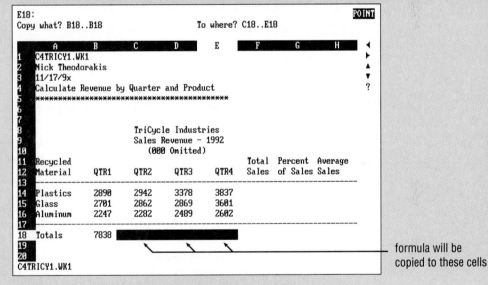

Figure 4-8
Highlighting the
cells where the
formula will be
copied

⑥ Press **[Enter]** to complete the command. See Figure 4-9 on the following page.

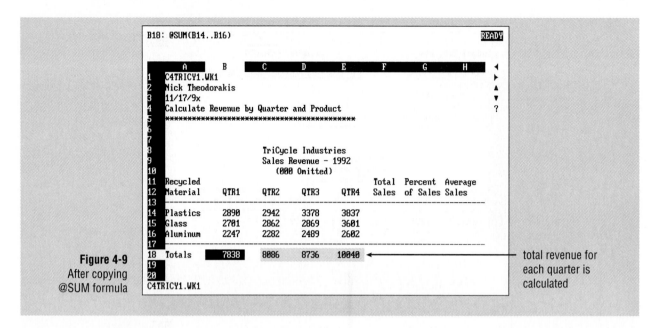

B18: @SUM(B14..B16)   READY

```
              A       B       C       D       E       F       G       H
1   C4TRICY1.WK1
2   Nick Theodorakis
3   11/17/9x
4   Calculate Revenue by Quarter and Product
5   ***************************************************
6
7
8                           TriCycle Industries
9                           Sales Revenue - 1992
10                             (000 Omitted)
11  Recycled                                      Total   Percent  Average
12  Material   QTR1    QTR2    QTR3    QTR4     Sales   of Sales Sales
13  ---------------------------------------------------
14  Plastics   2890    2942    3378    3837
15  Glass      2701    2862    2869    3601
16  Aluminum   2247    2282    2489    2602
17  ---------------------------------------------------
18  Totals     7838    8086    8736   10040
19
20
    C4TRICY1.WK1
```

total revenue for each quarter is calculated

Figure 4-9
After copying @SUM formula

Total revenue for each quarter has now been calculated. You entered the formula for the first quarter and then used the Copy command to copy that formula to the cell locations for quarters 2, 3, and 4.

Understanding Relative Cell References

How 1-2-3 copies a formula depends on whether you use relative cell references or absolute cell references in the formula. The concept of relative and absolute cell references is extremely important to your work with 1-2-3.

A **relative cell reference** is a cell or range of cells in a formula that 1-2-3 interprets as a location relative to the current cell. For example, in cell B18 you have the formula @SUM(B14..B16). 1-2-3 interprets this formula as "add the contents of three cells starting four cells above the formula cell." When you copy this formula to a new location, to cell C18, for example, you copy the relationship between the formula and the cell or range to which it refers. 1-2-3 automatically adjusts the addresses in the copied formulas to maintain the relationship. For example, if you copy the formula @SUM(B14..B16) to cell C18, 1-2-3 would interpret the formula as "add the contents of three cells starting four cells above the formula cell" and would adjust the formula automatically to @SUM(C14..C16).

1-2-3 treats cell references as relative references unless you specify that they are absolute. You will learn about absolute cell references later in this tutorial.

Naming Ranges

Kay also wants to know how much revenue TriCycle earned from recycling each material during 1992. To calculate yearly revenue, you will continue to use the @SUM function. Instead of using cell addresses inside the @SUM function, however, you will use range names in the formulas. Whenever you are working with a large worksheet, you should use descriptive words instead of cell addresses for ranges in a formula. Descriptive words are more meaningful in a formula, since they remind you of the purpose of the calculation. Thus, the formulas are easier to read and understand. 1-2-3 lets you assign descriptive names to individual cells and to cell ranges. You can then use these names in place of cell references when building formulas. For example, the formula @SUM(PLASTICS) is easier to understand than @SUM(B14..E14).

Let's assign range names to the range of cells representing quarterly sales for each recycled material: plastics, glass, and aluminum. Let's also assign a range name to the range of cells representing the four quarterly totals (B18..E18).

To assign the range name PLASTICS to the range B14..E14:

①　Move the cell pointer to B14, the revenue from recycled plastics in the first quarter.

②　Select /Range Name Create (**/RNC**).

You can now enter a range name of up to 15 characters.

③　Type **plastics** and press **[Enter]**. See Figure 4-10.

range name

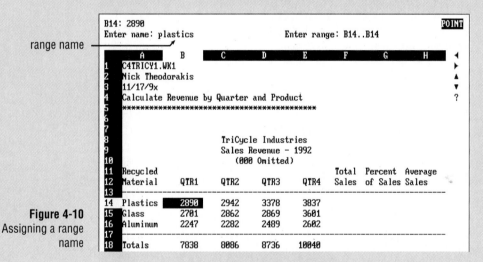

Figure 4-10
Assigning a range
name

```
B14: 2890                                                               POINT
Enter name: plastics                       Enter range: B14..B14

        A      B        C        D        E        F        G        H   ◀
 1  C4TRICY1.WK1                                                          ▶
 2  Nick Theodorakis                                                      ▲
 3  11/17/9x                                                              ▼
 4  Calculate Revenue by Quarter and Product                             ?
 5  ************************************************
 6
 7
 8                    TriCycle Industries
 9                    Sales Revenue - 1992
10                      (000 Omitted)
11  Recycled                                    Total  Percent  Average
12  Material    QTR1     QTR2     QTR3     QTR4  Sales  of Sales Sales
13  _____
14  Plastics    2890     2942     3378     3837
15  Glass       2701     2862     2869     3601
16  Aluminum    2247     2282     2489     2602
17  _____
18  Totals      7838     8086     8736    10040
```

You can use lowercase or uppercase letters. 1-2-3 automatically converts lower-case to uppercase.

④　Press **[→]** to highlight the range B14..E14. You don't need to anchor the cell pointer, because it is automatically anchored when you use the Range Name command.

⑤　Press **[Enter]**. You have just named the range B14..E14 PLASTICS.

Next, assign the range name GLASS to the revenue earned from recycling glass during the four quarters.

To assign the range name GLASS to the range B15..E15:

①　Move the cell pointer to B15, the revenue from glass during the first quarter.

②　Select /Range Name Create (**/RNC**).

③　Type **glass** and press **[Enter]**.

④ Press [→] to highlight the range B15..E15.

⑤ Press **[Enter]**. You have just named the range B15..E15 GLASS.

Now assign the range name ALUMINUM to the revenue received from recycling aluminum materials during the four quarters.

To assign the range name ALUMINUM to the range B16..E16:

❶ Move the cell pointer to B16, the revenue from aluminum in the first quarter.

❷ Select /Range Name Create (**/RNC**).

❸ Type **aluminum** and press **[Enter]**.

❹ Press [→] to highlight the range B16..E16.

❺ Press **[Enter]**. You have just named the range B16..E16 ALUMINUM.

Finally, assign the range name QTR_SALES to the revenue received from recycling all materials during the four quarters.

To assign the range name QTR_SALES to the range B18..E18:

❶ Move the cell pointer to B18, the revenue from all products during the first quarter.

❷ Select /Range Name Create (**/RNC**).

❸ Type **qtr_sales** and press **[Enter]**.

Notice the use of the [_] (Underscore) to connect words; spaces and hyphens are not recommended in range names, because 1-2-3 might misinterpret these symbols.

❹ Press [→] to highlight the range B18..E18.

❺ Press **[Enter]**. You have just named the range B18..E18 QTR_SALES.

If you select the Range Name Create command and then realize you want to highlight a range that starts in another location, press [Esc] to unanchor the cell pointer. Then move the cell pointer to the appropriate starting cell and press [.] (Period) to reanchor the cell pointer.

Range names can be up to 15 characters long, but they should not include spaces or the characters + * – / & { @ and #. The underscore character is often used to connect words together. Do not use range names such as Q1, because 1-2-3 will interpret these names as cell locations instead of range names.

Using Named Ranges in Formulas

Now you are ready to calculate total revenue earned by TriCycle Industries during 1992. In the previous steps, you created the range names PLASTIC, GLASS, ALUMINUM, and QTR_SALES. Assigning names to a range of cells makes formulas easier to create and interpret. You can use range names in formulas two ways: by choosing the one you want from a list of the previously named ranges or by typing the name of the range directly into the formula.

To obtain a list of range names while you are entering a formula, press [F3] (NAME) to display a list of range names created in the current worksheet. Highlight the range name you want and press [Enter]. The range name then is entered into the formula.

To use a range name in an @SUM formula by choosing from a list of range names:

① Move the cell pointer to F14, the cell in which you want total revenues from plastics for 1992 to appear.

② Type **@sum(**.

③ Press **[F3]** (NAME). This function key displays a list of all range names you have created for this worksheet. See Figure 4-11.

list of range names you've created and from which you can choose

Figure 4-11
Listing the range names by using the [F3] key

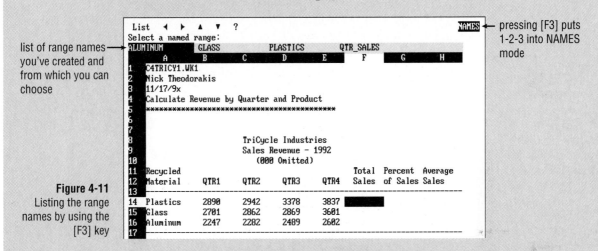

pressing [F3] puts 1-2-3 into NAMES mode

④ Move the cursor to the range name you want, PLASTICS, and press **[Enter]** to select it. Your entry should now look like that in Figure 4-12.

Figure 4-12
Selecting a range name to include in @SUM function

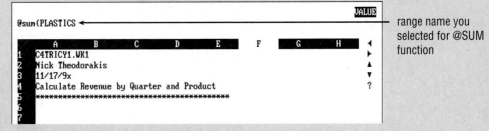

range name you selected for @SUM function

⑤ Complete the formula by typing **[)]** (Right Parenthesis).

⑥ Press **[Enter]**. 1-2-3 calculates the result, 13047, in cell F14. This is the sum of revenues earned from recycling plastics during 1992.

Alternatively, you could have typed in the range name, PLASTICS, directly after the left parenthesis in Step 2 and then omitted Steps 3 through 6. In Step 2 you would have typed **@sum(plastics)** and then pressed [Enter].

Now let's enter the @SUM formulas for glass, aluminum, and quarterly sales.

To continue entering @SUM formulas using the [F3] key:

① Move the cell pointer to F15, the cell in which you want total revenues from glass for 1992 to appear.

② Type **@sum(**.

③ Press **[F3]** (NAME). This function key displays a list of all range names you have created for this worksheet.

④ Move the cursor to the range name you want, GLASS, and press **[Enter]** to select it.

⑤ Type **[)]** (Right Parenthesis) and press **[Enter]**. 1-2-3 calculates the result, 12033, in cell F15. This is the sum of revenues earned from recycling glass during 1992.

⑥ Move the cell pointer to F16. Repeat steps 2 through 5 to enter an @SUM formula using the range name ALUMINUM to total revenue from aluminum in 1992. The result in F16 should be 9620. See Figure 4-13.

⑦ Move the cell pointer to F18. Repeat Steps 2 through 5 to enter an @SUM formula using the range name QTR_SALES to total revenue from all products in 1992. The result in F18 should be 34700. See Figure 4-13.

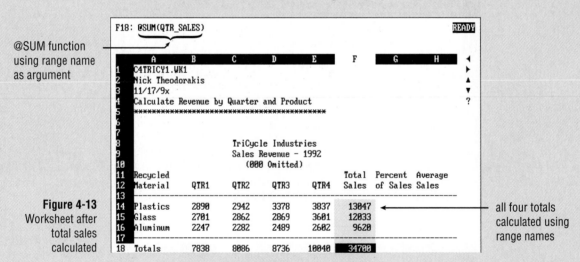

@SUM function
using range name
as argument

Figure 4-13
Worksheet after
total sales
calculated

all four totals
calculated using
range names

If you accidentally press [Enter] before typing the right parenthesis, 1-2-3 automatically beeps and moves to EDIT mode. You should then type [ )] (Right Parenthesis) and press [Enter].

Creating a Table of Range Names

If your worksheet contains several range names, a table containing each range name and its location might be helpful. You use the Range Name Table command to perform this task.

To create a table of range names, you move the cell pointer to the location where you want the range name table to begin. You then select /Range Name Table (/RNT) and highlight the range that will contain the table. Finally, you press [Enter] to complete the command. The range names and their corresponding addresses appear in the worksheet.

Be aware that the range name table is not updated automatically. If you add additional range names after you create the table, you must use the /Range Name command again to update the table.

Deleting Range Names

If you create a range name and then want to delete it, select /Range Name Delete (/RND). A list of the current range names appears in the control panel. Move the menu pointer to the name you want to delete from the list and press [Enter].

Copying Formulas with Absolute References

Nick has now calculated total revenue earned by TriCycle Industries during 1992, as well as individual revenues from plastics, glass, and aluminum. Next, Nick plans to calculate each material's percentage of total 1992 revenue. To calculate each material's contribution to total revenue, you divide the 1992 revenue for each material by total company revenue for 1992. For example,

$$percent\ contribution\ of\ plastics\ to\ total\ revenue = \frac{1992\ revenue\ for\ plastics}{total\ TriCycle\ 1992\ revenue}$$

To calculate the percent contribution of plastics to total revenue:

1. Move the cell pointer to G14.
2. Type the formula **+F14/F18** and press **[Enter]**. The result, 0.375994, appears in cell G14. See Figure 4-14.

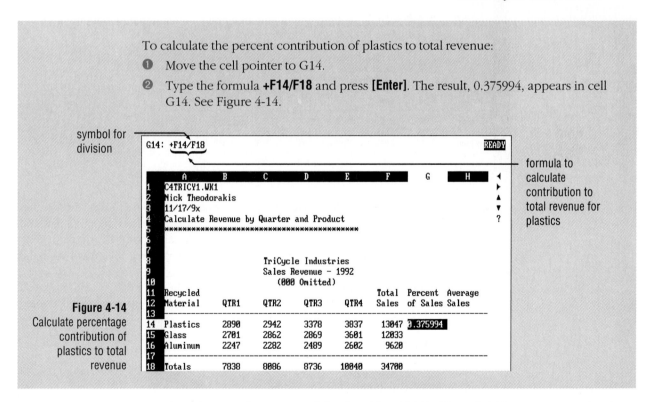

symbol for division

formula to calculate contribution to total revenue for plastics

Figure 4-14
Calculate percentage contribution of plastics to total revenue

Now that you have entered the formula +F14/F18 in cell G14, you can use the Copy command to copy this formula to other cells.

The steps that follow illustrate an approach that leads to incorrect results. We show these steps to demonstrate a common mistake made by many beginning students of 1-2-3, in the hopes of helping you avoid it.

To demonstrate a common mistake:

❶ Be sure the cell pointer is in G14, the cell that contains the formula to be copied. Select /Copy (**/C**). The control panel shows G14..G14 as the "Copy what?" range.

❷ Press **[Enter]**, since G14 is the only cell you want to copy.

❸ Move the cell pointer to G15, the first cell in the range to which you are copying.

❹ Press **[.]** (Period) to anchor the cell pointer. G15 is now the first cell in the range to which you are copying the formula.

❺ Highlight the range G15..G16 and press **[Enter]** to complete the command. Notice that ERR appears in cells G15 and G16. See Figure 4-15.

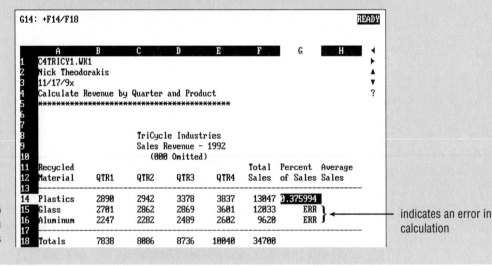

Figure 4-15
Common error in
copying formulas

indicates an error in calculation

Move the cell pointer sequentially to each cell that contains ERR and examine the formula in the control panel. Do you see what happened? The formula in cell G15 is +F15/F19, but what you want in G15 is the formula +F15/F18. You also have an incorrect formula in G16, +F16/F20 instead of +F16/F18. All the copied formulas have resulted in ERR appearing in the respective cells.

Why does ERR appear in these cells? When you copied the formula (+F14/F18) in cell G14, 1-2-3 assumed relative addressing and *adjusted* the cell references in the copied formula. The following formulas resulted:

Cell	Formula
G15	+F15/F19
G16	+F16/F20

When 1-2-3 calculated the glass and aluminum contributions using the formulas in G15 and G16, it tried to divide by zero (the values in cells F19 and F20 are both zero). Since division by zero is undefined, the message ERR appears in cells G15 and G16.

To calculate percentage contribution of each material, you need to use the following formulas:

Recycled Material	Formula	Description
Plastic	+F14/F18	$\dfrac{1992\ revenue\ for\ plastic}{total\ TriCycle\ 1992\ revenue}$
Glass	+F15/F18	$\dfrac{1992\ revenue\ for\ glass}{total\ TriCycle\ 1992\ revenue}$
Aluminum	+F16/F18	$\dfrac{1992\ revenue\ for\ aluminum}{total\ TriCycle\ 1992\ revenue}$

Notice that the cells in the numerators vary (F14, F15, F16), while the cells in the denominators are always the same, F18. When you copy the formula for percentage contribution to other cell locations, the cell addresses of the numerator should change relative to the cell formula. On the other hand, when you copy the cell address of the denominator to other cell locations, the cell address should remain unchanged. Thus, using relative referencing for the entire formula doesn't work. This is an example of a situation that requires absolute cell references.

Absolute Cell References

When you copy a formula, you sometimes want 1-2-3 to keep the original cell addresses in the copied formula. You do *not* want 1-2-3 to adjust the cell references for you. To keep the original cell or range reference constant, no matter where in the worksheet the formula is copied, you use an absolute reference. An **absolute cell reference** is a cell address or range name that *always* refers to the same cell, even if you copy the formula to a new location. To designate an absolute cell reference, you use [$] (Dollar Sign) to precede both the column letter and the row number or range name of the cell you want to remain unchanged. Thus, $F$18 is an absolute cell reference, whereas F18 is a relative reference. Initially, both reference the same cell location; however, if you copy the cell location $F$18 to another cell, the cell address in the new location remains unchanged, whereas if you copy the cell location F18 to another cell, the cell address in the new location is automatically adjusted to reflect its position relative to the original cell location.

To specify absolute cell references, you can either type the $ character before the column letter and row number when you enter (or edit) a formula, or you can use another of the 1-2-3 function keys, [F4] (ABS), the Absolute key. When you press the [F4] key while in EDIT mode, 1-2-3 inserts a $ character at the cursor location in the cell address in the control panel. You could also retype the formula using the $ symbol in the appropriate places, but using the [F4] key is usually faster and helps avoid entry errors.

Before you try using the absolute reference in your formula, let's erase the incorrect formulas in cells G15 and G16 that cause ERR to be displayed. When you type or copy an entry into the wrong cell, you can erase the contents of a single cell by moving the cell pointer to the cell you want to erase and pressing [Del].

To erase a cell using [Del]:

❶ Move the cell pointer to G15, the first cell to be erased, and press **[Del]**.

❷ Move the cell pointer to G16 and press **[Del]**. The formulas are erased from cells G15 and G16. See Figure 4-16.

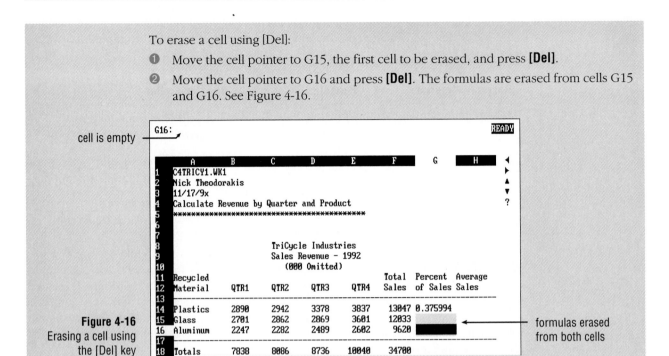

cell is empty

Figure 4-16
Erasing a cell using
the [Del] key

formulas erased
from both cells

Now let's correctly calculate the contributions to total revenue from glass and aluminum.

To use [F4] (ABS) to insert absolute cell references:

❶ Move the cell pointer to G14 and press **[F2]** (EDIT) to display the formula in the control panel. Notice that +F14/F18 appears in the second line of the control panel. See Figure 4-17.

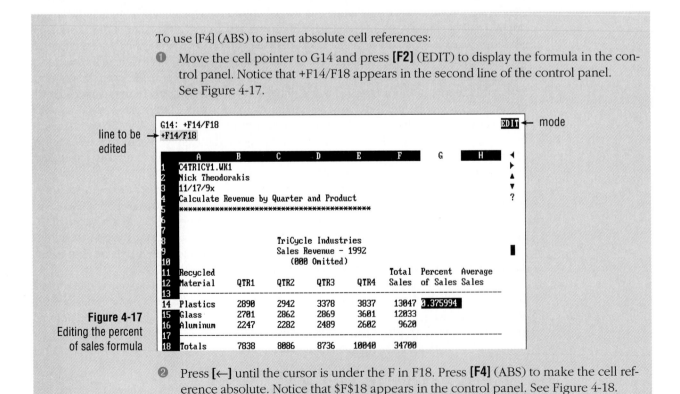

line to be
edited

mode

Figure 4-17
Editing the percent
of sales formula

❷ Press [←] until the cursor is under the F in F18. Press **[F4]** (ABS) to make the cell reference absolute. Notice that $F$18 appears in the control panel. See Figure 4-18.

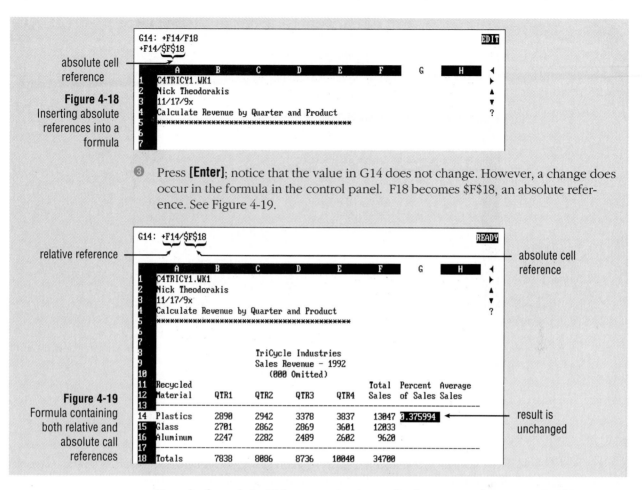

absolute cell
reference

Figure 4-18
Inserting absolute
references into a
formula

③ Press **[Enter]**; notice that the value in G14 does not change. However, a change does occur in the formula in the control panel. F18 becomes $F$18, an absolute reference. See Figure 4-19.

relative reference

Figure 4-19
Formula containing
both relative and
absolute call
references

absolute cell
reference

result is
unchanged

Now the formula in G14 uses an absolute cell reference to reference total 1992 revenues and a relative reference for each material's revenue. No matter what cell you copy the formula in G14 to, the cell reference $F$18 will not change. To demonstrate this process, let's copy the formula in G14 again to see what happens.

To copy G14 to G15..G16:
① Make sure the cell pointer is at G14 and select /Copy (**/C**).
② Press **[Enter]**, because G14 is the only cell you want to copy.
③ Move the cell pointer to G15, the first cell in the range to which you are copying.
④ Press **[.]** (Period) to anchor the cell pointer. G15 is now the first cell into which you want the formula copied.
⑤ Highlight the range G15..G16. This is the range of cells where the formula will be copied.

6 Press **[Enter]** to complete the command. The percent contribution of each material to total sales appears in cells G15 and G16. See Figure 4-20.

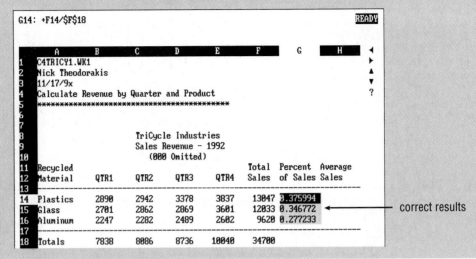

Figure 4-20
After copying
formulas with
absolute reference
to other cells

As a result of the Copy command, the following formulas appear in the control panel when you highlight cells G15 and G16:

Cell	Formula
G15	+F15/$F$18
G16	+F16/$F$18

Normally each material's contribution to total revenue is expressed as a percentage. In the worksheet, however, these values now appear as decimals. Let's change the contribution column so that all values will appear in Percent format. Numbers will then appear as percentages, that is, whole numbers followed by percent signs (%), for example, 15%. 1-2-3 multiplies the decimal number currently in the cell by 100 so that the number becomes a whole number. For example, .05 becomes 5%.

To format a range of cells to Percent format with one decimal place:

1 Make sure the cell pointer is in G14 and select /Range Format (**/RF**).

2 Select Percent (**P**).

3 Type **1** for the number of decimal places and press **[Enter]**.

4 Highlight the cells G14..G16 and press **[Enter]**. See Figure 4-21.

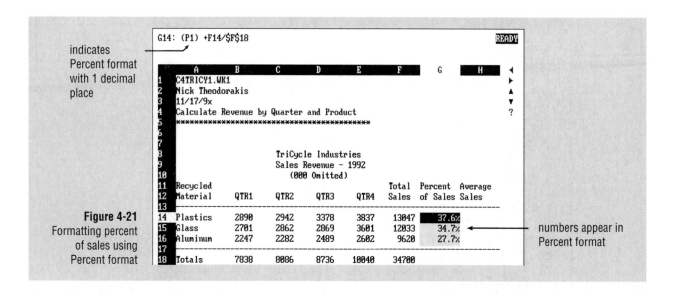

Figure 4-21
Formatting percent of sales using Percent format

indicates Percent format with 1 decimal place

numbers appear in Percent format

Using @AVG to Calculate Average Sales

Nick is ready to calculate the average quarterly sales for each recycled material during the year. To calculate the average, he can use the Lotus 1-2-3 statistical function @AVG. The format for this function is @AVG(*arguments*). The arguments for the @AVG function can be constants, cell references, and ranges.

To calculate the average sales for each material:

① Move the cell pointer to cell H14.

② Type **@avg(plastics)** and press **[Enter]**. See Figure 4-22. The average quarterly sales for plastics is 3261.75.

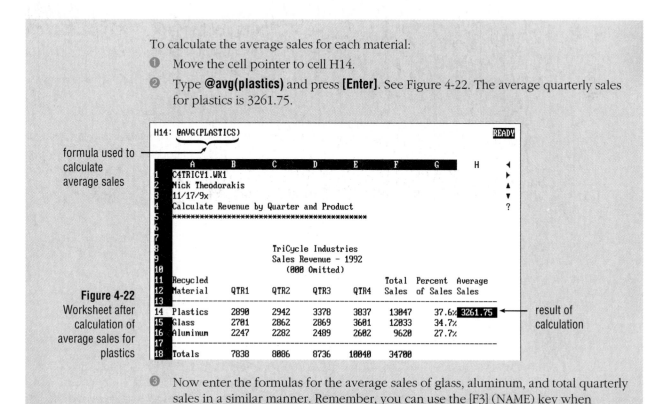

formula used to calculate average sales

Figure 4-22
Worksheet after calculation of average sales for plastics

result of calculation

③ Now enter the formulas for the average sales of glass, aluminum, and total quarterly sales in a similar manner. Remember, you can use the [F3] (NAME) key when entering the @AVG function if you can't recall the range name. When you are finished, your worksheet should look like Figure 4-23.

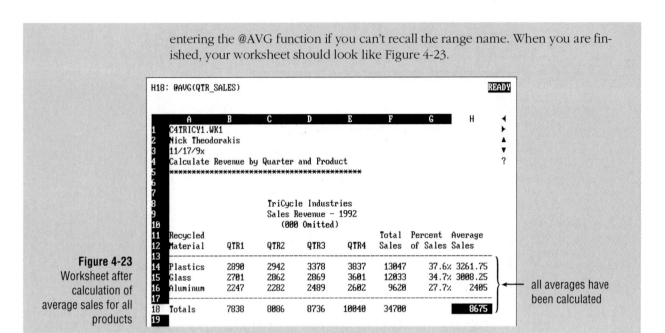

Figure 4-23
Worksheet after calculation of average sales for all products

Finally, let's format the average sales to the nearest dollar.

To format the average sales to the nearest dollar:
❶ Move the cell pointer to cell H14.
❷ Select /Range Format Fixed (**/RFF**).
❸ Type **0** (zero) and press **[Enter]**.
❹ Highlight the range H14..H18 and press **[Enter]**. The average sales are displayed to the nearest dollar.

The calculations are complete. All that remains is for Nick to save the worksheet and print the report.

To change the filename in cell A1 and to save the file:
❶ Press **[Home]** to move the cell pointer to cell A1.
❷ Type **S4TRICY1.WK1** and press **[Enter]**.
❸ Select /File Save (**/FS**). Save the worksheet as S4TRICY1.

Printing with Compressed Type

Larger worksheets are often too wide to fit on one printed page. What do you do if you want to show the entire worksheet on one page for easier interpretation? You can print more data on a page by instructing your printer to use compressed type. **Compressed type** is a smaller and more compact type. As a result, your printer can accommodate a 132-character line length instead of the normal 76 characters per line.

Let's adjust the margins and enter a setup string to print with compressed type. A **setup string** is a code sent to the printer to control the characteristics of the printed output.

Many dot-matrix printers use the code \ *015* to designate compressed type. (If you are using an HP LaserJet printer, the code \ *027(s0p16.66H* instructs the HP LaserJet printer to use a smaller type size. This code is case-sensitive, so make sure you enter it exactly as it appears here.) Check your printer manual or ask your instructor or technical support person for the correct code for your printer.

To set up compressed type for Epson printers:

❶ Select /Print Printer (**/PP**).

❷ Select Options Setup (**OS**) to choose the option to enter the code for compressed type.

❸ Type **** (Backslash) **015** and press **[Enter]** to enter the setup string. \015 may not work for your printer. If it doesn't, ask your instructor or lab assistant for the correct code for your printer.

❹ Select Margins (**M**) from the Options menu and then select Right (**R**). The right-margin option sets the maximum number of characters that can print on one line.

❺ Type **132** and press **[Enter]**. Your Print Settings dialog box should look similar to the one in Figure 4-24.

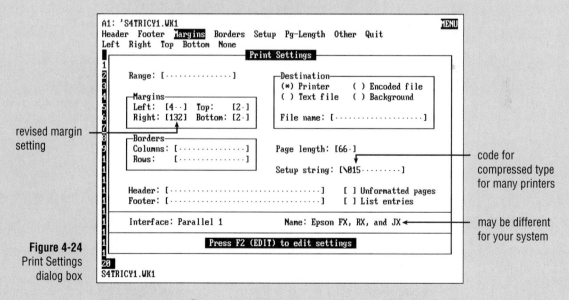

revised margin setting

code for compressed type for many printers

may be different for your system

Figure 4-24
Print Settings dialog box

❻ Select Quit (**Q**) to leave the Options menu, then select Quit (**Q**) again to leave the Print menu.

Now let's print the TriCycle revenue report. Be sure your printer is ready before you begin.

To print the TriCycle report:

① Select /Print Printer (**/PP**).

② Select Range (**R**).

③ Move the cell pointer to A8. Press **[.]** (Period) to anchor the cell pointer.

④ Highlight A8..H18, the cells that contain the report, then press **[Enter]**.

⑤ Select Align Go Page (**AGP**) to print the report. See Figure 4-25.

```
1-2-3 Spreadsheet Computing Series                    Nick Theodorakis




                         TriCycle Industries
                         Sales Revenue - 1992
                            (000 Omitted)

Recycled                                      Total   Percent  Average
Material     QTR1    QTR2    QTR3    QTR4      Sales   of Sales Sales
-----------------------------------------------------------------------
Plastics     2890    2942    3378    3837      13047   37.6%    3262
Glass        2701    2862    2869    3601      12033   34.7%    3008
Aluminum     2247    2282    2489    2602       9620   27.7%    2405
-----------------------------------------------------------------------
Totals       7838    8086    8736   10040      34700            8675
```

Figure 4-25
Final TriCycle
revenue report in
compressed type

⑥ Select Quit (**Q**) to return to READY mode.

⑦ Select /File Save (**/FS**) and save the worksheet again as S4TRICY1.

Printing Checklist

Look at your printed output and check the following:

- **Headings** – Does each listing contain a heading at the top that answers the questions who, what, or where?

- **Columns** – Are all column widths correct? Do any cells contain asterisks, meaning that the values are too wide to appear in the column?

- **Margins** – Are the margins adjusted evenly?

- **Accuracy** – Is all the information correct? Are the numbers accurate? Are all words spelled correctly?

- **Lines** – Do any blank lines appear in unintended places?

- **Appearance** – Is the print legible? Do you need to install a new ribbon or make any adjustments?

Very often you will not be satisfied with your first printing of the worksheet. Fortunately, computers simplify the task of making changes. If necessary, edit your worksheet, save the changes, and print again. Do not hand write corrections.

Printing with Range Names

Range names are often used in printing worksheets. If you are working with a large worksheet and have several different ranges to print, you can assign a range name to each range and then select the appropriate name when specifying the print range.

Clearing the Print Options

There are times when you might want to print more than one report from the same worksheet. For example, in addition to the report just printed, suppose you also wanted to print a summary that included only the total annual sales for each product. This second report would require a different print range and print options. You can use the /Print Printer Clear command to cancel some or all print settings and return the settings to the default settings.

To clear all the print settings:

❶ Select /Print Printer (**/PP**).

Now clear the settings.

❷ Select Clear (**C**).

The *All* option returns all settings to the default settings.

❸ Select All (**A**). See Figure 4-26. Notice that the dialog box indicates all settings have been erased or returned to the default setting.

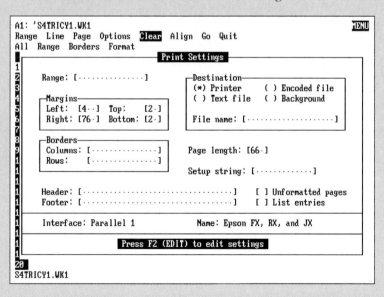

Figure 4-26
All print settings cleared

❹ Select Quit (**Q**) to leave the Print menu and return to READY mode.

Printing with the Borders Option

Nick decides that he also wants to print a summary report that excludes quarterly sales data. Figure 4-27 is Nick's design of this report.

Recycled Material	1992 Sales	Percent of Sales
Plastics	13047	37.6%
Glass	12033	34.7%
Aluminum	9620	27.7%
Totals	34700	

Figure 4-27
Nick's sketch of
summary report

The Borders option of the Print command allows you to add a range from your worksheet to the left side or on top of your print range. You can print row borders, column borders, or both. The column borders let you specify the range that is repeated on the left side of each page. If you specify row borders, the range is repeated at the top of each page.

Remember to exclude the border rows or columns from your print range.

To print the summary report using borders:

❶ Select /Print Printer Range (**/PPR**).

❷ Move the cell pointer to F11 and press **[.]** to anchor the cell pointer.

❸ Highlight the range F11..G18, the range containing total sales, and percent of sales, and press **[Enter]**.

❹ Select Option Borders (**OB**).

You want the column labeled Recycled Material to be a border for this report.

❺ Select Columns (**C**).

Next, indicate the range you want as a border.

❻ Move the cell pointer to A11, press **[.]**, and highlight the range A11..A18. Press **[Enter]**. See Figure 4-28.

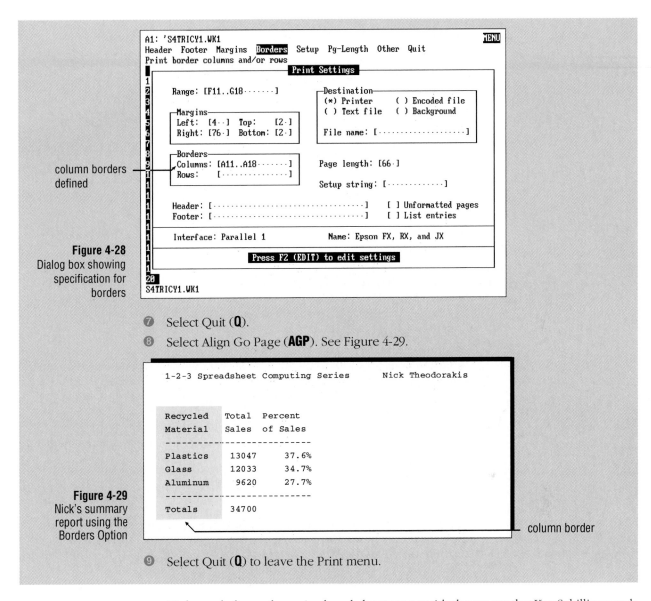

column borders
defined

Figure 4-28
Dialog box showing
specification for
borders

⑦ Select Quit (**Q**).

⑧ Select Align Go Page (**AGP**). See Figure 4-29.

Figure 4-29
Nick's summary
report using the
Borders Option

column border

⑨ Select Quit (**Q**) to leave the Print menu.

Nick now believes the revised worksheet can provide the reports that Kay Schilling needs
to use in her presentations at the quarterly meeting.

■   ■   ■

Exercises

1. Cell D13 contains the formula

    +D10+D11+D12

    After copying this formula to cells E13 and F13, what will the formulas be in cells E13
    and F13?

2. Suppose cell D5 contains the formula

    +A5*$B$5+C5

    What are the absolute and relative references in this formula?

3. Suppose you copy the formula in Exercise 2 to cells D6 and D7.
    a. What will the formula be in cell D6?
    b. What will the formula be in cell D7?

4. Suppose cell B10 has been assigned the range name SALES and cell B11 the range name COSTS.
    a. What formula would you enter in cell B12 to calculate profits using cell addresses?
    b. What formula would you enter in cell B12 to calculate profits using range names?

5. Retrieve the file E4FILE1 and do the following:
    a. Copy the column heading in row 1 to row 11. When you're done, the column heading will be in both row 1 and row 11.
    b. Print the range A1..D11.

6. Retrieve the file E4FILE2. Cell D8 contains the formula to calculate the value of the skates in inventory. The formula used is *units in inventory × unit cost* or (+B8*C8).
    a. Use the Copy command to copy the formula in cell D8 to cells D9..D14.
    b. Print the range A1..D14.

7. Retrieve the file E4FILE3 and do the following:
    a. Write a formula in cell C6 to calculate new salaries for employees based on a percentage increase applied to all employees. The percentage increase is stored in cell C1. The formula in cell C6 references the percentage increase stored in cell C1.

    The formula is *current salary × (1 + percentage increase)*.
    b. Use the Copy command to copy the formula in cell C6 to cells C7..C10. Check your results.
    c. Print the worksheet.
    d. Change the percentage increase to 5%. Print the worksheet.

8. Retrieve the file E4FILE4 and do the following:
    a. Print the 12-month forecast, range A3..M12 without changing the print options.
    b. Clear the print settings, then use the borders option to output the 12-month forecast. Use the range A5..A12 as the column border and B3..M12 as the print range.
    c. Clear the settings and use compressed type to print the range A3..M12.

Tutorial Assignments

Retrieve the worksheet T4TRICY1 and do the following:

1. Assign the range name PRINT1 to the range A8..H20. Print this area using the range name to specify the print range.

2. In cell A21 type the label Range Name Table. Beginning in cell A23 create a range name table.

3. Assign the range name PRINT2 to the range A8..H30. Does the range name PRINT2 appear in your range name table? Why or why not?

4. Save this worksheet as S4TRICY2.

5. Print the worksheet. Print the range A8..H30 using the range name PRINT2 to specify the print range.

Retrieve the worksheet T4KRIER1, a version of the final worksheet from Tutorial 2, and do the following:

6. Use the Copy command to copy the gross pay formula in D11 to the cells of the other employees.

7. Use the Copy command to copy the federal withholding formula (cell E11) to the cells of all other employees.

8. Use the Copy command to copy the net pay formula (cell F11) to the cells of the other employees.

9. Assign the following range names:
   a. GROSS_PAY to cells D11..D14
   b. TAXES to cells E11..E14
   c. NET_PAY to cells F11..F14

10. Calculate total gross pay, total taxes withheld, and total net pay using the @SUM function and the range names you assigned in Assignment 9.

11. Print the worksheet.

12. Save the worksheet as S4KRIER1.
    Retrieve the Balboa Equity Fund worksheet, T4BALBO1, and do the following:

13. Assign the range name FUND_SHARES to cell C36, the number of mutual fund shares, and assign the range name TOTAL_VALUE to cell D33, the total value of the mutual fund.

14. Calculate net asset value (NAV) (cell C37) using the range names in the formula instead of the cell locations.
$$NAV = \frac{TOTAL\_VALUE}{FUND\_SHARES}$$

15. Print the results using the *Borders* option. Use A36..C37 as the print range. Assign A21..A22 as row borders. Save your worksheet as S4BALBO1.

Case Problems

1. Employee Turnover Report

Each month the director of human resources for the public accounting firm of Armstrong, Black & Calzone turns in a report summarizing the number of employees who have left the firm. The data in this employee turnover report are valuable information to the senior partners of the firm, because they want to compare their turnover rates with previous periods and industry averages. If their rates are particularly high, they might decide to investigate the cause of the high turnover. Turnover can result from a variety of reasons, such as noncompetitive salaries, poor managers, lack of training, or poor hiring practices.

Do the following:

1. Enter the data from Figure 4-30 into a new worksheet.

Department	Number of Employees	Number of Terminations
Accounting	50	8
Finance	100	3
Marketing	100	5
Systems	50	12
Manufacturing	150	10

Figure 4-30

2. Calculate the number of employees in the company.

3. Calculate the total number of employees who have left the company (number of terminations).

4. Add a column labeled "Dept. Turnover (%)" and calculate the rate of turnover in each department as a percentage of the number of employees in the department. Use the following formula:

$$rate\ of\ turnover = \frac{number\ of\ employees\ who\ left\ each\ department}{number\ of\ employees\ in\ each\ department}$$

5. Add a column labeled "Company Turnover (%)" and calculate the rate of turnover in each department as a percentage of the number of employees in the company. Use the following formula:

$$rate\ of\ turnover = \frac{number\ of\ employees\ who\ left\ each\ department}{number\ of\ employees\ in\ company}$$

6. Include headings, formatting, and any other changes you think will improve the appearance of the final report.

7. Save the worksheet as S4TRNOVR.

8. Print the worksheet.

WYSIWYG Assignments

1. Attach WYSIWYG.

2. Add the following enhancements:
    a. Remove any dashed lines before you insert solid lines under column headings and above and below totals.
    b. Use a 14-point Swiss font for the report title line(s) and enclose the title in a drop shadow.
    c. Boldface the total row.
    d. Outline the entire report.

3. Save your worksheet as W4TRNOVR.

4. Print the entire worksheet on one page.

2. Leading Restaurant Chains

The managing editor of *Restaurant Happenings*, a weekly magazine, has asked his top writer, Gene Marchand, to research and write a lead article on the sales of U.S. restaurant chains. In researching the story, Gene first determines the U.S. sales for 1988 and 1989 (in millions of dollars) and then totals the number of individual stores in 1989 for each restaurant chain. As the publishing deadline approaches, Gene asks you — the office Lotus 1-2-3 whiz — to help him with this article. Gene wants you to use 1-2-3 to calculate the following four facts:

- industry totals for sales and number of stores
- percentage change in sales between 1988 and 1989 for each restaurant chain
- each restaurant's share of total industry sales in 1989
- average sales per store for each chain in 1989

Do the following for Gene:

1. Retrieve the worksheet file P4RSTAUR.WK1.

2. Calculate the four facts listed above.
   a. Calculate totals for sales in 1988, sales in 1989, and number of stores.
   b. Calculate percentage change in sales for each restaurant chain by using the following formula:

   $$\text{percentage change in sales} = \frac{(\text{chain's 1989 sales} - \text{chain's 1988 sales})}{\text{chain's 1988 sales}}$$

   c. Calculate each chain's share of total industry sales in 1989 by using the following formula:

   $$\text{chain's share of total industry sales in 1989} = \frac{\text{chain's sales in 1989}}{\text{total industry sales in 1989}}$$

   d. Calculate the average sales per store in 1989 by using the following formula:

   $$\text{average sales per store in 1989} = \frac{\text{chain's sales in 1989}}{\text{number of stores in chain}}$$

3. Add titles and dashed lines and format the numeric values to make the worksheet easier to read.

4. Save the worksheet as S4RSTAUR.

5. Print the results.

WYSIWYG Assignments

1. Attach WYSIWYG.

2. Add the following enhancements:
   a. Remove any dashed lines before you insert solid lines under column headings and above and below totals.
   b. Change the first line of the report title to a 24-point Swiss font. Use a 14-point Swiss font for the remaining report title lines.
   c. Boldface and italicize the row that contains totals.

3. Save your worksheet as W4RSTAUR.

4. Print the entire worksheet on one page.

3. Panther Oil Service, Inc.

Evonne Manfred is the owner and bookkeeper at Panther Oil Service, Inc., a small oil delivery and service company. Evonne keeps track of cash receipts using Lotus 1-2-3. Each week Evonne records customers' deliveries and payments in a worksheet.

Do the following:

1. Retrieve the file P4OIL. This worksheet is partially completed. Data on deliveries to customers have been entered, along with column headings for other items to be included in the worksheet.

2. Complete the worksheet by incorporating Evonne's calculations as shown in Figure 4-31.

Calculations

For each customer:

    Amount due = Gallons delivered × cost per gallon

    Balance owed = Amount due − (cash payment + discount taken)

Calculate company totals for:

    gallons delivered

    amount due

    cash payment

    discount taken

    balance owed

Calculate averages for:

    gallons delivered

    amount due

    balance owed

Notes on calculations:

a. Use the @ROUND function to round the <u>amount due</u> and <u>balance owed</u> to nearest cent.

b. <u>Discount taken</u> represents a cash discount taken by customer for prompt payment.

c. <u>Charge per gallon</u> is the same for each customer during the week.

Figure 4-31

3. Enter the customer payment data for the week 2/4/92 to 2/8/92 as shown in Figure 4-32.

Customer	Cash Payment	Discount Taken
Murphy	150.04	3.06
Higgins	50.00	
Belden	178.33	3.64
Breign	80.27	1.64
Connell	206.04	
Sabo	100.00	
Costelle	124.65	2.54
McNeal	163.13	3.33
Williams	191.92	3.92
Dean	54.57	
Daly	144.34	2.95
Walcott	155.84	3.18
Samelson	40.00	
Lishinsky	134.15	2.73
Longo	114.26	2.33

Figure 4-32

4. Improve the appearance of the worksheet: widen the columns, align column headings over numbers, format numeric columns, and add a report title.

5. Save the worksheet as S4OIL.

6. Print a cash receipts report that lists all customer information in the worksheet.

WYSIWYG Assignments

1. Attach WYSIWYG.

2. Add the following enhancements:
    a. Place a box around the Cost per gallon label and amount.
    b. Remove any dashed lines before you insert solid lines under column headings and above and below totals.
    c. Change the font of the first line of the report title to 24-point Swiss.
    d. Change the font of all other lines of the report title to 14-point Swiss.
    e. Boldface the column headings.

3. Save the file as W4OIL.

4. Print the entire report on one page.

4. Exchange Rates and Foreign Operations

As the world becomes "smaller," more and more companies operate in more than one country. A particular challenge for multinational companies is coping with doing business in different currencies. One interesting finance problem involves how to interpret financial results when different currencies are used. Typically, each country reports results in its local currency (dollar, mark, yen, franc, etc.). The challenge is to prepare a report that allows management to compare these results and accurately interpret them. Let's assume that a U.S. publishing company wants all the results of its different divisions converted to U.S. dollars.

Smithson Publishing International has divisions in England, France, Germany, and Italy. Quarterly each division reports data on sales revenue to corporate headquarters in the United States where the data are combined. Each division reports its sales in its local currency (Figure 4-33).

Figure 4-33

	Sales Revenue (Local Currency)			
Period	England (pound)	France (franc)	Germany (mark)	Italy (lira)
QTR1	270197	1943779	1282234	159887439
QTR2	272814	2218784	1385572	213441654
QTR3	346404	2760962	1372975	232303732
QTR4	375395	2711160	1458096	239693192

Since the data are reported in the currency of the local country, Smithson's top executives cannot accurately interpret these numbers. They cannot tell, for example, which division has the highest revenue or which division has the lowest. Thus, a staff assistant, Jim Newman, converts these foreign currencies to U.S. dollars. He collects data on exchange rates, which represent the price of one country's currency in terms of another. For example, if the exchange rate between the British pound and the U.S. dollar is 1:1.8505, for every British pound you would receive 1.8505 U.S. dollars.

Jim keeps track of the exchange rates between the United States and each of the four countries in which Smithson has divisions. At the end of each quarter, he enters the exchange rates into a second table (Figure 4-34).

Figure 4-34

	Exchange Rates			
Period	England (pound)	France (franc)	Germany (mark)	Italy (lira)
QTR1	1.8505	0.1672	0.5773	0.0007818
QTR2	1.7445	0.1613	0.5486	0.0007447
QTR3	1.5740	0.1413	0.5062	0.0006993
QTR4	1.6119	0.1568	0.5316	0.0007301

Using these two tables, Jim can generate a third table, which shows the sales revenue for Smithson's four divisions converted to U.S. dollars.

To convert the sales data to U.S. dollars, each quarter's sales revenue for a country is multiplied by the corresponding exchange rate. For example, in England sales in the first quarter were 270,197 pounds. At the end of the first quarter, the exchange rate between the British pound and the U.S. dollar was 1:1.8505. Therefore, first-quarter sales in England expressed in U.S. dollars would be

$$revenues \times exchange\ rate\ =\ converted\ amount$$

or in this case,

$$270,197 \quad \times \quad 1.8505 \quad = \quad \$500,000$$

Do the following:

1. Retrieve the worksheet P4EXCHNG.WK1. This file contains the data shown in Figures 4-33 and 4-34.

2. Create a third table that shows sales revenue expressed in U.S. dollars categorized by country and by quarter. Use the formula given above for converting currencies.

3. Also include in this table the calculation of total revenue by country.

4. Include in this table the calculation of total revenue by quarter.

5. Add titles and dashed lines, format the values, and make any other changes that will improve the appearance of the worksheet.

6. Save your worksheet as S4EXCHNG.

7. Print the three tables.

WYSIWYG Assignments

1. Attach WYSIWYG.

2. Add the following enhancements:
   a. Create a table (grid) effect for each table.
   b. Draw a double-lined outline around the entire report.

3. Save your worksheet as W4EXCHNG.

4. Print the three tables on one page.

Tutorial 5

Designing Professional Worksheets

Projecting Income

OBJECTIVES

In this tutorial you will learn to:

- Freeze titles
- Use the @IF function
- Protect cells
- Use windows
- Document a worksheet
- Print cell formulas
- Use a one-way data table
- Use the Data Fill command

Case: Trek Limited

Hillary Clarke is an accountant at Trek Limited, a manufacturer of fine luggage that has been in business for 55 years. Hillary works in the controller's office and reports to the controller, Stephan Akrawi. Stephan was so impressed with Hillary's work over the 14 months she has worked for him that he selected her to attend Trek's employee development workshop series.

Today is Hillary's first day back at her regular job after attending the workshop series. She is excited about the many skills she has learned, and she tells Stephan that she'd like to use some of them immediately. She is particularly excited about the workshop called "Financial Planning Using Lotus 1-2-3," because she thinks she can use what she learned to help Stephan with some of his projects. Last year Hillary assisted Stephan in updating Trek's Five-Year Plan, a collection of financial projections that help Trek's department managers make decisions about how to run the company. By making certain assumptions, such as that sales will increase 10% next year, the managers can plan, budget, and set goals accordingly. The plan includes the company's forecasts, or "best guesses," on what sales, expenses, and net income will be over the coming years.

In the past Stephan prepared the plan manually, but this year Hillary wants Stephan to use Lotus 1-2-3. She points out how much more helpful the plan would be if the department managers could perform what-if analyses. Department managers could make different assumptions about the financial data to see what results those assumptions would have on the company's finances. For example, what if sales went down 10% next year instead of up? What would the results be on profits or on expenses? What if the price of cowhide increased 5% over the next two years? How would that affect the cost of manufacturing?

How would it affect profits? What-if analysis using Lotus 1-2-3 could help managers make better decisions. They would not have to face the drudgery of numerous recalculations; they could easily, quickly, and accurately consider different alternatives by changing the data and then having Lotus 1-2-3 recalculate the formulas and totals. Thus, managers would spend more time and creative energy on decision making because they would not have to recalculate formulas and totals every time they asked, "What if?"

Stephan agrees with Hillary about using Lotus 1-2-3. He gives her the latest data that the accounting department prepared for 1992 (Figure 5-1). They agree that Hillary should design a Lotus 1-2-3 worksheet that reflects the Trek planning process. Then together they will perform some what-if analysis and show the department managers how they can use what-if analysis with 1-2-3.

Trek Limited Income Statement

	1992	Percent of Sales
Sales	$150,000	
Variable Costs:		
Manufacturing	75,000	50%
Selling	15,000	10%
Administrative	6,000	4%
Total Variable Cost	96,000	
Fixed Costs:		
Manufacturing	10,000	
Selling	20,000	
Administrative	5,000	
Total Fixed Cost	35,000	
Net income before taxes	19,000	
Income taxes	4,750	
Net income after taxes	$14,250	

Figure 5-1
Trek's accounting
department data

Hillary spends time studying the accounting department's data and begins to create her planning sheet (Figure 5-2a). After writing down her goal and her desired results, she considers what information she needs. She knows that, generally, the sales estimate is used as the starting point for projecting income. Why? Because production and selling are geared to the rate of sales activity.

My Goal:
    Develop a worksheet that easily tests alternative scenarios to help develop
    a five-year plan for Trek Limited

What results do I want to see?
    Projected income statements for 1993 to 1997

What information do I need?
    Information that can be changed:
        Sales estimate for 1993
    Information that remains unchanged:
        Annual growth rate in sales   (10%)
        Ratio of manufacturing costs to sales   (50%)
        Ratio of selling costs to sales   (10%)
        Ratio of administrative costs to sales   (4%)
        Fixed manufacturing costs   ($10)
        Fixed selling costs   ($20)
        Fixed administrative costs   ($5)

What calculations will I perform?
    1. sales first year = sales estimate for 1993
    2. sales subsequent years = previous year's sales × 110%
    3. variable manufacturing costs = 50% × sales estimate
    4. variable selling costs = 10% × sales estimate
    5. variable administrative costs = 4% × sales estimate
    6. total variable costs = variable manufacturing costs +
                                variable selling costs +
                                variable administrative costs
    7. total fixed costs =   fixed manufacturing costs ($10) +
                                fixed selling costs ($20) +
                                fixed administrative costs ($5)
    8. net income before taxes = sales – total variable costs – total fixed costs
    9. taxes = 25% × net income before taxes
    10. net income after taxes = net income before taxes – taxes

Figure 5-2a
Hillary's planning
sheet

Hillary decides to start her projections for 1993 sales at the same level as 1992, although she knows the managers will change this during their what-if analysis. Stephan suggests she build in a 10% increase per year in sales for 1994 to 1997. He believes sales will go up 10% annually as a result of a new line of luggage Trek Limited plans to introduce in 1993.

After looking at the sales side, Hillary turns her attention to costs. She must look at both variable costs and fixed costs. Variable costs are those that change in direct proportion to related volume. For instance, as sales volume goes up, variable costs such as materials, assembly labor, and sales commissions also go up. Fixed costs are costs that remain unchanged despite changes in related volume. For example, rent, property taxes, executive salaries, and insurance remain the same even when sales go up.

Once again, Hillary refers to the accounting department data in Figure 5-1. She decides to use the variable-cost percentages as the basis for calculating variable costs. For example, if sales were $200,000, the variable manufacturing costs would be calculated at 50% of sales, or $100,000. She also decides to use the fixed costs shown in the accounting data.

Next, Hillary considers the final group of calculations, net income. To calculate net income before taxes, Hillary calculates the difference between sales and the total of variable and fixed costs. She assumes taxes will be 25% of net income before taxes. Finally, she calculates net income after taxes, that is, net income before taxes minus income taxes.

Figure 5-2b is a sketch of how Hillary wants her worksheet to look. In this tutorial you will use Hillary's planning sheet and sketch to learn how to freeze titles, protect specified data, split screens, design and document your worksheet, and make use of data tables to ask what-if questions.

Trek Limited
Projected Income Statement
(000 omitted)

	1993	1994	1995	1996	1997
Sales	xxx	.	.	.	.
Variable Costs:		.	.	.	.
Manufacturing	xxx	.	.	.	.
Selling	xxx	.	.	.	.
Administrative	xxx	.	.	.	.
Total Variable Costs	xxx	xxx	xxx	xxx	xxx
Fixed Costs:					
Manufacturing	xxx	.	.	.	.
Selling	xxx	.	.	.	.
Administrative	xxx	.	.	.	.
Total Fixed Costs	xxx	xxx	xxx	xxx	xxx
Net Income Before Taxes	xxx	.	.	.	.
Income taxes	xxx	.	.	.	.
Net Income After Taxes	xxx	xxx	xxx	xxx	xxx

Figure 5-2b
Hillary's worksheet
sketch

Retrieving the Worksheet

Before you follow through on Hillary's plan, you will retrieve the worksheet she built based on her planning sheet and worksheet sketch and practice using the what-if capability of 1-2-3.

To retrieve the worksheet:

1. Select /File Retrieve (**/FR**).
2. Highlight the file C5TREK1.WK1. Press **[Enter]**.
3. Press **[PgDn]** to view the Projected Income Statement.

This worksheet contains the projected income statement for Trek Limited for the years 1993 to 1997 (Figure 5-3). All values are shown in thousands. For example, sales in 1993 are shown as 150, which represents $150,000. Also note that to simplify the numbers in this worksheet the cells were formatted to display zero decimal places. As a result, some totals do not appear to be correct. This is because the data are rounded whenever they appear on the screen.

```
                          Trek Limited
                  Projected Income Statement
                        (000 omitted)

                      1993    1994    1995    1996    1997
                    -----------------------------------------
Sales                 150     165     182     200     220
Variable Costs:
   Manufacturing       75      83      91     100     110
   Selling             15      17      18      20      22
   Administrative       6       7       7       8       9
                    -----------------------------------------
   Total Variable Costs 96    106     116     128     141

Fixed Costs:
   Manufacturing       10      10      10      10      10
   Selling             20      20      20      20      20
   Administrative       5       5       5       5       5
                    -----------------------------------------
   Total Fixed Costs   35      35      35      35      35

Net Income Before Taxes 19     24      30      37      44
Income Taxes            5       6       8       9      11
                    -----------------------------------------
Net Income After Taxes 14      18      23      28      33
                    =========================================
```

area of worksheet that appears on your screen

Figure 5-3 Contents of the entire worksheet

Demonstrating the What-If Feature

To demonstrate 1-2-3's what-if capability using Hillary's worksheet, let's suppose that you increase the sales estimate for 1993 from $150,000 (entered as 150) to $175,000 (entered as 175).

To use the what-if capability:

❶ Move the cell pointer to cell B28, sales for 1993.

❷ Type **175** and press **[Enter]**. Watch how the sales, costs, and net incomes change as a result of the change to 1993 sales. See Figure 5-4.

changed sales estimate

these costs are calculated as a percentage of sales

these costs remain fixed

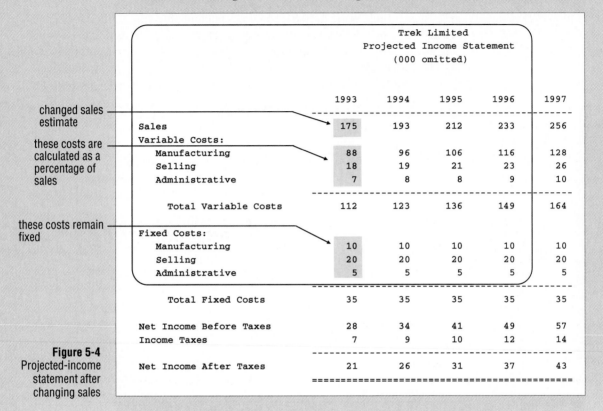

Figure 5-4
Projected-income
statement after
changing sales

Since the sales estimate for 1993 increased from 150 to 175, the variable costs, which are calculated as a percentage of sales, also increased. Net income also changed, since both sales and variable costs changed. The fixed costs, however, did not change.

The sales estimates for 1994 through 1997 also increased. Because sales are estimated to grow at 10% each year, changing the starting sales estimate for 1993 changes the sales for 1994 through 1997.

Scrolling on Large Worksheets **L 151**

Scrolling on Large Worksheets

Notice that the entire income statement does not fit on the screen — you cannot see the information for 1997. Also, the rows that follow "Administrative" in Hillary's worksheet sketch do not appear on the screen, even though she has typed them into her worksheet. To view this information, you use the cursor-movement keys to scroll down the screen. *Scrolling* is a way to view all parts of a large worksheet that cannot fit on one screen. For example, when you scroll down, a row previously unseen appears at the bottom of the screen and the row at the top disappears.

To scroll Hillary's worksheet:

❶ Press **[PgDn]** until Net Income After Taxes appears on the screen. Note that the column headings no longer appear on the screen. See Figure 5-5.

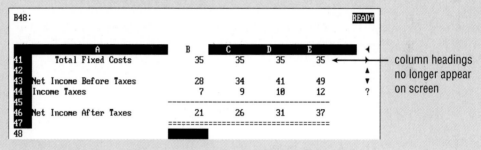

Figure 5-5
Scrolling Hillary's
worksheet

❷ Now move the cell pointer to cell A21.

The planning period for the company is 1993 to 1997, but 1997 does not appear on the screen. Let's scroll to the right to view the 1997 projections.

To scroll to the right:

❶ Press **[→]** until the 1997 column appears. Notice that the descriptive labels no longer appear on the left of the screen. This makes the worksheet data difficult to interpret. See Figure 5-6 on the following page.

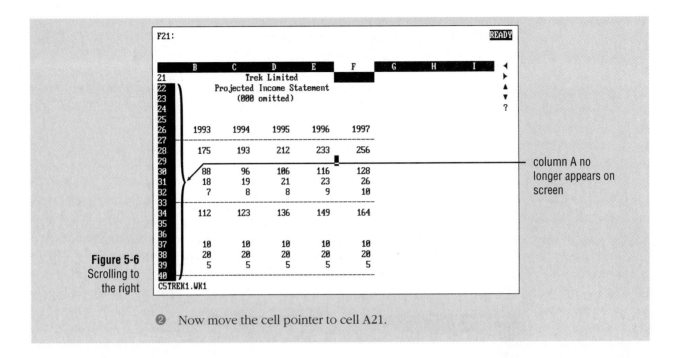

Figure 5-6
Scrolling to
the right

❷ Now move the cell pointer to cell A21.

Freezing Titles

As you move the cell pointer around a worksheet that is larger than the screen, you may find it difficult to remember row and column labels that may have disappeared. The Title command helps you keep your place on a large worksheet by "freezing" row and column titles on the screen; the titles then remain on the screen as you move within the worksheet. The Titles command allows you to freeze rows, columns, or both. If you choose *Horizontal*, you freeze all rows above the cell pointer on the screen. If you choose *Vertical*, you freeze all columns to the left of the cell pointer. If you choose *Both*, you freeze all rows above and all columns to the left of the cell pointer. In the next steps, you will freeze both the worksheet column headings and the account titles.

To freeze titles:
❶ Be sure cell A21 is in the upper left corner of the worksheet. Move the cell pointer to cell B28, the location below and to the right of the cells you want to remain on the screen.
❷ Select /Worksheet Titles (**/WT**). Your control panel should look like Figure 5-7.

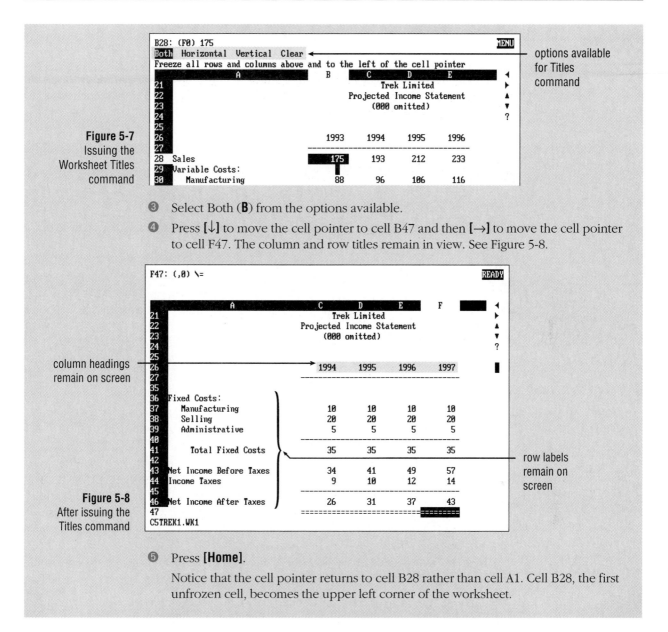

Figure 5-7
Issuing the
Worksheet Titles
command

③ Select Both (**B**) from the options available.

④ Press [↓] to move the cell pointer to cell B47 and then [→] to move the cell pointer to cell F47. The column and row titles remain in view. See Figure 5-8.

column headings
remain on screen

row labels
remain on
screen

Figure 5-8
After issuing the
Titles command

⑤ Press **[Home]**.

Notice that the cell pointer returns to cell B28 rather than cell A1. Cell B28, the first unfrozen cell, becomes the upper left corner of the worksheet.

Unfreezing Titles

Once you freeze an area of the worksheet, you cannot move the cell pointer into that area while you are in READY mode. You can, however, use the [F5](GoTo) key to move the cell pointer into the frozen area so you can make any changes to the headings or row labels.

If you need to unfreeze titles, you would select the command /Worksheet Titles Clear (/WTC). You would then be able to move the cell pointer into any area of the worksheet.

@IF Function

Now you are ready to follow Hillary's plan. The first thing Hillary wants to do is to see the effect of a poor sales year on net income. She assumes sales will be $75,000 (entered as 75) instead of $150,000 (entered as 150).

To consider the relationship between poor sales and income:

❶ Be certain the cell pointer is in cell B28.

❷ Type **75**. Press **[Enter]**.

❸ Move the cell pointer to cell B47 and look at the values in the rows for income taxes and net income after taxes. See Figure 5-9.

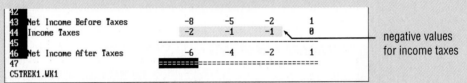

Figure 5-9
Incorrect calculations for income taxes

negative values for income taxes

Notice that income taxes appear as negative values for 1993, 1994, and 1995. This is not correct. Taxes should be zero whenever the net income before taxes is less than zero. How can we correct this?

❹ Move the cell pointer to cell B44. Look at the control panel and observe that the formula for calculating income taxes is +B43*0.25 (25% of net income before taxes). This formula is correct as long as net income before taxes is a positive number. If net income before taxes is a negative number, the worksheet should set income taxes equal to zero, not a negative value. What went wrong? Hillary represented the relationship between net income before taxes and income taxes incorrectly when she built her worksheet.

There are many situations where the value you store in a cell depends on certain conditions, for instance:

- An employee's gross pay may depend on whether that employee worked overtime.
- A taxpayer's tax rate depends on his or her taxable income.
- A customer's charge depends on whether the size of the order entitles that customer to a discount.

In 1-2-3 the @IF function allows you to make comparisons to determine which actions 1-2-3 should take. The @IF function has the following format:

@IF(*condition,true expression,false expression*)

The parenthetic expression can be interpreted to mean that if the condition is true, 1-2-3 is to execute the true expression; otherwise, it is to execute the false expression.

The @IF function has three components:

- A *condition* is a logical expression that represents a comparison between quantities. This comparison results in a value that is either true, indicated by a value of 1, or false, indicated by a value of 0.
- A *true expression* is a value or label stored in a cell if the condition is true.
- A *false expression* is a value or label stored in a cell if the condition is false.

An example may help to illustrate the format of an @IF function. Suppose you needed to determine whether an employee earned overtime pay, that is, whether he or she worked more than 40 hours in a week. This can be expressed as:

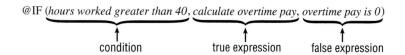

In this example, the condition is the comparison between the hours an employee works and 40 hours. The true expression is executed if an employee works more than 40 hours; then the condition is true and overtime pay is calculated. The false expression is executed if an employee works 40 hours or less; then the condition is false and overtime pay is 0.

The most common condition, a simple condition, is a comparison between two expressions. An **expression** may be a cell or range reference, a number, a label, a formula, or another @function. Besides expressions, a condition contains a comparison operator. A **comparison operator** indicates a mathematical comparison, such as less than or greater than. Figure 5-10 shows the comparison operators allowed in 1-2-3.

Type of Comparison	1-2-3 Symbol
Less than	<
Greater than	>
Less than or equal to	<=
Greater than or equal to	>=
Equal to	=
Not equal to	<>

Figure 5-10
Examples of comparison operators

A comparison operator is combined with expressions to form a condition. For example, say the hours worked are stored in cell D10; then the condition "*the number of hours worked is greater than 40*" would be expressed in 1-2-3 as @IF(D10>40...). Figure 5-11 on the following page illustrates several examples of conditional situations and how they can be expressed in 1-2-3.

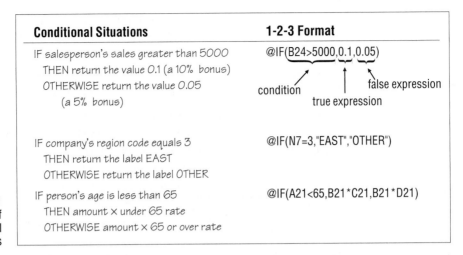

Figure 5-11
Examples of
conditional
situations

Conditional Situations	1-2-3 Format

IF salesperson's sales greater than 5000
   THEN return the value 0.1 (a 10% bonus)
   OTHERWISE return the value 0.05
      (a 5% bonus)
	@IF(B24>5000,0.1,0.05)
	condition true expression false expression

IF company's region code equals 3
   THEN return the label EAST
   OTHERWISE return the label OTHER
	@IF(N7=3,"EAST","OTHER")

IF person's age is less than 65
   THEN amount × under 65 rate
   OTHERWISE amount × 65 or over rate
	@IF(A21<65,B21*C21,B21*D21)

Let's now use the @IF function to correct Hillary's worksheet.

To use the @IF function to determine taxes:

❶ Make sure the cell pointer is in cell B44.

❷ Type **@if(b43>0,0.25*b43,0)** and press **[Enter]**. See Figure 5-12.

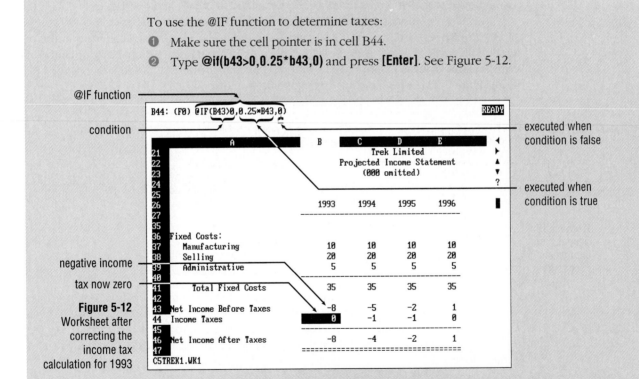

Figure 5-12
Worksheet after
correcting the
income tax
calculation for 1993

Do not include any spaces when you type this or any other @function and be sure
to separate each component with a comma. You can interpret this function as

IF the value in cell B43 is greater than 0
   THEN return the value .25*B43 to cell B44
   OTHERWISE return the value 0 to cell B44

Now let's copy this function to cells C44 through F44 so the correct formulas to calculate income taxes for the years 1994 to 1997 can be included in the worksheet.

To copy the function to cells C44..F44:

❶ Make sure the cell pointer is in cell B44.

❷ Select /Copy (**/C**). Press **[Enter]** since you are copying only the function in cell B44.

❸ Move the cell pointer to C44 and press **[.]** to anchor the cell pointer.

❹ Highlight the range C44..F44. Press **[Enter]**.

Notice that taxes are now zero. See Figure 5-13.

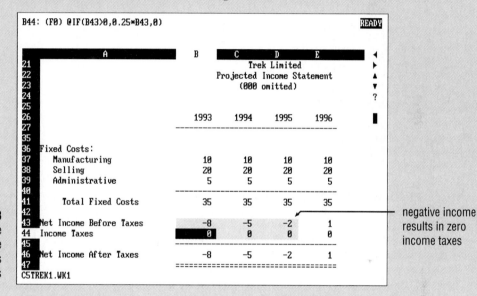

Figure 5-13
Worksheet after the corrected income tax calculation is copied to all cells

In addition to making changes to sales estimates, Hillary decides she wants to see how changes in the ratio of variable manufacturing costs to sales affects net income. To make this change, Hillary must change the formula for each cell that references variable manufacturing costs (B30, C30, D30, E30, F30). For example, she wants to change variable manufacturing costs from 50% to 52% of sales.

To change constants in a formula:

❶ Move the cell pointer to cell B30.

❷ Press **[F2]** (EDIT) to invoke EDIT mode.

❸ Change 0.5 to 0.52 and press **[Enter]**. The formula appears in the control panel as 0.52*B28, and the variable manufacturing costs in 1993 are 39.

Now copy the formula to C30..F30, where the formulas for variable manufacturing costs for the years 1994 to 1997 are located.

To copy the formula to C30..F30:

❶ With the cell pointer in B30, select /Copy (**/C**). Press **[Enter]**.

❷ Move the cell pointer to C30. Press **[.]** to anchor the cell pointer.

❸ Highlight C30..F30. Press **[Enter]**. See Figure 5-14.

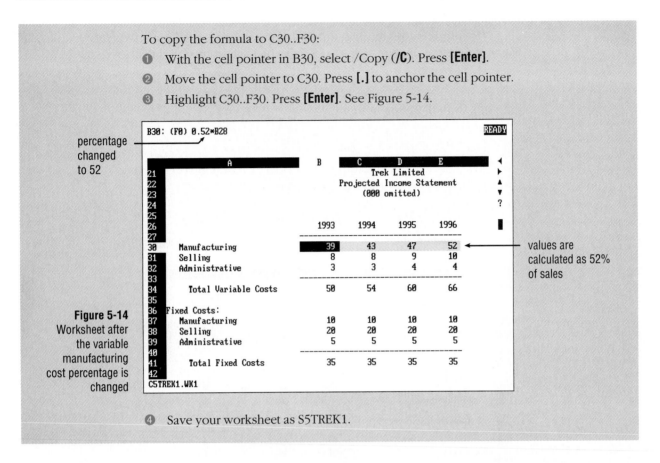

percentage
changed
to 52

Figure 5-14
Worksheet after
the variable
manufacturing
cost percentage is
changed

values are
calculated as 52%
of sales

❹ Save your worksheet as S5TREK1.

To change variable selling costs from 10% to 11% requires a similar process. But is there a way to change the variable costs that takes less time and avoids the possibility of errors that can occur with so many changes? Hillary thinks about how to revise the worksheet. She realizes that the more she uses numeric constants in her formulas, the less flexibility she has if she wants to change those values. Thus, she decides to completely revise her worksheet. She prepares a new plan and worksheet sketch. Figure 5-15 shows her revised plan, which includes these major changes:

- dividing the worksheet into three sections to clarify tasks — documentation, input, and calculation/output
- providing managers with five variables instead of one on which they can perform what-if analysis
- replacing constants in formulas with range names, such as GROWTH, that reference cells in the input area
- including the @ROUND function in formulas to avoid rounding errors

Now you can retrieve the new worksheet that Hillary has built.

My Goal:
  Develop a worksheet that easily tests alternative scenarios to help
  develop a five-year plan for Trek Limited

What results do I want to see?
  Projected income statements for 1991 to 1995

What information do I need?
  Information that can be changed:
    Sales estimate for 1991
  Information that remains unchanged:
    Annual growth rate in sales (10%)
    Ratio of manufacturing costs to sales (50%)
    Ratio of selling costs to sales (10%)
    Ratio of administrative costs to sales (4%)
    Fixed manufacturing costs ($10)
    Fixed selling costs ($20)
    Fixed administrative costs ($5)

Hillary now wants
to change this
information

What calculations will I perform?
  1. sales first year = sales estimate for 1991

  2. sales subsequent years = previous year's sales × 110%
      Sales growth rate

  3. variable manufacturing costs = 50% × sales estimate
      ratio of manufacturing costs to sales

  4. variable selling costs = 10% × sales estimate
      ratio of selling costs to sales

  5. variable administrative costs = 4% × sales estimate
      ratio of administrative costs to sales

  6. total variable costs = variable manufacturing costs +
                              variable selling costs +
                              variable administrative costs

  7. total fixed costs =   fixed manufacturing costs ($10) +
                             fixed selling costs ($20) +
                             fixed administrative costs ($5)

  8. net income before taxes = sales - total variable costs - total fixed costs

  9. *If net income before taxes > 0 then*
      taxes = 25% × net income before taxes
      Otherwise taxes = 0

Hillary will make
this a conditional
statement

  10. net income after taxes = net income before taxes - taxes

Figure 5-15
Hillary's revised
planning sheet

To retrieve a file:

❶ Select /File Retrieve (**/FR**).

❷ Highlight C5TREK2.WK1 and press **[Enter]**.

Notice in Figure 5-16 that Hillary has divided her new worksheet into three sections: documentation, input, and calculation/output. The **documentation section** contains information about the worksheet. Typically this section consists of the title of the worksheet, the filename, the name of the developer, the date it was prepared, the date it was last modified, and the purpose of the worksheet. Additional documentation might include information about the layout of various sections within the worksheet, the names and locations of named ranges, and instructions to the user. The most common location for the documentation section is the top left corner of the worksheet, where the information is immediately displayed when the worksheet is loaded.

A second section, the **input section**, contains the variables used in formulas that are likely to change. Sometimes the input section is said to contain the worksheet's *assumptions*, because the results of the worksheet are based on the values in the input section. For example, in Hillary's worksheet, the input section lists the variables a manager at Trek can change. The manager can ask what-if questions by changing the values in the input section and observing the changes in the projected-income statement. The values in the projected-income statement change because the formulas that calculate projected-income reference the cells in the input area.

A third section, the **calculation/output section**, performs the calculations. This section includes formulas and fixed data. In Hillary's case this section contains the formulas to calculate projected income over the five-year period. The formulas do not contain constants; instead they reference cells in the input area. The formulas often include range names to clarify their meanings.

Some worksheets divide the calculation/output section into separate sections. In those worksheets the output section summarizes the results from the calculation section and places them near the input section. That way you can immediately view the results of changing input values without having to search for this information in a different area of the worksheet.

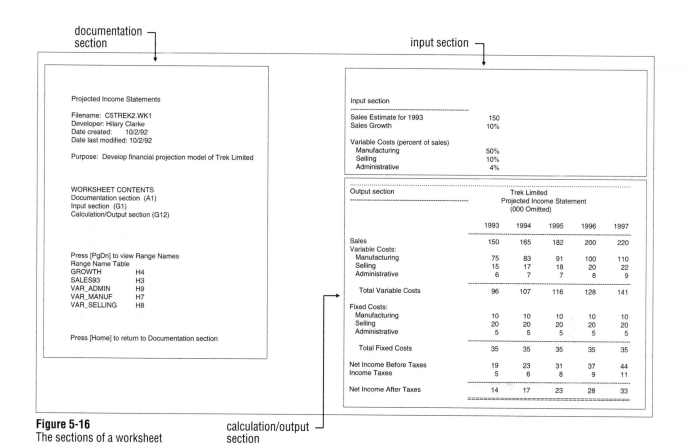

documentation section

input section

Projected Income Statements

Filename: C5TREK2.WK1
Developer: Hilary Clarke
Date created: 10/2/92
Date last modified: 10/2/92

Purpose: Develop financial projection model of Trek Limited

WORKSHEET CONTENTS
Documentation section (A1)
Input section (G1)
Calculation/Output section (G12)

Press [PgDn] to view Range Names
Range Name Table
GROWTH   H4
SALES93   H3
VAR_ADMIN   H9
VAR_MANUF   H7
VAR_SELLING H8

Press [Home] to return to Documentation section

Input section

Sales Estimate for 1993   150
Sales Growth   10%

Variable Costs (percent of sales)
  Manufacturing   50%
  Selling   10%
  Administrative   4%

Output section   Trek Limited
--   Projected Income Statement
                                       (000 Omitted)

                        1993   1994   1995   1996   1997

Sales   150   165   182   200   220
Variable Costs:
  Manufacturing   75   83   91   100   110
  Selling   15   17   18   20   22
  Administrative   6   7   7   8   9

    Total Variable Costs   96   107   116   128   141

Fixed Costs:
  Manufacturing   10   10   10   10   10
  Selling   20   20   20   20   20
  Administrative   5   5   5   5   5

    Total Fixed Costs   35   35   35   35   35

Net Income Before Taxes 19   23   31   37   44
Income Taxes   5   6   8   9   11

Net Income After Taxes   14   17   23   28   33
                      ==

Figure 5-16
The sections of a worksheet

calculation/output section

A Worksheet Map

A worksheet "map," similar to the one in Figure 5-17, can often accompany the worksheet to inform users about the organization of the worksheet. Such a map is especially helpful in a large worksheet that consists of many sections. The map identifies each section and the cell range of each section. With the worksheet map, users can quickly find different sections of the worksheet.

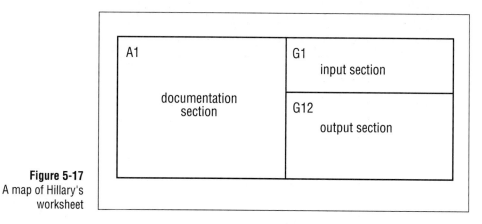

A1	G1
	input section
documentation section	G12
	output section

Figure 5-17
A map of Hillary's worksheet

Demonstrating What-If with the Revised Worksheet

Remember that Hillary developed this new worksheet because the previous worksheet was difficult to use for what-if questions. Let's try this new worksheet and see if it is any easier to use for this purpose.

To use the revised worksheet to change the variable percentage of manufacturing cost from 50% to 52% of sales:

❶ Press **[Tab]** to move to the input section. Then move the cell pointer to cell H7.

❷ Type **52%**. Press **[Enter]**. See Figure 5-18. You could also enter the value as .52.

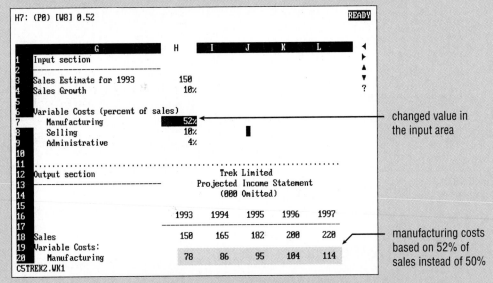

Figure 5-18
Using the revised worksheet to ask what-if questions

changed value in the input area

manufacturing costs based on 52% of sales instead of 50%

The variable manufacturing costs change from 75, 83, 91, 100, and 110 to 78, 86, 95, 104, and 114. Notice that we did not have to change formulas when we used this worksheet. When Hillary used the previous worksheet, she had to make changes to the formula every time a variable-cost percentage changed. The new worksheet is designed to transfer the input percentage to the calculation/output section, where the calculations are performed.

❸ Move the cell pointer to cell H20. See Figure 5-19.

no constant in
this formula

reference to the
input section
(cell H7)

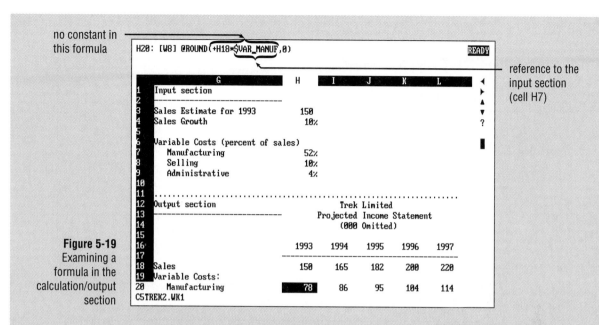

Figure 5-19
Examining a
formula in the
calculation/output
section

```
H20: [W8] @ROUND(+H18*$VAR_MANUF,0)                              READY

                G               H       I       J       K       L      ◄
 1  Input section                                                      ►
 2  ----------------------------                                       ▲
 3  Sales Estimate for 1993     150                                    ▼
 4  Sales Growth                10%                                    ?
 5
 6  Variable Costs (percent of sales)                                  █
 7      Manufacturing           52%
 8      Selling                 10%
 9      Administrative           4%
10
11  ........................................................
12  Output section                         Trek Limited
13  ----------------------------       Projected Income Statement
14                                          (000 Omitted)
15
16                           1993    1994    1995    1996    1997
17                           ----------------------------------
18  Sales                     150     165     182     200     220
19  Variable Costs:
20      Manufacturing          78      86      95     104     114
C5TREK2.WK1
```

Notice that in cell H20 the formula to calculate variable manufacturing costs uses a range name, VAR_MANUF, to reference the variable manufacturing cost percentage (cell H7). The variable manufacturing cost formula in cell H20 is @ROUND(+H18*$VAR_MANUF,0) instead of (.5*B28), which was the formula used in the previous worksheet. Cell H18 contains the sales estimate for 1993. Now all a user has to do is change the variable manufacturing-to-sales percentage in the input area, and the formula in cell H20 will automatically recalculate.

Hillary thinks the revisions she has made to the worksheet will help managers more easily ask what-if questions. For example, suppose a manager wants to see what would happen if the growth rate increased from 10% to 15%.

To ask "What if the growth rate for sales increased to 15%?":

❶ Move the cell pointer to cell H4, the input area for the sales growth rate.

❷ Type **15%**. Press **[Enter]**. You can also enter the value as .15.

Observe the results in the output section. See Figure 5-20 on the following page. Notice how sales in 1994 changed from 165 to 173. The revised sales estimates for 1994 also affected all the variable costs. The fixed costs, on the other hand, haven't changed. Net income before and after taxes has also changed. The increased growth rate also affects sales, variable costs, and income for 1995, 1996, and 1997.

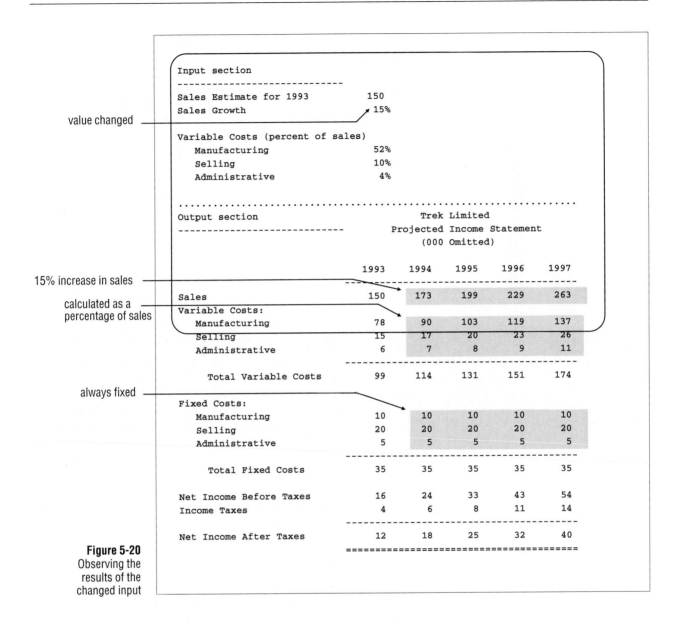

value changed

15% increase in sales

calculated as a
percentage of sales

always fixed

Figure 5-20
Observing the
results of the
changed input

Hillary is pleased with her work and decides to ask Stephan to try the revised worksheet. But Stephan wants to ask different what-if questions. He moves the cell pointer to cell I18 in the calculation/output section and changes the sales in 1994 to 200.

Hillary explains to Stephan that all changes to the worksheet must be made in the input section, not the output section. She thinks to herself that she must prevent Stephan or other managers from inadvertently making the same mistake. She remembers from her workshop that she can protect cells. She decides first to correct the error Stephan made and then to protect the formulas in cell I18 and any other appropriate cells from being changed. Let's make the same mistake Stephan made.

To make Stephan's mistake:

❶ Move the cell pointer to cell I18. Notice the formula @ROUND((1+$GROWTH)*H18,0) in the control panel.

❷ Type **200**. Press **[Enter]**. See Figure 5-21.

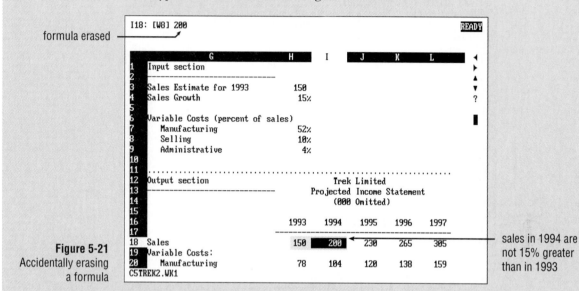

formula erased

sales in 1994 are not 15% greater than in 1993

Figure 5-21
Accidentally erasing a formula

Originally cell I18 contained the formula @ROUND((1+$GROWTH)*H18,0). When Stephan typed 200 in I18, he erased the formula and replaced it with the constant 200. The formula that was originally in this cell instructed 1-2-3 to increase sales for 1994 by the growth rate, currently 15%. Now that the formula is no longer in the cell, sales for 1994 do not reflect the anticipated 15% sales growth. Sales for 1994 are 200 and will remain 200 unless the formula is reentered in this cell.

Fortunately Hillary is able to use the Undo feature and restore the worksheet to its previous state.

❸ Press **[Alt][F4]** (UNDO). Cell I18 now shows 173, and the formula @ROUND((1+$GROWTH)*H18,0) appears in the control panel. If the Undo feature has not worked, type the formula @ROUND((1+$GROWTH)*H18,0) into cell I18.

Protecting and Unprotecting Ranges

Hillary learned in her workshop that what Stephan did is a common mistake. Accidentally erasing worksheet formulas occurs often, so she learned it is a good idea to protect certain areas of a worksheet from accidental changes. She learned a combination of commands with which she can first protect an entire worksheet and then unprotect the range or ranges in which she or other users need to enter or edit data. In the steps that follow, you will begin the process of protecting specific ranges in Hillary's worksheet by first protecting the entire worksheet.

To protect an entire worksheet:

❶ Select /Worksheet Global (**/WG**) to display the Global Settings dialog box, as shown in Figure 5-22. Notice that the global protection setting is not on.

protection is not on

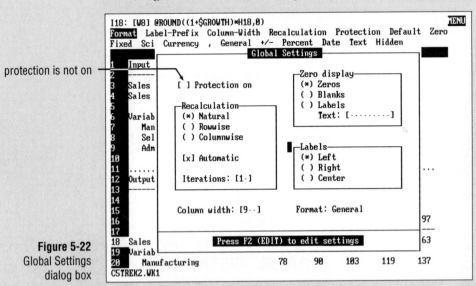

Figure 5-22
Global Settings
dialog box

❷ Select Protection Enable (**PE**) to turn on global protection. 1-2-3 then returns to the worksheet automatically.

❸ With the cell pointer in cell I18, type **200** and press **[Enter]**. You are now prevented from making a change to that cell.

The ERROR indicator in the upper right corner and the message "Protected cell" in the middle of the screen remind you that the cell is protected. Notice the control panel. The letters PR (protected) appear in the control panel whenever the cell pointer is on a protected cell. See Figure 5-23.

indicates this cell
is protected

mode indicator

error message

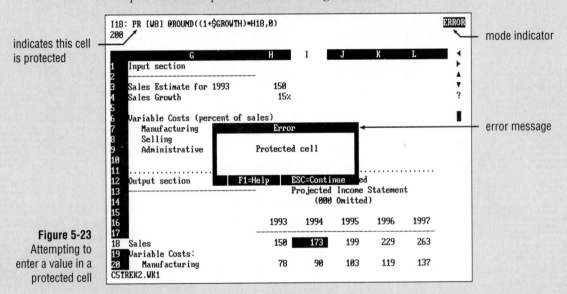

Figure 5-23
Attempting to
enter a value in a
protected cell

④ Press **[Esc]** to return to READY mode.

Move the cell pointer to any other cell in the worksheet and try to enter data or make a change. You'll find that you cannot make a change.

Currently every cell in the worksheet is protected. So what do you do if you need to enter values in some cell? In Hillary's worksheet, for example, we know that managers might want to ask what-if about data in cells H3 through H9. In the next steps, you will learn how to lift the protection, or unprotect, the range of cells that represents the input section of the worksheet.

To unprotect cells in a protected worksheet:

① Press **[Home]**. Press **[Tab]** and move the cell pointer to cell H3, the first cell to be unprotected.

② Select /Range Unprot (**/RU**).

③ Press **[↓]** to highlight the range H3..H9, the range of the input values.

④ Press **[Enter]**. The input area is now unprotected. See Figure 5-24.

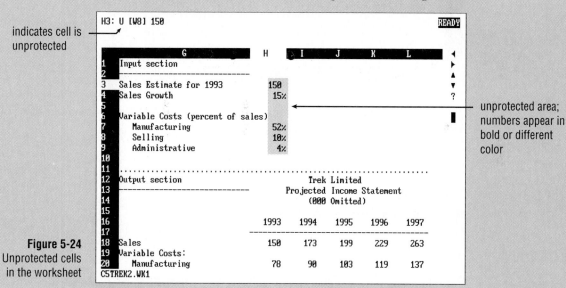

indicates cell is unprotected

unprotected area; numbers appear in bold or different color

Figure 5-24
Unprotected cells in the worksheet

You have now lifted protection from cells H3 to H9. The only area in the worksheet where you can make entries is the input area. Notice that the control panel's first line displays U (unprotected) whenever the cell pointer is in an unprotected cell. Another indication that protection is not in effect for these cells is that the values in these cells appear in boldface or in a different color.

To see if you can enter data in the input section, let's change the variable administrative costs to 5% in cell H9.

To make a change in cell H9:

① Move the cell pointer to H9, the cell for the variable administrative-cost percentage.

② Type **5%** and press **[Enter]**. You can also enter this value as .05. Notice that data can now be entered in unprotected cells.

③ Press **[PgDn]** to see the results. Variable administrative costs are now 8, 9, 10, 11, and 13 for the years 1993 through 1997. See Figure 5-25.

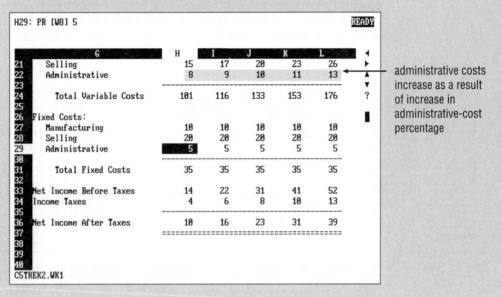

Figure 5-25
Change in administrative-cost percentage

administrative costs increase as a result of increase in administrative-cost percentage

If you decide to modify formulas or labels in the worksheet, remember that you will have to turn off protection. Let's try that.

To turn off protection:

① Select /Worksheet Global Protection (**/WGP**).

② Select Disable (**D**).

When you have completed the changes, you can turn on protection again by selecting /Worksheet Global Protection Enable (/WGPE). Let's keep the protection feature off for now.

Although adding protection to the worksheet is certainly an improvement, Hillary still is not satisfied. When changes are made in the input section, she has to press [PgDn] to see the results. She must then move the cell pointer back to the input section or press [PgUp] if she wants to make another change. Is there a way to have both the input and output sections appear on the screen at the same time?

Using Windows

To keep separate parts of the worksheet in view at the same time, you can use the Worksheet Window command. This command lets you view two parts of a large worksheet simultaneously, either horizontally or vertically. You can observe the results from one part of a worksheet while you make changes to another. You use [F6] (WINDOW) to move the cell pointer between the two windows.

In the next steps, you will split the worksheet into two windows — one for the input section and the other for the Projected Income Statement.

To split the screen into two windows:

❶ Press **[PgUp]**. Then move the cell pointer anywhere in row 8, the point where you decide to split the worksheet. For a horizontal window the rows above the cell pointer are placed in the top window. For vertical windows the columns to the left of the cell pointer are placed in the left window.

Next let's split the screen horizontally.

❷ Select /Worksheet Window Horizontal (**/WWH**). This command instructs 1-2-3 to split the screen horizontally into two windows, one above and one below the cell pointer. See Figure 5-26.

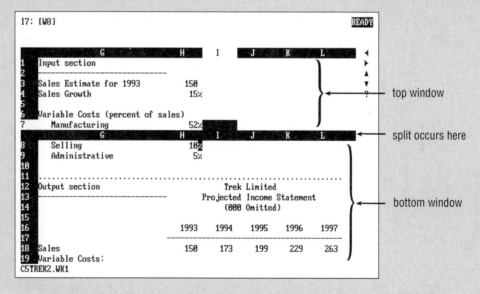

Figure 5-26
Splitting the
screen into two
windows

❸ Press **[F6]** (WINDOW) once to move the cell pointer to the bottom window. Press **[F6]** (WINDOW) again to switch back to the top window.

The Window key switches the cell pointer back and forth between the two windows.

④ If necessary, adjust your view of the worksheet so the cells G3 to H9 are visible in the top window.

⑤ Press **[F6]** (WINDOW) again to switch the cell pointer to the bottom window. Then press **[↓]** until row 37 is visible. Your screen should be similar to Figure 5-27.

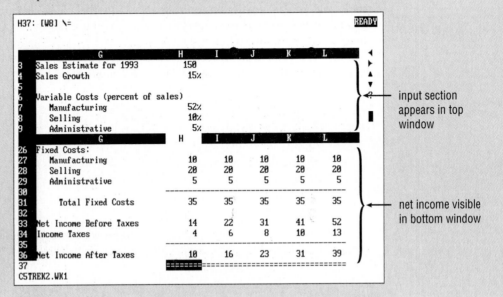

Figure 5-27
Worksheet
windows adjusted
to view the input
section and the net
income data

Now you can view, at the same time, part of the worksheet in the top window and part of the Projected Income Statement in the bottom window. Let's change the 1993 sales estimate to 225 and view the results.

To make a change and immediately view the results:

① Press **[F6]** (WINDOW) to switch to the top window.

② Move the cell pointer to cell H3, the location for the sales estimate.

③ Type **225** in cell H3. Press **[Enter]** and watch as the results of the change appear immediately. See Figure 5-28.

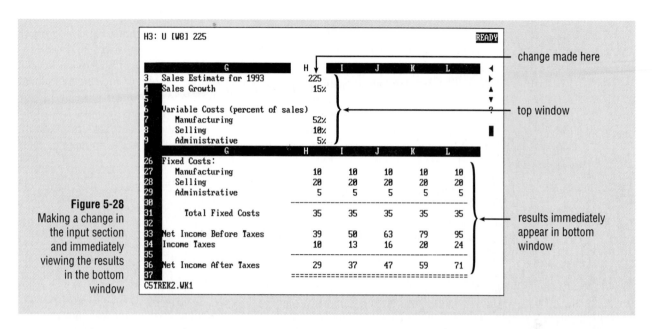

Figure 5-28
Making a change in
the input section
and immediately
viewing the results
in the bottom
window

It will be easier to perform other tasks in this tutorial if you first clear the windows.

To clear the windows:

● Select /Worksheet Window Clear (**/WWC**).

Hillary now thinks that the worksheet is getting closer to her ideal, but she still is not completely satisfied. Each time she tries new input values, she finds herself writing down the results on a sheet of paper. She wonders if there is a way to make more than one change at a time and see the results. Hillary decides to ask an experienced 1-2-3 user at her company. She explains the problem and is told to try the Data Table command.

Before using this command, Hillary decides to set her worksheet aside. She wants to develop and experiment on a new worksheet so she does not accidentally lose or destroy her current worksheet.

To save the worksheet:

● Select /File Save (**/FS**). Type **S5TREK2** and press **[Enter]**.

Printing Cell Formulas

So that she will be able to review the formulas in her current worksheet, Hillary prints the cell formulas that make up the current worksheet.

Printing the cell formulas is an option of the Print command. Using this option to create a printout of the cell formulas provides you with a record of the worksheet. It also allows you to see several formulas at once, thereby letting you see how formulas relate to one another. This is especially helpful if you are trying to find a problem in your worksheet. Instead of moving from cell to cell and viewing each formula in the control panel, you have a printout of all the formulas. By attaching this printout to the usual output from your worksheet, you add valuable backup documentation for the worksheet. Let's now use the print-cell-formula option of the Print command to print the worksheet's formulas.

To print the cell formulas:

❶ Select /Print Printer Range (**/PPR**).

❷ Move the cell pointer to G18, the first cell of the print range.

❸ Press **[.]** to anchor the cell pointer. Then highlight G18..L37 and press **[Enter]**. The print range consists of the cells in the calculation/output area.

❹ Select Options Other Cell-Formulas (**OOC**) to cause the range to print as cell formulas rather than as values. Notice the last setting, "List entries," in the lower left corner of the Print Settings dialog box, which now specifies that cell formulas will be output. See Figure 5-29.

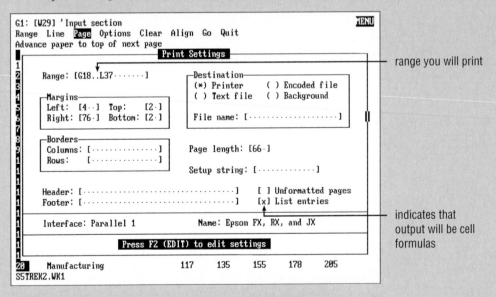

Figure 5-29
The Print Settings
dialog box

❺ Select Quit (**Q**) to leave the Options menu and return to the Print menu. Make sure the printer is ready.

❻ Print the cell formulas. Select Align Go Page (**AGP**). 1-2-3 prints a list of the cell address and cell formula for each cell within the specified range. See Figure 5-30. Notice in this figure that the second column shows the display format and the column width as well as the contents of each cell.

❼ Select Quit (**Q**) to exit the print menu.

display format, column width, and cell formula ——
cell address ——

```
G18: (G) [W29] 'Sales
H18: [W8] +SALES93
I18: [W8] @ROUND((1+$GROWTH)*H18,0)
J18: [W8] @ROUND((1+$GROWTH)*I18,0)
K18: [W8] @ROUND((1+$GROWTH)*J18,0)
L18: [W8] @ROUND((1+$GROWTH)*K18,0)
G19: (G) [W29] 'Variable Costs:
G20: (G) [W29] '   Manufacturing
H20: [W8] @ROUND(+H18*$VAR_MANUF,0)
I20: [W8] @ROUND(+I18*$VAR_MANUF,0)
J20: [W8] @ROUND(+J18*$VAR_MANUF,0)
K20: [W8] @ROUND(+K18*$VAR_MANUF,0)
L20: [W8] @ROUND(+L18*$VAR_MANUF,0)
G21: (G) [W29] '   Selling
H21: [W8] @ROUND(+H18*$VAR_SELLING,0)
I21: [W8] @ROUND(+I18*$VAR_SELLING,0)
J21: [W8] @ROUND(+J18*$VAR_SELLING,0)
K21: [W8] @ROUND(+K18*$VAR_SELLING,0)
L21: [W8] @ROUND(+L18*$VAR_SELLING,0)
G22: (G) [W29] '   Administrative
H22: [W8] @ROUND(+H18*$VAR_ADMIN,0)
I22: [W8] @ROUND(+I18*$VAR_ADMIN,0)
J22: [W8] @ROUND(+J18*$VAR_ADMIN,0)
K22: [W8] @ROUND(+K18*$VAR_ADMIN,0)
L22: [W8] @ROUND(+L18*$VAR_ADMIN,0)
H23: [W8] \-
I23: [W8] \-
J23: [W8] \-
K23: [W8] \-
L23: [W8] \-
G24: (G) [W29] '      Total Variable Costs
H24: [W8] +H20+H21+H22
I24: [W8] +I20+I21+I22
J24: [W8] +J20+J21+J22
K24: [W8] +K20+K21+K22
L24: [W8] +L20+L21+L22
G26: (G) [W29] 'Fixed Costs:
G27: (G) [W29] '   Manufacturing
H27: [W8] 10
I27: [W8] 10
J27: [W8] 10
K27: [W8] 10
L27: [W8] 10
G28: (G) [W29] '   Selling
H28: [W8] 20
I28: [W8] 20
J28: [W8] 20
K28: [W8] 20
L28: [W8] 20
G29: (G) [W29] '   Administrative
H29: [W8] 5
I29: [W8] 5
J29: [W8] 5
```

Figure 5-30
A printout of the cell formulas (continued on next page)

```
K29: [W8] 5
L29: [W8] 5
H30: [W8] \-
I30: [W8] \-
J30: [W8] \-
K30: [W8] \-
L30: [W8] \-
G31: (G) [W29] '      Total Fixed Costs
H31: [W8] +H27+H28+H29
I31: [W8] +I27+I28+I29
J31: [W8] +J27+J28+J29
K31: [W8] +K27+K28+K29
L31: [W8] +L27+L28+L29
G33: (G) [W29] 'Net Income Before Taxes
H33: [W8] +H18-H24-H31
I33: [W8] +I18-I24-I31
J33: [W8] +J18-J24-J31
K33: [W8] +K18-K24-K31
L33: [W8] +L18-L24-L31
G34: (G) [W29] 'Income Taxes
H34: [W8] @ROUND(@IF(H330,H33*0.25,0),0)
I34: [W8] @ROUND(@IF(I330,I33*0.25,0),0)
J34: [W8] @ROUND(@IF(J330,J33*0.25,0),0)
K34: [W8] @ROUND(@IF(K330,K33*0.25,0),0)
L34: [W8] @ROUND(@IF(L330,L33*0.25,0),0)
H35: [W8] \-
I35: [W8] \-
J35: [W8] \-
K35: [W8] \-
L35: [W8] \-
G36: (G) [W29] 'Net Income After Taxes
H36: [W8] +H33-H34
I36: [W8] +I33-I34
J36: [W8] +J33-J34
K36: [W8] +K33-K34
L36: [W8] +L33-L34
H37: [W8] \=
I37: [W8] \=
J37: [W8] \=
K37: [W8] \=
L37: [W8] \=
```

Figure 5-30
(continued from
previous page)

Data Tables

Now let's see how Hillary can use a data table to make more than one change at a time and see the results. She decides she wants to make several changes to estimated 1993 sales and observe how those changes will affect net income before taxes.

A data table is an area of the worksheet set up to show the results a formula generates each time you change a value in that formula.

Let's illustrate this concept using a bank loan as an example. Suppose you are considering borrowing $100,000 to buy a home. The bank requires monthly payments over 25 years. What if you wanted to know how much your monthly payments would be at various interest rates, such as 9%, 10%, 11%, 12%, and 13%? To show the relationship between the monthly payments and the various interest rates, you could use a data table such as Figure 5-31.

Interest Rate	Monthly Payment
9%	839.20
10%	908.70
11%	980.11
12%	1053.22
13%	1127.84

Figure 5-31
Monthly loan
payments at
different interest
rates

This figure shows how monthly payments increase as interest rates increase. The data table is a valuable tool because it allows you to try out several what-if questions at one time and observe their results. In the case of the monthly payments for the loan, you are saying:

What is the monthly payment *if* the interest rate is 9%?

What is the monthly payment *if* the interest rate is 10%?

What is the monthly payment *if* the interest rate is 11%?

What is the monthly payment *if* the interest rate is 12%?

What is the monthly payment *if* the interest rate is 13%?

Using a data table, you need only one formula to produce a table that shows the different results generated each time a new interest rate is substituted in the formula. When the value of only one variable in a formula is varied, the data table is referred to as a **one-way data table**.

One-Way Data Tables

The components and the layout of a one-way data table are shown in Figure 5-32 on the following page. As you can see, a one-way data table includes an **input cell** and a **table range.** The table range consists of four components: a **blank cell**, a **formula**, **input values**, and a **results area.**

The data table must contain these four components and be laid out as shown in Figure 5-32.

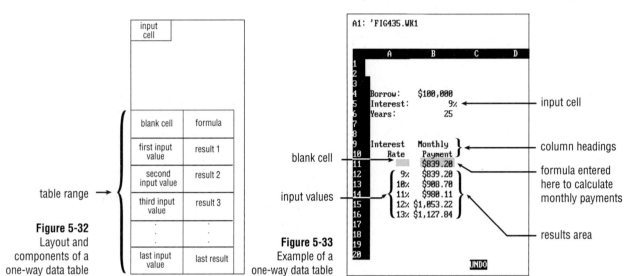

Figure 5-32
Layout and
components of a
one-way data table

Figure 5-33
Example of a
one-way data table

Figure 5-33 illustrates the components of the data table using a bank loan example. (You do not have a worksheet file for this example.) The components are defined as follows:

- The *input cell* is an unprotected cell that can be anywhere in the worksheet. It can be blank or can contain one of the input values. In the bank loan example, cell B5 is the input cell.

- The *blank cell* is a cell that does not contain data and is located at the intersection of the first row and the first column of the table range. In the bank loan example, cell A11 is considered the blank cell.

- The *formula* (or formulas) must be in the first row of the table range, starting at the second cell from the left. The formula contains a **variable**. A variable is a part of the formula for which different values can be substituted. In the bank loan example, the formula to calculate the monthly payments is in B11.

- The *input values* must be in the first column of the table range, starting immediately below the empty cell. The input values are the values that 1-2-3 substitutes for a variable whenever it performs the calculations specified in the formula. In the bank loan example, the interest rates in cells A12 to A16 are the input values that are substituted in the formula to calculate the monthly payments.

- The *results area* is the unprotected area below the formula and to the right of the input values. 1-2-3 enters the results of each calculation next to the input value it used. The results area should be blank when you first set up the data table because 1-2-3 writes over any data in this area when it calculates results. In the bank loan example, the results area is cells B12 to B16.

Setting Up a One-Way Data Table

Hillary now has her list of formulas and she has read how to use the Data Table command in her 1-2-3 reference manual. She draws a sketch that will help her visualize the planned changes in estimated 1993 sales and how these changes affect net income before taxes. Figure

5-34 is her handwritten sketch of how she wants her data table to look. Notice that she has followed the correct layout for a data table and has included all the required components.

		Sales	NIBT
Sales	xxx	blank cell	sales − (variable cost ratio x sales) − fixed costs
Variable cost percent	xx%	50	↑
Fixed cost	xx	75	
		100	
		125	
		150	Results here
		175	
		200	
		225	
		250	↓
		275	
		300	

Figure 5-34
Hillary's sketch for her data table

Now let's construct Hillary's data table. Begin by retrieving the file C5TREK3.WK1.

To retrieve the file:

① Select /File Retrieve (**/FR**). Highlight C5TREK3.WK1 and press **[Enter]**.

Your screen should now look like Figure 5-35. Notice that this file contains the input values that Hillary will use. Sales start at $50,000 (remember, the worksheets indicate the number of thousands), and variable costs are 64% of sales. Variable costs are the sum of variable manufacturing (50%), variable selling (10%), and variable administrative (4%) costs. Fixed costs are $35,000, the sum of fixed manufacturing ($10,000), fixed selling ($20,000), and fixed administrative ($5,000) costs.

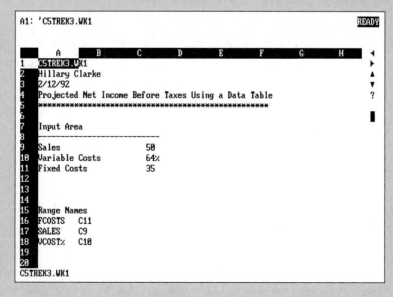

Figure 5-35
Hillary's retrieved worksheet

Your first step is to select a location in the worksheet to place the data table. The location of a data table can be any blank area of your worksheet. Let's use the cell range E8..F19.

Next, you must enter descriptive headings for the columns in the data table. Headings are *not* part of a data table, but you should enter them because they help you read the values in the data table. Hillary's sketch of the data table contains the headings you will now enter.

To enter headings for the data table:

❶ Move the cell pointer to cell **E7**. Type **"Sales** and press **[Enter]**. Notice that the label, Sales, is right-justified in the cell. That is because you typed the label prefix " (Quotation Mark) before you typed Sales.

❷ Move the cell pointer to F7 and type **"NIBT**, an abbreviation for net income before taxes. Press **[Enter]**.

Using the Data Fill Command

Now that you have entered the headings, let's enter the values in the input value section of the data table. Remember from the worksheet sketch that Hillary wants to see what will happen to NIBT as sales estimates increase in intervals of 25,000, starting at 50,000 and ending at 300,000 (remember, you type only the number of thousands, i.e., 50 for 50,000, 75 for 75,000, and so on).

You could enter each number — 50, 75, 100, and so on, up to 300 — in each appropriate cell, but that would be rather time consuming. Instead you can use a new command, the Data Fill command, to enter all the sales estimates at one time into the input value section of the data table. The Data Fill command lets you enter a sequence of equally spaced values into a range of cells, either in one column or in one row. To use the Data Fill command, you first need to understand four new terms:

- The **fill range** is the range you want to fill with a series of sequential values. In Hillary's case, the fill range is E9..E19.

- The **start value** is the first value you want to enter in the fill range. In Hillary's case, 50 is the start value.

- The **step value** is the increment between the values in the sequence. Hillary wants to increase sales estimates in increments of 25.

- The **stop value** is the value you want to use as a limit for the sequence. Hillary wants her data table to stop at 300. The default limit is 8191.

To use the Data Fill command:

❶ Move the cell pointer to E9. Notice that cell E8, the first cell in the data table, is empty.

❷ Select /Data Fill (**/DF**).

Now let's enter the fill range.

③ At cell E9, press **[.]** to anchor the cell pointer.

④ Highlight the cells E9..E19 and press **[Enter]**.

⑤ Type **50** to enter the start value and press **[Enter]**.

⑥ Type **25** to enter the step value and press **[Enter]**.

⑦ Type **300** to enter the stop value. Take a look at the control panel. See Figure 5-36.

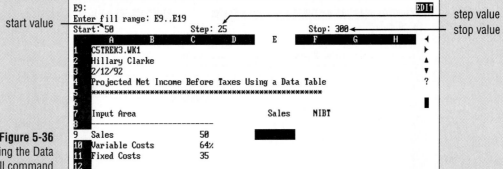

Figure 5-36
Executing the Data
Fill command

⑧ Press **[Enter]**. As you do, notice that the input values appear in column E of the data table. See Figure 5-37.

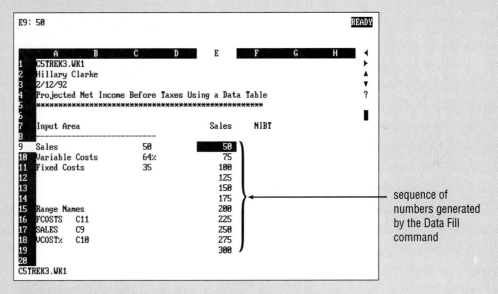

Figure 5-37
The worksheet after
executing the Data
Fill command

Now you should enter the formula to calculate net income before taxes (NIBT) into the formula section of the data table. Checking Hillary's sketch for her data table (Figure 5-34) you can see the formula is

$$sales - (variable\ cost\ ratio \times sales) - fixed\ costs$$

Be sure to enter this formula in cell F8, that is, to the right of the empty cell of the data table.

To enter the formula to calculate net income before taxes:

➊ Move the cell pointer to F8, the first row of the data table.

➋ Type **+sales–(vcost%*sales)–fcosts**. Press **[Enter]** and, as you do, notice that –17, the result of the calculation of this formula, appears in F8. See Figure 5-38.

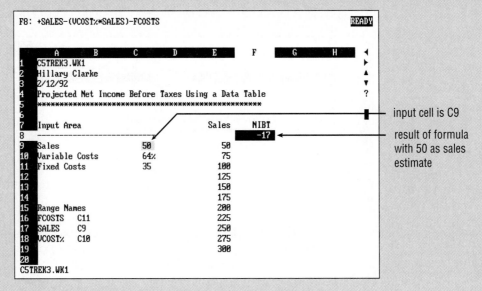

Figure 5-38
Formula to calculate the net income before taxes is entered

The components of the data table have been set up; now it's time to use the Data Table command.

To identify the cells that make up the table range of the data table:

➊ Select the command /Data Table 1 (**/DT1**) to set up a one-way data table. 1-2-3 prompts you to specify the data table range.

➋ Move the cell pointer to E8, the upper left corner of the table range.

➌ Anchor the cell pointer by pressing **[.]**.

❹   Highlight the range E8..F19. See Figure 5-39.

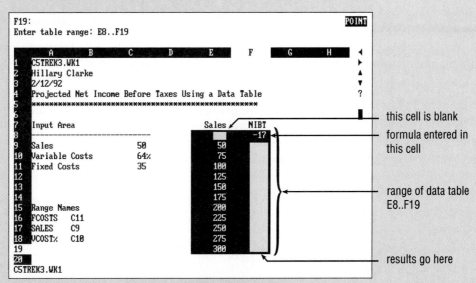

Figure 5-39
The process of
executing the Data
Table command

You have now defined the table range of the data table. Notice that the empty cell, E8, must be included in the range, but we have not included the column headings, which are in E7..F7.

❺   Press **[Enter]**.

Next, 1-2-3 prompts you to specify which cell will be the input cell. The input cell will contain the values from the input value section of the data table.

❻   Type **sales**. Press **[Enter]**. See Figure 5-40.

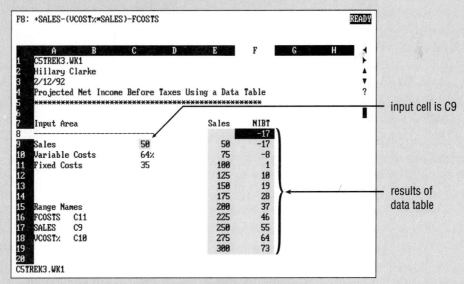

Figure 5-40
The worksheet
after executing the
Data Table
command

1-2-3 substitutes each value from the input section of the data table (E9..E19) into the input cell (C9), one at a time. Then using the formula in cell F8, 1-2-3 recalculates the formula using these input values and immediately displays the results in the results section of the data table (F9..F19). The data table is now complete, so let's save it.

⑦ Save the worksheet as S5TREK3.

Data tables can provide you even greater flexibility, because you can test the sensitivity of the results to various assumptions. Suppose, for example, that you believe the variable costs will increase from 64% to 66% of sales. With data tables, all you have to do is change the variable cost in cell C10 from 64 to 66 and then press [F8] (TABLE) to recalculate the entire table. Pressing [F8] repeats the last Data Table command you selected, in this case, Data Table 1. 1-2-3 uses the previous setting for the table range and the input cell.

Now let's see how Hillary can quickly change one value using the [F8] (TABLE) key and generate 11 new forecasts of NIBT.

To use [F8] for what-if analysis:

① Move to cell C10, type **66%**, a revised variable cost, and press **[Enter]**. You can also enter the value as .66.

No changes appear in the results area.

② Press **[F8]** (TABLE) to recalculate the table. See Figure 5-41.

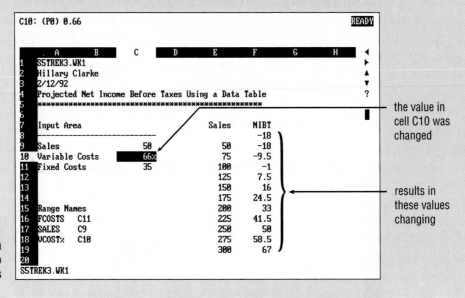

Figure 5-41
Results of data table using [F8] to recalculate results

Exercises

1. Which of the following @IF functions would work in a 1-2-3 worksheet?
   a.   IF(D–40>0,3,7)
   b.   @IF(D4–40>0 , 3, 7)
   c.   @IFD4–40>0,3,7
   d.   @IF(D4–40>0,3,7)

2. Write an English statement that explains what this @IF function says:
   @IF(C15<0,"LOSS","PROFIT")

3. Retrieve the file E5FILE1 and do the following:
   a.   Press **[Tab]**. Notice that the names of the countries in column A no longer appear on the screen. This makes it difficult to read the worksheet.
   b.   Write down the steps necessary to modify the worksheet so that when you press [Tab] the names of the countries remain on the screen.
   c.   Use your answer in (b) to actually modify the worksheet.

4. Retrieve the file E5FILE2 and do the following:
   a.   Use the @IF function in cells C4, C5, and C6 to determine a salesperson's commission based on his or her weekly sales. If weekly sales are above 10000, a 12-percent commission rate appears in column C; otherwise, a 7.5-percent commission rate appears in column C.
   b.   Print the worksheet and the cell formulas.

5. Retrieve the file E5FILE3 and do the following:
   a.   Use the @IF function in cells D3, D4, and D5 to check the value in column B. Display the word MALE or FEMALE in column D, depending on whether the code in column B is M (male) or F (female).
   b.   Use the @IF function in cells E3, E4, and E5 to place the phrase UNDER 21 or 21 AND OVER in cells E3, E4, and E5, depending on the age in column C.
   c.   Print your worksheet and cell formulas.

6. Identify the command you would use in each of the following situations:
   a.   You have a list of 100 customer names, addresses, and phone numbers. As you scroll down the worksheet, the column headings disappear from the screen.
   b.   Users of the worksheet keep erasing formulas accidentally.
   c.   You want an efficient way to do what-if analysis.
   d.   You want to see two different parts of a large worksheet at the same time.
   e.   You want to number cells in column A of your worksheet 1 to 500 without typing each number.

Tutorial Assignments

Before you begin these Tutorial Assignments, check your working copy of your data diskette. Be sure you have space to save the additional worksheet files you'll create in these assignments (at least 40,000 bytes). If not, save the files you need for this tutorial to another formatted diskette.

Retrieve the worksheet file T5TREK2 and do the following:

1. Build error checking into the input section. Do this by causing 1-2-3 to display the message "Error in input value" in cell I7 if the value entered for variable manufacturing

costs is greater than 1. Otherwise, be sure that 1-2-3 leaves cell I7 blank. *Hint:* Use the following logic to help you:

If value entered for variable manufacturing cost greater than 1
        Display "Error in input value"
Otherwise
        Display "   "

2.   Save the worksheet as S5TREK4.

3.   Enter the value 45 in cell H7 as the variable manufacturing costs. Print the input screen.

4.   Enter the value 45% in cell H7 as the variable manufacturing costs. Print the input screen.

Retrieve the worksheet file T5TREK3 and do the following:

5.   Change the fixed costs from 35 to 45 and recalculate the data table. Print your results.

6.   Reduce the variable costs from 64% to 60% and recalculate the data table. Print the results.

7.   Save the worksheet as S5TREK5.

Retrieve the worksheet file from Tutorial 3, T5BALBO1, and do the following:

8.   Protect the worksheet so the only cells that can be changed are the daily stock prices, cells C28..C31.

9.   Attempt to type 125 in cell B28 (you should not be able to). Enter the following prices in cells C28 to C31: 90, 70, 60, and 44, respectively. Save your worksheet as S5BALBO1.

Case Problems

1. Apex Auto Rental

Apex Auto Rental, a local car rental company, rents two types of cars: compact (Pontiac Sunbird) and luxury (Cadillac Seville). The current rental rates are shown in Figure 5-42.

	Current Rental Rates	
	Compact	**Luxury**
Charge/day	$38	$50
Charge/mile	$0.22	$0.32

Figure 5-42

1.   Develop a worksheet that calculates and prints customer bills. Your worksheet should be divided into the following sections:
   • A *documentation* section that includes a title, your name, date developed, filename, and purpose.
   • An *input* section to capture the customer billing data in Figure 5-43. Also include in the input area the rental rate table from Figure 5-42.

Name

Type of car (enter 1 if compact, 2 if luxury)

Number of days driven

Figure 5-43   Miles driven

- A *calculation/output* section in your worksheet for the customer bill. The bill should appear as shown in Figure 5-44.

Apex Car Rental

Name: $xxxxxxxxxxxxxxx^1$

Type of car: $xxxxxxxxxxxxx^2$

Days driven: xx^1

Miles driven: xxx^1

Amount due: xxxxx^3

^{1} Reference the data from the input area.

^{2} Enter the label Pontiac Sunbird if the code for type of car is a 1; otherwise, enter the label Cadillac Seville.

^{3} Amount due is based on the following calculation:

Figure 5-44   (*days driven* × *charge/day*) + (*miles/driven* × *charge/mile*)

2. Include features that you think will improve the appearance and use of your worksheet, for example, formatting, range names, cell protection, and more.

3. Use the data in Figure 5-45 to print a bill.

Name:	John Connolly
Type of car:	2
Days driven:	4
Miles driven:	525

Figure 5-45

4. Save your worksheet as P5APEX.

5. Use the data in Figure 5-46 to print a second bill.

Name:	Joe Dougherty
Type of car:	1
Days driven:	2
Miles driven:	125

Figure 5-46

6.   Suppose that Apex changes its rates to those shown in Figure 5-47. Update the rate schedule.

	New Rental Rates	
	Compact	**Luxury**
Charge/day	$40	$53
Charge/mile	$0.23	$0.35

Figure 5-47

7.   Use the data in Figure 5-48 to print a third bill based on the new rates.

Name:	Susan Solomon
Type of car:	1
Days driven:	1
Miles driven:	150

Figure 5-48

WYSIWYG Assignments

1.   Attach WYSIWYG.

2.   Add the following enhancements:
   a.   Remove any dashed lines you might have included in your worksheet. Replace them with solid lines under column headings and above and below totals.
   b.   Use a 14-point Swiss font for the report title line(s).
   c.   Boldface all descriptive labels in the rental bill in Figure 5-44.
   d.   Draw a line around the entire bill.

3.   Save your worksheet as W5APEX.

4.   Print the entire worksheet on one page.

2.   Loan Repayment Schedule

Occasionally businesses need to borrow money for new buildings, equipment, or other large purchases. If a business takes out a term loan, it must pay back the loan in installments over a specified period of time.

For example, assume Lockwood Enterprises borrows $10,000, payable over five years, at an interest rate of 16% per year on the unpaid balance. Each month Lockwood pays $243.18 to cover principal and interest. The principle is the amount of the loan still unpaid, and the interest is the amount paid for the use of the money.

Figure 5-49 is a partial repayment schedule that shows the monthly payments broken out into principal repaid (amount borrowed) and interest paid. If this table were carried out for 60 months (5 years × 12 months per year, or the life of the loan), it would show a remaining balance of 0 at the conclusion of the 60-month period.

Payment Number	Monthly Payment	Interest[1]	Principal Repayment[2]	Remaining Balance
0	0.00	0.00	0.00	10000.00
1	243.18	133.33	109.85	9890.15
2	243.18	131.87	111.31	9778.84
...				
60	243.18	3.20	239.98	0[3]

[1] Interest is equal to the monthly interest rate, .013333 (16% divided by 12 months), times the remaining balance from the previous period. For example, in month 1, interest equals $133.33 (.013333 × 10000). In month 2, interest equals $131.87 (.013333 × 9890.15).

[2] Principal repayment for each period is equal to the monthly payment ($243.18) minus the interest for the period. For example, in month 2, the monthly payment ($243.18) minus the interest ($131.87) equals the principal repaid ($111.31).

[3] Because of rounding, the result will not be exactly zero.

Figure 5-49

Do the following:

1. Develop a worksheet that prepares a complete loan payment schedule for this loan. At the bottom of the payment schedule, calculate the total payments and the total interest.

2. Your worksheet should be divided into the following sections:
   - A *documentation* section that includes a title, your name, date developed, filename, and purpose.
   - An *input* section that includes the amount borrowed, the interest rate, and the monthly payments.
   - A *calculation/output* section consisting of the repayment schedule shown in Figure 5-49.

3. Include features that you think will improve the appearance and use of your worksheet, for example, formatting, range names, cell protection, and other features.

4. Save the worksheet as S5LOAN.

5. Print the input section and the repayment schedule using these data.

6. What if the interest rate is 16.5% and the monthly payment is $245.85 on a $10,000 loan? Print the input section and repayment schedule using these data.

WYSIWYG Assignments

1. Attach WYSIWYG.

2. Add the following enhancements:
    a. Remove any dashed lines you might have included in your worksheet. Replace them with solid lines under column headings and above and below totals.
    b. Shade the input area.
    c. Boldface and italicize the column headings of the repayment schedule.

3. Save your worksheet as W5LOAN.

4. Print the entire worksheet on one page.

3. Predicting Demand for Mars Automobiles

Lynette Spiller, an economist working at HN Motor Company headquarters, has developed the following formula to estimate demand for HN's new line of Mars automobiles:

$$D \quad = \quad 100,000 - 100P + 2,000N + 50I - 1,000G + 0.2A$$

where

D	=	demand for Mars automobiles (in units)
P	=	price of Mars automobile (in dollars)
N	=	population in United States (in millions)
I	=	disposable income per person (in dollars)
G	=	price of gasoline (in cents per gallon)
A	=	advertising expenses by HN for Mars (in dollars)

The senior managers at HN are considering raising the price of Mars, but before they do, they want to determine how increasing the price will affect demand for this car. They ask Lynette to show how increasing the price in $100 increments from $10,000 to $11,000 will affect demand for the Mars.

Assume the following values when estimating demand:

N	=	250
I	=	$14,000
G	=	140 cents (do not enter as 1.40)
A	=	$1,000,000

Do the following:

1. Design a worksheet using the Data Table command to solve this problem. The data table should include a column for possible car prices beginning at $10,000, increasing in $100 increments to $11,000. The second column should show the demand for cars at each price.

2. Your worksheet should be divided into the following sections:
    - A *documentation* section that includes a title, your name, date developed, filename, and purpose.
    - An *input* section that includes the following variables: U.S. population, disposable income per person, price of gasoline, and advertising expenses.
    - A *calculation/output* section consisting of the data table.

3. Include features that you think will improve the appearance and use of your worksheet, for example, formatting, range names, cell protection, and other features.

4. Save your worksheet as S5MARS.

5. Print the input section and the results.

6. What if the gasoline price per gallon is $1.75 (enter as 175 cents)? Rerun the worksheet using the new price of gasoline. Print your results.

7. What if the gasoline price is $1.75 a gallon and the advertising budget is increased to $1,500,000? Print your results.

WYSIWYG Assignments

1. Attach WYSIWYG.

2. Add the following enhancements:
    a. Remove any dashed lines you might have included in your worksheet. Replace them with solid lines under column headings and above and below totals.
    b. Enclose the input area in a box using the Format Line Outline command.
    c. Boldface the column headings in the data table.

3. Save your worksheet as W5MARS.

4. Print the entire worksheet on one page.

4. Production Planning at QuikNails

QuikNails Manufacturing, makers of artificial fashion fingernails, anticipates selling 42,000 units of QuikNails in May. Currently the company has 22,000 units ready in inventory. The QuikNails plant will produce the additional product (20,000 units) during April to have enough product to meet the sales forecast for May. In addition to meeting May's sales forecast, the plant manager wants to have 24,000 units of QuikNails in inventory at the end of May for anticipated sales at the beginning of June. Thus, the QuickNails production requirement for April is the sum of the QuikNails units necessary to meet May sales estimates (20,000) plus the units needed to meet the desired ending inventory level (24,000).

The major ingredient needed to produce QuikNails is a chemical called Zinex. Assume the production department needs three gallons of Zinex to make one unit of QuikNails. Currently, the company has an inventory of 100,000 gallons of Zinex. The plant will use all of this raw material to meet its production requirement for April. It also needs 110,000 gallons of Zinex on hand at the end of April for production in May.

Sally Dolling is in charge of inventory control for both raw materials and finished products. She needs to inform senior management and the purchasing manager how much Zinex is required for current and future materials production. As Sally's assistant, you will develop a spreadsheet to help calculate the number of gallons of Zinex that she should tell the purchasing manager to buy in April for QuikNails to meet the production requirements. You decide to adapt the form that Sally has been using to develop her estimate for production and material requirements (Figure 5-50).

	Units
QuikNails Production:	
Monthly sales estimate for QuikNails	xxxx
<u>Less</u> QuikNails currently in inventory	.
Production needed to meet sales forecast	.
<u>Plus</u> QuikNails needed at end of month	.
Total QuikNails production requirement	xxxx
	Gallons
Zinex Purchases:	
Zinex needed to meet QuikNails production requirement	xxxx
<u>Less</u> Zinex currently in inventory	.
Purchases of Zinex required to meet QuikNails production requirement	.
<u>Plus</u> desired level of Zinex at end of month	.
Total Purchases of Zinex	xxxx

Figure 5-50

Design your spreadsheet so you can easily test alternative plans, such as different sales estimates and different inventory levels for QuikNails and Zinex.

Do the following:

1. Design a worksheet to calculate the production requirements of QuikNails and the amount of Zinex to purchase for the QuikNails manufacturing division.

2. Your worksheet should be divided into the following sections:
   - A *documentation* section that includes a title, your name, date developed, filename, and purpose.
   - An *input* section that includes the following variables: monthly sales estimate for QuikNails, QuikNails currently in inventory, QuikNails needed at end of month, Zinex currently in inventory, and desired level of Zinex at end of month.
   - A *calculation/output* section consisting of the form in Figure 5-50.

3. Include features that you think will improve the appearance and use of your worksheet, for example, formatting, range names, cell protection, and other features.

4. Use the following set of data:

Monthly sales estimate for QuikNails	42,000
QuikNails currently in inventory	22,000
QuikNails needed at end of month	24,000
Zinex currently in inventory	100,000
Desired level of Zinex at end of month	110,000

5. Save your worksheet as S5NAILS.

6. Print the input section and the results.

7. Print the cell formulas.

8. What if the sales estimates of QuikNails for May is revised to 50,000 units? Print your results.

9. What if sales estimates for May is 30,000 units? Print your results.

WYSIWYG Assignments

1. Attach WYSIWYG.

2. Add the following enhancements:
    a. Create a table (grid) effect for the input data.
    b. Draw a double-lined outline around the entire report.

3. Save your worksheet as W5NAILS.

4. Print the entire worksheet on one page.

Tutorial 6

Creating and Printing Graphs

Automobile Industry Sales: A Four-year Summary

OBJECTIVES

In this tutorial you will learn to:

- Start 1-2-3 and PrintGraph

- Create pie, line, bar, and stacked bar graphs

- Add titles, legends, and axis formatting

- Display bar graphs horizontally

- Add 3D effect to bar graphs

- Name and save graph settings

- Save graphs for printing

- Customize and use PrintGraph to print saved graphs

Case: McAuliffe & Burns

Carl Martinez majored in human resources in college and was particularly interested in labor relations. Thus, he was delighted when he landed a job as a staff assistant with McAuliffe & Burns (M&B), a leading consulting firm in Washington, D.C. M&B specializes in consulting to unions on labor relations issues.

When Carl began at M&B, his computer skills were not as polished as those of the other staff assistants. He knew how to use a word processor, but his spreadsheet skills were limited. But after M&B sent him to a two-day workshop on Lotus 1-2-3, Carl used Lotus 1-2-3 daily to prepare analyses for M&B's senior consultants. Over time Carl's skills with Lotus 1-2-3 improved dramatically, and he was promoted to a staff associate.

In his new job Carl is working for three senior consultants on a project for the United Auto Workers (UAW) union. Leaders of the UAW hired M&B to help them prepare testimony for upcoming Congressional committee hearings that will investigate whether the United States should establish import quotas for foreign cars.

Carl's first task is to research all automobile sales in the United States and gather data on unit sales by year and by company. After he gathers the data and creates a worksheet, Carl decides that he could present the data more effectively if he used the graphics function of Lotus 1-2-3. Carl is convinced that the data will make more of an impact on the Congressional subcommittee members if the UAW leaders show graphic representations of trends and markets. Carl plans to use a bar graph to show trends and a pie chart to show market shares. Figure 6-1a on the following page shows Carl's planning sheet for preparing his graphs. Figure 6-1b on the following page shows his sketches of the graphs he wants to create with 1-2-3.

Figure 6-1a
Carl's planning
sheet

My Goal:
  Prepare graphs showing market shares and trends of automobile sales
  in U.S. from 1987 – 1990

What results do I want to see?
  Bar graphs of sales from 1987 – 1990
  Pie chart showing market shares for 1990

What information do I need?
  Number of cars sold by year for General Motors, Ford, Chrysler, Honda,
  Toyota, and Nissan

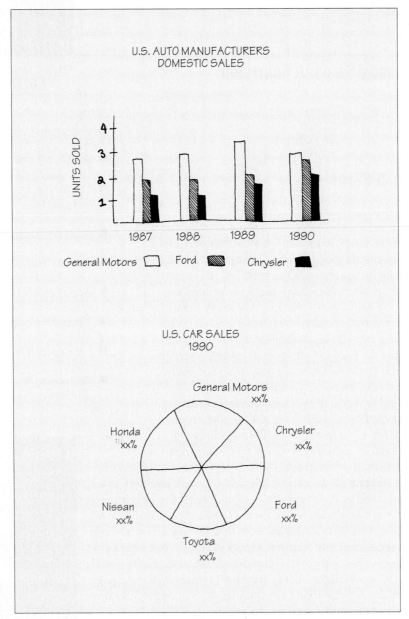

Figure 6-1b
Carl's sketches of
the graphs

This tutorial leads you through Carl's process of using graphs to analyze auto sales in the United States. After starting 1-2-3 from the Access menu, you will create a series of graphs to learn which type of graph is best suited to your data. Finally, you will print the graphs.

Introduction to Graphics

In business, graphics are used to represent one or more data series in a visually appealing and easily understood format. A **data series** is a single set of data represented by a line, a bar, or a pie. For example, a data series may include

- sales of a product by quarter (one data series)
- sales of three products by quarter (three data series)
- daily stock prices of a company over the past month (one data series)
- daily stock prices of two companies over the past month (two data series)

With your computer and 1-2-3, you can create graphs that will help you communicate your ideas quickly and easily. Lotus 1-2-3 includes a variety of graphs: bar graphs, line graphs, stacked bar graphs, pie charts, and XY graphs.

A **bar graph** consists of a series of vertical or horizontal bars. Each bar in the chart represents a single value from a set of values. The length or height of each bar is determined by the size of each value relative to all the other values. A bar graph is used to compare related data items during one time period or over a few time periods, such as four quarters. Bar graphs use the x axis, or horizontal axis, to classify data over regions, over time, over products, and so on. The vertical, or y, axis shows the quantity you are measuring, such as dollars, units sold, weight, or number of employees. For example, revenue at TriCycle Industries (Tutorial 4) could be represented by a bar graph that shows the relationship of sales of recycled materials by quarter (Figure 6-2a).

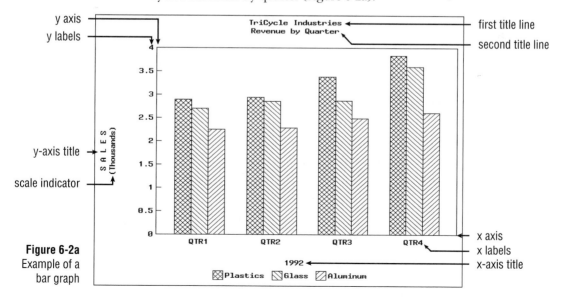

Figure 6-2a
Example of a bar graph

A **line graph** represents data with points and connects these points with a straight line. Line graphs are effective at showing trends in data over time. Each line represents one set of data, such as the daily stock prices of IBM. A line graph is a better choice than a bar graph to present a large number of data points over time. Figure 6-2b uses a line graph to show quarterly revenue for each recycled material at TriCycle Industries.

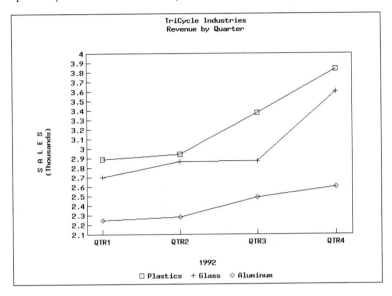

Figure 6-2b
Example of a
line graph

Stacked bar graphs show related data values on top of one another. These graphs show the components of several wholes. They are used to emphasize several totals and a breakdown of their components. For example, sales of each recycled material at TriCycle for the first quarter would appear on one bar, one material on top of the other (Figure 6-2c). A second bar would represent the same data for the second quarter. A third and fourth bar would show the sales of the last two quarters. This graph can compare total sales over several quarters, while also identifying the components that make up each quarterly total.

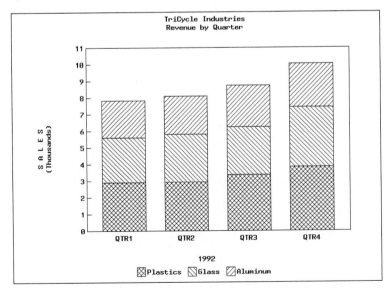

Figure 6-2c
Example of a
stacked bar graph

Pie charts are useful for showing how each value contributes to the whole. For example, the total 1990 sales at TriCycle are divided among plastics, glass, and aluminum (Figure 6-2d), each represented by a slice of the whole. The size of a slice depends on its component's value relative to the whole. When you want to express your data as percentages, consider using pie charts. You can emphasize one or more slices by using a cut, or "exploded," slice to draw the viewer's attention.

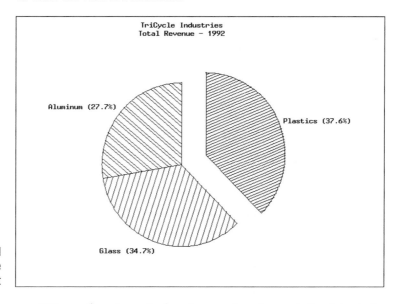

Figure 6-2d
Example of a pie chart

XY graphs, also called scatter graphs, show relationships between two variables. This type of graph shows how a change in one variable relates to another variable. For example, sales management at TriCycle graphed the relationship between the amount of recycled material in tons and sales revenue at TriCycle (Figure 6-2e). We will not cover XY graphs in this tutorial, but you should be aware that Lotus 1-2-3 can produce XY graphs.

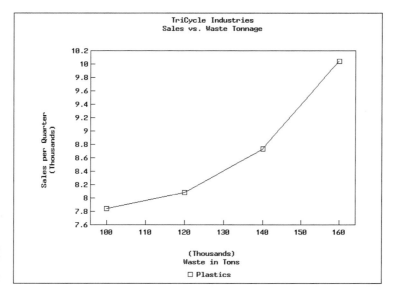

Figure 6-2e
Example of an XY graph

Mixed graphs combine lines and bars in the same graph. Lines are used to accent information in related bars. For example, Figure 6-2f on the following page shows how the quarterly revenue of each of TriCycle Industries' products, shown as bars, can be compared to average quarterly sales, shown as a line.

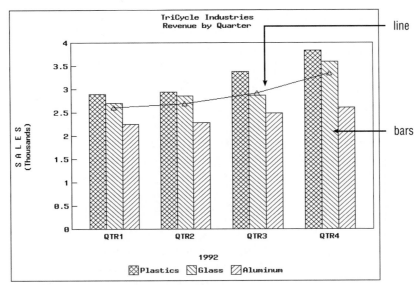

Figure 6-2f
Example of a
mixed graph

Creating a Bar Graph

Now let's retrieve one of Carl's worksheets that contains the number of cars sold in the United States from 1987 to 1990.

To retrieve this file:

❶   Retrieve the file C6AUTO1.WK1. See Figure 6-3.

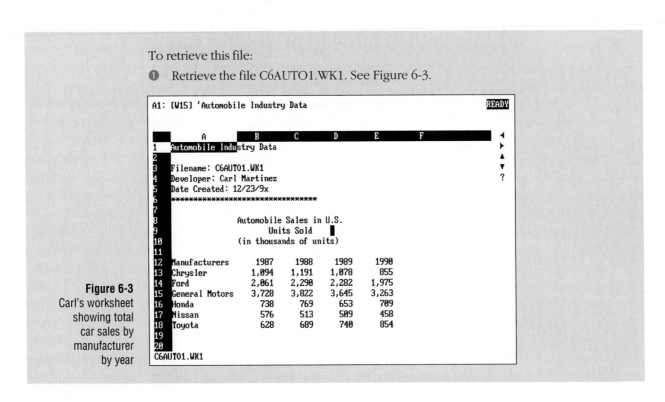

Figure 6-3
Carl's worksheet
showing total
car sales by
manufacturer
by year

Notice that the data in Figure 6-3 contain the number of cars sold annually in the United States from 1987 through 1990, broken down by manufacturer.

According to Carl's sketch, one of the graphs he wants to create is a bar graph showing car sales by manufacturer. Before creating the bar graph, you first need to learn about the Graph menu and the Graph Settings dialog box.

To create any graph in 1-2-3, you must use the Graph command. This command reveals the **Graph Settings dialog box,** in which you specify what data you want to graph and how you want to graph them. As you use the menu options available from the Graph command, 1-2-3 updates the Graph Settings dialog box.

To create a graph, you must specify the following:

- the type of graph you want
- the range of cells that represent the labels for the x axis
- the data series you plan to use in the graph

Carl plans first to compare graphically the total units sold by U.S. manufacturers (Chrysler, Ford, General Motors) over a four-year period (1987 to 1990) and then to compare these total U.S. units to units sold in the United States by Japanese manufacturers. Let's start by creating a bar graph of Chrysler's data that shows unit sales over a four-year period.

To create a bar graph of cars sold by Chrysler:

❶ Select /Graph (**/G**). 1-2-3 displays the Graph Settings dialog box.

❷ Select Type (**T**) and then select Bar (**B**) to indicate the type of graph you want to create — a bar graph. The graph settings now indicate the graph will be a bar graph. See Figure 6-4.

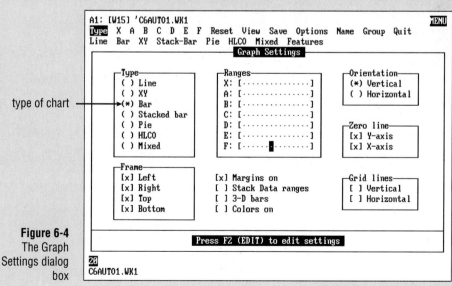

type of chart ──→

Figure 6-4
The Graph
Settings dialog
box

Next, specify the X data range, the worksheet range that contains the *labels* you want to place along the *x axis* (horizontal axis). Recall from Carl's sketch (Figure 6-1b) that you are using the years 1987, 1988, 1989, and 1990 as the x-axis labels.

③ Select **X** to specify the X data range. 1-2-3 reveals Carl's worksheet.

④ Move the cell pointer to cell B12, the first label to appear on the x axis. Press **[.]** (Period) to anchor the cell pointer. Then highlight the range B12..E12 and press **[Enter]** to specify the X data range.

Now use the same method to specify the first data series, sales of Chrysler cars from 1987 to 1990, to appear in the graph. The first data series is assigned to the A data range of your 1-2-3 Graph menu.

⑤ Select **A** to specify the A data range from the Graph menu. Move the cell pointer to B13, the cell containing Chrysler's sales data for 1987. Press **[.]** to anchor the cell pointer. Highlight B13..E13. See Figure 6-5a.

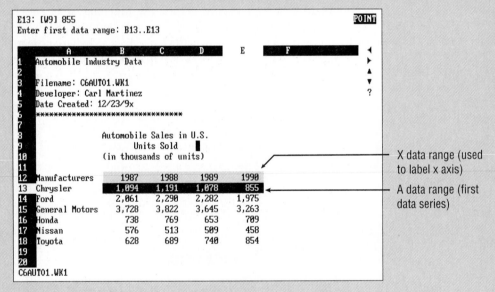

Figure 6-5a
Specifying the data range

⑥ Press **[Enter]**.

The Graph Settings dialog box now indicates the graph type and the X and A ranges you specified. See Figure 6-5b. You can graph up to six data series at one time. 1-2-3 uses the letters A through F to represent these data series.

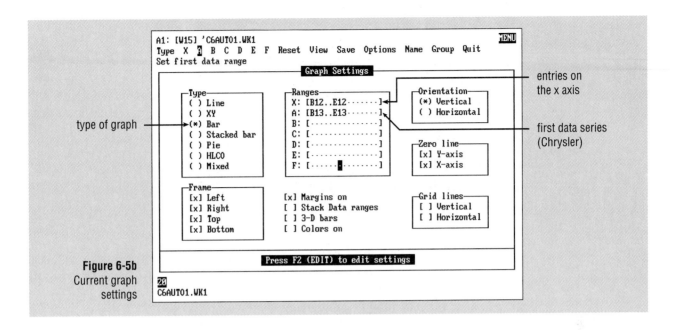

A1: [W15] 'C6AUT01.WK1   **MENU**
Type X █ B C D E F Reset View Save Options Name Group Quit
Set first data range

┌─────────────────────── Graph Settings ───────────────────────┐

type of graph ───→
┌─Type──────────┐   ┌─Ranges──────────┐   ┌─Orientation─┐
│ ( ) Line   │   │ X: [B12..E12······] │   │ (*) Vertical   │
│ ( ) XY   │   │ A: [B13..E13······] │   │ ( ) Horizontal │
│→(*) Bar   │   │ B: [·············] │   └────────────────┘
│ ( ) Stacked bar │ │ C: [·············] │
│ ( ) Pie   │   │ D: [·············] │   ┌─Zero line──┐
│ ( ) HLCO   │   │ E: [·············] │   │ [x] Y-axis │
│ ( ) Mixed   │   │ F: [······█······] │   │ [x] X-axis │
└───────────────┘   └─────────────────┘   └────────────┘

┌─Frame─────────┐
│ [x] Left   │   [x] Margins on   ┌─Grid lines──┐
│ [x] Right   │   [ ] Stack Data ranges │ [ ] Vertical   │
│ [x] Top   │   [ ] 3-D bars   │ [ ] Horizontal │
│ [x] Bottom   │   [ ] Colors on   └────────────────┘
└───────────────┘

┌─────────────── Press F2 (EDIT) to edit settings ───────────────┐

20
C6AUT01.WK1

entries on
the x axis

first data series
(Chrysler)

Figure 6-5b
Current graph
settings

Viewing the Current Graph

After you have chosen your graph type and specified the data ranges, you can view the graph on the screen.

To view the graph from in the Graph menu:

❶ Select View (**V**). The graph appears on the screen. See Figure 6-6.

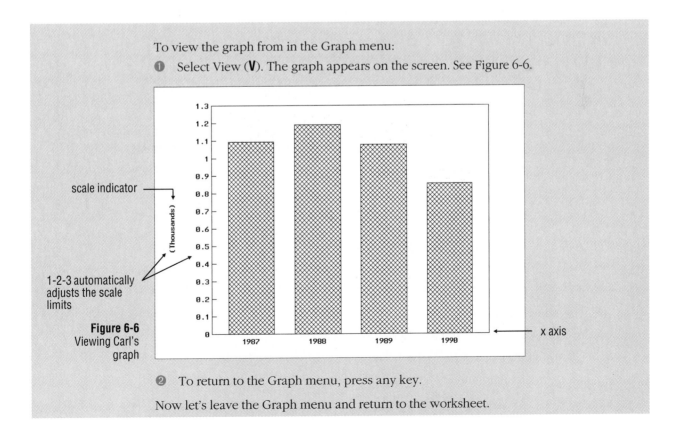

scale indicator ───→

1-2-3 automatically
adjusts the scale
limits

Figure 6-6
Viewing Carl's
graph

x axis

❷ To return to the Graph menu, press any key.

Now let's leave the Graph menu and return to the worksheet.

❸   Select Quit (**Q**). Now you are in READY mode.

In 1-2-3, the graph that appears on the screen when you enter the View command is called the **current graph**. You can also use [F10] (GRAPH) to display the current graph. This feature allows you to change data in your worksheet and quickly see the results in a graph.

To view the current graph by using the function key [F10]:

❶   Press **[F10]** (GRAPH). The current graph appears.

❷   Press any key to return to the worksheet.

If you press [F10] (GRAPH) when there is no graph type, no A data range, or no X data range specified in the dialog box, your screen will become blank. If that happens, press any key to return to the worksheet.

Adding Multiple Variables

Following Carl's plan, let's continue developing the graph by returning to the Graph menu and then adding the unit sales for Ford and General Motors, that is, the B and C data ranges, to the bar graph.

To add the B and C data ranges to the bar graph:

❶   Select /Graph (**/G**) to return to the Graph menu. The second data series, cars sold by Ford, will be assigned to the second, or B, data range.

❷   Select **B** to specify the B data range from the Graph menu.

❸   Move the cell pointer to B14, the cell containing Ford sales data for 1987. Press **[.]** (Period) to anchor the cell pointer. Highlight B14..E14. Press **[Enter]**.

The Graph Settings dialog box now indicates the graph type and the X, A, and B ranges you have specified.

Now specify the third, or C, data range, sales of General Motors cars from 1987 to 1990.

❹   Select **C**, for the C data range, from the Graph menu. You will assign the data for General Motors to this range.

Move the cell pointer to B15, the cell containing General Motors sales data for 1987. Press **[.]** (Period) to anchor the cell pointer. Highlight B15..E15 and press **[Enter]**.

The Graph Settings dialog box now indicates the graph type and the X, A, B, and C ranges you have specified. See Figure 6-7.

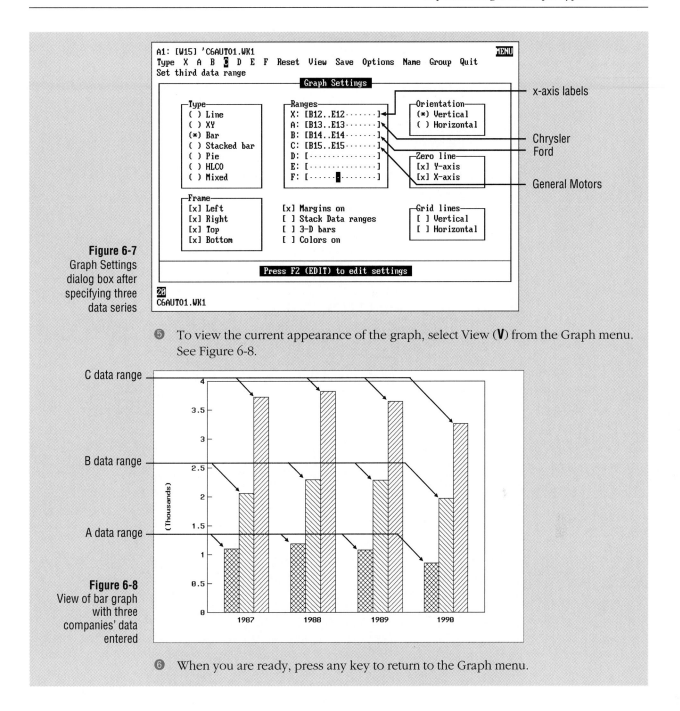

Figure 6-7
Graph Settings
dialog box after
specifying three
data series

⑤ To view the current appearance of the graph, select View (**V**) from the Graph menu.
See Figure 6-8.

Figure 6-8
View of bar graph
with three
companies' data
entered

⑥ When you are ready, press any key to return to the Graph menu.

Experimenting with Graph Types

Some types of graphs may be more appropriate for your data than others. You can
experiment with types of graphs by simply selecting another graph type from the Graph
menu. You can display the same data in different forms and see which form best presents

the information. Let's illustrate this concept by changing the graph you just created to a line graph and then to a stacked bar graph.

To change graph type to a line graph:

❶ Select Type Line (**TL**) and then select View (**V**). The data appear as a line graph. See Figure 6-9.

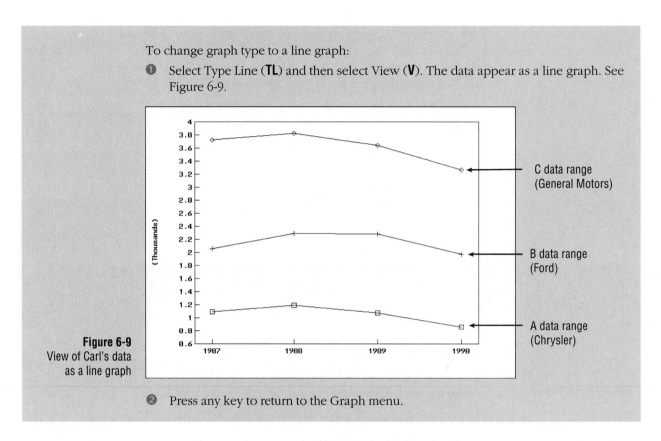

Figure 6-9
View of Carl's data
as a line graph

❷ Press any key to return to the Graph menu.

Now let's see how a stacked bar graph displays the data.

To display a stacked bar graph:

❶ Select Type and Stack-Bar (**TS**).

❷ Select View (**V**). See Figure 6-10.

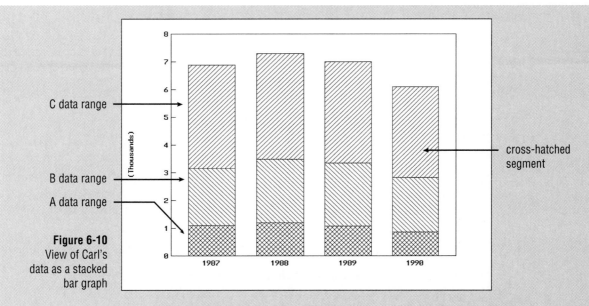

Figure 6-10
View of Carl's
data as a stacked
bar graph

1-2-3 displays the data as a stacked bar graph. This graph has a single bar for every value in the X data range, that is, a bar for each year. Each bar is made up of cross-hatched segments. Each segment of a bar represents the sales that each manufacturer contributed to total domestic sales in that year. Each bar viewed as a whole shows the total domestic sales in each year.

❸ Press any key to return to the Graph menu.

Carl decides that the relationships among the companies over the small number of time periods can best be shown by a bar graph. Let's return the graph settings to a bar graph.

To return the graph settings to those for a bar graph:

❶ Select Type Bar (**TB**).

❷ Select View (**V**). The bar graph appears on your screen.

❸ When you are ready, press any key to return to the Graph menu.

Carl decides not to try another popular type of graph, the pie chart, because it is not appropriate for the type of data with which he is working — data over time. A pie chart is more appropriate to show the relationship of the sales of each automobile company to total sales for a single year. You will create pie charts later in this tutorial.

Adding Titles and Legends

The current form of Carl's graph is difficult to interpret. What information does his graph represent? It has no title or labels to help anyone viewing the graph interpret the information. With 1-2-3 you can include a one- or two-line title and also label your x and y axes. Titles can be up to 39 characters.

Which bar in the graph represents General Motors sales? Ford sales? Chrysler sales? When you graph multiple data series, you should add a **legend** to identify the various lines in a line graph, the bars in a bar graph, or the segments in a stacked bar graph. The legend appears at the bottom of a graph below the x axis. You can add a legend of up to 19 characters for each data series.

Now you will add titles and legends to the bar graph you've created.

To add a title to your graph:

❶ From the Graph menu, select Options Titles First (**OTF**) to indicate you are entering the *first* line of the title. See Figure 6-11. A Graph Legends & Titles dialog box displays the options you specify.

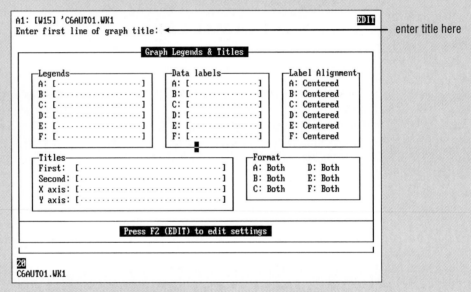

Figure 6-11
Graph Legends &
Titles dialog box

❷ Type **U.S. Auto Manufacturers**, the title of Carl's graph, and then press **[Enter]**.

❸ Select Titles Second (**TS**) to indicate you are entering the second line of the title.

❹ Type **Domestic Sales** for the second line of the title, then press **[Enter]**.

Now enter the information for each car company that will be contained in the legend.

To add legends to your graph:

❶ Select Legend A (**LA**) from the Graph menu. Then type **Chrysler** to specify the legend for the A data range. Press **[Enter]** to enter the legend setting.

❷ Select Legend B (**LB**) and type **Ford** for the legend for the B data range. Press **[Enter]**.

❸ Select Legend C (**LC**) and type **General Motors** for the legend for the C data range. See Figure 6-12.

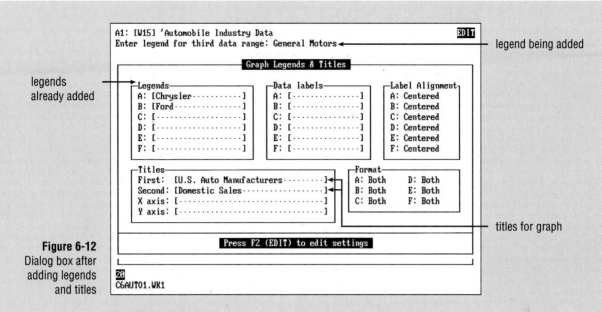

legend being added

legends already added

titles for graph

Figure 6-12
Dialog box after adding legends and titles

④ Press **[Enter]**.

⑤ Select Quit (**Q**) to leave the Options menu.

⑥ Select View (**V**) to display the graph with the title and the legends. See Figure 6-13.

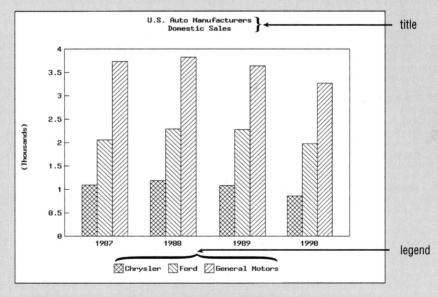

title

legend

Figure 6-13
View of Carl's bar graph with title and legends

⑦ Press any key to return to the Graph menu.

Adding Axis Titles

You can add titles for both the horizontal (x) and the vertical (y) axes. In the next steps you will add an axis title to improve the description of the y axis.

To add a y-axis title:

❶ From the Graph menu, choose Options Titles Y axis (**OTY**).

❷ Type **Units Sold**. Press **[Enter]**.

❸ Select Quit (**Q**) to return to the Graph menu.

❹ Select View (**V**) to see the revised graph. See Figure 6-14.

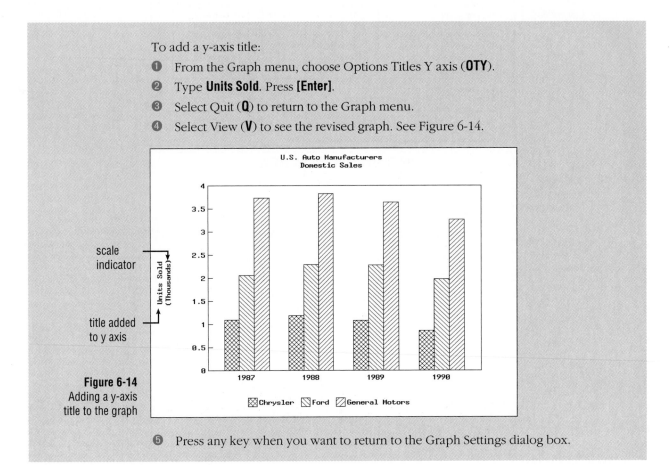

scale indicator

title added to y axis

Figure 6-14
Adding a y-axis title to the graph

❺ Press any key when you want to return to the Graph Settings dialog box.

Axis Scale Indicator

Carl has rounded the numbers in his worksheet to the nearest thousand, as indicated by the line in the worksheet (in thousands of units). For example, the 1990 entry for General Motors of 3,263 actually represents 3,263,000 units sold.

When you create a graph, 1-2-3 automatically scales, or adjusts, the values along the y axis based on the minimum and maximum values from the data series. When any of the y-axis values are above approximately 1,000, 1-2-3 scales the values that appear on the y axis, and automatically displays a scale indicator such as *Thousands* between the y axis and the y-axis title, as in Figure 6-14.

Sometimes the scale indicator may seem confusing. For example, in Figure 6-14, the y-axis title indicates thousands of units sold, but some of the numbers in the worksheet represent millions of units sold. The scale indicator is misleading. One solution is to suppress the display of the scale indicator and revise the y-axis title so it indicates the scale in millions of units sold. Let's do this for Carl's graph.

To remove the scale indicator from the y axis:

❶ Select Options Scale Y-Scale (**OSY**). See Figure 6-15. As the Graph Scale Settings dialog box indicates, the scale indicator is currently on.

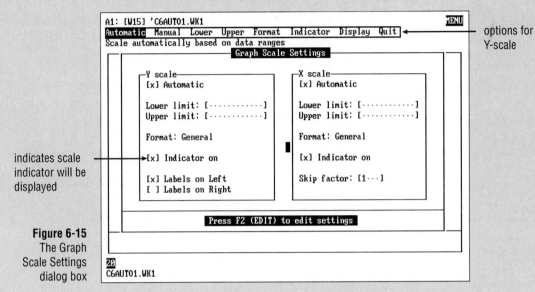

indicates scale indicator will be displayed

Figure 6-15
The Graph Scale Settings dialog box

options for Y-scale

A list of eight options appears in the control panel.

❷ Select Indicator (**I**).

To suppress the display of the scale indicator, choose No.

❸ Select No (**N**). The dialog box now shows that the indicator is off.

Now return to the Graph menu and view the graph.

④ Select Quit Quit View (**QQV**). See Figure 6-16. Notice that the scale indicator no longer appears on the graph.

indicator is suppressed →

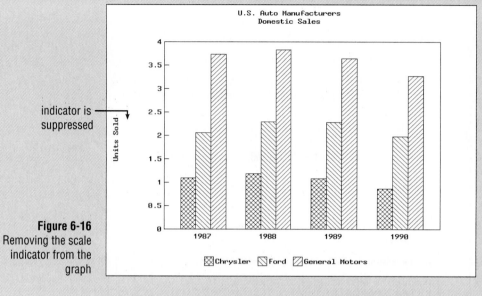

Figure 6-16
Removing the scale indicator from the graph

⑤ Press any key to return to the Graph Settings dialog box.

Now revise the y-axis title to include information indicating that the units sold are in millions.

To revise the y-axis title:
① Select Options Title (**OT**).

Next you need to change the y-axis title.

② Select y axis (**Y**).

The current title, Units Sold, appears in the control panel. Add the text "(in millions)" to the title.

③ Press **[Spacebar]** and type **(in millions)** and press **[Enter]**.

Now view the graph.

④ Select Quit View (**QV**). See Figure 6-17.

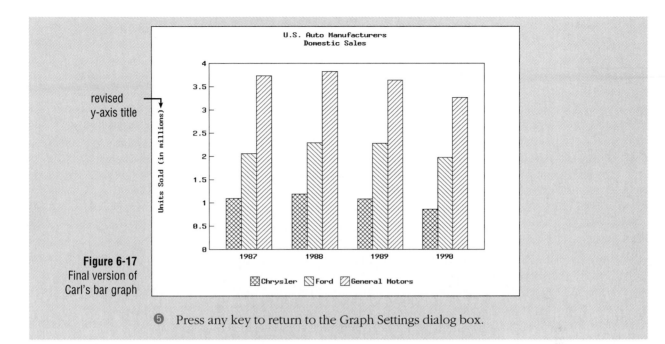

Figure 6-17
Final version of
Carl's bar graph

⑤ Press any key to return to the Graph Settings dialog box.

Naming the Current Graph

Carl plans to create several graphs within his worksheet. To have more than one graph available within your worksheet, you must assign a name to each graph. If you name this bar graph now, 1-2-3 stores all the settings needed to create this graph. Then whenever you want, you can view the graph without having to specify all the settings again.

Let's learn how to create named graphs in 1-2-3 by naming this bar graph BAR3. This name helps to describe the graph as a *bar* graph that compares *3* companies. Note that the bar graph is the current graph, because it is the one you have most recently entered.

To name the current graph:

❶ Select Name Create (**NC**). The Graph Settings dialog box appears on the screen, showing the settings that will be assigned to the named graph.

Figure 6-18a on the following page illustrates the current worksheet in the computer's memory.

You can enter a name of up to 15 characters. As with range names, spaces and certain characters are not recommended. It's often a helpful reminder to include the type of graph in the name you choose.

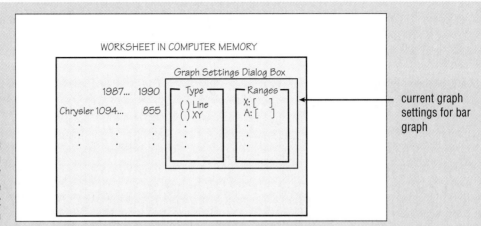

Figure 6-18a
Worksheet in
memory
immediately before
naming the current
graph

② Type **bar3** as the name of the graph and press **[Enter]**. You won't see any change in the graph settings; this name does not appear in the dialog box, but it does store the information found in the Graph Settings dialog box as part of the worksheet. Figure 6-18b shows that the current graph settings are now named BAR3 and stand as part of the worksheet within the computer's memory.

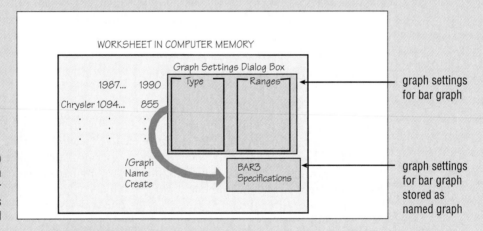

Figure 6-18b
Worksheet in
memory after
current graph has
been named

③ Select Quit (**Q**) to leave the Graph menu and return to READY mode. It is important to realize that when you name a graph you have not saved the graph specifications to disk. You have modified the worksheet only in the computer memory. To include a named graph as part of a worksheet file on disk, you must use the File Save command.

④ Save the worksheet file, which includes the named graph BAR3, as S6AUTO1.

Now when you save your worksheet, the settings for each named graph are saved as part of the worksheet. If you haven't named a graph, the settings for that graph will not be saved as part of the worksheet file. For example, earlier in the tutorial you created a line graph and a stacked bar graph. You did not, however, create a named graph for either of these graphs. Therefore, they were not saved as part of S6AUTO1.WK1. See Figure 6-18c.

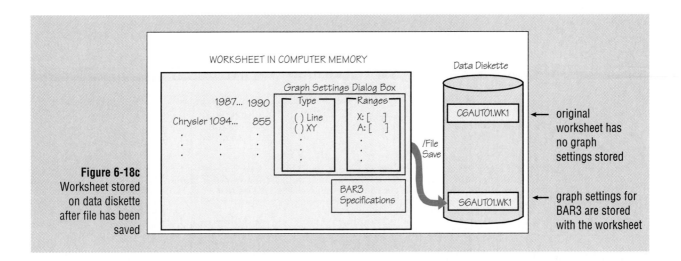

Figure 6-18c
Worksheet stored
on data diskette
after file has been
saved

Resetting Graph Settings

Once you have named a graph, you can define another graph. First, you may need to erase some or all of the current graph settings. You can erase the graph settings for the current graph by using the Graph Reset command.

To erase *all* the current graph settings:

❶ Select /Graph Reset (**/GR**). See Figure 6-19.

You can reset each setting individually, or you can reset the entire graph.

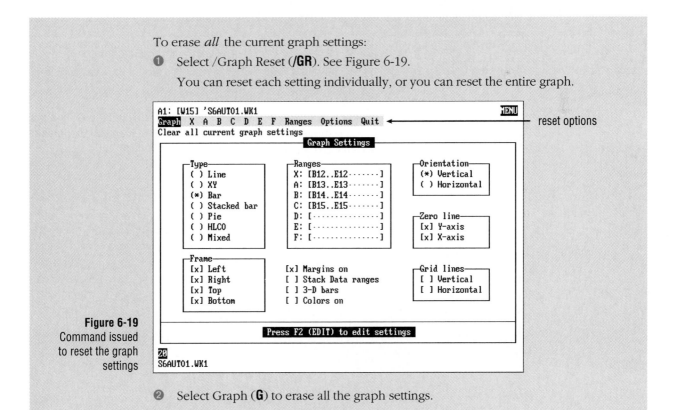

Figure 6-19
Command issued
to reset the graph
settings

❷ Select Graph (**G**) to erase all the graph settings.

The current settings disappear from the Graph Settings dialog box. See Figure 6-20.

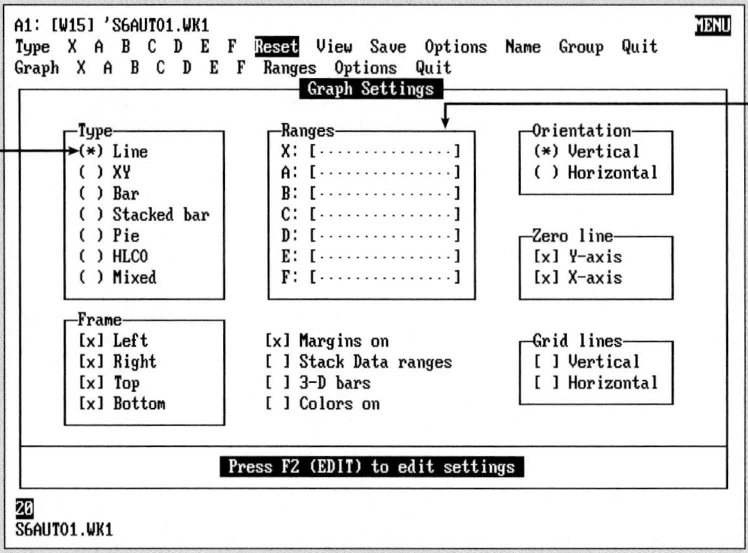

default graph type →

no data range →

Figure 6-20
Graph settings
reset

3. Select View (**V**). No graph appears because there are no current graph settings.
4. Press any key to return to the Graph Settings dialog box.

Even though the graph settings are cleared from the screen, the settings for BAR3 are still stored in memory as part of the worksheet. These settings are available by retrieving the named graph BAR3.

Retrieving a Named Graph

You were not able to view the bar graph after you erased the graph settings. However, since you have named your graph, the settings are still part of the worksheet. You can display the bar graph by selecting it from a list of named graph settings.

To view a named graph:
1. Select Name Use (**NU**). 1-2-3 displays the names of all the graph settings that are part of this worksheet. In this case, only one graph name appears because you have named only one so far in this tutorial.
2. With BAR3 highlighted, press **[Enter]** to view the graph. The bar graph appears on the screen. 1-2-3 has retrieved the graph settings for BAR3 that were stored as part of the worksheet and entered them as the current graph settings.
3. Press any key. The Graph Settings dialog box now contains the settings for the bar graph. See Figure 6-21.

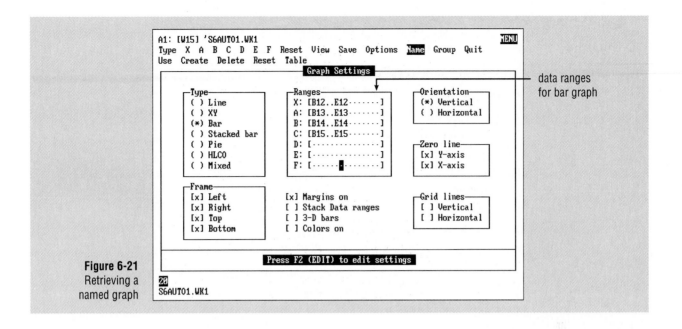

Figure 6-21
Retrieving a
named graph

Defining All Data Ranges Using the Group Command

Now Carl wants to create a bar graph that compares sales for all six companies. To create this graph, he can define each range one at a time as you did when you defined the previous graph. However, he can complete this task much more quickly. If he enters all the data for the graph in one continuous range (adjacent cells), he can use the Group command from the Graph menu to set the X range and all the data ranges for the graph in one step. Let's do this, but before you begin to specify the settings for this graph, let's clear the range settings for the current graph.

To clear the range settings for the current graph:

❶ Select Reset (**R**).

Reset only the range settings.

❷ Select Ranges (**R**). The range settings for X, A, B, and C ranges no longer appear in the Graph Settings dialog box.

❸ Select Quit (**Q**) to return to the Graph menu.

Now you can create the bar graph. Since the data are entered in adjacent cells, you can use the Group command to select a multiple graph range.

To create a bar graph using the Group command:

❶ Select Group (**G**).

Now identify the group range. The data in the first row become the X range, the data in the second row become the A range, the data in the third row become the B range, and so on.

❷   Move the cell pointer to cell B12.

❸   Press **[.]** (Period) to anchor the cell pointer, highlight B12..E18, and press **[Enter]**.

Now 1-2-3 asks how to graph the groups, Columnwise or Rowwise.

If you select Columnwise, the first column within the group will be the X range, and the remaining columns will be used as the data ranges. If you select Rowwise, the first row will be the X range, and the remaining rows will be the data ranges. Let's use Rowwise.

❹   Select Rowwise (**R**). See Figure 6-22.

ranges indicate a rowwise selection

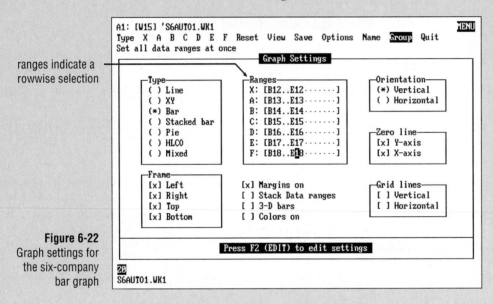

Figure 6-22
Graph settings for the six-company bar graph

Now view the graph.

❺   Select View (**V**). See Figure 6-23.

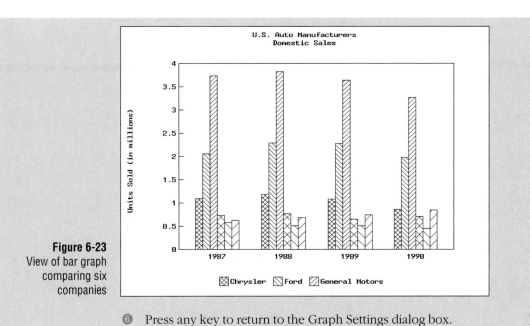

Figure 6-23
View of bar graph comparing six companies

⑥ Press any key to return to the Graph Settings dialog box.

Your legend is not accurate; it still reflects the settings from the previous graph. Let's correct the legend.

To add legends for the new graph:

① Select Options Legend (**OL**).

② Select Range (**R**).

Now identify the labels you want to use as legends.

③ Move the cell pointer to A13.

④ Press **[.]** (Period) to anchor the cell pointer, highlight the range A13..A18, and press **[Enter]**.

Next let's view the graph.

⑤ Select Quit View (**QV**). See Figure 6-24 on the following page. The legends now reflect the six bars.

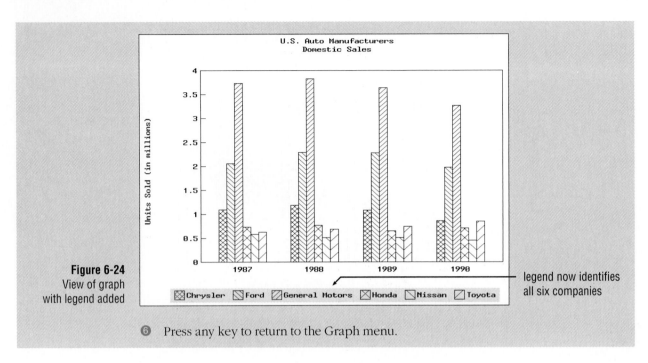

Figure 6-24
View of graph
with legend added

legend now identifies
all six companies

⑥ Press any key to return to the Graph menu.

The Features option from the Graph Type menu also allows you to change the appearance of your graph in other ways. You can use the Horizontal option to rotate the orientation of the graph, and you can use the 3D-Effect option with bar or stacked bar graphs to give an impression of depth in the chart. Let's examine these now.

Horizontal Bar Graphs

You can display a bar graph vertically or horizontally. The standard bar graph is typically displayed vertically. A horizontal bar graph rotates the graph so that it is displayed horizontally on the screen. When you use the Horizontal option, the graph's x axis runs vertically along the left side of the screen and the y-axis labels are along the top. Like a standard bar graph, this graph is used to compare and contrast values. You will use your personal preference to decide on the repositioning of the axes. Let's try the horizontal approach to see how you like it.

To change a vertical bar graph to a horizontal orientation:
❶ Select Type Features (**TF**).
❷ Select Horizontal (**H**).
❸ Select View (**V**). See Figure 6-25.

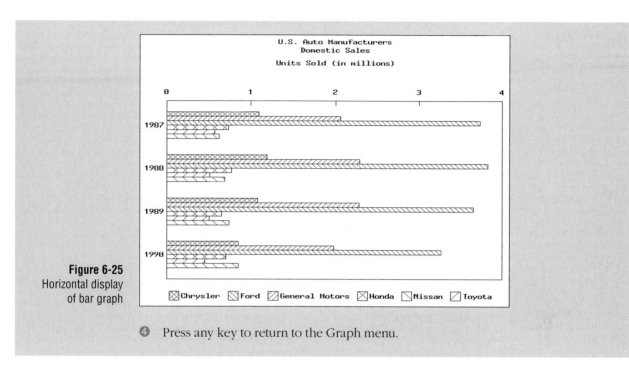

Figure 6-25
Horizontal display
of bar graph

④ Press any key to return to the Graph menu.

After looking at this version of the graph, Carl decides he prefers the vertical orientation. Let's change the graph back to the vertical orientation.

To return to the vertical orientation:
① Select Type Features (**TF**).
② Select Vertical (**V**).
③ Press **[F10]** (GRAPH). Notice that the bar graph is back to standard vertical orientation.
④ Press any key to return to the Graph menu.
⑤ Select Quit (**Q**) to return to the Graph menu.

3D Bar Graphs

1-2-3 allows you to enhance your bar, stacked bar, and mixed graphs to show a three-dimensional effect, which some people prefer to two-dimensional graphs. Let's add a three-dimensional (3D) effect to the current graph.

To add a 3D effect to a bar graph:
① Select Type Features (**TF**).
② Select 3D-Effect Yes (**3Y**).

❸ Select Quit View (**QV**). See Figure 6-26.

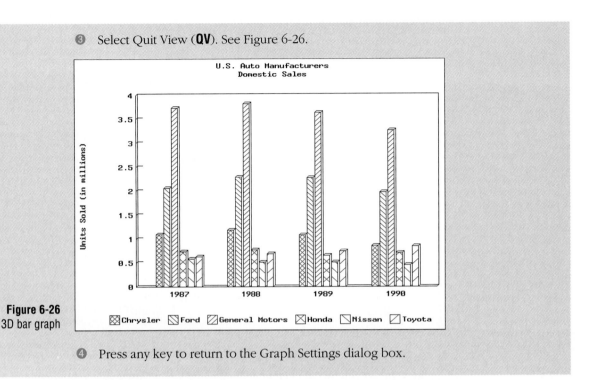

Figure 6-26
3D bar graph

❹ Press any key to return to the Graph Settings dialog box.

Which do you think is more attractive? Let's leave Carl's graph in 3D. You have now completed it, so let's name it.

To name the current graph:

❶ Select Name Create (**NC**). The Graph Settings dialog box appears showing the settings that will be assigned to the named graph.

Let's name the graph BAR6 to describe this file as containing a bar graph comparing the sales of the six companies.

❷ Type **bar6** as the name of the graph and press **[Enter]**.

❸ Select Quit (**Q**) to leave the Graph menu and return to READY mode.

❹ Save the worksheet again as S6AUTO1.

Creating a Pie Chart

Now that Carl has looked at automobile sales over time, he decides to focus on sales in a single year — 1990, the last year for which he has complete data. A pie chart is a useful way to visualize data for an entire year, because pie charts typically represent the relative contribution of each part to the whole. The larger the slice, the greater that part's percentage of the whole. When you create a pie chart, you need

- the set of values that represent the slices of the pie
- the set of labels that identify each slice of the pie chart

Before you can enter the settings for the pie chart, you must erase the bar graph settings.

To erase the current graph settings:

❶ Select /Graph (**/G**). Notice that the settings for the bar graph are the current settings.

❷ Select Reset Graph (**RG**). This erases the settings for the bar graph.

Selecting the A Range

Now Carl can begin to enter the settings for the pie chart.

To create a pie chart for the number of cars sold in 1990:

❶ Select Type Pie (**TP**). The pie chart becomes the current graph type. The A data range is used to indicate the set of values that represent the slices of the pie.

❷ Select **A**, the range representing the set of values in the pie chart.

❸ Move the cell pointer to E13, number of cars sold by Chrysler for 1990, and press **[.]** to anchor the cell pointer. Highlight E13..E18 and press **[Enter]**. See Figure 6-27.

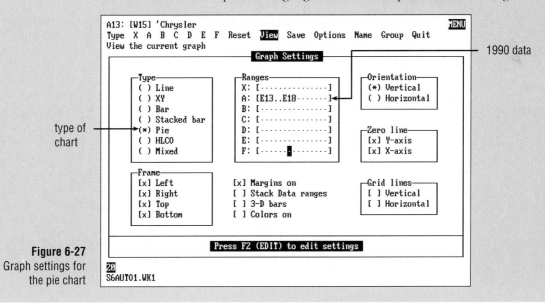

Figure 6-27
Graph settings for
the pie chart

④ Select View (**V**) to view the status of your graph. See Figure 6-28.

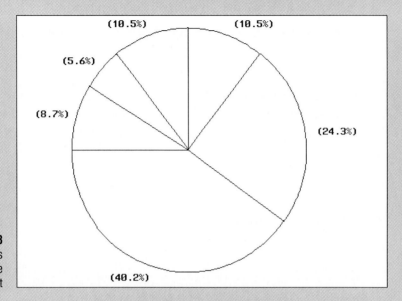

Figure 6-28
A view of Carl's
unlabeled pie
chart

⑤ When you are ready, press any key to return to the Graph menu.

Selecting the X Range

As you viewed the graph, you could not tell which car manufacturer was represented by which slice. Thus, you need to specify in the X range the labels that describe the slices. You will use the names of the car manufacturers in column A of the worksheet as the labels for the slices of the pie chart.

To label each pie slice:

① Select **X**.

② Move the cell pointer to A13, the cell holding the label Chrysler. Press **[.]** to anchor the cell pointer. Highlight A13..A18. Press **[Enter]**. Note that the labels in the X range correspond to the elements in the A range, that is, the first label in the X range will be the label of the first slice in the A range, and so on.

③ Press View (**V**) to view the pie chart. See Figure 6-29. Now you can identify each slice in the pie chart with a manufacturer.

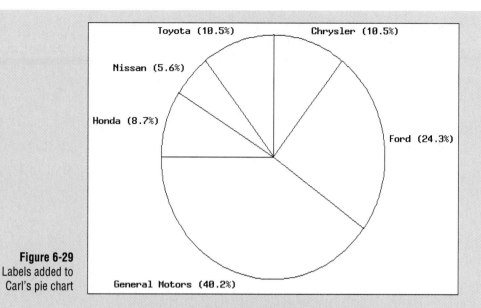

Figure 6-29
Labels added to
Carl's pie chart

❹ When you are ready, press any key to return to the Graph menu.

To help readers interpret your pie chart, you should add a title describing its contents. 1-2-3 allows you to include two title lines in the pie chart. Recall that Carl's sketch of the pie chart had a two-line title: U.S. CAR SALES, 1990.

To add a title to the pie chart:
❶ Select Options Titles First (**OTF**) to add the first line of the title.
❷ Type **U.S. CAR SALES**, then press **[Enter]**.
❸ Select Titles Second (**TS**) to add the second line of the title.
❹ Type **1990** and press **[Enter]**.
❺ Select Quit (**Q**) to leave the Options menu.
❻ Select View (**V**) to see the title you have added to the graph. See Figure 6-30 on the following page.

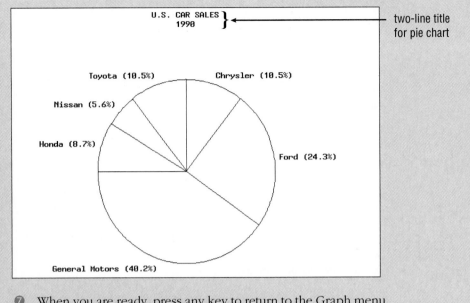

two-line title
for pie chart

Figure 6-30
A two-line title
added to Carl's
pie chart

❼ When you are ready, press any key to return to the Graph menu.

❽ Select Quit (**Q**) to leave the Graph menu.

Selecting the B Range

To make the pie chart easier to read, hatch patterns can be added to shade each slice of the pie chart. You use the B data range to add shading to your pie chart. The B data range is set up in your worksheet to correspond to the elements in the A data range. Each cell in the B range is associated with one cell in the A range. In each cell of the B range, you can enter a number between 1 and 7. 1-2-3 associates these numbers, when used in the B range of the graph settings for a pie chart, with different hatch patterns. A value of 0, 8, or a blank assigned to a cell in the B range indicates you do not want shading in the associated slice.

Let's use cells F13 to F18 to enter the shading codes. The first cell, F13, will identify Chrysler. The second cell, F15, will identify General Motors. The final cell, F17, will identify Nissan. In this graph you will assign shading to the slices for Chrysler, General Motors, and Nissan. The other cells, F14, F16, and F18, are automatically a value of zero, which 1-2-3 interprets to mean "no shading for this slice."

To assign hatch-pattern codes for slices of the pie chart:

❶ Move the cell pointer to cell F13, type **1,** and then press **[Enter]**. This code will assign a pattern to Chrysler's slice.

❷ Move the cell pointer to cell F15, type **2,** and then press **[Enter]**. This code will assign a different pattern to General Motors' slice.

❸ Move the cell pointer to cell F17, type **3**, and then press **[Enter]**. This code will assign yet another pattern to Nissan's slice. See Figure 6-31.

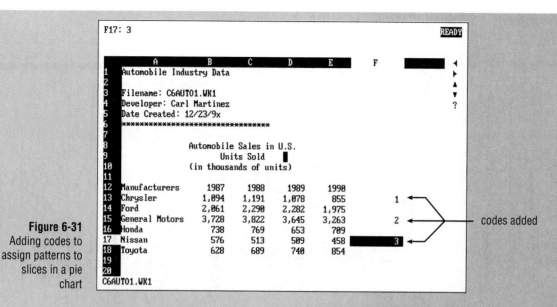

Figure 6-31
Adding codes to assign patterns to slices in a pie chart

Notice that the cells identifying Ford (cell F14), Honda (cell F16), and Toyota (cell F18) are blank. 1-2-3 interprets these blank cells as zero, and no hatched pattern will fill these slices of the pie chart. We have intentionally left these cells blank, because too many patterns make it difficult to distinguish slices.

For the shading to be included in the pie chart, the B range must be included in the graph settings.

To define the B range in the graph settings:

1. Select /Graph B (**/GB**).
2. Move the cell pointer to cell F13, the cell that corresponds to the first cell of the A data range. Press **[.]** [Period] to anchor the cell pointer. Then highlight the range F13..F18 and press **[Enter]**. The B range is now included in the graph settings. See Figure 6-32 on the following page.

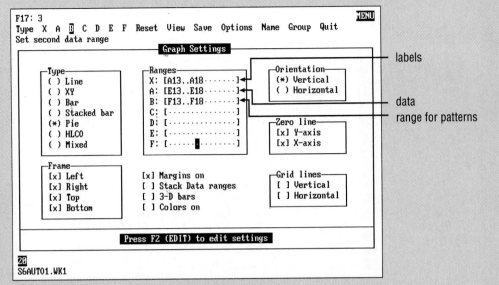

Figure 6-32
Graph Settings
dialog box with
the range for
patterns added

Be sure to highlight all cells in this range even though some may be blank. It's a good idea for the B data range to contain the same number of cells as the pie chart's A data range. This allows the shading assigned to each cell to correspond to the appropriate slice.

❸ Select View (**V**) to display the new pie chart. See Figure 6-33.

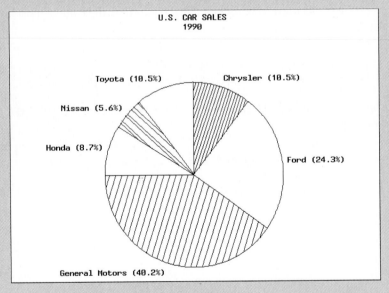

Figure 6-33
Carl's pie chart
with shading

❹ When you are ready, press any key to return to the Graph menu.

You can call even more attention to a slice of the pie chart by "exploding" it, that is, separating it from the rest of the pie. In 1-2-3 you indicate that a slice is to be exploded by adding 100 to whatever the value is in the B range. For example, if the value is 2, you would enter 102 in the B range.

The next steps show you how to set up and use the B data range for exploding a pie slice. Let's explode the slice that represents Chrysler.

First, leave the Graph menu:

❶ Select Quit (**Q**) to return to the worksheet.

❷ Move the cell pointer to F13, type **101**, and press **[Enter]**. See Figure 6-34.

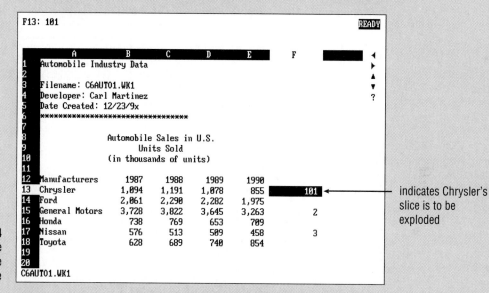

Figure 6-34
Adding the code to explode a pie slice

indicates Chrysler's slice is to be exploded

❸ Press **[F10]** (GRAPH) to view the pie chart. See Figure 6-35.

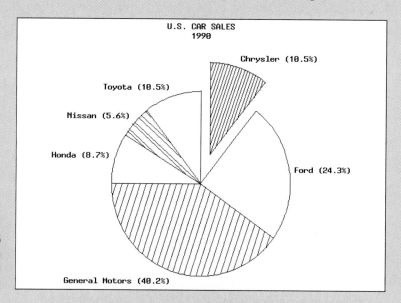

Figure 6-35
Carl's pie chart with shading and "exploded" slice

❹ When you are ready, press any key to return to READY mode.

Let's now assign a name to the pie chart so its settings will be stored with the worksheet.

To assign a name to the pie chart:

❶ Select /Graph Name Create (**/GNC**).

❷ Type **pie90**. Press **[Enter]**. Figure 6-36 shows that the current graph settings are now named PIE90 and are stored as part of the worksheet in the computer's memory.

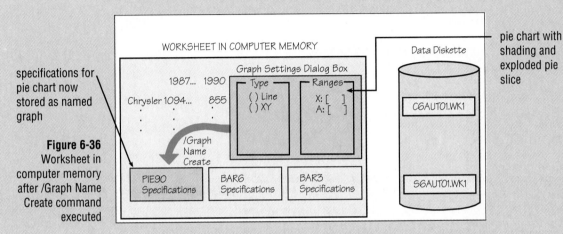

specifications for pie chart now stored as named graph

pie chart with shading and exploded pie slice

Figure 6-36
Worksheet in computer memory after /Graph Name Create command executed

❸ Select Quit (**Q**) to leave the Graph menu.

Save the worksheet file again.

❹ Select /File Save (**/FS**), press **[Enter]**, and select Replace (**R**). The current worksheet replaces the previous version of S6AUTO1.WK1. This saved worksheet now includes three named graphs: BAR3, BAR6, and PIE90. See Figure 6-37.

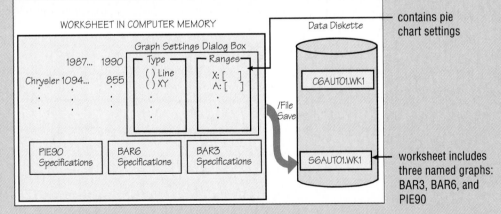

contains pie chart settings

Figure 6-37
Current worksheet replaces S6AUTO1.WK1 on data diskette after /File Save command executed

worksheet includes three named graphs: BAR3, BAR6, and PIE90

The use of the B range for shading and exploding slices applies to pie charts only. For other graph types the B range is used for data. Except for this special use of the B range, pie charts use only the X and A ranges.

Saving Graphs for Printing

In the previous section, you learned how to transform Carl's data into graphs. In this section you will print one of the graphs you created and named. To print a graph, you must take two steps: (1) save the graphs for printing with the Graph Save command and (2) print the graph with the Lotus PrintGraph program.

You must use a special command — the Graph Save command — to save a graph that you want to print. Saving the worksheet by using /File Save saves only *named* graphs for later *viewing*, but not for printing. The /File Save command does *not* create the type of files the PrintGraph program needs to print a graph. To save a graph for printing, *you must use the Graph Save command.* In the next steps you will learn how to save graphs specifically for printing.

To save a graph for printing:

❶ Select /Graph Name Use (**/GNU**) to list the named graphs. Next, retrieve BAR6, the graph you will print.

❷ Highlight BAR6. Press **[Enter]**. The second bar graph you created and named appears on the screen.

❸ Press any key to return to the Graph menu. The graph settings for the bar graph appear in the Graph Settings dialog box.

❹ Select Save (**S**) from the Graph menu. Only the current graph can be saved for printing.

Enter a name for the graph file. DOS limits the filename to eight characters, as it does for worksheet names.

❺ Type **p_bar6** and press **[Enter]**.

1-2-3 saves the graph in a file named P_BAR6.PIC; it automatically adds the extension .PIC. Each graph that you want to print must be saved as a separate .PIC file. See Figure 6-38.

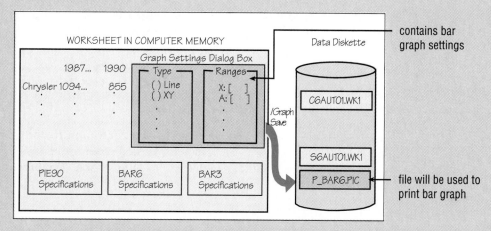

Figure 6-38
P_BAR6.PIC stored on data diskette after /Graph Save command executed

❻ Select Quit (**Q**) to return to READY mode.

❼ Select /File Save (**/FS**), press **[Enter]**, and select Replace (**R**).

Using PrintGraph

The **PrintGraph** program is a separate program that comes with 1-2-3 to enable you to print graphs. With PrintGraph you can print any graph you have previously saved with the Graph Save command.

> *Before continuing, check with your instructor or technical support person to see if PrintGraph is installed on your system. If it is installed, work through this section as usual. If PrintGraph is not installed, it can be installed using your copy of Lotus 1-2-3 software disks. Check with your instructor or technical support person or read the installation instructions that came with the software. If you are using Lotus 1-2-3 in a lab and PrintGraph cannot be installed, read this section, but do not press any keys.*

To start PrintGraph:

❶ Select /Quit Yes (**/QY**) to quit 1-2-3. You are now at the DOS prompt.

❷ Type **pgraph** and press **[Enter]**. The menu of PrintGraph commands appears at the top of the screen, and the current settings of PrintGraph appear below. Your screen should look similar to Figure 6-39.

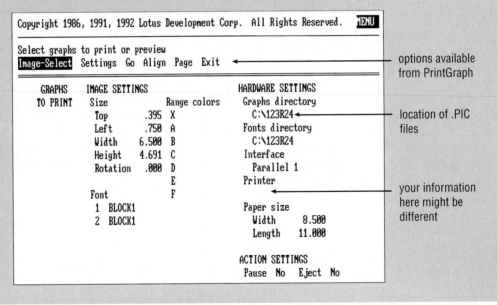

Figure 6-39
PrintGraph
settings

If this is the first time you have ever started PrintGraph, the program assumes that your graph (.PIC) files and font (.FNT) files are located either on a PrintGraph disk in drive A or, if you are using a hard-disk system, in your 1-2-3 directory. **Fonts** are the typefaces used to print the graph text.

Look at the rightmost column of the PrintGraph dialog box at the entries under Graphs directory and Fonts directory. You might need to adjust the disk/directory information for your Graph and Font directories and be sure your printer is specified properly. If necessary, ask your instructor or technical support person for assistance. The next steps show you how to change the PrintGraph settings in case the current settings are not correct for your system. Once you make and save these changes, you will not need to go through these steps again unless you make a change in your system.

To adjust the default PrintGraph settings, you first must specify the directory that contains the graph (.PIC) files so PrintGraph knows where to find your graphs:

❶ Select Settings Hardware Graphs-Directory (**SHG**).

❷ Enter the name of the directory or drive where you saved your graph (.PIC) files. Type **a:** (or the name of the drive that contains your graph [.PIC] files) and press **[Enter]**.

Next, specify the directory that contains the font (.FNT) files. PrintGraph needs to access these files to print your graphs.

❸ Select Fonts-Directory (**F**).

❹ Enter the name of the directory or drive where the fonts are stored.

Type **c:\123r23** and press **[Enter]** or check with your technical support person for the location of your fonts directory.

Finally, select a graphics printer to print your graphs.

❺ Select Printer (**P**) to display a list of installed printers.

If no printer names appear, rerun the Install program, as described in the Installation Guide.

❻ Follow the on-screen instructions. Press [↓] or [↑] to highlight the printer you want to use. Press **[Spacebar]** to mark your selection. Then press **[Enter]**. The # sign indicates the printer that you have selected for printing your graphs.

If you have a choice of low and high density, choose low density so your graphs will print more quickly. If you select high density, the quality of the graph will improve, but the graph will take longer to print.

❼ Select Quit (**Q**) to leave the Hardware menu and return to the PrintGraph menu.

❽ Select Save (**S**) to save these settings so they will appear automatically the next time you run PrintGraph.

These settings will remain as the current PrintGraph settings if you decide to print your graphs now.

Now you are ready to print the graph you saved as a .PIC file.

To print a single graph:

❶ Select Image-Select (**I**) from the PrintGraph menu to display an alphabetized list of all the graphs that have been saved for printing. See Figure 6-40.

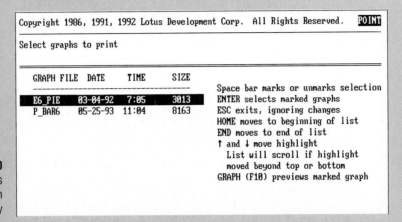

Figure 6-40
Lists of graphs
in the graph
directory

These are the files that you created with the Graph Save command and that 1-2-3 stored with a .PIC extension. Each file stores the description of one graph.

❷ With P_BAR6 highlighted, press **[Spacebar]** to mark your selection. The # sign indicates that a graph has been selected for printing. See Figure 6-41.

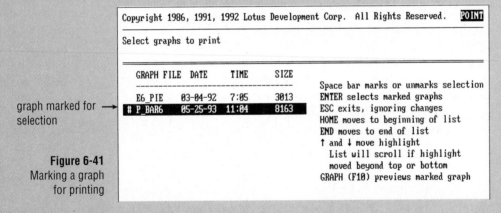

graph marked for →
selection

Figure 6-41
Marking a graph
for printing

If you change your mind about which graph to select, you can press [Spacebar] to unmark the selection.

❸ Press **[F10]** (GRAPH) to preview the graph. The bar graph appears on your screen. You should always preview a graph before you print it to make sure you have selected the graph you want to print. Press any key to leave the preview and return to the Select Graphs to Print screen.

❹ Press **[Enter]** to complete the selection process and return to the PrintGraph menu. Notice that a filename appears under the "Graphs to Print" section of the dialog box. See Figure 6-42.

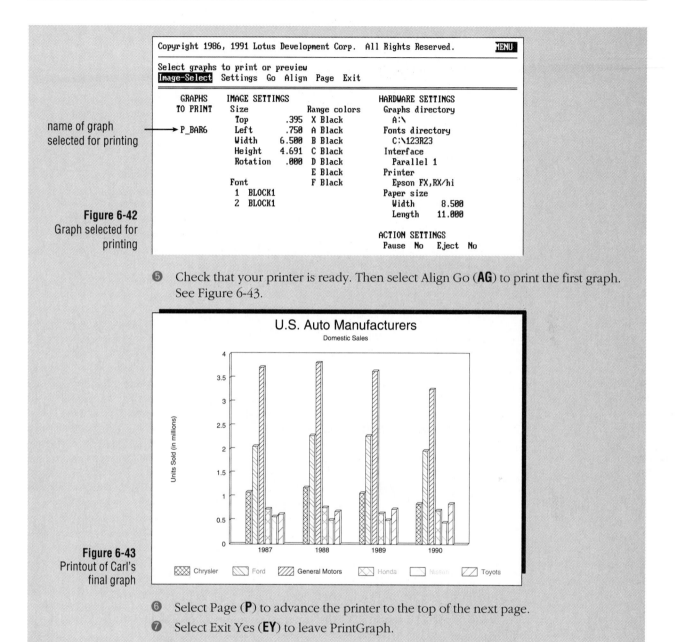

Figure 6-42
Graph selected for printing

name of graph selected for printing →

⑤ Check that your printer is ready. Then select Align Go (**AG**) to print the first graph. See Figure 6-43.

Figure 6-43
Printout of Carl's final graph

⑥ Select Page (**P**) to advance the printer to the top of the next page.
⑦ Select Exit Yes (**EY**) to leave PrintGraph.

Carl has now finished printing his graph, and he presents it to the senior consultants for their review. They are pleased with his work and decide to use this graph in their upcoming Congressional testimony.

Now that you have completed Tutorial 6, you can read Module 4, *Using WYSIWYG to Print and Enhance Graphs.* Check with your instructor.

Exercises

1. Use Figure 6-44 to identify the following components of a graph:
   a. type of graph
   b. x-axis labels
   c. y-axis title
   d. legends
   e. title
   f. x-axis title
   g. data series for projected sales
   h. scale indicator

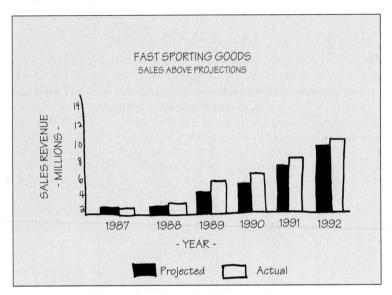

Figure 6-44

Retrieve the worksheet E6FILE1 and do the following:

2. Save the worksheet as S6FILE1.

3. Make the named graph PIE the current graph.

4. Change the value for first-quarter revenue from plastics from 2890 to 4890.

5. View the pie chart again. Did the appearance of the graph change? If yes, how did it change?

6. Make the named graph BAR the current graph. Is this graph based on the original data from the worksheet or the new data you entered in Exercise 4?

7. Save this worksheet as S6FILE1.

8. Erase the worksheet from the screen.

9. Your data diskette contains the file E6_PIE.PIC, which contains the pie chart that you viewed in Exercise 3. If you were to print E6_PIE.PIC, would the graph reflect the original data in the worksheet or the data after the change you made to the worksheet data in Exercise 4?

10. If you were to retrieve the worksheet S6FILE1.WK1 and view the graph named PIE, would the pie chart be based on the original data or the revised data from Exercise 4?

Tutorial Assignments

Before you begin these Tutorial Assignments, check your data diskette. Be sure you have space to save the additional worksheet files you'll create in these assignments (at least 30,000 bytes). If you do not have enough space, save the files that you need for these assignments to another formatted diskette.

Retrieve worksheet T6AUTO1.WK1 and do the following:

1. Create a pie chart that illustrates the market share of each of the six auto manufacturers for 1987.

2. Include a title on the pie chart.

3. Explode the slice that represents Honda.

4. Name this graph PIE87.

5. Save this graph as a .PIC file. Use the name P_PIE87.

6. Reset all the graph settings in this worksheet.

7. Prepare a bar graph that shows only the three Japanese companies' sales from 1987 to 1990.

8. Add a title and legends to this graph.

9. Name this graph BARJPN.

10. Save this graph as a .PIC file. Use the name P_BARJPN.

11. Change the graph to a stacked bar graph.

12. Name this graph STKJPN.

13. Save this graph as a .PIC file. Use the name P_STKJPN.

14. Save your worksheet as S6AUTO2.

15. Print the graph file P_PIE87.

Case Problems

1. Graphing Health Maintenance Organizations' Membership Data

Medical costs have risen dramatically over the last 10 to 15 years. Health maintenance organizations (HMOs) were created as an alternative to traditional health insurance to help decrease medical costs. HMOs provide a range of comprehensive health care services to people who pay an enrollment fee and become members. By joining an HMO, a member gains access to a team of doctors 365 days a year. Employers, labor unions, government agencies, and consumer groups often provide this type of medical coverage for their employees.

Figure 6-45 shows a table of the enrollment in HMO programs by major insurer.

Enrollment in HMOs	
Insurer	**Millions of members**
Blue Cross	15.5
Cigna	3.6
Aetna	2.5
Metropolitan	2.4
Prudential	2.2
Travelers	1.6

Figure 6-45

Use the data in Figure 6-45 to do the following:

1. Construct a pie chart.

2. Explode the Aetna segment.

3. Add appropriate titles and labels.

4. Name the graph PIEHMO.

5. Save the pie chart as a .PIC file. Use the name P_PIEHMO.

6. Save your worksheet as S6HMO.

7. Print the pie chart.

WYSIWYG Assignments

1. Attach WYSIWYG.

2. Retrieve the worksheet S6HMO.

3. Add the following enhancements:
   a. If your worksheet data do not include the title and the column headings shown in Figure 6-45, add them to your worksheet. Increase the title to 24-point Swiss font.
   b. Boldface the column headings.
   c. Draw a solid line under the column headings.
   d. Insert the current graph below your worksheet data.

4. Save your worksheet as W6HMO.

5. Print the entire worksheet on one page.

2. Sporting Goods Industry Trade Show

The Sporting Goods Manufacturers Association recently held a trade show for sporting goods retailers, where the manufacturers displayed their latest athletic goods. In preparation for the trade show the Sporting Goods Manufacturers Association sent out a press release about the show, including the data shown in Figure 6-46.

Sporting Goods Manufacturers' Sales by Category (in millions of dollars)		
	1991	**1992**
Apparel	11600	12645
Footwear	6950	7665
Golf equipment	1350	1285
Exercise	930	975
Camping	825	865

Figure 6-46

Use the data in Figure 6-46 to do the following:

1. Create a bar graph that compares the sales by category for 1991 and 1992.
2. Enter appropriate titles and a legend.
3. Name the bar graph BARSALES.
4. Create a second bar graph that adds a 3D effect to the bars in the current graph.
5. Name the 3D bar graph BAR3D.
6. Save each graph setting as a .PIC file. Save the bar graphs as P_BARSAL and P_BAR3D.
7. Save your worksheet as S6SPORT.
8. Print your graphs.

WYSIWYG Assignments

1. Attach WYSIWYG.
2. Retrieve the worksheet S6SPORT.
3. Add the following enhancements:
   a. Display the title in a font larger than that used for the text in the worksheet.
   b. Add a solid line under the title as shown in Figure 6-46.
   c. Shade the sales data column for 1992.
   d. Insert the named graph BAR3D to the right of your worksheet data.
4. Save your worksheet as W6SPORT.
5. Print the entire worksheet on one page.

3. Graphing Data on Cellular Telephone Subscribers and Revenues

Many people are using cellular telephones more and more in their business and personal lives. Figure 6-47 on the following page shows the changes in the number of cellular telephone subscribers in the U.S. and the revenue they generated from 1987 through 1991.

U.S. Cellular Telephones					
	1987	**1988**	**1989**	**1990**	**1991**
Subscribers (millions)	1200	2100	3050	5500	7500
Revenue (billions)	1600	2000	3300	4600	5900

Figure 6-47

Use the data in Figure 6-47 to do the following:

1. Create a horizontal bar graph that shows the growth in number of subscribers from 1987 through 1991.

2. Enter appropriate titles.

3. Name the bar graph BARSUB.

4. Create a second horizontal bar graph that shows the growth in revenue from 1987 through 1991. Enter appropriate titles.

5. Name the graph BARREV.

6. Save each graph setting as a .PIC file. Save the subscriber bar graph as P_BARSUB and the revenue bar graph as P_BARREV.

7. Save your worksheet as S6TELE1.

8. Print your graphs.

9. The 1991 data in Figure 6-47 were estimates. The actual data for 1991 were 8000 subscribers and 6800 in revenue. Change the data in your worksheet.

10. Save the revised .PIC file for the subscriber and revenue bar graphs. Name the files P_BARS and P_BARR, respectively.

11. Save your revised worksheet as S6TELE2.

12. Print your revised graphs.

WYSIWYG Assignments

1. Attach WYSIWYG.

2. Retrieve the worksheet S6TELE2.

3. Add the following enhancements:
    a. Insert the named graph BARSUB under your worksheet data.
    b. Add the comment "Cellular keeps growing" near the bar for 1991.
    c. Include an arrow that draws attention from the text to the 1991 bar on the bar graph.

4. Save your worksheet as W6TELE.

5. Print the entire worksheet on one page.

4. Using Line Charts to Analyze Stock Prices

Levon Smith, a stock analyst for the firm of Morris-Sorensen, specializes in recommending what computer industry stock investors should buy. Levon wants to analyze indexes and stock prices at the end of each month for 1990 to identify any trends. He has collected month-end data (Figure 6-48) on the following indexes and companies: Standard & Poor's 500 stock index, computer industry stock index, Digital Equipment Corporation, IBM, Apple Corporation, and Cray Research.

	S&P 500	Computer Index	Digital Equipment	IBM	Apple	Cray Research
Jan	297	205	118	130	44	64
Feb	289	213	120	130	37	61
Mar	295	195	104	121	34	60
Apr	310	189	97	116	40	59
May	321	191	90	114	49	59
Jun	318	190	86	115	50	58
Jul	346	195	90	116	40	56
Aug	351	193	105	120	45	55
Sep	349	181	104	119	46	54
Oct	340	170	84	110	50	45
Nov	346	164	84	101	47	42
Dec	353	190	80	102	45	40

Figure 6-48
Selected month-end index and stock prices

Retrieve the worksheet P6STOCK.WK1 and do the following:

1. Create a line chart of the month-end Standard & Poor's 500 and computer industry indexes. Remember to include a title and a legend. Name this graph LINE_MARKET.

2. Create a second line chart that includes the month-end stock prices for IBM, Digital, Cray Research, and Apple so Levon can observe the trend in stock prices for these companies. Remember to include a title and legends. Name this graph LINE_COMPANY.

3. Save each line chart as a .PIC file. Save the first line graph as P_LNEMRK and the second graph as P_LNECMP.

4. Save your worksheet as S6STOCK.

5. Print the graphs.

WYSIWYG Assignments

1. Attach WYSIWYG.

2. Retrieve the worksheet S6STOCK.

3. Add the following enhancements:
    a. Insert solid lines under the column headings.
    b. Boldface the column headings.
    c. Insert the named graph P_LNECMP under your worksheet data.
    d. Enclose the legends in a box.
    e. Draw a box around the worksheet data and graph.

4. Save your worksheet as W6STOCK.

5. Print the entire worksheet on one page.

5.   The U.S. Airline Industry

During the 1980s, the number of U.S. airline companies decreased. In the 1990s, however, international travel is expected to grow and exceed U.S. travel; thus, the remaining carriers are scrambling to increase their number of international routes. Figure 6-49 shows passenger revenues generated by international routes from 1985 through 1989 for five of the major carriers. These numbers are rounded to the nearest millions.

Passenger Revenues International Routes (in millions of $)					
Carrier	**1985**	**1986**	**1987**	**1988**	**1989**
American	400	472	672	884	1858
Continental	249	319	526	743	843
Delta	216	227	410	634	742
Northwest	936	1036	1362	1767	2051
United	114	802	1112	1514	1780

Figure 6-49

Use the data in Figure 6-49 to do the following:

1. Prepare a worksheet that incorporates the data in Figure 6-49 and adds an additional column representing average revenue for each carrier during the five-year period. Also add another row that provides total revenues for each year. Print this worksheet.

2. Prepare a 3D bar graph that compares passenger revenues for all five companies from 1985 through 1989. Remember to include the appropriate titles and legends. Name this graph 3DBAR.

3. Prepare a stacked bar graph showing the same data as Problem 2. Name this graph STACK.

4. Prepare a pie chart of passenger revenues during 1989 that includes all carriers. Name this graph PIE.

5. Save each graph as a .PIC file. Save the bar graph as P_65BAR, the stacked bar as P_65STK, and the pie chart as P_65PIE.

6. Save your worksheet as S6AIRLNE.

7. Print your graphs.

WYSIWYG Assignments

1. Attach WYSIWYG.

2. Retrieve the worksheet S6AIRLNE.

3. Add the following enhancements:
    a. Insert the named graph 3DBAR under your worksheet data.
    b. Add the comment "Big increase" so the text is near the bar for American Airlines 1989.
    c. Include an arrow that draws attention from the text to the 1989 bar on the bar graph.

4. Save your worksheet as W6AIRLINE.

5. Print the entire worksheet on one page.

Tutorial 7

Using a 1-2-3 Database

A Customer/Accounts Receivable Application

Case: Medi-Source Inc.

Medi-Source Inc. distributes supplies to hospitals, medical laboratories, and pharmacies throughout the United States. Files of all Medi-Source customers and accounts receivable data are available to department managers on the company's mainframe computer.

Joan Glazer, the manager of the credit and collection department, was recently reviewing these data and noticed that the outstanding balances of several Massachusetts and Rhode Island customers appeared to be higher than that of the average Medi-Source customer, which is approximately $6,000. She wants to study the accounts in these two states more carefully.

Joan asks Bert Spivak, the manager of the information systems department, to prepare several reports to help her analyze the data. Bert tells her that he and his programming staff are backed up on projects and will not be able to help her for four to six weeks. He suggests instead that he retrieve the Rhode Island and Massachusetts data from the mainframe database and provide her with a Lotus 1-2-3 file. Then she can analyze the data herself. Joan thinks this is a great idea. Bert says he'll have the data to her in two days.

While waiting for the data, Joan thinks about the analysis she will do. She decides to plan her project and makes a list of her goals, output, input, and calculations (Figure 7-1a on the following page). Joan realizes the worksheet will be large and will include several sections. As a part of her planning, she develops a sketch to help organize the overall design of the worksheet (Figure 7-1b on the following page). Note when you look at this figure that each section represents a screenful of information.

OBJECTIVES

In this tutorial you will learn to:

- Define the terms *field*, *record*, and *file*

- Sort a database

- Find records that match specified criteria

- Extract records that match specified criteria

- Use database @functions

My Goals:
  Review the Rhode Island and Massachusetts customer database to
  determine whether balances owed by customers in those states are
  higher than average Medi-Source customers.

What results do I want to see?
  List records in database by:
    customer name
    outstanding balance
    state, and within state by outstanding balance
  List customers with outstanding balances above Medi-Source average.
  Report of outstanding balances by state.

What information do I need?
  Subset of Medi-Source database – all RI and MA customer records

What calculations will I perform?
  Total outstanding balance by state
  Average outstanding balance by state

Figure 7-1a
Joan's planning
sheet

Columns A – H	Columns I – O	Columns P – V	Columns W – AD
Documentation Section	Customer Data ~~~~~~~ ~~~~~~~	Work Section ***Criteria Range	Report Section Medi-Source Inc. Amount Owed by State
			RI MA
			Total xx xx
		***Output Range:	Average xx xx
		~~ ~~~~~~~	

Figure 7-1b
Joan's sketch of
the sections of her
worksheet

In this tutorial you will learn some new database terms, learn how to arrange data into a meaningful order through sorting, search a database to locate and extract records that meet specific criteria, and use database @functions to perform statistical analysis on selected records within the database.

Introduction to Data File Concepts

Before you retrieve the Medi-Source file, you need to understand important terms that are critical to understanding and using computerized databases. These terms are field, record, and file.

A **field** is an attribute (characteristic) of some object, person, or place. For example, each item of data that Medi-Source tracks is referred to as a field. Customer ID, customer name, balance owed, and year-to-date sales represent attributes about a customer (Figure 7-2). Each represents a field. In 1-2-3 each of these fields is stored in a column of your worksheet.

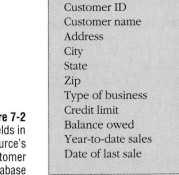

Figure 7-2
Fields in
Medi-Source's
customer
database

Customer ID
Customer name
Address
City
State
Zip
Type of business
Credit limit
Balance owed
Year-to-date sales
Date of last sale

Related fields are grouped together to form a **record**, a collection of attributes describing a person, place, or thing. In 1-2-3 each record is a single row that contains data for each field. For example, all the data about a customer such as Bristol Pharmacy are referred to as a record.

A collection of related records is called a **data file**. In 1-2-3 a data file is referred to as a **1-2-3 database**. In a 1-2-3 database the top cell of each column contains a **field name** that identifies the contents of the field. Figure 7-3 illustrates a 1-2-3 database. The database has fields for customer number, customer name, type of business, state, sales rep, balance owed, and year-to-date sales. The data about each customer make up a record. The 22 records in their entirety make up the customer database.

field names →

1-2-3 data file →

CUST#	CUSTNAME	TYPE	ST	REP	BAL_OWED	YTD_SALES
1	Bristol Pharmacy	P	RI	4	2,647.10	80,278.87
2	Nepco Labs	L	MA	4	3,274.25	6,866.25
3	EMG & EEG Labs	L	MA	4	12,583.97	31,685.19
4	Oaklawn Pharmacy	P	RI	4	4,513.21	5,176.26
5	St. Josephs Hospital	H	RI	3	47,113.50	4,451.68
6	Cape Psych Center	H	MA	3	31,509.10	44,173.24
7	Bioran Medical Lab	L	MA	3	2,799.12	11,927.84
8	Bayshore Pharmacy	P	MA	3	6,010.36	44,140.87
9	St Anne's Hospital	H	MA	3	1,009.53	2,431.80
10	Landmark Medical Center	H	RI	3	22,630.79	6,494.55
11	Lypho_Med Laboratory	L	RI	2	538.62	3,279.89
12	Gregg's Pharmacy	P	MA	2	2,052.70	3,771.28
13	Bradley Hospital	H	MA	2	9,430.72	32,451.95
14	Braintree Hospital	H	MA	2	36,609.80	75,562.35
15	Miriam Hospital	H	MA	2	14,800.44	24,510.04
16	Forgary Labs	L	MA	1	2,890.08	6,670.41
17	De Bellis Pharmacy	P	RI	1	2,715.35	85,063.85
18	Woman & Infants	H	RI	1	47,915.99	3,415.04
19	Depasquale Pharmacy	P	RI	1	4,214.50	39,727.98
20	Kent Hospital	H	MA	1	1,987.44	4,120.74
21	Butler Hospital	H	RI	1	31,215.67	21,144.05
22	Foster Blood Tests	L	MA	1	2,594.27	4,275.56

field →

record →

Figure 7-3
Medi-Source Inc.'s
customer data file

Retrieving the Worksheet

To retrieve the Medi-Source customer file (1-2-3 database):

❶ Retrieve the file C7MEDI1.WK1.

❷ Press **[Tab]** to view the 1-2-3 database. See Figure 7-4.

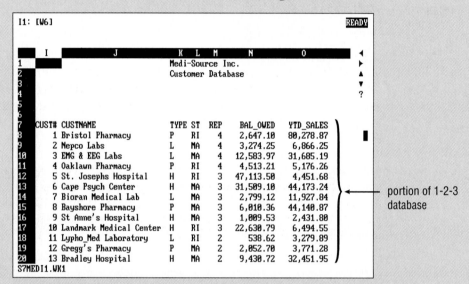

Figure 7-4
Database section
of Joan's initial
worksheet

Notice that each *row* in the database represents a customer record. The first row of the database, row 7, contains the field names. Field names *must* be in the first row of any database you use in 1-2-3 and must be unique.

❸ Press **[PgDn]** to view the remaining records.

❹ Press **[PgUp]** to return to the previous screen.

The field names in the Medi-Source customer database are:

Field	Description
CUST#	Unique identification number assigned to each customer
CUSTNAME	Name of each customer
TYPE	Code indicating the type of business, for example, P = pharmacy, L = laboratory, and H = hospital
ST	State abbreviation: RI = Rhode Island; MA = Massachusetts
REP	ID number of the sales representative assigned to make sales calls on this customer
BAL_OWED	Amount of money customer currently owes Medi-Source
YTD_SALES	Total sales to customer since the beginning of the year

Now that you are familiar with the Medi-Source customer file, you are ready to use it.

Sorting Data

The Data Sort command lets you arrange a 1-2-3 database in an order that you specify. For instance, you could arrange your data alphabetically by customer name or numerically by the amount of money the customer owes to Medi-Source.

Before performing the data sort, you need to understand three terms related to sorting data in 1-2-3: data range, primary key, and secondary key.

Data Range

The **data range** represents the records in the database you want to sort. This range usually includes all the records in the database. The data range does *not* include the field names of the columns, because the field names are merely labels and not part of the data you want to sort. You *must* be sure to include *all* the fields (columns) for the records you specify in the data range; otherwise, you will alter the relationships among data fields in the database.

Primary Key

A field that determines the order in which you sort the database is called a **sort key**. The **primary key** (primary sort key) represents the field (column) you want 1-2-3 to use to determine the new order for the database records. For example, if you want 1-2-3 to arrange the data by the amount customers owe Medi-Source, the primary key is the balance owed field (BAL_OWED).

Secondary Key

The **secondary key** (secondary sort key) represents a second field (column) by which 1-2-3 will determine the sort order within the primary sort key field. It tells 1-2-3 how to arrange the records if two or more records have the same primary key value. In other words, it acts as a tie-breaker. For example, you might select type of customer as the primary sort key and customer name as the secondary sort key. Thus, you could sort the data by customer type (such as hospital, lab, pharmacy) and within each customer type alphabetically by customer name. To explain this example further, all the hospital customers would appear first in alphabetical order, followed by an alphabetized list of laboratory customers, and finally the pharmacy customers would appear arranged in alphabetical order.

Sorting Using the Primary Key

Joan wants to sort the data alphabetically by customer name. Ordering the data by customer name will make it easier for her to locate a particular customer than will the current order of the database, which is by customer number.

To sort a data file by customer name:

❶ Select /Data Sort (**/DS**). 1-2-3 displays the Sort Settings dialog box. See Figure 7-5.

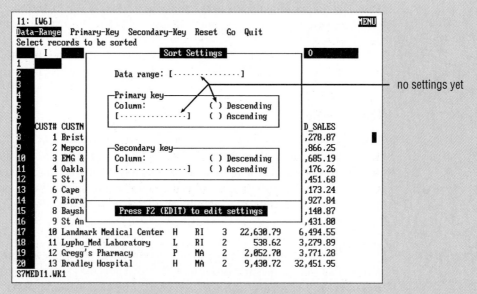

Figure 7-5
Sort Settings
dialog box

The dialog box indicates the settings for the data range, the primary key, and the secondary key. Currently there are no settings.

Now identify the area of the worksheet to be sorted, which 1-2-3 refers to as the data range.

❷ Select Data-Range (**D**). The worksheet appears on your screen.

❸ Move the cell pointer to the first cell in the data range, I8, and press **[.]** to anchor the cell pointer. Highlight I8..O29 and press **[Enter]**. See Figure 7-6.

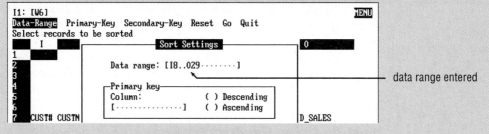

Figure 7-6
Area to be sorted
appears in dialog
box

1-2-3 enters I8..O29 as the data range in the dialog box. Remember that field names are not part of the data range and that every column in your database should be included in the data range.

Joan wants to sort the data by customer name, so next you need to specify CUSTNAME as the primary sort key.

❹ Select Primary-Key (**P**). Move the cell pointer to the first record in the customer name field, cell J8, and press **[Enter]**.

Actually you can move the cell pointer to any cell in column J to indicate that the primary sort key is customer name.

Next you specify the sort order.

⑤ Type **A** to specify ascending sort order and press **[Enter]**. See Figure 7-7.

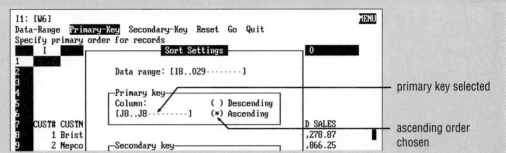

Figure 7-7
Information about primary key appears in dialog box

Ascending order for labels means arranging the data alphabetically from A to Z and numerically from lowest to highest number. Descending order for labels means arranging the data alphabetically backward, from Z to A, and numerically from highest to lowest number.

⑥ Select Go (**G**) to sort the database. When sorting has been completed, your screen should show the records alphabetized by customer name. See Figure 7-8.

```
I1: [W6]                                                         READY

      I              J            K  L  M      N          O       ◄
1                              Medi-Source Inc.                   ►
2                              Customer Database                  ▲
3                                                                 ▼
4                                                                 ?
5
6
7  CUST# CUSTNAME           TYPE ST REP   BAL_OWED   YTD_SALES
8       8 Bayshore Pharmacy   P   MA   3   6,010.36   44,140.87
9       7 Bioran Medical Lab  L   MA   3   2,799.12   11,927.84
10     13 Bradley Hospital    H   MA   2   9,430.72   32,451.95
11     14 Braintree Hospital  H   MA   2  36,609.80   75,562.35
12      1 Bristol Pharmacy    P   RI   4   2,647.10   80,278.87
13     21 Butler Hospital     H   RI   1  31,215.67   21,144.05
14      6 Cape Psych Center   H   MA   3  31,509.10   44,173.24
15     17 De Bellis Pharmacy  P   RI   1   2,715.35   85,063.85
16     19 Depasquale Pharmacy P   RI   1   4,214.50   39,727.98
17      3 EMG & EEG Labs      L   MA   4  12,583.97   31,685.19
18     16 Forgary Labs        L   MA   1   2,890.08    6,670.41
19     22 Foster Blood Tests  L   MA   1   2,594.27    4,275.56
20     12 Gregg's Pharmacy    P   MA   2   2,052.70    3,771.28
S7MEDI1.WK1
```

Figure 7-8
Records sorted by customer name in ascending order

⑦ Press **[PgDn]** to view the remaining customer records. Press **[PgUp]** to return to the beginning of the database.

Joan also planned to sort the customer data by balance owed, with customers having the largest outstanding balance appearing first, that is, in descending order. That way Joan can quickly identify the customers that have the higher outstanding balances.

To sort a data file in descending order by balance owed:

① Select /Data Sort (**/DS**). 1-2-3 displays the Sort Settings dialog box.

Because the range of cells to be sorted was previously entered and still appears in the Sort Settings dialog box, you do not have to select the data range again.

The next step is to change the primary sort key from CUSTNAME to BAL_OWED.

❷ Select Primary-Key (**P**). Move the cell pointer to cell N8 or any other cell in the BAL_OWED column and press **[Enter]**.

❸ Type **D** to specify descending sort order and press **[Enter]**. See Figure 7-9.

Figure 7-9
Dialog box indicates balance owed field to be sorted in descending order

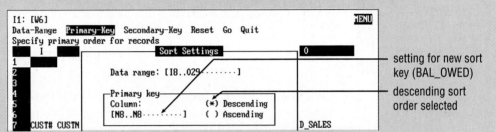

setting for new sort key (BAL_OWED)

descending sort order selected

❹ Select Go (**G**) to sort the database. When sorting has been completed, your screen should look like Figure 7-10. Notice that the customer having the highest balance owed appears first. The customer with the lowest balanced owed is last.

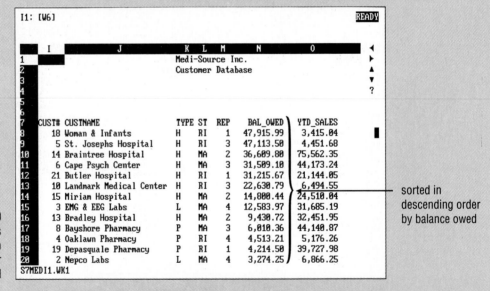

Figure 7-10
Customer records sorted in descending order by balance owed

sorted in descending order by balance owed

❺ Press **[PgDn]** to view the remaining customer records. When you have finished viewing the records, press **[PgUp]** to return to the start of the customer database.

Sorting Using a Secondary Key

You can organize data on more than one sort key. For example, Joan wants to organize the customers by state, and within each state she wants to arrange the customers in alphabetical order.

To sort the 1-2-3 database on two sort keys:

❶ Select /Data Sort (**/DS**). The Sort Settings dialog box appears.

Because the range of cells to be sorted was previously entered and still appears in the dialog box, you do not have to select the data range again.

Next specify ST (state) as the primary sort key.

❷ Select Primary-Key (**P**). Move the cell pointer to cell L8, the ST field, and press **[Enter]**.

❸ Type **A** to specify ascending sort order and press **[Enter]**.

Now specify CUSTNAME as the secondary sort key.

❹ Select Secondary-Key (**S**). Move the cell pointer to cell J8, the CUSTNAME field, and press **[Enter]**.

❺ Press **[Enter]** if A (ascending) already appears as the sort order for CUSTNAME. If D appears, type **A** and press **[Enter]**.

❻ Select Go (**G**) to sort the database. See Figure 7-11.

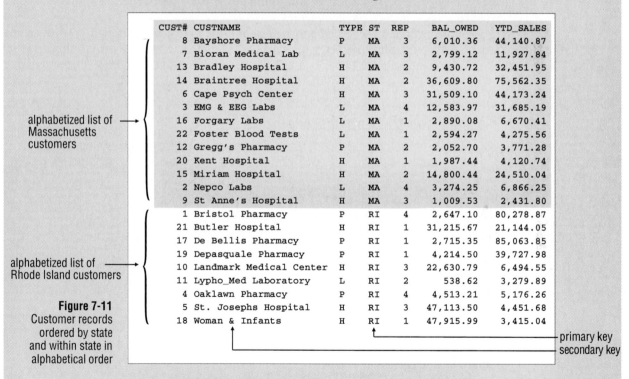

alphabetized list of Massachusetts customers

alphabetized list of Rhode Island customers

Figure 7-11
Customer records ordered by state and within state in alphabetical order

CUST#	CUSTNAME	TYPE	ST	REP	BAL_OWED	YTD_SALES
8	Bayshore Pharmacy	P	MA	3	6,010.36	44,140.87
7	Bioran Medical Lab	L	MA	3	2,799.12	11,927.84
13	Bradley Hospital	H	MA	2	9,430.72	32,451.95
14	Braintree Hospital	H	MA	2	36,609.80	75,562.35
6	Cape Psych Center	H	MA	3	31,509.10	44,173.24
3	EMG & EEG Labs	L	MA	4	12,583.97	31,685.19
16	Forgary Labs	L	MA	1	2,890.08	6,670.41
22	Foster Blood Tests	L	MA	1	2,594.27	4,275.56
12	Gregg's Pharmacy	P	MA	2	2,052.70	3,771.28
20	Kent Hospital	H	MA	1	1,987.44	4,120.74
15	Miriam Hospital	H	MA	2	14,800.44	24,510.04
2	Nepco Labs	L	MA	4	3,274.25	6,866.25
9	St Anne's Hospital	H	MA	3	1,009.53	2,431.80
1	Bristol Pharmacy	P	RI	4	2,647.10	80,278.87
21	Butler Hospital	H	RI	1	31,215.67	21,144.05
17	De Bellis Pharmacy	P	RI	1	2,715.35	85,063.85
19	Depasquale Pharmacy	P	RI	1	4,214.50	39,727.98
10	Landmark Medical Center	H	RI	3	22,630.79	6,494.55
11	Lypho_Med Laboratory	L	RI	2	538.62	3,279.89
4	Oaklawn Pharmacy	P	RI	4	4,513.21	5,176.26
5	St. Josephs Hospital	H	RI	3	47,113.50	4,451.68
18	Woman & Infants	H	RI	1	47,915.99	3,415.04

primary key
secondary key

❼ Press **[PgDn]** to view remaining customer records. When you have finished viewing the records, press **[PgUp]**.

Notice that all Massachusetts customers are grouped together, followed by all customers from Rhode Island. Within each state the customer records are alphabetized.

Data Query Command — Finding Records

Now that Joan has sorted the data, she wants to examine specific customer accounts. While sorting the data, she noticed that customers in the hospital category have outstanding balances that are high compared to customers in the lab and pharmacy categories. So she decides to examine these accounts first.

The Data Query command lets 1-2-3 select records that match certain criteria and finds (highlights) or extracts (copies) these records without examining every record in the database. Before 1-2-3 can find a record in the database, you must specify an input range and set up a criteria range. Let's discuss what we mean by these two ranges.

Input Range

An **input range** is the range of data that 1-2-3 will search when you query a 1-2-3 database. When you specify an input range to use with any Data Query command, you must *include the field names* as part of the range. This is unlike the data range in the Data Sort command, which does *not* include the field names.

You can assign a range name to represent the input range, although 1-2-3 does not require that you do this to execute the Data Query command. A range name allows you to specify the database without having to remember the exact cell locations of your database.

To assign a range name to the database:

❶ Move the cell pointer to cell I7, the upper left corner of the database. Remember, when you use the Data Query command, you *must* include the field names in the input range.

❷ Select /Range Name Create (**/RNC**).

❸ Type the name **database** and press **[Enter]**.

❹ Highlight the database cells I7..O29. Press **[Enter]**. The range name DATABASE has been assigned to this range of cells.

Again, note that the range includes the field names and the data records.

Criteria Range

The **criteria range** is a small area in your worksheet where you tell 1-2-3 which records to search for in the input range. This range must include at least two rows. The first row of the criteria range contains some or all of the field names from the database. The field names in the criteria range *must* be identical to the database field names. The rows below the field names in the criteria range include the search criteria.

The criteria range is often established below or to the right of the input range. Let's use cells P3 to V4. In the first row of the criteria range, you must enter the criteria field names. Because these names must be *identical* to the database field names, it is best to copy the database field names to the criteria range, so no difference can occur between the database field names and the criteria field names.

To copy the database fields names to the criteria range:

① Make sure the cell pointer is in cell I7, the location of the first database field name to be copied.

② Select /Copy (**/C**).

③ Highlight I7..O7. Press **[Enter]**.

④ Now move the cell pointer to cell P3, the location where you will place the field names for the criteria range. Then press **[Enter]**.

⑤ Press **[Tab]** so you can see that the database field names have been copied to the criteria range. See Figure 7-12.

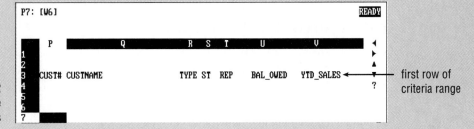

Figure 7-12
Criteria range
field names

Now enter the search criteria into the second row of the criteria range. Joan is searching for all hospital customers. To search for an exact match, enter the value or label you are searching for exactly as it appears in the database. Enter the criterion below the appropriate field name in the criteria range.

To enter the search criteria to find hospital customers:

① Move the cell pointer to cell R4, the location in the criteria range that stores the search criteria for the type of customer.

② Type **H** and press **[Enter]**. 1-2-3 considers lowercase and uppercase characters the same in the criteria range. See Figure 7-13.

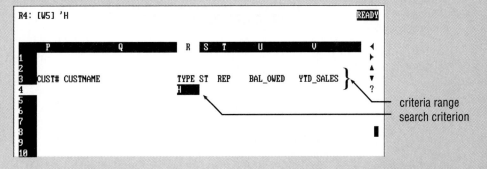

Figure 7-13
Criteria range
completely
specified

You can also assign a range name to the criteria range, although you do not have to do so to use the Data Query command. Assigning a range name allows you to specify the location of the criteria range without remembering the cell locations of the range.

To assign the range name CRITERIA to the criteria range:

❶ Move the cell pointer to P3, the upper left corner of the criteria range.

❷ Select /Range Name Create (**/RNC**).

❸ Type **criteria** and press **[Enter]**. Highlight the criteria range P3..V4. Press **[Enter]**. Now the criteria range P3..V4 has the name CRITERIA.

❹ To document that this range of cells is the criteria range, move the cell pointer to cell P2, type *****Criteria Range**, and press **[Enter]**.

Finding Records Using a Constant

Now that you have set up the input and criteria ranges, you can use the Data Query command to find (highlight) all hospital customers. The Find command is used to activate the search of the database records, finding each record that satisfies the criteria you specified in the criteria range.

To find hospital customers in the database:

❶ Select /Data Query (**/DQ**). The Query Settings dialog box appears. See Figure 7-14.

This dialog box lists the locations of the input, criteria, and output ranges. Currently no query settings are defined.

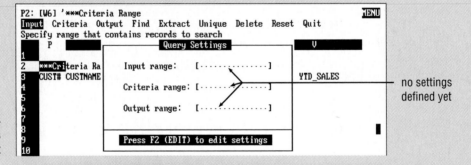

Figure 7-14
Query Settings
dialog box

To use the Find command, you must specify the locations of the input and criteria ranges. First, let's specify the input range.

❷ Select Input (**I**) to indicate the range of cells you want to search.

Enter the name of the input range.

❸ Type **database** and press **[Enter]**.

DATABASE, the range name you assigned to cells I7..O29, appears in the Query Settings dialog box.

Next, specify the criteria range.

❹ Select Criteria (**C**) to indicate the range of cells that contains the search criteria.

Enter the name of the criteria range.

⑤ Type **criteria** and press **[Enter]**.

CRITERIA, the range name you assigned to your criteria range, that is, cells P3..V4, appears in the Query Settings dialog box. See Figure 7-15.

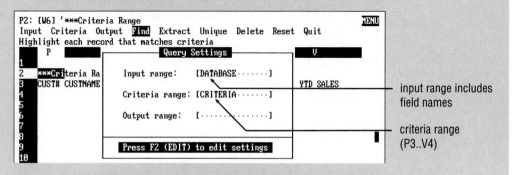

Figure 7-15
Query settings
specified

Now use the Find command to highlight the records that meet the search criteria.

To find all hospital customers:

① Select Find **(F)**.

1-2-3 highlights the first record that matches the criterion of TYPE equal to H. See Figure 7-16.

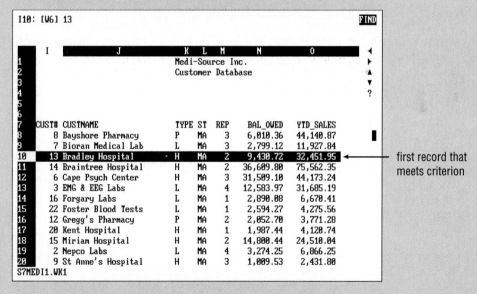

Figure 7-16
Finding all
hospital
customers

② Press **[↓]** to find the next hospital customer. Continue to press **[↓]** to find all hospital customers.

You can also press **[↑]** to search the database in the other direction.

③ Press **[Esc]** or **[Enter]** to return to the Data Query menu.

④ Select Quit **(Q)** to return to READY mode.

Finding Records Using a Search Formula

Remember that the average customer's outstanding balance is $6,000. This average was based on customers from all states in which Medi-Source does business. Now Joan wants to identify Rhode Island and Massachusetts customers who owe more than the average Medi-Source customer.

This query requires a search formula be included beneath the BAL_OWED field name in the criteria range. When you enter a formula as a criterion, you must begin the formula with a plus sign (+); otherwise, 1-2-3 will consider the entry as a label rather than a search formula. Follow the plus sign with the cell address of the field of the *first record* that appears immediately under the field name in the input range. Next in the formula you must include a comparison operator and a value 1-2-3 will compare against the cell address.

In the following steps, you will enter the search formula +N8>6000. This is the search criterion to find all customers who owe more than $6,000.

First, erase the search criterion from the previous query that still appears in the criteria range.

To erase the search criterion from row 4:

❶ Move the cell pointer to the second line of the criteria range, cell P4.

❷ Select /Range Erase (**/RE**).

❸ Highlight P4..V4 and press **[Enter]**. The row that stores the search criteria is now erased.

Now enter the new search criterion:

❹ Move the cell pointer to cell U4, the cell beneath the criteria field name, BAL_OWED.

❺ Type **+N8>6000** and press **[Enter]**. See Figure 7-17.

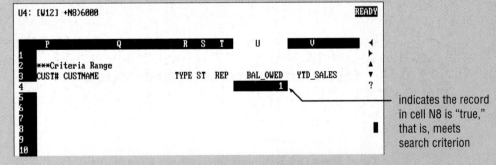

Figure 7-17
Specifying a
formula as the
search criterion

indicates the record
in cell N8 is "true,"
that is, meets
search criterion

Remember, you must place the + sign in front of the cell address; otherwise, 1-2-3 will treat the cell entry as a label. Also remember that you *must reference the first database cell* following the field name in the column you are searching.

Notice that a 1 appears in cell U4. When a condition containing a search formula is assigned to a cell in the criteria range, a 0 or a 1 will appear. The value in U4, the cell with the formula +N8>6000, depends on the value in cell N8. If the value in cell N8 is greater than 6000, the condition is true, and a 1 appears. If the condition is false, a 0 appears.

You can choose to have the formula appear in the criteria range instead of the value 0 or 1. This is often done because the formula is more meaningful to the user than a 1 or a 0. To display the formula in the cell, you use the Range Format Text command.

To display the formula in the cell:

❶ Make sure the cell pointer is at U4.

❷ Select /Range Format Text (**/RFT**).

❸ Cell U4 is the entire range, so press **[Enter]**. The formula for the search criterion now appears in cell U4. See Figure 7-18.

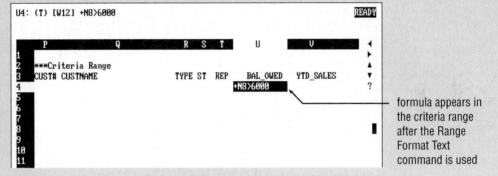

Figure 7-18
Displaying the
search formula in
the criteria range

formula appears in
the criteria range
after the Range
Format Text
command is used

Now Joan uses the Data Query Find command to highlight all customers with a balance above $6,000.

To use the Data Query Find command:

❶ Select /Data Query (**/DQ**).

The same input and criteria ranges that were used earlier in the tutorial now appear in the Query Settings dialog box. Because you defined the input and criteria ranges when you searched for hospital customers, you do not need to define these ranges again.

Once the input and criteria ranges have been defined, you can search the database records by using the Find command.

② Select Find (**F**).

1-2-3 highlights the first record with an outstanding balance greater than $6,000. See Figure 7-19.

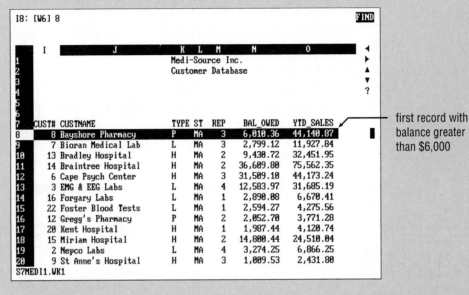

Figure 7-19
Finding customer records with balance owed greater than $6,000

③ Press [↓] to find the next matching record in the database.

Continue to press [↓] to find all customers with a balance above $6,000.

④ Press [**Esc**] and then select Quit (**Q**) to return to READY mode.

Data Query Command — Extracting Records

Joan has been using the Data Query Find command to highlight (locate) all records that meet her search criteria. Now she wants to copy customer records with balances greater than $6,000 to a different part of the worksheet. In this separate area of the worksheet she wants to list only those records that have balances above $6,000. This will make it easier for Joan to print or perform calculations on these records.

The Data Query Extract command lets you copy all records from the input range that match specific criteria in the criteria range to a location in the worksheet called the output range.

Before you use the Data Query Extract command, you must define the input range, the criteria range, and the output range.

Input Range

The input range identifies the location of the 1-2-3 database. This range includes the field names in addition to the records of the database. You specify this range by using the Input option of the Data Query command. The input range was defined when you used the Find command earlier in the tutorial, so you do not need to enter it again.

Criteria Range

The criteria range specifies the criteria you want 1-2-3 to use to extract records from the input range. You specify the criteria range by using the Criterion option of the Data Query command. Joan wants to extract records of customers with balances above $6,000. Because the search criterion is the same as that used earlier in this tutorial, you do not have to enter the search criterion again.

Output Range

The **output range** is an area of the worksheet where records from the input range that meet the search criteria are copied. The first row of the output range must contain field names that are identical to the field names in the input range. The Extract command copies all matching records into the output range beginning in the row below the field names of the output range. Because the Extract command erases all data values that were previously in these cells, it's best to choose an area of your worksheet that contains no data for the placement of the output range. Let's begin the output range in the range P7..V7.

There are two approaches to defining the output range. Usually you specify the row with the field names as the range of the output range. 1-2-3 uses as many rows below the output range as it needs to copy the records to this area. If you defined the output range in this manner, when you issue the Extract command, 1-2-3 automatically erases the contents of every cell below the output range up to the last row in the worksheet. Thus, when locating the output range in your worksheet choose an area that is not above any data.

As an alternative, when defining the output range, you can define its exact size. That is, when defining the output range, include the field names and a range of blank rows. The number of rows in the range depends on the number of records you think you will extract. When you define a *fixed length* output range and the output range is too small to hold all the extracted records, 1-2-3 extracts as many records as can fit in the output range. 1-2-3 also displays the error message "Too many records for Output range." If this occurs, increase the size of the output range and issue the Extract command again. The output range can include some or all of the field names from the input range. When you use the Data Query Extract command, 1-2-3 copies data only to the fields you specified in the output range. Joan wants to copy to the output range the complete record for all customers with balances over $6,000.

To copy the field names from the input range to P7..V7, the first row of the output range:

① Move the cell pointer to cell I7.

② Select /Copy (**/C**).

③ Highlight cells I7..O7, then press **[Enter]**.

④ Move the cell pointer to P7 and press **[Enter]**. The database field names appear in P7..V7.

⑤ Press **[Tab]** to see the copied field names.

⑥ Move the cell pointer to P6, type ***Output Range**, and then press **[Enter]**. This label helps identify this area of the worksheet. See Figure 7-20.

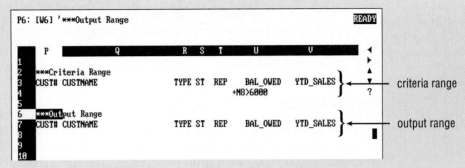

Figure 7-20
Ranges for extract

Although it is not required to extract records, you can assign a range name to the output range P7..V7. This allows you to specify the output range without remembering the cell locations.

To assign the range name OUTPUT to the output range:
① Move the cell pointer to the first field name in the output range, cell P7.
② Select /Range Name Create (**/RNC**).
③ Type **output** and press **[Enter]**.
④ Highlight the field names of the output range, P7..V7, then press **[Enter]**.
    The output range now has the name OUTPUT.

Before you can use the Data Query Extract command, you must specify the input, criteria, and output ranges. Because the input and criteria ranges were specified earlier in this tutorial, you do not need to enter them again. However, the output range has not been specified.

To specify the output range for the Data Query command:
① Select /Data Query (**/DQ**).
② Select Output (**O**), press **[F3]** (NAME), and highlight the range name OUTPUT, which is the output range. Press **[Enter]**. See Figure 7-21. The range name of the output range now appears in the Query Settings dialog box.

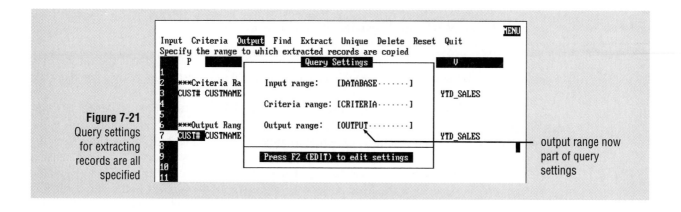

Figure 7-21
Query settings for extracting records are all specified

Extracting Records

Now that the input, criteria, and output ranges have been specified, you can use the Extract command. Joan wants to extract customer records with an outstanding balance above $6,000.

To extract records with a balance above $6,000:

❶ Select Extract (**E**).

1-2-3 copies to the output range all records from the database that meet the search formula you entered, in this case, customers whose balance is greater than $6,000.

❷ Select Quit (**Q**) to return to READY mode.

The extracted records appear below the row containing the output field names. See Figure 7-22. Notice that 1-2-3 has extracted only those records that meet the criterion, that is, only those customers whose outstanding balance is greater than $6,000.

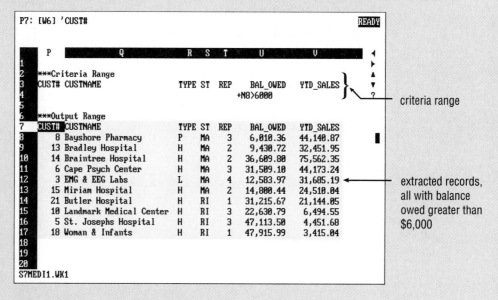

Figure 7-22
Records with balance greater than $6,000 appear in output range

❸ Save your worksheet as S7MEDI1.

Understanding Database @Functions

According to her plan, Joan wants a report that shows the total and average outstanding balances by state. One approach to calculating these statistics is to use the database @functions available in 1-2-3.

Lotus 1-2-3 has seven database @functions: @DAVG, @DSUM, @DMAX, @DMIN, @DCOUNT, @DSTD, and @DVAR. Each function calculates a value based on records in the database that match criteria in the criteria range. The database @functions differ from the corresponding statistical @functions, because the database @functions calculate statistics *only* for the records in a database that match the criteria you specify. For example, you would use @AVG to calculate the average balance owed for all the records in the database. You would use @DAVG to calculate the average balance owed for only those records that meet the criterion of being RI customers.

All 1-2-3 database @functions have the same format:

> *@function(input range, offset, criteria range)*

where *@function* is one of the following: @DAVG, @DSUM, @DCOUNT, @DMAX, @DMIN, @DSTD, or @DVAR and each database function consists of three arguments:

1. *Input range* is the range that contains the database, including the field names in the range definition. The range can be specified as a range name or as cell addresses.

2. *Offset* is the position number of the column in the database that is to be summed, averaged, counted, and so on. 1-2-3 assigns the first field in the database the offset number 0, the second field the offset number 1, and so on. For example, CUST# is the first column in the database and has the offset number 0; CUSTNAME is the second column, so it has the offset number 1; and BAL_OWED is the sixth column in the database, so it has the offset number 5.

3. *Criteria range* is an area of your worksheet where you specify the search criteria to determine which records you will use in the calculations.

Figure 7-23 summarizes the 1-2-3 database @functions.

@Function Name	Description	Example
@DAVG	Averages the values in the offset column that meet specified criteria	@DAVG(A11..G32,6,T25..T26)
@DSUM	Sums the values in the offset column that meet specified criteria	@DSUM(A11..G32,6,T25..T26)
@DMAX	Determines the largest value in the offset column that meets specified criteria	@DMAX(A11..G32,6,T25..T26)
@DMIN	Determines the smallest value in the offset column that meets specified criteria	@DMIN(A11..G32,6,T25..T26)
@DCOUNT	Counts the number of records in the offset column that meet specified criteria	@DCOUNT(A11..G32,6,T25..T26)
@DSTD	Calculates the standard deviation of the values in the offset column that meet specified criteria	@DSTD(A11..G32,6,T25..T26)
@DVAR	Calculates the variance of the values in the offset column that meet the specified criteria	@DVAR(A11..G32,6,T25..T26)

Figure 7-23
Database
@functions

Using Database @Functions

Joan wants to calculate separate statistics for Rhode Island and Massachusetts customers. She wants to know if there is a difference between the total and the average amount owed by customers in each state. Let's now prepare Joan's report. Place this report in the range W1..AB7. The headings and the labels for the report have already been entered in the worksheet.

Now calculate the statistics for the report. To calculate these statistics, you will use the database @functions @DSUM and @DAVG. Each function requires an input range, an offset range, and a criteria range.

The input range identifies the records to be used in calculations. You already defined this range earlier in the tutorial. The input range includes cells I7..O29 and has been assigned the name DATABASE.

You set up separate criteria ranges for each group of records on which you are performing calculations.

Let's first set up a criteria range at AA5..AA6 to use when you search for Rhode Island customers:

① Press **[Tab]** to move to the Report section of the worksheet. The title and the headings have already been entered.

② Move the cell pointer to cell AA5, the location of the criteria field name.

③ Type **ST** in uppercase letters and press **[Enter]**.

④ Move the cell pointer to AA6, the second row of the criteria range.

⑤ Type **RI** and press **[Enter]**. The criteria range for Rhode Island customers is complete.

Now assign a range name to the criteria range.

To assign the range name RICRITERIA to the criteria range AA5..AA6:

① Move the cell pointer to AA5.

② Select /Range Name Create (**/RNC**).

③ Type **ricriteria** and press **[Enter]**.

④ Highlight the cells AA5..AA6 and press **[Enter]**.

The criteria range has the name RICRITERIA.

Notice that the criteria range includes only one database field name. The criteria range does not have to include all field names in the database. It needs to include only the field names you intend to search.

Next, set up a separate criteria range at AB5..AB6 to search for customers in Massachusetts:

① Move the cell pointer to AB5, the location of the criteria field name of the second criteria range.

② Type **ST** in uppercase letters and press **[Enter]**.

③ Move the cell pointer to AB6, the second row of the criteria range.

④ Type **MA** and press **[Enter]**. The criteria range for specifying Massachusetts customers is complete. See Figure 7-24.

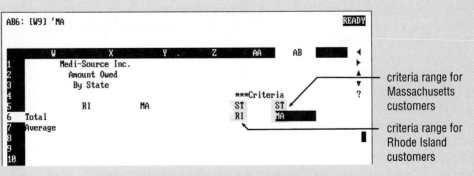

Figure 7-24
Criteria ranges to be used with database @functions

Now assign a range name to the criteria range.

To assign the range name MACRITERIA to the criteria range AB5..AB6:
❶ Move the cell pointer to AB5.
❷ Select /Range Name Create (**/RNC**).
❸ Type **macriteria** and press **[Enter]**.
❹ Highlight the cells AB5..AB6 and press **[Enter]**.

The criteria range has the name MACRITERIA.

Now that you have defined the input and criteria ranges, let's determine the offset number for the balance owed field. You recall that the offset is the position number of the column in the database that is to be summed, averaged, counted, and so on.

To determine the offset number for balance owed:
❶ Move the cell pointer to cell I7, the first field in the database.
❷ Starting with 0 for the first column, CUST#, count the columns to determine the offset number for column N, BAL_OWED. Your answer should be 5. See Figure 7-25.

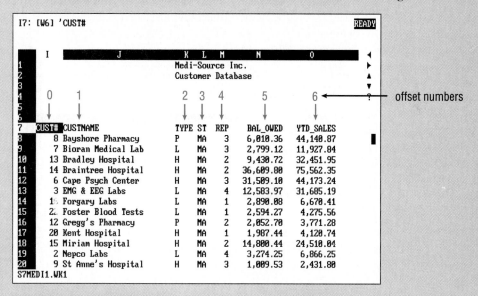

Figure 7-25
Determining the
offset number

Now let's use the database @functions to complete the report.

To use database @functions to calculate the statistics:

❶ Press **[F5]** (GOTO), type **w1**, and press **[Enter]**. The cell pointer is now in the section of the worksheet where you will average and total the outstanding balance by state. See Figure 7-26.

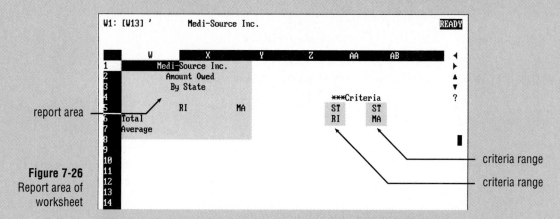

Figure 7-26
Report area of
worksheet

❷ Move the cell pointer to cell X6, under the cell labeled RI.

❸ Type **@dsum(database,5,ricriteria)** and press **[Enter]** to calculate the total balance owed by Rhode Island customers. The total, 163504.73, appears on the screen.

❹ Move the cell pointer to cell X7.

❺ Type **@davg(database,5,ricriteria)** and press **[Enter]** to calculate the average balance owed by Rhode Island customers. The average balance owed is 18167.192222. See Figure 7-27.

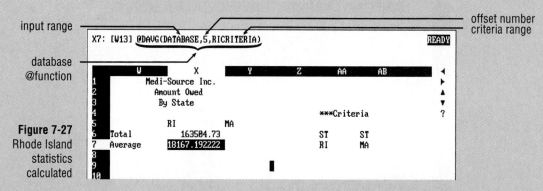

Figure 7-27
Rhode Island
statistics
calculated

❻ Move the cell pointer to cell Y6, under the cell labeled MA.

❼ Type **@dsum(database,5,macriteria)**. Press **[Enter]** to calculate the total balance owed by all Massachusetts customers. Massachusetts customers owe a total of 127551.78.

❽ Move the cell pointer to cell Y7.

❾ Type **@davg(database,5,macriteria).** Press **[Enter]** to calculate the average balance owed by Massachusetts customers. On average, Massachusetts customers owe 9811.675384.

The statistics for the report are complete. Joan, however, wants the amounts in the report displayed to the nearest dollar. Let's now format the values in X6..Y7 using Currency format.

To display the values in the report, using Currency format:

❶ Move the cell pointer to X6.

❷ Select /Range Format Currency (**/RFC**).

❸ Type **0** (zero) and press **[Enter]**.

❹ Highlight X6..Y7. Press **[Enter]**.

Your worksheet should look like Figure 7-28.

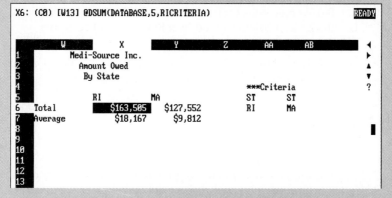

Figure 7-28
Joan's calculated information about Rhode Island and Massachusetts customers

Joan notices that the average outstanding balance for Rhode Island customers is $18,167 — nearly three times more than the Medi-Source customer average nationwide.

❺ Save your worksheet as S7MEDI1.WK1.

Exercises

1. The customer database that you used in this tutorial, C7MEDI1.WK1, contains how many fields? How many records?

2. To sort the customer names in Z-to-A order, you would use which sorting option?

3. Retrieve the file E7FILE1 and do the following:
   a. Assign the range name DATABASE to the range A3..E11.
   b. Sort the data on the field FNAME. Specify the range name DATABASE as the data range for the Data Sort command. Print your results. Explain what happened.

4. Retrieve the file E7FILE2 and do the following:
    a. Assign the range name DATABASE to the range A4..D11.
    b. Print this range.
    c. Sort the data on the field name FNAME in ascending order. Specify the range name DATABASE as the data range for the Data Sort command. Print your results. Explain what happened.

Answer Exercises 5 through 8 using the customer database you used in Tutorial 7.

5. List the steps you would follow to locate Kent Hospital in the customer database using the Find command.

6. List the steps you would follow to extract all Rhode Island customers using the Extract command.

7. What @function would you use to calculate the following statistics?
    a. the average sales for the year for sales representative #4
    b. the highest balance owed by a Rhode Island customer
    c. the number of pharmacies in the database

8. If you had used the database statistical function @DAVG(DATABASE,6, macriteria) in this tutorial, what statistic would you be calculating?

Tutorial Assignments

Before you begin these Tutorial Assignments, check your data diskette. Be sure you have space to save the additional worksheet files you'll create in these assignments (at least 85,000 bytes). If you do not have enough space, save your files for Tutorial 7 to another formatted diskette.

Retrieve the worksheet T7MEDI1.WK1 and do the following:

1. Sort the database by year-to-date (YTD) sales, with the customer having the lowest YTD sales appearing first. The database begins in cell I7. Save the file as S7MEDI2.

2. Sort the database in descending order using the field TYPE (type of customer) as the primary sort key. Save the file as S7MEDI3.

3. Arrange the customer database by type of customer (ascending order); within type of customer arrange the accounts with highest balance owed first. Print the sorted records.

Use the Data Query command for Assignments 4 through 7.

4. Copy the database field names to the first row of the criteria range, P3..V3.

5. Query the database to find all customers located in Rhode Island (code = RI). Save the worksheet as S7MEDI4.

6. Query the database to find all customers with average YTD sales above $50,000. Save the worksheet as S7MEDI5.

7. Query the database to extract and print all customers assigned to sales representative #4. Set up an output range beginning at P7..V7. Save the worksheet as S7MEDI6.

Complete Assignments 8 through 12 using the database statistical function @DAVG. Three criteria ranges have been partially set up in cells Z5, AA5, and AB5.

8. Calculate the average outstanding balance for hospitals. Complete the criteria range in Z5..Z6. Place your result in cell X6.

9. Calculate the average outstanding balance for labs. Complete the criteria range in AA5..AA6. Place your result in cell X7.

10. Calculate the average outstanding balance for pharmacies. Complete the criteria range in AB5..AB6. Place your result in cell X8.

11. Print this Outstanding Balance Report by Type of Customer.

12. Save your worksheet as S7MEDI7.

Case Problems

1. Human Resource Database

The human resource department of a small furniture manufacturer has developed a human resource database. The field names in this database are:

Field	Description
EMP#	Employee number
LNAME	Last name
FNAME	First name
BIRTH	Date of birth (yyyymmdd)
SEX	Code for sex (M = male; F = female)
MAR	Code for marital status (Y = married; N = not married)
DEP	Number of dependents
ANNSAL	Annual salary
HIREDT	Date employee hired (yyyymmdd)
XMPT	Exempt employee (X = exempt; N = nonexempt)
MED	Code for medical plan (F = family plan; I = individual plan; N = not on medical plan)
401K	401K retirement plan (Y = making contributions to plan; N = not making contributions to plan)
DIV	Division where employee works
JOBTITLE	Job title
PER	Payment method (H = hourly; M = monthly)

Retrieve the worksheet P7PERSNL and do the following:

1. Sort and print the database alphabetically by last name.

2. Sort and print the database by hire date in ascending order.

3. Sort and print the database by division and, within division, by salary in descending order.

4. Find all employees that have the family medical plan. The code is F.

5. Find all employees with one or more dependents.

6. Extract and print the records of all married employees.

7. Print a summary report showing salaries categorized by sex. Use the database @functions to prepare this report. Format the report as shown in Figure 7-29.

	Salaries — By Sex	
	Females	Males
Average	$ xxxx	$ xxxx
Maximum	$ xxxx	$ xxxx
Minimum	$ xxxx	$ xxxx
Count	xxxx	xxxx

Figure 7-29

8. Save your worksheet as S7PERSNL.

WYSIWYG Assignments

1. Attach WYSIWYG.

2. Add the following enhancements to the summary report:
   a. Replace any dashed lines with solid lines.
   b. Use a 14-point Swiss font for the report title line.
   c. Boldface the column headings.
   d. Draw a box around the entire report.

3. Save your worksheet as W7PERSNL.

4. Print the summary report.

2. The Top 50 U.S. Companies

Every year a leading business magazine publishes a list of the 50 largest U.S. companies and presents financial data about them.

Retrieve the worksheet P7TOP50. The field names in the file containing these data are as follows:

Field	Description
COMPANY	Name of company
INDUSTRY	Industry code
SALES	Sales revenue for the year
PROFITS	Net income
ASSETS	Total assets
EQUITY	Portion of assets owned by stockholders
MKT_VAL	Market value of company

Do the following:

1. Sort and print the database alphabetically by company.

2. Sort and print the database arranged by sales, with the company with the highest sales appearing first.

3. Calculate the rate of return (ROR) for each company. The formula is

$$ROR = \frac{profit}{equity}$$

Place this new field in column H and label the column ROR. Format using the Percent format with one decimal place.

4. Sort the database by ROR, with the company having the highest ROR appearing first. *Hint:* Think about your data range.

5. Print the database, which now includes the ROR field.

6. Extract and print all companies in the computer industry (industry code = 6).

7. Prepare and print a summary report that compares the average, the maximum, and the minimum sales for companies in the oil industry (code = 18) versus companies in the aerospace industry (code = 1). Use the database @functions to prepare this report. Format the report as shown in Figure 7-30.

Figure 7-30

Top 50 U.S. Companies Industry Comparison		
	Oil	Aerospace
Average sales	$ xxx	$ xxx
Minimum sales	xxx	xxx
Maximum sales	xxx	xxx

8. Save your worksheet as S7TOP50.

WYSIWYG Assignments

1. Attach WYSIWYG.

2. Add the following enhancements to the summary report:
    a. Replace any dashed lines with solid lines under column headings.
    b. Change the first line of the report title to a 24-point Swiss font. Use a 14-point Swiss font for the remaining report title lines. Adjust the column widths as appropriate.
    c. Boldface the column headings and report labels.
    d. Draw a box around the entire report.

3. Save your worksheet as W7TOP50.

4. Print the summary report.

3. Inventory of Microcomputer Software

A company that sells microcomputer software has just completed its annual physical inventory prior to preparing its financial statement. The data from this inventory were entered into a 1-2-3 worksheet.

Retrieve the worksheet P7SFTWRE. The field names for this inventory database include the following:

Field	Description
ITEM#	Unique number to identify each product
TITLE	Name of product
CAT	Category of software
COST	Cost to company per unit
QOH	Number of packages on hand (in inventory)
QOO	Number of packages on order
PRICE	Retail price of software package
YTD_SALES	Year-to-date sales

The codes for the category of software (CAT) are:

CO	=	Communications
DP	=	Desktop publishing
DB	=	Database
GR	=	Graphics
SP	=	Spreadsheet
WP	=	Word processing
UT	=	Utility

Do the following:

1. Print a list of current software products arranged by category and, within category, alphabetized by title.

2. Find the software products that have one or more units on order.

3. Extract and print the database (DB) software products.

4. Add two columns to the worksheet, Inventory Value, Cost (column I) and Inventory Value, Retail (column J). Calculate and print the total cost value and the total retail value for each inventory item. (*Hint:* You can use the following formulas: Inventory Value, Cost = QOH × COST and Inventory Value, Retail = QOH × PRICE.) Then total the value of the inventory for the entire company.

5. Calculate and print the total retail value of the inventory by software category. Be sure your report has a separate total for each of the seven category codes. Use database @functions to prepare this report. Format the report as shown in Figure 7-31.

Inventory - Retail Value	
By Software Category	
	Total Retail Value
Communication	xxxx
Desktop Publishing	xxxx
Database	xxxx
Graphics	xxxx
Spreadsheet	xxxx
Word Processing	xxxx
Utility	xxxx

Figure 7-31

6. Prepare a pie chart illustrating the same data that were calculated in Assignment 5. Create a PIC file named PIESOFT.

7. Save your worksheet as S7SFTWRE.

8. Print the pie chart PIESOFT using PGRAPH.

WYSIWYG Assignments

1. Attach WYSIWYG.

2. Add the following enhancements to the software category report:
   a. Change the first line of the report title to a 24-point Swiss font. Use a 14-point Swiss font for the second report title line.
   b. Create a table (grid) effect for the table.
   c. Insert the pie chart in the worksheet to the right of the software category report.
   d. Draw a double-lined box around the entire report and graph.

3. Save your worksheet as W7SFTWRE.

4. Print the revised report, including the graph, using the WYSIWYG Print command.

4. Checkbook Manager

Marvis Frazier wants to develop an electronic checkbook to record all checks and deposits. He decides that the checkbook should have the following columns:

Field	Description
TRANS	Code for transaction: D for deposit; P for payment
CHK_NO	Check number entered for checks; otherwise, blank
TRN_DATE	Date check was written or deposit made
DESCRIPTION	Payee or description of transaction
CAT	Two-character category code: FD = food; OF = office; UT = utilities; CL = clothing; MS = miscellaneous. If this transaction is not a check, leave the field blank.
AMOUNT	Amount of check, charge, or deposit
BALANCE	Running balance in checkbook
CLEARED	Status code: C when check returned with bank statement; O if outstanding (initially assign an O when check is entered in check register). If this transaction is not a check, leave the field blank.

Use the following data for the month of January:

TRANS	CHK_NO	TRN_DATE	DESCRIPTION	CAT	AMOUNT
P	4157	1/3/92	New England Telephone	UT	145.51
P	4158	1/5/92	Stop & Shop	FD	43.02
D		1/5/92	Deposit payroll check		850.28
P	4159	1/6/92	Staples	OF	24.00
P	4160	1/11/92	Federal Express	OF	9.00
P	4161	1/11/92	Narragansett Electric	UT	133.64
P	4162	1/12/92	Stop & Shop	FD	71.43
P	4163	1/16/92	Filene's	CL	79.99
D		1/16/92	Deposit dividend check		125.00
P	4164	1/16/92	O'Neil Oil Service	UT	170.41
P	4165	1/20/92	Stop & Shop	FD	83.83
P	4166	1/25/92	Federal Express	OF	39.00
P	4167	1/25/92	G. Fox	CL	50.00

Set aside a section above the balance column of the checkbook for the beginning balance. The balance at the beginning of the month is $514.25.

Marvis also lists the calculations he needs to perform:

Balance for first transaction:

if TRANS = D then BALANCE = *beginning balance + deposit*
if TRANS = P then BALANCE = *beginning balance – payment*

Balance for all other transactions:

if TRANS = P then BALANCE = *previous balance – payment*
if TRANS = D then BALANCE = *previous balance + deposit*

Do the following:

1. Create the checkbook worksheet.

2. Enter the data into your checkbook worksheet. Remember to assign a code of O (letter O) for all checks written during the month.

3. Marvis received his bank statement for the period ending January 28, 1992. The bank statement shows a balance of $736.61.
   a. There were three items in the bank statement that he has not entered in the check register: a monthly service charge of $6.25, a charge of $20 for new checks, and $3.73 in interest earned for the month. Include these items in the check register. Treat the service charge and the charge for new checks as payments and assign a miscellaneous expense (MS) code. Do not enter any check number in the CHK_NO column. Treat the interest earned as a deposit.
   b. The following checks were also included with the bank statement:

      4157, 4158, 4159, 4161, 4163, 4164, 4165, 4167

      Indicate in your check register that these checks have cleared by placing a code of C in the Cleared column.

4. Use the Data Query Extract command to copy all checks written during the month (CHK_NO greater than zero) to a separate area of the worksheet.

   After extracting the checks, sort them by category code in ascending order and within category code by date in ascending order. Total the checks written for the month.

5. Set aside another area of your worksheet to prepare the following summary report. Use the database statistical function @DSUM to calculate the totals in this report. Use Marvis' sketch shown in Figure 7-32 to help you lay out this report.

Figure 7-32

Expense Summary	
Code	**Total**
CL	xxxx
FD	xxxx
OF	xxxx
UT	xxxx
MS	xxxx
Total	xxxx

6. Include a section of your worksheet for a bank reconciliation report. The format is shown in Figure 7-33.

Bank Reconciliation Report

Ending balance shown on bank statement	xxxx
Add: deposits made after date of this statement	xxxx[1]
Subtotal	xxxx
Less: total of outstanding checks	xxxx[2]
Adjusted balance (should agree with checkbook balance)	xxxx

[1] Check to see if any deposits occurred after statement date. Enter amount. Enter zero for this month.

[2] Use @DSUM to calculate the total outstanding checks (code O).

Figure 7-33

---

7. Save your worksheet as P7CHECKS.

8. Print the checks-written report (the extracted records).

9. Print the expense summary report.

10. Print the bank reconciliation report.

11. Print the check register.

12. Include a worksheet map that describes the design of your worksheet.

13. Print all the cell formulas as documentation for this worksheet.

WYSIWYG Assignments

1. Attach WYSIWYG.

2. Add the following enhancements to the check register section of your worksheet:
   a. Create a table (grid) effect for the check register.
   b. Draw a box around the check register.
   c. Boldface the column headings.
   d. Remove the dashed lines under the column headings and replace them with solid lines.

3. Save your worksheet as W7CHECKS.

4. Print the revised report.

Tutorial 8

Creating and Using Macros

Case: Medi-Source Inc. Revisited

In Tutorial 7 you saw how Joan Glazer used 1-2-3's database capabilities to help her manage the credits and collections department at Medi-Source Inc. Joan has recently learned how to use macros to become an even more productive user of 1-2-3. To her, macros are stored keystrokes. For example, she created a macro to print the Massachusetts and Rhode Island customer database. With that macro she saved herself the time and the trouble of making over 15 keystrokes every time she wanted to print. She pressed only two keys, and Lotus 1-2-3 automatically printed the database.

Joan knows that, in addition to printing, she will need to save her 1-2-3 worksheet. She decides, therefore, that creating a macro to save this worksheet will be useful. Joan also plans to create a macro to create range names, because she frequently assigns range names to use with macros as well as for other 1-2-3 functions.

Joan will continue to use the macro for printing, and she now plans to create additional macros to make it easier for her to use the Medi-Source database. She decides first to prepare her planning sheet on creating these additional macros (Figure 8-1 on the following page).

OBJECTIVES

In this tutorial you will learn to:

- Plan a macro

- Create a macro

- Execute a macro

- Use LEARN mode

- Edit and debug a macro using STEP mode

Planning Sheet

My Goal:
   To simplify the use of the Medi-Source worksheet by creating macros

What results do I want to see?
   Customer database outstanding balance report

What information do I need?
   Customer database
   Macros

What macros do I want?
   Print customer database
   Save worksheet
   Name ranges
   Print Outstanding Balance by State report

Figure 8-1
Joan's planning
sheet

In this tutorial, you will first run a macro from the Medi-Source worksheet. Then you will add several macros to the worksheet. This involves planning, placing, entering, naming, and documenting each macro. Next, you will execute each macro. You will also use an alternative approach to creating macros, the LEARN mode. Finally, you will learn how to find errors in macros using the STEP mode and how to correct them.

What Are Macros?

A **macro** is a series of keystrokes and special commands stored in a worksheet as cell entries. Macros are most often created to automate frequently performed Lotus 1-2-3 tasks, such as printing a worksheet, naming a range, saving a worksheet, or formatting cells. Thus, macros save time. They also help less sophisticated users of 1-2-3 by making the worksheet easier to use.

A macro can be used to carry out a simple task and save a few keystrokes, such as printing a worksheet, or it can be used to help prevent typing or keystroke errors. For example, you can avoid errors by creating a macro that automatically moves the cell pointer to specified cells in a worksheet and automatically enters the date and time. Otherwise, you would have to move the cell pointer to the cells where you want to enter the date and time and then enter this information. A macro can also be designed to accomplish a series of more complex and repetitive tasks, such as preparing a weekly report that (1) lists all receivables over 30 days old, (2) sorts the list alphabetically by account, and then (3) prints three copies using compressed print — all in one macro — all automatically!

Retrieving the Worksheet

Joan has been using macros to make her work at Medi-Source more productive. For instance, she developed a print macro to simplify the printing of the Medi-Source database. Let's retrieve the database worksheet and run Joan's print macro.

To retrieve the worksheet and run the macro:

❶ Select /File Retrieve (**/FR**).

❷ Move the menu pointer to C8MEDI1.WK1 and press **[Enter]**. See Figure 8-2.

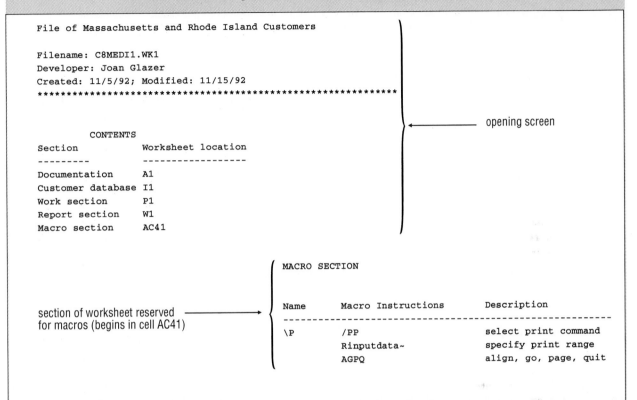

```
File of Massachusetts and Rhode Island Customers

Filename: C8MEDI1.WK1
Developer: Joan Glazer
Created: 11/5/92; Modified: 11/15/92
****************************************************************


          CONTENTS
Section              Worksheet location
---------            ------------------
Documentation        A1
Customer database    I1
Work section         P1
Report section       W1
Macro section        AC41
```

opening screen

section of worksheet reserved
for macros (begins in cell AC41)

```
MACRO SECTION


Name      Macro Instructions        Description
-------------------------------------------------------
\P        /PP                       select print command
          Rinputdata~              specify print range
          AGPQ                      align, go, page, quit
```

Figure 8-2
Part of Joan's initial worksheet

Joan named her printing macro \P and saved it with this worksheet. The \P macro automates printing of the customer database.

❸ Turn on your printer and make sure it's ready to print.

❹ Press **[Alt][p]** to run the macro named \P.

To run a macro that consists of a \ (Backslash) and a single letter, you press the [Alt] key in place of the \ (Backslash) and simultaneously press the letter.

⑤ The macro automatically prints the customer database. See Figure 8-3.

CUST#	CUSTNAME	TYPE	ST	REP	BAL_OWED	YTD_SALES
1	Bristol Pharmacy	P	RI	4	2,647.10	80,278.87
2	Nepco Labs	L	MA	4	3,274.25	6,866.25
3	EMG & EEG Labs	L	MA	4	12,583.97	31,685.19
4	Oaklawn Pharmacy	P	RI	4	4,513.21	5,176.26
5	St. Josephs Hospital	H	RI	3	47,113.50	4,451.68
6	Cape Psych Center	H	MA	3	31,509.10	44,173.24
7	Bioran Medical Lab	L	MA	3	2,799.12	11,927.84
8	Bayshore Pharmacy	P	MA	3	6,010.36	44,140.87
9	St Anne's Hospital	H	MA	3	1,009.53	2,431.80
10	Landmark Medical Center	H	RI	3	22,630.79	6,494.55
11	Lypho_Med Laboratory	L	RI	2	538.62	3,279.89
12	Gregg's Pharmacy	P	MA	2	2,052.70	3,771.28
13	Bradley Hospital	H	MA	2	9,430.72	32,451.95
14	Braintree Hospital	H	MA	2	36,609.80	75,562.35
15	Miriam Hospital	H	MA	2	14,800.44	24,510.04
16	Forgary Labs	L	MA	1	2,890.08	6,670.41
17	De Bellis Pharmacy	P	RI	1	2,715.35	85,063.85
18	Woman & Infants	H	RI	1	47,915.99	3,415.04
19	Depasquale Pharmacy	P	RI	1	4,214.50	39,727.98
20	Kent Hospital	H	MA	1	1,987.44	4,120.74
21	Butler Hospital	H	RI	1	31,215.67	21,144.05
22	Foster Blood Tests	L	MA	1	2,594.27	4,275.56

Figure 8-3
Printout of the
customer database
using the print
macro

Now let's look at the section of the worksheet where the print macro, \P, is located.

To examine the \P macro:

① Press **[F5]** (GOTO), type **ac41**, and press **[Enter]** to move the cell pointer to the area of the worksheet where Joan plans to store the macros. See Figure 8-4. Joan has labeled cell AC41 MACRO SECTION to identify this section of the worksheet.

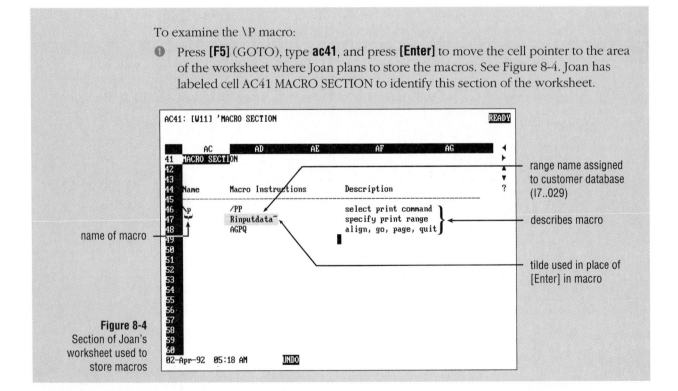

name of macro

Figure 8-4
Section of Joan's
worksheet used to
store macros

range name assigned
to customer database
(I7..O29)

describes macro

tilde used in place of
[Enter] in macro

❷ Move the cell pointer to cell AD46. Here you find the first cell of the actual macro, that is, the stored keystrokes. The complete macro is found in cells AD46, AD47, and AD48. The print macro is a series of keystrokes stored as a label. This macro contains the following stored keystrokes:

/PP	(cell AD46)	/print printer
Rinputdata~	(cell AD47)	Range INPUTDATA (I7..O29) press [Enter]
AGPQ	(cell AD48)	Align Go Page Quit

To run a macro, you must assign a range name to it. Joan has assigned the name \P to her print macro.

The keystroke [Enter] is represented in a macro by the ~ (Tilde). On many keyboards, the tilde is found in the upper left corner of the keyboard, to the left of the "1" key.

❸ Move the cell pointer to cell AC46. In this cell Joan has entered the name of the print macro. By including the name of the macro next to the stored keystrokes, she can easily identify the name assigned to the macro.

❹ Move the cell pointer to cell AF46, the first line of the description of the macro. The entire description is found in cells AF46, AF47, and AF48. Like cell AC46, these cells serve to document the macro.

As you have seen, the print macro automatically prints the customer database. This saves Joan some time and allows others who may be less familiar with 1-2-3 commands to print the worksheet.

Special Keys

Before you create your own macros, you need to know one more thing about them. Some keys require a special entry to represent the actual keystroke in the macro. As we've just seen, for example, the ~ (Tilde) represents the [Enter] key in Joan's print macro.

Function keys, cursor-movement keys, and other special keys are represented by the name of the key enclosed in braces. For instance, to represent pressing the [→] key in a macro, you would type {right}. To represent pressing the [Home] key, you would type {home}. To represent [F5] (GOTO), you would type {GOTO} followed by the cell address or range name of the location to which you want the cell pointer to jump, and you would type a tilde to end the macro. Figure 8-5 on the following page shows what you should enter in a macro to represent function keys, cursor-movement keys, and other special keys.

Action	Macro Entry
	Cursor-movement keys
Move cursor up one row	{UP} or {U}
Move cursor down one row	{DOWN} or {D}
Move cursor left one column	{LEFT} or {L}
Move cursor right one column	{RIGHT} or {R}
Jump to cell A1	{HOME}
Jump to intersection of first blank and non-blank cells	{END} + (arrow macro key)
Jump up 20 rows	{PGUP}
Jump down 20 rows	{PGDN}
Move left one screen	{BIGLEFT}
Move right one screen	{BIGRIGHT}
	Function keys
F2; edit current cell	{EDIT}
F3; list range names in POINT mode	{NAME}
F4; relative, absolute	{ABS}
F5; move cursor to specified cell	{GOTO}
F6; switch between windows	{WINDOW}
F7; repeat last /Data Query command	{QUERY}
F8; repeat last /Data Table command	{TABLE}
F9; recalculate the worksheet	{CALC}
F10; display current graph	{GRAPH}
	Other special keys
Press the [Enter] key	~
Press the [Esc] key	{ESC}
Press the [Backspace] key	{BS}
Press the [Delete] key	{DEL}

Figure 8-5
Special keys used
for macro
keystrokes

Creating the Macro

It takes time to plan and develop macros, but they can save you a great deal of time and effort.

The process of developing a macro involves several steps:

- planning the macro
- placing the macro
- entering the macro
- naming the macro

- documenting the macro
- saving the worksheet that includes the macro
- running and testing the macro
- debugging, or correcting any problems

Planning the Macro

One way to plan a macro is to write down on paper the keystrokes as you type them. For example, whenever Joan saves the Medi-Source worksheet, she presses the following keys:

Keystroke	Action
/	To call the Command menu
F	To select the File command
S	To select the Save command Prompt appears: "Enter name of file to save: filename"
[Enter]	1-2-3 displays the current file name and the Prompt appears: "Cancel Replace Backup"
R	To select Replace to update file

Thus, Joan writes these keystrokes on a piece of paper:

    /FS[Enter]R

This is the macro Joan wants to develop.

Placing the Macro

After planning the macro, you are ready to enter it. First, however, you must decide where to place it in the worksheet. The location of a macro should be in a part of the worksheet that will not be affected by changes made in the rest of the worksheet. One recommendation for the placement of macros is in an unused section of your worksheet, below and to the right of the current worksheet entries. Thus, your macros are not stored in an area that is likely to have data copied to it nor in an area in which you might insert or delete rows (Figure 8-6).

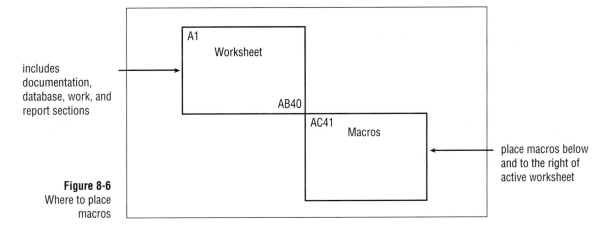

includes documentation, database, work, and report sections

A1
Worksheet
AB40
AC41
Macros

place macros below and to the right of active worksheet

Figure 8-6
Where to place macros

Joan has decided to enter the macros in an area beginning at cell AC41. She has placed the label MACRO SECTION in cell AC41 to identify this area of the worksheet.

Entering the Macro

You can enter a macro in one of two ways:

- By typing the keystrokes that represent the task (macro) as a series of labels directly into the worksheet cells.
- By having 1-2-3 automatically record your keystrokes as you perform the task. You use the LEARN mode, explained later in this tutorial, to do this.

A macro is stored in a cell just like a number, a letter, or a formula. However, in most situations a macro *must* be entered as a label. Thus, you begin a macro with a label prefix, usually the ['] (Apostrophe), and enter the macro in a column of one or more cells. Although a cell can hold up to 240 keystrokes (all 240 keystrokes won't appear in the cell unless the column width is increased, but they are stored in the cell), it is easier to understand a macro if only a small number of related keystrokes are entered in a cell.

Joan has planned her macro. She knows what keystrokes she needs to enter and where to place them. She is now ready to enter the macro by typing it in cell AD50.

To enter the macro worksheet:

❶ Move the cell pointer to cell AD50, the location of the keystrokes for this macro.

❷ Type **'/FS~R** and press **[Enter]**. The keystrokes for this macro appear in cell AD50. See Figure 8-7.

first character in macro is apostrophe

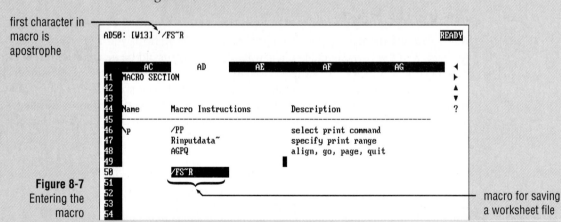

Figure 8-7
Entering the macro

macro for saving a worksheet file

Because macros are entered as labels, the first entry for a macro is a label prefix. If you do not begin the macro with a label prefix, the 1-2-3 command menu will appear on the screen. If this happens, press [Esc] and retype the macro with an apostrophe as the first character.

If you type the macro keystrokes incorrectly, just reenter the keystrokes or use [F2] (EDIT) to modify the macro entry.

Leave a blank cell below the last macro instruction to indicate the end of the macro.

Naming the Macro

Before you execute a macro, you must assign a range name to it. You can assign two types of range names to a macro:

- A \ (Backslash) and a single letter, such as \P
- A range name consisting of up to 15 characters

With either approach, you give the macro its name by using the Range Name Create (/RNC) command.

When you name a macro, you assign the range name to only the *first* cell of the macro. This is because 1-2-3 reads down the column of macro instructions until it reaches an empty cell; thus, you need name only the first cell.

Joan used the first type of name mentioned (Backslash plus a letter) to name her print macro (\P). For the macros you create in this tutorial, you will use the second approach, a range name with up to 15 characters. Although names such as \P are somewhat simpler to use, they can also be more difficult to remember. If you have several macros in a worksheet, you might forget which letter executes a particular task. By using a more descriptive name, you will be able to remember more about what your macro does.

It is a good practice to start each macro name with a Backslash (\) so you can distinguish the range names that represent macros from other range names you use in your worksheet. Joan decides to name this macro \SAVE; she feels this name should make the macro easy to remember.

To name the save macro \SAVE:

❶ Be sure the cell pointer is in cell AD50, the first cell of the macro. Select /Range Name Create (**/RNC**).

❷ Type the range name **\save** and press **[Enter]**.

❸ Press **[Enter]** to indicate you want to assign the name \SAVE to cell AD50.

Remember that you do not need to assign every cell in the macro to the range name. 1-2-3 will automatically move to the next cell below the current cell in the macro until it finds a blank cell, which indicates the end of the macro.

/Range Name Labels Right You could also use an alternative method to assign range names to macros. With this method you use the /Range Name Labels Right command to assign the name to the macro. To use this method you would place the cell pointer on the cell immediately to the left of the macro instruction. This is the cell where you'd find the documentation of the macro name. Next you'd use the /Range Name Labels Right (/RNLR) command to assign the range containing the macro names to the cells to the right of this range. The advantage of this method is that it ensures that you include the name of the macro next to the macro instruction for easy identification.

Documenting the Macro

Whenever you create a macro, a good habit is to include a label containing the macro's name in a cell to the *left* of the macro so you can easily see the name when you examine the macro. It is also a good idea to enter a short description of the macro's function to the *right* of the macro. In that way, you can see at a glance what the macro does. Documenting a macro is not required to make it work, but it is a good habit to develop because some macros can be quite complex and difficult to read. Good macro documentation will save you time and help you avoid confusion.

To document Joan's \SAVE macro:

① Move the cell pointer to cell AC50 and type the label **'\save**. Press **[Enter]**.

② Move the cell pointer to cell AF50 and type **save and replace a worksheet file**, then press **[Enter]**. See Figure 8-8.

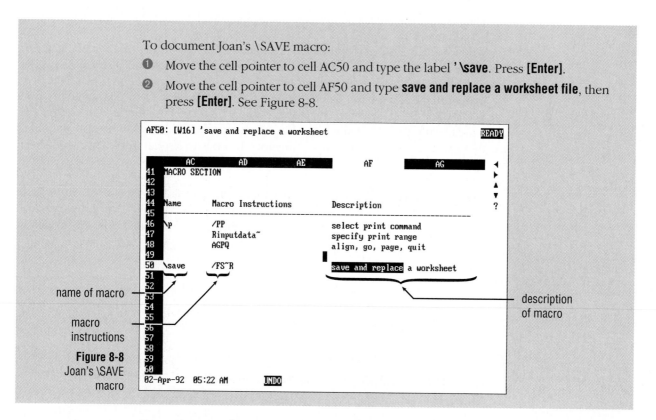

name of macro

macro instructions

Figure 8-8
Joan's \SAVE macro

description of macro

Running and Testing the Macro

Once you have entered and named your macro, you can run it. How you issue the command to run a macro depends on the type of name you assigned to the macro.

- If you named the macro with a backslash and a letter, you press the [Alt] key while pressing the letter of the macro name. You used this approach to run the print macro.

- If you named the macro with a range name of up to 15 characters, you use [Alt][F3] (RUN) and select the name of the macro you want to execute from a list of names that appears on the control panel.

When you run a macro, 1-2-3 reads the macro keystrokes starting with the first cell of the macro. When all the keystrokes in the first cell have been run, 1-2-3 continues reading down the column of cells, executing all keystrokes in each cell. It continues this process until it encounters an empty cell, which 1-2-3 interprets as the end of the macro.

As a general rule, you should save your worksheet prior to running your macro for the first time. This is a good habit to develop because *running a macro with an error could damage the data in a worksheet.*

Now let's save the current version of the worksheet before you test the macro you just entered.

To save your worksheet as S8MEDI1:

❶ Press **[Home]** and then move the cell pointer to cell A3.

❷ Change the filename in cell A3 from C8MEDI1.WK1 to S8MEDI1.WK1.

❸ Select /File Save (**/FS**).

❹ Type **s8medi1** and press **[Enter]**. The worksheet is saved.

Now you can test the macro to see if it is working correctly.

To run the \SAVE macro :

❶ Press **[Alt][F3]** (RUN) and then press **[F3]** (NAME). See Figure 8-9. A list of range names appears on your screen.

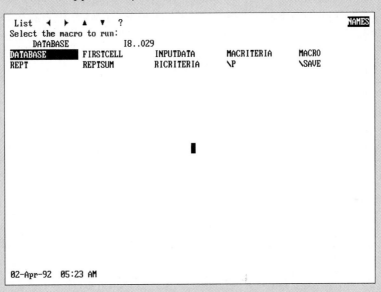

Figure 8-9
List of range names, including macros

❷ Make sure the menu pointer highlights the \SAVE macro.

❸ Press **[Enter]** to run the macro.

The macro runs and saves the current worksheet.

Interrupting a Macro

If you need to interrupt a macro during execution, press [Ctrl][Break]. 1-2-3 returns you immediately to READY mode. If the ERROR mode indicator flashes in the upper right corner of your screen when you press [Ctrl][Break], press [Esc]. This clears the error and returns you to READY mode.

Editing a Macro

Don't be surprised if your macro doesn't work the first time you execute it. When you typed the macro, you may have forgotten a tilde, included spaces, or entered the wrong command. The process of eliminating such errors is called **debugging**. If an error message appears when you run a macro, press [Esc] to return to READY mode. Then correct the macro by moving the cell pointer to the cell that contains the macro and do one of the following:

- Type over the current macro.
- Edit the cell of the macro that contains the error by pressing [F2] (EDIT) and changing the necessary keystrokes.

Creating Interactive Macros

Joan also planned to create a macro to create range names, because she frequently assigns range names to use with macros as well as for other 1-2-3 functions. She writes down the keystrokes required for assigning a range name to a range of cells:

Keystroke	Action
/	To call the command menu
R	To select the Range command
N	To select the Name command
C	To select the Create command Prompt appears: "Enter name"
Type range name	
[Enter]	1-2-3 prompts for range
Highlight range	
[Enter]	Indicates end of Range Name command

In looking over her notes, Joan realizes that the macro must pause to allow her to type the range name and the cells that represent the range. You can create macros that prompt you to enter data, enter a range name, or select a 1-2-3 command, and then the macro continues to run. A macro that pauses during its run is called an **interactive macro**.

To create an interactive macro, you use the Pause command, which is represented by {?}. You can enter {?} anywhere in your macro instruction. When 1-2-3 reads the {?} command, it temporarily stops the macro from running so you can manually enter a range name, move the cell or menu pointer, complete part of a command, or enter data for the macro to process. The macro continues processing when you press [Enter].

When you use {?} in a macro, you must complete the cell entry with a ~ (Tilde). This instructs 1-2-3 to accept your input.

Joan writes down the keystrokes required for the range name macro:

/RNC{?}~{?}~

This interactive macro selects /Range Name Create. At the first {?} command, the macro pauses so you can specify the name of the range. When you press [Enter], the macro continues to run. The macro encounters another {?} command and pauses again. This time you highlight the range of cells included in the range name. Press [Enter] again, to indicate that you want to end the pause. 1-2-3 then encounters the tilde and executes [Enter] to store the range. The macro is then complete.

To enter an interactive macro:

① Move the cell pointer to the macro area, cell AD52, the location where you will enter the interactive macro.

② To enter the macro, type **'/RNC{?}~{?}~** and press **[Enter]**. See Figure 8-10.

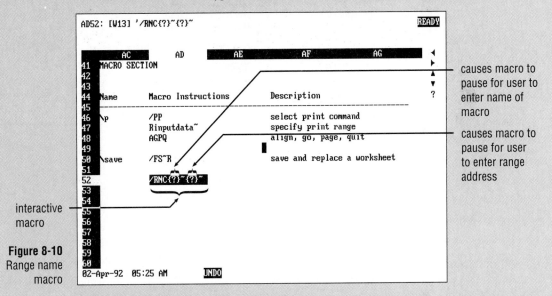

interactive macro

Figure 8-10
Range name macro

Now name the macro \NAME. You will select the Range Name Create command instead of using the \NAME macro, because you are still in the process of creating the \NAME macro.

③ With the cell pointer at cell AD52, select /Range Name Create (**/RNC**). Type **\name** and press **[Enter]**.

④ Press **[Enter]** to assign the range name to cell AD52.

Let's document the macro with a name and a description of what it does.

⑤ Move the cell pointer to cell AC52, type **'\name**, and press **[Enter]**.

⑥   Move the cell pointer to cell AF52, type **assigns range name** and press **[Enter]**. See
     Figure 8-11.

name of macro

Figure 8-11
Current entries in
macro section of
worksheet

description of macro

macro instructions

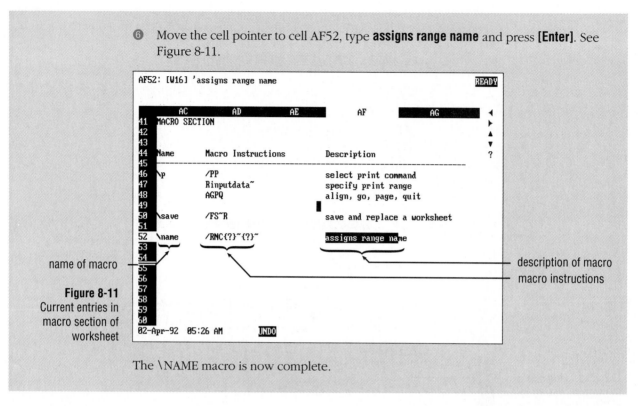

The \NAME macro is now complete.

Let's determine if the macro works properly. Again you need to save the current version
of the worksheet before you run the new macro for the first time. Use the \SAVE macro you
created earlier in the tutorial to save your worksheet.

To save your worksheet using the \SAVE macro:

❶   Press **[Alt][F3]** (RUN) and then press **[F3]** (NAME). Highlight \SAVE from the list of
     range names listed on the screen. Press **[Enter]**. The current version of the work-
     sheet has been saved.

You are now ready to test the \NAME macro. Let's do something that will save us time
as we work through this tutorial. Since this is a tutorial on macros, we'll be going to the macro
area frequently. Let's assign the name MACROS to cell AC41, so you can use this name with
the GOTO key [F5] to move directly to the macro area from any point in the worksheet.

To run the \NAME macro:

❶   Move the cell pointer to cell AC41.

❷   Press **[Alt][F3]** (RUN) and then press **[F3]** (NAME). Highlight \NAME from the list of
     range names listed on the screen. Press **[Enter]**. See Figure 8-12.

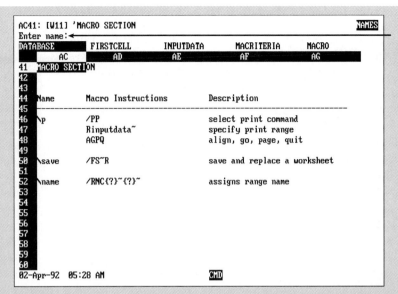

macro pauses
and waits for
you to enter
name of range

Figure 8-12
Running the
\NAME macro

The macro begins to run. When 1-2-3 encounters the first {?}, the macro stops running, and the prompt "Enter name" appears in the control panel.

Notice that the status indicator CMD appears at the bottom of the screen whenever a macro is interrupted.

Now specify the range name.

❸ Type **macros**. Press **[Enter]**.

The macro pauses, waiting for you to highlight the range of cells for the range name.

❹ Press **[Enter]** since the range of the macro is a single cell, AC41.

The macro continues to run until 1-2-3 encounters a blank cell, at which point it stops.

Let's verify that the \NAME macro worked properly.

To test the \NAME macro:

❶ Press **[Home]** to move the cell pointer to cell A1.

❷ Press **[F5]** (GOTO), type **macros**, and press **[Enter]**.

The cell pointer should now be at cell AC41.

LEARN Mode

Joan wants to create a macro that she can use to print a second report — the Outstanding Balance by State report.

As we mentioned earlier, Joan could type this macro directly into worksheet cells or she could use 1-2-3's LEARN mode. In LEARN mode 1-2-3 automatically records the keystrokes as it performs a sequence of 1-2-3 operations. The keystrokes are captured in a separate area of the worksheet called the **learn range**. Joan can then name the learn range and execute it as a macro whenever she chooses.

Let's use LEARN mode to create Joan's macro to print the Outstanding Balance by State report. When you use LEARN mode to create a macro, you must follow these steps:

- Decide where in the worksheet you want to put the learn range. The learn range must be a single column, long enough to contain all the keystrokes of the macro.
- Specify the learn range, using the Worksheet Learn Range command.
- Turn on LEARN mode to start recording all keystrokes.
- Perform the task you want 1-2-3 to record.
- Turn off LEARN mode to stop recording keystrokes.
- Assign a range name to the first cell in the learn range.
- Save the file.
- Run the macro.

Now let's follow these steps and use LEARN mode to create a macro that will print the Outstanding Balance by State report.

First, Joan decides to place the learn range in cells AD54 to AD58.

To specify the learn range and record the macro:

❶ Move the cell pointer to cell AD54 and select /Worksheet Learn Range (**/WLR**).

❷ Press **[.]** to anchor the cell pointer. Highlight the range AD54..AD58 and press **[Enter]**. The learn range is now defined.

Follow the next steps carefully, because once you turn on LEARN mode, every keystroke you make will be recorded. For example, if you press [Backspace] several times to correct typing errors, 1-2-3 will record the [Backspace] keystrokes.

Now turn on LEARN mode.

❸ Press **[Alt][F5]** (LEARN) to turn on LEARN mode. Notice that the status indicator LEARN appears at the bottom of your screen. See Figure 8-13.

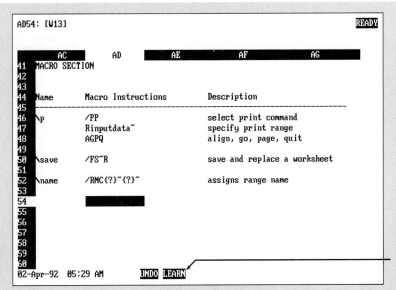

```
AD54: [W13]                                                    READY

          AC              AD          AE            AF              AG
41  MACRO SECTION
42
43
44  Name         Macro Instructions      Description
45  ─────────────────────────────────────────────────────────────────
46  \p           /PP                     select print command
47               Rinputdata~             specify print range
48               AGPQ                    align, go, page, quit
49
50  \save        /FS~R                   save and replace a worksheet
51
52  \name        /RNC{?}~{?}~             assigns range name
53
54
55
56
57
58
59
60
02-Apr-92  05:29 AM          UNDO LEARN
```

Figure 8-13
Creating a macro
using LEARN
mode

indicates LEARN
mode is on

The next step is to perform the tasks you want to record.

④ Check to be sure that your printer is on, then select /Print Printer (**/PP**).

⑤ Select Range (**R**), type **reptsum**, and press **[Enter]**.

⑥ Select Align Go Page Quit (**AGPQ**).

The Outstanding Balance Report begins to print.

Now you should turn off LEARN mode to stop recording the keystrokes.

⑦ Press **[Alt][F5]** (LEARN) to turn off LEARN mode. Notice that the status indicator LEARN no longer appears on the screen. Instead, the CALC indicator appears. If you don't turn off LEARN mode, 1-2-3 will continue to record your keystrokes and place them in the macro area.

⑧ Press **[Enter]** so the recorded keystrokes appear in the learn range. The CALC indicator disappears. With the cell pointer in cell AD54, the first cell in the learn range, view the keystrokes that 1-2-3 has recorded. See Figure 8-14.

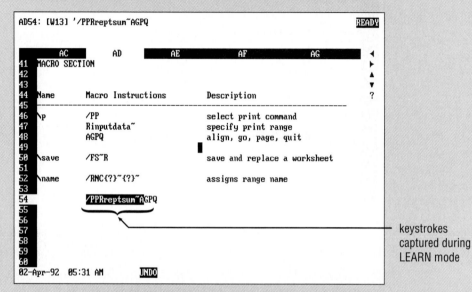

Figure 8-14
Macro created
using LEARN
mode

keystrokes
captured during
LEARN mode

If the macro looks correct, the next step is to specify a range name for it. On the other hand, if the macro needs corrections, you can edit it as you would any other cell.

Let's name the macro \PRINTREPT using the \NAME macro.

To name and document the macro:

① With the cell pointer in cell AD54, press **[Alt][F3]** (RUN) and then press **[F3]** (NAME). Highlight \NAME from the list of range names on the screen. Press **[Enter]**.

② Type **\printrept** and press **[Enter]** to enter the range name.

③ Press **[Enter]** to assign the range name to the first cell of the learn range.

Now let's document the macro.

④ Move the cell pointer to cell AC54. Type **' \printrept**, then press **[Enter]**. Move the cell pointer to cell AF54. Type **prints summary report** and press **[Enter]**. See Figure 8-15.

If you now wanted to create another macro using LEARN mode, you would have to reset the learn range to another range of cells (/Worksheet Learn Range); otherwise, the new macro would be added to the end of the existing macro.

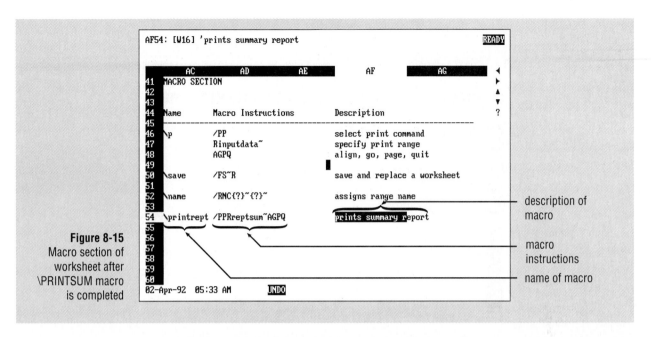

Figure 8-15
Macro section of
worksheet after
\PRINTSUM macro
is completed

Finally, let's run the \PRINTREPT macro to see if it works.

To run the macro:

❶ Make sure your printer is on.

❷ Press **[Alt][F3]** (RUN) and then press **[F3]** (NAME). Highlight \PRINTREPT from the list of range names on the control panel. Press **[Enter]**.

The Outstanding Balance by State report is printed.

❸ Save your worksheet as S8MEDI1 using the \SAVE macro.

Using STEP Mode to Debug a Macro

The first time you run a macro, it may not work as you intended. In a simple macro, you can easily identify errors by comparing the keystrokes in the worksheet with the keystroke entries you planned. In large macros, however, it is more difficult to identify errors, so Lotus 1-2-3 has a special feature to help you in debugging macros. This feature, called **STEP mode**, allows you to run a macro one keystroke at a time.

To demonstrate the use of STEP mode, let's run the \SAVE macro in STEP mode. First, we'll modify the \SAVE macro so it is intentionally incorrect; then we'll see how STEP mode can help us find the error.

To modify the \SAVE macro and intentionally enter an error:

❶ Move the cell pointer to cell AD50, the location of the \SAVE macro.

❷ Type **'/F~S~R** and press **[Enter]**. See Figure 8-16.

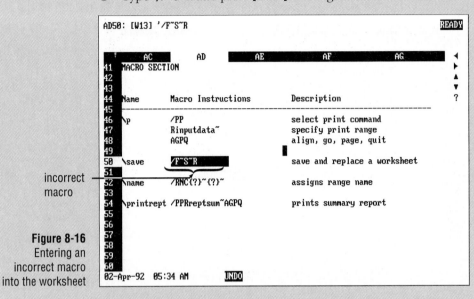

incorrect
macro

Figure 8-16
Entering an
incorrect macro
into the worksheet

Notice that a ~ (Tilde) appears between the F and the S. The correct macro is
'/FS~R.

Let's try to use this modified \SAVE macro.

To run the incorrect \SAVE macro:

❶ Press **[Alt][F3]** (RUN) and then press **[F3]** (NAME). Highlight \SAVE from the list of range names on the screen. Press **[Enter]**. See Figure 8-17.

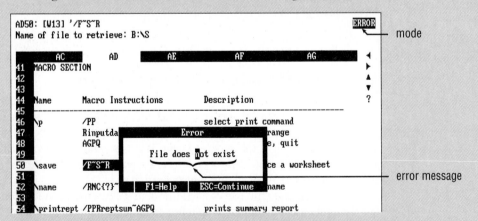

mode

error message

Figure 8-17
Attempting to run
incorrect \SAVE
macro

Notice that the mode indicator in the upper right corner has changed to ERROR and is blinking. This indicates something is wrong with your macro. In addition, the message appearing in the middle of your screen says that the "File does not exist."

❷ Press **[Esc]** to clear the error condition and return to READY mode.

What happened? Why did the macro stop running? If the reason is not obvious to you from looking at the macro keystrokes, you can use STEP mode to help debug the macro.

To use STEP mode:

1 Press **[Alt][F2]** (STEP). This turns on STEP mode. See Figure 8-18. Notice that the STEP indicator appears in the status line at the bottom of the screen.

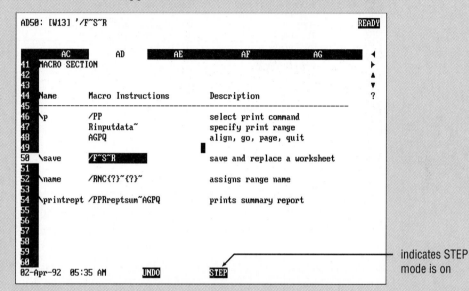

Figure 8-18
Turning on STEP
mode

indicates STEP
mode is on

To run a macro in STEP mode, you press any key to run the macro one keystroke at a time. That way, you can see each step the macro takes and perhaps determine the problem with the macro.

Now let's rerun the macro.

❷ Press **[Alt][F3]** (RUN) and then press **[F3]** (NAME). Highlight \SAVE from the list of range names on the screen. Press **[Enter]**. See Figure 8-19.

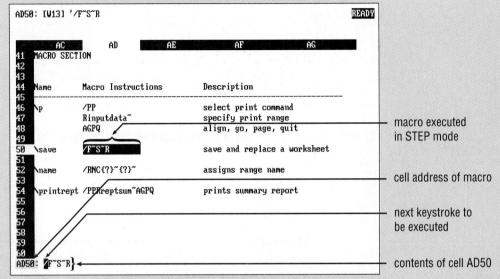

Figure 8-19
Macro appears in
status line

The cell address that contains the macro appears on the status line, along with the contents of that cell. The keystroke to be executed the next time you press a key is highlighted.

❸ Press **[Spacebar]**. This executes the first keystroke of the macro, the / (Slash). See Figure 8-20.

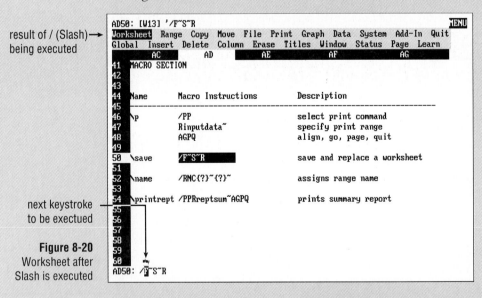

Figure 8-20
Worksheet after
Slash is executed

Notice that the Command menu appears in the control panel. In addition, in the status line, the keystroke that will be executed next, F, is highlighted.

❹ Press **[Spacebar]** once more to execute the next keystroke in the macro. See Figure 8-21.

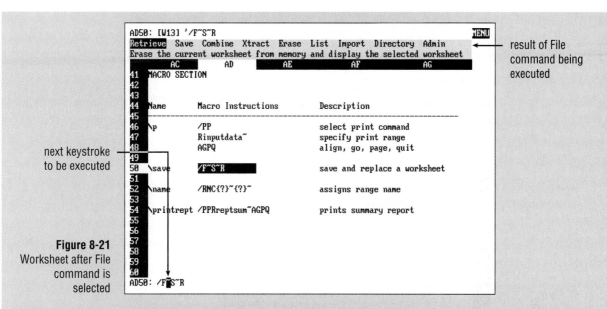

result of File command being executed

next keystroke to be executed

Figure 8-21
Worksheet after File command is selected

The File command from the Command menu is selected, and the File command options appear on the control panel. The Retrieve command is highlighted. Also notice that the ~ (Tilde) in the status line is highlighted. It is the next keystroke to be executed.

⑤ Press **[Spacebar]** once again. This runs the ~, that is, the [Enter] keystroke. See Figure 8-22. Since the Retrieve command was highlighted in the control panel, pressing [Enter] executes Retrieve rather than Save. The prompt "Name of the file to retrieve" appears in the control panel. Notice that the next keystroke to be executed, S, is highlighted in the status line.

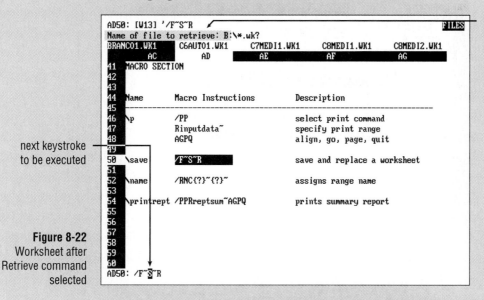

Retrieve command executed as a result of an erroneous ~ (Tilde)

next keystroke to be executed

Figure 8-22
Worksheet after Retrieve command selected

⑥ Press **[Spacebar]** again. S is entered as the name of the file to retrieve. See Figure 8-23.

next keystroke
to be executed

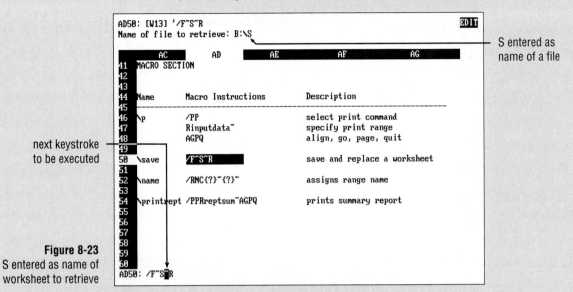

Figure 8-23
S entered as name of
worksheet to retrieve

S entered as
name of a file

The status line indicates the ~ (Tilde) will be the next keystroke to be executed.

⑦ Press **[Spacebar]**. 1-2-3 interprets the ~ as the [Enter] keystroke and attempts to retrieve a file named S. See Figure 8-24.

1-2-3 trying to
retrieve file
S.WK1

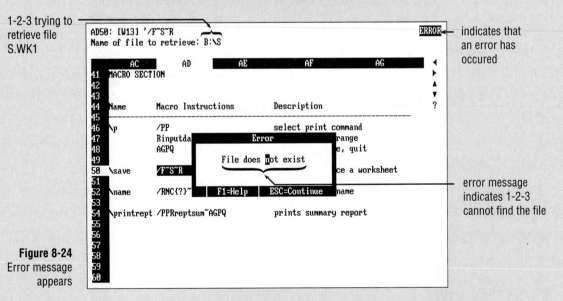

Figure 8-24
Error message
appears

indicates that
an error has
occured

error message
indicates 1-2-3
cannot find the file

1-2-3 doesn't find the file S.WK1 on your data diskette. The ERROR indicator appears in the upper right corner of your screen, and the error message "File does not exist" appears in the middle of the screen.

⑧ Press **[Esc]** to clear the error message and return to READY mode.

Once your worksheet is in READY mode, you can edit the macro.

⑨ Be sure the cell pointer is in cell AD50. Type **'/FS~R** and press **[Enter]** to correct the macro.

You are still in STEP mode, which means if you attempt to run another macro, 1-2-3 will continue to run the macro one keystroke at a time.

⑩ Press **[Alt][F2]** (STEP). This turns off STEP mode. Now the macros will run normally. The status indicator STEP disappears from the status line.

The Final Worksheet

As a final step in preparing the worksheet for her staff, Joan decides to create a section of the worksheet that will describe the various options of the worksheet. This section will also provide instructions that walk a user through the various steps to run these options. Figure 8-25 shows Joan's sketch of the instruction sections she plans to enter into her worksheet.

```
                    Menu Options
        Option      Description
        ---------   ------------------
        \PRINTDATA  Prints customer database
        \PRINTREPT  Prints Outstanding Balance by State report
        \SAVE       Saves worksheet
        \NAME       Names a range
        -------------------------------------
        Instructions:
                Press [Alt][F3] and then press [F3].
                Highlight name of option you want to execute.

                Press [Home] to return to instruction screen
```

Figure 8-25
Joan's sketch of
the instruction
section

To retrieve Joan's revised worksheet:

① Select /File Retrieve (**/FR**).

② Highlight C8MEDI2 and press **[Enter]**. See Figure 8-26 on the following page. The instruction screen appears immediately upon retrieval of the worksheet. This way, the first thing a user sees when retrieving the worksheet will be instructions on how to use the worksheet.

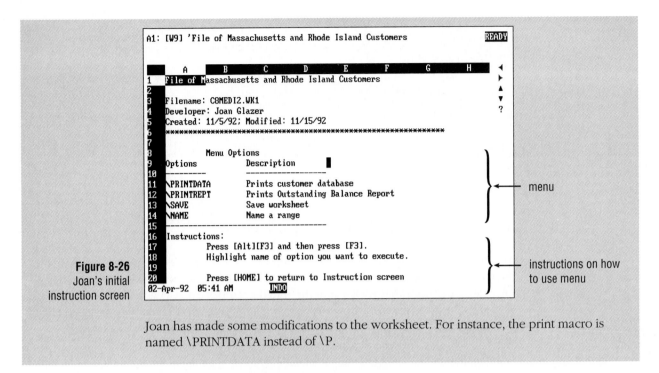

Figure 8-26
Joan's initial
instruction screen

Joan has made some modifications to the worksheet. For instance, the print macro is named \PRINTDATA instead of \P.

Let's try out the revised worksheet.

To print the customer database:

● Press **[Alt][F3]** (RUN) and then press **[F3]** (NAME). Highlight \PRINTDATA and press **[Enter]**. The customer database is printed.

Joan is satisfied with the worksheet and is ready to show it to her staff.

◼   ◼   ◼

Exercises

1. What keystrokes are used to do the following?
   a. run a macro
   b. turn STEP mode on and off
   c. turn LEARN mode on and off

2. What do you use in a macro to represent the following?
   a. pressing the [Enter] key
   b. a pause in the running of a macro
   c. pressing [F5] (GOTO) key
   d. the [Up] key

3. What do the following macros do?
    a. {GOTO}macros~ (*Note:* MACROS is a range name.)
    b. /RFF{?}~{?}~
    c. /RFC2~{END}{DOWN}~
    d. /C~{DOWN}~
    e. /PPOOCQQ

Tutorial Assignments

Before you begin these Tutorial Assignments, check your data diskette. Be sure you have space to save the additional worksheet files you'll create in these assignments (at least 30,000 bytes). If you do not have enough space, save your files for Tutorial 8 to another formatted diskette.

Retrieve the worksheet T8MEDI1.WK1. This worksheet contains the four macros created in this tutorial. Make the following additions or modifications to the macro area.

1. First, save this worksheet as S8MEDI2.

2. Modify the \SAVE macro so the cell pointer moves to cell A1 before the worksheet is saved. Save the worksheet using the revised \SAVE macro. What is the purpose of moving the cell pointer to cell A1 before saving the worksheet?

3. Create a macro as follows:
    a. Use the typing method to create a macro to set print settings to compressed print. This macro will set the right margin to 132 and the setup string to the code for compressed print used by your printer. For many printers, the setup string for compressed print is \015.
    b. Name this macro \COMPRESS.
    c. Document the macro.
    d. Save the worksheet as S8MEDI2.
    e. Run the \COMPRESS macro.
    f. Print the customer database using the \PRINTDATA macro.

4. Create a macro as follows:
    a. Use the typing method to create a macro that sets the print settings to normal print. This macro will set the right margin to 76 and the setup string to the code for normal print used by your printer. For many printers, the setup string for normal print is \018.
    b. Name this macro \NORM.
    c. Document the macro.
    d. Save the worksheet as S8MEDI2.
    e. Run the \NORM macro and then run the \PRINTDATA macro.

5. Create an interactive macro to sort the customer database. This macro should include the following steps:
    • Move the cell pointer to the first field name in the customer database. (The range name is FIRSTCELL.)
    • Select the Data Sort command.
    • Reset the sort settings.
    • Select the Data-Range option and assign the range name DATABASE as the data range.
    • Select the Primary-Key option.

- Allow the user to select the primary key. (This step is interactive.)
- Allow the user to type *a* or *d* for sort order. (This step is interactive.)
- Select the Go option to sort the database.
  a. Use the typing method to enter the sort macro.
  b. Name this macro \SORT.
  c. Document this macro.
  d. Save your worksheet as S8MEDI3.
  e. Run the \SORT macro and sort the customer database in descending order by balance owed.
  f. Run the \PRINTDATA macro to print the customer database.

6. Create a macro as follows:
   a. Use LEARN mode to develop a macro to format a range of cells using Currency format with zero decimal places. Move the cell pointer to the column you want to format before you execute the macro.
   b. Name this macro \CURRENCY0.
   c. Document the macro.
   d. Save the worksheet as S8MEDI3.
   e. Format the YTD_SALES column (O8..O29) using this macro.

7. Suppose that you want to view widely separated parts of your worksheet at the same time. You can use the Worksheet Windows command to accomplish this. Use LEARN mode to create the following macros. Remember to reset the learn range after creating each macro.
   a. Develop a macro to set up a horizontal window. Name this macro \WINDOWH. Document this macro.
   b. Develop a macro to set up a vertical window in your worksheet. Name this macro \WINDOWV. Document this macro.
   c. Develop a macro to clear the window settings. Name this macro \WINDOWC. Document this macro.
   d. Save your worksheet as S8MEDI3.

8. Print the macro section of your worksheet.

Retrieve the worksheet file T8MEDI2. This worksheet has two new macros in addition to the four that were originally in the T8MEDI1 worksheet.

9. The first new macro, \COLWIDTH, located in cell AD58, is supposed to change the column width. It doesn't work properly.
   a. Run the macro.
   b. Correct the macro.
   c. Save your worksheet as S8MEDI4.
   d. Run the corrected macro to increase the column width in column J from 25 to 28 characters.

10. The second macro, \DELRANGE, located in cell AD60, is supposed to allow you to select a range name to delete. When it runs, an error occurs.
    a. Run the macro.
    b. Correct the macro so it deletes any existing range name.
    c. Save your worksheet as S8MEDI4.
    d. Run the corrected macro and delete the range name \p.

e. Use the \NAME macro in the worksheet to assign the macro in cell AD48 the name \PRINTDATA.
f. Make the appropriate changes to the macro documentation.
g. Print the worksheet using the macro \PRINTDATA.
h. Save the worksheet as S8MEDI4.

Case Problems

1. Reporting on Word Processing Software

A marketing research firm has compiled data on the number of units the top six word processing software packages have shipped worldwide during 1989 (Figure 8-27).

Product	Units Shipped
WordPerfect	1,400,000
Microsoft Word	500,000
WordStar	345,000
Display Write	300,000
Professional Write	250,000
Multimate	200,000

Figure 8-27

1. Create a worksheet using the data from Figure 8-27.

2. Prepare a report that includes all the products and has the format shown in Figure 8-28.

	Add title	
Product	Units shipped	Market share
XXXXXXXXXXX	XXXXX	xx.x%
XXXXXXXXXXX	XXXXX	xx.x%
.	.	.
.	.	.
.	.	.
Total Units	XXXXX	

Figure 8-28

3. Create a pie chart of shipments by product. Name the graph PIE_SHIP.

4. Create a bar graph of shipments by product. Name the graph BAR_SHIP.

5. Create a macro to print the report. Name the macro \PRINT.

6. Create a macro to view the pie chart. Name the macro \PIEWP.

7. Create a macro to view the bar graph. Name the macro \BARWP.

8. Include in your worksheet an instruction section that will help anyone who uses the macros in this worksheet. This section should be the first screen that appears when a user retrieves the worksheet.

9. Save your worksheet as S8WORD.

10. Use the macro \PRINT to print the report in Assignment 2.

11. Print the macro section of your worksheet.

WYSIWYG Assignments

1. Attach WYSIWYG.

2. Add the following enhancements:
   a. Replace any dashed lines with solid lines under column headings and above and below totals.
   b. Use a 14-point Swiss font for the report title line(s) and enclose the title in a drop shadow.
   c. Boldface the total row.
   d. Insert the pie chart into the worksheet beneath the report.
   e. Create a macro to print the report and the graph on one page using the WYSIWYG print command. Name this macro \WYSIPRT.

3. Save your worksheet as W8WORD.

4. Print the entire worksheet on one page using the macro \WYSIPRT.

2. Tutorial 3 Revisited

Retrieve the worksheet P8BALBO1, the final version of the Balboa Mutual Fund worksheet from Tutorial 3, and do the following:

1. Modify the worksheet so that the first screen includes the information in Figure 8-29.

Macro Name	Description
\ERASE	Erase a column
\PRINT	Print fund report
\SAVE	Save the worksheet
[Place instructions on how to run a macro here.]	

Figure 8-29

2. Create a macro to erase the prices from the Current Prices column. You should be able to select (highlight) the range of cells to erase. Name the macro \ERASE.

3. Create a macro to print the Mutual Fund report. Name the macro \PRINT.

4. Create a macro to save the worksheet. You should be able to name the worksheet that you are saving. Name the macro \SAVE.

5. Save your file as S8BALBO1 using your save macro.

6. Enter the current prices for November 6, 199X, which were as follows:

IBM	92
Coca-Cola	68.50
Texaco	59
Boeing	49

   First, use your macro to erase the Current Price column. Then enter the new prices. Remember also to change the date.

7. Print the Net Asset Value report for November 6, 199X, using your print macro.

8. Print the macro section of your worksheet.

9. Save your file as S8BALBO2.

WYSIWYG Assignments

1. Attach WYSIWYG.

2. Add the following enhancements:
   a. Replace any dashed lines with solid lines under column headings and above and below totals.
   b. Use a 14-point Swiss font for the report title line(s) and enclose the title in a drop shadow.
   c. Boldface the total row.
   d. Shade the NAV and the number of shares components of this report.
   e. Create a macro to print the NAV report using the WYSIWYG print command. Name this macro \WYSIPRT. Include this macro name in your opening screen.

3. Save your worksheet as W8BALBO1.

4. Print the NAV report using the macro \WYSIPRT.

3. Tutorial 6 Revisited

Retrieve the worksheet P8AUTO1, the final version of the Automobile Industry Sales worksheet from Tutorial 6, and do the following:

1. Modify the worksheet so the that first screen includes the information in Figure 8-30.

Macro Name	Description
\BAR	View standard bar graph
\BAR3D	View 3D bar graph
\PIE	View pie chart
\PRINT	Print worksheet data
[Place instructions on how to run a macro here.]	

Figure 8-30

2. Create a macro to view the bar graph BAR3. Name the macro \BAR.

3. Create a macro to view the 3D bar graph BAR6. Name the macro \BAR3D.

4. Create a macro to view the pie chart PIE90. Name the macro \PIE.

5. Create a macro to print the automobile data. Name the macro \PRINT.

6. Save your worksheet as S8AUTO1.

7. Test all your macros.

8. Print the macro section of your worksheet.

WYSIWYG Assignments

1. Attach WYSIWYG.

2. Add the following enhancements:
   a. Insert the pie chart into the worksheet beneath the worksheet data.
   b. Create a macro to print the report and the graph on one page. Name this macro \WYSIPRT.

3. Save your worksheet as W8AUTO1.

4. Print the entire worksheet on one page using the macro \WYSIPRT.

Lotus 1-2-3 Modules

- **Module 1   Dialog Boxes**

- **Module 2   Using WYSIWYG to Enhance and Print 1-2-3 Worksheets**

- **Module 3   Using WYSIWYG to Enhance and Print Graphs**

- **Module   4 Using SmartIcons**

Module 1

Dialog Boxes

Components of a Dialog Box

A **dialog box** is a box in 1-2-3 that contains information about the current settings associated with a particular task. For example, whenever you print in 1-2-3 a Print Settings dialog box appears. You can change the print settings in this dialog box using either a keyboard or a mouse, or you can use the menu that appears above the dialog box to select commands to specify the settings.

If you interact directly with a dialog box (instead of selecting commands from the menu), you select settings by using different objects: option buttons, check boxes, text boxes, command buttons, pop-up dialog boxes, and list boxes. Let's review each of these objects.

Option buttons offer you a set of options, but you can select only one option at a time. You can identify the option buttons in a dialog box by looking for pairs of parentheses ( ). The option that is currently selected is marked by an asterisk in the parentheses. The unselected options have no asterisks in the parentheses. For example, the Graph Settings dialog box in Figure 1-1 on the following page illustrates option buttons and other dialog box features. The section of the dialog box marked Type has seven option buttons. The current selection, the line graph, is marked by an asterisk.

OBJECTIVES

In this tutorial you will learn to:

■ Use dialog box terminology

■ Use a dialog box with a keyboard

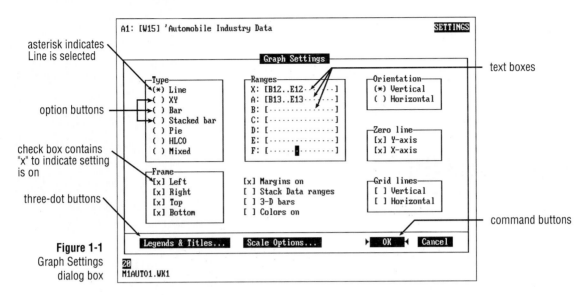

asterisk indicates Line is selected

option buttons

check box contains "x" to indicate setting is on

three-dot buttons

text boxes

command buttons

Figure 1-1
Graph Settings
dialog box

Check boxes are used for settings that can be on or off. A check box appears as brackets [ ]. If an *x* appears in the box, the setting is on. Unlike option buttons, more than one check box in a group can be selected at the same time. For example, as Figure 1-1 illustrates, all the settings that comprise the Frame of the graph are *on*. That means lines will appear on all sides of the graph.

Text boxes are boxes in a dialog box that enclose text in brackets; they are preceded by a descriptive label and a colon. The area within the brackets is where you enter or edit range names, numbers, cell addresses, or text. In Figure 1-1 the section of the dialog box marked Ranges contains several text boxes. When you select any text box in this section of the dialog box, you type in your settings.

Command buttons in dialog boxes are most often labeled OK or Cancel. When you have finished making your choices, you choose OK to accept the settings that currently appear in the dialog box. You choose Cancel if you want 1-2-3 to ignore the settings in the dialog box and continue to use the previous settings. Besides illustrating the OK and Cancel command buttons, Figure 1-1 illustrates an example of another command button that appears in the Graph Settings dialog box. The **three-dot buttons** are command buttons that contain ellipses (...) following the label. These buttons refer you to other dialog boxes that contain related settings. Figure 1-1 illustrates two three-dot command buttons: Legends & Titles and Scale Options, each of which is followed by ellipses.

Some tasks can't fit all their options in one dialog box. In those cases a **pop-up dialog box** appears over the initial dialog box when you select a particular option. A pop-up dialog box leads to further choices that do not appear in the initial dialog box.

List boxes display a list of available choices from which you can choose. If a list is too long to fit on one screen, you can scroll through the list.

Using Dialog Boxes

Before you can use a dialog box, you must activate it by pressing [F2] (EDIT) or by clicking anywhere inside the dialog box with a mouse.

Once a dialog box has been activated, you can select options by using the arrow keys and pressing [Spacebar] or [Enter], by typing the highlighted character of the option you want, or by clicking with the left mouse button.

Selecting Dialog Box Options Using the Keyboard

The Graph command illustrates a variety of settings you can change using the dialog box. You use the Graph command to create a graph. With this command you specify the data you want to graph and how you want to graph them.

The worksheet file M1AUTO1.WK1 contains a line graph of Chrysler's sales from 1987 to 1990. Let's retrieve this worksheet and try using the Graph Settings dialog box to change the line graph to a bar graph.

To retrieve a worksheet:

❶ Retrieve the worksheet file M1AUTO1.WK1. Select /File Retrieve (**/FR**).

❷ Highlight the file M1AUTO1.WK1 and press **[Enter]**.

The worksheet contains the settings for a line graph of sales of Chrysler automobiles.

❸ Press **[F10]**. A line graph appears. Press any key to continue.

Let's change the current graph to a bar graph.

❹ Select /Graph (**/G**). See Figure 1-2.

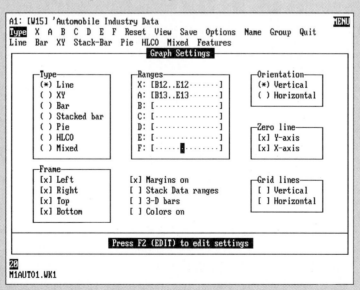

Figure 1-2
Graph Settings
dialog box

In addition to the Graph menu, the Graph Settings dialog box appears. Let's use the dialog box to change the line graph to a bar graph.

When the dialog box first appears on the screen, it is not active. Thus, you cannot make changes to the graph settings using the dialog box. To use the dialog box, you must activate it. Let's do that now.

To activate the dialog box:

❶   Press **[F2]** (EDIT). See Figure 1-3.

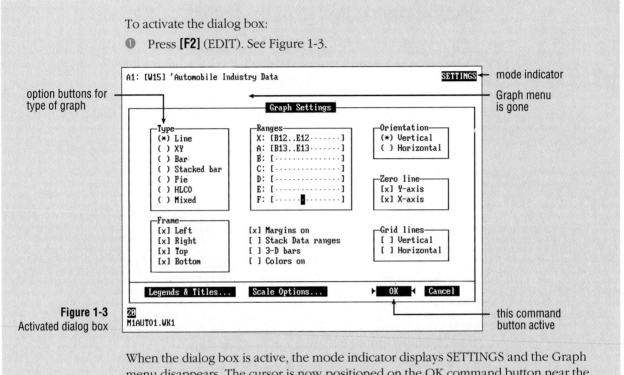

Figure 1-3
Activated dialog box

When the dialog box is active, the mode indicator displays SETTINGS and the Graph menu disappears. The cursor is now positioned on the OK command button near the bottom right corner of the dialog box. This button is active, which we know because it is highlighted or marked by arrows.

To help you distinguish among the options, one letter of each option is displayed in either a different color or a different intensity. To select an option, you either type the highlighted character or use the cursor-movement keys to highlight your choice in the dialog box and then press [Enter] or [Spacebar] to select it.

To change the line graph to a bar graph using the dialog box:

❶   Select Type (**T**). The option buttons within the Type group are activated.

❷   Select Bar (**B**) from the dialog box. See Figure 1-4. The asterisk indicates that you have selected a bar graph.

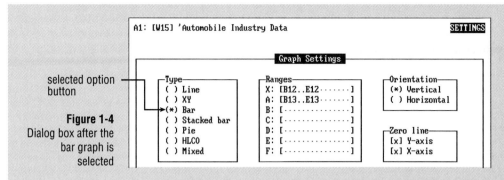

Figure 1-4
Dialog box after the
bar graph is
selected

selected option
button

If you wanted to, you could back out of that command by pressing [Esc]. But don't do that now because that would return you to the previous settings. Instead let's display the bar graph.

❸ Press **[F10]**. A bar graph appears. Press any key to continue.

You can now create a three-dimensional bar graph by turning on the 3-D bars check box.

To turn on the 3-D bars check box:

❶ Type **3**. See Figure 1-5.

check box
turned on

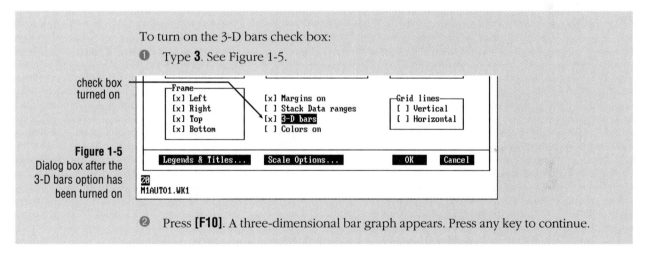

Figure 1-5
Dialog box after the
3-D bars option has
been turned on

❷ Press **[F10]**. A three-dimensional bar graph appears. Press any key to continue.

Now let's confirm the settings in the dialog box.

To confirm the settings in the dialog box:

❶ Press **[Tab]** until the command button OK is highlighted. Press **[Enter]**. The Graph menu appears in the control panel.

If you changed your mind, you could move the cursor to the Cancel command button and press [Enter] to reset all current graph settings to the previous settings.

❷ Select Quit (**Q**) to leave the Graph menu.

Dialog boxes provide information on a command's current settings. As you become an experienced 1-2-3 user, you may find using dialog boxes to change settings speeds up work, especially if you use a mouse.

Module 2

Using WYSIWYG to Enhance and Print 1-2-3 Worksheets

OBJECTIVES

In this tutorial you will learn to:

- Load and activate WYSIWYG

- Define fonts, typefaces, type sizes, and type styles

- Enhance worksheets with typefaces, type sizes, and type styles

- Enhance worksheets with lines and boxes

- Save worksheets that include WYSIWYG enhancements

- Print worksheets that include WYSIWYG enhancements

What Is WYSIWYG?

Every day business people read many pieces of paper. If your job is writing those papers, how can you make your work stand out? How can you make the spreadsheets you create catch and keep the reader's attention, be easy to read, and convey your ideas clearly and convincingly?

You can use a new feature of 1-2-3 called WYSIWYG. WYSIWYG enables you to enhance the appearance of your worksheets, databases, and graphs. WYSIWYG, pronounced *wizzy-wig,* stands for "**W**hat **Y**ou **S**ee **I**s **W**hat **Y**ou **G**et." As the acronym says, the worksheet you see on the screen closely resembles what you will see as printed output. WYSIWYG lets you use sophisticated features such as typefaces, type sizes and styles, lines, boxes, and shading to enhance your worksheet, making it easier to read and understand. Compare the worksheets in Figure 2-1 on the following page. Figure 2-1a shows the final version of the worksheet in Tutorial 3, and 2-1b shows the same worksheet enhanced with several WYSIWYG features. By the end of this tutorial you will have modified the worksheet shown in Figure 2-1a so that it looks like the worksheet in Figure 2-1b.

```
Balboa Equity Fund
Net Asset Value for November 5, 1992

Company                          # of   Current     Market
Name                            Shares   Price      Value
-------------------------------------------------------------

International Business Machines    100   $91.00   $9,100.00
Coca-Cola                           50    69.25    3,462.50
Texaco                             100    58.75    5,875.00
Boeing                             150    44.50    6,675.00
                                                 -------------
  Totals                                         $25,112.50
                                                 ============

Mutual Fund Shares                        2000
Price/Share (NAV)                        $12.56
```

Figure 2-1a
Pauline's
worksheet before
WYSIWYG

Balboa Equity Fund
Net Asset Value for November 5, 1992

Company Name	# of Shares	Current Price	Market Value
International Business Machines	100	$91.00	$9,100.00
Coca-Cola	50	69.25	3,462.50
Texaco	100	58.75	5,875.00
Boeing	150	44.50	6,675.00
Totals			$25,112.50

Mutual Fund Shares		*2000*
Price/Share (NAV)		*$12.56*

Figure 2-1b
Pauline's worksheet
after WYSIWYG
enhancements

You can do several things in WYSIWYG, for example:

- display text and numbers using a variety of typefaces, type styles, and type sizes
- draw lines, boxes, and grids around one or more cells to organize information in sections and blocks to give visual interest
- control the widths of columns and the heights of rows
- print worksheets and graphs on the same page
- annotate graphs with descriptive comments, lines, arrows, rectangles, and ellipses
- preview a worksheet before it is printed

In this module you will learn how to load and activate WYSIWYG; enhance your worksheet with different typefaces, type sizes, and type styles; draw lines and boxes; and print your worksheet using WYSIWYG's print command.

Loading WYSIWYG

When you load 1-2-3 Release 2.3, WYSIWYG is not automatically loaded because it is a separate program called an **add-in program**. WYSIWYG is automatically attached to 1-2-3 Release 2.4. If WYSIWYG is already attached, skip to "Accessing WYSIWYG" on page L 320. Before you can use the WYSIWYG features, you must attach the WYSIWYG program.

Let's attach the WYSIWYG add-in program.

To attach the WYSIWYG add-in program:

❶ Select /Add-in Attach (**/AA**). A list of add-in programs appears. See Figure 2-2.

WYSIWYG program

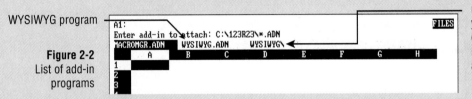

Figure 2-2
List of add-in
programs

names of programs; if you're using the commercial version, more names will appear

WYSIWYG.ADN is the program that contains WYSIWYG.

❷ Highlight WYSIWYG.ADN and press **[Enter]**. The extension ADN stands for **AD**d-i**N**.

Now choose how you want to access the WYSIWYG menu once WYSIWYG is loaded into memory. See Figure 2-3.

options ➞

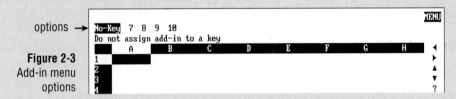

Figure 2-3
Add-in menu
options

If you choose *No-Key*, you press [:] to access the WYSIWYG menu.
If you choose *7*, you press [Alt] [F7] to access the WYSIWYG menu.
If you choose *8*, you press [Alt][F8] to access the WYSIWYG menu.
If you choose *9*, you press [Alt][F9] to access the WYSIWYG menu.
If you choose *10*, you press [Alt][F10] to access the WYSIWYG menu.

Pressing the colon key ([:]) is the simplest way to access the WYSIWYG menu.

❸ Select No-Key. The WYSIWYG worksheet appears.
❹ Select Quit (**Q**) to leave the add-in menu and return to READY mode. WYSIWYG is now attached to 1-2-3.

Like the 1-2-3 program and individual worksheets, the WYSIWYG program takes up computer memory. If you receive an error message when you try to attach WYSIWYG, it may mean that your computer does not have enough available memory to do so. See your instructor or technical support person for help if you are having trouble attaching WYSIWYG.

Accessing WYSIWYG

With WYSIWYG attached, you can access either the 1-2-3 main menu or the WYSIWYG menu. To display the WYSIWYG menu, you press [:] (Colon). To display the 1-2-3 main menu commands, you press [/] (Slash).

Now let's access the WYSIWYG menu.

To access the WYSIWYG menu:

① Press **[:]**. See Figure 2-4. When you access WYSIWYG, the WYSIWYG command menu appears. Notice that the mode indicator displays WYSIWYG.

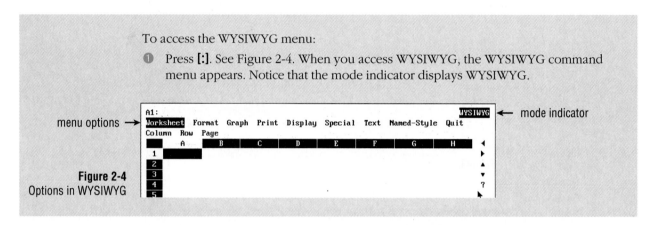

menu options →

← mode indicator

Figure 2-4
Options in WYSIWYG

Figure 2-5 summarizes the main menu options in WYSIWYG.

Option	Purpose
WORKSHEET	Sets column widths, row heights, and page breaks
FORMAT	Controls the appearance of your worksheets on screen and when printed
GRAPH	Adds, edits, and saves graphics in a worksheet range
PRINT	Creates printed copies of your worksheet or graph, including all formatting done with the WYSIWYG commands
DISPLAY	Controls how 1-2-3 displays the worksheet on the screen
SPECIAL	Copies and moves WYSIWYG formats from one range to another, imports formats and graphics from another format file, and exports formats and graphics to format files on another disk
TEXT	Enters and edits text in a range of cells as though the words were paragraphs in a word processor
NAMED-STYLE	Assigns names to commonly used formats

Figure 2-5
Summary of
WYSIWYG menu
options

Now return to READY mode.

To leave the WYSIWYG menu and return to READY mode:

① Select Quit (**Q**) from the WYSIWYG menu. You are back at READY mode. WYSIWYG is still attached . To access it again, you simply press [:].

If you are using a mouse, you can also display the WYSIWYG and 1-2-3 menus by moving the mouse pointer into the control panel on your screen. The menu that appears is the last one you used during the current 1-2-3 session. You can switch between WYSIWYG and 1-2-3 menus by clicking the right mouse button while the mouse pointer is in the control panel.

Introduction to Fonts

One way you can improve a worksheet's appearance is to enhance the appearance of the letters, numbers, and symbols. The appearance of letters, numbers, and symbols is determined by their typeface, type size, and type style. First, let's explore the meaning of typeface. The term **typeface** refers to a particular graphical design of letters, numbers, and symbols. Typefaces are designed for readability, to attract attention, or to set a mood. Each typeface has a name, which identifies a specific design of characters and symbols. Figure 2-6 illustrates the four typefaces that are included in the WYSIWYG program: Swiss, Dutch, Courier, and Xsymbol.

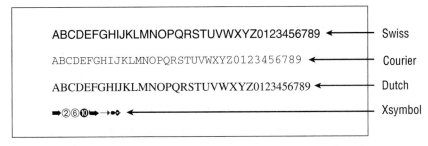

Figure 2-6
The typefaces available in WYSIWYG

Typefaces are classified as either serif or sans serif. **Serif** typefaces have small finishing strokes, called serifs, on the ends of the letters, and are often used in the body of a document or a report. **Sans serif** typefaces do not have these finishing strokes at the ends of letters and are commonly used for titles and headings. Dutch and Courier are serif typefaces, while Swiss is a sans serif typeface.

Type size refers to the height of the characters and is usually measured in units called points. A **point** is approximately 1/72 inch; thus, a 72-point typeface is approximately 1 inch high. The higher the point size, the larger the size of the characters. A 6-point type size might be appropriate for a footnote. The main body of text in a book ranges from 9 to 12 points. Headings typically are presented in 18 to 24 points. Figure 2-7 shows the Swiss typeface in three different type sizes: 6, 12, and 24 points.

Figure 2-7
Various type sizes in Swiss typeface

In WYSIWYG the term **font** refers to a typeface (a collection of characters, numbers, and symbols) in one type size. For example, 12-point Swiss is one font, 24-point Swiss is another font, and 12-point Dutch is a third font. WYSIWYG allows you to use up to eight fonts in a worksheet.

Type style is a variation within a font. The typeface remains basically the same, but the width, the weight, or the angle of the characters changes. Boldface, italic, and underline type styles are illustrated in Figure 2-8.

Figure 2-8
Various styles of
Swiss 12-point font

Enhancing a Worksheet with WYSIWYG

Now that you have learned about fonts, you are ready to use several WYSIWYG features to improve the appearance of Pauline's Net Asset Value worksheet. Let's retrieve a modified version of Pauline's final worksheet.

To retrieve Pauline's worksheet:

❶ Select /File Retrieve (**/FR**).

❷ Type **M2BALBO1** and press **[Enter]**. The worksheet's opening screen appears.

❸ Press **[PgDn]** to view the worksheet data. This version of Pauline's worksheet includes the changes requested in the Tutorial Assignments at the end of Tutorial 3, except that the dashed lines used for underlines have been removed. In WYSIWYG you can draw ruled lines without the lines occupying a separate row.

Notice that the worksheet appears in a font different from that in your worksheet in Tutorial 3. When WYSIWYG is attached, the worksheet characters appear in the WYSIWYG default font, which currently is 12-point Swiss.

Changing Typefaces

Many documents use two typefaces, one for headings and one for text. Pauline decides to use the Swiss typeface for her two-line title and then to convert the rest of the worksheet to Dutch typeface.

To change the body of the worksheet to 12-point Dutch font:

❶ Move the cell pointer to A25, the first cell in the body of the worksheet.

➋ Select :Format Font (**:FF**). A menu appears listing the eight fonts currently available for use within your worksheet. The fonts consist of Swiss, Dutch, and Xsymbol typefaces in various sizes. The first font that appears in the list is the default font. This font was used for each cell in the worksheet. See Figure 2-9.

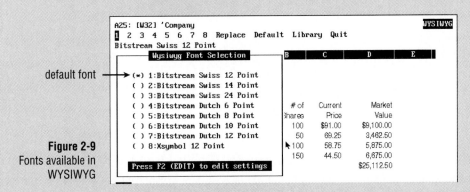

default font →

Figure 2-9
Fonts available in
WYSIWYG

To specify the 12-point Dutch font for a range of cells, you first select the number that precedes the typeface name and size you want.

➌ Type **7**, the number of 12-point Dutch font.

Now specify the cells of the worksheet that will appear in 12-point Dutch font.

➍ Highlight the range A25..D35 and press **[Enter]**. You are returned to READY mode.

The body of the worksheet now appears in 12-point Dutch. See Figure 2-10. Notice that the control panel displays "{DUTCH12}," a format code that indicates the font for the current cell is 12-point Dutch. If no format code appears in the control panel for a specific cell, the default font, font 1, is being used.

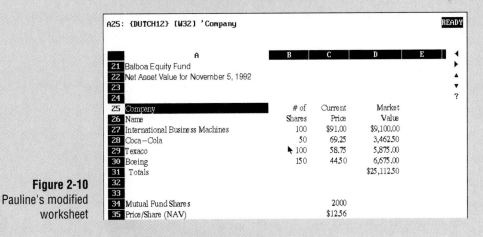

Figure 2-10
Pauline's modified
worksheet

Pauline's worksheet now has two fonts: the titles in 12-point Swiss and everything else in 12-point Dutch. Next, Pauline turns her attention to adjusting the type sizes.

Changing Type Size

Pauline wants the title lines of the worksheet to stand out. To accomplish this, she can display the titles in a larger font. She decides to use a 24-point Swiss font for the first title line. Let's try it.

To change the font of the first line of the title to a 24-point Swiss font:

1. Move the cell pointer to A21, the first heading line.
2. Select :Format Font (**:FF**). A menu of fonts appears.
3. Type **3** to choose the 24-point Swiss font.

Select the cells you want in this type size.

4. With cell A21 highlighted, press **[Enter]**. The title is displayed in 24-point Swiss, as shown in Figure 2-11. Notice that the height of row 21 is automatically adjusted to fit the size of the 24-point font.

Figure 2-11
Font of the first line of the title is changed

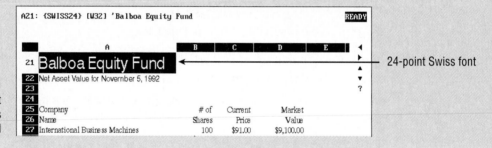

24-point Swiss font

Now let's change the font for the second line of the title to 14-point Swiss. Subtitles normally are displayed in a smaller type size than titles.

To change the font for the second title line:

1. Move the cell pointer to A22.
2. Select :Format Font (**:FF**). A menu of fonts appears.
3. Type **2** to choose 14-point Swiss.
4. With cell A22 highlighted, press **[Enter]**. The second line of the title is displayed in 14-point Swiss. See Figure 2-12.

Figure 2-12
Font of the second line of the title is changed

A22: {SWISS14} [W32] 'Net Asset Value for November 5, 1992   READY

	A	B	C	D	E
21	Balboa Equity Fund				
22	Net Asset Value for November 5, 1992				
23					
24					
25	Company		# of	Current	Market
26	Name		Shares	Price	Value
27	International Business Machines		100	$91.00	$9,100.00

column headings boldfaced

After adjusting the type size Pauline decides to try a type style to draw the reader's attention to various sections of the worksheet.

Changing Styles: Boldface

Several of the :Format commands add styles to a font. For instance, you can add boldface, underline, or italic styles. Pauline decides to set the column heading in a boldface style, to help differentiate the columns from the rest of the worksheet.

To boldface the column headings:

❶ Move the cell pointer to A25, the first cell of the column headings.

❷ Select :Format Bold Set (**:FBS**).

Next indicate the range of cells you want to boldface.

❸ Highlight A25..D26 and press **[Enter]**. In Figure 2-13 notice that the column headings appear in a darker type. Notice that the first line of the control panel indicates the format code for cell A25 is {DUTCH12 Bold} — 12-point Dutch boldface.

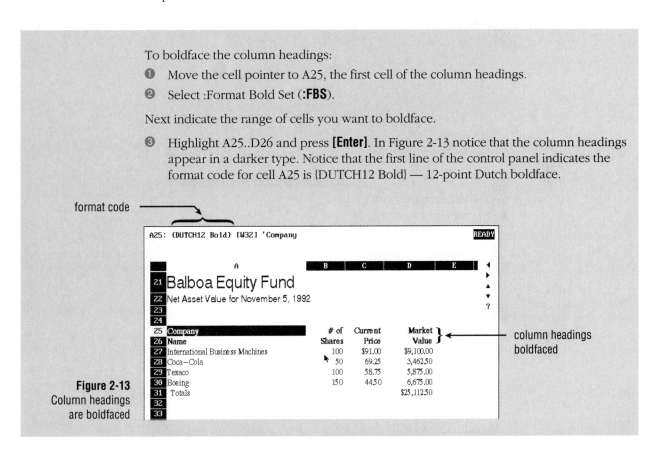

format code

Figure 2-13
Column headings
are boldfaced

column headings
boldfaced

Now that Pauline has boldfaced the column headings, she wants to draw a line under these headings to emphasize them and to make it easier for the reader to read the information contained in the columns.

Drawing Lines

You can add lines, borders, and boxes to your worksheet with the WYSIWYG :Format Lines command. By placing single, double, or thick lines around a cell or a range of cells, you can create different effects. For instance, you can use lines and boxes to add structure in a report, to create tables, or to group related items together. You can put lines on some or all sides of a cell or block of cells.

Pauline believes she can make her worksheet look more professional by adding lines under the column headings and before and after the total. Let's see how.

To draw a line underneath the column headings:

① Move the cell pointer to A26, the first cell of the range to be underlined.

② Select :Format Lines (**:FL**). See Figure 2-14.

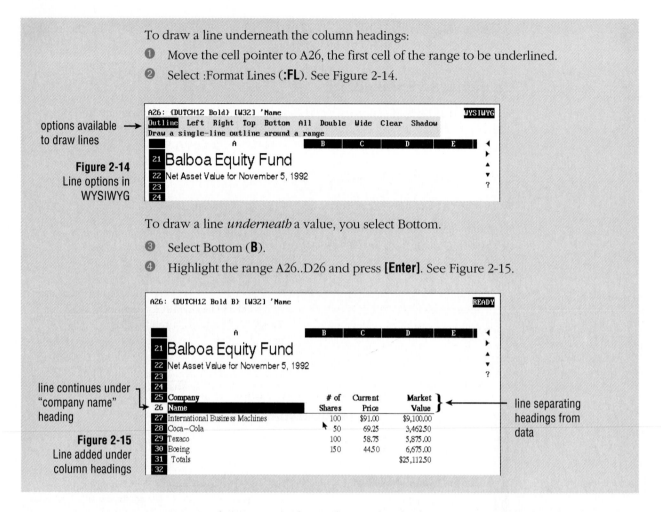

options available → to draw lines

Figure 2-14
Line options in
WYSIWYG

To draw a line *underneath* a value, you select Bottom.

③ Select Bottom (**B**).

④ Highlight the range A26..D26 and press **[Enter]**. See Figure 2-15.

line continues under
"company name"
heading

Figure 2-15
Line added under
column headings

line separating
headings from
data

Next Pauline wants to draw a line under the last company name listed in the Balboa Equity Fund to indicate that a total follows.

To draw a line:

① Move the cell pointer to A30, the first cell in the row to be underlined.

② Select :Format Line Bottom (**:FLB**).

Now specify the cells where the line will be drawn.

③ Highlight the range A30..D30 and press **[Enter]**.

A common way to indicate a final total in a worksheet is to place a double-ruled line under it.

To add a double-ruled line under the total market value:

❶ Move the cell pointer to D31, the cell where the double-ruled lined will be drawn.

❷ Select :Format Lines Double Bottom (**:FLDB**).

❸ With cell D31 highlighted, press **[Enter]**. See Figure 2-16. A double-ruled line now appears under the total.

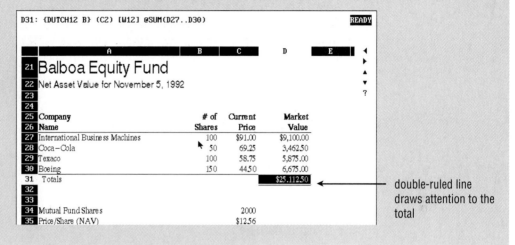

Figure 2-16
Double-ruled line
entered

double-ruled line
draws attention to the
total

Pauline is finished with her revision of the worksheet. She decides to save it.

Saving WYSIWYG Formats

When you save a worksheet that has been enhanced by WYSIWYG, your worksheet consists of two files: a WK1 worksheet file and a FMT format file. Both files have the same filename. Your data and the basic settings, such as column width, cell formats, and range names, are stored in the WK1 file. Your formatting information for the current worksheet, such as fonts, styles, and lines, are stored in a separate worksheet file with an FMT extension. For example, if you save the worksheet file on your screen as W2BALBO1, WYSIWYG automatically saves an associated file, W2BALBO1.FMT, in addition to the W2BALBO1.WK1 file that is saved. Let's save Pauline's worksheet.

To save a worksheet that includes WYSIWYG enhancements:

❶ Press **[Home]** to move to cell A1.

Now enter the filename of the worksheet in cell A1.

❷ Type **W2BALBO1.WK1** and press **[Enter]**.

❸ Select /File Save (**/FS**).

❹ Type **W2BALBO1** and press **[Enter]**. The two worksheet files are saved on your data diskette.

You should be aware of some additional points when you are saving files:

- WYSIWYG must be loaded in computer memory for the formatting information to be saved. If WYSIWYG is not loaded, your formatting changes will not be saved.

- Remember to save your worksheet whenever you make formatting changes, even if you didn't change the data, formulas, or relationships. If you don't, your formatting changes will not be saved.

- When you retrieve a worksheet that has both a WK1 and a FMT file and WYSIWYG is attached, you will see formatting on the screen. If WYSIWYG is not attached when you retrieve the file, you will not see any formatting. It cannot appear until you attach WYSIWYG.

Additional WYSIWYG Formatting

Pauline wants to see how a box with a drop shadow looks around the price/share calculation. Also, she wants to change the style of the text within the box to italic. Finally, she wants to give the stock portfolio section a grid-like look.

Preselecting a Range

Typically you specify a range of cells after issuing a command. However, what happens when you have several commands that affect the same range of cells? For example, suppose for a particular range you wanted to draw a box, change the font, and then italicize the text inside the box. In that case you would find it faster to **preselect the range** of cells before issuing any command. By preselecting a range you can issue several commands without having to respecify the same range each time you issue a new command.

Let's try it.

To preselect a range of cells:

❶ Move the cell pointer to A34.

❷ Press **[F4]** to anchor the cell pointer.

❸ Highlight the range of cells A34..C35. See Figure 2-17. Press **[Enter]**. You are returned to READY mode. The preselected range remains highlighted.

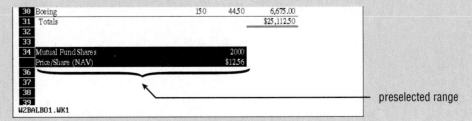

Figure 2-17
Preselecting a range

You can now issue a 1-2-3 or a WYSIWYG command, and you will *not* be prompted for a range; the preselected range will be used automatically. After you complete a command, the range remains selected. To cancel a preselected range, you press [Esc] or move the cell pointer to any other cell in the worksheet, but don't do that now.

Drawing a Box

You can use boxes to set off data from the rest of the text. Boxes are often drawn around a complete line of type to draw attention to a piece of information. Let's draw a box around Price/Share (the range that was previously shaded). You use the Lines Outline command to draw boxes.

To draw a box:

❶ Select :Format Lines Outline (**:FLO**). Remember that the range A34..C35 is pre-selected. A box (outline) appears around the preselected range of cells.

The price/share calculation is now boxed, but Pauline wants to add a drop shadow to the box. Let's see how she can complete this task.

Adding a Drop Shadow

A thick line along the bottom and up the right side of selected cells gives an effect called a **drop shadow** and results in the box having a three-dimensional appearance. You use the :Format Lines Shadow command to create a drop shadow.

To add a drop shadow:

❶ Select :Format Lines Shadow Set (**:FLSS**).

A drop shadow appears on the box. Next, Pauline decides to change the text inside the box to a different type style.

Changing Style: Italics

To focus attention on particular words or numbers, you can italicize them. Let's see if italics draw your attention to the text within the boxed area.

To italicize text:

❶ Select :Format Italics Set (**:FIS**). The text within the box is now italicized.

Adding a Grid

Now Pauline wants the section of the worksheet where the individual stocks are listed to appear as a grid, that is, a table with ruled lines. You can create a grid pattern for a table of data by adding lines to all four sides of several cells. Let's try it.

To draw a grid:

❶ Move the cell pointer to A27. As soon as you move the cell pointer in READY mode, 1-2-3 clears the preselected range. From now on you have to specify ranges as part of a command unless you preselect a new range.

You are now ready to add the grid lines.

❷ Select :Format Lines All (**:FLA**).

Next you need to specify the range for the grid.

❸ Highlight the range A27..D30 and press **[Enter]**. See Figure 2-18.

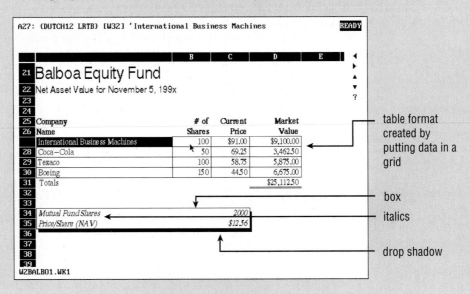

Figure 2-18
Adding a grid

Pauline likes this worksheet and decides to print a hard copy for her supervisor.

Printing with WYSIWYG

If a worksheet includes any WYSIWYG formatting options, you must use the print command *within* WYSIWYG if you want these enhancements to appear in your printout. In other words, WYSIWYG printing is independent of any printing you do using the 1-2-3 /Print commands. If you print using the 1-2-3 /Print command, your WYSIWYG enhancements will not be printed, even if you have attached WYSIWYG. To print your WYSIWYG enhancements, you must access the WYSIWYG printing option with the :Print command. The :Print command lets you print your worksheet exactly as you have formatted it on the screen.

Specifying a Print Range

To print in WYSIWYG, you must specify the range of cells you want printed. Even if you have previously selected a print range using the /Print Range command, you must now specify the print range for WYSIWYG — the print range from the /Print Range command is not transferred to WYSIWYG. Let's print the current version of Pauline's worksheet.

To set the print range:

❶ Select :Print (**:P**). A dialog box appears showing the current settings for WYSIWYG printing.

Next let's specify the range to be printed.

❷ Select Range Set (**RS**).

❸ Move the cell pointer to A21, the first cell in the print range, and press **[.]** to anchor the range.

❹ Highlight the range A21..D35 and press **[Enter]**. The range now appears in the dialog box. See Figure 2-19.

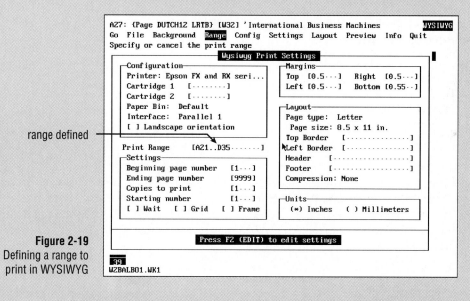

Figure 2-19
Defining a range to
print in WYSIWYG

You have now specified the print range.

Previewing a Document

Printing in WYSIWYG can take a long time. So before printing, you might want to **preview** the worksheet, that is, see exactly how the printed output will appear on the page before you actually print the worksheet. You use the Preview option to display your print range, one page at a time. The preview screen usually reduces the size of the worksheet. As a result you might not be able to read every character. But you can preview the page design to help you make layout and spacing adjustments. Let's preview Pauline's worksheet.

To preview a page:

❶ Select Preview (**P**). See Figure 2-20. You see the first page of the print range in reduced form on the preview screen. If you have more than one page to preview, you would press [PgDn] or [PgUp] to view the next or previous pages.

preview of output ────→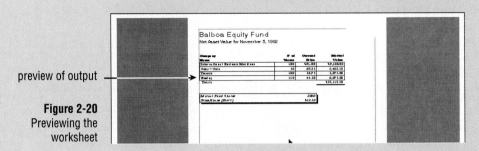

Figure 2-20
Previewing the
worksheet

❷ When you're ready to continue, press any key to return to the WYSIWYG print menu.

After previewing the worksheet, Pauline is happy with what she sees and is ready to print it.

Selecting a Printer

You must instruct WYSIWYG which printer to use to print the enhancements. Initially no printer is selected for use.

To select a printer:

❶ Select Config Printer (**CP**). See Figure 2-21. A list of installed printers appears. Depending on the printer you have installed, you may have several choices for the same printer. For example, if you are using an HP laser printer, you have three choices: high density, medium density, or extended capability. Extended capability prints the fastest, while high density gives you better print quality but takes longer to print.

list of printers;
yours may differ

Figure 2-21
WYSIWYG printer
list for Epson
printer

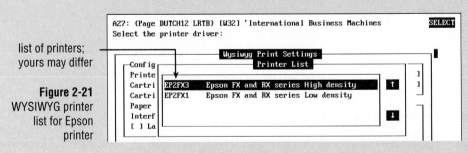

❷ Select the name of the printer that is correct for your current configuration. If you are not sure, check with your instructor or technical support person.

❸ Select Quit (**Q**) to return to the Print menu. You are ready to print.

Printing

Now that you have previewed the worksheet and selected the printer, you are ready to print.

To print the worksheet:

① Select Go (**G**). As the document is being printed, the mode indicator flashes "Wait." Depending on the formatting enhancements in your worksheet and the print density you selected, your output may take a few seconds to several minutes to complete. You can see the printing progress on the control panel.

After the worksheet has been printed, you are automatically returned to READY mode. If you have completed the work in this module, save the worksheet again.

To save a worksheet:

① Select /File Save (**/FS**) and press **[Enter]**.

② Select Replace (**R**). The worksheet replaces the previous version of W2BALBO1.WK1.

Remember that actually two files are replaced: W2BALBO1.WK1 and W2BALBO1.FMT.

Figure 2-22 shows the printed output that Pauline will give to her supervisor.

Balboa Equity Fund
Net Asset Value for November 5, 1992

Company Name	# of Shares	Current Price	Market Value
International Business Machines	100	$91.00	$9,100.00
Coca-Cola	50	69.25	3,462.50
Texaco	100	58.75	5,875.00
Boeing	150	44.50	6,675.00
Total			$25,112.50

Mutual Fund Shares	2000
Price/Share (NAV)	$12.56

Figure 2-22
Pauline's final printed worksheet

The Compression Feature

If you want to fit a large worksheet on one page, WYSIWYG can attempt to fit the print range onto one sheet of paper. WYSIWYG will automatically determine how much the worksheet needs to be reduced.

To reduce the size of a worksheet to fit on one page:

❶ Select :Print Layout Compression (**:PLC**).

Now instruct WYSIWYG to automatically compress the print range to attempt to fit it onto one printed page.

❷ Select Automatic (**A**). The dialog box appears, and you can select another option from the WYSIWYG menu.

A worksheet can be reduced to 15 percent of its original size. Very large worksheets, however, may not fit on a single page. If the print range is too large for the maximum reduction allowed, the worksheet will print on multiple pages.

❸ Select Quit (**Q**) to leave the layout menu and return to the WYSIWYG menu.

Design Guidelines

Now that you are ready to use WYSIWYG to enhance your worksheets, you should keep these points in mind:

- Use fonts to enhance your work. But don't overdo it — too many typefaces can make your worksheet confusing. Many users use only one or two typefaces in a document and then vary the type's size and style for emphasis.
- Use a boldface version of the font in your document to make column headings stand out.
- Use lines and shading to enhance legibility and to highlight certain parts of the worksheet.
- Don't cram every bit of data onto one page. Remember, proper use of white space helps make the page easier to read.

■   ■   ■

Exercises

1. If you're told to use a 10-point Dutch boldface font, what typeface is that? What type size? What type style?

2. Which is the larger font: 12-point Swiss or 24-point Swiss?

3. Is the font used in this sentence serif or sans serif?

4. Assume you have the files M2FILE.WK1 and M2FILE.FMT on your data diskette:
   a. What command would you issue to retrieve the worksheet?
   b. After you retrieve the worksheet, the format enhancements do not appear on your screen. Why would this happen?
   c. You retrieve the worksheet, and the WYSIWYG enhancements appear on the screen. You print the worksheet, but the format enhancements are not printed. Why would this happen?

5. Identify the WYSIWYG enhancements in Figure 2-23.

Quick Food Inc.
Fourth Quarter Sales

Region	Amount
North	$7,565
South	58,245
East	32,655
West	42,123
Total	$140,588

Figure 2-23

6. To activate the WYSIWYG menu, you press what key(s)?

7. Give the commands needed to do the following:
   a. To print your worksheet on one page
   b. To see how your printed output will look before you print
   c. To store your worksheet on your data diskette
   d. To draw a box around a range of cells
   e. To change the font of a title line

8. A worksheet cell contains the title "Sales Summary." This cell has been formatted, but you're not sure what typeface or point size has been used. Where can you look in the worksheet to get this information?

Case Problems

1. Twelve-Month Sales Forecast for International Food Brands, Inc.

International Food Brands, Inc., has completed a forecast of monthly sales for the upcoming year.

Do the following:

1. Attach WYSIWYG.
2. Retrieve the worksheet M2FORE.WK1.
3. Add the following enhancements:

    a.   Use a 14-point Swiss font for the title.
    b.   Boldface the column headings.
    c.   Place a ruled line underneath the column headings.
    d.   Italicize the names of the countries.

4.   Save your worksheet as W2FORE.

5.   Print the worksheet so the entire worksheet appears on one page.

2. Promotional Coupon for *Weekly Times*

Priscilla Burns is the circulation manager of *Weekly Times*, a newspaper serving three counties in New Hampshire. She has recently arranged for a promotional coupon to be inserted into next month's edition of *New Hampshire Magazine*, which sells in these counties. She has written the coupon, but she still must format it using WYSIWYG.

Do the following:

1.   Attach WYSIWYG.

2.   Retrieve the worksheet M2COUP.WK1.

3.   Add the following WYSIWYG enhancements:
    a.   Draw a box around the entire worksheet.
    b.   Use 14-point Swiss font for the text "Weekly Times."
    c.   Reverse the text "Weekly Times."
    d.   Use 24-point Swiss font for the heading "Super Discount Voucher."
    e.   Place a wide underline under the heading.
    f.   Use 12-point Dutch font for the body of the coupon (A5..G13).
    g.   Boldface the promotional message that begins "now you can receive..."
    h.   Add ruled lines above *NAME, STREET, APT. NO., CITY, STATE,* and *ZIP,* so there is space to enter this information on the coupon. Use 10-point Dutch font for these words.
    i.   Use 8-point Dutch font for the note "Offer good in U.S."
    j.   Put the data about payment terms in a grid format.

4.   Save the worksheet as the file W2COUP.

5.   Print the formatted worksheet.

Module 3

Using WYSIWYG to Enhance and Print Graphs

OBJECTIVES

In this tutorial you will learn to:

- Insert a graph into your worksheet

- Reduce the size of rows and columns

- Enclose a legend in a box

- Include text on a graph

- Draw arrows

- Print a graph and worksheet data on the same page

Graphs are effective tools for business communications. As you've seen in Tutorial 6, you can select from many different graph types, such as line, bar, stacked bar, pie, and XY graphs. You can add titles, legends, and other text information to a graph. You can also change the appearance of the graph, for example, by displaying bars with a three-dimensional effect or by exploding specific slices of a pie chart.

To communicate the message of your graph even more effectively, you can also use WYSIWYG. With WYSIWYG you can do such things as add boxes, lines, arrows, ellipses, and other shapes. You can prepare a report that contains both the graph and the data that support the graph. You can also print the graph without having to exit 1-2-3 and retrieve the PrintGraph Utility.

Compare the graphs in Figure 3-1 on the following page. Figure 3-1a shows one of the graphs Carl Martinez created while working on his project for M&B Consultants. Figure 3-1b shows the same graph inserted into the worksheet and enhanced with several of WYSIWYG's graphic features. As Figure 3-1b shows, you can use WYSIWYG's Graph commands to:

- display the current graph or a named graph in the worksheet next to the data on which it is based
- add explanatory text to your graph for clarity
- draw arrows to attract the reader's attention
- draw boxes to highlight a portion of the graph
- print graphs from within WYSIWYG

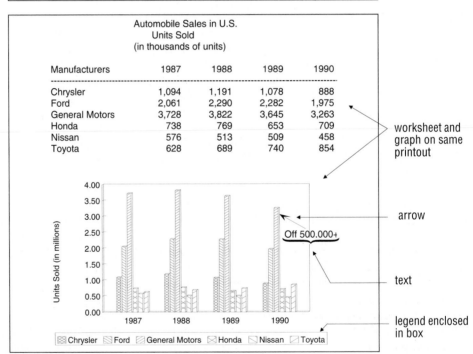

Figure 3-1a
Graph created with
1-2-3's /Graph
commands and
printed using
PGRAPH

Figure 3-1b
Graph enhanced
with WYSIWYG

Loading WYSIWYG

Remember that when you load 1-2-3, WYSIWYG is not automatically loaded — it is an add-in program. If WYSIWYG has not been loaded, see Module 2, page L 319 for instructions on how to attach WYSIWYG.

Adding a Graph to the Worksheet

Carl Martinez has created several graphs using 1-2-3's /Graph command. He now has WYSIWYG and wants to further improve the appearance of his graph, which will be included in the report being readied for the Senate subcommittee. Carl is ready to enhance one of these graphs using WYSIWYG's :Graph command. Let's retrieve one of the graphs from Tutorial 6, the bar graph that shows unit sales for the six automobile manufacturers from 1987 to 1990.

To retrieve Carl's worksheet:
1. Select /File Retrieve (**/FR**).
2. Type **M3AUTO1** and press **[Enter]**.
3. Press **[F10]** to view the graph.
4. Press any key to return to READY mode.

Be sure you understand that the WYSIWYG Graph commands *do not create graphs*. You use WYSIWYG commands *once you have already* created a graph using the Graph commands of the 1-2-3 main menu. Furthermore, after you create a graph you must first add the graph to the worksheet before you can enhance the graph using the WYSIWYG Graph commands. You use the Graph Add command to insert the current graph or a named graph into a range in your worksheet.

Carl realizes that he must first add the graph to his worksheet; he wants the graph to appear immediately below the worksheet data in the range A21..E35.

To add a graph to the range A21..E35 in the worksheet:
1. Select :Graph (**:G**). See Figure 3-2. A list of the 10 options available in the WYSIWYG Graph menu appear.

menu options →

Figure 3-2
Graph options in
WYSIWYG

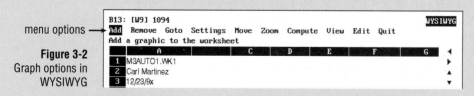

First add the graph to the worksheet.

2. Select Add (**A**).

You have five choices for the type of graph you can add. You can add the current graph, a named graph, a saved graph with a PIC extension, a special file called a Metafile (CGM extension), or a blank placeholder for a graphic that you can add later.

Add the current graph to the worksheet.

3. Select Current (**C**).

A graph added to your worksheet can be as large or as small as you want. The size of the range you specify determines the size of the graph in your worksheet. So let's now specify the range A21..E35.

④ Move the cell pointer to cell A21, the location where you want to insert the graph.

⑤ Press **[.]** to anchor the cell pointer. Now highlight A21..E35.

⑥ Press **[Enter]**. WYSIWYG automatically adds the graph to fit into the range you specified.

⑦ Select Quit (**Q**) to leave the WYSIWYG Graph menu and return to READY mode.

⑧ Press **[↓]** until you see the entire graph in the worksheet. See Figure 3-3. The graph appears immediately below the worksheet data.

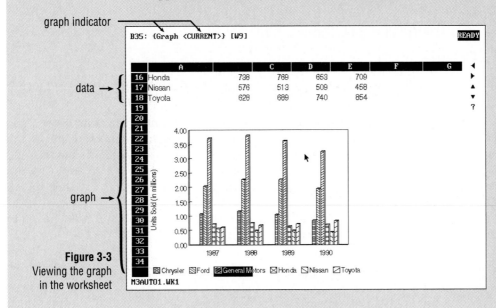

graph indicator

data →

graph →

Figure 3-3
Viewing the graph
in the worksheet

When the cell pointer is in the range occupied by the graph, the control panel displays a graph indicator in curly braces: either the name of the graph or the word CURRENT if a current graph was added to the worksheet.

Changing the Size of Worksheet Cells

You probably have noticed that in 1-2-3 you cannot view a graph and its supporting data on the screen at the same time. With WYSIWYG 1-2-3 can reduce or enlarge worksheet cells *on the screen* so you can see more or fewer rows and columns. The Display Zoom command reduces and enlarges the cells on the screen. Six options are available:

Option	Description
Tiny	Reduces cells displayed to 63% of normal size
Small	Reduces cells displayed to 87% of normal size
Normal	Displays cells at normal size
Large	Enlarges cells displayed to 125% of normal size
Huge	Enlarges cells displayed to 150% of normal size

Figure 3-4

Let's reduce the worksheet so you can view both the data and the graph in the worksheet area.

To reduce the size of the worksheet:

❶ Press **[F5]** (GOTO), type **A13**, and press **[Enter]** to position cell A13 in the upper left corner of the worksheet area.

❷ Select :Display Zoom (**:DZ**).

Select the size reduction.

❸ Select Small (**S**). See Figure 3-5.

reduction percentage

both data and graph fit in worksheet area

Figure 3-5
Reducing the on-screen image

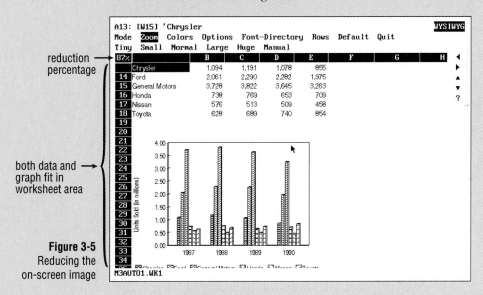

You are viewing the worksheet at 87 percent of its normal size. Notice that the zoom percentage appears in the upper left corner of your worksheet.

❹ Select Quit (**Q**) to return to READY mode.

To return the worksheet to normal size, use the Display Zoom Normal option.

Changing Worksheet Data and Updating the Graph

If WYSIWYG is attached and you change the data in your worksheet, 1-2-3 automatically redraws the graph in your worksheet to reflect those changes. You don't have to press [F10] (GRAPH) to see the graph, as you would if the graph were not added to the worksheet.

Let's assume an error was made when Chrysler's sales for 1990 were entered. Instead of 855 the value should be 2855. You'll make the change and observe how the graph in the worksheet changes immediately to reflect that change.

To observe how a change to the data affects the graph:

❶ Move the cell pointer to cell E13, the location of Chrysler's 1990 sales.

❷ Type **2855** and press **[Enter]**. Notice how the graph automatically changes to reflect the corrected data. See Figure 3-6.

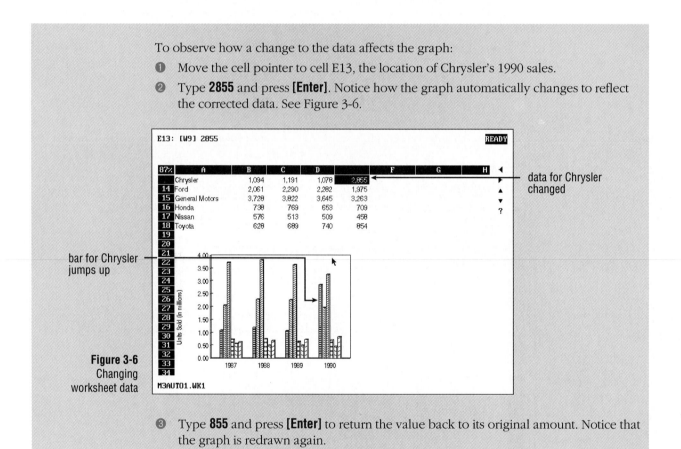

Figure 3-6
Changing worksheet data

❸ Type **855** and press **[Enter]** to return the value back to its original amount. Notice that the graph is redrawn again.

Carl could now use the WYSIWYG Print command to print the data and the graph on one page, but before he does this he wants to add a few enhancements to the graph.

Using the Graphics Editor

Once the graph has been inserted into the worksheet, you might want to add a variety of design elements, called **objects**, to enhance your graph. Objects include text, lines, arrows, rectangles, ellipses, and polygons. For example, you might want to point out or explain an unusually high or low point on the graph. Or you may want to draw a box around a legend. You can place objects anywhere on your graph.

To add geometric shapes, arrows, and text, you use WYSIWYG's graphics editor. The graphics editor provides a work area in which you can enhance your graph. A major component of the graphics editor is the graphics edit window. You transfer your graph from the worksheet to the graphics edit window. Once the graph is in the graphics edit window, you are ready to add various objects to the graph.

The graphics editor does not allow you to modify any part of the existing graph you created using the 1-2-3 /Graph commands. For example, you cannot modify such items as graph titles, X or Y axis labels, or legend text. To modify those items, you must use 1-2-3's /Graph commands.

Carl decides to draw a rectangle around the legend to help it stand out. He knows that before he can use the graphics editor, he must add the graph to the worksheet. Because he has already added the graph to the worksheet, his next step is to transfer the graph inserted in the worksheet to the graphics editor.

To transfer a graph to the graphics editor:

❶ Select :Graph Edit (**:GE**).

1-2-3 prompts you to identify the graph you want to transfer to the graphics editor.

❷ Move the cell pointer to any cell inside the graph's range, A21..E35, and press **[Enter]**. See Figure 3-7. The worksheet grid disappears and the graph appears in the graphics edit window, below the Graph Edit menu.

Graph Edit menu →

graphics edit → window

Figure 3-7 Graph transferred into WYSIWYG's graphics editor

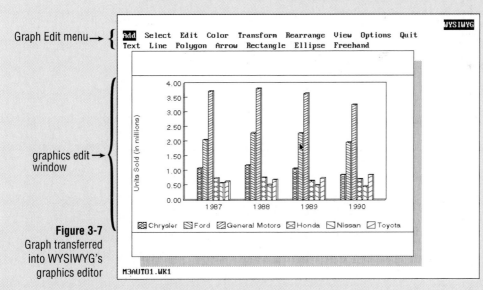

You are now ready to edit Carl's graph.

Adding Rectangles

Recall that Carl wants to enclose the legend in a box to make it stand out. To do this, he will add a rectangle to the graph. To draw a rectangle or any other object, you use the Add command from the graphics editor and indicate the upper left and lower right corners of the object.

To help you place the rectangle or any other graphic object exactly where you want it in the graphics edit window, 1-2-3 provides a way for you to know the exact location of the cursor in the graphics edit window. Whenever you add an object to a graph, a cursor appears as a set of crosshairs to indicate exactly where you are in the graphics edit window. In addition to the cursor, the edit window is divided into a grid of very tiny rectangles, 4096 across (X coordinate) by 4096 down (Y coordinate), as shown in Figure 3-8. The upper left corner of the edit window is designated as coordinate X=0, Y=0 and the lower right corner as coordinate X=4095, Y=4095. The X coordinate is always given first. This grid helps you align the object and keep track of its location as you add it to your graph. The X value is the number of tiny rectangles from the left edge of the window, and it helps you measure how far the cursor is from the left side of the window. The Y value is the number of tiny rectangles from the top of the graphics edit window, and it measures how far the cursor is from the top of the window. WYSIWYG reports on the exact location of the cursor as you move it around the graphics edit window.

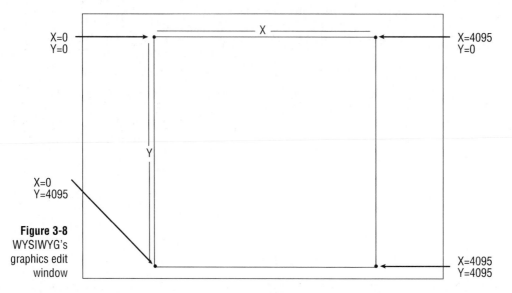

Figure 3-8
WYSIWYG's
graphics edit
window

To add a rectangle to your graph:

❶ Select Add (**A**). A list of objects appears. In this list are all the objects you can add to your graph. You can add text, lines, polygons, arrows, rectangles, ellipses, and freehand objects.

❷ Select Rectangle (**R**). See Figure 3-9.

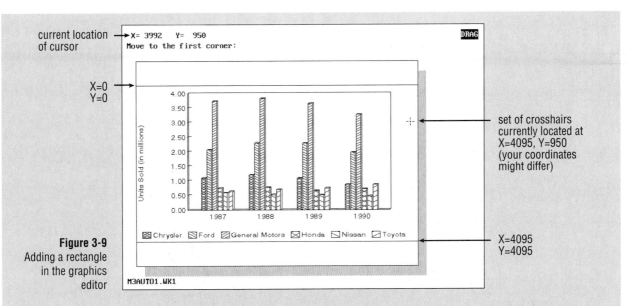

current location of cursor

X=0
Y=0

set of crosshairs currently located at X=4095, Y=950 (your coordinates might differ)

X=4095
Y=4095

Figure 3-9
Adding a rectangle in the graphics editor

The X and Y coordinates that appear in the control panel locate the exact location of the cursor in the graphics edit window.

Next specify the upper left corner of the area where you want the rectangle located.

❸ Press the arrow keys to move the cursor to the left and above the legend symbol for Chrysler. The exact position is indicated by the coordinates X=48, Y=3756. See Figure 3-10. The coordinates on your system may differ slightly from the coordinates listed in this module.

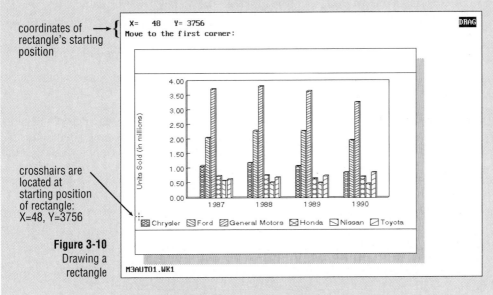

coordinates of rectangle's starting position

crosshairs are located at starting position of rectangle: X=48, Y=3756

Figure 3-10
Drawing a rectangle

❹ Press **[Spacebar]** to anchor the left corner of the rectangle.

Now 1-2-3 prompts you to stretch the box.

⑤ Press the arrow keys to move the cursor to the opposite corner of the rectangle, that is, to the right and under the word Toyota (X=3952, Y=4053). As you move the cursor, a rectangle, called a **bounding box**, stretches from the left corner of the rectangle to the position of the cursor. See Figure 3-11.

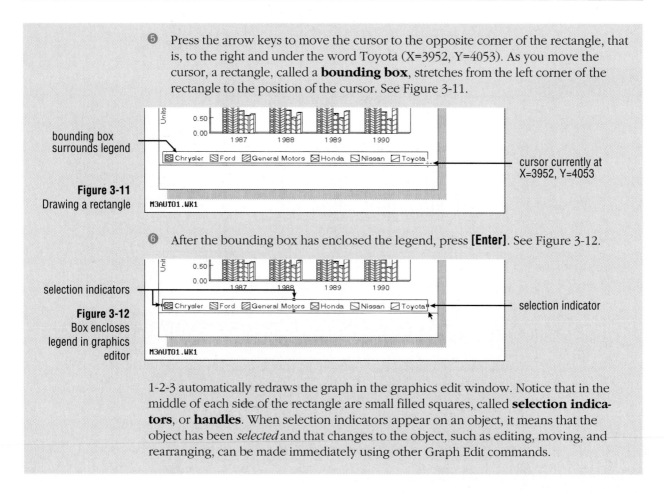

bounding box
surrounds legend

cursor currently at
X=3952, Y=4053

Figure 3-11
Drawing a rectangle

⑥ After the bounding box has enclosed the legend, press **[Enter]**. See Figure 3-12.

selection indicators

selection indicator

Figure 3-12
Box encloses
legend in graphics
editor

1-2-3 automatically redraws the graph in the graphics edit window. Notice that in the middle of each side of the rectangle are small filled squares, called **selection indicators**, or **handles**. When selection indicators appear on an object, it means that the object has been *selected* and that changes to the object, such as editing, moving, and rearranging, can be made immediately using other Graph Edit commands.

Carl decides that he doesn't want to make any changes to the lines of the rectangle.

Adding Text

The next enhancement Carl wants to make is to add a text message in the bar graph. Because he wants to focus the reader's attention on General Motors' loss of over 500,000 units, Carl will insert the message "Off 500,000+" next to the bar that represents General Motors' 1990 unit sales.

To add text to your graph, you must again use the graphics editor.

To add text to your graph:

① Select Add Text (**AT**). A prompt appears. See Figure 3-13.

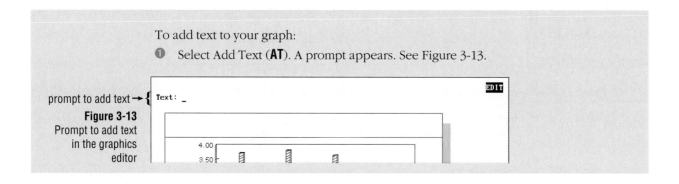

prompt to add text →

Figure 3-13
Prompt to add text
in the graphics
editor

Now you can type a single line of text, up to 240 characters, following the prompt for text.

❷ Type **Off 500,000+** and press **[Enter]**. See Figure 3-14 below. 1-2-3 initially places the text in the lower right area of the graphics edit window.

current coordinates of text

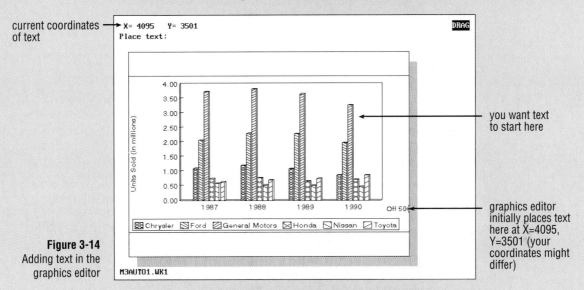

Figure 3-14
Adding text in the graphics editor

you want text to start here

graphics editor initially places text here at X=4095, Y=3501 (your coordinates might differ)

Next you need to instruct 1-2-3 where to position the text.

❸ Press the cursor keys until the text appears to the right of the 1990 bar for General Motors (X=3735, Y=1389). Don't worry if you can't locate the exact coordinates. Your results will be the same as long as your coordinates are close to these coordinates.

❹ After positioning the text, press **[Enter]**. See Figure 3-15.

options available to selected object

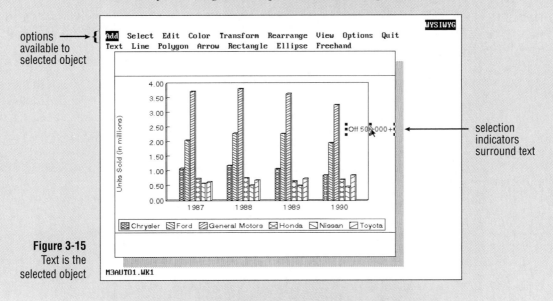

Figure 3-15
Text is the selected object

selection indicators surround text

The graph is automatically redrawn in the graphics edit window, and selection indicators surround the text. As before, these indicators let you know that the text has been selected and that you can immediately perform another operation on the text such as moving it, editing it, or changing its font.

Adding Arrows

Carl next wants to draw the reader's eye from the message to the bar that shows the decline in General Motors' sales. He decides to add an arrow at the end beside the text message.

To add an arrow to your graph, the graphics editor must be loaded. In this case the graphics editor is already loaded, so you are ready to add the arrow.

To add an arrow to your graph:

❶ With the graph in the edit window of the graphics editor, select Add Arrow (**AA**).

Now move the cursor to the location where the text begins.

❷ Move the cursor to just above the "50" in "500,000" (X=3647, Y=1261), where the end of the arrow will begin. See Figure 3-16.

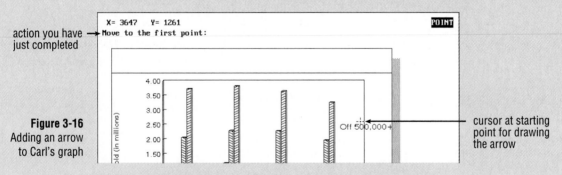

Figure 3-16
Adding an arrow
to Carl's graph

❸ Press **[Spacebar]** to anchor the starting point of the arrow.

❹ Press the arrow keys up and to the left to move the cursor toward General Motors' bar for unit sales in 1990. As you press the arrow keys, watch as a line appears, stretching from the first point of the line to the cursor. Position the cursor at the end of the line (X=3335, Y=964). See Figure 3-17.

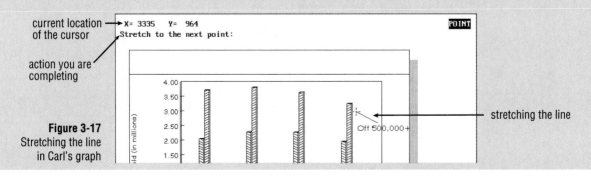

Figure 3-17
Stretching the line
in Carl's graph

⑤ Press **[Enter]** to complete the line. The arrowhead is drawn and the Graphic menu appears again. When you draw an arrow, 1-2-3 points the arrowhead toward the last point you specified.

Note the selection indicator on the arrow. As before, this indicates that the arrow is the selected object, and you can immediately make a change to it. For instance, you might change the width of the line.

Carl decides that he likes the arrow just as it is and no changes are needed.

⑥ Select Quit (**Q**) to leave the graphics editor and return to READY mode. See Figure 3-18.

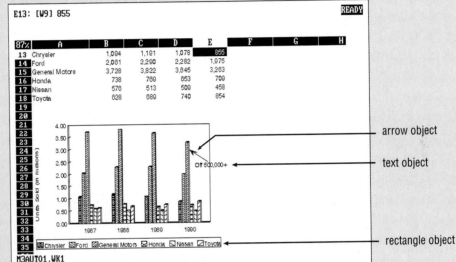

Figure 3-18
Current version of
graph in worksheet
with three objects
added

⟶ arrow object

⟶ text object

⟶ rectangle object

Saving the Graph

Recall that when you save a worksheet that has been enhanced by WYSIWYG, your worksheet will consist of two files: a WK1 worksheet file and an FMT format file. Both files have the same filename. Your data and basic settings, such as column width, cell formats, and range names, are stored in the WK1 file. Your formatting information for the current worksheet, such as fonts, styles, lines, added graphs, and enhanced graphics, are stored in the FMT file. Let's save Carl's worksheet.

To save a worksheet that includes WYSIWYG enhancements:

❶ Press **[Home]** to move the cell pointer to cell A1.

Enter the name of the file you will use when saving the worksheet.

❷ Type **W3AUT01.WK1** and press **[Enter]**.

Now save the file.

❸ Select /File Save (**/FS**).

❹ Type **W3AUTO1** and press **[Enter]**. Both the WK1 and FMT files are now saved.

Printing Graphs in WYSIWYG

WYSIWYG provides a way to print your worksheet and graph that is simpler than using 1-2-3's PrintGraph utility. When you add a graph to your worksheet with the Graph Add command, you can use the WYSIWYG Print commands to print a graph by itself or print a graph along with the worksheet data. To print in WYSIWYG, you must specify the range of cells you want printed.

Carl decides to print the bar graph on the same page as the automobile sales data. He looks at the data and the graph, and sees that the range he wants to print is A7..E35.

To set the print range:

❶ Select :Print (**:P**). A dialog box appears showing the current settings for WYSIWYG printing.

❷ Select Range Set (**RS**).

❸ Move the cell pointer to A7, the first cell in the print range, and press **[.]** to anchor the print range.

❹ Highlight the range A7..E35 and press **[Enter]**. The range now appears in the dialog box. See Figure 3-19. You have now specified the print range.

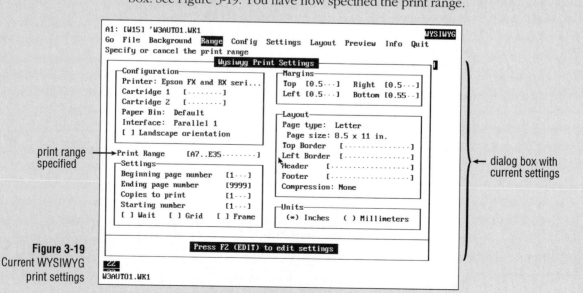

Figure 3-19
Current WYSIWYG
print settings

Next you must instruct WYSIWYG which printer to use to print the graph and the data. If no printer appears in the dialog box, you must select one.

To select a printer:

1 Select Config Print (**CP**). A list of installed printers appears.

2 Select the name of the printer you want to use and press **[Enter]**. If you are not sure, check with your instructor or technical support person.

3 Select Quit (**Q**) to return to the Print menu. You are ready to print.

Printing in WYSIWYG can take a long time. So let's preview the output before actually printing the worksheet.

To preview a page:

1 Select Preview (**P**). See Figure 3-20.

preview of data and graph

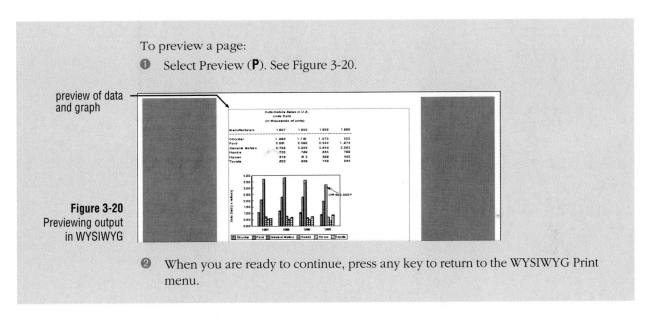

Figure 3-20
Previewing output in WYSIWYG

2 When you are ready to continue, press any key to return to the WYSIWYG Print menu.

After previewing the worksheet, Carl is happy with what he sees and is ready to print it.

To print the data and their graph:

1 Select Go (**G**). As you are printing your document, the mode indicator flashes "Wait." Depending on the formatting enhancements in your worksheet and the printer you selected, your output may take a few seconds to several minutes to complete.

If you are using diskettes to store your data files, you might encounter the message "Error writing file" when you try to print in WYSIWYG. If this happens, place another formatted diskette in the drive and try again.

After the worksheet has been printed, you are automatically returned to READY mode.

Figure 3-21 shows the printed output that Carl will give to his supervisor.

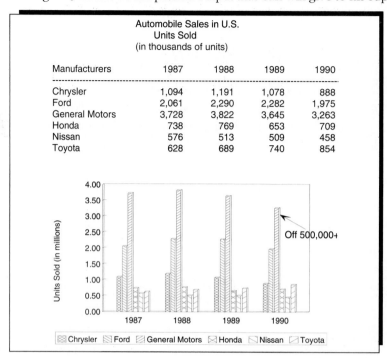

Figure 3-21
Carl's final output

Exercises

1. What types of graphs can you add to a worksheet using WYSIWYG?

2. What WYSIWYG commands or actions would you choose to accomplish each of the following?
    a. insert a graph into a worksheet
    b. reduce the size of worksheet cells
    c. add rectangle to a graph
    d. print a hard copy of your data and supporting graph on one page

3. You have just completed a graph using the /Graph command. What steps are necessary to add text inside a box to the graph?

4. You have just added a pie chart to your worksheet using WYSIWYG. Before you have a chance to add some enhancements to the pie chart, you have to stop working. You decide to complete your work tomorrow. What should you do to make sure you can begin your work from the point where you left off today?

5. How would you print each of the following graphs?
    a. a bar graph you added to your worksheet
    b. a bar graph you added to your worksheet but did not enhance with a boxed-in legend

Case Problems

1. Coles Investments

Ian Coles owns an investment research firm. Each month he prepares a newsletter for his clients. This month he is recommending that investors consider investing in pharmaceutical companies. He feels drug companies are recession resistant and offer above-average growth. He is in the process of completing a graph that will be included in his newsletter. Help Ian complete the graph.

Do the following:

1. Attach WYSIWYG.

2. Retrieve the worksheet M3INVEST.WK1.

3. Insert the current graph into the worksheet.

4. Save the worksheet as W3INVEST.

5. Print the data and the graph on one page.

2. Inflation Is Under Control

The Center for Business and Economics at Ashland University publishes a quarterly newsletter about business and economic conditions in the region that is mailed to over 150 businesses. One part of the report deals with consumer prices. Rory Jones is in the process of completing a graph on the U.S. inflation rates since 1981. Help him complete the graph.

Do the following:

1. Attach WYSIWYG.

2. Retrieve the file M3INFLA1.WK1.

3. Use WYSIWYG to insert the current graph to the right of the data in the range D5..H16.

4. Print the data and the graph on one page.

5. Add the following footnote at the bottom left corner of the graph:
   Source: U.S. Department of Labor

6. Display the footnote using an 8-point Dutch font.

7. Add the comment "Inflation Slowed" near the mark for 1991.

8. Include an arrow that draws attention from the text to the 1991 point on the line graph.

9. Save your worksheet as W3INFLA1.

10. Print the graph with its enhancements.

Module 4

Using SmartIcons

What are SmartIcons?

If you are using Lotus 1-2-3 Release 2.4, you can take advantage of a powerful new feature called SmartIcons. **SmartIcons** are graphic images that represent 1-2-3 commands or functions such as retrieving and saving files, formatting data, and printing worksheets. They provide a faster and easier way to access 1-2-3 commands than 1-2-3's menu system.

You can access SmartIcons with a keyboard or a mouse, but mouse users benefit more because complex operations can be executed with one click of the mouse button.

SmartIcons can be used with or without WYSIWYG. Figure 4-1 on the next page shows what SmartIcons look like on your screen.

OBJECTIVES

In this tutorial you will:

- Learn the definitions of SmartIcon, icon, and palette

- Load the SmartIcons add-in program

- Use a SmartIcon to retrieve a worksheet

- Use a SmartIcon to format a range

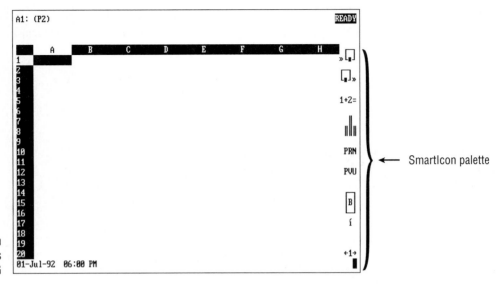

Figure 4-1a
SmartIcons
without WYSIWYG

SmartIcon palette

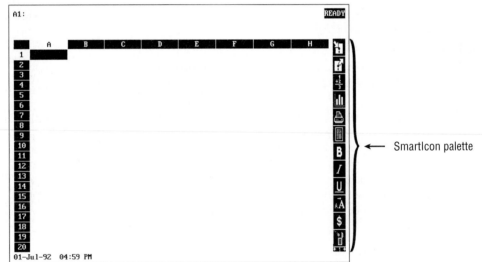

Figure 4-1b
SmartIcons with
WYSIWYG

SmartIcon palette

SmartIcons are grouped into columns called **palettes**. The icons in Figure 4-1 appear on palettes found to the right of the worksheets. In all, 1-2-3 Release 2.4 offers 77 icons grouped on several palettes. 65 of these icons are predefined Lotus commands or functions; 12 icons are user-defined and can be assigned to macros. The total number of palettes depends on the resolution of your screen and whether WYSIWYG is attached.

In this tutorial, you will learn how to load, access, and use SmartIcons.

Loading the SmartIcons Program

SmartIcons is an add-in program that is separate from the 1-2-3 program. You must attach the SmartIcons program before you can use SmartIcons. It is possible to run the SmartIcons and WYSIWYG programs at the same time; doing so will enhance the appearance of the icons, as in Figure 4-1b. However, since not all computers have enough memory to run both programs at once, we will assume in this tutorial that WYSIWYG is not attached. If WYSIWYG *is* attached on your system, the instructions in this tutorial will work, but the SmartIcons will look different on your screen.

If you do not see a SmartIcons palette on the right side of your screen, follow these steps to attach the SmartIcons add-in program. If SmartIcons appear on your screen the program is attached and you can go to "Using SmartIcons" on page L 358. Do not confuse SmartIcons with mouse icons. If your screen displays only a set of four triangles and a question mark along the right side, SmartIcons are not attached and you should follow the instructions for attaching them.

To attach the SmartIcons add-in program:

① Select */Add-in Attach* (**/AA**). A list of add-in programs appears. See Figure 4-2.

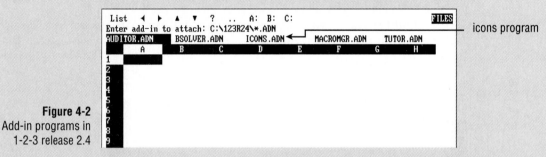

icons program

Figure 4-2
Add-in programs in
1-2-3 release 2.4

ICONS.ADN is the name of the SmartIcons program.

② Highlight ICONS.ADN and press **[Enter]**. The extension ADN stands for **AD**d-i**N**.

Once the SmartIcons program is loaded into memory, choose how you want to access the icon palettes using the keyboard. See Figure 4-3.

options →

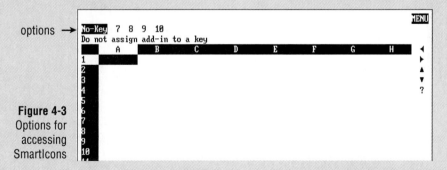

Figure 4-3
Options for
accessing
SmartIcons

If you choose *No-Key*, you cannot access the SmartIcons using the keyboard. You must use a mouse.

If you choose *7*, you press [Alt] [F7] to access the SmartIcons.

If you choose *8*, you press [Alt][F8] to access the SmartIcons.

If you choose *9*, you press [Alt][F9] to access the SmartIcons.

If you choose *10*, you press [Alt][F10] to access the SmartIcons.

③ Highlight 7 and press **[Enter]**.

④ Select *Quit* (**Q**) to leave the add-in menu and return to READY mode. The SmartIcons program is now attached to 1-2-3. Your screen should be similar to Figure 4-1a or 4-1b.

Using SmartIcons

Pauline wants to see how the worksheet will look if all of the values that represent currency are formatted as currency. We'll use SmartIcons first to retrieve a worksheet file, then to format a range as currency.

Using SmartIcons to Retrieve a File

First, let's use a SmartIcon to retrieve Pauline's final worksheet.

To retrieve Pauline's worksheet using the keyboard to access SmartIcons:

❶ Press **[Alt][F7]** to access SmartIcons. See Figure 4-4. Notice that the top icon is high-lighted and that a brief description of its function appears in the control panel.

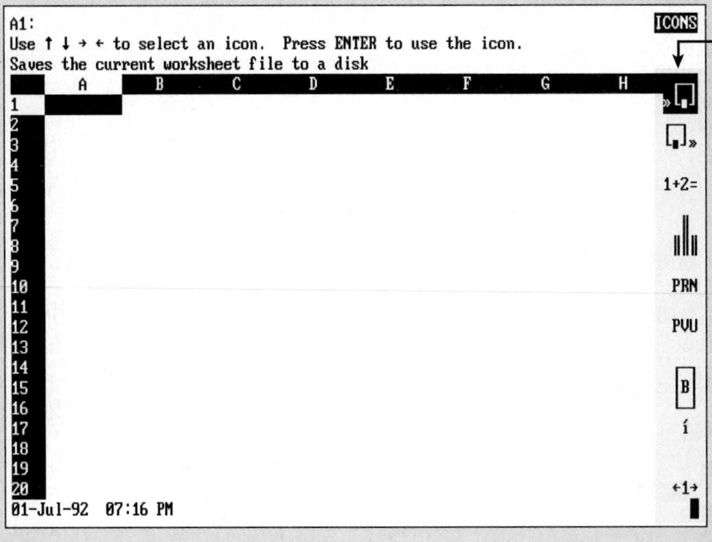

description of the → save icon's function

palette area

Figure 4-4
Accessing the
SmartIcons program

If you have a mouse, you can access SmartIcons by moving your mouse pointer anywhere into the palette area.

❷ Press **[↓]** once to highlight the next icon. A description of the highlighted icon is dis-played on the control panel. See Figure 4-5.

If you have a mouse, you can see a description of a SmartIcon by holding down the right mouse button while you move the mouse pointer over that icon.

If the second icon on the current palette is not the retrieve file icon, continue pressing **[↓]** until the retrieve file icon is highlighted.

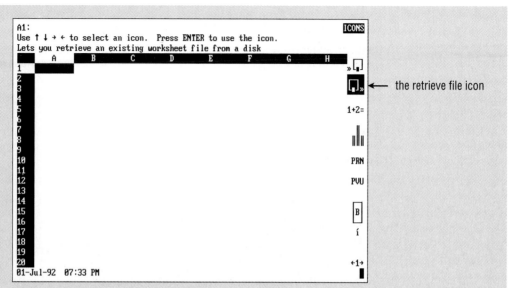

the retrieve file icon

Figure 4-5
Highlighting the
retrieve file icon

Now let's actually select the SmartIcon.

③ Press **[Enter]**. A list of your worksheet files appears on the screen.

If you have a mouse, you can select SmartIcons by clicking the left mouse button while your mouse pointer is on that icon.

④ Highlight the file M4BALBO1.WK1 and press **[Enter]**.

⑤ Press **[PgDn]** to view the worksheet data. See Figure 4-6.

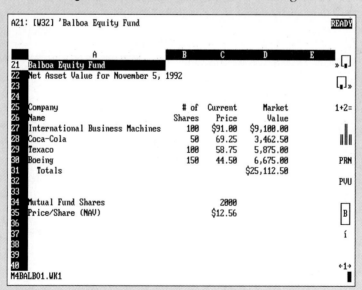

Figure 4-6

Formatting a Range as Currency

Before Pauline can change the format to currency, she needs to specify the range of cells that she wants to format.

To specify the range of data:

❶   Move the cell pointer to cell C28.

❷   Press **[F4]** to anchor the cell pointer.

❸   Highlight the range C28..D30 and press **[Enter]** to select them.

Because many SmartIcons perform their actions on a *range* of cells, learning how to prese-lect ranges is important. If the range you want to specify is a single cell, just move the cell pointer to the cell on which you wish to perform the action, then access SmartIcons.

Now that the range of data is specified it can be formatted. Pauline knows that the $ icon formats a selected range to currency with 2 decimals, but she can't remember on which palette she saw that icon.

To display another icon palette:

❶   Press **[Alt][F7]** to access SmartIcons.

❷   Move to the next palette by pressing **[→]**. See Figure 4-7.

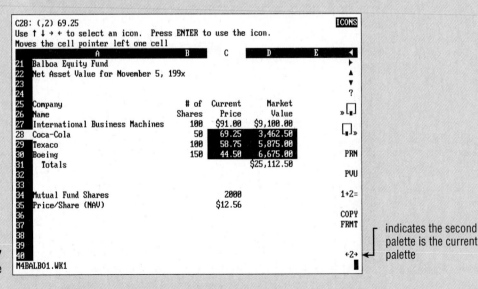

Figure 4-7
Second icon palette

indicates the second palette is the current palette

The current palette is indicated by the number at the bottom of the palette area. To move to the previous palette, you would press [←].

If you have a mouse, you can move to the next palette by clicking the left mouse button on the arrow to the right of the palette number at the bottom of the palette

(See Figure 4-7). To move to the previous palette, click on the arrow to the left of the palette number.

In text mode, the currency format SmartIcon is not on the second palette. Let's look on the third palette.

❸ Press [→] to display the third palette. See Figure 4-8. The currency icon is on the third palette.

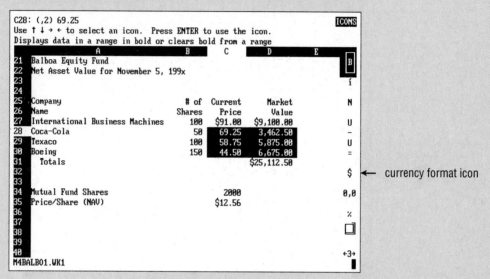

Figure 4-8
Third icon palette

← currency format icon

If the currency format icon is not on your third palette, use the [←] and [→] keys to search the other palettes until you find it.

Now format the range as currency format.

To select the currency format SmartIcon:

❶ Use [↓] to move the highlight to the currency format icon ($) and press **[Enter]**.

The values within the specified range change to currency format. See Figure 4-9.

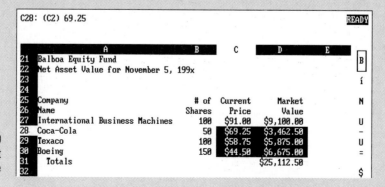

Figure 4-9
Currency format
applied to the range

Pauline decides the added dollar signs make the worksheet look cluttered. She decides to remove the currency format.

To turn off the currency format:

❶ Press **[Alt][F7]** to access SmartIcons.

Because the range C28..D30 remained highlighted after you selected currency format the first time, you do not have to preselect it again.

❷ Highlight the currency format icon and press **[Enter]**. The data changes back to general format. See Figure 4-10.

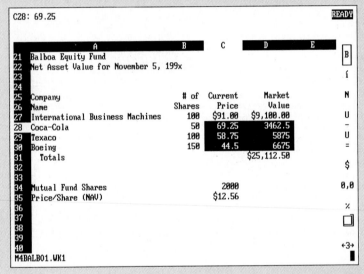

Figure 4-10
Range format
changed back to
general format

Reselecting the icon reverts the selected range to the Worksheet's global format. If you want the range to have two decimal places again, you would need to type /Range Format Fixed (/RF F), then press [Enter] to accept 2 as the number of decimal places.

Descriptions of the SmartIcons

Now that you know what SmartIcons are and how to use them, refer to Figure 4-11 to see a description of the SmartIcons. Some icons work only when WYSIWYG is attached. The icons in the first column are the icons that appear when WYSIWYG is attached. The icons in the second column are the icons that appear when WYSIWYG is not attached. Remember that by navigating through the palettes yourself, you can view descriptions of the icons and experiment with what they do.

Icons in WYSIWYG mode	Icons in text mode	Description
	»	Saves the current worksheet file to a disk.
U	U	This icon can only be used with WYSIWYG attached. Adds a single underline to data in a range or removes a single underline.
U	U	This icon can only be used with WYSIWYG attached. Adds a double underline to data in a range or removes a double underline.
$	$	Formats values in a range with 2 decimal places, the default currency symbol, and the default thousands separator or restores the global format in the range.
0,0	0,0	Formats values in a range with the default thousands separator and no decimal places or restores the global format in the range.
%	%	Formats values in a range as % (percent) with 2 decimal places or restores the global format in the range.
AA	2→2	This icon can only be used with WYSIWYG attached. Displays data in the highlighted range in the next available type style and/or point size.
AA	FGRD	This icon can only be used with WYSIWYG attached. Displays data in the highlighted range in the next available color.
A	BGRD	This icon can only be used with WYSIWYG attached. Displays the background of the highlighted range in the next available color.
		This icon can only be used with WYSIWYG attached. Draws an outline around a range and draws a drop shadow below and to the right of the range or removes an existing drop shadow and outline.

□	This icon can only be used with WYSIWYG attached. Draws a single-line, double-line, or wide outline around a range or clears the outline, depending on the current type of outline.
###	This icon can only be used with WYSIWYG attached. Adds light, dark, or solid shading to a range or removes the solid shading, depending on the current type of shading in the range.
←L	Left-aligns labels in a range.
←C→	Centers labels in a range.
R→	Right-aligns labels in a range.
ALGN TEXT	This icon can only be used with WYSIWYG attached. Centers text in a text range, aligns text evenly at both the left and right of a text range, right-aligns text, left-aligns text, or clears the alignment settings for a range, depending on the current alignment setting.
+ROW	Inserts one or more rows above the highlighted range.
+COL	Inserts one or more columns to the left of the high-lighted range.
−ROW	Deletes all rows in the highlighted range.
−COL	Deletes all columns in the highlighted range.
—— --- ——	Inserts a page break in the row that contains the cell pointer.
¦ ¦ ¦	This icon can only be used with WYSIWYG attached. Inserts a page break in the column that contains the cell pointer.
A→Z	Sorts a database in ascending order (A through Z and smallest to largest values), using the selected column as the sort key.
Z→A	Sorts a database in descending order (Z through A and largest to smallest values), using the selected column as the sort key.

FILL — Fills the highlighted range with a sequence of values.

CALC — Recalculates all formulas in the worksheet.

DATE — Enters a number that corresponds to the current date and time in the current cell. If the cell is formatted with a date format, the date appears in the cell in that format. If the cell is not formatted with a date format, the date appears in the cell in the default date format. If the cell is formatted with a time format, the time appears in the cell in that format.

CRCL — This icon can only be used with WYSIWYG attached. Circles the data in the highlighted range. 1-2-3 creates the circle by adding a graphic to the highlighted range.

ZOOM — This icon can only be used with WYSIWYG attached. Enlarges the size of displayed cells and their contents to 125% or 150% of their normal size; reduces the size of displayed cells to 63% or 87% of their normal size; or displays cells at their normal size, depending on the current display size setting.

STEP — Turns on STEP mode, which executes macros one step at a time for debugging.

RUN — Lets you select and run a macro.

◀ — Moves the cell pointer left one cell.

▶ — Moves the cell pointer right one cell.

▲ — Moves the cell pointer up one cell.

▼ — Moves the cell pointer down one cell.

? — Starts the 1-2-3 Help system in READY mode.

Moves the cell pointer to cell A1. Equivalent to pressing HOME.

Moves the cell pointer to the lower right corner of the active area (the rectangular area between cell A1 and the lowest and rightmost nonblank cell in the worksheet).

Moves the cell pointer down to the intersection of a blank and a nonblank cell. Equivalent to pressing END ↓.

Moves the cell pointer up to the intersection of a blank and a nonblank cell. Equivalent to pressing END ↑.

Moves the cell pointer right to the intersection of a blank and a nonblank cell. Equivalent to pressing END →.

Moves the cell pointer left to the intersection of a blank and a nonblank cell. Equivalent to press END ←.

GOTO   Lets you move the cell pointer to a specified cell or range.

FIND   Lets you find or replace specified characters in labels and formulas in a range.

UNDO   Cancels your previous action or command if the undo feature is on.

DEL   Erases the highlighted range.

Lets you retrieve an existing worksheet file from a disk.

1+2=   Sums values in the highlighted range, if you include empty cells below or to the right of the range; or, if the highlighted range is blank, sums values in the nearest area of data and places the results in the highlighted range.

Graphs the contents of the highlighted range or the data immediately adjacent to or surrounding the cell pointer. This icon displays the QuickGraph dialog box, which lets you change the settings for graph type, orientation, colors and 3-D effect and lets you graph data in columns or rows. If the cell pointer is not currently in an area that contains data, this icon lets you make changes to the current graph settings and displays the current graph.

This icon can only be used with WYSIWYG attached. Adds the current graph to the highlighted range in the worksheet.

	VIEW GRPH	Displays the current graph. Equivalent to pressing F10 (GRAPH).
	EDIT TEXT	This icon can only be used with WYSIWYG attached. Lets you enter or edit text in a text range.
	PRN	Prints the range you specified with /Print Printer Range or :Print Range or, if no print range is specified, prints the highlighted range.
	PVU	This icon can only be used with WYSIWYG attached. Displays a preview of the range you specified with /Printer Printer Range or :Print Range or, if no print range is specified, displays a preview of the highlighted range.
	COPY	Lets you specify a range to copy the highlighted range to.
	MOVE	Lets you specify a range to move the highlighted range to.
	COPY FRMT	This icon can only be used with WYSIWYG attached. Applies the WYSIWYG formats of the highlighted range to a range you specify.
	REP DATA	Copies the contents of the current cell of the highlighted range in all other cells in the range.
B	B	This icon can only be used with WYSIWYG attached. Displays data in a range in bold or clears bold from a previously formatted range.
I	i	This icon can only be used with WYSIWYG attached. Displays data in a range in italic or clears italic from a previously formatted range.
N	N	This icon can only be used with WYSIWYG attached. Clears all WYSIWYG formatting from a range and restores the default font.
	+ ∎ ∎→	Adds an icon to your custom palette.
	∎ − ∎→	Removes an icon from you custom palette.

Moves an icon to another location on your custom palette.

Displays descriptions of user icons U1 through U12, lets you assign one or more macros and descriptions to one or more user icons, and lets you copy the text of one or more macros to the worksheet so you can debug the macros.

Runs the macro you assigned to user icon U1. The SmartIcons add-in includes 12 user icons, labeled U1, U2, and so on through U12.

Lotus 1-2-3 Index

Praise for Patricia Davids and her novels

"[A] lovely romance between two strong-willed, intelligent people."
> —*RT Book Reviews* on *The Doctor's Blessing*

"Davids' deep understanding of Amish culture is evident in the compassionate characters and beautiful descriptions."
> —*RT Book Reviews* on *A Home for Hannah*

"Quaint characters and tender moments combine in this…sweet tale."
> —*RT Book Reviews* on *A Hope Springs Christmas*

Praise for Anna Schmidt and her novels

"Schmidt's story lets readers into the Amish world and teaches how they live and love."
> —*RT Book Reviews* on *Hannah's Journey*

"A poignant story of two people who…embrace their love."
> —*RT Book Reviews* on *Second Chance Proposal*

"Schmidt knows what readers expect…and delivers on all levels."
> —*RT Book Reviews* on *Gift from the Sea*

After thirty-five years as a nurse, **Patricia Davids** hung up her stethoscope to become a full-time writer. She enjoys spending her free time visiting her grandchildren, doing some long-overdue yard work and traveling to research her story locations. She resides in Wichita, Kansas. Pat always enjoys hearing from her readers. You can visit her online at patriciadavids.com.

Anna Schmidt is an award-winning author of more than twenty-five works of historical and contemporary fiction. She is a three-time finalist for the coveted RITA® Award from Romance Writers of America, as well as a four-time finalist for an RT Reviewers' Choice Award. Critics have called Anna "a natural writer, spinning tales reminiscent of old favorites like *Miracle on 34th Street*." One reviewer raved, "I love Anna Schmidt's style of writing!"

CONTENTS

THE DOCTOR'S BLESSING

Patricia Davids

To Terrah in Kansas City
and to Rachel in Poland, Ohio.
Bless you both for all your help. This book
is dedicated to nurse-midwives everywhere.
Women helping women bring healthy babies
into loving families.

USA TODAY Bestselling Author

PATRICIA DAVIDS

The Doctor's Blessing

&

ANNA SCHMIDT

Hannah's Journey

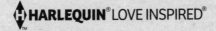

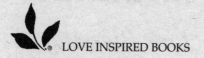

LOVE INSPIRED BOOKS

Recycling programs for this product may not exist in your area.

ISBN-13: 978-0-373-20972-9

The Doctor's Blessing and Hannah's Journey

Copyright © 2017 by Harlequin Books S.A.

The publisher acknowledges the copyright holders of the individual works as follows:

The Doctor's Blessing
Copyright © 2010 by Patricia MacDonald

Hannah's Journey
Copyright © 2011 by Jo Horne Schmidt

www.Harlequin.com

Printed in U.S.A.

My little children, let us not love in word
or in tongue, but in deed and in truth.
—*1 John* 3:18

Chapter One

"Amber, you won't believe who's here!"

The agitated whisper stopped Amber Bradley in her tracks halfway through the front door of the Hope Springs Medical Clinic. She glanced around the small waiting room. The only occupant was her wide-eyed receptionist standing at her desk with one finger pressed to her lips.

Amber whispered back, "I give up, Wilma. Who's here?"

The tiny, sixtysomething woman glanced toward the hallway leading to the offices and exam rooms, then hurried around the corner of her desk wringing her hands. "Dr. Phillip White."

Oh, no. Amber closed the door with deliberate slowness. So the ax was going to fall on their small-town clinic in spite of everyone's prayers. What would they do now? What would happen to their patients? Her heart sank at the prospect.

Please, dear Lord, don't let this happen.

Composing herself, she turned to face Wilma. "What did he say? Is Harold worse?"

"He said Harold is the reason he needs to meet with us, but he wanted to wait until you were here before going into details."

Dr. Harold White was the only doctor in the predominantly Amish community of Hope Springs, Ohio. Four weeks earlier, he'd taken his first vacation in more than twenty years to visit his grandson, Phillip, in Honolulu. While there, a serious accident landed the seventy-five-year-old man in intensive care.

Wilma leaned close. "What do you think he's doing here?"

"I have no idea."

"You think he's here to close the office, don't you?"

Amber couldn't come up with another reason that made more sense. Harold's only relative had come to close the clinic and inform them that Harold wouldn't be returning.

At least he was kind enough to come in person instead of delivering the news over the phone.

Amber had been expecting something like this since she'd learned the extent of Harold's injuries. Chances were slim a man his age could make a full recovery after suffering a broken leg, a fractured skull and surgery to remove a blood clot on his brain. Still, Harold hadn't given up hope that he'd be back, so neither would she.

Summoning a smile for her coworker, Amber laid a hand on Wilma's shoulder. "When I spoke to Harold last night, he assured me the clinic would stay open."

"For now." The deep male voice came from behind them.

Wilma squeaked as she spun around. Amber had a better grip on her emotions. Wilma hurried away to the safety of her oak desk in the corner, leaving Amber to face the newcomer alone. She surveyed Harold's grandson with interest.

Dr. Phillip White was more imposing than she had expected. He stood six foot at least, if not a shade taller. His light brown hair, streaked with sun-bleached highlights, curled slightly where it touched the collar of his blue, button-down shirt. His bronze tan emphasized his bone structure and the startling blue of his eyes.

He was movie-star gorgeous. The thought popped into Amber's brain and stuck. She licked her suddenly dry lips. When had she met a man who triggered such intense awareness at first glance? Okay, never.

Rejecting her left-field thoughts as totally irrelevant, Amber tried for a professional smile. Moving forward, she held out her hand. "Welcome to Hope Springs, Dr. White."

His grip, firm and oddly stirring, made her pulse spike and her breathing quicken. He held her hand a fraction longer than necessary. When he let go, she shoved her hands in the front pockets of her white lab coat, curling her fingers into tight balls.

Striving to appear unruffled, she said, "Your grandfather speaks of you frequently. I never saw him so excited as the day he learned of your existence."

His expression remained carefully blank. "I'm sure my happiness was equal to his."

Little warning bells started going off in Amber's brain. He wasn't here to make friends. Her smile grew stiff. "Of course, it can't be every day a grown man discovers he has a grandfather he never knew about."

Up close, Phillip's resemblance to Harold was undeniable. They shared the same intense blue eyes, strong chin and full lips. But not, it seemed, Harold's friendly demeanor. Still, she cast aside any lingering doubts that the whole thing was a hoax. They were obviously related.

She said, "Isn't it strange that both of you became family practice doctors. It must be in the genes. I'd love to hear the whole story. Harold was vague about the details."

A cooler expression entered Phillip's eyes. "It's a personal matter that I'm not comfortable discussing."

Oops! It seemed she'd stumbled on a touchy subject. "I'm sorry Harold's holiday with you ended so badly."

"As am I." His lips pressed into a tighter line.

Amber indicated their receptionist. "I take it you've met Mrs. Nolan? Wilma has worked for your grandfather since he came to Hope Springs over thirty years ago."

He nodded in Wilma's direction. "Yes, we've met."

"And I'm Amber Bradley." She waited with bated breath for his reaction. She knew Harold had told his grandson about their collaborative practice.

Phillip's expression didn't change. "Ah, the midwife."

There it was, that touch of disdain in his voice that belittled her profession, dismissed her education and years of training as if they were nothing. She'd heard it before from physicians and even nurses. It seemed young Dr. White didn't value her occupation the way his grandfather did.

She stood as tall as her five-foot-three frame allowed. "Yes, I'm a certified nurse-midwife. It's my vocation as well as my job."

"Vocation? That's a strong word."

"It is what it is."

Was that a flicker of respect in his eyes? Maybe she had jumped the gun in thinking he disapproved.

Bracing herself, she asked the unspoken question that

hovered in the air. "What brings you to Hope Springs, Dr. White?"

He glanced around the small office. "Harold is fretting himself sick over this place."

Amber tried to see the clinic through Phillip's eyes. The one-story brick building was devoid of frills. The walls were painted pale blue. The chairs grouped around the small waiting room had worn upholstery. Wilma's desk, small and crowded by the ancient tan filing cabinets lined up behind it, didn't make much of a statement.

Their clinic might not look like much, but it was essential to the well-being of their friends and neighbors. Amber wouldn't let it close without a fight.

"Harold shouldn't worry," she said. "We're managing."

"Grandfather's doctors can't keep his blood pressure under control. He's not eating. He's not sleeping well. He needs to concentrate on his recovery and he's not doing that." Deep concern vibrated through Phillip's voice.

A pang stabbed Amber's heart. "I know Harold's concerned about us, but I didn't realize it was affecting his health."

"Unfortunately, it is. The only way to relieve his anxiety was to find someone to cover his practice. In spite of my best efforts to hire temporary help, I've had no success. Clearly, working in a remote Amish community is not an assignment most physicians are eager to take on. In the end, I had to obtain a temporary license to practice in the state of Ohio. I'm here until the tenth of September or until a more permanent solution can be found."

"You're taking over the practice?" Amber blinked hard. While she was delighted they were going to have a physician again, for the life of her she couldn't understand why Harold hadn't mentioned this tidbit of information. It ranked above bad hospital food and clueless medical students, the subjects of their conversation last night.

Her shock must have shown on her face. Phillip's eyes narrowed. "Harold did tell you I was coming, didn't he?"

Amber glanced at Wilma, hoping she'd taken the message. Wilma shook her head. Amber looked back at Phillip. "Ah, no."

"I shouldn't be surprised. His mind wanders at times. This is additional proof that he is incapable of returning to work."

Amber wasn't sure what to think. Harold sounded perfectly rational each time she'd spoken to him on the phone. Could he fool her that easily?

Compelled to defend the man who was her mentor and friend, she said, "Perhaps his pain medication muddled his thinking and he forgot to mention it. He will bounce back. He loves this place and the people here. He says working is what keeps him sane."

Phillip didn't look convinced. "We'll see how it goes. For now, I'm in charge of this practice."

He jerked his head toward the parking lot visible through the front Plateglass window. A gray horse hitched to a black buggy stood patiently waiting beside the split-rail fence that ringed the property. "Do we put out hay for the horses or do their owners bring their own?"

His satire-laden comment raised Amber's hackles. The Amish community was tight-knit and wary of outsiders. Harold had earned their trust over thirty years of practicing medicine by respecting their ways, not by poking fun at them.

She crossed her arms over her chest. "I thought you were joining some big practice in Honolulu. I'm sure Harold told me that before he left."

"Under the circumstances my partners have agreed to let me take a two-month leave of absence."

Wilma finally found the courage to pipe up. "But what if Dr. Harold isn't back in two months?"

"Then I imagine he won't be back at all. In that case, the clinic will be closed until another physician can be found. I'm aware there is a real shortage of rural doctors in this state, so you ladies may want to think about job hunting."

Wilma gasped. Amber wasn't ready to accept Phillip's prediction. The community needed this clinic. She needed Harold's support for her nurse-midwife practice. The people of Hope Springs needed them both.

She chose to remain calm. There was no use getting in a panic. She would put her faith in the Lord and pray harder than ever for Harold's recovery.

Phillip didn't seem to notice the turmoil his words caused. He said, "I found the coffeepot but I can't find any coffee."

His abrupt change of subject threw her for a second. Recovering, she reached in her bag and withdrew a package of Colombian blend. "We were out. I stopped at the store on my way here."

"Good. I take mine black. Just bring it to my office."

Was he trying to annoy her? Everyone was equal in this office. That was Harold's rule. The person who wanted coffee made it and then offered it to the others. He never expected anyone to wait on him. And it wasn't Phillip's office anyway. It still belonged to Harold.

"When can we begin seeing patients?" The object of her ire glanced at his watch.

Wilma advanced around the corner of her desk with a chart in hand. "There is a patient here to see Amber now."

His frown deepened to a fierce scowl. He pinned Amber with his gaze. "You're seeing patients?"

Amber knew the legal limits of her profession. She didn't care for his tone.

Her chin came up. "I *am* a primary care provider. I do see patients. If you mean am I seeing obstetrical patients, the answer is no. I haven't been since Harold left. Edna Nissley is sixty-nine. She's here for a blood pressure check and to have lab work drawn."

"I see." His glower lightened.

"People knew Harold was going to be gone, so our schedule has been light. Those patients outside my scope of practice have been sent to a physician in a neighboring town."

"Plus, we painted all the rooms except Harold's office and had the carpets cleaned," Wilma added brightly.

Amber continued to study Phillip. He was a hard man to read. "Someone had to be here to refer patients and fax charts to other doctors. We haven't exactly been on vacation. We've both traveled a lot of miles letting people know what has happened."

He raised one eyebrow. "Wouldn't a few phone calls have been easier?"

Smiling with artificial sweetness, Amber said, "It would if our patients had phones. The majority of our clients are Amish, remember?"

"Edna is waiting in room one," Wilma interjected.

Amber started to walk past Phillip but stopped. She

pressed the bag of coffee into his midsection. "I take cream and one sugar. Just leave it on my desk."

Phillip took the bag. "I'll let you get to work, Miss Bradley, but there will be changes around here that you and I need to discuss. Come to my office when you're done."

Amber didn't like the sound of that. Not one bit.

Chapter Two

Phillip watched Amber's stunning blue-green eyes narrow. She was right to worry. He wasn't looking forward to the coming conversation. He'd rather see the charming smile she'd greeted him with earlier than the wary expression on her face at the moment.

She was pretty in a small-town-girl kind of way. Her pink cheeks and slightly sunburned nose gave her a wholesome look. She wasn't tall, but she had a shapely figure he admired. He knew from his grandfather that she wasn't married. Seeing her, he had to wonder why.

Phillip had listened to his grandfather singing the praises of Nurse-Midwife Bradley for the past year but this woman was nothing like he'd imagined. He had pictured a plump, gray-haired matron, not a pretty, petite woman who didn't look a day over twenty-five.

Her honey-blond hair was wound into a thick bun at the nape of her neck. How long was it? What would it look like when she wore it down?

Intrigued as he was by the thought, it was her blue-green eyes that drew and held his attention. They were the color of the sea he loved. A calm sea, the kind that made a man want to spend a lifetime gazing over it and soaking in the beauty.

Such romantic musings had to be a by-product of his jet lag. He forced his attention back to the matter at hand. He was going to be working with Miss Bradley. He had no intention of setting up a workplace flirtation. Besides, he'd be lucky if she was still speaking to him by the end of the day.

He didn't believe in home deliveries. In his opinion, they were too risky. She wasn't going to be happy when she learned his stance on the subject.

He hefted the coffee bag. Perhaps it was best to give her this small victory before the confrontation. "Cream with one sugar. Got it."

He left her to see her patient and retreated to the small refreshment room beside his grandfather's office. Making coffee took only a few minutes. As he waited for the pot to fill, he studied the array of mugs hanging from hooks beneath the cabinet. Which one belonged to Amber?

He ruled out the white one that said World's Greatest Grandma in neon pink letters. Beside it hung two plain black mugs, one with a chipped lip. Somehow he knew those belonged to his grandfather. That left either the white cup with yellow daisies around the rim or the sky blue mug with *1 John* 3:18 printed in dark blue letters.

1 John 3:18. He pulled down the mug. He didn't know his Bible well enough to hazard a guess at the meaning of the passage, but he filed it away to look up later.

Studying medicine, working as a resident and then setting up a practice had consumed his life. All of which left him time to eat or maybe sleep, but rarely both. Even his surfing time had dropped to almost nothing. Bible study had fallen by the wayside, but it looked as if he'd have some free time now. How busy could he be in a small town like this? The next two months stretched before him like an eternity.

He'd do his best while he was here. He knew how much this place meant to his grandfather. Taking over until things were settled was the least he could do. After all, it was his fault Harold wasn't here.

Putting aside that painful memory, Phillip carried the blue mug to the coffee dispenser. If this wasn't Amber's cup, at least it was clean. He filled it, then added the creamer and sugar. Taking down the grandmother mug, he filled it, too. After stuffing a couple of sugar and creamer packages in his pocket, he carried the cups to the front desk.

Wilma was on the phone, so he set her cup on the corner and held up the condiments in a silent query. She shook her head and mouthed the words, "Just black." She reached for the mug, took a quick sip, then continued her conversation. That left him with Amber's cup in hand.

He'd already discovered the clinic layout when he'd arrived early that morning. He knew Amber's office was the one beside his grandfather's, while two exam rooms occupied the opposite side of the short hallway.

Entering her office, he took note of the plain white walls devoid of pictures or mementos. The starkness didn't seem to fit her vibrant personality. Her furniture was another story.

Her desk was a simple-yet-graceful cherrywood piece with curved legs and a delicately carved matching chair. Her computer sat on a small stand beside the desk, as if she couldn't bear to put something so modern on such a classic piece. Everything about the room was neat and tidy. He liked that.

After setting her cup on a coaster at the edge of her desk, he returned to his grandfather's office. Nothing in it remotely hinted at neat or tidy.

Stacks of medical journals, books and file folders sat on every flat surface. Some had meandered to the floor around his grandfather's chair. The tall bookcases on the back wall were crammed full of textbooks. A number of them had pieces of paper sticking out the tops as if to mark important places.

Harold's computer sat squarely in the middle of his large oak desk. On either side of the monitor were two pictures. Phillip reached past the photo of himself standing by his surfboard to pick up a framed portrait of a young man in a marine dress uniform.

He'd seen this picture before. One like it hung in his grandfather's house where he'd spent the night last night. A third copy sat in a box at the back of his mother's closet. The young marine was the father he never knew.

Phillip searched the face that looked so much like his own. All his life he'd aspired to be a person his father would have been proud of. He got good grades, played baseball, learned to surf, things his mother told him his father had done or wanted to do. His dad was even the reason he'd become a physician.

As a child he'd hungered for any crumb of information his mother would share about his dad. Those crumbs were all too rare. Whenever he would ask questions about his father, her reply was always the same: it was too painful to talk about that time of her life.

He could understand that. Much of his early life was painful to talk about, too.

Engrossed in the past, he didn't hear the door open. He thought he was alone until Amber spoke. "You look like him."

He set the picture back in its place. "So I've been told."

Amber moved to stand at his side. "I can see it in the arch of your brow and your square chin, but especially your eyes."

"Did you know he was killed in action?"

"I asked Harold once what happened to his son. He said he didn't want to talk about it. I never asked again."

"My father was killed in some third world country trying to rescue American citizens who'd been kidnapped."

"You must be very proud of him."

It was hard to be proud of an image on paper. Yet it had been the picture that led Phillip to his grandfather. Finding Harold had been like a gift from God.

What Phillip still didn't understand was why his mother had kept his grandfather's existence a secret for more than thirty years. She'd been furious when he announced he had contacted Harold. She wouldn't say why.

Many of his questions about his father had been answered in the long phone conversations he and Harold had shared, but like his mother, Harold refused to talk about his relationship with his daughter-in-law. It seemed the reason for the family breakup might never come to light.

Amber cleared her throat. "You wanted to talk to me?"

Her voice broke his connection with the past and catapulted him into the present. Face-to-face with a task he knew would be distasteful.

How was she going to take it? He hated scenes. His mother had made enough of them in his life.

He lifted a stack of medical journals from a chair and

added them to a precarious pile on the desk. "Please, have a seat."

When she did, Phillip hesitated a few seconds, but quickly decided there was no point beating around the bush. Pulling out his grandfather's chair, he sat behind the desk and faced her. "I've been doing some research on Ohio midwifery."

A look of surprise brightened her eyes. "That's great. It's very important that I resume my practice as soon as possible. I have four patients due this month. Without Harold available, I've had to send them to a clinic that's twenty miles from here. That's a hardship for families who travel by horse and buggy. I can't tell you how relieved I am to be getting back to my real work."

He hated knowing he was about to crush her excitement. "You have a collaborative practice agreement only with my grandfather, is that correct?"

"Yes, but I can easily modify the agreement, listing you as my primary backup. I'll print off a copy ASAP. You can sign it and I can start seeing patients again."

"I'm afraid I can't do that."

A puzzled look replaced the happiness on her face. Then she relaxed and nodded. "Yes, you can. In this state, I'm not required to partner with an OB/GYN. I can legally work with a Family Practice physician."

"I'm aware of that. I'm telling you I won't sign such an agreement. I strongly believe the safest place for a woman to labor, give birth and recover is in a hospital or a well-equipped birthing center near a hospital."

Amber shot to her feet. "Are you serious? Do you know what this means?"

Sitting forward, he steepled his fingers together. "It

means you can't legally deliver babies or treat patients as a midwife unless you agree to do so in a hospital."

It took less than a second for the storm brewing behind her stunning eyes to erupt. She leaned forward and braced her arms on the desktop. Each word could have cut stone. "Your grandfather and I have worked diligently to get the Amish women in this community to use a certified nurse-midwife instead of an illegal lay midwife. There are still numerous Amish midwives practicing under the radar in this area. Some of them are highly skilled, but some are not. I have the equipment and training to handle emergencies that arise. I'm well qualified. I've delivered over five hundred babies."

"All without complications?"

Her outrage dimmed. Caution replaced it. "There have been a few problems. I carry a cell phone and can get emergency services quickly if they're needed."

"I'm sorry, this isn't open for discussion. As long as I'm here, there will be no home deliveries. However, I'd like you to remain as my office nurse. We'll talk later about you handling hospital deliveries."

Pushing off his desk, she crossed her arms. "Does Harold know you're shutting down my practice?"

He thought he was being patient with her, but now he glared back. "I don't intend to worry my grandfather with the day-to-day running of the office nor should you. His recovery depends on decreasing his stress level."

"Oh, rest assured, I won't go tattle to him. But you're making a big mistake. You can't change the way the Amish live by dictating to them. If I'm not doing home deliveries, someone else less qualified will."

Spinning on her heels, she marched out of the office, slamming the door behind her.

Clenching his jaw, Phillip sat back. He had hoped Miss Bradley would be reasonable about this. It seemed he was mistaken. Too bad. He wasn't about to back down on this issue. No matter what the lovely nurse-midwife wanted.

Chapter Three

"If that man thinks I'm gonna lay down and take this, he has another think coming!"

Three days after her first unhappy meeting with Phillip, Amber was still fuming. They had been working together getting the clinic back up and running full-time, but things remained tense. He refused to alter his stance on home births.

Amber sat at a back booth in the Shoofly Pie Café with her friend, Katie Lantz, across from her. Katie was dressed in the traditional Plain style with a solid green dress, white apron and a white organdy prayer *kapp* covering her dark hair. Amber knew outsiders would never suspect Katie had once lived in the English world. The room was empty except for the two women.

"What can you do about it?" Katie's lilting voice carried a rich Pennsylvania Dutch accent. She took a sip of hot tea from a heavy white mug.

"I'm thinking." Amber drummed her fingers on the red Formica tabletop.

"You'll lose your license if you deliver babies, *ja*?"

"*Ja*. Unless I find another doctor who'll support me."

Katie brightened. "Why not ask Dr. Drake over in Haydenville?"

"Because Doctor Drake, great doctor that she is, is a DO, a Doctor of Osteopathic Medicine. The state requires my backup to be a Family Practice physician or OB/GYN. Most clinics and MDs won't partner with a midwife who does home births. They don't want to pay the huge malpractice insurance fees that go along with it. Dr. Harold is one of the few physicians who'll take the risk."

"Because the Amish do not sue."

"Right."

"This is not so easy a problem to solve." Katie tapped her lower lip with one finger.

Propping an elbow on the table, Amber settled her chin on her hand. "I wish I could talk to Harold about it."

"Why can't you? It is his office. He should have some say in how it is being run."

"The last thing he needs is to hear his beloved long-lost grandson and I are at loggerheads. In that respect, Phillip is right. Harold doesn't need more stress. When he's better and comes home, things will get back to normal. In the meantime, I'll keep looking for a doctor who'll partner with me. Until then, I'll have to bear with Dr. Phillip while I work on changing his mind."

"I have met your doctor. He had lunch here yesterday. He's a handsome man."

Amber rolled her eyes. "Is he handsome? I hadn't noticed."

"For an Englisher, he's not bad. Those dark eyes are hot."

"They're blue, and a good Amish woman should not say a man is 'hot.'"

Katie giggled. "I am Amish, I am not dead. If you know what color his eyes are, you've been looking, too."

"Okay, I noticed he is a nice-looking man, but handsome is as handsome does. What he's doing isn't handsome."

"You're right. Elam's sister, Mary, will be so upset if she must go to the hospital to have this baby. She didn't have a good experience there with her first child."

Elam Sutter was a special someone in Katie's life. He and his mother, Nettie, took her in when she had returned from the English world destitute and pregnant. That act of kindness had blossomed into love for the pair. His sister, Mary Yutzi, had only recently become a patient of Amber's.

"Elam's mother convinced Mary you would do a better job. For less money, too."

A smile tugged at the corner of Amber's mouth. "I'm glad Nettie Sutter thinks I do good work. Thank her for the recommendation."

It had taken years but Amber was finally finding acceptance among the majority of the Amish in the area. People like Nettie Sutter were the key. Older and respected, their word counted for a lot with the younger women in the community.

Amber took a sip of her tea, letting the warmth of the gourmet blend soothe away some of her irritation. "Two of my expectant mothers have appointments today. I'll let them know what's going on when they come to the office. As for the rest of my clients, I can visit their homes on Sunday to explain things and prepare them."

"It is our church Sunday. Everyone will be at Levi

Troyer's farm. It will save you some miles if you come there after the service."

"Thank you. If you're sure it's all right, I'll drop in. Of course, I might not need to. In this tight-knit community, the word may have spread already."

"*Ja*, you could be right."

"How is Elam, by the way?" Amber smiled in spite of her unhappiness as a blush bloomed in Katie's cheeks.

A soft smile curved her lips. "He is well."

"And the wedding? When will it be?"

Katie's eyes grew round. "What?"

Amber started laughing. "The whole countryside is talking about how much celery Elam planted this year. It won't come as a surprise to anyone when you have the banns read."

Creamed celery was a traditional food served at every Amish wedding. Leafy stalks of it were also used to decorate the tables. When a family's garden contained a big crop of celery, everyone knew there would be a wedding in the fall.

Blushing sweetly, Katie dropped her gaze. "We don't speak of such things before the time comes."

Amish marriage banns were read only a few weeks before the wedding. Until then, the engagement was kept a secret, sort of. Speculating about who would be getting hitched during the months of November and December was a popular pastime.

Amber said, "I'm sorry to tease."

Katie glanced around, then leaned close. "Not all of the celery is for Elam and me."

"Really?" Amber was intrigued. Elam lived with his widowed mother. All his sisters and older brothers were already married.

Sitting back, Katie smiled. "I will say no more."

"Now you've got me curious. Is someone courting Nettie?"

"Perhaps, but she isn't the only one with a new beau." Leaning forward, Katie tipped her head toward her boss. Emma Wadler was busy cleaning behind the counter.

"Emma and who?" Amber whispered.

Katie refused to comment. Knowing when to give up, Amber said, "I'm sure you and Elam will be very happy together."

"And Rachel."

"That's right, we can't forget little Rachel. She was my five-hundredth delivery. Did I ever tell you that?"

"No. Looking back all those months ago, I thought it was the worst night of my life. I was unwed, homeless and without family. I didn't see how things could get much worse. I couldn't see it would become the best night of my life. I met Elam, I met you, my friend, and I had a beautiful baby girl. *Gott* has a plan for us even when we can't see it."

"If you're trying to tell me God will take care of my troubles, I already know that. But I can't sit idly by. I've got to take action. Get my own ox out of the well, if you will."

Katie stirred a drizzle of honey into her tea. "I might be able to help."

"How?"

"Perhaps I should talk with some of Elam's family before I say anything. This may be a matter to bring before the church district."

Frowning in concern, Amber said, "I don't want you to do anything that will cause trouble for you, Katie. I know you recently took your vows and were baptized into the Amish Church."

"Don't worry about me. Worry about the women who are depending on you."

They were the reason Amber was upset, not for herself. She glanced at her watch. "I should get back to the office. Dr. Phillip is trying to organize some of Harold's files. Truthfully, they need it. Harold has a terrible time putting things in their place."

"A day with the *furchtbar* Dr. Phillip and old files. Sounds like poor fun to me."

"He's not terrible. I'm wrong to make him sound that way. The community needs a doctor while Harold is gone and Phillip has put his own career on hold to come here."

"*Ja*, we do need a doctor."

"Even if he's a wonderful doctor, I just can't like him. He's so different from Harold," Amber muttered, knowing it made her sound like a petulant third grader.

Rising, Katie chuckled. "We must forgive those who trespass against us, Amber."

"I know," she admitted. "I'm working on it."

"And I also must get back to work."

"I haven't asked before, but do you like your job here at the Inn?" The café was part of the Wadler Inn, run by Emma and her elderly mother.

"Emma is a good woman to work for. Her mother enjoys watching Rachel while I work. It does fine for me now."

"Until you marry and become a stay-at-home wife and mother."

Grinning, Katie nodded. "*Ja*, until then."

Amber paid her bill and headed for the door. Being

a wife and mother was something she'd always wanted, but it hadn't come her way.

Not that it was too late. She was only twenty-nine. So what if most of her Amish clients that age already had three or four children? Meeting an eligible man who wasn't Amish was as likely as finding hen's teeth in Hope Springs.

As she opened the door, Amber saw Phillip coming out of the hardware store across the street. He caught sight of her at the same moment. She either had to be civil or pretend she was in a hurry and rush away. Tough choice.

Phillip halted at the sight of Amber framed in the doorway of the Shoofly Pie Café, an unappetizing name if he'd ever heard one. Once again he was struck by how lovely she was. Today she wore a simple yellow dress with short sleeves. Her hair hung over her shoulder in a single braid that reached her waist. Now he knew how long it was. Obviously, she hadn't cut it in many years. It was a nice touch of old-fashioned feminine charm.

They stood staring at each other for several long seconds until a man with a thick black beard and a straw hat stopped in front of Phillip. Realizing he was blocking the door, Phillip stepped out of the way. By the time he looked back, Amber was on her way down the sidewalk heading toward the clinic. He sprinted after her, cutting between two buggies rolling down the avenue.

He and Amber had both been doing their jobs at the clinic, but it didn't take a genius to see she was still upset. Her icy stares and monosyllabic replies weren't going unnoticed by their patients. Somehow he had to find a way to break through her anger. Phillip couldn't handle the practice by himself. There was more to medicine than treating symptoms.

Good medicine had physical, emotional and spiritual components. Amber had what he didn't yet have in Hope Springs. A familiarity with the people he would be treating and knowledge of the inner workings of the town.

He needed to reach some kind of common ground with her if she could get past his stance on home deliveries. As much as he hated to admit it, he needed her help to keep his grandfather's clinic running smoothly.

Besides, the last thing he wanted was to tell Harold that he'd driven away the irreplaceable Miss Bradley. During their brief phone conversation last night, Harold once again sang her many praises. If Phillip didn't know better, he might have thought the old man was playing matchmaker.

After crossing the street at a jog, Phillip reached Amber's side and shortened his stride to match hers. "Morning, Miss Bradley."

"Good morning, Doctor."

"Are you on your way to the office?"

"Yes."

He glanced at his watch. "You're a little early, aren't you?"

"Yes."

In spite of the warm summer sun there was no sign of thawing on her part. He said, "We didn't see many patients yesterday. Can I expect our patient load to be so light every day?"

"No."

This didn't bode well for the rest of the day. "The weather has been agreeable. Are summers in Ohio always this nice?"

"No."

Getting nowhere, he decided to try a different tack.

Phillip saw an Amish family walking toward them. The man with his bushy beard nodded slightly. His wife kept her eyes averted, but their children gawked at them as they passed by. One of them, a teenage boy, was a dwarf. A group of several young men in straw hats and Amish clothing walked behind the group. None of the younger men wore beards.

When they were out of earshot, Phillip asked, "Why is it that only some Amish men have beards?"

He waited patiently for her answer. They passed two more shops before she obliged him. "An Amish man grows a beard when he marries."

"Okay, why don't they have mustaches?"

"Mustaches were associated with the military in Europe before the Amish immigrated to this country so they are forbidden."

"From what I understand, a lot of things are forbidden… TV, ordinary clothes, a car."

She shot him a sour look and kept walking.

That was dumb. Criticizing the Amish wasn't the way to mend fences. "Sorry, that was a stupid remark. Guess I'm nervous."

She kept walking, ignoring his bait. Either she had great patience, grim determination or a total lack of curiosity about him.

He gave in first. "I'm nervous because I know you're upset with me."

"Ya think?" She didn't slow down.

Spreading his hands wide, he waved them side to side. "I'm getting that vibe. People say I'm sensitive that way."

Had he coaxed a hint of a smile? She looked down before he could be sure.

"Amber, we've gotten off to a bad start. I know you must blame me for Harold's injuries. I blame myself."

She stopped abruptly. A puzzled frown settled between her alluring eyes. "Why would I blame you for Harold's accident?"

Chapter Four

Stunned by Amber's question, Phillip could only stare. She didn't know? How was that possible? More to the point, once she found out would it kill any chance of a better working relationship? He had opened a can of worms and didn't know how to shut it. She was waiting for his answer.

"Harold hasn't told you how the accident happened?" Phillip cringed at the memory.

"He said he foolishly stepped into the path of an on-coming car."

Phillip stiffened his spine, bracing for the worst possible reaction from Amber. "I was driving that car."

When the silence lengthened, he expected an angry or horror-filled outburst. He didn't expect the compassion that slowly filled her eyes.

Encouraged, he forged ahead. "It was the last night of his visit. We'd had an argument. I dropped him off at his hotel. I was angry and waiting impatiently for a chance to pull out into the heavy traffic. When a break came, I gunned it."

He'd never forgive himself for what happened next. "I

should have been paying more attention. I should have seen him, but he rushed out from between two parked cars right in front of me. I couldn't stop."

She laid her hand on his arm. "That must have been terrible for you."

"I thought I killed him." Phillip relived that terrifying moment, that horrific sound, every time he closed his eyes.

Quietly, Amber said, "Thank you for telling me. I can understand how hard it was for you. I want you to know I don't blame you. An accident is an accident. Things happen for a reason only God knows."

Phillip's pent-up guilt seeped out of his bones, leaving him light-headed with relief. "Now, can we work together without those frosty silences between us?"

He knew he'd made a mistake when her look of compassion changed to annoyance. "I don't blame you for what happened in Hawaii. I do blame you for making me feel marginalized and ridiculed for my career choice. For brushing aside my years of training and my skills as if they were nothing. I'm proud to be a nurse-midwife."

Taken aback, he snapped, "Wait a minute. I did not ridicule you. I stated my opinion about home childbirth. An opinion that is shared by the American Medical Association, as I'm sure you know."

"And so far, not upheld by the courts, as I'm sure *you* know. Childbirth is not a medical condition. It is a normal, natural part of life." She started walking again.

Catching up with her, he said, "But it can become a medical emergency in a matter of minutes. I'm sorry we can't agree on this. However, if we're going to be working together we need to agree on some other important issues."

She shot him an exasperated look. "Such as?"

"That my grandfather's practice is important to him. Both you and I are important to him. He wouldn't want us at odds with each other."

He detected a softening in her rigid posture. Finally, she admitted, "That's true."

"Right. We can also agree that the clinic needs to run smoothly, that I don't know where to buy groceries in Hope Springs and I haven't found a barbershop. Can you help a guy out?"

She did smile at that. "The grocery store is at the corner of Plum and Maple. Take a left at the next block and go three blocks east. The barbershop backs up to our building. Go through the alley to Vine Street. It'll be on your left. And yes, the clinic needs to run smoothly. Our patients deserve our best."

"Thank you."

"You're welcome."

It was grudgingly given, but he'd won a small victory. "I also don't know what labs Mrs. Nissley had done. I couldn't find her chart."

"I was checking her hemoglobin A1c. She's a diabetic. Ask Wilma for any charts you can't find. She has her own system of filing because so many of our patients have the same names."

"Why is that?"

"Most Amish are descendants of a small group who came to this country in the seventeen hundreds. It is forbidden to marry outside of their faith so very few new names have come into the mix."

By now they had reached the clinic. He held open the door and she went in ahead of him. To his surprise he saw they already had a waiting room full of people. Word was getting around that there was a new doctor in town.

It seemed that more one-on-one time with Amber would have to wait. He should have walked more slowly.

She leaned over and said quietly, "Something you should know. The Amish don't run to the doctor for every little thing. They are usually quite sick when they come to us. When they find a 'good doctor,' they send all their family and friends to him."

"And if I'm not a good doctor, in their opinion?"

"We'll lose Amish clients very quickly and we'll be out of business in no time. So, no pressure."

"Right. No pressure."

The day passed quickly. True to Amber's prediction, many of the patients Phillip treated had been putting off seeing a doctor since his grandfather's departure. Two bad cuts had become serious infections. A young mill worker with a gash on his arm and a high fever had to be sent to the hospital in Millersburg for IV antibiotics.

After that, he saw a young Amish woman who'd come to see Amber for her prenatal visits. After he explained the current situation, his patient got up and left his exam room without a word. In the waiting room, she spoke to a second expectant mother. The two left together. Amber followed them outside and talked with them briefly.

Was she smoothing things over or throwing gasoline on the fire?

His next patient was a three-year-old Amish girl with a severe cough. The shy toddler was also a dwarf, and she wanted nothing to do with him. She kept pushing his stethoscope away each time he tried to listen to her chest.

Mrs. Lapp, her worried mother, apologized. Amber moved forward to help restrain the child. "Doctor, Helen doesn't speak English yet. She won't learn it until she goes to school. The Amish speak Pennsylvania Deitsh at home, a German dialect."

Glancing up at her, he said, "I thought it was Dutch."

"It's commonly called Pennsylvania Dutch but that's an Americanization of the term *Deitsh*," Amber replied.

He said, "Don't hold her down, it will only frighten her. What we need is a little help from Doctor Dog."

Reaching into a drawer on the exam table, he withdrew a hand puppet, a fuzzy brown dog with floppy ears, a white lab coat and a miniature stethoscope around his neck. Looking down at the toy, Phillip said, "Dr. Dog, I'd like you to meet Helen Lapp."

"Hello, Helen," the puppet chirped in a falsetto voice as he waved one stubby arm.

Phillip heard Amber giggle behind him. Helen sat up with a hesitant smile on her face.

The puppet scratched his head with his paw. "What's wrong with you, Helen? Are you sick?"

Helen's mother translated for her. The girl nodded, never taking her eyes off the toy.

Swinging the puppet around to face himself, Phillip asked in his puppet voice, "Aren't you going to make her better, Dr. White?"

"I'm trying but Helen is afraid of me."

"She is?" Turning to face the little girl, Dr. Dog asked, "Are you afraid of Dr. White?"

Her mother asked her the question in Pennsylvania Dutch. Helen glared at Phillip and nodded.

Dr. Dog rubbed his nose. "But you aren't scared of me, are you?"

When her mother stopped speaking, Helen shook her

head. Reaching out tentatively, she patted the dog's head then giggled. Her laughter quickly became a harsh cough.

Dr. Dog asked, "Can I listen to your chest?"

Helen leaned back against her mother but didn't object. Using Dr. Dog to grasp his stethoscope, Phillip listened to the child. When he was done with the exam, Dr. Dog thanked Helen, shook hands with her and her mother, then returned to his drawer. Helen continued to watch the drawer as if he might pop out again.

As Phillip wrote out a prescription for Helen, Amber leaned close. "Very clever."

More pleased than he should have been by that simple compliment, he continued with his work. Helen had him deeply concerned.

Turning to her mother, he handed her the prescription and said, "I hear a loud murmur in Helen's heart, a noise that shouldn't be there. I'd like for her to see a specialist."

The woman stared at the note in her hand. "Will this medicine make her better?"

"I believe so, but she needs to see a heart doctor. I'll have Amber make an appointment. I believe Helen's heart condition is making her cough worse."

The mother nodded. Relieved, he looked to Amber. She said, "I'll take care of it."

He saw several more townspeople after that with assorted coughs and colds. Then two young Amish brothers came in with poison ivy from head to toe. Their mother explained her usual home remedy had failed to help.

He asked for her recipe and jotted it down. He then ordered a steroid shot for each of the boys. Afterward, he gave their mother a prescription for an ointment to be used twice a day, but encouraged her to continue her own treatment, as well.

When they left, Amber remained in the room.

"Yes?" He kept writing on the chart without looking up.

"Why didn't you have her discontinue her home remedy? It clearly isn't working."

"There was nothing in it that would interfere with the medication I prescribed. It should even give the boys some added relief. Mostly, it will make her feel better to be doing something for them." He snapped the chart shut. "What's next?"

His final patient of the day turned out to be an Amish woman with a badly swollen wrist.

Amber stood by the counter as Phillip pulled his chair up beside the young Mrs. Nissley. Her first name was Martha. She held her arm cradled across her stomach.

Phillip said, "May I see your wrist, please?"

Taking it gently, he palpated it, feeling for any obvious breaks. "Tell me what happened."

"The dog scared my *Milch* cow, and she kicked. She missed the dog but hit me."

He winced. "Sounds painful."

"*Ja.* That it is."

He admired her stoicism. "You're the first cow-kick victim I've treated in my career. In spite of that, the only way to be certain it isn't broken is to get an X-ray. Are you related to Edna Nissley?"

"Which Edna Nissley?"

He struggled to find a description since they dressed alike and seemed so similar. "She's an older lady. Short, kind of stout. Oh, she drives a gray horse."

"That is my husband's uncle's wife. The other Edna Nissley is the wife of my husband's cousin William. Little Edna Nissley is the daughter of my husband's youngest brother, Daniel."

"Okay." A confusing family history if he'd ever heard one. He glanced at Amber. "I'll need AP and Lateral X-rays of the left wrist. Mrs. Nissley, is there any chance you may be pregnant?"

"*Nee.* At least, I don't think so."

He looked at Amber. "Make sure she wears a lead apron just in case."

"Of course."

Ten minutes later he had the films in hand. Putting them up on the light box, he indicated the wrist bones for his patient to see.

"I don't detect a break. What you have is a bad sprain and some nasty bruising. I'll wrap it with an elastic bandage to compress the swelling. Rest it and ice it. I want you to keep the arm elevated. Is there a problem with doing any of those things?"

"Can I milk the cow?"

He tried not to smile. "If you can do it with one hand or with your toes."

She grinned. "I have children and a helpful husband."

"Good. Here's a prescription for some pain medication if you need it. See me again if it isn't better by the end of the week."

When Mrs. Nissley left he saw the waiting room was finally empty. A glance at his watch told him it was nearly four in the afternoon. More tired than he cared to admit, Phillip retreated to his grandfather's office and sank gratefully into Harold's padded, brown leather chair. If his seventy-five-year-old grandfather kept this kind of pace, he was hardier than Phillip gave him credit for.

After only five minutes of downtime, a knock sounded at his door. Sighing, he called out, "Yes?"

Amber poked her head in. "I have a ham sandwich. Would you like to share?"

His stomach rumbled at the mention of food, reminding him he'd had nothing but one cup of coffee since he'd left the house that morning. "I'd love a sandwich. Thank you."

She entered and whisked a plate from behind her back. "I thought you might say that."

He took her offering and made a place for the paper dinnerware on his desk. "Why don't you and Wilma join me?"

"Wilma has gone home."

"Then will you join me?" He held his breath as he waited for her reply.

Amber hesitated. It was one thing to work with Phillip. It was a whole other thing to share a meal with him.

He said, "Don't tell me you've never joined Harold for a late lunch."

"Of course I have."

"Then what's the problem? Afraid I'll bite or afraid you won't be able to resist stabbing me with a knife?"

"All I have is a plastic fork, so you're safe on that score."

"Good." He lifted the upper slice of bread and peered inside. "You didn't lace this with an overdose of digoxin, did you?"

"And slow your heart until it stopped?" She snapped her fingers. "Wish I'd thought of it. Then Dr. Dog could take over. Thanks for the idea."

Grinning, Amber left the room and returned to the

break room to get her half of the sandwich. It seemed Dr. Phillip had a sense of humor. It was one more point in his favor. The most impressive thing about him, good looks aside, was how he dealt with patients.

During the long, exhausting day he had listened to them. He discussed his plans of care in simple terms. And he was great with children. She liked that about him.

He could be a good replacement for Harold. If only she could change his mind about her midwife services.

Looking heavenward, she said, "Please, Lord, heal Harold and send him back to us quickly. In the meantime, give me the right words to help Phillip see the need the Amish have for my work."

With her plate in hand, she returned to his office. She saw he'd been busy clearing off another spot on the opposite side of the desk. She pulled over a chair and sat down. Closing her eyes, she took a deep breath then silently said a blessing over her meal.

"Sitting down feels good, doesn't it?" Phillip asked.

She nodded. "You can say that again."

"Is the clinic normally this busy?"

"We serve a large rural area besides the town. Today was busier than usual but not by much."

He took a big bite of his sandwich. "This is good," he mumbled with his mouth full.

"I picked it up at the café this morning."

"Okay, I have to know. Why is it called the Shoofly Pie Café?"

"You've never heard of shoofly pie?"

"No."

"Wait here." Rising, Amber returned to the break room and pulled a small box from the bottom shelf. Returning to Phillip's office, she set it in front of him with a pair of plastic forks.

He popped the last bite of sandwich into his mouth and cautiously raised the lid of the box. Swallowing, he said, "It looks like a wedge of coffee cake."

"It's similar. No dessert in the world says 'Amish' like shoofly pie. It's made with molasses, which some people say gave it the name because they had to shoo the flies away from it. It's a traditional Pennsylvania Dutch recipe but it's served in many places across the South."

"Interesting."

"Try some." She pushed it closer.

He shook his head.

"Are you a culinary chicken, Dr. Phillip?"

"It must be loaded with calories. I don't indulge in risky behaviors."

"That from a man who surfs the North Shore of Oahu?"

His eyes brightened. "You follow surfing?"

"A little." And only since Harold told her it was his grandson's favorite sport.

Phillip sat back and closed his eyes. "The North Shore is perfection. You should see the waves that come in there. Towering blue-green walls of water curling over and crashing with such a roar. The sandy shore is a pale strip between the blue sea and lush tropical palms. It's like no place else on earth."

"I'd like to see the ocean someday," she said wistfully.

His eyes shot open in disbelief. "You've never been to the seashore?"

"I once saw Lake Erie."

"Sorry, that doesn't count. What makes you stick so

close to these cornfields?" He picked up the fork and tried a sample of pie.

"I was born and raised in Ohio."

"That's no excuse." He pointed to the box with his fork. "This is good stuff."

"Told you. I was raised on a farm in an Amish community about fifty miles from here. My mother grew up Amish but didn't join the church because she fell in love with my father, who wasn't Amish. They owned a dairy farm. That means work three hundred sixty-five days a year. I don't think I traveled more than thirty miles from our farm until I was in college."

"What made you go into midwifery?"

"I always wanted to be a nurse. I liked the idea of helping sick people. Becoming a CNM wasn't my first choice. I was led to become a nurse-midwife by my older sister, Esther. You would have liked her."

Thoughts of Esther, always laughing, always smiling, brought a catch to Amber's voice. He noticed.

"Did something happen to her?" he asked gently.

"Unlike mother, Esther longed to join the Amish church. She did when she was eighteen. After that, she married the farmer who lived across the road from us."

"Sounds like you had a close-knit family."

"Yes, we did. Esther had her first child at home with an Amish midwife. Everything was fine. Things went terribly wrong with her second baby. The midwife hesitated getting Esther to a hospital for fear of repercussions. By the time they did get help, it was too late. Esther and her baby died."

"I don't understand. How would that make you want to become a midwife?"

"Because a CNM has the skills, training and equipment to deal with emergencies. There are a lot of good lay midwives out there, but as a CNM I don't have to be afraid to take a patient to the hospital for fear of being arrested for practicing medicine without a license. I can save the lives of women like my sister who want to give birth at home because they truly believe it is the way God intended."

"Had your sister been in the hospital to start with, things might have turned out differently."

He didn't get it. She shouldn't have expected him to. "Maybe, or maybe God allowed Esther to show me my true vocation among her people."

Amber helped herself to the small bite of pie he'd left. "My turn to ask a question."

"Why won't I allow you to do home deliveries? I don't believe it's safe."

She leaned forward earnestly. "But it is. Home births with a qualified attendant are safe for healthy, low-risk women. Countries where there are large numbers of home births have fewer complications and fewer deaths than here in the United States. How do you explain that if home births aren't safe?"

"The American College of Obstetricians and Gynecologists do not support programs that advocate home birth. They don't support individuals who provide home births."

"Is that for safety reasons or financial ones? I'm taking money out of their pockets if my patients deliver at home."

"You think the majority of doctors in the ACOG put money before the safety of patients? I doubt it. We could argue this point until we're both blue in the face. I'm not changing my mind."

Frustrated, Amber threw up her hands and shook her head. "This isn't a whim or a craze. This has been their way of life for hundreds of years. At least listen to some of the Amish women who want home births. Hear their side of the story. This is important to them."

All trace of humor vanished from his face. "What part of *no* don't you understand, Miss Bradley?"

They glared at each other, the tension thick enough to cut with a knife.

Suddenly, Amber heard the front door of the clinic open. A boy's voice yelled, *"Doktor, doktor, komm shnell!"*

She leapt to her feet. "He says come quick."

Chapter Five

Phillip jumped to his feet and followed Amber out to the office lobby. An Amish boy of about eight began talking rapidly. Phillip couldn't understand a word. He looked at Amber. "What's he saying?"

She shushed him with one hand until the boy was done. Then she said, "Their wagon tipped over in a ditch. His mother is trapped."

"Did he call 911?"

She gave him a look of pure exasperation. "How many times do I have to tell you? They don't have phones."

Running back to his office, Phillip grabbed his grandfather's black bag from a shelf beside the door. Returning to the lobby, he saw Amber had a large canvas bag slung over her shoulder.

He said, "I'll get the car. Try to find out from him how badly she's hurt and where they're located so we can get EMS on the way."

Taking the boy by the hand, Amber followed Phillip out the door and climbed into his black SUV. She said, "It's Martha Nissley, the woman we treated today. They overturned near their farm. It's a quarter of a mile from the edge of town. Should I drive?"

"You navigate and try to keep the boy calm. Is he hurt?"

She spoke briefly to the boy in Pennsylvania Dutch. He shook his head. To Phillip, she said, "I don't think so. He's just out of breath from running and from fright. Turn left up ahead and then take the right fork in the road."

Phillip did as instructed. He wanted to hurry but he knew he had to drive safely. He'd heard horror stories from his grandfather about buggy and automobile collisions on the narrow, hilly roads.

"There, that's the lane." Amber pointed it out to him as she was dialing 911 on her cell phone.

Topping a rise, Phillip saw a group of four men freeing the horses from the wagon. Both animals were limping badly. The wagon lay on its side in a shallow ditch. Phillip pulled to a stop a few yards away.

Turning to Amber, he said, "Make the boy understand he needs to stay in the car."

"Of course." After giving the child his instructions, Phillip and Amber got out.

Martha was lying facedown in the ditch, trapped beneath the wagon. A man knelt beside her. Phillip assumed he was her husband.

Only the broken spokes of the front wheel were keeping the wagon from crushing her completely. The rear wheel bowed out dangerously. If either wheel came off, she wouldn't stand a chance.

He knelt beside her. "Martha, can you hear me?"

"Ja," she answered through gritted teeth.

"Where are you hurt?"

"My back burns like fire. I can't move my legs."

His heart sank. "All right, lie still. We'll get you out."

"Where is my boy, Louis? Is he okay?"

"He's sitting in my car. I told him to stay there."

"Goot." She began muttering what he thought was a prayer. Amber scrambled down in the ditch beside them. Quickly, she checked Martha's vital signs. Then, to Phillip's horror, she lay down and wiggled as far under the overturned wagon as she could.

After a minute, Amber worked herself backward and Phillip helped her gain her feet. He said, "Don't do that again."

"Martha's bleeding profusely from a gash on her left thigh. I couldn't reach it to put pressure on it, but it's bad."

He wanted to wait for the fire department and EMS. They'd likely have the Jaws of Life to lift the vehicle. But if she were hemorrhaging as badly as Amber thought, time was of the essence. "Okay, we'll have to get the wagon off of her."

Phillip turned to the men gathered around. The one kneeling beside Martha rose and joined them. "I'm David Nissley, Martha's husband. We were afraid to move the wagon and do Martha more injury."

"You were right. However, we need to move it now."

Mr. Nissley pointed up the lane. "My boy, Noah, is coming with the draft team."

What Phillip wouldn't give for a forklift or at least a tractor…something he knew had enough power and wouldn't bolt in fright and pull the heavy wagon on top of his patient. He considered trying to use his SUV but there was no room to maneuver on the narrow road.

He said, "We need some way to brace the wagon in case that wheel comes off."

"We can use boards from there." Amber pointed to the white painted fence running alongside the road. An instant later, Mr. Nissley and the men were dismantling the boards by using their heavy boots to kick them loose from the posts.

Phillip watched the activity impatiently. "Once we have it braced so it can't fall back, we'll try pulling it off her."

A boy of about fifteen came racing down the road with a pair of enormous gray horses trotting at his heels. Sunlight gleamed off their shiny flanks as their powerful muscles rippled beneath their hides. They made a breathtaking sight.

The boy quickly backed them into position. They stood perfectly still as they waited for their harnesses to be hooked to the wagon. Feeling dwarfed by the massive animals, Phillip decided a tractor wouldn't be necessary.

He turned back to Mrs. Nissley just as Amber was once again working herself under the broken vehicle, this time with her bag. He caught her foot. "What do you think you're doing?"

Her voice was muffled. "Once the weight comes off her leg, someone has to put pressure on that gash. It's oozing bright red blood."

"You think it's a severed artery?"

"I do."

He didn't like the danger she was putting herself in. He let go of her ankle because he knew she was right. The weight of the wagon on Martha might be stemming the flow of blood. Once it came off, she could bleed out rapidly.

Mr. Nissley alternated between speaking comforting words to his wife, directing the men making braces and instructing his son on the best way to attach the horses to the rig.

In less than five minutes, they were ready. Mr. Nissley spoke briefly to his wife, then took the reins from his son.

The boy said, "I can do it, Papa?"

"Nee, das ist für mich zu tun."

Phillip looked at Mrs. Nissley for an explanation. "He said, 'This is for me to do.' If it falls back, he doesn't want my son blaming himself."

Another man called the boy over to help with the braces. Mr. Nissley coaxed the big horses forward. The wagon creaked ominously but lifted a few inches. The men standing by instantly moved in with the fence boards to prop it up. Squatting beside Amber's feet, Phillip prepared to drag her out of harm's way if need be.

The wagon inched upward with painful slowness, but finally Martha was free. Amber was already staunching the flow of blood with a heavy pad as the team dragged the broken wagon across the road. Phillip rushed to help secure the pad with a heavy elastic bandage. Amber was right. It was arterial blood. Martha would have bled to death if they'd delayed any longer.

The Amish woman was conscious but pale. Phillip said to Amber, "What supplies have you got in your bag?"

"IV supplies, pain medication, sterile drapes, suture, anything you'd need for a regular delivery. I'm going to start an eighteen gauge IV with Ringer's Lactate."

"Once that's done give her a bolus of morphine if you've got it. Martha, are you allergic to any medications?"

"*Nee.*"

All color was gone from her cheeks and her breathing was shallow. Phillip's concern spiked. She was going into shock.

"Amber, hurry with that IV."

"Should we try to turn her over?" Amber asked as she rapidly assembled her equipment, donned gloves and started prepping Martha's arm for the needle.

"I'd rather wait for EMS and their backboard." Phillip grabbed his stethoscope from his bag and listened to Martha's lungs through her back. They were clear of fluid. One thing in her favor.

Amber slipped the IV line in and started the fluids. Gesturing to one of the men nearby, she gave him the bag to hold.

After handing over the reins of his horses to his son, Mr. Nissley returned to his wife's side. Once there, he sat beside her and simply held her hand without saying a word.

Relief ripped through Phillip when he heard the sound of a siren in the distance.

Within minutes, the ambulance arrived on the scene, followed by a sheriff's department cruiser. Standing beside Amber, Phillip felt her grasp his hand as they loaded Mrs. Nissley aboard.

Louis jumped out of Phillip's SUV and raced to his mother's side. She patted his head and told him not to worry. One of his sisters took his hand and coaxed him away. Mr. Nissley climbed in beside Martha. Soon they were on their way to the hospital in Millersburg, red lights flashing.

Together, Phillip and Amber watched the vehicle disappear in the distance. As the adrenaline drained away, Phillip grew shaky. Looking down, he noticed Amber still gripped his hand.

Following Phillip's gaze, Amber realized her fingers were entwined with his. Suddenly, she became aware of the warmth traveling up her arm from where they touched. It spread through her body in waves and made her skin tingle like a charge of static electricity.

Their eyes met. An intense awareness rippled around them. Her breath froze in her chest. Her eyes roved over his face, soaking in every detail and committing it to memory.

Sweat trickled down his cheek. His hair was mussed, his clothes dirty. None of that diminished the attraction drawing her to him.

Behind her, someone spoke and a discussion about where to take the wagon broke out. She let go of Phillip's hand and wrapped her arms across her chest. It had to be the adrenaline ebb. Holding his hand surely wasn't making her weak in the knees, right?

He said, "I should follow them to the hospital. She's my patient, after all."

Amber struggled to get herself together. "We'll need to make arrangements for the family to travel there, too."

Phillip reached into his pocket and pulled out his cell phone. "Who shall I call?"

"Samson Carter has a van service." She gave him the number and after someone answered, he handed the phone to the oldest Nissley boy. When the boy was finished with the call, he handed the phone back and then gave instructions to his younger brothers and sisters. Already, the neighbors who had come to help were busy repairing the fence. The sheriff was interviewing them.

"Will these kids be all right?" Phillip asked quietly as they made their way toward his SUV.

Walking beside him, Amber nodded. "Yes. Word will spread quickly, and they will be smothered with help. Men will come to do the chores and women will come to take charge of the house. An Amish family never has to worry about what will happen to them in an emergency. It's a given that everyone in the Church will rally around them."

"That's good to know. Martha shouldn't have been driving that big wagon with her arm in a splint."

"She wasn't driving. Her son was."

"That little one who ran to our clinic?"

"Yes, but it wasn't his fault. Some teenage boys driving by in a pickup threw firecrackers under the wagon and spooked the horses."

He stopped. "Does the officer know that?"

Amber glanced over her shoulder. "I doubt it. They won't talk to the authorities about it. They will forgive whoever has done this. It is their way."

"Someone should tell the officer. Can you get a description of the vehicle from them?"

"No. They won't talk to me about it. I'm an outsider, like you."

"But you've lived here for years."

"That makes no difference. I'm not Amish."

The sheriff came over to them. Tall and blond, with eyes only a shade lighter than Amber's, he smiled at her fondly. "Hey, cuz. Can you give me any information about what happened here?"

"Hi, Nick. I can tell you what I overheard but not much else." She relayed her story while he took notes.

After a few minutes, he put his notepad away. "Thanks. Not much chance of solving this but I'll give it my best shot. How about you, Doc? Can you add anything?"

"Sorry, no."

Amber said, "Dr. White, this is Nicolas Bradley, my cousin. Nick, this is Harold's grandson. Phillip's taking over the clinic until Harold gets back."

The two men shook hands. Nick said, "Sorry we didn't meet under better circumstances. Ordinarily, this is a pretty quiet place. If you'll excuse me, I've got to get back to work. Amber, see you later."

As he went to finish interviewing the witnesses, Amber turned to Phillip. "We should get to the hospital."

Reaching out, he gently brushed some dirt from her cheek. "I should get to the hospital. You should get home."

Her heart turned over and melted into a foolish puddle.

Don't do this. Don't go falling for a man who'll be gone in a few weeks.

It was good advice. Could she follow it?

Drawing a quick breath, she forced her practical nature to the forefront. This rush of emotion was nothing more than a reaction to their working together during a crisis. It would soon fade.

With a logical explanation for her irrational feelings, Amber was able to smile and say, "Dr. White, you can't find your way to the grocery store. How are you going to find your way to Millersburg?"

He looked as if he wanted to argue. Instead, he nodded toward his car. "Get in."

Chapter Six

Phillip tried to concentrate on the road ahead, but he couldn't ignore the presence of the woman seated beside him. Her foolish bravery, her skill and quick thinking under pressure impressed him to no end. He saw now why his grandfather valued her so highly.

He said, "You did a good job back there."

"Thanks. It's not the first horse-drawn vehicle accident I've been to. Although there's usually a car involved."

"If they're so unsafe, why do the Amish continue to use their buggies?"

"It's part of being separate from the world. It's who they are. Turn left at the next corner. You handled yourself well. Your grandfather would be proud of you."

"I hope so."

"He means a lot to you, doesn't he?"

Phillip glanced at her. "Yes. More than you can know. How did you end up working for him?"

"Long story."

"Longer than the drive to Millersburg?"

Her smile slipped out. "Probably not."

"So tell me."

"When I finished my nurse-midwife program, I started looking for a place to set up my practice. I knew I wanted to do home deliveries among the Amish. I know you don't approve. Rest assured, you aren't the only doctor who feels that way."

"But my grandfather sees things differently."

"Yes. I began talking to Amish families at local farmers' markets and other gatherings. It was at the produce market in Millersburg that I heard about your grandfather. He's held in very high regard in the Amish community."

"He's devoted more than thirty years to these people. They should think highly of him. I'm sorry. Go on." He might not approve of their lifestyle, but he had to remember she did.

"I came to Hope Springs and explained to Harold how I wanted to practice. He was delighted. We both knew it wouldn't be easy building a practice for me, so he hired me to work as his office nurse, too. Those first couple of years he mentored me every step of the way."

"I envy you knowing him so well and working so closely with him." Surprised that he'd admitted that out loud, he checked for her reaction.

"Your grandfather has taught me so much. The Amish say if you want good advice, seek an old man. It is true—but don't tell Harold I called him old."

Phillip laughed. "It will be our secret. I wish I could get him to act his age."

"How is he supposed to act?"

"The man is seventy-five years old. He should be retired and enjoying his golden years."

She waved a hand, dismissing his assumption. "If Harold is able, he'll be back. We need him."

Phillip needed him, too. He'd longed for a father figure all his life. His mother's string of "Uncles" who lived
with them over the years hadn't filled that need. If anything, they made it worse. Meeting Harold in person had
finally started to fill the hole in Phillip's life.

All he'd wanted was to spend more time with his
grandfather. Their weeklong visit had been drawing to
a close far too quickly. Phillip's suggestion that Harold
think about relocating to Hawaii had been met with an
unexpectedly harsh response.

His grandfather had made it *abundantly* clear that
his place was in Hope Springs. Harold's anger seemed
entirely out of proportion to the suggestion. Phillip still
didn't know why. Was he wrong to want his grandfather
near him for what few years the man might have left?
Were these backward Amish more important than Harold's own flesh and blood?

Phillip glanced at Amber. "Harold has given enough
of his life to this backwater burg. He deserves a few years
of peace and relaxation."

Her smile faded, replaced by a puzzled frown. "I think
that's up to Harold to decide."

Phillip reined in his sudden anger because he knew
she was right. For the rest of the ride, neither of them
spoke. When they pulled into a parking space outside the
hospital's ER, Phillip turned off the engine. Sitting with
his hands still gripping the steering wheel, he said, "I'm
sorry I snapped at you. I have issues with my family but
that's no reason to take it out on you."

She stared at him for a long moment. The spark of annoyance in her eyes gradually died away.

"You're forgiven. Care to talk about what happened
between you and Harold in Hawaii? I'm getting the impression that something is seriously bothering you."

"So you're a mind reader as well as a midwife?"

She waved her hands back and forth. "Some people say I'm sensitive that way."

He chuckled at his own line being thrown back at him. "I appreciate the offer, but I've got to deal with things in my own fashion."

Reaching out, she laid her hand over his where it rested on the steering wheel and asked gently, "Are you sure that's best?"

The touch of her hand made his heart stumble, miss a beat and then race like it did when he was surfing into the pipeline at Oahu. And like being inside the curl of a giant wave, Phillip knew he'd just entered dangerous waters.

His next move could shoot him into the clear or send him headlong into a painful battering.

Amber meant her touch to be comforting, an offer of friendship. It turned into something more in an instant. The warmth of his skin sent her heart racing. She couldn't tear her gaze away from his. What was he thinking? Did he feel it, too, this strange and wonderful chemistry that sparked between them? On some purely feminine level, she knew he did.

The attraction both thrilled and frightened her. She'd never reacted to any man this way, and she'd been in a few relationships over the years.

The ambulance pulled out of the ER bay as they sat staring at each other. Phillip slowly withdrew his hand. Looking out the window, he said, "We should go in and find out how Martha is faring."

Embarrassment flooded Amber to her very core. Did he think she was making a pass at him? She'd only known him a few days. He was her boss. Nothing had been further from her mind, but that might not be the way it looked to him. She quickly opened her car door and got out.

Inside the ER doors, the charge nurse came to greet them. "Hello, Amber. I heard about your excitement."

"Yes. Give me pregnant women and crying babies any day. Gloria, this is Dr. Phillip White, Harold's grandson. Dr. White, this is Gloria Bender. She's the head of the ER department."

The two shook hands. Gloria said, "Dr. White, I received the notice just this morning that you've been granted privileges here."

"Excellent. Where is Mrs. Nissley and who's seeing her?"

"Dr. Kline was on duty when Mrs. Nissley came in. X-rays confirmed a spinal fracture. She's been taken to MRI to assess the complexity of her injury. The two of you did a good job stabilizing her in the field. It made our work much easier."

Wearily, Phillip rubbed a hand over his face. "Thanks. Do we know yet if her spinal cord is compressed or if it is severed?"

"I haven't heard. Dr. Kline started her on steroids to reduce any swelling. I know he wants to speak to you as soon as he's done. His plan is to take her straight from MRI to surgery where he'll clean out and close the gash on her leg. If she needs spinal surgery, she'll be airlifted to Akron." Glancing at her watch, she noted, "They should be finished in about thirty minutes."

"Thank you." He sighed heavily. Amber could sense his frustration.

Gloria returned to her office, leaving them alone once more. Phillip's face mirrored the same worry running through Amber. If Martha's spinal cord was severed, she'd never walk again.

He said, "Thirty minutes. Guess that leaves us enough time to get a cup of coffee."

"It's not gourmet, but the coffee in the cafeteria here is drinkable. Let me tell Gloria where we'll be and then I'd like to wash up first."

He smiled and looked her over. "Good idea. You've got grass in your hair."

"What?" she squeaked as her hands flew up and brushed at her scalp.

"Come here." He pulled her over and plucked the offending blades from where they'd lodged in her braid.

She kept her gaze riveted to the floor.

I'm not going to blush and babble like a teenage girl with a crush on the top jock. I'm a professional and I can act like one.

Phillip took a step back. "There, I think that's all of it."

"Thank you." Without looking at him, she made her escape to the ladies' room, where she splashed water on her heated face.

Staring into the mirror for a long time, she said, "I can't hide in here forever. I'm going to be working with the man. I've got to get a handle on my emotions." Standing up straight, she added, "Right? Can do!"

Bucked up by her personal pep talk, Amber exited the room.

Phillip also took the time to wash up and sternly remind himself that he and Amber shared a professional relationship. He couldn't allow it to become anything else.

Unfortunately, it was easy to forget that when he looked into her compelling eyes. Determined to stick to his professional standards of behavior, he left the washroom.

Amber was waiting for him but avoided looking him

in the eyes. Together, they walked out of the ER and took the elevator to the lower level of the hospital.

Stepping out, they walked without speaking down a short hallway to a wide set of double doors. Amber pushed one open to reveal a small, cozy room where a dozen round tables were covered with red-checkered tablecloths. Several Amish men sat at one of the tables near the back of the room. They glanced up, then resumed their quiet conversation.

Phillip said, "This doesn't resemble any hospital cafeteria I've eaten in and I've eaten in plenty."

"It is homey, isn't it?"

The smell of fresh-baked bread and fried chicken filled the air. A young Amish woman wearing a dark maroon dress under a white apron with a white organdy cap on her head stood behind the low counter.

Amber approached her. "Hello, Barbara."

"Hello, Amber. How's Martha Nissley doing?"

"She's still in surgery. Can we get a couple cups of coffee?"

"Sure. Have a seat anywhere and I'll bring some out."

Phillip realized he was hungry. The half sandwich he'd shared with Amber hadn't been enough to fill the void in his midsection. He pointed to a chef's salad under glass in the serving area. "Let me have one of those and give Miss Bradley anything she'd like."

"I'll take one of your wonderful cinnamon rolls, Barbara."

"Icing or no icing?"

"Are you kidding? The icing's the best part."

Phillip eyed her petite figure in surprise. "It's refreshing to meet a woman who isn't afraid of a few calories. Shoofly pie and now a cinnamon roll?"

Amber giggled. "Oh, Barbara doesn't put any calories in her rolls, do you?"

Smiling shyly, the Amish waitress shook her head. "Not a one."

While she went to get their order, Phillip led the way to a table near the back corner. As he sat down, the elder of the two Amish men approached him. Phillip recognized him as Martha's husband.

"I thank you both for your kindness to my wife today. *Gott* was *gut* to send you in her hour of need."

Phillip nodded. "You're welcome. I'm glad we were still in the office when your son arrived. He must have run like the wind."

"He wanted to help his mama. He felt bad about the accident but it wasn't his fault. Also, I want to tell you we are praying for your grandfather. He has done much for the Plain People hereabouts. We praise *Gott* for bringing him to us."

A lump rose in Phillip's throat, making it hard to speak. He had been harsh in his judgment of these people and he had been wrong. "Thank you."

Barbara arrived with their food. Mr. Nissley nodded to them and returned to his own table. After Barbara set the plates down, Amber asked her, "How is your Grandmother Zook doing? Is she taking her heart medication like she should?"

"Mammi is *gut*. She has more energy every day."

After the waitress left, Phillip watched Amber dig into her steaming roll. "Do you know everyone around here?"

"Not everyone, but many of the Amish. I delivered Barbara's two youngest sisters."

"It must be odd." He cut a hard-boiled egg in half and forked it into his mouth.

"What?"

"Knowing everybody. Having them know you."

"Why do you think that's odd?"

He shrugged. "It just is. Can I try of bite of your roll? It looks good."

"Sure." She pushed her plate toward him. When he'd cut himself a generous piece, she said, "I take it you've never lived in a small town?"

"I've lived in three or four. Just not for long."

"You moved around a lot?"

"Yes, you could say that." He couldn't count on both hands the number of schools he'd attended before his mother settled in Hawaii and he started college.

After taking a sip of coffee, Amber glanced at the large round clock on the wall behind him. "Gloria said thirty minutes. That was ten minutes ago. We should hear something soon."

He closed his eyes as he savored his sample of roll. "There are some very good cooks around here. Is it difficult working among the Amish?"

"It can be challenging. Many don't readily accept an English midwife."

Puzzled, he glanced at her. "English?"

"It's what they call anyone who isn't Amish."

"I used to think my grandfather's Amish stories were exaggerations."

She grinned at that. "Harold is a talented storyteller. I don't doubt he has embellished some things."

"The Amish really don't allow their children to go past the eighth grade in school?"

"That's true."

"It's hard to believe anyone in this day and age is opposed to higher education."

"They aren't opposed to it. They just don't want it for their children. They believe in on-the-job training for skills that will keep their family and community together. They aren't all farmers, you know. Many are successful small-business owners. Their work ethic and craftsmanship skills are second to none. Employers love to hire the Amish. They work for less and work hard."

"You sound like you approve of this."

She cocked her head to the side. "Don't you believe in freedom of religion?"

"Of course I do."

"Do you believe a person has the right to choose his own lifestyle?"

"Yes." He didn't like feeling he was in the wrong somehow.

"The Amish lifestyle *is* their religion. They do not separate the two."

Her intenseness reminded him of his mother's Pomeranian standing guard over his food dish. Phillip wasn't looking to get bitten. He'd had enough trouble for one day. "I defer to someone who knows them better than I ever will."

After they finished eating, they returned to the ER waiting area and were soon joined by Dr. Kline. Shaking hands with the big, burly man in blue scrubs, Phillip immediately had the feeling that Martha was being well taken care of.

"Good news. The spine isn't severed. A bone fragment is compressing it. That's why she can't move her legs. I've already placed a call for an airlift to Akron."

Dr. Kline continued with a description of Martha's injuries. Phillip conferred with him over some of her interim care and then left the hospital knowing she was getting the best possible treatment.

As he walked to his SUV with Amber at his side, he said, "My grandfather told me the Amish don't believe in health insurance. How are Martha and her family going to pay for her care?"

"It's true that they don't believe in insurance of any kind. If a man gets insurance, that means he doesn't have faith in God's protection. Whatever happens is God's will. On the flip side of that, they don't sue for bad outcomes. Such a thing is also *Gottes Wille.*

"As far as the Nissleys are concerned, the Church community will take up a collection for them. A notice will be sent to the Amish newspaper and donations will come from all over. Their bills will be paid."

Phillip had to admire people who cared so well for their own. While he thought they were some of the most backward people on the planet for refusing modernization, he had to admit that their sense of community was impressive.

The drive back to Hope Springs was made in silence. They were both too tired to make small talk. The only time Amber spoke was when she gave him directions to her home. It was nearly dark when he pulled up in front of her house.

She hesitated before getting out. Taking a deep breath, she said, "I'm glad you came to Hope Springs. We needed you."

"It's not the type of medicine I want to practice, but I'll admit it isn't boring."

Turning to face him, she asked, "What type of medicine do you want to practice?"

He sensed her unwillingness to leave, and it made

him feel good. "I want to practice cutting-edge medicine. I want the newest and best equipment and procedures available for my patients."

"We don't have that here."

"No, but you've got mighty big horses." That coaxed a tiny smile from her. She looked beautiful in the fading light.

She acted as if she wanted to say something else. Instead, she abruptly got out. She gave a little wave and said, "Good night, Dr. White. See you on Monday."

He watched her walk inside the white, narrow, two-story Victorian and felt a sharp sense of regret. He'd missed his chance to escape her dangerous undertow. He was well and truly in for a nasty dunking. Amber Bradley was as beautiful as the sea and every bit as dangerous to his peace of mind. Shifting his SUV into reverse, he backed out of her drive, determined not to think about her the rest of the night.

He hadn't gone half a block before the memory of her last little smile slipped into his mind and stayed there.

Chapter Seven

Beside Amber's front door, Fluffy sat waiting to get in. She picked up the overweight white cat. "How did you get out?"

A yellow tabby darted past her feet and raced down the steps. Amber recognized Ginger, her neighbor's cat. Apparently, she had broken up a feline tryst.

Inside her house, Amber put the cat down and flipped on the kitchen light. Crossing the room, she dumped her purse on the table. Fluffy began rubbing against Amber's legs. She picked up the big cat again and cuddled him close, taking comfort from his happy, rumbling purr.

"Did you see the guy in the car? This is nuts, Fluffy. I don't understand why I'm so attracted to that man. He's standing in the way of my life's work. One minute I want to strangle him, the next minute I'm wondering what kissing him would be like. What is wrong with me?"

Putting the cat down, Amber puttered around her cheery yellow kitchen. She had only one object in mind, to get so tired that she couldn't think about Dr. Phillip White anymore. On the one hand, she was furious with him for stopping her midwife practice. On the other hand, she was honest enough to admit she was deeply drawn to him.

Why, she had no idea. Sure, he was a good physician, but she'd met plenty of those. He wasn't the best-looking man she'd ever met. Close maybe, but looks weren't everything. Phillip had more going for him. Even if he didn't understand the Amish, he seemed willing to learn. Could he learn to love this place as she did?

She banged her hands on the countertop. "Stop obsessing about him!"

Her shout startled Fluffy and sent the long-haired white cat dashing out of the room.

"Great. Now you'll be stuck behind the sofa, and I'll spend the night listening to you yowl. One more mark against the oh-so-handsome Dr. Surfer Boy," she shouted after the cat.

Fluffy's ample girth made it impossible for him to turn around and get out of his favorite hiding place. He would simply yowl until someone moved the heavy sofa away from the wall or pulled aside the even heavier bookcase that blocked one end of his tunnel.

Ignoring her cat, Amber began vigorously scrubbing her kitchen sink. Unfortunately, the exercise only took a couple of minutes. Next, she washed the kitchen floor. Another ten minutes gone. By now, Fluffy had started mewing loudly. "All right, I'm coming."

After freeing her pet, Amber glanced at the clock. It was time to call Harold. Settling herself in her favorite chair, she dialed the long-distance number.

Each day she called and got an update from Harold to share with his friends. The entire county was praying for his recovery. He was improving slowly but not as quickly as he wanted.

As she listened to the phone ring, she wondered what she could tell Harold that wouldn't upset him. Should she mention that things in Hope Springs weren't the same without him?

It was true, yet if the accident hadn't occurred, Amber never would have met Phillip.

There was no way she was going to tell Harold she might be falling for his grandson. Even a hint of that would have him planting a whole garden of celery. She had stopped counting the number of times he'd told her she needed to find a husband and raise some kids of her own.

Like it was as simple as picking out a ripe melon at a roadside produce stand.

Amber wasn't opposed to finding a man who could win her heart and soul, but she didn't want one who lived in Hawaii. She wanted someone who loved this community the way she did.

When Harold answered at last, she knew what she would do. She'd fill Harold in on the things happening in Hope Springs. That was the truth. She could only hope that he wouldn't dig deeper.

"Keep it about the work," Phillip muttered as he entered his grandfather's house and closed the heavy oak door behind him. Sure, Amber was cute, intelligent, quick thinking and dedicated. What was so unusual about that?

"Okay, she's the kind of woman any man would want to know better, but she's completely off-limits."

Talking to himself about it sure wasn't a good sign. With the pressures of school and setting up his practice, the only relationships he'd had in the past few years were uncomplicated. Short-term relationships where both parties wanted nothing deeper than an occasional movie date, a dinner partner or someone to go surfing with. Amber was anything but uncomplicated.

He'd ruled out taking a wife a long, long time ago. Too many times as a kid he'd seen his mother weeping uncontrollably when her latest lover left her brokenhearted. He'd seen it often enough to know he'd never risk doing that to any woman. If his father had lived, would it have been different? He would never know.

At least his mother was happy now, or as happy as she could be. Her current husband, Michael Watson, was a good and decent man. After spending years with one toad after another, she'd finally found her prince. However, the emotional toll of her former life stayed with her. She suffered from a deep-seated fear of abandonment.

His mother met Michael when Phillip was a junior in high school. Michael provided the things she desperately longed for—safety, security, a nice home and a man who loved her. Although Phillip wasn't sure she truly loved Michael in return, she worked hard to be a good wife.

Phillip owed his stepfather a great deal. Without Michael's help, med school would have remained a pipe dream. Phillip never would have come to know God without his stepfather's gentle encouragement. That had been Michael's greatest gift, but one Phillip had let slide recently. He would remedy that while he was in Hope Springs.

He glanced at the clock above his grandfather's mantel. With the five-hour time difference, his stepfather should be getting home from work in another twenty minutes. That left Phillip enough time to check on his grandfather first.

After dialing the number to his grandfather's room in the rehab hospital in Honolulu, Phillip settled himself on the sofa and waited for Harold to pick up. When he finally did, he was anything but cordial.

"It's about time you called. How are things? I want to know what's going on."

"Things are fine. Like they were yesterday when I spoke to you. I came to Hope Springs so you would stop worrying. If you're not doing that, I might as well go home and get a little surfing in."

"And then what would become of my people?"

It was a good question. One Phillip hesitated to suggest an answer for, but he did anyway. "You could advertise for a partner or for someone to take over the practice."

"Ha! Don't you dare try to sell my practice out from under me. I'll fight you every step of the way."

"I'm not trying to sell your clinic out from under you. It's just that I've seen how much work is involved here. You're not a spring chicken anymore."

"There's a little crowing left in this old rooster. I'll be back there before you know it."

"I hope so. I really do. How's the physical therapy going?"

"They just like to torture people here. I might have fractured my skull but my mind still works."

"I can tell. What did you do today? Besides grump at the therapists." Harold chuckled. Phillip was happy to hear that sound again.

"I've been putting square pegs in round holes. I picked up numerous small objects and transferred them to different types of containers. Joy, joy. I went up three steps with my crutches but that was all I could manage. I can't seem to make my legs work right."

"Harold, that's a lot more than you could do a week ago. What did your doctor have to say?"

"He says I can't come home yet. What does he know?"

"He's one of the best in Honolulu. He knows a lot. You're making progress."

"Maybe so. It's just hard to be here and not there. Everyone writes, though. I've gotten lots of mail. So tell me, who did you see today?"

After describing the patients he'd seen in the clinic and their conditions, he recounted Martha Nissley's accident.

"Yes, Amber told me about that. It's a shame. Martha kept house for me years ago, before she was married. I don't know why some teenagers think it's fun to torment the Amish. They are such gentle people. They'd never hurt anyone. I will pray for her recovery."

"The family wouldn't make a police report."

"It's their way."

"That's what Amber told me."

There was a long pause on the line, then Harold asked, "How are the two of you getting along?"

"Fine." Phillip wasn't about to get into details when he wasn't sure what his feelings were.

"Yes, that's what Amber said, with exactly that same tone in her voice."

Phillip felt like a college freshman pumping his best friend for information about the cute girl in English class. "What did she have to say about me?"

"Nothing much."

"Oh." He hoped he didn't sound as disappointed as he felt.

"She did mention you were a nice-looking guy."

"She did?" That was promising.

"I think what she actually said was that you look a lot like me."

"Gray-haired and wrinkled? Oh, joy!" he replied with teasing sarcasm.

Harold laughed out loud. "Tell me what you think of her."

"Are you going to repeat this conversation to her?"

"Maybe."

"Then I'm not telling you a thing. Except she's a very good nurse. She's brave, incredibly foolish, stubborn to a fault and—"

"And what, Phillip?"

He searched for the right word but came up short. "I don't know. Sweet."

"She's pretty as the day is long, too. Don't you think?"

Now Phillip was sorry he'd gotten himself into this conversation. "I hadn't noticed."

The sound that came through the phone had to be a snort. "Didn't know you were thickheaded, boy."

"Okay, she's cute, but being a skilled nurse is a lot more important to me."

"She's the best midwife I've ever worked with."

Phillip decided it was best to avoid that topic. "Is there anything you need, Harold?"

"No, your stepdad has been here every day to check on me and bring me some decent food. Some of this Hawaiian stuff is good. Have you had poi?"

Phillip chuckled. "Many times."

He hesitated a moment, then asked, "Has my mother been to see you?"

"No, and she won't."

"Don't you think it's about time one of you told me what happened between you?"

A long silence followed Phillip's question. Finally, Harold said, "That's between her and me."

"It certainly affected me. We could have known each other for thirty additional years. I could have learned so much more about my father from you!" He was almost shouting as his resentment surged to the forefront.

Calmly, Harold said, "Phillip, you have to let go of your father. Nothing you learn can bring you closer to him or bring him back. All you can do is live your life for God and others and pray you will see him in heaven."

Sighing heavily, Phillip struggled to gain control of his raw emotions. It was hard to admit, but he said, "I know you're right."

"But you can't accept it."

"Not until I know why my mother kept me away from you all these years. Nothing you tell me can be worse than the things I imagine."

"I wouldn't be too sure of that. Tell Amber I'm thinking of her and hoping Sophie Knepp has an easy delivery. The poor woman has already lost two of her seven children before they turned two."

"You're changing the subject, sir."

"Yes, I am. Good night, Phillip." The line went dead.

Chapter Eight

By Sunday morning Amber had complete control of her emotions. Her feelings for Phillip were a silly infatuation and nothing more. Once she had spent a few more days working with him, this odd attraction would die a natural death. They had bonded because of their danger-filled rescue of Martha Nissley. It was a common occurrence between people in tension filled situations. Such intense emotions rarely lasted. Satisfied that she understood what was going on, she headed with light steps toward the Hope Springs Fellowship Church.

It was a beautiful summer morning. Late July could be frightfully hot in Ohio but the temperature had been mild lately. The sky was clear except for rare fleecy clouds floating past.

They reminded her of Fluffy. The cat who was most likely curled up at home asleep on Amber's blue sofa. A few white hairs on the furniture were a small price to pay for such a loving companion. Looking toward the white spire of the church silhouetted against the sky, Amber allowed the peace she always felt on this day to soak into her soul.

That peace lasted until she reached the church steps. At the top of them, Phillip stood talking to Pastor Finzer as he greeted his flock. Her hope to slip inside unnoticed was dashed when the minister caught sight of her.

"Amber, look who's joining us this morning."

She nodded in their direction and slowly climbed the steps. "Pastor, good morning. Dr. White, nice to see you."

Beaming a bright smile at the two of them, the friendly young pastor said, "We're delighted to have Dr. White as a visitor to our church while he's in town. I'm sure Amber will introduce you around, Phillip, and help you feel at home. Won't you, dear?"

"Of course." The smile on her face was fake. She hoped neither of the men realized it.

As they passed through the doors, Phillip leaned down and softly said, "Sorry about that. I know you didn't want to get stuck with me on your day off."

Was that how he was feeling? That he was stuck with her? She couldn't hide the sting of disappointment she felt. "Don't worry, Dr. White. I'll find somebody to pass you off to quickly."

"That wasn't what I meant."

Amber spied the perfect candidate sitting to the left of the aisle. Stopping beside an ample woman in a pink suit with a matching pink hat, Amber said, "Mrs. Curtis, how lovely to see you're feeling well enough to attend church today."

"Thank you, Amber dear. I struggled this morning. I don't know how I managed, but the Lord gave me strength."

"Mrs. Curtis, I'd like you to meet the new doctor in town. Dr. White, this is Gina Curtis. She's one of your grandfather's most frequent visitors."

"Dr. White, do have a seat." Gina scooted over to make room for him, her eyes bright with interest.

After he sat she said, "You know, I've been having this terrible pain in my neck. What do you think it could be? Oh, and my left heel hurts dreadfully when I stand up in the mornings. What can cause that? Your grandfather has never been able to figure out what ails me."

Amber felt a little ashamed, but if Phillip was going to be practicing in Hope Springs, he had to take the good with the bad. He might as well get his first meeting with Gina over with. She'd stop listing her ailments as soon as Pastor Finzer began the service.

Amber suspected the spinster harbored a secret crush on the good-looking blond preacher who was at least thirty years her junior.

Amber started to turn away, but Phillip grasped her wrist. "Please, sit with us."

It wasn't so much a request as a command. Unless she wanted to make a scene by twisting away from his firm grip, she had no choice. With another false smile in place, she said, "I'd be delighted."

He stood to let her in the pew. "I doubt it," he muttered as she slipped past and sat down

Gina leaned forward to look past Amber. "Isn't this cozy?"

"Very," Phillip replied, a twinkle of amusement in his eyes.

Amber took her punishment like a big girl. For the next ten minutes she listened to Gina's litany of complaints and answered the odd medical question aimed her way. Phillip got the brunt of them. Between Mrs. Curtis's painful heel, clicking knee, sciatica and the nervous twitching of her right eye that only happened during the late show, she put Phillip through his paces.

Amber glanced his way once and saw his eyes about to glaze over. Taking pity on him, Amber turned to Gina. "How is your nephew in Cleveland getting along? Didn't he have surgery not long ago?"

"Oh, honey, you don't *even* want to know the things that went wrong for Gerald. First, they checked him into the wrong wing of the hospital."

Before Amber had to hear the entire story, Pastor Finzer entered and the congregation rose to its feet. Opening her hymnal to the first song, Amber softly joined in the singing. She couldn't carry a tune very well, but the Lord only asked for joyful noise. Phillip had no such trouble. His deep baritone rang out clear and strong.

She had been surprised to see him standing on the church steps earlier. He hadn't struck her as a religious person. The moment the thought crossed her mind she amended it. *She* wasn't being very Christian this morning.

Determined to do better, she gave her full attention to the sermon when it started. Pastor Finzer spoke eloquently on suffering for being a Christian and the prejudice that existed in their own small town.

Once or twice, well, okay, four or five times, she glanced at Phillip out of the corner of her eye. He was listening intently, not fidgeting or yawning as a few others in the congregation were doing. It warmed her heart to know he was truly listening to God's word.

Since first meeting him, she had cast Phillip in the role of a villain because his decision played havoc with her career. He wasn't a bad guy, and she owed him an apology.

When the closing hymn began, he glanced down at her and smiled. She smiled back before she could stop herself. Clearly, it was time to admit that she liked this man in spite of their professional differences.

When the service ended and they began filing out, Amber saw her chance to separate Phillip from Mrs. Curtis when the woman stopped to compliment Pastor Finzer on his sermon. Grabbing Phillip's hand, Amber tugged him toward the corner of the building. Once they were out of sight, he pulled her to a stop.

"Miss Bradley, you should be ashamed of yourself."

"I am. I'm so sorry. She's one of our town characters."

"Remind me to look up late show twitching tomorrow so I can at least sound like I know something."

"Okay, but I warn you, it will be her left shoulder that hurts or her right thigh the next time you see her. Gina's ailments travel from one place to the next."

He nodded. "She must be lonely."

Tipping her head to the side, Amber said, "You're right. She is. Her family is gone or moved away."

"She needs a hobby or, better yet, a cause."

"A cause?"

"Yes, doing something for others helps diminish our own troubles."

"Very wise. Did Harold teach you that?"

"No, my stepfather. He got my mother involved in raising money for a women's shelter shortly after they were married."

"Sounds like a worthy cause."

"It is."

"What's your cause?" She was curious about every aspect of his life.

"Me? Getting my practice up and running and hitting the beach when I can."

Disappointed, she said, "Not very altruistic."

"Maybe I'm trying to maintain the stereotype of surfers as self-centered thrill seekers."

She raised her eyebrows. "I'm familiar with stereotyping."

Grinning, he said, "I thought you might be. If you must know, I'm on the board of a private relief agency called Surf Care. It's an agency that combats diseases inside the prime surfing areas of Indonesia."

"I've never heard of it."

"I'm not surprised. A friend of mine, a doctor named Jake Taylor, started Surf Care. Jake wanted to show our thanks to the people of Indonesia for allowing us to surf in their islands. Jake was horrified at the poverty and suffering he saw when he first traveled there. He quickly saw that ninety percent of the suffering could be prevented with simple medications."

"That's very noble of him, and of you."

"Thanks. We've been working together on the project since day one. To date, we've raised more than one million dollars for treatment teams and supplies."

He had surprised her once more. In a good way.

Tipping his head, he regarded her intently. "So what is your cause, besides mothers and babies?"

"I'm active in my Ohio midwifery chapter, and I foster animals for the local Humane Society."

"No kidding? Are you like a dog whisperer person?"

"No, I'm the woman with the food bowl."

He laughed. The masculine sound of pure joy sent a thrill straight to her heart. Still chuckling, he asked, "How many animals do you have?"

A number of other families were gathering in the area so they began walking toward a small footbridge that arched over the stream behind the church.

Amber said, "I've had as many as four. Right now I have one. A big white cat named Fluffy."

"How original." Humor danced through his voice. His smile brightened his often-stern face and made him even more attractive.

Shaking her head, Amber said, "I didn't name him. The shelter did."

"How does fostering an animal work?"

"The shelter has a limited amount of space. When they have more pets than they have room for, they send them to foster families. Sometimes they stay a week, sometimes a month, but they always go back and then to good homes."

They had reached the bridge and Amber stopped to lean on the wooden railing. The water in the small stream slipped like quicksilver over and around the stones in its race down the hillside from its birthplace in the bubbling spring that had given the town its name.

Phillip stopped beside her and leaned his forearms on the rail, too. "This is a pretty little spot."

"It's one of my favorites."

Amber kept her gaze on the water. How did he do this? How could he twist her around so easily? Each time they were together she started out annoyed with him, and for good reason. Then before long she was sharing a sand-wich or cinnamon roll or her favorite spot with him and wishing their time together wouldn't end. It was perplex-ing in the extreme.

He turned around and leaned against the railing.

"I've found some very lovely things to admire in Hope Springs."

She stared at her hands. "Now you're making fun of us. Hawaii is much more beautiful."

"Each place has its own unique beauty, just as each person does."

Surprised, she gazed up at him. "That's so true."

Their eyes locked, his darkened with emotion. "Yes. There are some very, very lovely things in Hope Springs."

He slowly lowered his head toward her. Amber knew he was going to kiss her. Her heart began to race.

Chapter Nine

It could have been the sun on her upturned face, or the wind that toyed with a few wisps of her hair at her temples that made Phillip want to kiss her. It could have been the secluded bridge with the sound of the brook babbling underneath and the smell of mossy rocks and pine needles in the air.

It could have been anything, but it wasn't just anything. It was those beautiful mermaid eyes looking up at him. Eyes a man could get lost in.

He bent toward her slowly, giving her time to realize what was happening. That was his mistake.

She leaned toward him a fraction. He sensed her willingness and tilted his head to meet her. Abruptly, she pulled back and took several steps away. A rosy blush flooded her cheeks with color.

She looked down, her hands fluttering nervously as she gestured toward the church. "I have to get going. I...I need to visit my clients today and tell them I won't be delivering their babies."

Spinning around, she hurried away from him and back up the grassy lawn toward the building.

Heaving a heartfelt sigh, he leaned against the rail again. "Phillip, old boy, you messed that up big-time."

Amber ran to her car without stopping. She didn't care about the odd looks being thrown her way by the congregation members still visiting near the church steps. She had to get away.

Why had he tried to kiss her? Did he think that was what she wanted?

Okay, maybe it was. The thought of what it would be like to kiss him had entered her mind, but she was sure she'd been careful not to let on. Hadn't she? Had he seen through her pretense? Oh, please, no.

Reaching the sanctuary of her blue station wagon, Amber quickly started the engine and drove home. When she pulled into her own driveway, some of her panic started to fade. She turned off the engine and sat in the quiet car. Leaning forward, she rested her forehead against the steering wheel.

How was she going to face him again? How was she going to work with him after this? She sat back slowly and pressed her fingertips to her lips.

What *would* it be like to kiss him?

Would it have been as wonderful as she imagined? Closing her eyes, she relived those moments. The way the sunlight brought out the highlights in his hair. The way his blue eyes matched the color of the sky beyond. She'd never forget the quiet way he said, "There are some very, very lovely things in Hope Springs."

She knew by the way he was gazing at her that he wasn't talking about scenery. He'd been talking about her.

"He thinks I'm lovely." No one had ever said that before. Reaching up, she turned the rearview mirror to see her reflection. What she saw couldn't be described as beauty.

She had nice hair when she kept the curl contained. It was a light blond color that was as common as dirt among the Amish communities. Her nose was short and turned up at the tip. A classical beauty wouldn't be caught dead with a nose like that. Her eyes were a muddle of blue and green without being either. If she had her way, she'd have dark, mysterious eyes like her friend Katie Lantz.

"Oh, skip it. I'm not lovely. He was playing with me."

Readjusting the mirror, she shook her head at her own foolishness. He was a good-looking man who found himself stuck in a tiny town with nothing to do. It was no wonder he decided to set up a flirtation to ease the boredom.

Well, she would not be his plaything. She was better than that. She would let him know the next time she saw him that he'd stepped over the line. She got out of the car and slammed the door shut.

With purposeful steps she marched toward her front door. When she reached the porch, she opened the door and saw Fluffy waiting by his food bowl. The cat let out a mournful meow. "Fluffy, you won't believe what that man tried to do today."

The cat meowed again and circled his bowl. It was clear he didn't care what was troubling his human companion. Tossing her purse on the kitchen table, Amber opened a cabinet and pulled out a can of cat food. As the opener ran, she tried to think of something scathing to say.

About what? About an almost, maybe kiss? She was more mature than that.

No. She wouldn't mention a thing to Dr. Phillip. She'd carry on as if nothing *had* happened because nothing had happened. He hadn't kissed her.

"That's right. He didn't kiss me."

As she knelt beside Fluffy's bowl, the cat rubbed against her legs.

Spooning the salmon-flavored food into the dish, Amber said, "Maybe he'd simply been leaning forward to scratch his knee, and I completely misread his intentions."

How embarrassing would it be to rake him over the coals for something he hadn't done or intended to do?

Banging the spoon against the edge of the bowl to get the last morsel out, she said, "Nothing happened and that's that."

Rising to her feet, she drew a deep breath. "Good. Now I need to let my clients know that I won't be seeing them until Harold is back or until I can change Phillip's— I mean *Dr. White's* opinion about home births. I'll go to work as usual at the office. I won't say a thing unless he says something because nothing happened."

Looking down, she said, "Do you hear me, Fluffy? Nothing happened."

The cat didn't stop eating to reply.

By Monday morning, Phillip had an adequate apology prepared and rehearsed. It had taken most of a sleepless night to compose, but he felt he'd achieved the right tone of repentance mixed with a touch of humor. Although he wasn't eager to deliver it, he found he *was* eager to see Amber again.

At eight o'clock, he left his grandfather's house and walked with quick steps the two blocks the office. As he rounded the last corner, he stopped in surprise. The parking lot in front of the office was filled with horses and buggies. A crowd of Amish people stood grouped near the front door.

Had there been some kind of epidemic outbreak to bring so many people in at once? As he walked toward the door, one elderly man with a long gray beard stepped forward and approached Phillip.

"I am Bishop Zook. May I have a word with you, Dr. White?"

"What's going on, Bishop? Are these people sick?"

"No. We've come today to ask you to reconsider your decision to stop Nurse Bradley from delivering our babies."

Phillip looked over the sea of Amish faces, both men and women, waiting for his reply. Many of the women had children at their sides or babies in their arms. None of them were smiling.

Amber had put them up to this. And to think he'd lost sleep planning to apologize for wanting to kiss her.

Shaking his head, he said, "I'm sorry, Bishop Zook. On this issue I cannot change my mind. The safest place for a woman to have a child is in the hospital."

The bishop eyed him silently for a long moment. "A high court of Pennsylvania upheld our right to have our children at home and to use midwives."

"This is Ohio, not Pennsylvania, sir."

"We are a peaceful people, Doctor. It is not our way to make trouble. Your thinking on this matter jeopardizes our way of life. We must be separate from the world, a peculiar people set apart by our faith. Home births are natural and in keeping with God's design."

"I understand and admire your religious principles, but I have principles of my own. They won't allow me to change my mind on this issue. Amber won't be delivering babies. I will. Your women will have to go to the hospital or birthing clinic in Millersburg."

"I am sorry you feel this way, Doctor. We will no longer be needing your services." Turning around, he spoke to the crowd in Pennsylvania Dutch, leaving Phillip clueless as to what he was saying. Whatever he said, it started a buzz of low conversation in return.

"What's going on here?"

Phillip spun around to see Amber standing a few feet away. "Oh, like you don't know."

"Sorry?" She stepped closer, a frown making a deep crease between her brows.

"Now you're going to try to tell me you didn't arrange this mob?"

"What are you talking about?"

He pointed to Bishop Zook. "Ask him."

"I will. I'm sure he'll at least be civil in his answers."

Walking past Phillip, she stopped beside the bishop. They spoke in low tones and in the language Phillip couldn't understand, but it was easy to see Amber was becoming upset.

Phillip crossed his arms over his chest and waited. If she hadn't arranged this, he might have thought she was pleading with the church elder. After a few more minutes, the bishop turned and walked away. One by one, the buggies drove out of the parking lot until only one man was left standing by the door. It was David Nissley, Martha's husband.

The look of indecision on his face moved Phillip to approach him. "Mr. Nissley, how is Martha?"

"Some better. She can move her legs now. Again, I wish to offer my thanks for your help that day. I say this now because I will not speak to you again." He turned away, climbed into his buggy and left.

Phillip turned to Amber. "What does he mean?"

"It has been decided that you are an outsider who seeks to disrupt their ways. They will no longer have communication with you or do business with you."

"I'm being shunned?"

Amber shook her head. "Only someone who departs from the teaching of the Amish faith is shunned. You're being avoided. I can't believe this. The Amish make up over fifty percent of our patient base."

"You can't believe this? Aren't you the one who arranged it?"

She rounded on him with a deep scowl. "Why would I arrange this?"

"Payback because I won't sign your collaborative practice agreement."

"Are you serious? You think I'd do this?"

"Did you or did you not visit your clients and tell them I stopped you from making home deliveries?"

"I did. But I didn't plan this."

They were still glaring at each other when Wilma drove in and parked her old sedan beside the front door. She got out and gave them a funny look. "What's going on?"

"I'm being shunned," Phillip said, daring Amber to correct him.

Wilma shook her head. "You can't be shunned. You aren't a member of the Amish faith."

He blew out a huff of pure frustration. "Okay, I'm being avoided."

Wilma looked at Amber. "For real?"

Nodding, Amber said, "For real."

"That's not good." Wilma pressed her hands to her face. "That's *really* not good. The Amish are half our patients. We aren't going to be able to make our expenses if they stop coming to the clinic. We're barely making it as it is. Why, we could be broke in a matter of weeks."

Phillip walked over and laid a hand on her shoulder. "Don't panic, Wilma. I'm sure this is a bluff on their part. People can't do without medical care."

Amber walked past them, shaking her head. "You underestimate the Amish, Dr. Phillip. Word will spread and the Amish will stop coming here. They've resisted changes that threaten their way of life for hundreds of years. They aren't going to make an exception for you."

Normally shy Wilma surprised Phillip when she shook off his hand and shouted at him, "You're trying to shut this place down, aren't you? Is that what you want? Well, you might get it. Then see how proud Harold is of you."

Chapter Ten

When Amber arrived at the clinic the following morning, the walkway was lined with Amish women, most of them her clients. Almost all of them had their children with them. Katie Lantz stepped forward. She held her four-month-old daughter in her arms.

Katie said, "We have come to show our support for you. Dr. White must allow you to continue your work among us. It is God's will."

Amber's hopes that Phillip hadn't arrived yet were dashed. She glanced toward the clinic and saw him staring out the window in her direction. His usual frown was back in place.

Turning to Katie, Amber reached out to touch Rachel's little bare feet where they stuck out of her blanket. "*Danki*, Katie."

Mary Yutzi, Katie's future sister-in-law, patted her round stomach. "We know you have a good place in your heart for our babies."

Another woman said, "You have done so much for us, Amber. We wish to give back."

Although she didn't know if their tactics were helping

or hurting, Amber was deeply moved by their support. Tears stung her eyes. Glancing around at the women, she said, "My thanks to each of you. I can't tell you what this means to me."

After delivering their promises of prayers and well wishes, the women left and Amber walked inside. Phillip, black coffee mug in hand, was still standing by the window.

He said, "You have a lot of friends."

"Yes, I do."

"Another group was waiting outside my house this morning. They gave me copies of the Pennsylvania court decision allowing their midwife to continue practicing in that state."

"It was a huge victory for their way of life. Many hundreds of Amish showed up on the courthouse steps in support of the midwife on trial."

"For practicing medicine without a license, I believe."

"Yes, but the court ruled—"

He threw up his hands. "I know how the court ruled. You still claim you had nothing to do with these assemblies?"

Fisting her hands on her hips, Amber shouted, "I did not arrange this! What part of that don't you understand?"

Shocked, he took a step back. "Isn't this out of character for the quiet and simple Plain People?"

Crossing her arms, she reined in her anger and tried to sound reasonable. "Not really. When something threatens their teachings or way of life, they are willing to take peaceful action. When the states tried to make them send their children to high school, many were jailed for refusing to comply. They took their case all the way to the U.S. Supreme Court and won."

Phillip took a sip of his coffee. Then without another word, he walked back to his office and shut the door.

Amber had no idea if he believed her claim or not.

By Friday afternoon, Amber knew the boycott of the clinic had become the talk of the town. Several non-Amish patients canceled their appointments to show their support of their neighbors.

None of the merchants in town wanted to upset the Amish by taking Phillip's side. Most employed Amish men and women and many of their businesses depended on either the Amish themselves or the tourists who came to see them.

Even the mayor made a visit to Phillip asking him to reconsider. He stressed how the Amish were good for tourism and how tourism was good for the entire community. As far as Amber could see, Phillip remained unmoved.

Reluctantly, Amber admired the way he stuck to his principles in the face of so much pressure.

By late afternoon on Friday, the one patient that showed up was Gina Curtis. After taking her vital signs, Amber listened to her describe her usual recurring, traveling pains and made a few quick notes on her chart. Phillip was waiting outside the door when she left the room. She didn't speak to him as she handed over the chart.

Still annoyed over the fact that he believed she had set up the confrontation with the Amish, she tried her best to ignore him. Seating herself on the corner of Wilma's desk, she noticed that Wilma's long face matched her mood.

"How tight are the expenses, Wilma?"

"We've had very little income since Harold left. Our checking account is almost empty."

"But the business has a reserve fund, doesn't it?"

"Only enough to run the place for another month. You know how Harold is about his charities."

"He'd give away the shoes off his feet."

"And his smelly socks, too." Wilma leaned forward. Worry set deep creases between her eyebrows. "What are we going to do?"

It was the same question that had been keeping Amber up at night. She gave Wilma the only answer she had. "We're going to pray and we're going to hold on until Harold gets back."

"What if he doesn't come back?"

"He has to. He just has to."

Amber heard the exam room door open and stood up.

Phillip came down the hall with a look of deep concentration on his face. "I want to set up an appointment for Mrs. Curtis with a rheumatologist. Is there one Harold normally uses?"

"Dr. Abe Snider in Akron," Amber said.

"Fine. See how soon they can get Mrs. Curtis in."

He started to turn away but Amber wanted more of an explanation. "Why are you sending Gina to a rheumatologist?"

He stopped and looked over his shoulder. "Because I suspect she has fibromyalgia. I think she's been dismissed as a crackpot for years instead of getting the workup she deserves."

Amber stared at him, aghast. "Are you insinuating your grandfather inadequately treated one of his patients?

How dare you. Harold loves the people of this town. He'd do anything for them."

Phillip stared at the chart in his hands for a long moment, then looked at her. "I'm not insinuating anything. I'm flat-out telling you. This woman has the symptoms of a real disease and she's been left untreated. Because she complains a lot doesn't mean she isn't sick."

Amber was speechless. Phillip handed her the chart. "I've ordered lab work, and I'm starting her on some medication for her pain."

Turning to Wilma, he said, "I want to see Gina back in three weeks to assess if the medication helps her. Please put her on the schedule."

With that, he walked away and left Amber staring openmouthed behind him.

"Harold is a fine doctor," Wilma stated emphatically. "He's been the salvation of this town for more than thirty years."

Still staring down the hall, Amber replied quietly, "Our only salvation is the Lord."

"You know what I mean."

"I do, Wilma. I'm going to be in my office for a while. Call me if you need anything."

Walking down the hall, Amber paused outside the exam room door. She heard muffled voices but she couldn't make out what they were saying. Turning aside, she entered her office and sat at her computer.

For the next thirty minutes, she did an extensive search for information on fibromyalgia. After reading through the literature and surfing the websites, she conceded Phillip might be right.

Some of the stories from patients were heartwrenching. Many had been ignored by their physicians and made to feel like they were crazy or simply attention seekers. After proper treatment many had drastically improved lives.

Turning off her computer, Amber sat with her chin in her hand and her elbow on the desktop. Surely Harold had done a proper workup on Gina Curtis before deciding she was a hypochondriac. Amber thought back over the years the woman had been coming to the clinic and couldn't recall one.

Had Harold been negligent? As hard as that was to accept, the idea stuck in Amber's mind and couldn't be dislodged. She idolized Harold. To know that he might have let Gina suffer all this time was enough to make her feel sick to her stomach. She rose from her desk and walked down the hall to Phillip's office.

His door was open. He was seated at the desk studying a spreadsheet on Harold's computer and making notes. He glanced up as she entered.

Looking around, she said, "I see you've made some inroads in taming the disorder."

Waving to the stack of folders on the corner of the desk, he shook his head. "I've still got a long way to go."

Picking up a journal that had fallen to the floor, Amber rolled it into a tight cone. "You know Harold will complain for months that he can't find anything."

"Then we will be even. I can't find anything in here now."

She walked over and sat in the chair across from him. "Have you had an update on Martha Nissley?"

"They were able to repair the fractured spine and she has recovered some use of her legs."

Amber chewed the corner of her lip, then asked, "Do you think Harold blew off Gina's symptoms?"

Phillip rubbed his forehead. "I don't know. I can't find evidence that he sent her for a workup, and Gina says she's only seen Harold. Ignoring complaints from people with this disease is more common that you think because of the vague and changing symptoms they have."

"So I've learned as I've been reading. I feel horrible about this."

Leaning back in his chair, Phillip gazed at her intently. "I'm not saying you and Harold are entirely to blame. These textbooks must be more than twenty years old. Many of the journals look like they've never been opened. I can't tell if he's done any online research."

Unrolling the journal in her hand, she stared at the cover. "He hates using the computer. He told me he'd rather have real paper in his hands. There were never enough hours in the day to catch up on his reading."

"I'm sure there weren't. From what I've seen of this practice, I can't imagine how a seventy-five-year-old man could manage it by himself."

Rolling his eyes, he gave her a half smile. "This week being the exception, of course. Has Harold ever tried to get a partner?"

"We had a young resident drop in last year and ask about joining us but Harold turned him down."

"Do you know why?"

Shrugging, she said, "I assumed Harold didn't think there was enough work for the both of them."

"That might be true now."

Amber gritted her teeth and decided it was best to get it out in the open. "When I said I had nothing to do with the meeting Monday, that may not have been the entire truth."

His eyebrows rose. "Oh?"

"I didn't organize it, but I may know who did. I have a friend, an Amish woman whose baby I delivered a few months ago. She told me she thought she could help by bringing it to the attention of the Church elders."

"And you didn't try to dissuade her?"

"I don't remember the exact conversation. I don't believe I encouraged her. She may have seen it differently."

He waved aside her confession. "What's done is done. My intention was to keep my grandfather's practice going in the event that he could return." He tapped the computer screen. "It looks like I may run it into the ground instead."

Leaning closer to see what he was pointing out, she asked, "What is that?"

"Harold's financial records."

"He did his financials on the computer? That's surprising."

"Wilma does them for him. I nearly had to threaten her with bodily harm to get the password."

"I can imagine. Is it as bad as she says?"

"It is. Harold has taken out a large bank loan using this place as collateral."

Amber was stunned. "Why?"

"It appears he bought a fifty-one percent interest in the Wadler Inn."

"He owns part of the inn? He never mentioned that. I know he takes most of his meals at the café. He likes their cooking. When did he do this?"

"Five years ago."

"Five years ago was when Mrs. Wadler's husband died."

"Maybe he was trying to help out an old friend's

widow. Anyway, the loan payment is what's hurting us the most."

Tapping the desk lightly with her journal, Amber gathered her courage and said, "I know this must sound like blackmail, but if you'd allow me to resume my deliveries it would solve a lot of problems."

He sent her a sidelong glance. "You're right. It does sound like blackmail."

Her shoulders drooped. "You don't know how important this is to them."

There had to be some way to make him understand.

Chapter Eleven

As Phillip stared at Amber, she suddenly jumped to her feet. "We need to take a trip."

"We do?" What was she up to now?

"Yes, we do. You need to meet someone who can tell you what being Amish really means." There was new excitement in her voice.

"I think I already know," he replied drily.

"No, you don't. You've been on the outside looking in. We're going to take a drive to an Amish farm about thirty-five miles from here."

"Won't they shun me, too?"

"They're not from the same church district as the Amish in this area. When I explain why we've come, they'll be happy to educate you."

"What if we get a patient in?"

"Wilma can call us and we'll be back in forty minutes or less."

This was a waste of time. "I don't see what good it will do. I'm not going to change my mind."

Crossing her arms, she gave him a challenging stare. "Okay, then why not come with me? What have you got to lose? The Plain People mean a great deal to your grandfather. Why not learn why?"

Phillip stared at her thoughtfully. What *did* his grandfather see in these people? Why had he chosen to remain here instead of living near Phillip and making up for thirty-four years of lost time with his only living relative?

Maybe Amber was right. Maybe it would be worthwhile to understand them better.

If his stepfather were here, Michael would be telling him to keep his heart open to God's whispering. Perhaps this was one of those times.

"Okay. I'm game," he admitted slowly.

Within ten minutes they were traveling northeast on a winding rural highway in Amber's beat-up station wagon. As they left the town limits, they had to slow down for an open-topped buggy. The high-stepping horse pulling it looked like a thoroughbred trotter.

When the opportunity arose, Amber pulled out and passed the buggy. Phillip said, "That animal looks more like a racehorse than a farm horse."

"He may have been on the track at one time. The Amish frequently buy trotters and pacers who can't make the grade on the racetracks. They've already been trained to pull racing carts. It's a short step to teaching them to pull the family buggy. The one we just passed most likely belongs to a young man of courting age. A high stepper and an open buggy are cool."

"The Amish version of a sports car?"

"Sort of." She smiled at him and he relaxed.

Glancing covertly at Amber as she drove, Phillip realized their on-again, off-again battle was starting to take its toll on him. He was friendless in a strange land.

Amber was the one person he'd met that he wanted to count as a friend—and perhaps even something more.

They continued down the highway, slowing occasionally to follow behind a buggy or horse-drawn cart until it was safe to pass. Outside his window he saw farm after farm dotting the rolling landscape of fields and pastures. For the most part, the houses were white and the barns were red. It was easy to tell which farms belonged to the Amish. The lack of power and phone lines was a dead giveaway.

After traveling in silence for a quarter of an hour, he turned in the seat to face her. "What should I know about the Amish?"

"Wow, there is so much it's hard to know where to begin. They immigrated to this country, mostly from Germany and Switzerland in the seventeen hundreds to avoid religious persecution."

"I thought they were Dutch."

"Because their language is called Pennsylvania Dutch?"

"That might lead a person to believe they came from Holland."

"The common explanation was that they were known as the Pennsylvania *Deutsch*, or 'German,' and that the word *Deutsch* morphed into Dutch over time. What they speak is a form of German."

"You speak it, too."

"It was spoken in my home when I was growing up."

"Was it hard growing up in an Amish community not being Amish?"

"Not really. Like most kids I accepted my home life as normal. I knew I dressed differently than my cousins and that I went to a different school. That didn't matter when we were playing together."

"Makes sense."

"Back to your history lesson. In nineteen hundred there were about five thousand Amish in America and Canada. Currently, there are over two hundred thousand. Ohio and Pennsylvania have the largest settlements. We have about three hundred seventy-five church districts among the dozen or so different types of Amish."

Intrigued in spite of himself, Phillip asked, "What do you mean different types? Aren't they all one religion?"

"Yes and no. They range from ultraconservative like the Swartzentrubers who live without gas, electricity or indoor plumbing and don't even allow cushioned chairs in their homes, to the Beachy Amish. They use electricity and drive cars. However, the cars must be black. They paint the chrome bumpers black so they don't appear 'fancy' or worldly."

"You're kidding, right?"

"Nope. If you're Amish and you must use a computer for your business and your church group doesn't allow it, you can join a more progressive group."

"Do they switch?"

"Not very often. Okay, here we are." She slowed the car, turned onto a gravel lane and drove up to a large, rambling white farmhouse.

An elderly Amish woman sat on a rocker on the front porch surrounded by three young girls of varying ages. They all had large pans in their laps.

The woman's face brightened into a big smile when Amber got out of the car. Putting her pan aside, she held out her hands. Amber raced up the steps and sank to her knees beside the woman. "Hello, *Mammi*."

"My English granddaughter finds time to visit me at last. I thought I was going to have to get a driver to take me into Hope Springs to look for you."

Phillip walked around the hood of Amber's car and stood beside the steps.

Amber laid her hand on her grandmother's arm. "I'm sorry. I will come more often, I promise."

"You must not forget us while you are out in the English world. Who have you brought with you? Your young man perhaps?" She eyed Phillip hopefully. He knew his face had to be turning red.

Amber giggled like a schoolgirl. The sound was adorable. "No, *Mammi*, don't go planting extra celery for me. This is Dr. Phillip White. We work together. Phillip, this is my grandmother, Betsy Fisher."

Betsy studied him with interest. "I thought your doctor was old, like me."

"This is his grandson."

Phillip stepped forward. "How do you do, madam? It's a pleasure to meet you."

"You will stay to supper, *ja*?"

"Unless we get called back for an emergency, I'd love to. I'm finding Amish cooking is full of hidden delights."

"*Gut!* Amber, your *Tante* and *Onkel* should be home soon. They've gone to market."

Amber glanced from Phillip to her grandmother. "I've brought Phillip here today so you can talk to him about Amish ways."

Betsy's eyes brightened. "What is it about our ways that you would like to know?"

"Many things."

She spoke in German to the young girls who were

watching the adults intently. The girls set their pans on the floor and went into the house.

Betsy looked at Amber for a few seconds, then said, "Go and help your nieces prepare supper, Amber. They have many questions for you about living in the English world."

"Yes, *Mammi*." Rising, Amber kissed her grandmother's cheek, then followed the younger girls into the house.

Turning her sharp gaze back to Phillip, Betsy scrutinized him long enough to make him squirm. Finally, she patted the chair beside her. When he sat down, she handed him a pan. "Have you snapped beans before?"

"No, but I'm a fast learner."

She chuckled warmly. "A man willing to learn a woman's task is a man I like. Ask your questions, Phillip."

Chapter Twelve

Amber visited with her young cousins in the spacious kitchen but kept an eye on Phillip and her grandmother through the big window overlooking the porch. Could her grandmother make him understand that the Amish weren't some strange cult but simply Christians that didn't separate their everyday lives from their faith?

She glanced at her watch. They had been out there for almost thirty minutes.

Taking a sip of tea that had been made for her, Amber blew out a long breath. If her grandmother couldn't make Phillip see how important having a home birth was for an Amish woman, Amber didn't know who could. She glanced out the window again and saw the rocker was empty. Her grandmother and Phillip were nowhere in sight.

"Is he your *boo-friend*?" Lilly, the youngest cousin asked.

Turning her attention back to the three girls ranging in age from seven to twelve who were seated around the table with her, Amber shook her head. "No. He is most definitely not my boyfriend."

The girls were like stair-step carbon copies of each other with blond hair, inquisitive blue eyes and ready smiles for the English cousin they rarely saw.

"Mammi Fisher fears you will become *en alt maedel.* Will you?" Ruth, at twelve, was in charge of her younger sisters while their parents and brothers were gone.

Amber summoned a smile. Trust kids to ask the most embarrassing questions. "If I find the right man, I'll get married someday."

"Are there no good English men? My friend Kara's *dat* needs a new wife. Kara's *mamm* died last year. Kara has only four brothers and sisters." Ruth looked hopeful.

"Please tell Kara I'm sorry for her loss but I'm not interested in getting married right now. Besides, I'm not Amish. Kara's *dat* would not marry me."

"Mammi says you could be Amish if *Gott* wished it." Rhoda, the nine-year-old, left the table to check on the roast simmering in the oven. The mouthwatering smells of perfectly seasoned beef with roasting carrots and onions filled the kitchen and set Amber's stomach rumbling.

She said, "I believe I'm following the path He has chosen for me."

The door opened and Betsy came in, followed by Phillip. He had three large pans full of snapped beans stacked in his arms. Amber jumped up to help him by taking one. "This is the trouble with visiting my family. They find work for everyone."

"I don't mind. I can add bean snapper to my résumé now." He was smiling and seemed less tense than he'd been at the start of this journey.

After helping him set his burdens on the counter,

Amber showed him where to wash up, then waited for him in the living room.

When he returned, she gestured to an empty chair. "Was my grandmother able to answer your questions?"

"She's a very wise woman. Do you know she is worried about you? She wishes you lived closer to home so she could see you more often." There was a touch of longing in his voice that Amber didn't understand.

"I know she worries about me. She doesn't understand I have my work and I love what I do. The Amish view being a wife, a mother and a helpmate to her husband as the only roles for women. Has she helped you see how important my work is?"

"She gave me a lot to think about."

The sound of a buggy coming into the yard sent the girls scurrying outside to help. Amber and Phillip were soon engulfed in introductions as she presented her mother's youngest sister, Maryanne, and her stoic husband, Tobias. While he and his two teenage boys stayed to visit with Phillip, it was easy to see they weren't entirely comfortable with an outsider in their home. When the conversation lagged, Amber leaned over and whispered to Phillip, "Do you like baseball?"

He gave a slight nod.

"So does Tobias," she said with a nod in his direction.

Giving her a thankful wink, Phillip straightened on the sofa and asked, "How do you think the Cleveland Indians will do this year?"

Tobias's face turned bright red. His oldest son sat forward in his chair. "Their pitching staff is deep and they can field a ball. I think they'll do well this year."

"Nee." Tobias shook his head. "They've got good hitters but no consistency."

The conversation quickly turned to local Amish teams and then to the sport Phillip enjoyed. He tried to explain surfing, but it was clear the idea of zipping along in front of a wave on a long board seemed silly to these stoic men. Fortunately, Maryanne came in to announce that supper was ready.

When everyone was seated in the kitchen, Tobias clasped his hands together at the head of the table. The entire family did the same and closed their eyes for his silent blessing over the meal.

He cleared his throat when he was finished. It signaled everyone to begin serving themselves and passing the food to their guests.

For Amber, watching Phillip enjoy her family's home cooking made the trip worthwhile. The roast, fork-tender, was done to perfection, as were the warm dinner rolls served with homemade strawberry jam and fresh butter.

Phillip sat beside Lilly. She watched his every move with wide eyes, especially when he began laying a few of his string beans aside at the edge of his plate. After careful examination of each bean, he chose to eat some and save some. Finally, it was too much for her.

"What are you doing? Are de beans *faul*?" Lilly eyed her own critically.

"Bad," Amber translated.

Pointing to his stack with his fork, Phillip said, "These are my friends. I met them today when I was snapping with your grandmother."

A few chuckles came from the adults at the table, including Amber.

Lilly looked at him in disbelief. "You can't be friends with a bean."

"I can't?"

"*Nee*, and you can't tell 'em apart, neither."

"Are you sure?" He picked up one. "This looks an awful lot like one I snapped today."

"I'm sure."

Phillip tossed the bean in his mouth. "Well, he tastes good, even if he was my buddy."

Lilly put her hands on her hips. "Are you funning me?"

Smiling, he nodded. "*Ja*, just a little."

Lilly looked at her papa. *"Der Englischer ist ab im kopf."*

That made everyone laugh. Amber, seated across from Phillip, explained. "She said you are off in the head. Crazy."

Phillip laughed, too.

When the meal was nearing its end, Betsy brought an applesauce cake to the table. Phillip held up his hand. "It smells wonderful, but I'm too full. Thank you, no."

Cutting a slice, she placed it on his plate. "You must try this. It is my special recipe."

Sighing, he lifted his fork and took one small bite. His eyes grew as round as silver dollars. Swallowing, he said, "This is the best stuff I've ever had."

Seeing her grandmother's delight, Amber was glad she had talked Phillip into coming here.

Later on the way back to Hope Springs, they traveled in companionable silence, both too stuffed to need conversation. The setting sun painted the sky with bands of gold and turned the bottom of the clouds a beautiful pink. When they passed a small cornfield, a flock of black birds rose in unison and wheeled across the sky, circling back and coming to rest again in the place they'd left.

Amber watched them settle in her rearview mirror and

knew she was like those birds. No matter where she traveled in life, she would always come back to this place. It saddened her to think that Phillip would be flying away and might never return.

As they were nearing the outskirts of Hope Springs, he said, "I had a wonderful time today."

"I'm glad."

"Meeting your family has changed my perception of the Amish in many ways."

"For the better or for the worse?"

"For the better. But I haven't figured out one thing."

"What?"

"Without TV or radio, how do they keep up on the baseball scores?"

Amber started giggling. "The Amish do love baseball. You'll find games being played in all the districts during the summer. While interest in such worldly things is forbidden, you can find many of the young boys gathered around a radio in someone's store when a professional game is on, with the occasional elder shopping near by. The local newspapers have a sports section for those not willing to risk the censure."

"Ah."

"Dr. White—"

"Please, call me Phillip."

"Very well, Phillip."

"I know what you're going to ask. I'm afraid the answer is still no."

Deflated, Amber didn't know how to respond. She was out of arguments. Driving into the clinic parking lot, she stopped the car and turned toward him. "I'm still glad you enjoyed your visit with my family."

"They have a special charm, don't they? Not only

your family but all the Amish. They coexist peacefully in a world that is anything but peaceful. They turn their backs on the basic modern inventions most Americans can't live without, yet they thrive and are happy in their small world."

"Everything they do, everything in their daily lives, is a direct reflection of how they interpret the Bible."

"It's very thought-provoking. Your grandmother's explanation for why they don't use electricity made a lot of sense."

"I imagine she said if electricity comes to a house then all sorts of things come with it, things that pull a family apart. Instead of spending the evening together, they turn on the TV and tune out what is happening around them. Another person may go away to listen to the radio or use a computer. Still another chats on the phone instead of with the family."

"Right, and before long it isn't a family anymore. It has become a group of strangers living in the same house. I've seen the truth of that in my own life, but I still couldn't live the way the Amish do."

"Nor could I, but my respect for their culture is bone-deep."

After a long pause, he said, "I see you inherited your wisdom and strength from your grandmother."

Looking down, Amber shook her head. "I'm not sure I have wisdom, but I do have stubbornness."

"I've noticed, but you are passionate, too, in your defense of these people. I think that's a rare thing."

His soft tone made her look up. When she did, he reached out and gently touched her cheek. "Thanks for a great evening."

Blushing, she shrugged. "And I didn't even have to cook."

Don't get sappy. Don't read more into his touch. Don't think about kissing him. He's your boss.

Looking away, she noticed a light still on in the clinic. "Wilma must be working late."

He withdrew his hand. "Does she do that often?"

"Once a month or so she stays late to catch up on filing and to get old charts ready to be shipped to the storage facility."

"Maybe we should give her a hand after goofing off most of the day."

"Maybe we should." Anything to escape the close intimacy of sitting in the car with him. The scent of his sandalwood cologne stirred her, making her anxious to get away.

Quickly, she pushed open the car door and got out. As she headed for the clinic, he fell into step beside her. When they entered, they found Wilma sealing several cardboard boxes with packing tape. Her disapproval when she caught sight of them was all too easy to read.

Amber felt like a teenager who'd been caught coming home after curfew.

Phillip didn't look troubled in the least. Glancing at the files stacked on her desk and the number of boxes, he said, "I didn't know you had this much work to do. You shouldn't have to work late."

"I've been managing this office for thirty-four years. Your grandfather never complained about my working late."

"I'm not complaining. I hate to see you doing this by yourself. You should have called us to come back."

"Then you should keep your cell phone turned on."

"What?" Reaching for the phone in his pocket, he lifted it up to the light. "It's dead. Wilma, I'm so sorry. Did we have patients? You should have gotten me by calling Amber."

"No patients, just phone calls."

As if on cue, the telephone on the desk rang. She answered it, spoke briefly, then held it out toward Phillip. "It's your grandfather. Again. And he's not happy."

Chapter Thirteen

Phillip picked up the phone. "Harold, is something wrong?"

"I'll say there is! What on earth do you think you're doing, running my practice into the ground?"

Phillip held the phone away from his ear until the shouting decreased in volume. It was then he caught Wilma's self-satisfied smirk. When she realized he was staring at her, she began working industriously.

Speaking into the phone once more, Phillip said, "Harold, I'd rather have this conversation in my office. I'm going to put you on hold."

Some muttering started. Phillip ignored it and pushed the button. Amber moved to stand beside him, a look of worry clouding her eyes. "Is he all right?"

"Once he's finished reading me the riot act, I think he will be."

"Do you think he's heard about the Amish avoiding us?"

"That would be my guess. Go home, both of you. I'll lock up."

"But I have work to finish," Wilma said.

He scowled in her direction. "It can wait."

"Very well." Rolling her eyes, she gathered her purse and headed for the front door.

His annoyance faded as he transferred his gaze to Amber. "You go home, too. I can handle this."

"Are you sure?"

He wasn't. He wanted her to stay. He wanted her help in calming Harold. He just wanted her near him.

For a moment, he wavered, but in the end realized this trouble was of his own making. His principles were under fire. He was the one who needed to face the music.

"Go on home, Amber. I'll be fine."

Amber left the building reluctantly. Looking over her shoulder, she said, "I hope Harold isn't too upset."

"Oh, he is." Wilma confirmed Amber's fears.

"You talked to him?"

"Yes. Someone had let him know how things were being handled here. I spoke the truth when he asked me about it."

"You told him we were being boycotted? Why would you do that? You know he needs to rest and recuperate."

Wilma dismissed Amber's concern with a wave of her hand. "Harold already knew. I just wish Surfer Dude Doc had never found Harold. Things were fine the way they were. Don't worry, Amber. I have a feeling you'll be seeing patients again in no time."

Wilma got into her car and drove off, leaving Amber staring after her. Torn between leaving and staying to hear what Phillip had to say, Amber decided it was best to go home. Phillip and Harold deserved their privacy. She drove back to her house with a million questions swirling through her brain.

When she reached home, the cat greeted her at the door. As usual, Fluffy was more interested in his bowl being filled than granting affection. Keeping his mistress company went by the wayside when there was kibble available. When his belly was full, he'd be all about purring and wanting attention.

Tossing her handbag on the dining room table, Amber checked her message machine. It showed a big fat zero. It seemed she wasn't as popular as Dr. White.

In the kitchen, she put the kettle on and grabbed a box of tea from the cupboard. She was pouring the hot water into her cup when her doorbell rang.

When she opened the door, she saw Phillip standing on her steps. In her heart, she had been hoping he would come.

Looking tired and frustrated, he said, "I didn't know where else to go."

She took a step back. "Come in. I just made some chamomile tea. Would you like some?"

"Sounds great, thank you." He followed her into the kitchen and took a seat on one of the bistro chairs at her small round glass table near the bay window.

Fluffy came over to investigate the new visitor. Purring loudly, he wound in and around Phillip's ankles. Phillip picked him up and scratched behind his ears, a maneuver Fluffy loved.

"If he bothers you I can put him up." Amber fixed Phillip his tea and carried it to him.

"No, I like cats. Is this the well-named Fluffy?"

"It is. Of all the animals I've fostered, I like him the best."

Handing Phillip his cup, she sat down opposite him. "What did Harold have to say?"

Phillip put Fluffy on the floor. "The gist was that if I can't run his clinic any better than this, I need to go back where I belong."

"That was harsh and not like Harold."

Propping his elbows on the table, Phillip said, "I spoke to his primary doctor after Harold hung up on me. His doctor says he's been improving rapidly when he isn't worried about his patients here. His doctor and I are both afraid this may trigger a setback."

"Oh, no. I was worried about that, too."

"So you weren't the person who called and updated him on our troubles."

Scowling, she retorted, "No."

"I didn't think so."

Somewhat mollified, Amber said, "It wasn't Wilma, either."

"Rats. She was at the top of my list."

"It doesn't matter who called him."

"Maybe not, but I'd like to find out who it was."

"If you leave, we'll go under anyway."

"It seems we can't stay afloat with or without me. I came here to help my grandfather. I owed him that much. I'm even beginning to understand why he feels so protective of these people, why he loves the simplicity and peaceful lives they lead. But instead of helping him out, I've made things worse."

She wanted to take Phillip's hand, to reach out and hold him and offer him comfort, but she didn't dare. She had no idea where such a move would lead. Her attraction to this man was simply too strong. The last thing she wanted was for him to find out how she felt.

After taking a sip of her tea, she asked, "What are your plans? Will you leave?"

"That may depend on you."

Taken aback, she frowned. "What do you mean?"

He hesitated and suddenly she knew. Happiness surged through her veins. "You're going to sign a collaborative practice agreement with me."

"Yes, but before you start doing the happy dance, I've got a few restrictions."

Her scowl came back. "Such as?"

"I'll allow home births as long as I'm in attendance. If I'm going to be ultimately responsible for these women and their babies, I want to be there."

This was the last thing she expected. "Let me get this straight; I can do home deliveries, but you have to be there?"

"Yes."

"What about my prenatal and postnatal visits, the birthing classes I hold here and my seeing women at the clinic?"

"All those things can continue. After every delivery, I want to see both mother and baby at the clinic within two days."

"Harold liked to see them at two weeks unless there were problems. Remember, these women have to come by horse and buggy, not in a comfortable car."

"All right, I'll compromise and say one week."

Rising, she carried her cup to the sink and poured out her tea. "What makes you think you're more capable of delivering a baby than I am?"

"I'm an MD."

Spinning around, she glared at him. "How many babies have you delivered?"

"Fifty-four."

"Fifty-four compared to my five hundred and two.

You're asking me to give up my autonomy, to project the image that I can't do my job. Why would I want you tagging along?"

"So that you *can* do your job. Being a midwife is what you love, isn't it? I'm offering you the opportunity to get back to it."

Crossing her arms, she leaned back against the sink. "*Will* you let me do my job? Or will you interfere if you see something you don't like?"

"You can do your thing as long as no lives are endangered. If we can't agree on this, it won't matter anyway."

He was right. Amber considered her options. If she didn't work with Phillip, she would remain out of business until Harold returned. *If* he returned.

She had to admit she'd known for some time that Harold needed a partner. He was getting on in years. Finding another doctor who allowed home deliveries would take time. Time she would not have if the clinic went under.

Staring at the tips of her shoes, she said, "Dr. White, I accept your proposal under one condition."

"What's that?"

She looked up. "That you begin searching for someone to take over the practice in the event Harold can't return."

"I've been doing that."

"I don't mean temporary help."

"You mean someone with the same Amish-friendly philosophy that Harold has?"

"Yes."

"I can't guarantee we can find someone or that he or she will permit home deliveries."

"I'll face that when I come to it. This town needs a full-time doctor."

They were both silent for several long seconds. Amber

suspected they were thinking the same thing. She asked, "Shall we arm wrestle to see who gets to mention this to Harold?"

A touch of humor glinted in Phillip's eyes. "I'm good with that."

"I was kidding."

"I'm not."

She leveled her most serious gaze at him. "Your mission, Dr. White, should you accept it, is to convince your grandfather that he needs a partner."

"Will this message self-destruct in five seconds?"

"No. I will be here to remind you constantly that God never gives us more than we can bear." A smile tugged at the corner of her lips.

"I still think the suggestion would be better coming from you."

"No."

He crossed his arms. "From both of us then."

"Maybe, but you first," she insisted.

Rolling his eyes, he said, "I've already mentioned something like that once."

"And how did that go over?" she asked with interest.

He shook his head. "Not well."

Her smile vanished. "You'll simply have to keep after him. If he doesn't agree, our clinic could be without a doctor in a few more years. I pray that doesn't happen for a long time, but I have to be practical."

"I'm not sure you know what you're asking me to do."

Chapter Fourteen

Phillip knew Amber was right. Harold needed to start looking for a partner or someone to replace him. Since their last conversation on the subject ended with Phillip accidentally running Harold down with his car, he wasn't eager to broach that subject again. His relationship with his grandfather was tenuous at best. It might not survive many more blowups. And he wanted it to survive.

Amber said, "If you are going to be seeing my patients, you need to get up to speed on their cases. I'll get their files for you."

He hated giving in on this. He'd hate himself more if Harold had a serious setback following his angry outburst tonight. It had never been Phillip's intention to ruin Harold's health, his business or his standing in the Amish community. Yet in the past month he had accomplished just that.

Coming out of her office, Amber handed Phillip a heavy box. "If you look at my outcomes, you'll see how safe giving birth at home is for low-risk pregnancies."

He shook his head. The woman did not give up.

"You've won. What more do you want? Is that everything?" He gestured toward the box.

"Yes, even those patients I sent to the hospital because of complications. What I want is for you to accept what I do. Wait a minute. Before you leave, let me get a few other things for you."

She sat down at her desk and booted up her computer. A few minutes of searching gave her a dozen articles in favor of home deliveries with qualified nurse-midwives in attendance. Handing them to him, she said, "If you won't believe me, maybe you'll believe the data from other experts in the field. Say you'll at least read these."

He looked at the loaded box he held. "Sure, in my spare time."

"It won't be that bad. I've put the charts of the women who are due first on the top."

"Good. So, how do we get the word out?"

"It won't take long. I'll make a few calls."

He cocked his head to the side. "I thought you said they don't use phones."

"No, but the businesses they use do. We can start by putting a notice in the paper and notes up at the grocery and feed stores."

"I can see the headlines tomorrow. Dr. Phillip White Crumples Under Pressure."

Her gaze turned sympathetic. "I realize you're doing this only because Harold insisted, but I do want to thank you."

It was hard to resist her when she was being nice. "I'll admit I've been curious about how you handle the whole thing at someone's home."

"I'm sure your questions will be answered within a

few days. I have women due the end of this week and two due the following week."

He patted the top of the box she'd given him. "Then I'd better get my homework done."

"If you have any questions I'll be happy to answer them. I plan to make this very easy on you." They walked together to her front door.

"Why, after the grief I've given you so far?"

"Because I believe in what I do, and I want you to feel the same way. Birth at home is a beautiful, spiritual experience."

He thought simply looking into her eyes was a beautiful, spiritual experience. He stopped trying to kid himself. He was falling hard for this woman.

The last thing he'd expected to find in Ohio was someone like Amber Bradley. He deeply admired her grace, her humor, her dedication to the Amish people, her skill as a nurse and her profound faith.

Leaving Hope Springs was going to be much harder than he'd anticipated.

It didn't take long for word to get around that Amber was back in business. The first person Amber told was her friend Katie. After several moments of rejoicing in the lobby of the Wadler Inn, Katie declared that she'd be happy to pass on the news.

On Monday afternoon, Bishop Zook arrived at the clinic and had a brief chat with Phillip. Amber was not included. Phillip looked surprised by the fact that she wasn't being asked to sit in. She wasn't. Men dominated Amish society. Only men held Church offices and could work outside the home. Unmarried women could hold jobs to help support the family, but once a woman married she stayed at home.

The bishop, satisfied that Phillip was willing to allow home births, left to share the news with the rest of the Church district. That evening, Amber resumed prenatal visits with her expectant mothers.

Phillip accompanied her. She knew it was important for the families to meet him prior to the big day, but spending so much time alone with him as they traveled the back roads of the county began wearing on her nerves. Each hour she spent with him made it increasingly difficult to maintain a professional attitude. The one thing helping her was the knowledge that he didn't agree with what she was doing.

Sunday morning rolled around on the first day of August with the good soaking rain so many farmers had been praying for. In church, Amber made a point of sitting with Nick and several of her cousins during the service. Looking over her shoulder, she saw Phillip come in.

Nick leaned over to whisper, "I see your special friend is here."

Slanting a glance at her handsome cousin, she caught his mischievous grin and made a face. "He's not my anything, Nick."

"That's not what I've been hearing."

Okay, who had been talking? "Not all gossip in Hope Springs is true, you know."

Nick glanced toward the back of the church then crossed his arms. "The man might think you're avoiding him."

Amber focused her attention on the sanctuary where a large stained glass window depicting a shroud-draped cross was set high in the wall. Instantly, she felt guilty.

*It's not that I'm avoiding Phillip, Lord. It's just that…
Okay, I'm avoiding him.*

Being in Phillip's constant company was making her
wish for things that could never be. He was charming
and funny. He loved kids. In spite of their many differences, it would be so easy to fall for the guy.

She hadn't fallen for him, but she could feel herself
stumbling.

*Remember, he isn't staying in Hope Springs. He has
a life waiting for him in Hawaii.*

She had a wonderful life here. A life she had always
wanted. So why didn't it feel as wonderful as it once had?

During the service, she prayed for the strength to keep
a level head and her heart intact. After church was over
and they all went outside, she remained with her cousins, exchanging small talk and getting updated on family matters. The sun had come out and the air smelled
fresh-washed and sweet. She saw Phillip standing off to
the side of the church steps. He looked lonely by himself, and very handsome in his charcoal gray suit and
pale green dress shirt.

Amber wavered and nearly went to talk to him. The
arrival of the mayor saved her. As the tall, lanky public
servant pumped Phillip's hand and loudly expressed his
gratitude, Amber made a quick escape.

Her respite lasted until Monday. At least they were
busy through the morning, which left them little time
together. In the afternoon, Phillip sat down with her to
finish reviewing the charts of her clients.

Amber was leery that he would be critical of her methods. She knew she did good work, but this collaboration
could prove to be difficult if they didn't see eye to eye
on the basics.

Closing the last chart, he looked up at her. "You're very thorough. The only patient I question as low-risk is Sophie Knepp."

"Why? Everything about this pregnancy has been great."

"She has lost two children."

"From what Harold and the family told me, those little girls died at the age of two from medical problems. It was before my time here. Her last two pregnancies have gone without a hitch."

"Still, I'm not comfortable with doing a home delivery with her."

"Will you be comfortable with any of them?" Amber snapped. She didn't mean to be snippy but the words were out before she could stop them.

He sat forward in his chair and crossed his arms on the desktop. "You think I'll find something wrong with all your patients?"

"No. I'm sorry I said that."

"We've got some trust issues here, don't we? Maybe we should begin addressing those."

Leaning back in her chair, she studied him intently. "I want to believe you've got my back here but it's a little hard. I know you've been forced into this and it goes against what you believe. Besides that, you aren't invested in these patients because you'll be leaving in a few weeks."

"Fair enough. The only thing I can do is to let my actions speak for me."

Just then her cell phone rang. Opening it, she spoke briefly with the caller and then hung up.

Looking at Phillip, she said, "Here and now you should know this isn't about us anymore. From now on, our focus must be making sure our clients have a wonderful birthing experience."

"And safe."

Nodding, she echoed him. "And safe. Agreed?"

"Absolutely."

Amber rose to her feet. "Well then, you're about to see your first home birth. That call was from a neighbor of Mary Yutzi. She's in labor and we need to go."

He picked up the phone. "Wilma, do I have any more patients scheduled this afternoon?"

Amber grinned. He was going to find balancing office work and delivering babies to be a real time challenge.

He said, "Cancel Mrs. Curtis and reschedule her for tomorrow morning."

Hanging up the phone, he rose. "Let's go welcome a new child of God into this world."

As soon as they arrived at the Yutzi farm, Phillip watched Amber quickly set up her equipment. Mary was still walking the floor with her hands pressed to the small of her back. Her husband was holding her elbow and speaking softly to her as he walked by her side.

After examining her, Amber smiled. "You've got a ways to go yet."

Getting up from the bed, Mary looked at Amber. "But you will stay, *ja*?"

"I'll stay. Dr. Phillip and I can make ourselves at home. Why don't you take a walk outside? It's a beautiful day."

With her attentive husband at her side, Mary went out the front door.

Amber said, "Walking will move her labor along more quickly."

She removed her gloves and washed while Phillip checked over her supplies.

"Clamps, suction bulb, Ambu bag, oxygen, IV fluids, Pitocin, a baby scale. You've got a whole delivery suite here." He sounded impressed.

"There's more in the car if I need it. Are you feeling less apprehensive about this?"

"Maybe. Cleanliness isn't an issue here. This home is as neat as a pin."

"That's true for most Amish homes."

It wasn't long before Mary and her husband returned. Phillip stood in the bedroom doorway and watched as Amber helped her lie down. When Mary was comfortable, Amber listened to the baby's heartbeat with her fetoscope. "Everything sounds fine. How are your contractions?"

"Uncomfortable and about every two minutes." She glanced repeatedly at Phillip with a slight frown on her face.

"Good. It won't be long now," Amber reassured her.

Walking over to Phillip, she asked, "Would you like to help?"

"You seem to have everything under control."

"You look like you're ready to jump in at any second."

"I am."

"I'll tell you what you can do to help. I find reading from the Bible will often calm my mothers."

"And nervous doctors, too?"

Smiling, she nodded. "Yes, you, too. I hand out an instruction packet on diet and exercise and what new moms need to expect on my first prenatal visit with a client. The packet also contains some of my favorite Scripture passages."

"Do you do that because they are Amish?"

"No, I do it because I have been called by God to be a nurse-midwife. Praising His name and reading His word while a new life is coming into the world just seems right."

"Would one of your favorite Scriptures be *1 John* 3:18?"

"Yes, how did you know that?"

"Your coffee cup told me. 'My little children, let us not love in word or in tongue, but in deed and in truth.'"

Her eyes softened. "Exactly."

"Would you like me to read to you, Mary?"

"Ja."

Amber said, "I think it would make us less nervous than having you hovering in the background."

He looked about the room. "Do you have a Bible I can use?"

"How good is your German?" Amber asked with a know-it-all grin.

He adored her smile. "I now know *Doktor, doktor, komm schnell* and *Der Englischer ist ab im kopf.*"

Mary and her husband chuckled at that.

Amber slipped past him in the doorway. "I have my Bible in my bag. I'll get it."

When she came back, she handed it to him. Happily, it was an English version. She said, "Read anything you like."

Settling himself on a wooden chair by the bedroom window, Phillip started reading as Amber coached Mary in her labor, checked her progress and kept a good eye on the baby's condition without seeming intrusive.

Later, when it grew dark outside, Mary's husband lit the gas lamp on the bedroom wall. Phillip moved to make use of the soft, warm glow.

Throughout the evening, Mary asked for numerous readings and he was happy to oblige. In amazement, he watched as Mary labored with her husband at her side in the quiet stillness of their own bedroom and by the light of a single lantern. It was a surreal experience for Phillip who had attended many deliveries under bright hospital lights with numerous medical personnel in the room.

At 12:09 a.m. Anna Yutzi arrived, weighing seven pounds, three ounces. She was twenty inches long and as bald as a rock.

"A beautiful and healthy girl," Phillip said after examining the baby. He gave the weighed and measured infant back to her smiling parents. He had usurped Amber's job, but the chance to hold such a precious child wasn't to be missed.

"*Ja*, she is our gift from God. My mother will be excited to have her first granddaughter," Mary replied, never taking her eyes from her baby's face. Her gentle smile warmed Phillip's heart.

It took another hour or so to clean up and make sure both mother and baby were comfortable. Mary's husband assured them Mary's mother would come to stay as soon as she heard the joyful news.

Phillip knew it was the man's way of saying that he and Mary wanted to be alone.

Amber said, "I'll check in on you tomorrow."

"And I'd like to see you in the office in about a week," Phillip added.

As he followed Amber outside to her car a little after two o'clock in the morning, he noticed at once the full white moon shining down on them. A soft breeze stirred the night air and carried to him the scent of roses from Mary's garden and the smell of corn ripening in the fields. He drew in a deep, cleansing breath and blew it out slowly.

"Tired?" Amber asked.

"A little. You?"

"A lot."

"Want me to drive?"

She turned and leaned against the car door, then slipped her hands into her scrub top pockets. "First tell me what you thought of this home birth. How did it compare to your hospital deliveries?"

At a loss for words, he simply shook his head.

"Come on. You must have some opinion. What did it feel like?"

Moving to stand beside her, he rested his hip against the car, too. "It was amazing. To see their all-embracing faith, their absolute trust in God's will, was humbling. There is beauty and serenity in every birth but this was special. Mary was so quiet, I've never seen a laboring woman stay so calm."

"You will find that's the norm among Amish women."

"Really?" He studied her upturned face. Her eyes glittered in the moonlight. Her hair glowed from the touch of moonbeams. Her skin looked flawless and pure. He beheld her ethereal beauty that was so much more than skin-deep.

This time, he wasn't going to mess up. Cupping her chin in his hand, he bent down and kissed her before she could turn away.

Chapter Fifteen

The world stood still around Amber. The full moon faded away and the stars winked out. The wind died to a soft sigh. Only it wasn't the wind she heard. That wistful sound formed in her own mind. The wonder of the moment swept her away from everything she'd ever known and into enchantment.

Phillip's lips were firm yet gentle as they moved across hers. The rasp of his whiskers on the tender skin around her mouth sent a thrill racing over her, making her want to draw closer. She leaned into the kiss and her arms crept up to encircle his neck.

Nothing in the world existed except the two of them and this wonderful feeling of rightness. Her hands moved up his neck to tangle in his hair. He was a very good kisser.

It took a while but Amber's common sense finally reasserted itself. As hard as she tried to stay in the glorious moment, reality seeped in. It was a wonderful kiss. It was a doomed romance. She couldn't let this go any further.

Moving her hands to Phillip's shoulders, she pushed gently. He loosened his embrace but didn't release her entirely. The kiss lasted one more heart-stopping second before he pulled away.

Drawing a ragged breath, he cupped the back of her head and tucked her face against his neck. "Wow."

It felt marvelous to rest in his embrace. He was so warm and strong and vital. It was the kind of moment she'd dreamed of but never thought would become a reality. She didn't want to lose this marvelous feeling but the sensation was fading. She had to get the two of them back on solid footing.

"Phillip, if you say something stupid like 'I'm sorry,' I'll kick your shin."

He chuckled. The sound reverberated deep in his chest beneath her ear and made her smile. "Amber, of all the things running through my mind right now, *I'm sorry* is not even on the horizon."

"Good."

Where did this leave them? It changed nothing and it changed everything.

"Does this mean we've resolved the trust issues between us?" he asked.

"I'm working on it." If only it were that easy. One kiss and everything became rosy. *Not.*

He leaned back so he could see her face. Amber looked up, hoping her heart wasn't shining in her eyes. Before she could think of anything else to say, he released her and stepped away.

"I think it's time I drove you home."

Without his arms around her, the night air felt cold. She crossed her arms as a shiver ran down her spine. "If you aren't going to kiss me again, we should go."

He paused in the act of opening the car door. "Oh,

Amber. Talk about temptation. You've been one since the first day I came to Hope Springs."

His comment pleased her feminine side to no end, but it didn't narrow the chasm that existed between them.

"Okay, home it is," he conceded.

Once in the car, Amber hoped things would return to normal. Her hopes were in vain. He said, "What are we going to do about this?"

What could they do about it? The answer was painfully clear to her. "Nothing."

His gaze jerked toward her. "What's that supposed to mean?"

"Don't get me wrong. It was a wonderful kiss."

"That was the impression I had at the time. Now I'm wondering if I misread something."

"You didn't. It just can't happen again."

By the sudden deep silence, Amber knew he understood. Finally, he said, "It won't."

"We have to work together. You're my boss. Besides that, you're leaving in a few weeks. If we jump headlong into a relationship, we'll end up hurting each other."

"I thought I was practical. You've got me beat hands down. But answer me this, what if we allowed this relationship to take its natural course and see where it leads?"

He had no idea how much she longed to have that happen. One kiss from him was not enough. It would never be enough. That didn't change anything. "Okay, you tell me how this might play out differently."

"We could enjoy each other's company when we aren't working. You know, spend time together. We could get to know each other. Who knows, we might find this is the real deal for both of us."

"And then what? You'd settle down in Hope Springs for the rest of your life? You'd be happy being a family doctor to the Amish and skip the part where you practice cutting-edge medicine with the latest technology?"

She hated driving home the point, but it was a pipe dream to think what they had between them could ever be more than a breathless kiss in the moonlight.

"You're right," he admitted.

"Of course, I'm right."

He gave in so easily. That hurt a little. He could have offered a few more arguments.

Okay, maybe it was better that he hadn't. This way she could make believe it was nothing more than a simple flirtation.

By now they had reached the edge of town. It didn't take much longer to reach her house. When he pulled up to the curb in front of her home, she turned in her seat to see his face better. Trying to convince herself it hadn't been an important moment didn't cut it. She had to admit the truth. "I'll never forget tonight, Phillip."

Reaching out, he tenderly stroked her cheek with the back of his knuckles. "Neither will I, Amber. Neither will I."

Phillip didn't want her to go. The delight he'd felt when he held her in his arms was stronger than anything he'd experienced before. She fit so perfectly.

Perhaps those feelings had been caused by the heightened emotions they both shared following Mary's delivery. Perhaps it was because Amber was a remarkable, beautiful woman.

Whatever the reasons, he knew once she stepped out of the car they had to go back to their roles of doctor and nurse. Working side by side, never touching the way he touched her now.

She said, "I should go."

He withdrew his hand. Other than locking the doors and driving away with her, he couldn't think of any way to stop her from leaving.

Silently admitting defeat, he tried for a normal, friendly tone. "Then I'll see you tomorrow at the clinic."

"You mean today at the clinic."

She was right. Dawn was still a few hours away, but he wasn't in any rush to get home. Sleep would be very hard to come by. He would relive that tender kiss many times before he slumbered. Probably for many nights to come.

"Don't forget, Gina Curtis will be in first thing," she reminded him.

Shaking his head, he said, "I've never seen a person so happy to find out there was actually something wrong with her."

"Poor Gina. I feel terrible for dismissing her complaints so callously."

"What happened in the past can't be changed. What we do from now on is what's important. Get some sleep, Nurse Bradley. I'll need you at your best today."

"Are you sure you don't want me to drop you off at your place?" she asked.

"No, a walk will do me good. It's only a few blocks. Besides, it not like Hope Springs has much of a criminal element."

He got out and came around to her side of the car. Opening the door, he handed her the keys as she got out. "I'll expect you at eight sharp."

"Yes, Doctor," she replied smartly and walked up the steps to her house.

She never looked back. He knew because he waited at the curb until she entered her front door, until the downstairs lights finally went out and until her upstairs bedroom window went dark. Only then did he walk away.

At the corner, he stopped and looked back. How was he going to stay away?

Chapter Sixteen

After a sleepless, very short night, Amber arrived at the clinic determined to revert to her normal working relationship with Phillip. The last thing she needed was for things to be strained between them.

By the middle of the morning she knew it wasn't working.

There were all those little things that sparked memories of the kiss. Like when he handed her a cup of coffee when she arrived and their hands touched for a brief moment. The current of attraction that ran between them zinged like lightning. It grew more powerful with each passing moment.

Not long afterward, she came face-to-face with him in the break room door. She froze, unable to move as she stared into his expressive eyes. He was thinking about the kiss, too.

He found the presence of mind to step back and allow her to leave. If he hadn't, she'd still be standing there longing to find out if a second kiss would be as wonderful as the first.

Several times throughout the morning she looked up

to find him staring at her. Once, he had the sweetest smile tugging at the corner of his mouth. The next time, he wore a faraway sad look, as if he'd lost something important. Was she important to him? She was afraid to ask. Afraid that he would say yes. Afraid he would say no.

A little before noon, Amber's phone rang. Phillip, having finished with their last patient of the morning, stopped outside her door to wait as she answered it.

It was the husband of Sophie Knepp. Excitement sent Amber's pulse skipping. She loved delivering babies and was grateful God had chosen her for this special work.

After assuring Elijah Knepp that she would be there within the hour, she closed her phone, looked at Phillip and grinned. "Ready to help me bring another child into the world?"

He glanced at the schedule board. "We've got three more patients to see this afternoon."

Sitting back in her chair, she shrugged. "Clue number one as to why Harold lets me do my own deliveries. Not enough hours in the day. I can do this on my own," she offered.

"That's not the agreement we signed."

She smiled sweetly. "Can't blame a girl for trying."

He struggled not to smile but lost the battle. "I'll get Wilma to reschedule. Give me five minutes. Will this one last all night, too?"

"That's not likely. It's baby number five for Sophie Knepp. She's not due for three more weeks, but her other babies have come this early. They did fine."

"Knepp? I remember reading her chart. She's not a candidate for home delivery. She's high-risk." All levity vanished from his face.

Amber bristled. "In my professional assessment, she is not a high-risk mother."

"Then professionally we disagree."

"Yes, I believe we do." To think she'd been feeling sorry for him less than an hour ago.

"Call the Knepps back. Tell them to make arrangements for Mrs. Knepp to go to the hospital in Millersburg. I'll meet them there."

"Yes, Doctor," she snapped. Annoyed, Amber flipped open her phone and poked in the numbers.

After eight rings, she hung up. "There's no answer. It's likely that Elijah called from one of the rural phone booths shared by several of Amish families in his area."

"I thought they didn't use phones."

"Not in their homes. Some who need phones for their businesses share a freestanding booth located centrally to their farms."

"So how do we contact him and tell him about the change of plans?"

"Wilma will know if they have a neighbor with a phone who can deliver that message. If not, one of us will have to go out there." Amber picked up her desk phone and asked Wilma to see what she could find out.

Hanging up, Amber glared at Phillip. "She's looking into it."

"Good. Keep me informed."

Something in his tone pushed her over the edge. "Yes, Dr. White, of course, Dr. White. I shall keep you informed of the situation without delay, Dr. White. How could you think otherwise?"

Turning back to her computer, she said, "Now, if you will excuse me, I have work to do."

She pulled out her keyboard and began typing up her

notes from her last delivery. He didn't move. He simply stood in the doorway staring at her. Try as she might, she couldn't ignore him.

With an exasperated huff, she looked up. "Yes, Dr. White, is there something else? Some other mistake I've made that needs to be pointed out?"

"Amber, please."

"Please what? Please don't be annoyed that you can't trust my judgment? You know what? You're right. That little episode of *bad judgment* on my part last night proves your point."

Taking a step toward her, he said, "We need to talk about that."

Nope. That was the last thing she wanted. What if she blurted out how much she enjoyed it?

"I have nothing to say to you. Now, this is still my office. I have work to do. Close the door on your way out." Pushing the print button on the machine at the side of her desk, she focused on the noisy clatter as her notes were transferred to paper.

He didn't reply. When she looked up from her task, her door was closed. Phillip was standing inside with his arms folded across his chest. The look on his face said he wasn't going anywhere.

Phillip had no idea how to handle Amber when she was in a mood like this one, but he couldn't leave until they had reached some kind of understanding. She had become too important to him, and he had hurt her.

Trusting God to bring him the right words, he crossed the room and pulled a chair over beside her. He sat down and took her hand. "I'm sorry."

"For what?" She tried to pull away. He held on.

The catch in her voice made him want to kick himself for upsetting her. "I'm sorry for a lot of things. For kissing you last night, not in the least."

"If you're expecting a repeat, you're not getting one."

He chuckled. "How can you be so cute even when you're mad at me?" She opened her mouth but shut it quickly. He turned her hand over and began stroking her palm with his thumb. "*Now* you're speechless?"

"I can't very well say I'm not cute because I am. That doesn't make me less irritated with you."

Her tone, if not her words, showed she was somewhat mollified. It was hard to believe she hadn't pulled her hand away and slapped him. That gave him hope.

"Let's get things out in the open. Maybe then we won't have to tiptoe around each other for the next few weeks."

"That's not necessary."

"I think it is. From my point of view, we were both elated by the beauty of Anna's birth. The moonlight and the scent of roses were utterly romantic. You are a beautiful woman. One thing led to another and we kissed. It wasn't wrong. It was an expression of joy. I'd repeat the event in a heartbeat."

The tension left her shoulders and the wary expression disappeared from her eyes. A shy smile tugged at the corner of her oh-so-kissable lips. "That wasn't exactly an apology."

"No, and I won't offer one. I don't regret that I kissed you. I do regret it's making it difficult for us to work together. Believe it or not, I do understand boundaries."

"You're giving our interlude too much credit. We had trouble working together before then."

Letting go of her hand, he sat back with a grin. "Okay, you're right about that, but we are making progress."

"I know I'm right. I'm right about a lot of things. Including Sophie Knepp."

Leaning forward, he rested his forearms on his knees and clasped his hand together. "Let's say you are right and her delivery goes off without a hitch. Is it really going to make a difference to this Amish community to have one mother deliver at a hospital just to be on the safe side? Come on, are these people so fragile or so autocratic that they can't accept this?"

He watched the internal struggle going on behind her expressive eyes. Finally, she shook her head.

He sat back. "I've reviewed your charts. I have agreed with all your assessments except this one. Doesn't that prove I think you know your stuff?"

"Maybe."

"Not maybe. Yes or no?"

"Okay, yes, you believe I know my stuff."

"And you will agree that I know my stuff?"

"Maybe."

Shaking his head in exasperation, he said, "Yes or no, Amber?"

"Yes, you're a skilled doctor who has the best interests of his patients in mind."

"Thank you."

"You're welcome."

Reaching out, he took her hand again. "Does this mean we can kiss and make up?"

She yanked her hand away. "In your dreams, buster."

How right she was. She'd been invading his dreams for some time now. He didn't see it stopping anytime soon.

There was a knock at the door. Wilma looked in. "I got hold of the Knepps' neighbor who went right over to give them your message. He just called me back on his cell phone. He was still at their house. Sophie says it was false labor. Elijah jumped the gun by calling. She says she's sorry to have alarmed you."

"Thank you, Wilma."

Rising, Phillip looked at them both. "We've got forty minutes before our next patient. How about lunch at the Shoofly? It's on me."

"I've already had my sandwich," Wilma replied. She left the room, but she made a point of leaving the door open.

Phillip turned to Amber. "What about you? Have you forgiven me enough to join me for lunch?"

"Only if we go Dutch."

It was always small victories with her. Independent, stubborn and passionate about her work, he wouldn't have her any other way. "Dutch it is."

Leaving Wilma to hold down the fort, Phillip walked beside Amber as they traversed the few blocks to the café.

He fought the urge to hold her hand the entire way. He kept his hands inside his lab coat pockets instead.

The day was sunny and warm, but the breeze made it bearable. At the café, the interior was cool and filled with appetizing aromas that made his mouth water. He hadn't realized how hungry he was.

Katie came forward to greet them. "*Willkommen.* I'm afraid we don't have a table for you, but the wait should not be long. Our special today is pork chops with fresh peas and home-baked dinner rolls."

"Sounds wonderful, Katie. What's for dessert?"

Katie grinned, "We have raisin pie. I know you want a slice of that."

"Oh, yes I do."

Phillip nudged Amber with his elbow. "Let's have lunch first before you go diving into dessert."

"All right, but we don't have time to wait for a table. It took us ten minutes to walk here."

"We have some fried chicken ready. I can make you a quick picnic," Katie offered.

"Is that all right?" Phillip asked Amber. He loved the outdoors and the sun on his face. He suspected Amber was the outdoorsy type but he didn't know for certain.

To his delight, she said, "Sounds great. We can eat at the park. It's a block from the clinic."

He liked the sound of that. Amber was being practical. He saw it as the perfect opportunity to spend some quality time with her. Their brief but so-very-sweet kiss left him longing for more. He smiled at the prospect of a repeat.

A hint of wariness crept into her eyes. He wiped the grin from his face. It wasn't like he was planning to kiss her again. He wasn't. Absolutely not. No way.

He turned his attention to the rest of the room. From their spot by the door, he saw the place was indeed packed with a dozen or so English tourists, and numerous Amish families at the other tables.

Phillip leaned toward Amber. "I didn't think the Amish ate out."

"Sure they do. They come for special occasions like birthdays or simply to enjoy a break from home cooking on market day."

At the nearest table, Phillip noticed that two of the children where dwarfs. "I've seen a disproportionately large number of little people since I've arrived."

"The Amish, because of intermarriages, suffer from

many inherited diseases such as the dwarfism that those children have."

"For people who don't believe in health insurance, some inherited diseases must place a huge burden on the families."

"They don't see it as a burden. They accept it as God's will. They consider the children who are affected to be gifts from God."

"As they are."

"I'm glad you think so. I've noticed you are very good with the children who come to the clinic."

He folded his arms across his chest. "I almost went into pediatrics."

"Why didn't you?"

"I've wanted to be a family practice doctor since I was ten years old." Memories of his unhappy childhood slipped out to taint the day.

"So young? Did something happen that pushed you in that direction?"

Staring into her sympathetic eyes, Phillip struggled with a difficult decision. Normally, he deflected questions about his early life. Plenty of people had looked down on him in the past. Deeply ashamed of the way he'd grown up and of his mother's behaviors, he preferred to keep those times bottled away.

Amber was someone who made him want to share even the ugly parts of his life. There was something about her that made him believe he could trust her—made him believe that she would understand.

Was he right? Could he take that chance?

Chapter Seventeen

Katie returned with their box lunches, giving Phillip a chance to ponder his options. Some inner part of him wanted to share everything about himself with Amber. He had guarded his past so closely for so long, he wasn't sure he could talk about it now. It existed like a bad dream in the back of his mind.

With their lunches and ice-cold bottles of soda in hand, they left the Shoofly and started back toward the clinic. Flashing a sidelong glance at her, he half hoped she would forget about her question.

She hadn't. After taking a sip of her cola, she went right back to the subject. "What happened that made you want to become a doctor?"

He walked in silence for several yards, unable to bring himself to talk about it.

She cast a worried glance his way. "I'm sorry. I didn't mean to pry."

He opened his mouth to say it was a personal matter he didn't care to discuss. That wasn't what came out. "When I was ten, my mother and her current boyfriend had a birthday party for me. I can't remember his name.

She had so many men in her life that they all run together in my head."

Looking down, he expected to see repugnance. He saw only sympathy in her beautiful eyes. "I'm sorry, Phillip. I can't imagine what that must have been like for you."

Suddenly, it was as if the floodgates of his emotions broke open. His unhappy past came pouring out. "It was so hard. A new town every few months, a new 'Uncle' just as often. I was always the new kid at school who didn't fit in, who wore dirty clothes. It didn't pay trying to make friends because I knew I'd be leaving."

"Yet you turned out to be a responsible, caring adult. You became a physician, which is no easy task."

"That was due in large part to my stepfather. When I was fifteen, God brought a great guy into our lives. A man who saw how sad Mom was and helped her find a better life. Michael is a devout Christian. He showed me God's blessings in my own life. He made me realize I didn't have to shoulder my burdens alone. I still have a ways to go in being a good Christian, but I'm trying to get there. It was Michael's generosity that allowed me to go to medical school, although I did receive some academic scholarships."

By this time they had reached the park. They found a picnic table in the shade of a pear tree and sat down. The park was deserted except for a few squirrels chattering as they raced from treetop to treetop. The faint breeze smelled of newly mown grass. Phillip opened his box just as Amber held out her hand and bowed her head. He grasped her hand and did the same.

She said, "We thank You, Lord, for the food that nourishes our body. Grant us Your comfort and Your grace as we work to do Your will. Amen."

"Amen," Phillip echoed. Slowly, he released her hand.

"What happened on your birthday?" She took a bite of her drumstick. Her gaze didn't leave his face.

Drawing a deep breath, he said, "Mom's boyfriend asked me what I wanted to be when I grew up. She told him I was going to be a doctor like my father planned to be. It was the first I'd heard that my dad wanted to be a doctor. I cornered her later that night before she and what's-his-name went out to party. I asked her what kind of doctor my dad wanted to be. She hemmed and hawed, but finally told me he wanted to be a family doctor."

"Your father must have wanted to be like his own dad. I'm sure Harold would be happy to know that."

Phillip took a drink, then said, "You once asked me how Harold and I found each other."

"I remember. You said it was personal. I respect that."

"I want to tell you now. Sometimes, when I'm in my grandfather's house, I try to put myself in his place. I try to imagine what it would be like to live alone in that small house for thirty-four years. I stare at the walls and wonder what made him give up a lucrative practice in Boston to come to Hope Springs. I wonder what makes him stay. Did he ever tell you what brought him here?"

"No, and I never asked. By the time I began working here he was already a fixture, like the clock in the town square. I didn't even know he came from Boston. Perhaps it was the death of his only son that made him leave."

He shrugged. "Mother rarely talked about my father although I pestered her for information about him from the time I could talk. I was certain if he had lived my life would have been different. I thought my mother would have been happy. That we would live in a house instead of rented trailers and abysmal run-down apartments."

"It's easy to understand that you wanted to know him."

"That's the easy part. The rest is weird."

"How so?"

"My mother never showed me a picture of my dad. Yet she kept it all those years. Through all the moves and all the crummy boyfriends. When I found it, I didn't know who he was. I turned it over. On the back of the picture he'd written, 'To my wife Natalie with all my love, Brendan.' I was shocked."

"What did she say when you asked her about it? She had to know how much you wanted to learn things about him."

"She gave no explanation other than to say it was a personal item and for me to put it away."

"That is weird. Perhaps it was too painful for her to look at."

"That was always her excuse. Once I knew my dad had been in the military, I started searching his military records for some clues about what kind of man he was. That was how I found out about Harold. He was listed along with my mother as kin. My mother told me that my dad was an orphan, that he had no family."

"Why would she do that?"

"I don't have a clue. She's very good at avoiding uncomfortable situations. From the moment I learned of my grandfather's existence, I spent every free minute and every free dime I had trying to track him down. I looked online, combed through old newspaper articles and public records. It was slow going. I finally hired a private detective in Boston to do the legwork for me."

"And that's how you found Harold?"

"The P.I. was a good investment. Within a week, he sent me Harold's current address and the phone number of this clinic. I can't begin to describe the emotions going through me at that moment."

"To finally find your father's father must have been wonderful."

"My fingers were cold as icicles when I dialed the number. My heart was beating so hard I thought I might stroke out."

Every word of that first conversation remained imprinted in Phillip's mind. After explaining who he was and how he'd found Harold, Phillip waited for his grandfather's reaction.

Amber said, "I imagine Harold was delighted to hear from you."

"His reaction wasn't exactly what I'd hoped for. Harold was hard to convince. Who could blame him? To have me pop up out of nowhere after thirty-four years must have been a shock. I told him about the military records and the P.I. I left my phone number with him, then I hung up and waited."

"He may have sounded hesitant when you were on the phone but I saw him when he came out of his office after speaking to you. There was such joy on his face. He didn't share his news until a few days later but I knew something big was up."

"That's because he hired a P.I. to check me out first."

Her eyes widened. "Really?"

"He's a smart man. A week after our first contact Harold called me. We began a tentative long-distance relationship. After nearly a year of emails and phone conversations, Harold announced he was ready to meet me. We both know how that turned out. I ran him down with my car."

Reaching out, Amber laid a hand on his arm. "You never intended to hurt him, Phillip. It was an accident. You have to stop blaming yourself."

Her gesture of comfort was exactly what he needed. A sense of peace settled in his bones. "You're right. I can't blame myself forever."

Amber withdrew her hand. The warmth between them cooled as she concentrated on her pie. Words didn't seem adequate but she needed to say something. "Thank you for sharing your story with me. I feel honored."

"Thank you for listening."

They finished their meal in silence. As they gathered their trash and disposed of it, he glanced at his watch. "Time to get back to work."

And time to shift back into her professional mode. If only Phillip didn't make it so hard for her to maintain that persona.

Having him share his unhappy childhood memories with her touched her deeply. Little by little he was creeping into her heart in a way she knew would lead to heartbreak. He'd be leaving in a few weeks. She simply had to get a grip on these emotions.

If only he weren't such a wonderful person. Sure, they disagreed about a few things, important things. She could get downright angry with him but it never lasted long. He had a way of smoothing over the rough spots and making her like him all over again.

Besides being charming, he was wonderful with patients, especially the children. He attended the same church she did. He had strong Christian beliefs. He was growing to accept and care about the Amish and their ways.

Okay, he's an almost perfect man. My mother would fall over backward with joy if I brought him home.

So why had the Lord brought such a wonderful man into her life if he wasn't going to stay? It was a question she couldn't answer. The ways of the Lord were not for her understanding.

Back at the office, they went through the rest of the day together without any more blowups or exchanged confidences. A little before five o'clock, they were in the lobby getting ready to close for the night.

Phillip said, "I still have to make my rounds at the hospital in Millersburg. I should get going."

"And I need to see Mary and her baby."

"Let me know how they're doing." He held up one hand. "Not because I don't trust your professional expertise. Because I'd like to know how they're getting along."

Amber couldn't help smiling. "I'll call you later tonight."

He stopped on his way to the door and glanced back. "I'll look forward to that."

Just then, the phone rang. Phillip waited as Wilma picked up. After exchanging a few pleasantries with the caller, she covered the mouthpiece with one hand. "It's Harold. He'd like to speak to both of you."

Amber exchanged a worried glance with Phillip. He said, "We'll take it in my office. Thank you, Wilma. You can go home."

"I always miss the good stuff," she grumbled as she gathered her purse.

"I'll fill you in tomorrow morning," Amber promised.

"You'd better." She walked out the door, leaving Amber and Phillip alone.

Amber turned to face him. "Ready to accomplish your mission?"

Stuffing his hands in his pockets, he asked, "What mission?"

"Don't play dumb. Harold needs a partner. You get to tell him."

"I can't believe I gave in to you."

She gave him a playful push toward his office. "Don't worry. I'll be right there beside you."

"You'd better be."

In the office, Phillip pressed the blinking light on the phone and set it to speakerphone mode. Leaning his hip against the corner of the desk, he said, "Hello, Grandfather. How are you?"

"Better than these morons give me credit for. If I were home I'd be doing great."

Speaking up, Amber said, "Harold, I'm sure they know what's best for you."

"Enough about me. How is my practice?"

"It's busy," Phillip said with a questioning look at her.

"And Amber is back to work as a nurse-midwife?"

"Yes," she said quickly. "Mary Yutzi had a little girl last night. Seven pounds, three ounces and twenty inches long."

"Wonderful. What did they name her?" He sounded truly relieved and happy.

"Anna." Phillip answered.

Harold chuckled. "Nettie must be over the moon to finally get a granddaughter. Give Mary my congratulations."

Amber perched on a chair by the desk and leaned to-

ward the speaker. "I will. I'm going out to the farm tonight to check on her and Anna."

Looking at Phillip, Amber nodded toward the phone.
He closed his eyes and said, "We've been busy here."

"You mean since the boycott ended."

Phillip flinched. "Even before the boycott, I was
amazed at the number of patients you see."

Harold replied, "Of course we're busy. There's a shortage of rural doctors, or haven't you heard that in Hawaii?"

"I've heard. I was simply wondering if you had considered taking on a partner?"

"Ha! Find me one who'll work for peanuts, see patients without insurance and make visits to homes without electricity, and I'll take him on. It has to be a man,
though. No offense, Amber."

She grinned. "None taken. I know Amish men won't
use female doctors."

Phillip said, "Let me be clear. You are okay with me
advertising for a new physician to work with you?"

There was a long silence on the phone. Amber finally
asked, "Harold, are you still there?"

"Yes."

"What do you think about Phillip's suggestion?"

"So the pair of you think I can't do the job, anymore,
is that it?"

"No!" they said in unison.

Phillip closed his eyes. "You aren't a young man anymore. These people deserve to have your knowledge and
skills passed on to someone who can help them far into
the future. If you had died, what would have happened
to them?"

"Don't think that hasn't crossed my mind, but I'm not ready to hang up my stethoscope."

"Phillip didn't say that you were," Amber replied, trying to be reasonable.

"All right. Go ahead and advertise. You won't find anyone."

Phillip winked at Amber. "Then you should do as your doctors tell you so you can get back here and get to work soon."

"Everyone sends their love and prayers," Amber added.

"Give them my thanks." Harold's tone held a pensive quality that troubled Amber. The line went dead before she could ask him what was wrong.

Phillip rubbed his jaw thoughtfully. "Do you remember the name of the resident who wanted to join this practice?"

"I still have his card somewhere." What was it that Harold hadn't said? Amber couldn't get his tone out of her mind.

Springing to his feet, Phillip said, "Great. Maybe the guy is still interested in working here. I can't believe Harold agreed. That was easy."

Amber continued to stare at the phone. "I'm not so sure."

Chapter Eighteen

Phillip couldn't believe how quickly the days were flying by. When he'd first agreed to spend two months in Ohio, it had seemed like a prison sentence. He couldn't imagine being away from his beloved ocean for so long. Now he wished he had more time to spend with Amber.

They had done one more delivery together, a first baby for a non-Amish couple. In spite of Phillip's worries, Amber conducted the whole experience so that both the young woman and her nervous husband had a happy and successful birthing experience.

As Amber and Hope Springs worked their way deeper into his heart, it became increasingly clear why Harold refused to give up medicine in this place. There was something so soothing and rich about the way these people lived.

He sat in his grandfather's kitchen, absently tapping a pen on the table. He didn't have to leave. He could be the man to work with his grandfather.

Tempting as the thought was, he knew it wouldn't work. This wasn't the kind of medicine he saw himself doing into his seventies. He imagined himself working in the finest modern medical center, diagnosing diseases and treating his patients with the best tools available.

Coming to Hope Springs had clarified one issue for him. It was the sick children that called to his soul. Sick children like little Helen Lapp with her bad heart. If anyone deserved the finest care, it was children like her.

Wilma was waiting for him when he reached the clinic. Not once since arriving in Hope Springs had he beaten the woman to the office. He wasn't sure that she didn't sleep there. She said, "The Lapp family is here as you requested."

"Good, thank you. Please hold my calls."

He had little Helen's report from the cardiologist. He had asked for a family meeting to discuss it.

In his office, he found Mr. and Mrs. Lapp waiting for him. They looked like any other Amish couple he might pass on the street. She wore a dark blue dress and apron. On her head she wore a dark bonnet with a wide brim.

Her husband had on a dark suit and held his black felt hat in his hands. They could have been any Amish couple in Hope Springs except for the intense worry in their eyes.

Phillip sat behind his desk. "How is Helen?"

"Some better," her mother answered.

"As I'm sure Dr. Yang discussed with you, Helen has a heart defect called an atrial septal defect."

Her father nodded. "*Ja*, she will need surgery soon to fix her heart."

"Yes. In studying her cardiologist's report, I see that her disease is genetic in nature. Do you know what that means?"

They looked at each other and shook their heads.

"She has Ellis-van Creveld syndrome. That means

your future children are at risk for the same type of dwarfism and heart defects."

"But I have two fine sons," Mr. Lapp insisted.

"I know. I merely wanted you to be aware of the risks for any other children. Your sons need to know that their children may have the same problems."

"It was *Gottes Wille* that our daughter was born this way. We accept that." Mrs. Lapp spoke at last. She sat with her hands clasped tightly in front of her, her knuckles white with tension.

Her husband nodded. "If He sends us more children like Helen, we will accept that, too."

Phillip sat back in his chair. "We have no way to cure Helen. Surgery isn't a complete fix. Any colds or coughs can quickly turn serious for her, so please don't hesitate to come see me if she becomes ill again."

"Danki, Doktor." Rising, Mr. Lapp nodded, then walked out the door. His wife hung back.

Looking at Phillip, she asked, "What can be done so that my sons don't have such children?"

"They can be tested for the defective gene. If they don't carry it, their children will not have Helen's disease."

She took a step closer. "And if they do carry it?"

"In that case, the way to prevent them from having a child with her defect would be to screen the women they wish to marry to see if they carry the gene."

"If they both have this gene?"

Sighing deeply, he said, "Their children will have a one in four chance of having Ellis-van Creveld syndrome."

"So God decides?"

"Yes. I'm not an expert on this disease, Mrs. Lapp. If

you'd like, I can make an appointment for you to see a genetic specialist."

"No." She left his office and caught up with her husband waiting outside.

Phillip watched them leave and knew they both carried heavy hearts. The specialist believed Helen had only a fifty-fifty chance of reaching adulthood. Phillip prayed God would give them the strength and comfort they needed to deal with such devastating news.

Turning back to his desk, he stared at the books in his grandfather's case. Pulling down one with numerous bits of paper sticking out, he read the title. *Noted Patterns of Human Malformation.*

Leafing though the pages of the text, Phillip saw Harold had made dozens of comments in the margins, mostly dates and occasional names.

"Are you looking for something special?"

He turned at the sound of Amber's voice. She was standing in the doorway. She had on her usual pale blue scrubs and white lab coat. He heard Wilma call out a question to her. Turning around, she stepped into the hall to answer. When she did, he saw that her hair hung to her hips in a shimmering honey-colored curtain. The sight robbed him of breath.

When she turned back to face him, he closed his mouth and asked, "What did you say?"

"I asked if you were looking for something special?"

He focused his gaze on the books. "I was looking for some texts on genetics."

She joined him by the bookcase and reached for a book on the upper shelf. "I'm not sure what Harold has in here. He never alphabetizes anything."

The clean citrus fragrance of her hair slipped around

him like a soft Hawaiian breeze. He leaned back to scope her hair out again.

Yep. Every bit as glorious up close.

She should have flowers in it, the way the island women wore them. It was easy to picture her walking beside him on the beach, her hair flowing in the wind. He itched to feel its softness. To let it glide though his fingers.

Suddenly, she whipped her head around to stare at him. "What?"

He took a step back and crossed his arms. "Nothing."

"You were staring at me."

"No, I wasn't." Even to his own ears he sounded like a kid caught with his hand in the cookie jar.

She arched one brow. Her look said she wasn't buying it.

"Okay, I was admiring your hair, that's all."

Grasping a lock in her hand, she frowned at it. "When I left the house this morning it wasn't dry so I had to leave it down. I'll put it up before I see patients."

"You don't have to do that. It's very lovely."

Her cheeks took on a rosy hue. "Thank you."

He couldn't help himself. Reaching out, he brushed a strand from her shoulder in a soft caress.

Amber sucked in a quick breath at his touch. Her hair *had* been damp when she left the house, but she could have put it up after she arrived. She never wore it down. It was always confined in a braid or bun. Today had been different. For some inexplicable reason, she wanted Phillip to see it down.

Now she realized she was being vain. Taking a step away from him, she swept it into a rope and began coiling it. "My mother never cut her hair. She called it a hangover from her Amish life. I adopted the habit."

"You don't have to put it up." He sounded sorry to see her do so.

"It's dry now."

"Have you ever cut it?"

Continuing to wind, she said, "It gets trimmed. It pleases mother and my grandmother that I keep it long."

Pulling several large hairpins from her pocket, she slipped them in and patted the roll. "There. Good to go."

"You should wear it down more often. It's beautiful."

He did like it. A thrill of happiness made her smile.

"Amber, have you ever thought of working somewhere else?"

"Like where?"

"Hawaii, for one place." A question hovered in his eyes, a hope that secretly pleased her. She had thought about seeing his island home, but she wasn't ready to admit that.

She turned back to the bookcase. "I sunburn too easily. Genetics, you say? I don't see anything but what you're holding. You can always use the computer to look something up. I know our dial-up can be slow and frustrating."

"I'll drive to Millersburg after work and do some research at their medical library. I need to check on Martha anyway. Are any of your patients in labor?"

"Not a one."

He opened the book and held it out to her. "Do these dates and names mean anything to you?"

She studied the textbook for a few minutes. "I'm not sure." Pointing, she said, "This could be the Zook boy who died two years ago. He had some developmental difficulties from birth."

"What kind of difficulties?"

"I'm not sure."

"He wasn't one of your patients?"

She shook her head. "No, he was born in the hospital in Millersburg. They were visiting family there when she went into premature labor. He never left the hospital."

Turning to a new page, he asked, "What about this one?"

Checking, she shook her head. "Before my time."

"It says Knepp. Could it be one of Sophie Knepp's girls?"

"It could be. We have a lot of Knepps in this state."

He carried the book back to his desk and sat down. It was clear he was deep in thought.

"Your next patient is in room one," she reminded him.

"Fine. Thank you. I'll be there in a minute."

She started to leave but he suddenly spoke again. "Do me a favor, will you? Ask Wilma to get some old charts from storage."

"Sure. Which ones?"

"The one for this Zook boy, and see if she can find a Knepp with this birth date." He scribbled it down and handed her the note.

"It may take a few days. We store our closed charts out of state."

"Tell her to get them as soon as she can."

Throughout the rest of the morning, Phillip remained distracted. He was always attentive to his patients, but in between clients he shut himself in the office.

At noon, Amber stuck her head in to see if he wanted

to get some lunch. He didn't, and she went away feeling more disappointed than she should have.

When they closed up that evening, she watched him walk across the parking lot and turn the corner.

"You'll have to get used to that," Wilma said as she came to stand beside Amber.

"Get used to what?"

"Him being gone."

"I know he's leaving soon." It was hard to imagine this place without him. He'd become so much a part of her life. Pushing open the door, she walked to her car and drove home feeling more depressed than she had since she'd first learned of Harold's accident.

At home, Fluffy was waiting eagerly for his food bowl to be filled. Amber obliged the cat then made herself a light supper. She spent the rest of the evening catching up on her midwife journal, reading and trying not to think about Phillip. Or how much she would miss him when he went away.

On an impulse, she went to the computer and began clicking through some of the travel sites that featured Hawaii. She'd always thought the rolling hills, fertile fields and pristine white farmsteads of the Amish made Hope Springs a beautiful place. It paled in comparison to the exotic beauty of the islands embraced by the blue-green sea.

What man in his right mind would give up a home and a practice there to relocate to this wide spot in the road? No, she might wish he would stay but he wouldn't. This wasn't the kind of medicine he wanted to practice. She understood and respected that to the fullest. Phillip would leave in a few more weeks.

Unless Harold asked him to stay.

Was that what Harold had been thinking when he agreed to getting a partner? Was that idea the odd quality she detected in his voice? If it was, he might be in for a heartbreak as big as hers.

Fluffy chose that moment to leap onto Amber's desk in search of some affection. Pulling the cat close, Amber sighed. It was time to stop denying it. She had fallen hard for Dr. Phillip White.

"Do you want to hear how foolish I am, Fluffy? I may not get stuck behind the sofa but I'm a fool anyway. I've fallen in love with Phillip. Stupid, huh?"

The cat meowed softly as if in agreement.

It was foolish. A wonderful kind of foolishness. She'd never felt like this about anyone. She suspected the attraction was mutual. Even if it were, it wouldn't make a difference.

"He didn't come here looking for a relationship, Fluffy. He's doing his grandfather a favor, that's all. He came out of guilt, not because he wanted to work in an Amish community."

Fluffy remained silent this time.

"You're right. I'm going to do myself a favor by forgetting we had this conversation."

Raising the cat to look into his face, Amber said, "I hope you can keep a secret. I'm going to bed now and I'm not going to cry myself to sleep. I'll save that for the night he leaves."

It seemed like she'd barely closed her eyes when her doorbell began ringing incessantly. She glanced at the clock. It was a few minutes after three thirty in the morning.

The doorbell chimed again. Slipping into her robe,

she pulled it tight and padded barefoot down the stairs. It was likely that one of her expectant mothers needed her.

Turning on the porch light, she pulled aside the lace panel on the tall window that flanked her entryway.

To her surprise, she saw Elijah Knepp standing outside, his straw hat in his hand. She pulled open the door. "Elijah, what's wrong?"

"It is Sophie. Her time has come."

Amber's heart sank. "Elijah, I can't deliver her. Sophie must go to the hospital in Millersburg."

His brows snapped together in a worried scowl. "We do not wish the hospital."

"I'm sorry, but this is what Dr. White says must happen. Didn't you get his message last week?" She couldn't force anyone to accept medical care. She could only hope to persuade them to agree.

"*Ja*, we got the message. But it is not what we wanted. If you say we must, we will. Her time is close."

"Thank you. Let me grab her chart. The hospital will want it. Why don't you leave your buggy here? I'll drive you back to the farm and take both of you into the city. You can make arrangements for someone to get the buggy home in the morning."

"*Danki*. I will unhitch Dobby."

"You can put him in the side yard."

It wouldn't be the first Amish buggy to be parked in her drive overnight. She'd had a small area privacy fenced at the side of the house for such occasions.

Racing back upstairs to change, Amber wished with all her heart she could give Elijah and Sophie the kind of delivery they wanted. Being able to do home deliveries again was the one good thing that would happen when Phillip left.

Perhaps the only good thing. She would to cling to that bit of comfort.

Chapter Nineteen

The ringing of Phillip's cell phone woke him at a quarter to four. Picking it up, he mumbled, "Dr. White here."

"Phillip, this is Amber."

Her voice brought him wide-awake. "What's up?"

"I'm on my way to Sophie Knepp's home. She's in labor. Her husband came to get me."

He sat up and swung his legs over the side of the bed. "Okay. What's the plan?"

"I'm going to pick her up and drive her to the hospital. Why don't you meet us there?"

"Sounds good. How long?"

"It'll take me at least fifteen minutes to get out to the farm. I'd say we should be in Millersburg in forty minutes."

"All right. I'll meet you there."

Hanging up the phone, he headed for the shower. He couldn't be sure of his grandfather's motivation for allowing Amber to do home births, but if it meant more hours of sleep, it wasn't such a bad idea.

After a quick shower, he dressed and jumped into his car. He did think Sophie was a high-risk patient, but his conscience pricked him. She might not get to experience the calm, spiritual birth that he'd seen with Amber's other home delivery patients. Even so, it was better to be safe than sorry.

Halfway to Millersburg, he dialed Amber's number while he was stopped at a stop sign. It went straight to her voice mail. He left a brief message asking for an update, then snapped his phone shut and drove on. At the parking lot of the hospital, he placed another call to her number with the same results.

Why wasn't she picking up? What was wrong?

Up on the OB floor, he checked in with the night shift charge nurse. The young woman in pink scrubs smiled at him brightly. "How may I help you?"

"I'm Dr. Phillip White. I'm expecting a patient soon. Nurse-midwife Bradley is bringing her in. What room is she going to?"

"This is the first I've heard of an admission, Dr. White."

"Miss Bradley hasn't notified you?" He glanced at his watch. It had been almost an hour since he'd spoken to her last.

"No sir, but we have room six ready. Can I have the patient's name?"

"Sophie Knepp," he replied absently.

"Do you have her chart with you?"

"No. Excuse me a moment." He walked away from the desk and tried Amber's number once more. There was still no answer.

Driving on the dark roads required all Amber's concentration. In places it was rough and bumpy. It was easy to get lost on some of these twisting lanes. When they finally pulled up to the farmhouse, Mr. Knepp got out first and hurried toward the house. Pausing to grab her bag from the front seat, Amber noticed her phone on the car floor. Picking it up, she dropped it in her jacket pocket and followed Elijah inside.

It took her five seconds to see that Sophie was well into her labor. Her face, sweat streaked and red from exertion, filled with relief when she caught sight of Amber. "The baby is coming."

There was no way Amber was going to put her in a car and risk a delivery on the roadside somewhere between here and Millersburg. Smiling to reassure her, Amber said, "Hi, Sophie. It looks like you've done most of the work already."

Sophie's only answer was heavy breathing as another contraction took hold.

Pulling her phone from her pocket, Amber started to dial Phillip's number, but her phone screen remained blank.

Surprised, she tried again. "This isn't out of my service area. I should still get a signal."

She tapped the phone against her palm. Nothing. She tapped it harder. Still nothing. It couldn't be the battery. She'd put a new one in two days ago. Maybe it had broken when it fell out of her bag.

Sophie spoke up. "I do not want to go to the hospital."

Amber shook her phone again. "I'm sorry, we talked about this. The doctor feels it's best that you do."

Sophie, wide-eyed, shook her head. "There is no time."

Amber slipped her useless phone in her pocket, then took off her jacket and looked for a place to lay it. Elijah took it from her. She muttered her thanks and started laying out her things. Babies didn't care what doctors wanted. They came in their own good time. This one was going to arrive very soon. She needed to get ready.

For another hour, Phillip waited by the hospital maternity desk, drumming his fingers, turning down offers of coffee and pacing. His first instinct was to rush out to the Knepp farm, but he knew he'd never find his way in the dark. He wasn't sure he could remember the way in broad daylight.

He'd spent more time enjoying Amber's company than memorizing the twisting roads when they'd made prenatal visits to her clients. If he hadn't been so smitten with her he'd be more effective now in tracking her down. That irony wasn't lost on him.

When a second full hour had gone by, he couldn't wait any longer. Something was up. She wouldn't blow him off like this. Maybe she'd had an accident. His mind shied away from that thought, but he knew something had gone wrong.

Returning to the desk, he leaned on the counter and spoke to the charge nurse. "How do I contact the sheriff?"

The nurse dialed the emergency number and handed him the phone. When dispatch answered, he quickly explained the situation. After being asked to wait, he impatiently held the line, his fear growing by leaps and bounds. Finally, a man's voice came on.

"This is Nick Bradley. You think something has happened to Amber?"

"She hasn't shown up at the hospital, she's not answering her phone. Did she call 911?"

"We've got no record of that. Stay at the hospital, Doc. I'm on my way. I'll pick you up out front."

Amber was loading her supplies in the back of her station wagon when she saw the flashing lights coming up the lane. Oh, dear. Phillip had pulled out all the stops to find her. At least she knew he cared.

When the sheriff's car stopped beside her and an officer got out, she gave him a little wave. "Hi, Nick."

She saw Phillip emerge from the cruiser's passenger side door. Her heart did a funny little flip-flop at the sight of him. He was a tall, lean silhouette against the blood-red sunrise; she couldn't see his face.

The sheriff said, "You okay, cuz?"

"I'm fine, Nick. Sorry you were sent on a wild goose chase."

"When someone tells me my little cousin is missing, I don't take that lightly. What's the story?"

"Yes, Amber. What is the story?" Phillip asked coming up behind Nick.

"It was the weirdest thing. I called you on my cell phone and told you I was on my way here. When I arrived, I tried to notify you, but my phone didn't work. I think it broke when it fell out of my bag."

Nick gestured toward the house. "Everything go okay?"

"Sophie and her new daughter are fine. They were settling down to sleep when I left. Phillip, I was going to call you as soon as I got to a phone. Thanks for sending the cavalry after me. Even if I didn't need it."

He approached and stood close. Softly, he said, "I'm just thankful you're okay."

His voice vibrated with deep emotion. He held out

his hand. She took it and he squeezed tightly, as if he'd never let go. Amber wanted to throw her arms around him and reassure him with a kiss. Having her eagle-eyed cousin observing them kept her from doing something so foolish.

Nick opened his cell phone and held it up. "I've got cell service here. I wonder why you can't get it?"

"It wasn't that I didn't have service. The thing was dead. It wouldn't work."

Suddenly, her phone began ringing. Both men looked at her in surprise.

Amber dug it out of her pocket, her surprise equal to the men standing beside her. She opened the phone and said, "Hello?"

"Honey, are you all right?" It was Wilma.

"I'm fine."

"I heard the sheriff's office is looking for you."

"They found me."

"Thank the Lord for that. Where are you?"

Amber saw a scowl begin to darken Phillip's face. "Wilma, I'll give you the details when I get to the office. I've got to go."

Closing the phone, she looked Phillip straight in the eye. "It was not working an hour ago. At least the delivery went off without a hitch. I told you it would."

A remote expression turned his face to stone. "You had to do it your way, didn't you? You had to prove I was wrong."

"What?" Was he implying she deliberately didn't take Sophie to the hospital?

"I never thought you'd risk her life to make a point." Disappointment filled his voice.

Amber stood toe-to-toe with him. "If I planned to attend her at home, why did I call you in the first place?"

"Beats me, but it's clear your phone works. I've seen people devoted to their jobs, but you take the cake, Amber. What if something had gone wrong?"

Anger sent her pulse pounding. Crossing her arms, she glared at him. "Nothing did go wrong, so I was *right* all along."

"Whoa." Nick stepped in between them. "There'll be no bloodshed on my watch. It makes too much paperwork."

Seething, she said, "Don't worry, Nick. I wouldn't waste my time trying to knock some sense into Dr. White. There's no room in that brain with his overgrown ego taking up so much space."

Phillip's jaw tightened and his eyes narrowed. For a second, she thought she'd gone too far. When he spoke his voice was like ice. "Take the day off, Miss Bradley. We'll manage without you at the office."

"Fine. I'd love to." Marching to her car, Amber got in, slammed the door and started the engine. Her anger began draining away and tears rushed in to fill the void.

How could he think she would play such a trick on him? She pressed the heels of her hands into her stinging eyes to stem her tears. It didn't help.

It had been such a beautiful birth. The calmness, the joy on their faces when they saw their little girl. From their rushed start to the peaceful finish, it had gone without a bit of trouble.

Phillip would have robbed them of one of the most precious moments of their lives because he didn't trust *her* judgment. He didn't believe in her skill. He believed she was capable of underhanded deceit and lying to his face.

Slamming the car in gear, she backed up to turn around in the narrow yard. When she had the car straight, she saw Mr. Knepp coming out of the barn with his oldest son. Each of them carried pails full of frothy milk.

Rolling down her window, she said, "I'll be happy to take your son into town so he can bring your buggy back but I must leave now."

She heard Phillip call her name. She ignored him.

Setting his pails down, Mr. Knepp spoke quietly to his son, handed him something, then spoke to her. "*Danki*. Walter will go with you."

Again she heard Phillip call her name. She refused to look that way. She had no intention of letting him see she was crying.

Walter raced around to the passenger side of the car, eager to ride in the normally forbidden automobile. When he got in, she said, "Buckle up."

After he complied, she stomped on the gas and tore down the dirt lane. She left her window rolled down so the warm air would dry the tears on her cheeks.

Walter, at sixteen, loved everything about cars. He chatted happily on the way to town and changed the radio station a dozen times. Amber didn't mind. It saved her from having to make conversation.

When they reached her home, she got out feeling as if her entire body were made of lead. She couldn't remember the last time she felt so disconnected. Her tears were done but they'd brought on a pounding headache.

Walter went to get the horse and she waited until he returned and harnessed the animal. When he climbed into the buggy, she stepped up to the driver's side. "Please remind your mother that I will be back tomorrow to check on her and your new sister."

"My *dat* asked me to give you this." He held out a note.

She opened the slip of paper. It was a brief apology for disabling her phone. She looked up at Walter in shock. "Your father tampered with my phone?"

"*Mamm* did not want to go to the hospital. *Dat* took your battery out when you weren't looking and put it back before you were ready to leave. He does it to my phone whenever he finds it."

Lifting his pant leg to show his boot, he pulled a cell phone out of his sock. "I hide it better now, and I keep a spare battery in the barn."

The Amish never ceased to amaze her. She knew that their teenagers often ventured outside the Church rules to use modern gadgets such as phones and radios. Without electricity in their homes, they had to find an English friend or neighbor who would charge the battery-powered devices for them.

While parents often turned a blind eye to such behaviors, Mr. Knepp had apparently learned how to silence his son's unwanted intrusion in his home. The Knepps belonged to the Swartzentruber Amish, the most conservative group. Walter would soon have to give up his worldly ways or face growing Church disapproval of him and his family.

Walter said, "*Dat* is sorry if you were upset."

"Tell your father he is forgiven." There was nothing else she could do.

"*Danki*, I will." He slapped the reins and sent the horse trotting out into the street.

Amber stared at the note. She had proof that she hadn't lied about her phone. When Phillip saw this he'd realize how wrong he'd been.

Suddenly angry, she crumpled the note and tore it

into shreds. Phillip shouldn't need a note to prove she was honest. What an idiot she'd been to think she was in love with him. He didn't trust her. How could she love a man like that?

That answer was simple. She couldn't.

Chapter Twenty

"How long are you going to keep giving me the silent treatment?"

Phillip watched as Amber ignored his question, laid the patient chart he'd asked for on his desk and walked out of the room. Apparently, she could be silent a little longer.

Wilma, standing on the other side of his desk, tucked her pencil behind her ear, crossed her arms and scowled at him. "I don't know what you did. I've never seen her this upset."

Shooting her a sour look, he asked, "What makes you think I'm to blame?"

"Because you're a man."

There was no point arguing with her logic. He was beginning to think he had liked Wilma better when she was a timid mouse. Who knew she could become a spitting cat when her friends were in trouble? "Just order those forms and check to see if we have more printer ink somewhere."

"Yes, sir." She rolled her eyes and started to leave, but stopped at the door and turned around.

"What now?" he demanded.

Pointing at him, she said, "Don't be crabby with me, young man. I'm old enough to be your grandmother. I deserve some respect."

She was right. He folded his hands and made himself smile. "I'm sorry, Mrs. Nolan. What is it you wanted to tell me?"

"That young Mennonite doctor who was here last year called after you left last night. He wants to come interview for the position."

Phillip's spirits shot skyward. Maybe he could get Harold the partner he needed. "That's great. Thank you, Wilma. I'll give him a call and we can set something up."

"Maybe he'll be smart enough not to go around upsetting the Amish, Harold and everyone else." She closed the door behind her when she left.

Phillip's elation popped like a balloon hitting a thorn tree. It had been like this for three days. Amber spoke to him only when necessary. Wilma never missed a chance to deliver a jab. If this was how his last three weeks were going to go, he honestly didn't think he could take it.

How was he supposed to run a clinic with a nurse who wouldn't speak to him? Maybe he should have handled the whole thing differently.

He had cooled off considerably by the time Nick Bradley dropped him at the office after leaving the Knepp farm. After all, Amber had been found safe and sound. Mrs. Knepp and her daughter seemed fine. He had checked on them before he left the farm. He'd almost called Amber then to apologize but his pride had held him back. He wasn't wrong. She was.

How often had she insisted Sophie Knepp wasn't a high-risk patient? Unable to change his mind on the subject, she'd gone behind his back and delivered the woman at home anyway. What he didn't understand was why Amber wouldn't admit she'd turned her phone off on purpose. She'd been found out. She had nothing to gain by pretending anymore.

Unless she was telling the truth.

That nagging voice at the back of his brain was getting louder by the hour. He hadn't known Amber very long but she didn't seem like an underhanded person. She was warm and witty and devoted to the people of her community.

Okay, there had been that time at church when she'd seated him with Gina Curtis. That had been a little sneaky but it was nothing compared to this. Was his ability to read a person that messed up?

If she had told the truth, what could he do at this point? He'd already called her a liar. In front of her cousin, no less. Would she even accept his apology?

He glanced at his watch. It was almost four and it was time to end this standoff. They had to work together. He would eat crow. One wouldn't hurt him. There were plenty more out in the cornfields.

He pressed the intercom button. "Wilma, ask Amber to step in here, please."

"Can't."

Letting go of the button, he muttered a few unkind words under his breath, then asked. "Why not?"

"She's with Sophie Knepp and her new baby."

"Sophie wasn't scheduled to come in until Monday. Is something wrong?"

"Oh, yes."

He rose and headed for the door. Before he reached it,

it flew open. Amber stood in the doorway with a look of panic on her face. "You need to come quick."

"What's the matter?"

"It's Sophie Knepp. She's hallucinating and muttering that God is taking another child away. She won't let me see that baby."

"Is her husband with her?"

"Yes."

They crossed the hall and Phillip saw Amber wasn't exaggerating. Sophie sat plucking invisible things from the baby's blanket and throwing them away as fast as she could. She kept muttering the same phrase over and over.

Quietly, he asked Amber, "What's she saying?"

"That leaves are falling and covering her baby. She has to keep them away or her baby will be buried."

Phillip looked at her husband. "When did this start?"

"This morning. She picked up the baby and started crying. I couldn't get her to stop." He stood against the wall turning his straw hat around and around in his hands. He looked worried to death.

Phillip sat on a stool and moved in front of her. "Sophie, I'm Dr. White. Do you remember me?"

She didn't answer, didn't make eye contact. He moved closer slowly and touched her hand. "Sophie, I need to see your pretty little girl."

She stopped picking and started crying. Carefully, he withdrew the swaddled child. Laying the baby on the exam table, he opened the blankets. The child looked asleep. To his relief she was clearly breathing. She was also very jaundiced.

He looked at Mr. Knepp. "How long has her skin been so yellow?"

"Since two days after she was born."

Amber broke in. "I told you to contact me if the baby's jaundice got worse."

"When we saw the whites of her eyes were yellow, too, we knew God was taking her from us as He did our first children."

Puzzled, Phillip asked, "You've had other children with jaundice?"

"Twin girls who both died before they were two years old. Then we had strong sons and more healthy daughters. Why has God put this burden on us again?"

Sophie sat rocking herself and staring into space.

Phillip said, "Elijah, your wife is very sick. This is a rare thing called postpartum psychosis. She needs to be hospitalized, but she will get better."

The man nodded without looking convinced. Phillip turned to Amber. "Call an ambulance, then call the hospital and tell them we need a mental health assessment for Sophie. After that, call the Peds unit and tell them we need triple phototherapy lights for this little one. I also want a total bilirubin level STAT along with standard admission lab."

"Yes, Doctor."

He asked, "Mr. Knepp, do you understand what jaundice is?"

When the man shook his head, Phillip explained. "This is a common thing in newborns. Jaundice refers to the yellow color of the skin and whites of the eyes caused by excess bilirubin in the blood. Bilirubin is a chemical produced by the normal breakdown of red blood cells. We all have a little in our blood. Normally, bilirubin passes through the liver and is excreted as bile by our intestines. This yellow color occurs when bilirubin builds up faster than the baby's liver can break it down and pass it from the body. We treat it by putting the child under a special light. If the level is very high, we may have to do an exchange transfusion. To do that, we take out some of the blood with the high concentration and put in blood with normal levels."

"Will she die from this as our other children did?"

"I'll do everything I can to make sure that doesn't happen."

Within thirty minutes, both Knepp patients were on their way to the hospital. Phillip was getting into his car to follow the ambulance when Amber came running up to him. She grasped his arm in a tight grip. "I have to know, Phillip. Did I miss something? The jaundice was barely visible the day after birth. I told them to bring her in if it got worse."

The look in her eyes tugged at his heart. He didn't want to answer her. He wanted to pull her into his arms, kiss her and tell her everything would be all right, but that might be a lie.

Home deliveries weren't safe. Maybe she hadn't missed anything at the birth, but a woman and her baby need round-the-clock observation for two days after a delivery. Most state laws require a mother and her new-born to stay in the hospital at least that long.

He had tried to make that point. Amber had made it for him.

When Phillip didn't answer, Amber's heart sank. "I saw them the day after delivery and nothing looked out of the ordinary. Lots of newborns have mild jaundice."

She bit her lip as she waited for him to say something, anything.

"Amber, there are too many unknowns for me to start

guessing now. We need some solid information. Let's run some lab tests and find out why the baby is so jaundiced at four days old."

"Sophie's blood type is O positive so it can't be an RH incompatibility. Sepsis? The baby didn't act sick or look dehydrated. Maybe it's an ABO problem. And what about Sophie?" Amber knew she was babbling. She couldn't help herself.

He gripped her hand. "Calm down. You'll drive yourself nuts doing this. Postpartum psychosis can occur anywhere from one to three months after delivery. I've not heard of a case starting four days after birth, but I haven't researched it. Were the signs there when you saw her? We may never know. The best thing that could happen is happening now. They're getting the treatment they need."

She withdrew her hand. "You're right."

"Do you want to come with me to the hospital?"

Shaking her head, she stepped back. "I'd only be in the way."

"All right, I have to get going. I'll fill you in when I get back."

After he drove away, Amber went back inside the clinic. Wilma, getting ready to close up, slipped her purse strap over her shoulder. "Is everybody okay?"

"Sophie was sedated enough to go calmly. Elijah looked like a zombie. I don't think he knows what's hit him. The baby was sleeping quietly in the car seat the EMS brought."

"Dr. White will find out what's wrong. Don't worry."

"You think he's a good doctor, don't you?"

"As good as Harold. Maybe better."

Turning around, Amber began pacing across the lobby as she racked her mind for every little detail. "For a baby to get that jaundiced so fast, it must have been worse than I thought when I saw her last. Why didn't I pick up on that?"

"Amber, you're a great midwife. You love your patients. You'd never hurt them."

Pressing her hand to her forehead, Amber closed her eyes. "I remember checking her nose. I always push lightly on the tip of their noses to see what color their skin was underneath. I do that on all newborn checks."

"See? What did I tell you?"

"I was so mad that day. Did my anger at Phillip cloud my judgment? Did I want to be right so badly that I fooled myself into thinking everything was fine? That baby could have permanent brain damage if her jaundice causes kernicterus."

"What does that mean?"

"If the levels of bilirubin in her blood rise high enough to cross the blood-brain barrier, the bilirubin can enter her brain cells and damage them."

Wilma took Amber by the shoulders. "Some things are out of our control. We are human. Only God is perfect. Beating yourself up is not helping. Go home and get some rest."

Dropping her arms to her side, Amber nodded. "I will. First, I need to call Harold."

"That reminds me. The charts Dr. White wanted were delivered a little while ago." Returning to her desk, Wilma picked up a large package and brought it to Amber.

Taking it, Amber said, "I'll see that he gets them."

After Wilma left, Amber retreated to her office and put a call through to the rehab hospital in Hawaii. When Harold came to the phone, she started crying. It seemed

like she was always crying. How many tears did she
have left?

"Amber? What on earth is wrong? Get a hold of yourself. Has something happened to my grandson?"

The fright in his voice forced her to gain a modicum
of control. "Phillip…I mean, Dr. White, is fine. It's nothing like that."

"Thank heaven. Then what is it?"

After blotting her face and blowing her nose, she was
able to relate the event of the afternoon with only a few
hiccups.

He said, "Another yellow baby for Sophie. I'm so, so,
sorry to hear that. The twins she lost were such beautiful little girls."

"What was the cause of death?"

"I'm not sure. It had to be some kind of liver disorder, but all the liver function studies were normal. It was
very puzzling. Both Sophie and Elijah said they had family members who had lost children from the same thing.
They knew the girls were going to die. I tried everything.
Phototherapy and blood transfusions worked for a while,
but once we stopped them the jaundice came back. There
was nothing left to do but let them take the girls home
to die. We accepted it as God's will."

"That must have been awful for Sophie. Seeing this
baby getting jaundice may be what triggered her psychosis."

"I imagine you're right."

"I'll let Phillip know what you've told me. I'll pray
this isn't the same thing."

"I'll do the same. All those tears over Sophie's illness,
that's not like you, Amber. What's going on?"

"We need you back," she moaned, then pressed her

fingers to her lips. She had no intention of telling him that his grandson was breaking her heart.

"I'm getting better by leaps and bounds."

"Are you? Honestly?"

"Okay, now you've got me worried."

"Don't be. Things are…okay here. I'm tired. I miss you."

"Are you sure there isn't something else you want to tell me? Are you and Phillip still not getting along? Wilma told me he accused you of doing deliveries without his consent. I'm gonna have to have a talk with that boy."

"No," she said promptly. "Just…just get well soon. Everyone misses you."

"Okay." He didn't sound convinced but he hung up.

Amber settled the handset back in the cradle and lowered her head on her folded arms. She did miss Harold. Things were okay at the clinic. It was only her heart that was broken.

She'd seen the look in Phillip's eyes. The look that said she had messed up big-time. Exactly the way he had expected.

Sitting up, she dried her face on her sleeve. After leaving her office, she locked up the building and got in her car. She didn't drive home.

Chapter Twenty-One

When Phillip pulled into his grandfather's driveway it was well after eleven o'clock at night. He'd had a long day and an even longer evening.

Getting out of the car, he headed for the front steps. Someone rose from the wrought iron bench that circled the maple in the front yard and came toward him. He saw it was Amber when she stepped into the light coming from the front porch.

She had her hands clenched tightly in front of her. "How are they?"

"Both of them are doing better."

He heard her sigh of relief. "I'm so glad."

They stood staring at each other like strangers in the near darkness. How had their relationship gotten so out of whack?

"Amber, you should go home."

"I needed to know how they are."

He walked toward the bench and sat down. She joined him but left some distance between them.

Running his hand through his hair, he said, "Sophie has been admitted to the psychiatric unit. Little Grace had a bilirubin level of twenty-six milligrams per deci-liter. We did an exchange transfusion and got it down to sixteen."

"That's still a long way above a normal of four."

"She'll stay under triple lights for now. We're doing a workup to see if this is an infection. It doesn't look like it."

"Will she have brain damage from such a high level?"

"You mean will she want to be a doctor when she grows up?" He didn't get the smile he was hoping for.

"Phillip, please. Tell me."

"She's lethargic but she isn't showing the more se-rious symptoms of kernicterus. They'll check her bili level again at midnight. I came home to get a change of clothes. I'll be spending the night at the hospital."

She nodded slightly. "I talked to Harold about So-phie's other children who died. He thinks it was some kind of liver disorder."

"All Grace's liver studies are normal. You know that in some cases the reason for a high bilirubin is never found and the child recovers. Grace was a little dehydrated. I think she'll be fine in a few days. Stop worrying."

"I can't help feeling guilty."

He hated to add to her burden, but he didn't believe in sugarcoating the truth. "To have a bili level this high this soon after birth, she had to have had some symp-toms when you saw her."

Clasping her arms across her middle, Amber stood. "I'm so sorry. I thought it was ordinary newborn jaun-dice. I should have gone back to see her again."

"Amber, mistakes happen." He rose and reached for her. She stepped away. She wouldn't look at him.

"You'll stop all my home births, won't you?" She sniffed and wiped her face with the heels of her hands.

"I have to. You know that." He hated giving her this news on top of everything else.

She gave a short, quick nod. "I knew you would."

Picking up a mailing envelope, she held it out to him. "These are the old charts you wanted."

He took them, wondering what he could say to make this whole thing better. No words came to him.

She said, "Thanks for giving me an update on Sophie and Grace. I'll see you on Monday."

Before he could stop her, she vanished into the darkness.

Phillip kept close tabs on Grace overnight. Her bilirubin levels dropped as expected. With no sign of infection or other underlying problems, he thought he'd be able to send her home in a few days.

By early in the morning, he was able to gradually drop the number of blue lights to one. Her level stayed low and steady. He went home.

He wanted to call Amber then, but he wasn't sure what to say. In spite of being exhausted, he slept poorly. The phone rang shortly after six thirty the next morning. The news was good. Grace's levels were much lower.

He'd had the nursing staff take the lights off for six hours and recheck her. She might have some rebound but he didn't expect much.

Waiting was the hardest, so he called to get an update on Sophie. The report he got for her was good. Sophie continued to improve with medication, but she remained under the care of her psychiatrist. It might be several more days before she could be reunited with her baby.

Getting dressed, Phillip got ready to go into work, eager to see Amber and find out how she was doing. The answer, as it turned out, was not well.

She came in to work but remained aloof and withdrawn. He missed her smile more than he missed the sea. When he tried to talk with her, she found something to do elsewhere.

A little after one o'clock, Wilma came toward him with a sheet of paper in her hand. "The hospital called over these lab reports for you."

"Thank you."

Just then Amber came out of the exam room. She muttered, "Excuse me." Then she slipped between them and went into her office and shut the door without another word.

He stared after her. "Wilma, what are we going to do with her? I hate to see her like this."

Patting his arm, Wilma said, "She'll come around. She feels responsible. She's going to have to learn to live with that. Medicine is not for the faint of heart."

"Amen to that."

"How are you doing?"

"Me? I'm fine."

"Are you?" Wilma nodded toward Amber's door. "I ask because you've got the same hangdog look on your face that she's wearing."

As Wilma walked away, he glanced at the lab report in his hands. Grace's bilirubin level had shot back up. Her jaundice had returned.

This was not right. Puzzled, he went to his phone and called the pediatric unit with orders to restart the lights and retest her in six hours.

Sitting at his desk, he noticed the old chart files he'd

been too busy to review. He opened them and began to study them.

The first chart he picked was the child named Knepp. As it turned out, it wasn't one of Sophie's children. The parents were Otto and Norma Knepp. Their child had died at eighteen months from persistent jaundice. As he read the lab reports and notes by his grandfather, he became more and more intrigued. It was as if he were reading Grace's chart. The similarities were too close to ignore.

There was a soft knock at his door. Amber looked in, staring at a point over his head. Each time she couldn't bring herself to look him in the face, another piece got shaved off his heart. He had no idea how to mend it.

She said, "I'm getting ready to leave. Do you need anything before I go?"

A kiss, a hug, a smile. I want you back, Amber. How do I do that? Help me, God. Help me find a way through this wall she's put up between us.

He glanced at the chart in his hands. Medicine was her life. Somehow, the answer was in their work.

"Amber, do you remember a child of Otto and Norma Knepp who died about eight years ago?"

He saw the hesitation in her face, but her curiosity won out. "I do. The funeral was held the day after I arrived here. Why?"

"I started reading this old chart and found that this Knepp child died of severe jaundice at eighteen months of age."

Amber stepped inside the room. He wanted to shout for joy. Instead, he kept his gaze down. She asked, "Was it liver failure?"

Leafing though the chart, he said, "Not according to

these lab reports. Do you know if Otto and Elijah are related?"

"I believe they're first cousins. Actually, I think Norma and Sophie are second cousins." She came to peer over his shoulder at the papers he held.

His heart raced at her nearness. It was a struggle to keep his voice level. "Sophie's twins, this child and now Grace, all related. This suggests we are dealing with some kind of inherited disorder."

"Like what?"

"I'm not sure. Maybe something like Dubin-Johnson or Rotor's syndromes, maybe—" He spun around to the computer and began typing.

Pulling a chair up, she sat beside him. "Maybe what?"

His frustration at the slow speed of the dial-up connection was offset by Amber's nearness. He wouldn't care if it took an hour to get online as long as she stayed beside him.

Nudging him with her elbow, she repeated, "Maybe what?"

"Maybe it's Crigler-Najjar Syndrome."

Her eyebrows shot up. "Why does that sound familiar?"

"It's a very rare recessive genetic defect. The actual incidence is less than one case per one million live births."

"One in a million?" she repeated. "And you think we've had four suspected cases in our town? That's kind of a stretch."

"No, it's not. There are only about two hundred cases of Crigler-Najjar Syndrome in the world. There are nearly forty cases in the United States. Care to guess where the majority of those are found?"

He saw the lightbulb come on. She leaned toward him eagerly. "A recessive gene disorder would occur more frequently in a population with limited common ancestors."

"Bingo. Old Order Amish and Mennonite communities." The computer finally connected. She bumped him with her elbow to gain access to his keyboard.

Happily, he allowed it, grinning like a schoolkid. This was the woman he'd come to love, determined, smart and eager to help. She typed quickly and pulled up the website for the Pennsylvania Clinic for Special-Needs Children.

Tapping the screen with her finger, she said, "This is where they're doing wonders with genetic research among the Amish. They are working on treatments and, someday, maybe even cures."

"How do you know this?" He stared at her in amazement.

"I read everything I can about my mother's people. This is the contact information for the clinic." She pointed to a number scrolling at the bottom of the screen.

Leaning close to look, he inhaled the clean, citrus scent of her hair and the fragrance that was uniquely her own. It sent his head swimming. He reached for the mouse at the same time she did. His hand covered hers.

Her gaze flew to his face, those beautiful mermaid eyes widened with wonder. He'd never wanted to kiss anyone so badly in his whole life.

Never had Amber wanted a man to kiss her as much as she wanted to be kissed by Phillip. He knew it. She saw it in his gaze.

He was so close. If she moved a fraction of an inch toward him it would be the impetus he needed. The temptation was so great it formed a physical ache in her chest.

"Amber." He breathed her name into the air with such longing.

Turning her face away, she concentrated on keeping her wild emotions in check.

He squeezed her hand. "Tell me you feel the way I do about you. Tell me I'm not imagining this...thing we have."

"Phillip, there's no future for us."

Taking her chin in his hand, he tipped her face toward him. "Are you sure about that?"

"Maybe," she whispered, wishing for some way to keep this wonderful man in her life.

His tender smile was her undoing. Closing her eyes, she raised her lips to his. His kiss, featherlight at first, slowly deepened as his hands cupped her face. This was how it was meant to be between two people in love.

Pulling away at last, he drew a ragged breath. "You rock my world, Amber. We can work this out, darling. I know we can."

"How? Do you give up your dreams or do I give up mine? How long before one of us starts to feel cheated? To wonder if it was worth it? I won't do that to you. I won't do it to myself."

How she wanted to snatch her words out of the air and take them back. She couldn't because they were the truth.

"I understand." His voice grew rough as he withdrew his hand in a soft caress. "I don't like it, but I understand."

Clenching her jaw, she refused to acknowledge the stinging behind her eyes. She forced her attention back to the computer screen. "This may not be what Grace has."

When he didn't say anything, she chanced a glance in his direction. He stared at her with a lost, sad look in his eyes.

After a moment, he blinked hard, then focused on the computer and took control of the mouse. "I'll have to do some further research on this disorder, but I think we're on to something."

He clicked through to information and symptoms of the disorder. "It says high levels of unconjugated bilirubin in the presence of normal liver function is characteristic of CNS. That's exactly what I've found with Grace. The cause of CNS is a missing liver enzyme. That explains a lot."

Amber forced herself to concentrate on the computer screen and not on her breaking heart. A child needed their help. "Grace's liver functions normally, but without that specific enzyme, the production of bilirubin in the blood can't be controlled by her body."

"Right. Nothing we've tested for so far could detect that."

One more click brought up the picture of a child resting in a crib under intense blue lights. A mirror on one side of the crib reflected the light around the sleeping infant.

Phillip said, "The current treatment is twelve hours of phototherapy a day for their entire lives. With the type 1, which sounds like Grace's illness, patients will die before they are two years old without these special blue lights."

Amber couldn't imagine trying to sleep one night under such intense lamps, let alone a whole lifetime.

He leaned closer to the screen. "These people are doing some fascinating work. In rural Pennsylvania, of all places. How strange is that? They've identified more than thirty-five different diseases that Amish children can be born with. Wow. What I wouldn't give to tour their facility."

"Is there anything else that can be done for Grace?"

"Sorry, I got off on a tangent for a second. It says a liver transplant provides the only known cure."

Sitting back, he shook his head. "A transplant exchanges one set of problems for another. Costly antirejection drugs, infections, a whole host of other potential complications."

"But it can save her life?"

He looked at her. "Yes. Would the Amish consent to a liver transplant for one of their children?"

"Harold told me they won't accept heart transplants. I do know someone who had a kidney transplant. Yes, I believe most of them would allow it. They're not opposed to modern medicine."

Rubbing his chin with one hand, he studied the screen. "She would need home phototherapy lights like the ones in the picture in order to survive until she's old enough for a transplant."

Amber sat back with a sigh. "I see one big hurdle with that."

"What?"

"The Amish have no electricity in their homes."

"That is a big problem. Would they make an exception for this?"

"I'm not sure. What is the likelihood of matching Grace for a liver?"

"We're getting ahead of ourselves. First we need to confirm that this is what she has." He picked up the phone and began dialing.

"Who are you calling?"

"The physicians at the Pennsylvania Clinic for Special Needs Children. I want to pick their brains."

Rising to her feet, she stared down at him with pride and sadness. She deeply admired his intensity, his knowledge and his desire to help patients. He was a fine doctor. She would be sorry to see him leave—for that reason and many others.

As she headed for the door, he softly called her name. When she looked back, he said, "Thank you."

She gave him a half smile and a short nod. He was a good man but he wasn't the man for her.

The eagerness in his voice as he spoke with the genetic specialist and the questions he fired off proved to her he'd never be happy practicing small-town medicine. His vocation lay in another direction.

Her calling was here among the Amish. Only, how could she be happy in Hope Springs without Phillip?

Chapter Twenty-Two

At the sound of her phone ringing, Amber laid aside her duster to answer it. Even a telemarketer would be a welcome break from her Saturday morning housecleaning. How did things get so dirty in a week?

Snatching up the portable handset, she pressed it to her ear. "Hello?"

"Amber, I'm glad I caught you." The cheerful voice belonged to Jennifer Hart, the director of the county animal shelter.

A sinking sensation hit the pit of Amber's stomach. Crossing to her kitchen table, she parked herself on one of the chairs. "What's up?"

"We have room at the shelter now for the cat you are fostering."

Oh, no. Amber knew this day was coming, but she still wasn't prepared. "Jennifer, I don't mind keeping Fluffy a little longer. I've been thinking about adopting him myself."

"We've had an inquiry about him from our website. A family in Toledo believes he's the cat they lost when they were on vacation. They're driving down to see him tomorrow. I'm sorry, Amber. Is there any way you can bring him in today?"

Fluffy had a family searching for him. Adopting him was out of the question now. Amber fought back sudden, unexpected tears. What was wrong with her? She should be thrilled for her pet and the unknown family. "Sure. I can bring him in."

Ten minutes later, Amber could barely see the front door for her tears. She didn't want company but the persistent knocking would not stop. Setting her now-damp cat down off her lap, she wiped her swollen eyes with a paper towel and jerked open the door. "Yes?"

It was Phillip. Why did it have to be him?

"Amber, you're crying. What's wrong, honey?"

Sympathy was the last thing she needed. She started boo-hooing again.

Without another word, he stepped inside and took her in his arms. One hand cupped the back of her head and tucked her face against him. The other arm held her tight as she cried out her heartbreak. Softly, he swayed and rocked her as if she were a child. Over and over, he murmured that it would be okay.

No, it wouldn't.

Her sobbing slowed to an occasional hiccup, but she didn't move. She simply rested in the gentleness of his embrace, soaking in his masculine smell and warmth. He would be gone soon. When he was, she would remember this moment of kindness for a long, long time.

He leaned back to look down at her. "What happened?"

"It's just the last straw." She fought back a new flood of tears.

Slipping a finger under her chin, he raised her face to his. "What was the last straw?"

"The Humane Society wants Fluffy back. I have to take him there this afternoon." Her lip started quivering.

"I'm so sorry. Can't you adopt him?"

"He has a family already."

"You're his family."

"No, the family that lost him wants him back. I knew I wouldn't keep him but I didn't know how attached I was going to get, either."

That, in a nutshell, was what was wrong with her whole life. The things she loved were gone or going away. Her practice, unless Harold came back, her cat, this wonderful man—it wasn't fair.

Moving out of his arms was the last thing she wanted to do. She forced herself to do it anyway. "What are you doing here, Phillip?"

"I need your help."

Rubbing her cheeks with her palms, she cleared her throat and tried to look like a calm, reasonable woman instead of a wreck. "Sure. What do you need me to do?"

"I'm meeting with Elijah Knepp and some of his Church elders at five o'clock tonight. I'm sorry for the short notice. We were right about Grace having Crigler-Nijjar syndrome. I got confirmation this morning."

"Oh, no. I hoped we were wrong." Her heart ached for Grace and her parents. Returning Fluffy paled in comparison to such heartrending news.

"Elijah was at the hospital this morning. Sophie has been released. Both of them came to see the baby. When I explained what Grace would need to go home, they said no. Can you believe that?"

Putting her own troubles aside, she gestured toward

the living room. "Have a seat. Let me wash my face and we can talk about this."

"I'm sorry to bring this to you but I didn't know who else could help."

After Amber made herself presentable, she joined Phillip in the living room. Agitated, he paced back and forth in front of her bay window. Taking a seat in one of her chairs, she asked, "Can I get you something to drink? A soda? I have iced tea made."

He stopped pacing and turned around. "No, I'm fine. Tell me why these people won't allow electricity in their home to save their child's life."

How could she explain it to him? "Phillip, the Amish believe they are commanded to be separate from the world. Literally. Having power lines come to their home makes them connected to the world at large."

"Grace will die without those lights."

"We all die. The Amish understand that and accept it in a way that is foreign to many people. They know that Grace will be in a better place, a place without pain or want. They love their child as any parent loves their child, but they believe they will be with her in heaven. She will not be lost to them."

He turned to stare out the window. "You were supposed to help. How can I argue against that when it is what I believe as a Christian?"

She rose and moved to his side. "I'm not suggesting we give up. I'm simply saying we have to work within their system."

Rubbing the back of his neck, he asked, "How do we do that?"

"Do you know why my phone didn't work the night Sophie gave birth?"

"Why?"

"Because Elijah slipped the battery out when I wasn't looking and put it back in before I left."

Looking stunned, he pressed the fingers of one hand against his temple. "Okay, two questions. Why? And how did he know *how* to do that?"

"The why was because Sophie didn't want to deliver at the hospital. He knew how because his son uses a cell phone. The cell phone operates on a battery and is not connected to landlines so some Amish are accepting them."

"That seems contradictory."

"Welcome to the Amish world. What we need is a way to provide the power for Sophie's light without electric lines to the house." Amber started pacing.

"A generator?" he suggested.

"That may not work. The Knepps belong to an ultra-conservative church district that doesn't allow the use of gas."

"How do the Amish feel about solar power?"

Returning to her chair, Amber sat forward and laced her fingers together around her knees. "Solar might be okay. It's light from God to power the world. Maybe that's the right angle. If their Church elders don't agree to the lights, then Sophie and Elijah will have to abide by that decision or be shunned."

"It doesn't seem right." He shook his head in frustration.

"For the Amish, it is not about the individual. It is about the good of the whole."

"Then the good of the whole is the angle I need."

"I'd say so."

He sat in the armchair opposite her. "Let's think this through."

Folding her jean-clad legs under her, she stared at the floor. "My mind is a blank."

"I'm sorry. I know you're upset about your cat. I shouldn't have come running to you."

She waved aside his concern. "I don't have to leave for a while yet. I'm glad you came."

He rose and started pacing again, his brow furrowed in concentration. She didn't envy him his task. His words today might mean the difference between life and death for little Grace.

Turning to her, he said, "I think I've got an idea. Listen to this."

Phillip arrived at the home of Elijah Knepp at five minutes before five o'clock. On the porch, he saw eight straw hats hanging from pegs along the side of the house. He took a second to wonder how each man found his own hat when he left. They looked identical to him.

The elders were already waiting for him inside. Seated in a semicircle, the men all wore dark suits or pale blue shirts under dark vests. Most wore wire-rimmed glasses. All had gray beards that reached to the middle of their chests.

After the introductions were made, Phillip took a seat. "Thank you for meeting with me today."

The man on the end said, "It is a serious thing you are asking Elijah to do. It is forbidden."

"I understand that. I do not ask lightly. Without these special lights, his daughter will die. As did his first daughters and in the same way."

"It was *Gottes Wille*," said one on the other end.

"He had need for my daughters to be with Him in Heaven," Elijah replied, his voice heavy with sorrow.

His suffering was painful to watch. Phillip had no doubt he loved his child. "Grace has a terrible disease, but one that can be treated by the very first gift God gave the world. *Genesis* 1:3-4, 'And God said, Let there be light: and there was light. And God saw the light, that it was good: and God divided the light from the darkness.'"

A stern-faced man in the middle said, "We know the Bible."

"Forgive me. What I want to show you is that God has given us the knowledge to understand how His gift, His light can save Grace."

Pulling a prism from his pocket, Phillip moved to where the sunlight was streaming in the south window. Holding the glass to the light, he threw a rainbow on the opposite wall.

"Light is made up of all these colors. The blue you see is the color that will make Grace better. Blue fluorescent lamps generate specific wavelengths of light that help break down the chemical in her blood, the bilirubin. As the light shines on her skin it changes the bilirubin into water-soluble components that are excreted."

He put the prism back in his pocket. Did they understand or was he talking over their heads? "If Grace could stay outside all day, without clothes on, all year 'round, and let God's light touch her skin, her jaundice would be controlled. You men know what it is to be outside all day summer and winter."

"It would not be possible for a child to live like this." The elder on the end stroked his beard.

Phillip knew he was reaching them. "That's right. That's why we take the blue light and bring it inside and let the sick children sleep under it at night. By using a solar panel, we can change sunlight into electricity to run the lights."

"But this will not cure her," Elijah said mournfully.

Phillip returned and sat on the edge of his seat. "No, but work is being done in the Amish community in Lancaster County, Pennsylvania, to understand this disease and find a cure. It will be found, but not in time to help Grace. Right now, the only cure for her will be a liver transplant when she is old enough to have one."

Elijah's bishop, who had been sitting quietly among the other elders, spoke up at last. "You have given us much to consider. Thank you for coming."

He was being dismissed. Deflated, Phillip tried one last thing. "Because this defective gene comes from both her father and mother, we know there will be more children with this disease in your community. We have already seen it in Elijah and Sophie's families. When the children of those families grow up and marry, they will pass this gene along to their children and their grandchildren. More Amish children will be sick. It is within your power to save them by using the first gift God gave the world. How can you turn your backs on them?"

He held his breath as he waited for their reply.

Wilma was already at the clinic when Phillip arrived there early on Monday morning. To his surprise, Amber was there, too.

He knew he'd never tire of seeing her face. The thought that he'd be leaving in two weeks was as painful as a knife in his heart. How could he leave her? How could he not?

His new partners in Hawaii were eagerly awaiting his

return. Their busy practice needed him there full-time. They had been generous in granting him a two-month leave, but he couldn't ask them for more time.

Harold was progressing so well that he'd be able to return in a month or so. The clinic might have to close for a few weeks, but it would survive until Harold's return. It might even prosper if Harold took on a partner of his own.

Phillip wondered if Amber would be as sorry to see him go as he was to leave.

"Well?" Wilma demanded. "What did they decide?"

"I don't know. I haven't heard." He came into the room and parked himself on the corner of her desk. Amber moved to settle herself close beside him.

"When will you hear?" she asked.

"I'm not sure. Soon, I hope."

Amber laid her hand on his arm. "What if they say no?"

"I won't think like that."

Smiling, she nodded. "God brought you here for this reason."

He had such a short time left in Hope Springs. He was going to make the most of every minute with this wonderful woman. He had a lifetime worth of memories he needed to make.

"But what if they do say no?" Wilma asked.

"If they say no, I have a tough choice ahead of me. I'll either have to release the child from the hospital to go home and die, or I can petition the court to have her removed from her parents' custody. In that case, she would go to foster care, but at least she'd be getting the treatment she needs. I'm sure the Amish would take us to court over such a move. They might even win."

Amber's hand tightened in a gesture of sympathy. "What will you do?"

He gave her a soft smile. "I honestly don't know."

The clatter of hooves outside announced the arrival of a buggy. Phillip stood and waited with his heart pounding as Elijah Knepp walked in. The farmer pulled his hat from his head. "I must speak with you, Phillip White."

"Please, come to my office." Phillip led the way and when they were inside the room, he offered Elijah a chair.

"*Nee*, I must get back to my fields. I wish to tell you the Church elders have come to a decision regarding Grace."

"I see." Phillip swallowed hard. "What was their decision?"

"Grace may have the lights."

Phillip's mouth dropped open in relief. Rounding the corner of his desk, he slapped the man on the back. "That's great news."

Elijah grinned. "*Ja*. It is *goot*. My Sophie is happy today."

"I'm sure she must be. I don't want you to worry. I'll take care of getting the equipment ordered."

"My Church will pay for what is needed."

"Fine. As soon as it's installed in your house, Grace can come home." Phillip knew he was grinning like a fool, but he couldn't stop.

At the door, Elijah said, "My thanks for your efforts to help my daughter and my wife. You have been a gift from *Gott* to my family."

Pulling open the office door for him, Phillip said, "I'm glad I could help."

Elijah looked down at his hat and then back to Phillip. "This cure they are looking for, you will help them find it?"

"I'm afraid I must leave that to more qualified doctors." What he wouldn't give to be part of that battle.

As the man walked away down the hall, Phillip stared after him. He did want to be a part of finding answers and cures, not waiting for others to do the work. He'd never be content to send grieving parents out his door without being able to give them hope.

Suddenly, he realized he'd been heading down the wrong career path.

Perhaps this had been God's purpose in bringing him to Hope Springs. To show him where his true calling lay. Not in family medicine like this, but in genetic research.

Amber once said God used her sister's tragedy to reveal her true calling. In his heart, Phillip knew he was being called, too. Not to follow in his father's footsteps, but to forge a new path for himself.

I'm listening, Lord. I'm finally listening.

Excitement percolated through his body. He'd need a new degree. It would mean more years of study. He knew just where to make it happen. At his alma mater, the University of Hawaii at Manoa.

The door beside his office opened. Amber peeked out. "Well?"

Wilma came rushing down the hall. "Don't keep me in suspense."

Phillip stepped back into his office. The women crowded in. Holding his arms wide, he grinned. "They said yes."

Happy screams almost raised the roof. Phillip found himself the center of a group hug and joyful jumping.

Wilma broke away first. "I've got to call my husband.

We've been praying about this all weekend." She dashed out of the room and headed for her desk.

Shyly, Amber smiled at Phillip and placed both her hands on his chest. "You done good."

"With your help." His heart turned over and he pulled her close. She had become as important to him as breathing. How could he live without her?

He loved her. He loved her with all his heart. Would she leave this place and come with him to Hawaii if he told her that? He braced himself to find out.

The outer door of the office opened. Expecting Wilma, he looked over Amber's head and his mouth dropped open.

Harold, leaning on crutches, stood in the doorway scowling at them. "Don't let me interrupt. On second thought, what's going on here?"

With a squeal of delight, Amber tore away from Phillip to embrace his grandfather. "Harold, I'm so glad you're back. Why didn't you tell us you were coming?"

Wilma squeezed through the door behind them shaking with excitement. She, too, threw her arms around the man. "God has answered my prayers. It hasn't been the same without you."

He hugged both women close. "I'm happy to be back. I don't think I'll ever leave this town again."

"Good," Wilma stated firmly, patting his chest. "Now, maybe things can get back to normal around here."

Phillip stood back, allowing them their long-awaited reunion. Finally, his grandfather looked up and met Phillip's gaze over the women's heads. Harold said, "That's my plan. I'm here to make sure that things get back to normal as soon as possible."

Chapter Twenty-Three

Amber walked slowly toward Phillip's office the following morning. The door stood open.

Harold's office, she corrected herself. It would take some time to get used to that again. She stopped in the doorway and watched the man she had come to love more than anyone in her life. Busy packing his few belongings, he didn't see her.

The dreaded moment was here at last. She wouldn't cry. She wouldn't. "You're leaving?"

He looked up. His eyes were filled with the same pain and longing that was tearing her heart to shreds. "Yes."

"When?" She took a step inside the room.

"I've got a flight out of Cincinnati at two o'clock. I can make it if I hurry."

"Today?" He heard the despair in her voice because he stopped packing and came to take her in his arms. Huddled against his chest, she said, "I don't want you to go."

If she told him that she loved him, would he stay? Did she have the right to ask him?

He whispered, "You could practice as a CNM in Hawaii. It's a beautiful, special place."

Those were the words she both longed and dreaded to hear. "There are no Amish in Hawaii."

The strength ebbed out of his embrace. "Why are they so important to you?"

"I don't really know—except I believe this is where God wants me to be." She looked up. "Why don't you stay? You know Harold could use the help."

"Not according to him. He's in a rush to get back in the saddle. I'm in the way. I've changed things."

"He's bluffing. He does need help, especially now. He can barely walk."

"Even if I didn't have commitments in Hawaii, I wouldn't stay longer."

"Of course. It was silly of me to ask."

He held her at arm's length. "Let's not make this any harder than it already is. We knew from the start that I was only here for a short while."

Her throat ached with unshed tears. "Somehow, I forgot that."

Gently, he stroked her cheek. "So did I. I never meant to hurt you, Amber."

"I know that."

"You are the most amazing person I've ever met in my life. Knowing you has been an honor. I've learned so much from you about the Amish, about birthing babies and a great deal about myself. If you ever change your mind, you'll be welcome in Hawaii."

"I thought we weren't going to make this harder than it already is?" Her voice caught on the last word and she pressed a hand to her lips as she struggled not to cry. "I'd love to see your island, but Harold is going to need me more than ever. I can't run out on him now."

"No, and I shouldn't ask you to do that." Defeat laced his words. She stepped away from him and wondered why life had to be so difficult.

Just then, her cell phone rang. As much as she wanted to ignore it, she couldn't. One of her patients needed her. The longer she stayed with Phillip the harder it became to say goodbye.

Holding up the phone, she said, "I have to take this."

She silenced the ringing and put the party on hold. Taking another step away, she said, "Have a wonderful flight. I know you'll be a great doctor in Hawaii. Send me a postcard of the ocean."

She turned and ran before the tears started falling again.

Phillip pressed his fingertips to his eyes to ease the burning pain behind them. Why had God allowed him to find the most perfect woman in the world only to put her out of reach?

A tap at the door made him look up. Harold stood in the doorway. "May I come in?"

"It's your office." Phillip turned away to finish putting his few personal belongings in his carry-on case. The last item to go in was Doctor Dog. Phillip drew his hand over the puppet's silky ears before putting him away.

Harold cleared his throat nervously. "I'm hearing good things about what you did while you were here. I'm a little sorry now that I rushed back."

Phillip glanced at his grandfather with concern. "Are you well enough to be back to work?"

Holding out his leg cast, Harold said, "I'll need some physical therapy when this comes off, but they tell me I'll be as fit as ever. The old noggin gets headaches. Hopefully, those will fade." Stepping close, Harold said, "I know you didn't have an easy time here, but I'm proud of the way you handled yourself. Your father would have been proud of you, too."

"I hope someday I can become as good a doctor as he hoped to be."

Harold drew back, a puzzled frown on his face. "Your father never wanted to be a doctor."

Stunned, Phillip stared at his grandfather. "Wait a minute. What are you saying?"

"My boy wanted to be a musician from the time he could reach the piano keys. I know you idolized him, but he drifted from club to club playing his saxophone and guitar. He was always broke, never had a decent place to live. I prayed for him. I paid for his college but he blew that, too."

"Why didn't anyone tell me this?" It was like Phillip's world had tipped off its axis.

"Was it your mother who told you Brendan wanted to be a doctor?"

"Yes."

"What else did she tell you about him?"

"That he loved baseball."

"I wouldn't say he loved it, but he enjoyed Little League."

"And did he surf?"

"As far as I know, he never tried it."

Phillip sat down, his knees suddenly weak. His entire life he'd done things because he believed they were the things his father wanted to do. It had all been a lie. Why?

He thought back to those times. When his mother

wanted him to play ball, he refused at first. Telling him his father had loved the sport had changed his mind. Shortly after that, she began dating his coach.

She'd never brought up the subject of surfing until they moved to California. She had hooked up with more than one beach bum during those years.

He looked up at Harold. "Why did my father join the Marines?"

"Your mother should tell you that."

Phillip stood and picked up his bag. "This time she will."

He started to leave, but Harold grabbed him in a fierce hug and clung to him as if for dear life. "I'm going to miss you, my boy. I love you, more than I thought possible. I loved your father, too. Remember that and don't think badly of me."

"I could never think badly of you."

Sniffing once, Harold straightened. "It was great getting to know you. Thank you for everything you've done to keep this practice going. It's all I have left in the world."

Pulling a card from his pocket, Phillip handed it to him. "This is the number of a young doctor who'd like to go into practice with you. You should give him a call. The Amish deserve to have someone here after you're gone. Hopefully, that won't be for many years so you can train him up the way you want."

Harold took the card. "God bless you, Phillip."

"And you, too, sir." With a nod of goodbye, he walked out to the lobby. Wilma rose from her desk and came around to shake his hand and wish him well.

Out in the parking lot, he tossed his bag on the front

seat of his car, then glanced toward the building once more. Amber stood at the window in the first exam room. She raised her hand and pressed it to the glass.

He raised his hand briefly in return, then got into his car and drove away.

His flight was long and tedious, giving him plenty of time to rehash every decision he'd made in Hope Springs. Right or wrong, he still wasn't sure. He put his pain and unhappiness in God's hands. The Lord had a plan for his life that he couldn't see yet. He had to believe that.

After seventeen hours in a cramped airline seat, he was more than happy to get off the plane. To his surprise, his mother was waiting near the gate.

"Mom! I wasn't expecting you." He gave her a quick hug.

"When my baby is gone for two months, do you think I wouldn't want to see you the moment you got off the plane? Tell me about your stay in that frightful place."

Petite, with an artfully styled riot of red curls that wasn't her natural color, Melinda Watson tried never to look her age, yet tonight she looked much older than he remembered. There were carefully disguised dark circles under her eyes.

He wasn't ready to talk about his time in Ohio. "Mom, what I want is a hot shower and to sleep for a week."

"I thought you could use a lift back to your apartment."

"I could have grabbed a cab. Where's Michael?"

"I didn't tell him you were coming today. I thought you and I could visit for a while."

"All right. Let me get my bags." He was tired, but he

didn't want to dampen her happiness. Besides, he had questions he needed to ask her.

"Marvelous." She clapped her hands together. "Why don't we have dinner at the Maui Fire? I hear it's the hot new place."

After catching his bags off the carousel, he followed his mother outside into the warm, tropical evening air. He could smell the sea. For the first time in his life it didn't make him want to pick up his board. It reminded him of Amber…and her sea-green eyes glistening with tears.

How was he going to function if he couldn't cross the airport parking lot without missing her so much his heart felt like a jumble of broken glass?

His mother continued to chat aimlessly on the drive. Watching the familiar sights of high-rise hotels and waving palm trees, he couldn't help comparing the glitter and glitz to the simple rolling hills and plain white farmsteads of the Amish countryside.

"You're very quiet," she said, sneaking a peek at him.

"I'm tired."

"A good dinner will perk you up in no time."

He didn't want food. He wanted answers. "Why did you tell me my father wanted to be a doctor?"

"Because he did!"

"Was that before or after he wanted to form his own rock band?"

She didn't answer. Instead, she slowed the car and turned into the parking lot of one of the popular beaches, stopping the car where they faced the ocean. The waves came sweeping in, each topped with a whitecap of foam. His stomach was churning in much the same fashion.

After rolling down the windows, she turned the car off. Gripping the steering wheel, she stared straight ahead. "Phillip, I wasn't a very good mother when you were young. I know that. I do."

She turned to gaze at him. "But I've been a good mother since I met Michael, haven't I? I love you. You know that, don't you?"

"You've always done your best, Mom. I love you, too."

"I know how excited you were to find your grandfather, but he isn't a good man. Believe me, I know."

Phillip drew a deep breath. Was he finally going to get to the bottom of this? "He is a good man, Mother. He's kind and devoted to the Amish and his community."

"Well, he wasn't always that way. Your father and he never got along. Nothing Brendan did was good enough for Harold. Finding out that Brendan and I were planning to get married infuriated him. I wasn't good enough for his only son." Scorn dripped off her every word.

Phillip wasn't sure he liked where this conversation was leading. "Some parents have trouble accepting their child's new spouse at first. It normally changes over time."

"Harold didn't want his son tied down with a family at such a young age. He knew Brendan couldn't handle it, that it would destroy his life. We were only nineteen and I was pregnant. We were as poor as dirt, living in Brendan's van half the time. Oh, Brendan's father had plenty of money. He could have helped us but he wanted his son to earn his own way."

Phillip tried to imagine what his mother had gone through back then. "I'm sorry things were so difficult for you. I never knew."

"And I never wanted you to know but there's no point in hiding it any longer. Your grandfather came to me and offered me a lot of money."

Phillip's heart sank. "He paid you to leave my father?"

"He paid me to get rid of you."

The blood rushed to Phillip's brain and sent his head pounding. "I don't believe it!"

Calmly, she replied, "It's true. When Brendan found out, he flipped. He and your grandfather had a terrible fight. Brendan told his old man he'd find a way to support his wife and a child. Then he stormed out of the house and stopped at the first recruiting station he could find."

"That's why he joined the Marines?"

"Yes. We were married before he shipped out and he was killed three months later. It's your grandfather's fault that your father is dead."

Leaning his head back against the seat rest, Phillip listened to the waves and struggled to digest all the information he'd been given. Had he wanted his grandfather to be a wonderful man so badly that he'd been blind to Harold's faults? Perhaps that had been true, at first.

Phillip realized that he'd spent his life longing for something he could never have. He'd never have his father watch him at a ball game or sit in the audience at his graduation. Maybe he'd gone to medical school because he thought that was what his father would have wanted, but medicine was where Phillip belonged. It was his vocation.

Images of Amber slipped through his mind, quieting the turmoil inside him. Amber knew where she belonged in life. Now he finally did, too.

He couldn't stay in Hawaii. He had to confront his grandfather, to find out if this was the truth or more of his mother's manipulations.

Then he needed to tell Amber that he loved her. He'd been a fool to leave without telling her how he felt. If she returned his love, somehow he would to find a way to keep her in his life.

He looked at his mother. "Thanks for telling me this, Mom. I'd like to go to your house now. There are some important things I want you and Michael to hear together."

Chapter Twenty-Four

Phillip got out of his rental car in front of Harold's home late on a Saturday afternoon. It had been almost three weeks since he'd left Hope Springs. Because it was the weekend, Phillip was reasonably sure Harold would be in. He hadn't called in advance. He wasn't sure what he was going to say now that he was here. After knocking, he waited outside the door.

Thumping of crutches and grumbling on the other side alerted him before Harold yanked it open. The elderly man's annoyed expression changed to happiness, then to guarded surprise. "Phillip. What are you doing here?"

What was he doing here? What did he hope to learn? The truth? Or more carefully crafted secrets? "I need to talk to you."

The light died in Harold's eyes. His face went ashen. "Your mother told you, didn't she?"

"I want to hear your side of the story."

The man seemed to grow older in front of Phillip's eyes. "Then you'd better come in. I can't be up long or this miserable leg begins to swell."

Following his grandfather inside, Phillip sat on the

sofa and waited until Harold settled himself in his recliner. He sighed loudly as he grimaced and leaned back. "Thought you might like to know that Martha Nissley got to come home."

"That's great. How is she doing?"

"She got all the feeling back in her legs. Looks like she'll make a full recovery."

"That's great to hear." Phillip nodded toward Harold's walking cast. "How are you managing at the clinic?"

"I get around in a wheelchair for the most part. That young whippersnapper, Dr. Zook, is helping a lot."

"I'm glad to hear he took the job."

"He's got his head on straight, but don't tell him I said so."

"I'll leave that to you. I'm sure he'd like a little encouragement." Any would be more than Harold had given Phillip.

Harold dismissed the idea with a wave of his hand. "I don't need to give him pats on the back. Amber and Wilma do it for me."

"How is Amber?" Phillip was almost afraid to hear the answer but he was dying for any information about her.

"She has changed. She's not herself, although she tries to be. Some of the light has gone out of her."

Phillip dropped his gaze to his feet. He was to blame. "She's a wonderful, strong woman. I'm sure she'll be fine."

"You didn't come here to talk about Amber, did you?"

Raising his head, Phillip stared at Harold. "I came to get some straight answers."

"All right. Ask away."

Phillip hesitated. His mother had lied to him and manipulated him so many times in the past. Why should he trust what she'd told him about Harold? Would it alienate his grandfather to be accused of such horrible motives? Was that her plan all along?

Well, he hadn't come all this way for nothing. "Is it true you tried to bribe my mother to get an abortion and to leave my dad?"

Harold closed his eyes. "Stupidest mistake I ever made. I had no idea how much Brendan loved her. What a terrible fight we had when he found out."

"At least they wanted me." Phillip couldn't keep the bitterness out of his voice.

Harold folded his hands across his abdomen. "Did your mother tell you she took the money?"

Phillip blinked hard. Why wasn't he surprised? No wonder she hadn't wanted him to contact Harold. "She left that part out."

"I never dreamed Brendan would enlist. I always thought we'd be able to mend things between us. Then he was killed. You are so like him. Looking at you is like looking into my past."

"Why didn't you take care of us after he died?"

"When Brendan was killed, your mother blamed me. At his funeral, the only time we saw each other again, she told me she'd gone through with the abortion and she never wanted to see me again. You have to understand. I held her responsible for my son's death instead of accepting my share of the blame. I didn't know and didn't care where she went after that."

Phillip struggled to find the words for what he was feeling. "We lived a hard life. She drank heavily. She got into drugs. I can't count the times we were evicted from one rattrap or another. I can't count the number of men she brought home. If it hadn't been for Michael, I don't know what would have happened to us."

"Believe me when I tell you I'm glad your mother has found some happiness. I came to realize Brendan's death and the loss of his child was my punishment for putting my own desires ahead of his love. In spite of what you think, I was doing what I thought was best for my son. Had I known about you, I would have moved heaven and earth to find you."

Seeing the sincerity in his grandfather's eyes, Phillip felt he had the truth at last. "I believe that."

"After your father died, I couldn't stay in Boston. Everything reminded me of him and my horrible mistake. My wife had died when Brendan was five. There was nothing to keep me there. I sold all I had and came here. I hoped to find forgiveness and peace working among these simple and faithful people."

Phillip wasn't done with his questions. "When I suggested you retire and come live near me, why did you become so upset?"

Harold rubbed his jaw with one hand. "Because I was terrified my sins would come to light. I didn't want to lose you the way I lost your father."

"When you ran in front of my car, why were you trying to stop me?"

"I realized I couldn't come back to Hope Springs and live among the Plain People with that terrible secret in my heart. I had to tell you the truth." The corners of his mouth quirked upward. "I honestly had no intention of getting run down."

"I thank God each day you weren't killed."

"I thank God He has given me the chance to right the terrible wrong I did you and your mother."

Harold struggled to stand. Phillip moved to assist him. When he was on his feet and steady, he gripped Phillip's arm and looked into his eyes. "Can you forgive me?"

Phillip had the truth now. More than he wanted to know. It was all so sad and so unnecessary. He had it within his power to lay a lifetime of unhappiness to rest, for both of them.

Phillip covered his grandfather's hand with his own. "Yes, I can."

The old man's eyes closed and he swayed. Frightened, Phillip quickly helped him into his chair. "Are you all right, Grandfather?"

"I'm fine. I'm fine for the first time in a long while. Thank you."

"Can I get you something?"

"Great-grandchildren."

Phillip's worry slipped away. Relief made him smile. "I was thinking along the lines of a glass of water."

Harold sat up and took a deep breath. "That would be nice, too. You are going to marry Amber, aren't you? She loves you. You're a fool if you don't know that."

Amber was bone-tired by the time she returned home. The delivery had gone well. Both mother and child were happy and healthy. She should have been thrilled, but all through the long hours of labor she kept thinking about the time she and Phillip spent with Mary and her family. Remembering their time together was still painful but she didn't cry as often anymore.

After parking in her driveway, Amber walked toward the house with lagging steps. Everything took more energy since Phillip had gone. Walking, eating, getting out of bed, it was all so hard to do. How much longer would this malaise affect her? It already felt like a lifetime had passed since he went away.

At the steps, she heard a meow from the end of the porch. For a second she thought it was Fluffy, then she remembered that her cat was gone, too. It had to be one of the neighborhood cats.

Fluffy was back with the family who loved him. At least that had ended well. When Amber reached the front door, she heard a second meow.

Turning to see whose cat had come for a visit, she froze in shock. Phillip sat in her wicker chair with a box at his feet. Afraid to blink in case he vanished, she kept staring, trying to make herself believe it was true.

Rising to his feet, he said, "Hello, Amber."

He wasn't a figment of her imagination. Her heart thudded painfully against the inside of her chest. It took every ounce of self-control she possessed to keep from flinging herself into his arms. "Phillip? What are you doing here?"

He smiled but she saw the uncertainty in his eyes. "I had to see you again."

Looking away before he could read the longing on her face, she fumbled to get her keys out of her purse. Finally, she found them and attempted to open her lock. When they tumbled out of her shaky fingers she knew there was no use pretending she was okay.

She closed her eyes and leaned her head against the door. "I can't do this again, Phillip."

In a few steps he was beside her, not touching her, but surrounding her with his masculine warmth. "I'm sorry. I had to see you."

Bending down, he picked up her keys. She stayed strong until he placed them in her palm and tenderly closed his fingers over hers. He whispered, "I've missed you, Amber."

His soft words were her undoing. She melted into his arms as he gathered her close. "Oh, Phillip, I've missed you so much."

"I love you. I never want to leave you again."

"I can't bear it, Phillip. I can't stay here without you."

Brushing her damp cheeks with his knuckle, he asked in surprise, "You would come to Hawaii?"

"Yes, if you want me. I can't be more unhappy there than I've been here these past three weeks."

"My poor darling. I don't want you to be unhappy anywhere. I don't want you to give up the things you love most."

She buried her face against his chest. "I love you the most. So we are right back where we started from because I know you will never be happy practicing small-town medicine."

He rocked her gently in his embrace. "We're not exactly back where we started from. I know that I love you and I know that you love me."

"True."

Leaning back, he looked down at her. "I have something for you."

"What?" Wiping her face with both hands, she took a step back, already missing the warmth of his body and the comfort of his arms around her.

Picking up the box by the chair, he held it out. "Open it. Doctor's orders."

As she started to take the top off, she heard a tiny meow. It was then she noticed the holes poked in the sides of the box. Phillip said, "I know you miss Fluffy."

The moment the top came off, a white kitten raised

its head over the lip. Amber gasped in delight. "Oh, he's beautiful."

Phillip looked quite pleased with himself. "I'm glad you like him. He's all yours. No one is going to take him back."

"He's just what I've been needing. What a wonderful gift. Thank you."

"I'm not done." Phillip put the top on the box and took it from her. The kitten protested as he set it aside. Drawing a deep breath, he withdrew several packets from his jacket and offered them to her.

Puzzled, Amber took them. Tilting them toward the porch light she saw they were celery seed packets. Her lip quivered as she pressed a hand to her chest. "Oh, Phillip."

He dropped to one knee in front of her. "Amber Bradley, will you marry me?"

Speechless, she stared at him as happiness strummed the cords of her heart. Joy unlike anything she'd ever known sent her blood humming. On the heels of that intense joy came a quick downer dose of common sense.

She bit her lower lip. What should she do? If she said yes, one of them would have to give up their dreams. Yet how could she bear to say no and lose his wonderful love? Finally, she said, "Maybe."

He sat back on his heel. "Maybe? I thought your only choices were yes or no."

"I want to marry you, but I'm afraid."

"Of what?" He rose to his feet and took her in his arms once more.

"I'm afraid I'll be miserable away from the Amish and I'll make you miserable, too." If they could only stay this way forever, encircled in each other's arms, surrounded by love.

He took her face in his hands. "I don't want you to come to Hawaii. I want you to stay here."

In a flash, she realized he was giving up his dream for her. "You can't resign from your practice in Hawaii."

"I already have."

"But you won't like practicing medicine here. You know you won't."

"I'll be happy wherever you are, but you're right. I wouldn't be content practicing general medicine. Anywhere."

"Then I don't understand."

"I have been mistakenly trying to fulfill my father's dreams, not my own. God brought me to this town to meet the most wonderful woman in the world." He flicked the tip of her nose with his finger.

She chuckled. "I'm glad you think so."

"And He brought me here to show me my true calling. I'm going to be a pediatrician in a new diagnostic center for children with special needs that will open in Hope Springs sometime in the next few years."

He wasn't kidding. She knew by the joy in his voice. "A new clinic here?"

His eyes danced with eagerness. "I've just come back from Pennsylvania and their genetic research facility for special needs children. It's a wonderful place. They are doing cutting-edge genetic research among the Amish there. Besides research, they treat children with all types of inherited diseases and they don't limit their service to just the Amish. They are eager to find out more about the Knepp baby and her parents, and they want to develop a second clinic in this area."

"You and Dr. Dog will make wonderful pediatricians. But that means you'll have to go back to school."

"Believe me, I've been looking into it. There's a combined human genetics and pediatric residency at Cincinnati Children's. It's only three hours away. We can see each other on my days off. It's a five-year program, but I'll be board certified in both genetics and pediatrics when I'm done. I've already applied. So, you can see why I'm going to need a wife with a good job."

Pulling back, she asked, "You're okay with me continuing as a nurse-midwife here?"

"Honey, I know you give your patients the very best of care. I know that because I've seen your passion and your skill. I may never be convinced that home deliveries are best, but I will support *you* one hundred percent."

Circling his neck with her arms, she smiled softly. "Oh, I think in fifty or sixty years I can get you to come around."

"What method of persuasion will you be using?" He tightened his hold and gave her a heart-stopping grin. The love in his eyes sent a tingle clear to her toes.

Leaning close, she whispered, "Kisses, lots of kisses."

Phillip pulled back a little. "Does this mean you've changed your maybe to a yes?"

"Yes, yes, yes," she whispered as she drew his face to hers. The heady feel of his arms and his lips sent her heart tripping with delight.

As their lips touched, Amber sent up a silent prayer of thanks. God had truly brought a wonderful man into her life.

After that, she gave Phillip her full and undivided attention.

* * * * *

HANNAH'S JOURNEY

Anna Schmidt

To those who have dared
follow the beat of the different drummer.

For Yahweh has heard the sound of my weeping,
Yahweh has heard my pleading.
Yahweh will accept my prayer…
—*Psalms* 6:8–9

Chapter One

Sarasota, Florida, May 1928

Levi Harmon pushed aside the piles of bills littering his desk and swiveled his high-backed, leather chair toward the series of leaded glass-paned doors that led outside to the front lawn. The room had been designed as a solarium, but Levi had seen little use for such a space and instead had located his Florida office in the room with its tiled terrazzo floor, its arched doors opening to the out-of-doors that he loved so much. After all, what was the use of being rich if not to live as you pleased?

He walked out onto the terrace and leaned against the stone railing. Before him the lawn stretched green and verdant past the swimming pool and rose garden, past the mammoth banyan trees that he'd insisted the builder spare when constructing the mansion and on to the gate-house that was a miniature version of the mansion itself. He'd worked hard for all of this and had thought that by now he might be sharing it with a wife and children, but work had consumed him and he had never found a woman that he thought suited to the kind of vagabond life he'd chosen.

He'd come outside to think. Perhaps he should take a walk along the azure bay that most of the mansion's rooms looked out on. That always calmed him whenever business worries piled up. And indeed, they had begun to pile up—not just for him but for many men who had taken the cash flows of their businesses for granted these past several boom years. He had started down the curved stairs to the lawn when he noticed a woman he did not recognize walking up the driveway.

She moved with purpose and determination, her strides even, her tall slender frame erect, her head bent almost as if in prayer. As she came closer, he saw that she wore a dark gray dress with a black apron and the telltale starched white cap that was the uniform of the Amish women. How was it possible that she had not been stopped at the gate, detained there while the gatekeeper made a call to the house?

At that same moment he heard the phone in the foyer jangle. He moved back to the open office doorway and continued watching the woman even as he half listened to his butler, Hans, hold a quiet conversation with the gatekeeper. The woman was even with the pool when Hans came onto the terrace to deliver his report.

"She is Mrs. Hannah Goodloe," Hans said.

"She's Amish—probably lives out near the celery fields," Levi said impatiently. "What business could she possibly have here?"

"She would not say, but insisted on speaking with you personally. Shall I…"

Levi waved him away and went inside, rolling down the sleeves of his white shirt as he retrieved his jacket from the hall tree in his office. "Show her to the Great Hall," he said as he ran his fingers through his copper brown straight hair.

"Very good, sir," Hans murmured, but his words came with little approval. "May I remind you, sir, that your train…"

"I know my schedule. This won't take long."

"Very good, sir."

Levi listened to the tap of his butler's leather heels crossing the marble foyer to take up his post at the massive double front door. By now she should have reached them and yet neither the bell nor the door knocker sounded. Had she changed her mind?

He crossed his office and peered outside. No sign of her retreating. Assuming she was standing on the front steps, perhaps gathering her courage, he could simply walk around to the front of the house and encounter her there. But for reasons he did not take the time to fathom, it seemed important that this woman—this stranger— enter his house, see the proof of all that he had accomplished, marvel at the beauty of his self-made world in spite of her religion's stand against anything deemed ostentatious.

And even as the chime of the front doorbell resonated throughout the house, Levi thought not so much of the present, but of a time when he was not so different from this plain-living woman who now stood at his door.

Just by coming to the winter home of the circus impresario, Hannah had probably violated several of the unwritten laws of the Ordnung followed by people of her faith. In the first place, the minute the gatekeeper had

turned his back to make the call to the mansion, she had
slipped past him and started her walk up the long drive.
Surely that was wrong. But she had to see the only man
capable of finding her son.

All the way up the drive, she kept her eyes on the
ground half expecting to hear the gatekeeper running to
catch up with her as she followed the pristine, white-shell
path until it curved in front of the massive house itself.
Only then did she glance up and her breath caught. The
house soared three stories into the cloudless blue sky,
its roof lined with curved terra-cotta tiles sparkling in
the late-morning sun. Curved iron balconies hung from
large arched windows on the second and third stories,
and everywhere the facade of the house had been fes-
tooned with ornate carvings, colorful tiles and stone figures that were as frightening as they were fascinating.

Hannah dropped her gaze and started up the front
stairs, avoiding the detailed iron railing that lined either
side of the wide stairway and refusing to be tempted to
admire the tiered fountain where water splashed like
music. Even the stairs were a rainbow of colorful marble in pink and purple and pale green. She supposed that
for a man like Levi Harmon—a showman known for his
extravaganzas and exotic menagerie of animals from
around the world—a little purple marble was to be expected. She sucked in her breath, straightened her spine
and prepared to knock.

But the massive wood door was covered by a gate, a
barricade in filigreed iron that boasted twin medallions
or perhaps coats of arms where she might have expected
the obvious door handle to be located. Perturbed more
than amused at this need for such material grandeur,
Hannah took a step back and studied the house. De-

termined not to be daunted in her mission, she made a detailed study of the entrance. After all, the man entertained guests, did he not? Surely those people had to at some point enter and exit the house.

The doorbell was housed in the uplifted hand of a bronze sculpture of a circus clown located to the right of the door. Hannah took a deep breath, uttered a short prayer begging God's forgiveness for any misdemeanor she might be committing and pressed the button. When she heard a series of muffled bells gong inside the grand house, she locked her knees rigidly to keep them from shaking and waited for the doors to open.

"Good morning, Mrs. Goodloe," a man dressed in a black suit intoned as he swung open the inside door, and then opened the wrought-iron screen for her. "Please come in. Mr. Harmon is just completing some business. He asks that you wait for him in here."

The small man of indeterminate age led the way across a space that by itself was larger than any house she'd ever seen. Hannah avoided glancing at her surroundings, but could not miss the large curved stairway that wound its way up to the top of the house, or the gilt-framed paintings that lined the walls.

"Please make yourself comfortable," the man was saying as he led her down three shallow steps into a room easily twice the size of the space they had just left. He indicated one of four dark blue, tufted-velvet sofas. "Mr. Harmon will be with you shortly."

"Is that…" Hannah stared across the room at a wall of polished brass pipes in a range of sizes and the large wooden piece in front of them.

"The Butterfield pipe organ? Indeed," the man reported with obvious pride. "Mr. Harmon purchased that when they demolished the old Butterfield Theatre in London. He had it taken apart, labeled, then shipped here to be reassembled. It makes the most wondrous sound."

"I see." She had no idea what he was talking about. She had simply been taken aback to see an enormous pipe organ in a private home.

"Actually, the organ was Mr. Harmon's gift to me, ma'am." And then as if reminding himself that he was not to offer such information, he cleared his throat. "May I offer you a cool glass of water, ma'am?"

She had walked the five miles from her father-in-law's house near the celery fields down Fruitville Street, and then along the bay to the Harmon estate. But she had not come on a social call. "No, thank you," she replied as she perched on the edge of one of the sofas and folded her hands primly in her lap.

Seconds later, the silence surrounding her told her that she was alone. If she liked she could walk around the grand room, touch the furnishings, peer at the many framed pictures that lined the tops of tables and even satisfy her curiosity to know what the bay might look like seen through one of the multicolored panes of glass in the sets of double doors that lined one wall. But an Amish person was never truly alone. One was always in the presence of God and as such, one was always expected to consider actions carefully.

Hannah focused on her folded hands and considered the rashness of her action in coming here. But what other choice did she have? Caleb was missing and she had every reason to believe that he had run away. Oh, she had been foolish to think that taking him to the circus grounds the day before would somehow dampen his romantic ideal of what circus life was like. She had thought

that once the boy saw the reality of the dirt and stench
and hard work that lay behind the brightly colored posters, he would appreciate the security and comfort of the
life he had. She had even thought of promising him a
visit to his cousins in Ohio over the summer as a way
of stemming his wanderlust. But when she had gone to
his room to rouse him for school this morning, he hadn't
been there and his bed had not been slept in.

She laced her fingers more tightly together and forced
herself to steady her breathing. She would find Caleb
even if she put herself in danger of being shunned to do it.

"Mrs. Goodloe?"

She'd heard no step on the hard, stone floor and yet
when she looked up, Levi Harmon was standing at the
entrance to the oversize room. He was a tall man, easily
topping six feet. He looked down at her with eyes the
color of the rich hot chocolate her mother used to make.
"I understand there is a business matter we need to discuss," he added as he came down the shallow stairs, and
took a seat at the opposite end of the sofa she already occupied. "I must say I am curious," he admitted, and his
eyes twinkled just enough to put her at ease.

"My son, Caleb," she began and found her throat and
mouth suddenly dry. She licked her lips and began again.
"My son, Caleb, is missing, Mr. Harmon. I believe that
he may have run away."

"Forgive me, ma'am, but I hardly see…"

"…With your circus," she added, and was relieved to
see his eyes widen with surprise even as his brow furrowed with concern.

"It would not be the first time," he said more to himself than to her as he stood and walked to the glass doors,

keeping his back to her. "What does your husband think happened to the boy?"

"My husband died when Caleb was four. He's eleven now. This past year he has…" She searched for words. "There have been some occasions when he has tested the limits that our culture sets for young people."

"He's been in trouble," Levi Harmon said.

"Nothing serious," Hannah hastened to assure him. "Then last month I found one of your circus posters folded up and hidden under his mattress. When I asked for an explanation, he told me that he wanted to join your circus. He had actually spoken to one of the men you employ to care for the animals."

"And what did you say in response to this announcement?"

"I tried to make him see that the poster was nothing more than paint on paper, that it made the life seem inviting but it was not real. That nothing about the circus is real."

She saw him stiffen defensively. "Oh, I know that it's your livelihood, Mr. Harmon, and I mean no disrespect. But for people like us—for a boy like Caleb—it's a life that goes against everything we believe."

"What happened next?"

Hannah was surprised that he did not question her further, but rather seemed determined to get at the root of her story. This was the part that was hardest for her because in the seven years since her husband had died, she and Caleb had never had a harsh word between them. "He became quite unlike himself," she said almost in a whisper. "He was sullen and stayed to himself. I went to our bishop but he said that time was the great healer."

"And you believed that?"

"For a while," she admitted. "But when nothing changed I decided to go against the bishop's advice and take action."

He turned to look at her. "What did you do?"

"I took Caleb to your circus, Mr. Harmon."

Levi tried and failed to disguise his shock that she would do such a thing. "You saw the show?"

"No. I took him to the grounds after the matinee yesterday. I wanted him to get a glimpse of what living the life of a circus worker would really be."

"My performers and crew are well cared for, Mrs. Goodloe. They have chosen this life for any number of reasons and…"

"I did not mean to imply otherwise, sir. However, a young boy's eyes are often clouded by the color and excitement associated with that life—the parades and the applause and such." She stood up and moved a step closer as if she needed to make her point and yet the tone of her voice remained soft and even solicitous. "I wanted Caleb to see that a life of traveling from place to place could be a difficult one."

He could find no argument for that. Instead, he turned the topic back to her reasons for coming to him. "That matinee was our last show of the season down here," he said. "At this moment the company is on its way to our headquarters in Baraboo, Wisconsin, with stops along the way, of course."

"And I have reason to believe that my son is on that train," she said. "I have come here to ask that you stop that train until Caleb can be found."

"Mrs. Goodloe, I am sympathetic to your situation,

but surely you can understand that I cannot disrupt an entire schedule because you think your son…"

"He is on that train, sir," she repeated.

"How can you be so certain?"

"Because besides the fact that Caleb was not in his bed when I went to wake him this morning, there were two other things missing from his room."

Levi waited but she had his full attention. He had never met a woman whose outward demeanor was so gentle, even submissive and at the same time, her eyes reflected an inner strength and certainty that she would not back down.

"About the time he began to have problems within the community he began wearing an old hat he found once. A fedora, I believe it's called. That hat was not on its usual peg this morning."

"So, the boy went out and wore his hat," Levi said, resisting the patronizing smile he felt about to reveal.

"That's true," she said, "but he had also taken a jar of coins that he's been saving for months now, adding to it almost weekly after taking on odd jobs for others in the community."

Levi flashed back to his own packing the day he decided to run away. He, too, had taken money carefully squirreled away for months as he planned his escape. "Still, neither of those items ties my circus to his plan. He could have just…left."

She smiled and it was unsettling how that simple act changed everything about her. Suddenly, she looked younger and more vulnerable and at the same time, so very sure of herself. "Caleb would never leave without a plan," she said. "From the time he was four or five, Caleb has planned his days. Then it was that he would spend the morning at play and then have the noon meal with his grandfather before spending the afternoon helping out at his uncle's carpentry shop. Once he entered school he would write out a daily schedule, leaving it for me so that I would not worry."

"Am I to assume there was no schedule this morning?"

"No. Just this." She produced a lined piece of paper from the pocket of her apron and handed it to him. In a large childish script the note read,

Ma,
Don't worry. I'm fine and I know this is all a part of God's plan the way you always said. I'll write once I get settled and I'll send you half my wages by way of General Delivery. Please don't cry, okay? It's all going to be all right.
Love, Caleb

"There's not one word here that indicates…"

"He plans to send me part of his wages, Mr. Harmon. That means he plans to get a job. When we were on the circus grounds yesterday, I took note of a posted advertisement for a stable worker. My son has been around horses his entire life."

Once again, Levi found it difficult to suppress a smile. "I believe that posting was for someone to muck out the elephant quarters," he said and saw that this was news she had not considered.

"Oh. Well, Caleb also saw that posting although he tried hard to steer me in the opposite direction and frankly, it did not occur to me that there might be a connection until I arrived at the grounds before coming here and saw the sign lying in the sawdust where the tent had been."

"And on that slimmest of evidence you have assumed that your son is on the circus train that left town last night?"

She nodded. She waited.

Levi ran one hand through his hair and heaved a sigh of frustration. "Mrs. Goodloe, please be reasonable. I have a business to run, several hundred employees who depend upon me, not to mention the hundreds of customers waiting along the way because they have purchased tickets for a performance tonight or tomorrow or the following day."

She said nothing but kept her eyes—a startling and unexpected shade of forget-me-not blue, he realized—focused squarely on him.

"Tell you what I'll do," he said without the slightest idea of how he might extricate himself from the situation. He stalled for time by pulling out his pocket watch, glancing at the time and then snapping the embossed silver cover shut and slipping it back into the pocket of his vest. "I am leaving at seven this evening for my home and summer headquarters in Wisconsin. Tomorrow, I will meet up with the circus train and make the remainder of the journey with them. If your boy is on that train I will find him."

"Thank you," she said, her head slightly bowed so that for one moment he was unclear whether or not her gratitude was directed at him or to God. She lifted her gaze to his and touched the sleeve of his suit jacket. "You are a good man, Mr. Harmon."

"There's one thing more, Mrs. Goodloe."
Anything, her eyes exclaimed.
"I expect you to come with me."

Chapter Two

"You can't…that is…why…I could not possibly.…"

"Those are my terms, Mrs. Goodloe. Assuming you are correct and your son is traveling with my circus, then it is my duty to find the boy and return him to you. However, as I mentioned, I have a business to run and other people who must be considered. Once the boy is found it would only be right for you to take charge of him from that point forward."

Without her being aware of moving, Hannah suddenly realized that Levi Harmon had escorted her back into the foyer where his servant stood by the door. "Hans, please make sure that Mrs. Goodloe has all of the information she needs to meet us at the railway station tonight." He turned back to Hannah then and took her hand between both of his. "I wouldn't worry, Mrs. Goodloe. The likelihood is that by the time you are reunited with your son he will be more than happy to come home, and any concerns you might have about his wanderlust will have been cured."

"Shall I call for your car to take Mrs. Goodloe home?" Hans asked.

"I…" Hannah searched for her voice which seemed to have been permanently silenced by her shock at the recent turn of events.

"Mrs. Goodloe and her people do not travel by motorized vehicle," Levi explained. "Unless, of course, the situation is an unusual one." His eyes met hers just before he entered the room off the foyer and closed the door.

The man called Hans seemed every bit as nonplussed as Hannah was. "I believe we have a bicycle," he said. "Would that be all right?"

"Thank you, Mr. Hans, but I walked here and I can walk back." Squaring her shoulders and forcing herself not to so much as glance at the closed door where Levi Harmon was, she marched to the open front door.

Hans scurried to open the iron gate for her. "It's simply Hans, ma'am," he said.

Hannah paused and looked at him. "You have no last name?"

"Winters," he managed, "but…"

"Thank you for your kindness, Mr. Winters."

"Mr. Harmon's private car will be attached to the train leaving for Atlanta at 7:02 this evening, ma'am. You really only need to pack a single valise. Everything you may need will be provided. Mr. Harmon is extraordinarily good to his guests." His voice was almost pleading for her to not think too badly of his employer.

"Thank you, Mr. Winters." She shook his hand. "It was my pleasure to make your acquaintance." She started down the drive and, although she refused to look back, she was suddenly certain that Hans Winters was not the only one watching her go.

By the time she reached the edge of the celery fields with their cottages in the background, it was midafternoon. The five-mile walk had given her ample time to consider the possibilities before her—and to pray for guidance in choosing correctly.

Instead of stopping at her small bungalow, she went straight to her father-in-law's bakery. As she had suspected, he was still there—as was his eldest daughter Pleasant, who had helped him run the business since the death of her mother. Hannah frowned. She had hoped to find Gunther Goodloe alone. Pleasant was the antithesis of her name. A spinster, she seemed always to look on the dark side of any situation. Hannah could only imagine how she might react to the idea that Hannah needed to travel—by train—to find Caleb.

Hannah took a deep, steadying breath, closed her eyes for a moment to gather her wits, then opened the door to the bakery.

"We're closed," Pleasant barked without looking up from her sweeping.

"Hello, Pleasant. Is Gunther in the back?"

"Where else would he be?"

Hannah saw this for the rhetorical question it was and inched past her sister-in-law. Her father-in-law was a short and stocky man with a full gray beard that only highlighted his lack of hair. "Good day to you," Hannah called out over the clang of pans that Gunther was scrubbing. She took a towel from a peg near the back door of the shop, and began drying one of the pans he'd left to drain on the sideboard.

"The boy took off, did he?"

Hannah nodded.

"Any idea where he went?"

"Yes." She inhaled deeply and then told her father-in-law her suspicions.

"The circus? Well, he wouldn't be the first." He shook the water from his large hands and then wiped them on a towel that had once been a flour sack. "Do you want me to go down there and fetch him home?"

"You can't. The circus company left before dawn."

Gunther raised his bushy eyebrows but said nothing.

"I went to see Mr. Levi Harmon," she admitted.

"Why would you do such a thing on your own, Hannah? Why wouldn't you have come to me—or the bishop—right away and let us handle this?"

"Because Caleb is my son."

"Nevertheless…"

"It's done," she interrupted, "and now we must decide what to do next."

"What did Harmon have to say? He can't have been any too pleased to have you accusing him of harboring a runaway."

"I didn't accuse him of anything. I simply asked for his help in bringing Caleb home. He leaves this evening and plans to meet up with the company tomorrow and travel the rest of the way back to Wisconsin with them."

"So if Caleb is with the company, he'll send him back?"

Hannah swallowed. "He's agreed to look for Caleb."

"And if he finds him?" Gunther looked at her with suspicion.

There was no use beating about the bush. She met his gaze. "He expects me to come with him and bring Caleb home myself."

"You cannot travel alone, child." The older man ran his hand over the length of his gray beard.

Hannah held her breath. He was not saying she shouldn't go.

"I think this is a matter for the bishop to decide," he said finally. He took down his hat from the peg by the side door. "Pleasant? Hannah and I will be back shortly."

Pleasant cast one curious glance at Hannah and then returned to her sweeping. "I'll be here," she said.

They found Bishop Troyer at home and Hannah stood quietly by the front door while Gunther explained the situation. The two men discussed the matter in low tones that made it difficult for Hannah to hear. Twice the bishop glanced directly at her, shook his head and returned to the discussion. *I should have simply agreed to go with him*, she thought and then immediately prayed for forgiveness in even thinking such a thing. *But this is my son—my only child and I...*

"Hannah? The bishop would like a word with you."

Her legs felt like wood as she crossed the room and took a seat on the hard straight-backed chair opposite Bishop Troyer. She folded her hands in her lap more to steady them than to appear pious and kept her eyes lowered, lest he see her fear.

"This is indeed an unusual circumstance, Mrs. Goodloe, but at the core of it all is the undeniable fact that a boy—one of our own—is missing. And although you may be right in surmising that he has run away with the circus, we must be sure."

Hope tugged at her heart and she risked a glance at the kindly face of the bishop. His brow was furrowed but he was not frowning, just concentrating, she realized. He was trying to work out a solution that would serve the purpose of finding Caleb and bringing him home without going too far afield from the traditions that governed their community.

"It seems to me that Mr. Harmon's offer is a kind and generous one."

"Oh, he is a good man, Bishop, I'm certain of that," Hannah blurted.

This time there was no mistaking the frown that crossed both the bishop's face and her father-in-law's. Gunther cleared his throat and when she glanced at him, he shook his head as if warning her to remain silent.

"I have given my permission for you to take this journey as long as your father-in-law and your sister-in-law, Pleasant, travel with you."

Hannah's heart fell. "But the bakery," she whispered, knowing there was no one else Gunther would trust with his business.

"I have some time," the bishop replied, "as well as some experience in managing a business. I have offered to watch over the store while you are away."

She could hardly believe her ears. The bishop's offer was beyond anything she might have imagined possible. She glanced at Gunther who had offered the bishop a handshake—a contract in their society as binding as any piece of paper.

"Well, child, we must go. You said the train will leave at seven?"

Hannah nodded, unable to find words to express her joy and relief.

"Then come along. You and Pleasant can see to the packing while the bishop and I go over some of the particulars of managing the business for a few days."

Levi had spent the rest of the day in his office tending to the mountain of paperwork in preparation for vacating the Florida house for his more modest home in Wisconsin. For the next few weeks he would conduct his business from his private railway car. The Florida staff would see to the closing of his Sarasota residence and the opening of his home in Baraboo. With the exception of Hans who would travel with him, others of his household staff would travel directly to Wisconsin while he and Hans caught up with his company and made the scheduled stops with the circus for performances along the way.

He'd tried not to think about the Goodloe woman. He was fairly certain that she would not—could not—meet his demand that she travel with him to find her son. It had been ridiculous to even suggest such a thing and yet there had been something about the way she had looked at him as he dismissed her and returned to his office that made him uncertain.

The boy had run away and perhaps had inherited his wanderlust from his mother. It was intriguing to think that she was the parent with the adventurous streak. Over the years he had spent living the circus life, never once could he recall a female running away to join the troupe. Of course, Mrs. Goodloe was not exactly planning to join the traveling show. She simply wanted to find her son. But would she defy the counsel of her community's elders to accomplish that? He doubted it.

And he had no more time to give to the woman's problem. No doubt the boy had stowed away on the train. No doubt he would be discovered. No doubt that by week's end he would be back in his own bed. Levi knew that his managers would see to that. Besides, he had other far more serious matters to consider. How was it that when his circus had just completed its most successful season yet in terms of sold-out performances, the numbers did not reflect that? Expenses had risen to be sure but it seemed impossible that the cost of feeding and housing a menagerie of exotic animals and a hundred-plus performers and crew could explain such a disparity in revenue.

"Your car is waiting, sir," Hans announced with a meaningful glance at the nineteenth-century, gilded French clock that dominated the narrow marble mantel of the fireplace. The manservant was dressed in traveling clothes and holding Levi's hat as well as his own.

Levi gathered the papers he would need and stuffed them into the valise that Hans had brought to him earlier. "I should change," he muttered irritably and then wondered why. It was unlikely that there would be anyone at the station to see him off. Levi was a generous supporter of many charitable groups throughout this part of Florida, but he was known to be a reclusive man and most people had learned to respect that—even though they openly commented on the paradox that a man known for his extravagant entertainments and lavish lifestyle should be so protective of his personal privacy.

"Let's go," he told Hans as he headed for the door.

The weather had deteriorated. The air was steamy with humidity and the sky had gone from blue to a steel gray that held the promise of rain. He thought of Hannah Goodloe, imagining her walking back to the small Amish community east and north of the train station. For reasons he could not fathom, he felt the desire to make certain she arrived home before the rain began. He should have insisted on having his driver take her back. Surely she was there by now. Surely she had taken precautions for the weather.

At the station his private railway car was attached to the train that regularly made the run from Sarasota to Tampa and then from there to points north. Once the train reached Jonesville on the Florida/Georgia border, his car would be disconnected from the regular train and attached to his circus train. By the time they reached Baraboo, they would have performed in a dozen towns across half a dozen states and it would be June in Wisconsin.

"All aboard!" the conductor bellowed as Levi strode the length of the hissing and belching train to where his car waited. He passed clusters of passengers that had gathered on the platform to say their goodbyes and board the public cars. Not one of them paid the slightest attention to him but he could not help scanning their faces to see if she had come after all.

"Ridiculous," he muttered, but while Hans handed the rail attendant Levi's valise, Levi looked back, down the length of the now almost deserted platform.

"Board!" The conductor's call seemed to echo and exaggerate the fact that she was nowhere in sight.

"Sir?" Hans stood at his elbow waiting for him to mount the filigreed metal steps to enter his car.

Levi nodded and climbed aboard but took one last look back. And there, out of the steam and fog, he saw three figures—two women and a bearded man—consulting with the conductor who pointed them in Levi's direction.

He felt a strange sense of relief that bordered on victory. She had come after all and apparently with her family's blessing, assuming her two companions had accompanied her to see her off. "Make sure the guest stateroom is prepared," he said to Hans as he stepped back onto the platform and walked toward the trio. "Mrs. Goodloe," he said, removing his hat and smiling broadly.

"Mr. Harmon, may I introduce my father-in-law, Gunther Goodloe, and my late husband's sister, Pleasant."

It was only when the older man shifted a worn cardboard suitcase from one hand to the other in order to accept his handshake that Levi realized they were all three carrying luggage. "I see you came prepared to stay for some time, Mrs. Goodloe. However, if your son is…"

"My father and sister-in-law will be accompanying me on the journey, Mr. Harmon. The conductor tells us that the regular seating is filled and I apologize for not notifying you sooner of the extra passengers, but…"

Levi turned his attention to the man. "I assure you, sir, your daughter-in-law will travel in comfort and there is no reason at all for you to…"

"Our bishop has given his permission for this unusual trip," Gunther Goodloe said in a gentle but firm tone, "and he has done so only on the understanding that our Hannah will not make this journey alone." He smiled and shrugged as if he'd just made some observation about the inclement weather.

"I see." He could feel Hans watching him nervously, waiting for instruction. He could see the conductor checking his pocket watch and casting impatient looks in his direction. "Well, come aboard then and let's get you all settled in." He waited while the threesome climbed the stairs and then turned to Hans. "Prepare my quarters for the gentleman. The two women can stay in the larger guestroom."

"Very good, sir." Hans knew better than to question his boss, although the question of where Levi would sleep was implicit in the look he gave his employer. He walked to the far end of the car and boarded from there. Levi was well aware that while he was giving his guests the grand tour of the viewing room, the dining room and the parlor, Hans would be organizing the staff to prepare the rooms.

Once Levi had left the ladies and Gunther Goodloe to rest before dinner in their staterooms, he let out a long sigh of relief. The older man made him nervous. Not intentionally, of course. Gunther was the epitome of polite reserve, but it was that very reserve that brought back memories Levi had thought he'd long ago laid to rest. Memories of his late father—a man who, like Gunther, said little in words but spoke volumes with his half smile and expressive pale blue eyes. And his grandfather, whose strict household where Levi had lived after his parents died had been the deciding factor in his decision to run away.

"Mr. Harmon?"

Levi had been so lost in the past that he had not heard the young widow come in. Of course, even within the quiet of his luxurious car, there was always the steady rumble of the train moving over the tracks. He fixed a smile on his face and turned to greet her. "I trust everything is to your liking, Mrs. Goodloe?"

"It's very…" She hesitated, studying the pattern of the Oriental rug that carpeted the combination dining and sitting room. She drew in a deep breath, closed her eyes for an instant, then met his gaze directly. "I'm afraid that the accommodations simply won't do," she said. "Not at all. My family and I simply cannot stay here."

Chapter Three

"We are on a moving train, Mrs. Goodloe." His head was throbbing. Would these people never be satisfied?

"I appreciate that," she replied without a hint of the sarcasm he'd infused into his comment. "I only thought that my father-in-law could perhaps share whatever accommodations Mr. Winters uses."

"Mr. Winters? Hans?"

"Yes. I am thinking that his accommodations are... plainer and would be more comfortable for my father-in-law."

"And where would you and Miss Goodloe stay?"

Her brow furrowed slightly. "I hadn't thought that far ahead," she admitted. "It's just that Gunther—Mr. Goodloe—seemed troubled by his surroundings. He's of the old school and..."

"You and your sister-in-law are not?" Levi felt the twitch of a smile jerk at one corner of his mouth. He could see that she had not considered this in her zeal to assure her father-in-law's comfort, but after a moment she offered him a tentative smile.

"We can perhaps make do if you would agree to certain minor changes that would allow Pleasant to feel more at ease."

"What kinds of changes?"

"If we might have some plain muslin cloth—perhaps some linens that are plain, we could cover some of the more…" Her voice trailed off.

Levi closed his eyes in a vain attempt to get control of his irritation and found himself thinking about the room he had given the women for the night. The cabin had ample room for two. A sofa upholstered in Parisian brocade that folded out into a bed and an upper berth. Above the cabin door hung a painting from his collection in a thick gilded frame. The dressing table was stocked with a variety of toiletries in elegant crystal bottles, each set into a specially designed compartment to keep it secure when the train was in motion. The lighting in the room came from wall sconces that sported laughing cherubs and the floor was outfitted with a thick sheepskin rug. For people like the Goodloe family, he could see that the place might come across as anything but "plain."

"Could we not do the same for Mr. Goodloe in my room?"

"I suppose. It's just that he's beginning to think that we made a mistake in accepting your kind and generous offer." To his shock her eyes filled suddenly with tears. "Oh, Mr. Harmon, I want so much to find my son and bring him home but if my father-in-law decides we've made a mistake and the train stops to take on more passengers and…"

A woman's genuine distress had always been Levi's undoing. "Hans!"

The manservant appeared immediately. "Sir?"

"Mr. Goodloe will be bunking in with you for the

duration of our trip. I apologize for any inconvenience but it's necessary."

"Very good, sir. I'll see to it at once. Will there be anything else?"

"Yes, while we are at dinner, please see that Mrs. Goodloe's stateroom is refurbished. Remove anything that shines or glitters or smacks of flamboyance. Use plain linens to make up the beds and see if you can locate a couple of those rag rugs you use at the mansion for wiping our feet inside the garden entrance to put by each bed."

"Yes, sir."

"And cover the paintings and mirrors," Levi added as Hans hurried off to do his bidding. "They are bolted to the walls," he explained when he saw Hannah's puzzled look.

"I'll go and let the others know. May God bless you, Mr. Harmon." She was halfway down the narrow corridor when he called her back.

"Mrs. Goodloe?"

This time her face was wreathed in a genuine and full-blown smile that took his breath away. He had intended to reassure her that her son would be found and before she knew it, she and her family would be safely back home. But the attraction that shot through him like a bolt of adrenaline before a tightrope walker steps out onto the wire for the first time made him react with the same philosophy by which he had lived his entire life. *Never let the other person believe he—or she—has won.*

"I am a businessman," he began, and saw her smile falter slightly. "I rarely if ever do anything without expecting something in return." The way her spine straight-

ened almost imperceptibly and her chin jutted forward
with just a hint of defiance fascinated him.

"I thought you had invited us here as your guests, sir."

"That's true."

"Then what is your price?"

"I would like to know your given name and be allowed
to call you by it when we are alone."

Her lips worked as if trying to find words. Her eyes
widened. And then to his delight she burst out laughing.
"Oh, that's a good one, Mr. Harmon. You had me going
there for a moment."

"I'm serious."

She sobered. "My name is Hannah."

"Hannah," he repeated. "Well, dinner will be served
in fifteen minutes, Hannah. And I assure you that the
food will be plain enough even for your father-in-law."
He turned away, busying himself by flipping through
a stack of messages Hans had left for him on the sideboard. He was aware that she remained standing in the
doorway to the corridor but he refused to turn around.

"I'll tell my family," she said, and then added in the
lowest possible tone to still be heard clearly. "Thank
you, Levi."

All the way back to her room, Hannah sent up pleas
for forgiveness. From childhood on she had been known
for her impish personality. But she was a grown woman
now—a mother, a widow. Surely such mischievous behavior was beneath her. Levi Harmon could have turned
her away at the door of his lavish Sarasota estate. He
could have thrown up his hands and informed her that
Caleb's running away was hardly his concern. He could
have done so many things other than what he had done—

shown her kindness. And yet the way he had strutted about just now as if he owned everything within his view—which, of course, he did—nevertheless irritated her. And there was another cause for prayer. She sometimes suffered from a lack of patience when it came to the quirks of others. Her mother had often suggested that she look on the qualities of others that frustrated her as habits beyond their control. Such people were to be pitied, not scolded, she had advised. But her mother had never met Levi Harmon who did not inspire pity on any level.

She turned the engraved silver knob of the room she was to share with Pleasant and found her sister-in-law staggering about the cabin bumping up against the furnishings as the train rocked from side to side, and yet clearly reluctant to touch anything. Her eyes were clenched tightly shut, fingers knitted together as she murmured prayers in the dialect of Swiss-German they always used in private. She was earnestly beseeching God's mercy and deliverance from this place that was surely the devil's own workshop.

"Pleasant?" Hannah caught her sister-in-law as the train rounded a curve. Although the woman was three years younger than Hannah's age of thirty-two, she looked older. Her face was lined with anxiety. "It's all going to work out," Hannah assured her in their native tongue as she led her to the upholstered bench that was bolted to the floor in front of the dressing table.

They sat together with their backs to the mirror and the array of bottles and jars that filled the insets on top of the ornately curved dressing table. Hannah kept her arm around Pleasant's shoulders as they rocked in rhythm to the train's movement. "I spoke with Mr. Harmon. He's going to do his best to see that we are more comfortable."

"So much temptation," Pleasant muttered, glancing about with wild-eyed worry.

"Not if we refuse to be drawn to it," Hannah said.

There was a soft knock at the door and Hannah got up to answer it.

"Oh, miss," a young woman in a starched uniform exclaimed. "I thought you would be at supper and Hans said that I should…" She clutched a large bundle of plain linens to her chest.

"Let me take those," Hannah urged, reverting to English. She engaged in the brief tug-of-war it took to persuade the woman to release them. "These will do just fine. Please thank Mr. Winters for us and thank you, as well. I'll get started and while we're at supper you can finish, all right?"

The maid nodded then bowed her way out of the room, closing the door behind her. Hannah immediately began covering the large full-length mirror with one of the sheets. As if in a trance, Pleasant got up and unfolded another cloth to drape over the dressing table. "I suppose we could use the bench," she said, speaking German once again and looking to Hannah for approval.

"Absolutely," Hannah agreed as she covered the seat's tufted satin with a plain muslin pillow case. "We'll leave these for the maid," she decided as she knelt on the sofa and pulled down the upper berth. It was made up with satin linens and a silk coverlet and Hannah suspected the sofa bed was similarly garbed.

To her surprise, Pleasant giggled. "The maid," she exclaimed with glee.

Hannah saw her point. For two Amish women to be discussing what they could leave for the maid to finish was ludicrous. She started to laugh and soon the two of them were toppled on to the sofa holding their sides as their giggles subsided and then started all over again.

A knock at the door finally sobered them.

"Daughters?"

"Yes, Father," Pleasant replied as both women sprang to their feet and Hannah smoothed the covers.

"Mr. Winters tells me that supper is served."

Hannah glanced up at the taller, thinner Pleasant and straightened her sister-in-law's prayer cap that had slipped sideways when they lay on the bed. Pleasant cupped her cheek and within the look the two women exchanged more tenderness and sisterly concern than either had felt for the other in all the years Hannah had been married to Pleasant's brother. "Coming," they answered in unison.

Levi's idea of a simple supper was a three-course meal as opposed to the five-course meal his staff would normally serve. He surveyed the cold cuts, the potato salad, the dark rye bread sliced into thick wedges waiting on the sideboard. They would begin the meal with barley soup and end it with one of his cook's delicious key lime pies. It was the last of those he would enjoy for some time, Levi suspected as he turned to see that Hans was preparing to pour a dark lager into tall glasses.

"Our guests do not indulge," he said.

"But they are of German descent. I thought that this particular lager would…"

Levi shrugged. "Start with water and offer tea or milk."

Hans hesitated. "For you, as well, sir?"

"Yes." He turned as he heard the trio coming down the corridor, murmuring to each other in the Swiss-German they'd been raised to speak among their own. He wondered if it would surprise them to realize that he understood every word and decided he would leave them in the dark about that, at least for now. He didn't want to raise their curiosity regarding his past or how he had come to learn their language. "Welcome," he said jovially, indicating that Gunther should take one end of the table and then ushering the two women to the banquette built into the car against the windows.

In German, the woman Pleasant—who seemed to be anything but—murmured a comment about the magenta, tufted-velvet cushioning. She took her seat but did so with an expression she might have worn had she been asked to sit on a hot stove. Hannah gave him an apologetic smile and sat next to her sister-in-law.

Within seconds, a steaming bowl of soup had been served at each place and yet the three of them sat staring down at their bowls. Levi snapped open his white linen napkin and tucked it under his chin into the collar of his pristine white shirt. Still, they made no move, so he picked up his spoon.

"Shall we pray?" Gunther stretched out his hand to Pleasant who in turn took Hannah's hand.

Dumbly, Levi stared down at Hannah's hand extended palm-up to him and Gunther's large work-worn palm stretching to cover the extra space from one end of the small dining table to the other. Levi put down his spoon, stretched to meet Gunther's rough fingers and then placed his palm on top of Hannah's. Her head was bowed but he saw her eyes shift to focus on their joined hands.

Gunther frowned when he observed that connection but then closed his eyes and the four of them sat in silence with heads bowed for several long moments. In spite of the lengthy time allotted for a simple mealtime grace, Levi couldn't complain. He was far too busy analyzing the sensation of touching Hannah's palm. Her skin was smooth and warm and once, when her fingers twitched, he responded automatically by wrapping his fingers around hers. Hannah's breath quickened but she did not glance his way.

Gunther's head remained bowed for so long that Levi could no longer see steam rising from the soup. At last, the older man ended the prayer by looking up and reaching for his napkin. Instantly, Hannah slid her fingers from Levi's. She busied herself unfolding her napkin and placing it across her lap, then waited for her father-in-law to take the first spoonful of soup before dipping her spoon into her bowl.

"My family and I are indebted to you, Mr. Harmon, not only for your assistance in finding my grandson, but also in respecting our ways."

"Not at all. I should have thought about the rooms I offered and their furnishings."

There was a period of silence broken only by the clink of sterling soup spoons on china bowls and the rhythmic churning of the train's wheels on metal tracks.

"How is it you know of our ways?" Gunther asked after a time. "After all, we Amish have not been in Florida for long."

Levi saw Hannah glance at him and understood by her expression that it was a question she had wondered about, as well.

"My company travels all over the Midwest and eastern states of America, sir. That includes Pennsylvania where I believe there is a large established community of Amish?"

"Several of them," Gunther agreed and seemed satisfied with the response.

"How did you come to reside in Florida, sir?"

Gunther smiled. "My son was something of an adventurer. He and a friend had traveled to Florida during the time of their *Rumspringa*. That's the time when…"

"I'm familiar with the tradition," Levi said. When Hannah gave him a curious glance he added, "Isn't that the time when parents permit—even encourage—their young people to explore the outside world before making their commitment to your faith?"

"That's right," Gunther said.

All three members of the Goodloe family were regarding him with interest, so Levi turned the conversation back to the original topic. "So your son came to Florida and…"

"When he returned, he could talk of nothing else. The weather. The possibility of growing crops year-round. The opportunities." Gunther shook his head and smiled at the memory. "Even after he and Hannah had married and he had joined my bakery business, he would bring it up from time to time."

"So you just picked up and moved?" Levi directed this question to Hannah, but it was Gunther who replied.

"As I said, we were in the bakery business and one night there was a fire. We lost everything. A few years earlier his mother had died and I had remarried. My second wife was from another Amish community in another state. They did things differently there and she was having some problems settling in. My son saw it all as God's sign that we should start over someplace else."

"Did you buy land then in Sarasota?"

"No. We did what we knew best. My son and I opened a bakery." Gunther looked a little wistful for a moment and murmured, "It was all seeming to work out until…"

"My husband was killed when the wagon he was driving was struck by a motor vehicle," Hannah said softly.

"My only boy," Gunther said, his voice quavering.

Everyone concentrated on finishing their soup, then Hans directed the removal of the soup bowls and the serving of the cold cuts and side dishes. Levi was well aware that neither of the women had contributed to the limited conversation. It was going to be a long supper. He waited until everyone had been served then turned his attention to Hannah. "Tell me about your son," he said.

Again, the slightest frown of disapproval from the old man, but Hannah appeared not to notice—or perhaps chose to ignore it.

"I have told you that his name is Caleb. He is eleven years old though tall for his age. He has blue eyes and his hair…" She paused as she appeared to notice Levi's hair for the first time. "His hair is like corn silk," she murmured and quickly averted her eyes to focus on her food.

"Do you think he might have changed into clothing that is less conspicuous?"

"Perhaps."

"Where would he get such clothing?" Pleasant asked and then immediately glanced at her father and lowered her eyes.

Hannah shrugged. "I am only guessing. I mentioned the English hat. His Amish hat was still on its peg." Her eyes glittered with tears that Levi guessed she would be far too proud to shed in his presence. They were tears of worry and exhaustion and he had to force himself not to cover her hand with his and assure her it would all turn out for the best. For after all, hadn't it turned out that way for him after he'd run away to join the circus when he was only a few years older than Caleb was?

"I'm sure that the boy will turn up," Gunther said as he pushed the last of his potato salad onto his fork with the crust of his bread. "We thank you for your hospitality, sir." He placed his napkin on the table and pushed back his chair.

Levi knew that he should simply permit the supper to end so he could attend to the work he'd brought on board with him and yet he wanted more time. Why? Because of the lovely young widow? Or because he was for the first time seeing the effect that his running away must have had on his grandmother?

"Now that you've told me of your bakery, Mr. Goodloe. I'd be curious to have your opinion of my cook's key lime pie. Would you be so kind as to try it?"

"My daughter is the baker, sir."

Pleasant's cheeks flamed a ruddy brick red as Levi signaled Hans to clear and serve. "And you, Mrs. Goodloe? Do you also contribute to the wares available at your father-in-law's bakery?"

"My daughter-in-law handles the housework for our family," Gunther replied before Hannah could open her mouth. "She is an excellent cook and has been a good influence on my younger daughters."

Levi noticed that Pleasant's scowl deepened. "You have sisters then, Miss Goodloe?"

"Half sisters," she corrected, but said no more.

"Pleasant's mother died when Pleasant was just coming of age. After a time, I remarried so that she would have a mother."

"And these other daughters are the product of that marriage?"

"Ja."

"So they have stayed at home with their mother?" Gathering information from these people was like organizing a menagerie into a parade.

"Sadly, their mother died in childbirth."

"I am doubly sorry for your losses, sir," Levi said.

Gunther smiled at Hannah. "Our Hannah has become like a mother to my younger girls," he said. "God has blessed us."

"I see." Levi would hardly have called the loss of two wives and Hannah's husband a blessing, but he knew better than to debate the point.

"We have indeed been blessed. I only hope God sees fit to bless us yet again by leading us to Caleb," Hannah said in a barely audible voice.

Levi hadn't realized that he had continued to study Hannah far beyond the casual glance her comment might have indicated until Gunther cleared his throat and made a show of tasting his first bite of the pie. The two women followed his lead and all three smiled at Levi as if they had just tasted the best key lime pie ever made.

But Levi had turned his thoughts back to the situation at hand. Here was Gunther, an experienced entrepreneur in his own right, and while Levi did not hold with divine intervention, he had to admit that Gunther had come along at a time when he could use the opinion of a fellow businessman. He needed someone he could trust, someone who had no interest in his business, to review the ledgers for the past season. A fresh set of eyes. But he dismissed the idea as ludicrous. How would an unschooled, Amish baker possibly find what he had not been able to uncover himself?

He looked up and realized that once again Gunther had laid his napkin aside and this time he was standing. The two women had followed suit. Levi scrambled to his feet. "Forgive me," he said. "I'm afraid that at about this time of night my mind often goes to the business of the day past and that to come tomorrow."

"You are worried?" Gunther's eyes narrowed in sympathy.

Levi shrugged. "Always. A great many people rely on me, sir."

"And who do you rely on, Levi Harmon?"

The older man's pale blue eyes were kind and concerned. It struck Levi that if his father had lived, he would be about the same age as this man was now. He felt his throat tighten with the bile of loneliness that he had carried with him from the day his parents had died. Instead of responding to Gunther's question, he motioned for Hans to join them.

"Hans, I believe our guests are ready to retire for the night. Will you show Mr. Goodloe to your quarters?"

"If you don't mind," Gunther added, directing his comment to Hans.

"Not at all, sir. I took the liberty of moving your belongings to my cabin while you were enjoying your supper."

"Then we'll say good night." Gunther waited while the two women nodded to Levi and Hans and walked down the corridor to the guest room. Then he clasped Levi's shoulder. "May God be with you, Levi Harmon."

And as he watched Hans lead the older man to the plainer quarters, Levi understood that Gunther had not missed the fact that Levi had avoided answering his question. The fact was Levi had no response, for since he'd been a boy, there had been no one to watch over him.

Chapter Four

Hannah found sleep impossible that night. Her mind reeled. Where was her son and had he indeed run off with the circus, or was she on some wild goose chase while Caleb was out there somewhere alone? Every clack of the wheels might be taking her farther from him.

She sat on the edge of the upper berth that she'd insisted on taking. Below her, Pleasant's even breathing seemed to have fallen into a rhythm that matched the rumble of the train. Outside the window, Hannah saw the silhouette of telephone poles standing like sentinels in the fields. As the train rounded a bend, the noise flushed a flock of large blackbirds and they scattered into the night sky. The window faced east and she could see the breaking of dawn on the horizon.

"Please keep him safe until I can come for him," she prayed as she watched the sky turn from black to charcoal and then pink. "He is my life," she added and closed her eyes tight against the memory of the long, lonely years that had passed since her husband's death. Years when her only solace had been Caleb.

Perhaps that was it. Perhaps she and others had put

so much pressure on him in the absence of his father. How often had she heard someone remind him that he was now the man of the family? How often had someone suggested that she needed his support and help more than ever because all she had was him? Perhaps his need for freedom wasn't that at all. Perhaps it was more a need to be what he was—a boy. A child.

Oh, how she wished she might talk to someone—a male who might understand the workings of a young boy's mind. Perhaps Mr. Winters, she thought.

Outside the cabin door she heard footsteps. Given the early hour, she assumed it would be Hans Winters, up before dawn to see to the needs of his master and the guests. She eased herself down from the upper berth, taking care not to wake Pleasant and got dressed as quickly as she could, given the need to fumble blindly for the black straight pins that held the skirt and bodice of her dress in place. Once properly dressed, she wrapped her hair—grown now to past her waist—round and round her hand and coiled it into the casing of her prayer cap.

When she slipped into the passageway, she paused for a moment listening for sounds. That way led to Hans's quarters and the kitchen. The opposite way led to the observation room and dining room. She heard the clink of silver and assumed Hans would be setting the dining table for their breakfast.

"May I help you?" she asked as she entered the opulent room. It would be the perfect opportunity to engage the servant in conversation. The two of them working together to prepare the room for breakfast.

But instead of Hans, she found herself facing Levi. He was sitting at a small drop-down desk on one side of the large sideboard, stirring a cup of coffee. "Not unless you've a head for figures," he grumbled.

Actually, I do, Hannah thought but understood instinctively that the circus owner would no doubt laugh at the very idea that she might be able to solve whatever problem that he clearly could not. Still, if the idea brought a smile to his face that would certainly be preferable to the scowl that darkened his deep-set eyes at the moment. "I apologize," she murmured, turning to go. "I assumed that Mr. Winters…"

"Kitchen," he grumbled, turning his attention back to the ledger before him.

The table was already set so she turned to go. But she had retreated only two steps before he stopped her. "I'm sorry. Is there a problem, Hannah?"

"Not at all," she said brightly.

"You slept well?" He seemed to be studying her features closely.

"Not really," she admitted, knowing that her face surely showed the effects of her restless night. "But it was not the accommodations," she hastened to assure him. "The berth was quite comfortable and the rhythm of the train's movement was a little like rocking a child."

A smile tugged at the corners of his mouth. "Upper or lower?"

"Upper," she replied and felt her cheeks flush at the impropriety of this particular topic. "Well, I'll leave you to your work," she said.

"Why were you looking for Hans? It's not yet dawn and if there's no problem with your accommodations…."

She took a moment to consider her options. Levi was a man—younger than Hans and perhaps more likely to remember what it had been like to be a boy of eleven. "I am worried about my son," she admitted.

"If he took off with my crew, Hannah, we will find him and until we do, I assure you that he is in good company. No harm will come to him."

"But what if he didn't? What if he just ran away? What if he got to the circus grounds too late and your company had already left and he just decided to go off on his own?" The thoughts that she had successfully held at bay through the long night now came tumbling out. "What if even now with every mile we go I am moving farther and farther from him? Perhaps I was too hasty in my assumption. Perhaps I should…"

Levi pushed the ledger aside and indicated that she should take a seat on the end of the tufted settee closest to the dining chair he had pulled over to the desk. "It seems to me that you have ample reason to believe that your son is with my company. From what you have told me, the boy is a planner and as such he would have timed his departure so that he did not run the risk of missing the train."

"But…"

"And even if he did miss it, we are going to know that within a matter of hours. We are scheduled to arrive in Jonesville just after breakfast. The company will be doing two shows there today—a matinee and an evening performance. If Caleb is with them we will find him."

"And if not?"

"Then I will see that you and your family are on the next train back to Sarasota and I will personally notify the authorities there to begin the search for your son. One step at a time, Hannah." He stood up and poured a second cup of coffee from the silver coffeepot on the sideboard and handed it to her. "Drink this," he said. "You're running on nerves and you're going to need your strength for the day ahead, whatever it may bring."

"Thank you," she murmured as she took a sip of the hot strong brew. "You've been more than kind to us. I assure you that we'll be out of your way soon." She took a second sip. "Do you recall—I mean, Caleb is a boy of eleven and he's had so much responsibility thrust upon him since the death of his father. It occurred to me that this business isn't really about joining the circus at all."

"It's about finding his way," Levi said. "Testing himself—and you."

"In what way is he testing me?"

Levi shrugged. "He may not realize it but he wants to see if you will come after him and, if you do, whether or not things will be different for the two of you once you find him."

"I love him," Hannah whispered and her voice quaked.

"Enough to one day let him go?"

"He's eleven," she protested.

"I said one day, Hannah. Don't make the mistake of making this boy your reason for living. Don't try to mold him into some kind of replacement for the life you thought you would have with your husband."

"I wouldn't. I don't," she said firmly and stood up. Flustered with irritation at his assumption that he knew anything at all about her or her life, she started to hand him the coffee cup then thought better of it and placed the cup and saucer on the silver tray that held the coffee service on the sideboard. "Thank you for the coffee," she said. "I expect Pleasant will be awake by now—she's used to rising early for the baking...." She started toward the passageway just as the train lurched around a curve.

Surefooted as a tiger, he steadied her before she could fall, his hands grasping her upper arms and remaining there until she regained her balance.

"Thank you," she whispered and pulled away.

Levi stood watching her hurry along the corridor that ran the length of his private car. It wasn't until she opened the door to her cabin and disappeared that he realized he'd been holding his breath and clenching his fists as if somehow that might keep the warmth of touching her from running away as she had.

"It's not the same," he muttered as he turned back to the desk, slammed shut the ledger and then retrieved his suit jacket from the back of the chair. But the picture of Hannah's son striking out in the middle of the night, slipping away from the only house he'd probably ever known as home and heading off into the unknown stirred memories of Levi's own youth that he had thought long since forgotten.

Suddenly, he recalled with graphic clarity the combination of fear and exhilaration he'd felt that night. Equally as strong came the memory of his doubt and regret after he'd been on the road for only a day. "It was different for me," he muttered as he poured himself a second cup of coffee. "I was fourteen."

He heard the sound of conversation in the passageway, drained his coffee and turned to face whatever this day might bring. Gunther Goodloe was speaking in low tones in his native tongue as he led Hannah and Pleasant to the dining room.

"Good morning, Mr. Goodloe. I trust your accommodations were satisfactory?"

"Yes, thank you for allowing the change." He indi-

cated that the two women should take the places on the
settee where they had sat for supper the evening before.

"Please take my place, sir," Levi urged, holding out
the chair for the older man. "You'll have a better view
of the passing scenery from here," he added, knowing
full well that he had decided upon the change in seating abruptly so that he would not have to touch Hannah
again during morning prayers.

On cue Hans appeared with a tea cart loaded with
covered sterling serving dishes. He lifted the cover on
the first and offered a selection of sausages and bacon
to the two women, then Mr. Goodloe and finally Levi.
He repeated this process with a chafing dish filled with
steaming scrambled eggs, then another with a selection
of breads and rolls, and finally offered each guest butter
and jam. Meanwhile, the maid traveling with them filled
glasses with milk and offered coffee and tea.

Through all of this Levi kept up a running conversation about the countryside they were traversing. "I'm
afraid the boom times ended for Florida after the hurricane of '26," he said.

"And yet your business seems to be thriving," Gunther replied.

"Even in hard times people need to be entertained,"
Levi replied. "Perhaps especially in hard times." Knowing it was inevitable, Levi extended his hands to Pleasant and Gunther. "Shall we pray?"

It took a moment before he realized that because he
had extended the invitation, the others were waiting
for him to bow his head. Forgetting that Amish grace
was said in silence, he cleared his throat and murmured
thanks for the food and the company and then added,

"And may today bring Hannah the news she needs to know that her son is safe. Amen."

When he looked up he was surprised to see Gunther frowning and Hannah blushing. For her part, Pleasant had focused all of her attention on the food before her and he couldn't help but wonder what law of propriety he had just broken. Was it the prayer? He hadn't prayed in years and yet thought he had done a passable job of offering grace before a meal. And then he understood his mistake. It was bad enough that he had offered the prayer aloud, but he had also singled Hannah out for special attention and called her by her given name.

"I apologize, sir," he said, refusing to ignore the situation. "It's just that we are all concerned about your grandson and I suppose that has made me feel a particular closeness to your family. Nevertheless, I was too familiar just now. I hope you will forgive my lapse in manners."

"Not at all," Gunther replied. "We are in your world now. I am honored that you have shown such concern for my grandson's well-being. If you are more comfortable calling us by our given names, then that's the least we can do." He drank a long swallow of his milk. "I have noticed that Mr. Winters is distinctly uncomfortable with such formality," he added.

"You are very observant, sir. And very kind."

He saw that Gunther took the compliment in stride without acknowledging it. Instead, he evidently decided that a fresh round of introductions was in order. "And so we are the Goodloe family. I am Gunther and my daughter is Pleasant and as you have observed, Caleb's mother is Hannah."

"And I am Levi." He shook hands with Gunther then smiled at Pleasant whose lips were pursed into a worried pucker as if unsure of what to make of all this. Finally, he looked at Hannah who met his gaze directly.

"And my son is Caleb," she said softly. "And today, God willing, we shall find him and not trouble you further, Levi."

As promised, they arrived in the small town of Jonesville an hour later. On the way into town the train slowed and then paused as Levi's private car was moved to a siding next to a large field. From her position on the observation deck at the back of the car, Hannah could see dozens of workers, some hammering in the long stakes that would hold the huge circus tent in place. Other workers performed the same task as a dozen smaller tents went up on the property.

"That one is the cooking tent and next to it the dining tent," Levi told them as Gunther, Pleasant and Hannah leaned out over the scrolled and turned-brass railing of the deck for a better view. "Wardrobe," he continued, "dressing rooms, makeup, props."

"It's like a city in itself," Hannah observed and she was beginning to understand how such activity might have captivated Caleb. "It's so colorful and…"

"Exciting," Pleasant whispered. Then she glanced at her father and added, "If you enjoy that sort of thing."

"So many people," Hannah said as she scanned the throng of workers for any sign of her son.

"We'll find him," Levi said quietly. Then in a more normal tone he added, "Care to watch the unloading of the wagons, Gunther? I promise you it's worth every minute of your time."

"I wouldn't mind getting off this train and stretching my legs on firm ground a bit," Gunther replied.

Levi opened the small gate that led to three steps and disembarked. From the ground he held out a hand to Pleasant. "Ladies," he invited as he escorted them safely to the ground. Then he waited for Gunther to navigate the short flight of steps before beginning the tour.

"There are forty flatcars for transporting the wagons," he said as he headed toward a siding where the line of cars with their cargo of painted and gilded circus wagons waited. "A wagon can weigh as much as six tons," he added, and Hannah saw that her father-in-law was intrigued in spite of his reservations about coming too close to this outside world.

"You use Belgians to do the heavy work," Gunther noted, nodding toward a matched pair of large black horses dragging a ramp into place at the end of one flatcar.

"Belgians, Percherons, Clydesdales," Levi replied. "They serve double duty as both work horses and performance animals. But the men will handle the actual work of taking the wagons off the flatcars."

The four of them watched in silence as the work crew set a ramp in place at one end of the flatcar. Then a crew member took hold of the wagon's tongue and carefully steered the wagon toward the ramp.

"This is where things get tricky," Levi said. "If he loses control and the wagon starts to roll too quickly then we risk injuring a worker. So that man there—a 'snubber'—will control the speed using that network of ropes and capstans."

Hannah held her breath as the unwieldy wagon gained speed and threatened to topple over on its way down the ramp. Safely on the ground another member of the crew hitched it to the team of horses, climbed aboard and drove it across the lot. Then the process began all over again.

"It's a lot of work," Gunther observed.

"Especially when you realize that after tonight's performance we'll simply reverse the process and move on to the next town."

"Are those the tents for housing the animals?" Hannah asked, recalling the notice for a stable boy that she and Caleb had seen on the grounds in Sarasota.

"Yes. Gunther, why don't you and Pleasant go over there to the dining and cook tents and see if there's any sign of the boy while Hannah and I check out the animal tents?"

Before Gunther could object, Levi had started off toward a large tent where Hannah could see horses and elephants stabled. Without a backward look she followed him.

While Levi spoke with the men working the area, she searched for Caleb. Methodically, she checked every stall and gently prodded every pile of hay that looked bulky enough for a boy to be hiding under with the toe of her shoe. Nothing.

She had searched the large open-aired tent from one end to the other and found no sign of her son. Now she stood at the entrance to the tent looking out across the circus grounds, wondering where he might be and praying that she had not made a mistake in guessing that he had left with the circus.

"Mrs. Goodloe?"

She turned at the sound of Levi's call. He was walking toward her with another man. The sun was behind them, streaming in from the far end of the tent and both men were in silhouette, and yet there was something about

Levi's confident stride that made her know him at once. The other man was a stranger. She focused on Levi, willing him to break free of the shadows and give her the news she'd prayed to hear—that Caleb had been found.

Chapter Five

"Mrs. Hannah Goodloe, this is my accountant and business manager, Jake Jenkins."

"Very pleased to make your acquaintance, ma'am," the small wiry man gushed. He was dressed in a business suit and held a bowler hat that he kept tapping against his thigh in a nervous cadence. "I understand your son is missing?"

"Have you seen him?" Hannah was well aware that she had dispensed with the niceties of meeting someone new and gotten directly to the point. But all through the night and especially in the bright light of day, she had felt that time was of the essence. Either she would find Caleb today or...

"I may have."

Hannah's heart beat in quick time. "Where is he?"

"Now, ma'am, I said I might have seen the boy. There was a kid on the grounds in Sarasota yesterday morning as we were loading the last of the wagons. Most everyone was already on board but I saw him hanging around the livestock car."

"Did he board the train, Mr. Jenkins?" Hannah

thought that she might scream if the man insisted on stretching out his story any further.

"I'm not sure."

"But back there you said…" Levi's voice was tight, as if each word were an effort.

"I said I might have seen the kid, Levi. You know how it is. We get kids hanging around all the time—granted, usually not at that hour of the morning, but still…"

"Where did you last see him?" Hannah asked, suddenly unable to swallow around the lump of fear in her throat.

"I hollered at him to get going and he ran off toward the front of the train—up where the sleeping cars are. He could have just kept going or he could have boarded one of those cars."

"Let's go," Levi said, taking Hannah's elbow and ushering her past the dapper little man. "Maybe he's still there—maybe he fell asleep and…"

"He could never sleep through all of this," Hannah replied as she practically ran to keep up with his long strides. "Besides, he's an early riser and…"

"Let's just be sure."

But after a thorough search of the sleeping, dining and stock cars there was no sign of Caleb. Levi even spoke to the local authorities to see if they might have spotted a boy obviously on his own in town.

"I've alerted the authorities in Sarasota," Levi told the family when they had all returned to his private car where Hans had prepared lunch for them. "And Hans can arrange for your trip home. However, I'm afraid the earliest train is tomorrow."

"It's God's will," Pleasant murmured, and Hannah shivered at the very idea that God would be so cruel as to allow a boy to wander alone over yet a second night while his mother was miles away.

"Or man's failure," Levi added quietly. "I'll question my business manager again, Hannah. Perhaps there's some detail he forgot, something that might offer more information."

"Thank you," Hannah replied and stood up. "Please excuse me," she murmured and did not wait for their permission.

Outside she wandered the circus lot, oblivious to the growing throng surrounding her as people gathered for the matinee performance. But as she found her way around the enormous tent away from the main entrance and the smaller sideshow tents and ticket wagon, she began to consider her surroundings through the eyes of her son.

The dining tent was mostly empty now. Only a few of the waiters were left, lounging at one of the tables, cigarettes dangling from their lips as they took a well-deserved break. She followed the sounds of chatter and found herself in what Caleb had described to her as the "backyard" of the circus.

"See, Ma," he'd explained excitedly, "it's not so different from home if they have a backyard."

Hannah watched as a parade of elaborately outfitted animals and performers lined up for their grand entrance into the tent. "The big top, Ma," Caleb had corrected her when she referred to it as a tent on their tour. "Because it's the biggest."

"The big top," she murmured as she trudged on. She had no idea where she was headed. She only knew that she had to find a quiet place where she could think. She had noticed a little creek near the tracks on their way in. Perhaps…

"Watch it, honey." Hannah glanced up to find that she'd nearly run straight into a highly made-up woman wearing a skintight leotard, tights and a sheer flowing skirt covered in sequins.

Immediately, she averted her eyes. "So sorry," she murmured. "Forgive me, please," she added as she and the woman engaged in a kind of dance as one moved one way and the other moved in unison so that they were still blocking each other.

"Hey," the woman said, "you're the mother of that missing kid, aren't you?"

The mention of Caleb took precedence over anything that might have proved embarrassing about being so close to a woman like this. She met the woman's gaze and saw that beneath the layers of mascara and eye shadow, the woman had eyes that were kind and concerned.

"Yes," she admitted.

"Thought so. Look, honey, you didn't hear it from me but some of us were talking and we're pretty sure we saw the kid. Blond hair, right? Looks like it's been cut by using a bowl as a cap?"

Hannah nodded, unable to breathe for the rush of hope she didn't want to allow herself to feel.

"Skinny kid but taller than most. White shirt, suspenders holding up high-water black pants?"

"What are high-water…"

"Too short for him," the woman explained.

"Yes," Hannah said, her excitement building. "Where…when…"

"All I can tell you is that kid was on the train last

night—like a shadow he was." She chuckled. "Now you saw him and now you didn't."

"And now?"

The woman's laughing eyes sobered. "Haven't seen him since we got here, honey," she admitted. "And from the chatter in the dining tent earlier, neither has anyone else. We figured he must have moved on but then I saw you searching this morning and…well, I'm a mother myself and when I ran into you just now, it seemed like I was supposed to tell you what I knew even if…"

"May I know your name?" Hannah asked.

The woman's eyes narrowed, then she shrugged. "Sure. That's me there." She pointed to the painted side of a large float where the words *Lily Palmer, The Girl in the Gilded Cage* were emblazoned in gold script.

Hannah heard the band sound a fanfare and slowly the parade of people and animals started forward. "Gotta run, honey," Lily shouted as she dashed off to climb aboard her float. Hannah watched as the woman nimbly climbed up the side of a three-tiered scaffolding and into an oversize gilded birdcage. From her perch up high, Lily waved at Hannah. "Keep the faith, honey," she shouted and Hannah realized that she was smiling, and that her breathing was coming in gasps of excitement rather than panic. She waved back to Lily and then headed back to Levi's private car to share the news with the others.

"I thought you said you saw the kid." Levi fumed later that afternoon as he and Jake went over the orders Jake would need to place at each stop on their way north.

"I told you I saw a kid, Levi. Blond hair, Amish looking duds—seemed to match what you described. Don't shoot the messenger, okay?"

Jake and Levi had been friends for years. They had both been stowaways and after spending several months riding the circus train and doing odd jobs, Jake had left to find his fortune in Chicago. A couple of months after Levi inherited the Brody circus from his mentor Jasper Brody, Levi contacted his old friend and the two had worked together ever since. He'd quickly realized that Jake's talents were exactly the right complement to his own. The man had a head for business, plus he was a crowd-pleaser. That meant he was great at negotiating favorable deals for the myriad list of goods and supplies that it took to keep a circus running.

In the process the two of them had become good friends. Jake's naturally outgoing personality was a perfect complement to Levi's reticence and as the years had gone by, Levi had been more than happy to let Jake handle the public and promotional parts of running a circus.

"I just hated to disappoint her," he said by way of apology for snapping at his friend.

Jake shrugged. "You've gone above and beyond the way I see it. It's hardly your concern if the boy decided to take off."

"He's younger than most," Levi said absently.

"Maybe there was trouble at home. Maybe his ma— or maybe his grandpa—were…"

"They're good people, Jake."

His friend shrugged. "I'm just saying. A boy doesn't take off for no good reason."

"She thinks he fell for the glamour," Levi said and then both men laughed. For both understood that life on the road with the circus was about as glamorous as shoveling elephant dung at the end of the parade.

"Then there's nothing to worry about," Jake said,

clapping Levi on the shoulder. "Give the kid a couple of days—a week at most—and I guarantee you he'll be begging us to send him back—if he's here at all, that is."

"You looked everywhere? Spoke to everyone?"

Jake sighed and nodded. "Lily and some of the gals thought they spotted him on board last night but there was no sign of him. More likely they were all falling asleep when I was chasing the kid and they looked outside, spotted him then dreamed he was running through their sleeping car."

"Why'd you chase him?"

"Because the train was about to move and he was dodging in and out between cars. The last thing we needed was for a kid to get crushed as we were leaving town. Business is bad enough without adding that to the mix."

Levi couldn't debate that point. "I don't get it," he said, his attention now firmly back on the figures he'd been studying for days now. "Our last performances in Sarasota were sold out and yet…"

"You gave all those tickets to that charity thing, remember?" Jake reminded him. "You'll see. Things will start to look better now that we're on the road. Besides, you aren't exactly hurting, Levi."

"You know it's not about my personal fortune," Levi snapped. "We employ so many people, Jake. I'm responsible for their welfare—not to mention the welfare of their families. With the way the economy took a nosedive in Florida these past couple of years, I don't want to have to start letting people go."

"Trust me, my friend. Everyone knows you're going to do the right thing when it comes to taking care of the company. Whatever happens, everybody knows that when Levi Harmon gives you his word, it beats any official piece of paper you might ever hold in your hand." Jake gathered up the orders. "I'll go send these so the supplies are waiting at the next stop. And stop worrying!"

Levi smiled for the first time since he'd sat down with his friend. Somehow Jake had always had a way of putting a new face on things—a more positive face—and Levi was grateful for that.

Supper that evening was a somber affair. Levi was tired from the stresses of the day. Attendance for the matinee had been good but people had not spent the extra money for the sideshows and cotton candy and popcorn that they usually did. Although the wealthy classes were still thriving, these were hard times for ordinary folks and it did not look as if things were going to get much better for some time.

But the real gloom that hung over the gathering was the fact that there had been no sign of the boy. Hannah kept her eyes lowered as she methodically sipped her soup. Levi doubted she was even aware that she was taking in nourishment. Gunther kept glancing at his daughter-in-law and sighing heavily. Only Pleasant seemed to be enjoying the meal.

"Excuse me, sir." Hans entered the dining area with his usual catlike grace. He was holding a piece of yellow paper.

"A telegram?" Levi asked, reaching for it.

"Yes, sir. It's from Miss Ida."

Hannah looked up for the first time, her eyes flickering with some interest.

"Ida Benson," Levi explained to his guests. "She's my personal secretary. She headed straight back to Wisconsin once the company arrived here yesterday."

Levi read the short message. Then read it again. He glanced at Hannah, then handed her the telegram. "It's good news," he said softly.

Hannah felt as if everyone must surely be able to see the beat of her heart under her caped dress. It was hammering away so hard that she thought she could actually feel the blood rushing through her veins. Her hand shook slightly as she accepted the telegram.

Amish runaway in my cabin. Stop. Just crossed into Indiana. Stop. Please instruct. Stop. Ida

She read the words again. *Amish runaway.* "It's Caleb," she whispered as if to assure herself, then she turned to her father-in-law and handed him the wire. "It's Caleb," she repeated as relief washed through her like a cleansing dip in the Gulf. She grasped Pleasant's hand as they waited for Gunther to scan the words.

"Could be," he said cautiously.

"Must be," Pleasant said firmly. "Now what?"

All eyes turned to Levi.

"There are several options," he began slowly. "Miss Benson could put the boy on the next train back to Sarasota or she could get him a ticket to meet us tomorrow at our next stop in Georgia."

"She could not accompany him?" Gunther asked.

"Miss Benson has a great deal of work to do once she reaches Wisconsin," Levi explained. "That's why she has traveled back ahead of the rest of us."

"Someone else, then." Pleasant's tone was less a question than a demand.

"There is no one else. Miss Benson is traveling alone."

"You said there were several options," Hannah reminded him. "Allowing Caleb to travel alone seems risky to me."

"And yet, Hannah, he has been traveling alone since the night he ran away."

"That's my point. Caleb ran away and he hates to fail at anything so if he's put on a train alone my concern is that he will decide to make another attempt and that this time we will have no Miss Benson to watch over him."

Levi slowly removed his reading glasses and set them on the pristine, white tablecloth as he leaned back in his chair and ran one large palm over his face. He looked so weary and certainly the last thing he needed right now was this. Hannah hated adding to his worries, but this was her son.

"I suppose," he began, then looked from her to Gunther to Pleasant before continuing. "I suppose that I could instruct Ida to take the boy with her, get him settled with a farm family she knows in Baraboo and keep an eye on him until you can all get there."

"Baraboo?" Pleasant asked, her eyes suddenly alive with interest.

"Yes. It's the town where we have our summer headquarters," Levi replied. "Do you know it?"

To Hannah's shock, Pleasant blushed scarlet and returned her attention to her soup. "I…no…just a curious name."

"How soon would we get there?" Hannah asked.

"By commercial train, two to three days depending on when we can get you tickets."

Hannah glanced at her father-in-law and saw him frown. She was well aware that he was calculating the expense. "I could go and you and Pleasant could return to Sarasota," she suggested.

"Absolutely not," Gunther thundered. "The very idea of you traveling alone…"

"Or you could continue as my guests and arrive back in Wisconsin in two weeks," Levi suggested. "That way you will only encounter the expense of the return trip. In the meantime, I assure you that Caleb will be quite well-provided for and perhaps have the time to consider the error of his actions. The family I spoke of is Amish. The woman is a close friend of Miss Benson's."

Now all eyes swiveled to Gunther's place at the opposite end of the table from Levi. *Please*, Hannah prayed silently.

Gunther cleared his throat but said nothing.

"We could send word to your people in Sarasota," Levi suggested. "Let them know the trip will take longer than expected."

"I also have a business to run," Gunther reminded him and the women, and Hannah steeled herself to stand her ground. Under no circumstances was she going to allow Caleb to travel alone and risk losing him again.

She was just about to make her case when Pleasant spoke up. "Oh, Father, you know how Bishop Troyer loves taking charge." She turned to Levi, explaining, "He's up in years and has little to occupy him beyond church business these days."

"He's competent?" Levi asked Gunther.

"Exceptionally so," Gunther agreed. "But, daughter, while I agree that he can manage the business itself, who would you suggest do the baking?"

Pleasant opened her mouth then closed it. She clearly had not considered that.

"I will go with Levi to Wisconsin and fetch the boy. You two girls will return to Sarasota as planned in the morning." He nodded once and flattened both palms against the table as if that made everything final.

Hannah could feel Levi watching her. Well, what did he expect her to do? This was her father-in-law and in the absence of her husband, the head of the family.

But Caleb is your son—your only child.

She closed her eyes tightly against the warring loyalties within her then said quietly, "If you think that best." Then she folded her napkin and pushed away from the table. "Will you excuse me? I'd like to take a walk before bedtime."

To her shock, Pleasant also pushed back from the table. "I'll come with you," she announced.

Hannah sighed. She needed some time to think, but Pleasant was right behind her and as soon as both had stepped off the train, Pleasant took her arm. Her sister-in-law was silent for a bit and then leaned in close, glancing back toward Levi's private car as she whispered, "I think I might know a way Papa will agree to have us all travel to Baraboo."

Chapter Six

Once again the grounds were alive with activity as the company prepared for the evening performance. Levi had explained that the activity would go on long into the night as the crew dismantled the big top, loaded up the animals and wagons and prepared to move on to the next stop. There they would repeat the entire process all over again as they would half a dozen times on the way back to Baraboo. It was so noisy on the circus grounds that Hannah was certain she must have misunderstood Pleasant's astonishing comment.

"Hannah? Did you hear what I said?"

She fought her irritation at Pleasant's sudden and surprising decision to join her in her walk. "No. The noise."

Pleasant pulled Hannah toward the creek, away from the clatter. "I don't mean to pry but…"

Hannah steeled herself for what was to come for when Pleasant said she didn't mean to pry, prying was just what she did. "Go on," she said. *Get it out so we can move past it.*

"Well, of course you're Caleb's mother—his only living parent. I'm just his aunt, but if he were my child, I would want to go and fetch him myself. I would want to be there. I would want to hear what he had to say for himself—why he would put me and the rest of the family in such…"

Hannah couldn't help it. She burst into tears. "Of course, I want to go to him," she blubbered. "How could I not? I have been so frightened for him, so very worried that perhaps…" She couldn't begin to finish that thought. All of the awful possibilities of what might have happened to her child that had gone through her mind these past two days.

"There, there," Pleasant soothed as she put her arm around Hannah's shoulders. "I didn't mean to upset you so. Of course, you've been worried and of course, you would go to him tonight if you could."

Hannah sniffed back tears and tried to compose herself. They had stopped next to a live oak tree drooping like a willow with Spanish moss. "Then why…"

Pleasant pursed her lips and glanced around as if half expecting someone to be listening in on their conversation. "Do you remember Mr. Noah Yoder from last winter?"

Hannah was so confused by the sudden shift in conversation that she shook her head.

"Of course you do," Pleasant pressed. "He came down to visit his uncle and to see about possibly buying land and starting a produce farm?"

"Vaguely," Hannah said, recalling a small jovial young man who had developed a habit of appearing at the bakery every morning at opening time, and again in the afternoons when Pleasant was cleaning up for the day. "He used to come to the bakery for fresh hot rolls every morning and buy up the leftover rolls at the end of the day."

"That's him," Pleasant said, a smile softening her usually stern features, a look that Hannah had never before witnessed.

"As I recall, he decided against buying land and returned to…" Her eyes widened in understanding. "Baraboo, Wisconsin," she whispered.

"Don't you see, Hannah, if we could just persuade Father that it's only right for you to be the one to see Caleb first then he would insist on traveling with you and if he won't let you travel alone then he certainly would not allow me to return home alone and…"

"Slow down," Hannah said but she was beginning to see the possibilities in Pleasant's chatter. "So if the three of us traveled on to Wisconsin then you might…"

"I could possibly see Mr. Yoder again—I mean Levi said there's an Amish community nearby where Caleb will stay until we can get there and how many Amish communities can there be in such a place and if Mr. Yoder is there, then…"

"But what about the bakery?"

"I thought of that and perhaps it's time my half sisters stepped in to help. After all," she continued, "there are two of them to share the baking and the housework and all."

"Lydia is just seventeen," Hannah reminded her, but Pleasant only shrugged.

"Why couldn't she do the work, or perhaps the two of them working together? I mean it would be no different if I suddenly took ill, would it? They'd have to step in then."

"You've thought all this through in just a matter of minutes?" Hannah was impressed. No wonder her sister-in-law had been so quiet when they first started their walk.

"I've been thinking about it—not really daring to hope, of course—since we first boarded the train. And then when Levi mentioned Baraboo earlier it was like a sign. Don't you think so, Hannah? Don't you think that perhaps God has given me this opportunity to travel there and perhaps to…" She waved her hand in the air, unwilling to finish her hope aloud.

"But your father has decided," Hannah reminded her, knowing she did not have to add that once he made up his mind Gunther did not like being second-guessed.

Pleasant looked crestfallen, but then brightened. "Perhaps Levi could help. He likes you, Hannah. He would certainly understand how badly you want to see your child. Yes, he's the one I shall speak with and then he can persuade Father. I'll do it right now before I lose my nerve," she announced, and turned on her heels and marched straight back to Levi's private car.

Levi had just learned that the Stravinskys were leaving his employ and staying in Florida. It wasn't that uncommon in his business for people to come and go, but Igor Stravinsky and his wife, Maria, as well as Igor's brother, Ivan, had been with him almost from the beginning. Igor and Ivan had handled the stock of ring or performance horses, grooming the animals and polishing their silver or brass trappings until they glittered. Maria had done everything from mending to designing costumes for the company. Igor had apologized for the inconvenience but pleaded old age even though he was only in his midforties. Maria had admitted that she wanted time to enjoy a home of her own. Together the brothers had pooled their money and bought a small business in central Florida. They had thought the deal would not be finalized for several weeks but the owner of the shop had taken ill and unless they took over immediately the shop would have to be closed until they could.

"I don't like leaving you in the middle of the trip back and all," Igor told him, "but what can we do?"

It was clear to Levi that the decision had not been an easy one for the trio and he was touched by their loyalty. "I wish you well," he said as he walked out onto the observation platform of his railroad car with Igor. "Stay in touch, my friend," he added, and accepted the bear hug the older man gave him before running down the three metal steps and racing off to get ready for his last performance and to tell his wife and brother the news.

Pleased for them in spite of the inconvenience their leaving meant to his business, Levi could not help feeling a little envious. What might it be like to settle down in one place? *You chose your path*, he reminded himself and went back inside to work out the logistics of filling three holes in his company.

He was going over the roster of employees, trying to decide how to shift people around so that they would be covered at least until they got home to Baraboo when Hans cleared his throat.

"Miss Goodloe to see you, sir."

"Hannah?" Levi ignored the quickening of his heart. He'd been worried about her after the conversation at supper was all. He could see that she was upset and why wouldn't she be?

"It's *Miss* Pleasant Goodloe, sir."

Levi stifled a groan. He'd had little contact with Gunther's daughter but her demeanor always set him on edge.

"Very well," he said and stood up to put on his suitcoat. "Show her in."

The woman seemed unusually nervous and vulnerable.

"How can I help you, Pleasant? Has something happened?" He suddenly worried that one of the townspeople Jake often hired to help out with the backstage work might have accosted the woman.

She drew in a deep breath, squeezed her eyes closed for a couple of seconds and then blurted out a speech she had apparently been practicing. "Hannah needs your help in convincing my father that it is she who should be the first to reunite with Caleb. After all, she is the parent—the only parent—and if she is not there, well, what does that say to the boy? That she has no authority, that's what it says. So she must be the one to go and fetch him from Wisconsin and since my father is opposed to women traveling alone, I will just have to go along as well because…"

Well, well, well, Levi thought as he stifled a smile. *For whatever reason, Miss Pleasant Goodloe was not yet ready to go home. Perhaps young Caleb was not the only member of this family that had entertained dreams of a different life?*

She continued to prattle on making her case, grabbing short breaths between phrases and leaving him no possible entry into the conversation. Finally, completely winded and unable to find the words to add to her plea, she stopped talking and looked at him, her eyebrows raised like question marks.

"And what does Hannah—Mrs. Goodloe—think of your idea?"

"Hannah will not go against my father's decision,"

she replied. "However, she was sobbing inconsolably before and well, how would you feel if your only son had run away, been found hundreds of miles away and you were going to have to wait for weeks to see him again?"

"I see your point," Levi mused, having only heard the part about Hannah crying. He fingered the papers on his desk, his eyes coming to rest on the place where he had marked through the names of the Stravinskys and placed blank lines next to their positions. "Do you sew, Pleasant?"

"Of course I sew," she snapped.

"And Hannah?"

"Amish women are well-skilled in the things necessary to run a household, Levi. Cooking, sewing…"

"And your father appeared to have a solid knowledge of horses when we toured the grounds," he said more to himself than to her.

Pleasant tapped one foot impatiently. "I fear, sir, that you have lost track of our conversation. Will you help us persuade my father or not?"

Levi looked at her. The woman was speaking to him firmly and yet she was wringing her hands as if her very future depended upon his answer. "I believe I just might be able to be of service, Miss Goodloe. However, my plan involves you and Mrs. Goodloe working for me— in my circus."

Pleasant pressed her fist to her mouth. "Never," she whispered, clearly horrified at the very idea.

"Then I can't help you." He turned his attention to the papers on his desk, stacking them and replacing the cap on his fountain pen.

"What sort of work?"

"Sewing," he replied, still not looking at her. "Mending. The costumes take quite a beating in every performance."

Silence. He tapped the stack of papers against the leather blotter and waited.

"We wouldn't have to…"

"If you like, you could do the work in your cabin. You wouldn't have to have any contact at all with the performers if that's what worries you."

"I see. It might work."

"Is that a 'yes,' Miss Goodloe?" he asked as he turned to face her.

She hesitated only a second, again closed her eyes tightly as if entreating God to show her the way, then nodded. "Yes," she whispered. "If you can convince my father to let us come to Wisconsin with you, then yes."

Levi smiled. "Very well. I'll speak to your father right away. Good night, Miss Goodloe."

Pleasant practically curtsied she was so happy with the news. "Thank you," she repeated as she backed her way down the hall. "Oh, thank you so much."

Levi was well aware that whatever Pleasant's reasons for coming to him, they had less to do with helping her sister-in-law than they did with facilitating a visit to Wisconsin for herself. Whatever her purpose, if he could convince Gunther to let the two women stay on, it meant he would see more of Hannah and, surprisingly, that thought made him feel an emotion he had long ago abandoned. Levi felt happiness.

When Pleasant had taken off to talk to Levi, Hannah had hurried to catch up with her. But then she had seen Lily outside the women's dressing tent having a cigarette. Lily had shown her a kindness and Hannah felt it only fair to let her in on the good news that Caleb had been found. To her surprise, Lily had hugged her hard as tears streamed down her cheeks.

"Oh, honey, that is just grand—just fabulous news. I am so happy for you." Then she'd brushed away her tears and asked about the plans for a reunion, frowning when Hannah told her of the current plan for Gunther to travel to Wisconsin while she and Pleasant returned home.

"But it should be you he sees first," Lily had protested.

Hannah had to admit that she agreed but what was she to do? In her world the men were the heads of households and in the absence of her husband, her father-in-law had every right to make the decision. Then she remembered Pleasant's idea and glanced toward the railroad car where she could see Levi pacing as Pleasant laid out her case, hands aflutter and voice rising enough that the sound carried out to the grounds.

"I should go," she told Lily. "Thank you again for your concern."

"We mothers have to stick together," Lily said as she hugged Hannah again and then hurried away, wiping away tears.

By the time Hannah reached Levi's private car, Pleasant had left the room and he was standing at his desk studying a typed sheet of names.

"Levi?" She was stunned when he turned to her with a smile that lit up his handsome but usually brooding features.

"Ah, Hannah. I've just had a most interesting conversation with your sister-in-law. It seems that we may have come up with a plan that will be mutually beneficial to all parties concerned."

"I don't understand."

He chuckled. "No, I suppose not. Give me time to speak privately with Gunther and then I can explain everything."

"My father-in-law does not take kindly to having his decisions questioned once he's made up his mind," Hannah cautioned.

"Nor do I. But I believe I may be about to offer a proposition—a business proposition that may interest him." He shrugged. "If the result of that is that the three of you continue to travel with the show all the way to Wisconsin, then I can understand where that would be a bonus for you."

The man actually winked at her.

"I…we…"

"By the way," Levi continued, "I fully understand why you would want to go on to Wisconsin and be reunited with your son. What's Pleasant's agenda?"

"Agenda?"

"What's in it for her?"

"She…" Hannah felt her irritation at the twists and turns of this conversation getting the better of her. "Can't she just want the best for me?"

Levi nodded. "She might but that's not her main goal. Pleasant is a woman who looks out for herself."

"In our culture we look out for each other," Hannah snapped.

His features darkened once again to the more familiar solemn demeanor she had come to expect from him. "Not always, Hannah," he murmured. "Not always."

In the silence that fell like a curtain between them, she could hear the brass trumpets of the circus band announcing the grand march that opened the evening show. "If you'll excuse me, Hannah, I want to be sure everything is going well with the opening," he said, moving toward the observation platform. "After that I'll speak with Gunther. Have a good evening."

Upon returning to their shared cabin, Hannah had insisted that she and Pleasant prepare for the journey back to Sarasota the following morning. The plan was that the two women would be taken to the public train station before dawn to await the southbound train while the circus train—this time pulling Levi's private car—moved north into Georgia.

But Pleasant refused to give up. She sat on the edge of her berth, gripping the muslin coverlet and murmuring prayers in the language they had learned as children.

An hour passed, and through the open window they could hear the laughter and oohs and ahs of the audience at the big top as the show moved from act to act. Another hour passed, and they could hear the finale and the applause and the excited chatter of the patrons as they left the show and headed home. And with every passing moment, Pleasant's assurance faded and Hannah released the kernel of hope that she had dared to plant.

"We should get some sleep," she said.

Pleasant nodded and pushed herself to her feet.

The knock at their cabin door startled them both.

"Daughters?"

Pleasant pressed her fist to her mouth to stem the flood of giggles that threatened to escape. Clearly, she thought her prayers had been answered.

Hannah was not so sure and when she opened the cabin door and saw her father-in-law standing in the narrow passageway, his brow knitted into a frown, she was positive that Levi's conversation with him had not gone well.

"We have a dilemma," he said. "Please come so we

may discuss this." Without another word he headed for the sitting room.

Pleasant practically pushed Hannah down the hallway in her eagerness to follow.

"Sit down, please," Gunther said as he remained standing—and pacing. Levi was nowhere in sight.

"What is it?" Hannah asked softly.

"Our friend, Levi, has a problem. One that he has asked for our help in addressing." As he told them the story of the Stravinskys leaving Levi's employ, Hannah could barely concentrate because Pleasant was squeezing her hand so tightly that she thought her fingers must surely crack and break.

"So we will help our friend who has shown us such kindness. We will all travel the rest of the way to Wisconsin and during the trip, Pleasant, you will mend and sew as needed and I will see to the ring horses. It is only right," he added, as if trying to assure himself that he had not gone back on a decision. Rather, he had made a new plan—one that served a fellow man.

"And what shall I do to help?" Hannah asked.

"Levi had thought to have you both tend to the costumes although he only needs one. He asked if I could think of some other task for you, Hannah. I told him that you had taken charge of the office duties and accounting in the bakery back home. He seemed both surprised and pleased at that news. He wants you to serve as his secretary while Miss Benson is in Wisconsin."

Hannah let out a squeak of protest. "But…"

"It's only right that we should do whatever we can to help Levi now that he is the one in need," Gunther continued.

But as his secretary I will be called upon to spend

time with him—time alone without the buffer of you and Pleasant. Hannah could not seem to find the words to convey these thoughts to Gunther. Instead, she said nothing, wondering why the idea of spending time alone with Levi was so upsetting to her when clearly it was not an issue for her father-in-law.

Chapter Seven

Hannah spent yet another sleepless night as she lay awake listening to the sounds of the workers dismantling the tents and loading the wagons and livestock. Sometime well after midnight, she felt the train begin to move and in minutes faced the fact that instead of boarding a public train for the trip back home, she was heading north to be reunited with her wayward son. The idea of seeing Caleb again cheered her, but she could not seem to control her anxiety at what working with Levi might mean.

What would he expect of her? And more to the point, was she up to the job? Keeping books for her father-in-law was one thing. His business was relatively simple. Over the past couple of days, she had been amazed at the complexities of running a circus. Levi employed so many people, some salaried and some paid by the hour. Still, they all needed to be paid. And then there was feeding them—not to mention feeding and caring for the animals and…

What did lions and tigers and elephants eat? she wondered. "And where does one purchase such items?" she muttered aloud. She imagined herself filling out orders for tons of wild animal food which led to imagining herself writing up correspondence as Levi dictated. She bolted upright. What if Levi expected her to use the typing machine that she'd seen Jake Jenkins pecking away on when she'd walked past the railroad car that served as the traveling circus's office?

But remembering Jake in that other car—in that more public place—was reassuring. Surely she would carry out her work as Levi's secretary from a desk there. She even recalled seeing an empty desk when she'd returned Jake's jovial greeting the previous afternoon.

She lay down again and this time she slept. It might not be so bad after all, she decided. At least it would make the time go more quickly and before she knew it, they would arrive in Wisconsin and she would see Caleb.

Levi sat on the private observation platform at the very rear of the train watching the shadowy scenery fly by. What had he been thinking suggesting that Hannah work as his secretary? Gunther had suggested both women take Maria's place in the costume shop and surely that would have been the wisest choice. After all, Maria was an experienced and talented circus seamstress. Sewing sequins back onto velvet or satin costumes was a far cry from what he imagined the usual sewing tasks might be for an Amish woman. Surely between the two of them they could muddle through until the company reached Baraboo and he could start interviewing potential replacements for Maria.

But, no, almost the minute Gunther had suggested the idea, Levi had rejected it. "I wonder if Mrs. Goodloe might not be qualified to assist me in the absence of my secretary, Miss Benson. I find that I have a great deal of work to get done before we get home to Wisconsin and while I can certainly instruct Miss Benson by way of letters and telegrams, it would be so much more efficient if I could simply handle things from here."

In his eagerness to repay Levi's kindness to his family, Gunther had readily agreed. He'd spent the next several minutes singing Hannah's praises. "The woman is remarkable with figures," he told Levi. "And she writes a fine hand, as well. I'm sure she could be a great help to you, Levi." Then he had smiled and added, "Frankly, her handiwork with a needle leaves something to be desired according to my daughter. Not that she can't sew a seam or mend a tear—it's just her stitches are not as small and tight as Pleasant's are."

What were you thinking? Levi wondered, propping his feet on the brass railing and closing his eyes as the warm May breeze rushed over his face. But instead of the blackness he sought in shutting out the passing world, he found himself visualizing Hannah.

Plain or not, she was one of the most beautiful women he'd ever seen. Her competitors had the advantage of enhancing their best features and concealing their lesser ones with cosmetics. Lily, for example, was by any man's standards, a beauty. But then he had never seen Lily without rouged lips and cheeks highlighted with fake color and eyelashes that had been artificially embellished.

Hannah wore no makeup and yet her lashes fanned her cheeks when she looked down—as she did far too often—and her cheeks glowed pink with the natural brush of the sun's kiss. Her lips were full and a soft rosy pink and every feature was set off perfectly by her skin—a soft golden color that was, no doubt, the result of days spent coming and going in the Florida sun.

He tried to imagine her hair and thought of the gold satin gown that Lily always wore for her entrance. Hannah's hair reminded him of that luxurious satin. She wore it in the traditional Amish style, pulled tight away from her face and wound into a bun under her prayer cap. What might it be like to see that hair falling freely down her back? he wondered. Would it come to her waist? Would it fall straight like a waterfall, or cascade its way down her back with natural curls and ringlets like a brook thawed after the winter, finding its way over rocks?

Levi pushed himself to a standing position, adjusting to the sway of the train as naturally as a ship's captain might adjust to the pitch and fall of a ship's deck. "Enough," he muttered, banishing the thought of Hannah Goodloe from his thoughts. "She's not for you so get some sleep."

But that night Levi did not enjoy the kind of dreamless sleep that comes from sheer exhaustion. That night he dreamed of Hannah Goodloe and by morning, he had made up his mind that she would be reassigned immediately to the costume department.

But Hannah had been dressed before the train pulled on to the siding near the field where the circus would set up. The instant she felt it roll to a stop, she quietly left the cabin and hurried along the passageway to the rear exit from Levi's private car. The morning was cool so she wrapped her head and shoulders in a shawl as she walked quickly along the length of the train.

All around her people had already sprung into action, unloading wagons and hitching them to teams so they could be pulled to the circus grounds several blocks away. The dining and cooking tents were already up, having arrived on a separate train that had left Jonesville even as the evening performance was going on. Hannah could smell eggs and bacon frying and gallons of coffee brewing in anticipation of feeding the cast and crew. Several dozen local people had already gathered at the site—some to watch and some hoping to help out and perhaps pick up some extra money. Automatically, Hannah scanned their faces for any sign of Caleb. Although she knew he was safe in Wisconsin, somehow she couldn't help looking for him.

Finally, she reached the steps leading into the car reserved for the female performers. She wanted some advice and she thought she knew exactly who would be her wisest choice as a counselor and confidante. A woman on her way back to her berth pointed to a private cabin at the opposite end of the car near the galley kitchen.

Hannah tapped lightly on the frosted glass of the narrow door. "Lily?" she whispered so as not to disturb others who were still sleeping. "Are you awake?" She opened the door a crack.

"Coasting," Lily grumbled. "Who's that?" She rolled over and blinked several times as she adjusted her eyes to the light and to the unexpected sight of Hannah standing next to her. "What's happened?" she demanded as she rolled to a sitting position and reached for her robe.

"Nothing," Hannah assured her. "I'm sorry I woke you. It's just that…I mean if you could spare me a few minutes…"

"It isn't your son, is it? I mean, nothing's happened to the kid?"

"No. As far as I know he's fine—safe in Baraboo."

"Could you keep it down?" a voice from down the way grumbled. "I'm trying to sleep."

Lily thrust her feet into feathered slippers as she wrapped her robe tightly around her and tied the sash, then motioned for Hannah to follow her. In the small galley kitchen she filled two stained mugs with coffee and handed one to Hannah. "Speak," she commanded as she took a long swallow of the hot liquid and closed her eyes as it made its way down her throat.

Hannah told her of the plan for her to work for Levi while her in-laws also worked, but in other parts of the circus.

"Sounds like you got the better end of that deal," Lily said. "What's the problem?"

And suddenly Hannah was completely at a loss for words. What was she going to say? That she couldn't work so closely with Levi because… *Because why?*

Because you are drawn to him. Because there is an attraction there that you recognize because it's what you once felt for your husband when you first met him. Because…

"Hannah?" Lily had set her mug aside and was patting Hannah's shoulder and peering at her with curiosity. "Is it because Levi—I mean he hasn't made any—you know—advances or anything, has he?"

"Oh, no," Hannah rushed to reassure her and when she saw the relief in Lily's eyes, she realized for the first time what a fool she was being. Levi would hardly be interested in someone like her when there were women as beautiful as Lily around. After all, he could have his pick of any number of women—not just the performers, but women in the towns where the circus traveled, high-society women in Sarasota. What had she been thinking?

She smiled at Lily. "I'm just having a case of nerves,"

she said. "I've never worked for anyone but my husband and father-in-law. This is going to be so different and…"

"Levi is a good and patient man. If he's asked for you to step in for Ida while we're on the road, then take that as a compliment. Ida is like his right arm. She does everything for him, knows where everything is, can almost do what he wants before he even knows he wants it. Ida and Hans keep Levi on track."

Hannah blurted the first thing that came to mind, "Sounds like a wife."

Lily burst into laughter so raucous that several sleepy-eyed women poked their heads out of their berths and shouted at her to keep it down. "Ida might be like his wife, but I think Levi's taste in women runs to someone a lot younger and prettier—like you, honey." She pinched Hannah's cheek and drained the last of her coffee. "You'll be fine. The boss is way too much of a gentleman to cause you any problems, okay?"

"Thank you."

Lily yawned and stretched. "Let me throw on some clothes and let's go see what the cook's fried up for breakfast."

"I should…" Hannah started to say that she should get back to Levi's private car for breakfast with her in-laws and Levi, but then thought better of it. If they were going to work for Levi then why should they receive special treatment? "Lily, are there any extra berths in this car?"

"A couple of third berths," she replied, pointing to a row of top berths where even lying down a person's nose would be only inches from the ceiling. "Why?"

"I was just thinking that maybe Pleasant and I should move in here—I mean now that we're working for the circus."

Lily stopped midstride. "Okay, let me get this straight.
You have your own private quarters in Levi's luxuriously
appointed car, your meals served up by his personal cook,
your needs attended to by Hans and you want to trade
that for this?" She swept her arm in an arch to take in
the cramped, stuffy surroundings.

Hannah shrugged. "It only seems fair."

"Well, I'd pay to be a fly on the wall when you have
that conversation with Levi, honey."

Once Levi Harmon made up his mind about something he liked to take action and move on. The problem
was that he could not seem to locate Hannah to tell her
of his decision to put her to work with Pleasant in the
costume shop.

She had not appeared for breakfast and neither Pleasant nor Gunther had seen her. Pleasant remembered hearing her go out quite early and surmised that she had
gone for one of her usual walks. "She starts every morning that way," Pleasant told him. "And more often than
not ends the day with a walk, as well. Of course, since
we've been traveling with you, she's had that schedule
disrupted a bit, but my guess is that if there's a stream
or river nearby you'll find her there."

Gunther had offered to go looking for his daughter-in-
law, but Levi needed the older man to get started working with the rest of the crew. He would be checking the
horses, replacing a shoe if necessary and making sure
the horses and their harnesses were in perfect order for
the day's parade and two performances. "I'll go," Levi
said as he dabbed the corners of his mouth with his linen
napkin and laid it aside. "Pleasant, if you would be so
kind as to report to the costume tent. The head seam-

stress, now that Mrs. Stravinsky is gone, is Ruth Davis. She can show you what needs to be done before this afternoon's matinee."

He'd looked everywhere when he saw Hannah talking to the box-office manager. She glanced up as if she had somehow sensed his nearness, said a few words to the box-office manager and hurried toward him.

"Good morning," she said a little out of breath. "I think I lost track of time. I was talking to some of the cast and crew, wanting to learn as much as possible about how things work. I mean, Levi, it's actually quite exciting, isn't it? It's like a small community in and of itself but one that moves around."

Her cheeks were flushed and her smile radiated the excitement of her discovery.

"And so perhaps you begin to understand the appeal for young Caleb," he said, and knew in that instant that he would not forbid himself the opportunity—however brief—to be closer to her by working with her. There was something about her that made him look forward to the day. Perhaps it was her innocence, that naiveté that came with discovering a world you never knew existed. He'd been living in the midst of it for so many years that in spite of his wealth and material comforts, life had lost all of its freshness for him.

Her expression sobered. "What I know is that I have suffered the sin of prejudice, Levi. I had judged these people and their lifestyle without once taking the time to understand. It's not a life I would choose, but I see now that these are good people whose hopes for themselves and their families are not so very different from my own."

He started to walk back to the outside of the big top

toward the backyard of the circus and she fell into step with him. "And what will you do if your son's infatuation with the life has not yet been satisfied?" he asked.

"I don't know," she admitted.

"I mean Caleb is what? Eleven, you said?"

"Almost twelve."

"Then he has some time."

He saw her peer up at him curiously. "Time?"

"Well, as I understand it, a boy does not make a final decision to follow the ways of the Amish until he's maybe fourteen?" He had taken this conversation too far and soon she would start to raise questions he wasn't prepared to answer. Questions like how it was that he knew so much about the Amish life. He cast about for some way to change the subject. "Ah, there's Jake. Good. You can go over the accounting procedures with him while I see how your father-in-law is adjusting to his new duties." He walked ahead of her, hailing his friend. He had almost said too much. He had almost opened the door to the past. What was it about this woman that made him want to do that? He'd had dealings with other Amish before—trading with them as the circus traveled from town to town. But of course, he had never actually had members of that faith traveling with him. He had never had to face the daily reminder of what he had run away from all those years ago. Not until Hannah Goodloe had walked up to his front door and into his life.

Chapter Eight

The business office was housed in a converted passenger car, although any resemblance between that space and Levi's private car ended there. The seats and overhead berths had been removed and in their place were three large oak desks on the window side of the car, and behind them a wall of enclosed shelving filled with files and ledgers and office supplies.

"That's Ida's desk there," Jake Jenkins said. "The middle one is for our twenty-four-hour guy, Chester Tuck, and that last one near the payroll window is mine."

"Mr. Tuck really works twenty-four hours a day?" Hannah asked.

Jake scratched his slicked-back hair and frowned. Then he exploded into laughter. "No, not at all. It's a circus term for the lead guy. Chester is the one member of the staff who travels ahead of the rest of the company to make sure everything's ready for us when we arrive. Usually, that's a day ahead, like he got here yesterday while our first train section arrived this morning. See?"

"It's confusing but yes, I think I understand. Mr. Tuck

works with the townspeople but always in the next town on the schedule."

"That's pretty much the idea. He's hardly ever here. Or if he is, he tends to be here at night while the show's going on, catching up before he heads out to the next town," Jake said as he sat down in a scarred wooden swivel chair and plopped both of his feet on top of his desk. "So, what's Levi got in mind for you?"

Hannah didn't like his tone or the way one of his eyebrows arched suggestively. "Filing. Correspondence," she replied as she considered the items on Ida Benson's desk. A compartment filled with pencils, a stack of unused paper, a spiral-bound notebook, two bottles of ink—one black and one red—and two fountain pens resting on an onyx stand. The typewriter sat on a separate metal stand to one side of Ida's desk chair.

"You know how to type?" Jake asked as Hannah ran her fingers over the keys.

"No," she admitted, noticing for the first time that the letters were not in alphabetical order as she might have expected. The squeal of Jake's chair as he stood and came toward her startled her and she jumped as if she'd just had a terrible fright.

"Sorry. Didn't mean to scare you." He reached around her and took down a straw hat from the brass hook behind her. The hat looked brand new. Jake was definitely a man who took pride in his looks, she thought. "I have to go out for a while. In the meantim—" he plopped a wire basket piled high with papers on the desk "—you can start filing these." Near the doorway he pulled open a file drawer and pointed. "Each invoice goes into a folder in here—these are paid," he said. "So animal food goes under 'feed,' people food goes under 'kitchen' and so on.

Pretty straightforward," he assured her as he put on the hat, checked his appearance in a small mirror hanging by the door and left.

"When do you think Levi…that is, Mr. Harmon will return?"

Jake shrugged. "He'll be back soon enough. If you want to impress him, get that filing done." He waved then turned a corner and was gone.

Hannah stood at the door for a minute longer scanning the grounds for any sign of Levi. After all, supposedly she was working for him. Shouldn't he be the one giving her tasks to complete?

But there was no sign of him. Outside the railroad car, the grounds teemed with activity and Hannah was struck once again with how very much the circus was like its own little neighborhood. People coming and going, attending to their work, calling out greetings to each other. It felt like…home. It was nothing like she had imagined, and the idea that Caleb had traveled that first night with these good people gave her such a sense of relief that she found herself humming an old hymn as she turned to attend to her work.

Levi had made his escape so abruptly that he realized now that he had failed to give Hannah any proper instructions. Well, Jake could show her the ropes. His friend and business manager certainly knew as much about what Ida did day-to-day as Levi knew.

But that really wasn't the point. There was something about the Amish woman that made him want to run as far and fast away from her as possible and yet at the same time, he was drawn to her like the moths that fluttered around the spotlights at the evening performances.

True to his nature, Levi was determined to solve the mystery of his attraction to Hannah Goodloe—an attraction that he suspected she would agree was impossible. Okay, so she was a natural beauty. That much he'd already determined. And she was a person of conviction and strength—two traits he had always respected in others. But there were plenty of beautiful women and most of his friends and employees had been chosen on the basis of their strength of character. So what was it?

Her unavailability? Was that the attraction? For some men—like Jake Jenkins—that would have been the draw. The sheer challenge of the chase. But Levi wasn't like that. Men like Jake tended to view women as objects set before them for their personal pleasure—objects that could be replaced. The one thing that was missing in Levi's life was a woman with whom he could share the fortune and lavish lifestyle that he'd worked so hard to build. Someone whose eyes would light up with delight as he showered her with jewels and gifts and showed her places she had only read about in books.

Hannah Goodloe was not that woman. She was of the "plain" tradition—a tradition that set no value on material things. And suddenly it clicked. Hannah Goodloe's attraction for him was that she had found contentment in the very life that he had cast aside all those year earlier. A life that he had cavalierly rejected as too boring and restricting.

Relieved that he finally understood why he was drawn to the woman and could safely dismiss the idea of any romantic attraction, Levi headed back across the circus grounds to the payroll car. He could work with her now that he understood her and he would simply ignore the obvious question of why Gunther and Pleasant Goodloe did not stir the same fascination within him that Hannah did.

Hannah made quick work of the filing project then looked around for other ways to make herself useful. She found cleaning supplies in a corner of the car near the sink. Using a feather duster, she went over Ida's desk—now hers, she supposed—and then Chester's desk, which was bare except for a wire basket attached to one corner and filled with papers similar to those she had just filed.

The basket was labeled "Invoices to be paid" so she carefully dusted around them so as not to disturb the order. But the top invoice caught her eye. It was from a feed company in Jonesville, Florida—the town they had just left. She had filed a similar invoice in the paid drawer—similar in more than just the letterhead it was printed on. The amount for the bill struck her as odd.

"Seventy-nine dollars and ninety-seven cents," she murmured, remembering that she had noted the same reversal of numbers on the filed invoice. She carried the invoice from Chester's desk over to the file cabinet and compared it to the one marked "paid." They were identical—date, list of items ordered, amount—everything. "Why would there be two…?"

"I apologize for being away so long," Levi said as he climbed the two metal steps to the entrance and filled the car with his presence.

Unnerved that she'd been caught snooping into matters that were certainly none of her business, Hannah slammed the file drawer shut as soon as she heard his voice, and by the time he'd entered the car, she was back dusting Chester's desk.

"I see you found something to occupy yourself," Levi said, nodding toward the feather duster. "Where's Jake?"

"He said something about an errand. I did the filing he gave me and then—well, I found the duster and broom and thought…"

"Hannah, I don't expect you to clean," Levi said.

"I don't mind," she replied. "In fact, I find it soothing. Besides, you keep money in here for the payroll, right?" She had noticed the large heavy safe that practically filled one end of the long car.

Levi's eyes widened. "We do. I don't see…"

"It just occurs to me that if only you and I and Mr. Tuck and Mr. Jenkins have access to this car, it would be a kind of safety measure. If it's just the three of us—and you, of course—then there's no temptation for someone coming in."

To her surprise, Levi grinned and then laughed out loud. Oh, the things laughter did for his features. It took her breath away how handsome he was when he smiled.

"It's just a suggestion," she huffed, offended that she had been the cause of his laughter.

"And a good one it is," he agreed. "I didn't mean to laugh, Hannah. It's just that you're the last person I would have thought might imagine anyone trying to steal something."

"Why?"

He shrugged. "You're Amish."

"We are Amish, Levi, not angels. As among any people, there are those who lose their way. Some young men broke into the bakery just last fall. They nearly tore the place apart looking for money, not knowing that Gunther always carried the day's receipts home with him after closing."

"Were they arrested?"

"It is not our way to turn our own transgressors over to outside authorities. The two young men were brought to the bishop by their families and it was handled within our community."

"They were shunned," Levi guessed, and she could not help but notice that it was not a question.

"They were banned and when they saw and admitted the error of their ways and promised to change, they were forgiven."

"And where are they now?"

"One of them works for my father-in-law and the other works on his family's celery farm."

"They came back even though…?"

"Everyone deserves a second chance, Levi," she said softly. "Our ways offer that."

He took the feather duster from her and placed it and the broom back on their hooks. "Either way, I do not expect you to clean, Hannah. If you feel the urge to do so in order to think through some issue you may be dealing with, then I suppose it would be cruel to stop you. But you are here in the capacity of interim secretary, and I suspect you will have plenty to do between now and when we reach Wisconsin in a few weeks."

"I don't know how to use that contraption," she blurted nervously, pointing to the typewriter.

"I prefer letters written in longhand for my correspondence. Anything else can wait until we reach Baraboo," Levi replied. "What else?"

Hannah glanced around the space. "I don't know— not until you tell me what you expect."

"Hannah, this is not a test. Gunther wants—no, he needs to feel as if the three of you are somehow making a contribution in repayment for the journey to collect your son. I am just trying to honor that."

"Then why not put me to work with Pleasant in the wardrobe department?"

To her surprise, another smile tugged at the corners of his mouth. "The fact is that I was told that your sewing skills are not exactly…that you are far better at figures and filing and the like."

"It's true," she admitted. "I mean, Pleasant's stitches are tiny and so wonderfully straight and mine…" She shrugged and risked a glance up at him.

"Actually, I'm relieved," Levi said. "I find that at the moment, I need the services of a good and efficient secretary far more desperately than I need another pair of sewing hands. So, will you help me?"

It occurred to Hannah that he was very good at his work. For what was the circus business after all, except one of persuading others to part with their hard-earned money to experience something that would be over in a couple of hours with nothing to show for it but memories? That kind of persuasion came so naturally to him that it no doubt took very little to turn those talents of persuasion into talents for making others feel needed. She studied his expression for any sign that he was trying to trick her. But instead, she saw that his eyes were almost pleading. She didn't know why, but Levi Harmon was counting on her, beseeching her to accept his offer.

"Very well," she said, and was quite positive that his expression shifted at once to one of relief and then as quickly to one of business.

"Excellent. Now let me show you the basic routine. Every morning, there will be several messages that have come in during the night. I'll need you to sort through…"

And so it went for the better part of an hour. As Levi instructed, Hannah made notes in the spiral-bound notebook. These files were kept separate. Those were ready to be disposed of as soon as she had updated the ledger. Jake would give her this. Chester would need her to see to something else. She began to have a deep respect for Ida Benson's ability to keep it all running smoothly.

Still, it was invigorating. For one thing, it took her mind off Caleb and her worries about the boy. For it had occurred to her that bringing him home to Florida would not solve the problem. He had run away—more to the point he had run toward another lifestyle. And now having experienced a bit of that lifestyle herself, she could understand why circus life had been attractive to her son. How was she going to make sure that he didn't resent returning to the community and culture that he had abandoned?

"What is it, Hannah?"

She'd allowed her thoughts to wander and failed to notice that Levi had stopped talking.

"Nothi…" But she was incapable of lying. "I was just thinking about my son," she admitted. "I apologize. It seems that even though I know he is safe, I can't stop worrying about him. I'm sure you never gave your mother cause for such concern, Levi." She was trying to lighten the moment, but the dark shadow that crossed his eyes told her she'd failed.

"My parents died when I was just a little older than Caleb is now," he said.

"I'm so sorry. That must have been so very painful. Both of them?"

He nodded. "There was a tornado. My grandfather had insisted that my father go out to the barn and secure the animals. When he didn't come back, Ma made all us kids go into the cellar and then she went after him. The tornado hit the barn and it collapsed, killing them both."

"Oh, Levi, how awful for you—for all of you."

He picked up the story as if she hadn't spoken, as if he needed to tell it all and be done with it. "My sisters went to live with an aunt and uncle in Iowa. My younger brother and I went to live with our grandparents." He studied her for a long moment as if trying to decide whether or not to tell her more. "And then," he said softly, using his forefinger to push a wisp of her hair back into place, "the circus came to town and when it left—just like Caleb—I went with it."

Chapter Nine

Levi watched her incredible blue eyes grow large with shock. "You?"

He nodded.

"But your grandparents—your siblings…"

"They were all happy with the life they had. Three of them were too young to truly miss our parents. My eldest sister was being courted by a boy she'd met in Iowa. I had never really taken to life on the farm even when my parents were alive. But Matthew was a natural. He followed our grandfather around like a puppy, soaking up every facet of the farm life."

"How old were you when you left and what did your grandparents say when they found out where you'd gone and didn't anyone try to find you or bring you home?"

The questions poured out of her and he knew that in place of him she was seeing her own son. Instead of comforting her, he had only added to her worries. "It's not the same, Hannah. My situation and Caleb's are completely different."

"I don't see how. You were what—twelve?"

"Fourteen—old enough to begin to think of being

out on my own. Old enough that others expected me to take an interest in the farm that I would one day inherit."

"Even so," she conceded reluctantly, "it was circus life that drew your interest and made you decide to leave."

He really couldn't argue that point, but he had to try. "Look, there's more to the story than just a boy out for an adventure. Just take my word for it. My circumstances were nothing like Caleb's."

"I don't see so much difference. Caleb's father is dead and…"

"But he has you and he has Gunther."

"And you had your grandparents," she pointed out.

"Not the same," he said, and gazed out the open door of the payroll car. "Ah, here's Jake." Relieved to have a buffer that would prevent Hannah from questioning him further, Levi did not even think of wondering where his friend had disappeared to, or what might lie behind the scowl he wore in place of his usual hearty smile.

"I was just going through the routine with Hannah," Levi explained. "I think we're going to have to keep her busy with filing and correspondence, Jake. I found her cleaning the place when I got back."

"Oh, that won't do, Mrs. Goodloe," Jake said. "Miss Benson is quite dedicated to the cause of making sure women hold what she likes to refer to as 'their rightful place in the world.' And that means if you have been given the post of secretary, you have not—at least in Ida's world—been handed the position of cleaning lady along with it."

"But…"

Levi held up one professorial finger to Jake, interrupting her. "I'm afraid we may have to remind Ida that in

Mrs. Goodloe's world, the role of women first and foremost is that of making a home for others."

"Ida will try to change your mind on that one," Jake told Hannah. "Trust me, she thinks the world would be a good sight better run if women handled business and politics and men were relegated to cleaning and cooking."

Levi saw that Hannah was becoming alarmed at this discussion, but he was also relieved that it had at least taken her mind off her son. "Don't pay too much attention to what my friend here says. He does tend to embellish the situation."

Jake grinned. "You meet Ida," he instructed Hannah, "and then decide if every word I just spoke isn't the truth." He walked the length of the car and settled into his desk chair as he pulled a stack of papers toward him.

"That reminds me," Hannah said. She picked up the top paper from the basket on Chester's desk and showed it to Jake. "When I was dusting I saw this. It's a duplicate of the one you had me file earlier and I was just wondering…"

Levi watched as Jake snatched the invoice from Hannah's outstretched hand and studied it. "No, I paid this," he muttered as he rifled through the pages of an oversize ledger. "Yep, here it is right here." He pounded the notation several times with his forefinger, then glanced up at Levi.

"I'm sure you did," Levi said. "Chester might just like to keep his own copies of each invoice. I think he told me once that it helps when he's negotiating with a new vendor to be able to show what price we've gotten from others."

Jake seemed unconvinced. "I guess. Anyway it's paid—says so right here." He tapped the ledger page again and then closed the book and smiled up at them. "Well, getting close to matinee time. You should come see the show, Hannah. I mean if you're going to work here, shouldn't you know how the folks we're paying earn their money?"

Hannah smiled. "It is not…"

"…Your way," Jake finished for her. "Got it."

Levi frowned. He didn't like Jake making light of Hannah's lifestyle. And although she seemed unperturbed by the comment, Levi felt keenly protective toward her, wanting to be sure that she was not offended. "What Jake means is…"

"It's all right," she assured both men. And then with a twinkle in her eye added, "It is our way to have very thick skins when dealing with the outside world."

Jake exploded into laughter and nearly tipped his chair over backward. "She's a winner, this one, Levi. Can we keep her and get rid of Ida? I think she's going to be like a ray of sunshine around here."

Levi saw that Hannah was about to protest such an idea. "He's kidding," he told her. "Better get used to it. Jake is a great kidder, especially with anyone prone to taking his outrageous comments seriously."

"Does Miss Benson take you seriously?" Hannah asked.

"Extremely," Jake assured her.

"Well, if someone who is seemingly so well-educated can be fooled by your humor, I can see that I will have to watch myself."

"Wise move," Levi said.

"But no fun at all," Jake added as he pushed himself away from the desk and headed for the exit. "Showtime," he said. "You kids have a good evening now." And he was gone.

"He makes you smile," Hannah noted.

And it was true. Levi's usually somber mood could always be relieved by an encounter with Jake. "He's my best friend—almost like a brother to me."

"You've known each other for some time, then?"

Levi smiled. "We were stowaways together on the circus train."

"Jake ran away as well?"

"There I was thinking I was so smart, hiding out in one of the baggage cars when all of a sudden a voice grumbles, 'This is my hiding place, kid. Find your own.'"

"You must have been frightened," Hannah guessed.

Levi chuckled. "I was. I mean, the voice was deep like a grown man's would be but my choice was to stay put or jump from a moving train. So I decided to stay put and before I knew it, I fell asleep."

"What happened?"

"When I woke up, Jake was sitting next to me chewing on a piece of jerky. It wasn't until he offered me a piece and muttered something about how he expected to be paid for the food that I put it together. That deep voice from the night before belonged to this skinny little kid who had to be at least a couple of years younger than I was."

"And the two of you became the best of friends," Hannah said, her smile radiant. "That's lovely, Levi."

"Friends and coworkers."

"So when you bought the circus…"

"Actually, I inherited it from the former owner. By that time Jake had gone his own way again—staying in Chicago for a time. The first thing I did once I took over was get in touch with him and ask him to come work with me."

"And neither of you ever married?" She blushed after asking the question. "I apologize. That is really none of my business."

"Jake came close. Me? I never even got close."

"I imagine it's difficult to maintain a relationship if one travels so much of the time," she said.

I could make it work with the right woman, he thought as he looked down at her. She was standing near the desk she would occupy and suddenly busied herself with re-arranging the pens and other supplies Ida had left there.

"Hannah," he murmured more to test the feel of her name on his lips than to say anything.

She glanced up.

He reached over and twisted one string of her prayer cap around his forefinger. She did not waver from meeting his gaze. He leaned forward slightly and she remained as still as a flower on a windless day.

"Hannah," he whispered and her eyes drifted closed.

Levi was going to kiss her, Hannah thought and realized the greater surprise was that she was going to permit him to do so. *What's happening to me?*

"Hannah," he said softly. "Open your eyes and look at me."

She did as he asked and almost had to look away when she saw that the indecision she felt was mirrored in his gaze. "This is impossible, you know."

"Yes," she whispered and bowed her head.

He placed his forefinger under her chin and gently

lifted her face to meet his. "You are so very beautiful," he said, his voice husky and completely lacking in the self-assurance she had come to expect from him.

Her heartbeat quickened and she prayed for forgiveness that his compliment had meant so much to her, had made her think of ways that a kiss shared with him might not be impossible after all.

With determination she took a step back so that his finger slipped free of contact with her skin. "It is not our way to speak of such things," she said.

"Ah, but it is your way to speak the truth and that was all that I was doing." He picked up his hat and moved past her to the doorway. "Did Jake show you how to lock up?"

Confused by the abrupt shift in his demeanor, she nodded and showed him the keys that Jake had given her. The music coming from the big top told her that the matinee was already half over. During dinner the night before, he had told them that he liked to be at the back entrance to the big top when the show ended so that every performer passed by him as they exited the tent.

"Was there anything you wanted me to do yet this afternoon?" she asked, forcing her voice to reflect his professional business tone.

"No. Just take your time getting to know the files and procedures we went over. If Jake isn't back by the time you finish, be sure to lock up. I'll see you at dinner."

"Yes," she murmured, but he was already gone. She watched as he strode quickly across the large circus lot and it wasn't until he had disappeared around the side of the ticket wagon that she realized that all the while she had been gently stroking the place where he had touched her chin.

* * *

Levi could not believe that he had almost allowed himself to surrender to the feelings for Hannah Goodloe that he now realized had been planted that first day she'd come to his home in Sarasota. What was he thinking? Any real relationship between them was impossible.

He watched as Lily mesmerized the crowd with her acrobatics on the swing high above them. He and Lily had had a brief romance a few years earlier when he'd first hired her, but both had admitted that they were not well-matched for anything long lasting. They had ended the romance amicably and remained good friends. It was obvious to Levi that Lily's heart belonged to Jake. Too bad his friend was too much of a ladies' man to realize what he was missing.

All around him, performers and exotic animals lined up for the grand finale where they would enter the tent one last time and parade around the perimeter of the ring to thunderous applause, whistles and stamping feet. It was a moment that never grew old for Levi and whenever he was traveling with the company, it was a moment he tried not to miss.

But you would gladly have missed it today and every day from now on if Hannah had not stepped away.

The truth of that thought struck him like a thunderbolt. Behind him, elephants trumpeted their impatience to get moving while lions roared in agreement. But Levi barely heard them as he considered the idea of what he might be willing to sacrifice to win Hannah's affections.

"Hey, boss man!"

Levi turned to see Fred Stone waddling toward him. Fred was the lead clown for the company and at the moment he was in full costume—baggy pants and oversize clown shoes that slapped the ground with each step. His red hair had been frizzed into a halo and he was wearing his whiteface makeup with the exaggerated red lips turned down. Fred was one of the most cheerful people Levi knew, but his act was that of the sad clown and it won the hearts and cheers of audience members every performance.

"Heard the Amish kid turned up in Baraboo," Fred continued. "Good news for the pretty little widow I'd say."

"She's very relieved," Levi agreed.

"So, you gonna have Ida ship the kid back down to meet us on the route or what?"

"His mother is going with us to Baraboo," Levi replied.

Fred nodded slowly. "Makes sense but I'd think she'd want the fastest way possible to get the boy back in the fold."

"I'm sure she does, but we have commitments along the way and her father-in-law is against her traveling alone so this seemed the best option under the circumstances. Ida's watching over the boy."

"Did she take him out to the farm?"

Only four people in the company were aware that Levi stayed in close touch with his younger brother. Fred, Hans, Ida and Jake. Matthew had inherited their grandfather's farm and lived there with his wife and five children. "The door's always open," he had told Levi more than once. "As Ma used to say, 'you can always come home.'"

"Levi?" Fred was looking at him curiously.

"Yeah. The boy's with Matt," Levi said. "Better get in

there," he added with a nod toward the parade that had
begun to move into the tent for the finale.

"Going," Fred said as he slap-footed his way to the
rear of the line. "She's a nice lady," he called. "The
Amish widow. Lily and the girls say she's top drawer."

Too good for the likes of me, Levi thought and men-
tally vowed to keep his association with Hannah on a
strictly business level now that she was technically working for him.

But later, after he was delayed by a vendor insisting
that he had not been paid for the goods delivered earlier
that day, Levi arrived at the dinner table to see that the
only available seat was next to Hannah.

"Ah, Levi, Hans had suggested we start without you,"
Gunther said. "We were just about to say grace."

Gunther was holding Pleasant's hand who in turn
was holding Hannah's. In order to complete the circle he
needed to take Gunther's free hand as well as Hannah's.
He grasped Gunther's calloused hand but then hesitated.

Slowly and without meeting his eyes, Hannah slipped
her fingers over the back of his hand. She was barely
touching him and yet he felt a warmth radiating from
that contact that made it impossible not to want to turn
his palm face up and entwine his fingers with hers.

"Shall we pray?" Gunther intoned and as he and Pleasant closed their eyes, Levi risked a look at Hannah. Her
eyes were as wide open as his were and did not waver as
she met his gaze. To his surprise, she seemed to be trying to come to some decision about him.

Levi was not used to being judged by others. With his
wealth and position in the community, more often than
not, others sought to get something from him. But Hannah was different. When Hannah looked at him it was

not for the purpose of trying to find the best way to curry his favor. No. Levi knew that expression because he'd seen it often enough staring back at him from his shaving mirror. Hannah Goodloe was trying to figure him out.

Chapter Ten

Gunther was not pleased. And Hannah was surprised to realize that Pleasant was no more anxious to move out of Levi's luxurious private car than Gunther was to approve the idea of the two women traveling with the other women of the company.

"But now that we are employees," she argued, "it seems only fair that we have no better accommodations than the others. You were right to ask to stay with Hans when we first arrived, Gunther. Pleasant and I should have done the same."

"But Hans is different," Pleasant protested.

"How so?" Hannah asked, genuinely perplexed by the idea.

"He's—well, that is, his work is more…"

"These people are good people, Hannah," Gunther interrupted. "I realize that. But they have chosen a profession that does not fit with our ways. They don't mean to, I'm sure, but their ways could pose unnecessary temptations before you and Pleasant."

"I don't see how."

"As one example there's the issue of making themselves up every day. Taking great pride in how they look to others."

"They are performers," Hannah argued.

"And yet I see the women continuing to wear their makeup when not performing. And the way they dress…" Gunther shook his head.

"And what does it say for us that we continue to live here? Is that not also prideful?" She saw that Gunther was wavering and pressed her point. "It's only for a week," she said. "Then we'll be in Wisconsin."

"Your daughter-in-law makes a good point," Levi said as he stepped out onto the observation platform where the Goodloes had been holding their conversation.

Hannah could not believe what she was hearing. Levi confused her so—the way he looked at her when he thought she wasn't aware and the ways he seemed to find to be near her. Jake had commented twice on how much more often Levi was showing up unannounced in the payroll car during the day. Now this. As if he couldn't wait to be rid of them—of her.

"It would be a great help to me if you would agree to the new arrangements, sir," Levi continued. "When people are living in such close quarters as this company does and when the stresses of the daily schedule begin to wear on them, there can be problems. Right now I just need to keep a lid on everything until we can reach Wisconsin and folks can spread out a bit for the next few months."

"I cannot see how my daughters moving in with the women of the company will make much difference," Gunther said.

"Oh, but it will. It will also help to have the three of you take meals with the rest of the company. You see, while it is not your way to give in to petty jealousies, that particular malady runs rampant in a situation like this. If your daughter and daughter-in-law were to show that they expect no special treatment, it would calm the rumblings of several ladies who are beginning to think they deserve more."

"I suppose there's no real harm," Gunther said more to himself than to the others. "There's no fraternizing between the sleeping cars?"

"I don't allow that," Levi assured him. "In fact, it's grounds for dismissal and believe me, Lily Palmer would be the first to raise the alarm."

All eyes were riveted on Gunther as he wrestled with his decision. "And we'll reach Wisconsin in a week?"

"Ten days," Levi corrected.

"We're still going to offer grace before meals," Gunther said in a tone that showed he was daring Levi to cross him on that point.

"I would expect so, sir."

Hannah saw that her father-in-law had run out of arguing points and yet she held her breath waiting for his final answer.

"All right then," Gunther said. "Let's get you two women packed up and moved in while the others are doing the matinee. The less fuss there is surrounding this, the better."

"Very wise," Levi said. "I'll leave you to your packing, then." He extended a hand to Gunther. "Thank you, sir."

Solemnly, the two men shook hands while Pleasant practically fled down the passageway to their cabin and Hannah wondered why she felt such sadness that she would no longer be sharing her meals with Levi. After all, hadn't she begun this campaign for the real purpose of distancing herself from him?

"Yes, thank you, Levi," she said, determined to put her regrets behind her. She had no clue why he had been so supportive. Perhaps she had misread his interest in them—in her. *Sheer vanity*, she thought, and prayed silently for the will to resist such worldly ways in the future.

It was done. The solution to his problem with Hannah Goodloe had been provided by the woman herself. Probably an indication that she was alarmed at the growing attention he paid her. Levi could not believe it when he overheard her making a case to move with Pleasant to the women's sleeping car.

He hadn't intentionally listened in on the family discussion, but after all, this was his private car—his residence when traveling. They were his guests and also his employees now. Yes, he had every right to eavesdrop on such a conversation. And when it had looked as if Gunther would stand firm against the idea, he had stepped in.

Relieved to have spent his last sleepless night thinking of Hannah just two doors away from his own cabin, he left the Goodloe women to their packing and headed over to the resting tent where performers waited for their act to be called. Lily was there as he had expected.

"The Goodloe women are moving into the women's dorm car," he said, grateful that for the moment, Lily was the only performer in the tent.

Lily paused in the series of stretches she routinely performed as a warm-up for her act and glanced up at him. "And hello to you, too, Levi."

He ignored her sarcasm. "You'll make sure they have what they need?"

"That depends."

"On what?" he snapped impatiently.

"On whether you want them to be settled in as one of the gang or as special."

"You know what I mean. They are different—their ways are different and I just don't want…"

"We're not going to embarrass them, Levi," Lily interrupted. "Or you."

"That's not…"

"Then stop acting like it is. If you want us to put on a show for Hannah and Pleasant then I'm afraid you're going to be disappointed. We're all tired and anxious to get back home to Wisconsin. I'm pretty sure Hannah understands *our ways*."

"Are you mocking me?"

"A little bit. Sometimes you need to get down off your high horse."

Levi smiled. "All right, I deserved that."

Lily went back to her stretching. "Jake tells me that Hannah's caught on to stuff real quick over in the office."

"He's right. In just a couple of days she's already done all the filing and caught up with the ledger entries. I may have to start looking for things to keep her busy over the next ten days."

"Don't be too hard on her, Levi. You're the one who's gone sweet on her, not the other way around." He opened his mouth to protest but Lily wasn't done. "Oh, don't give me that look. You're as transparent as a pane of glass when it comes to trying to hide your feelings."

Levi perched on the edge of a chair, his hands hanging between his knees as he watched her finish her warm-up exercises. "It's that obvious?"

"To me," Lily said. "I doubt others have noticed. Everybody's pretty single-minded about getting through each day and getting home right now, so they're fairly wrapped up in themselves."

"It's an impossible situation," he muttered.

"You like her. She likes you. Pretty simple, really."

"She's Amish."

Lily sat up and wrapped a towel around her neck. "So were you once upon a time."

If she had suddenly announced that she was off to join a nunnery, Levi could not have been more shocked. "How do you…"

"Everybody knows, Levi. You're hardly immune to gossip and speculation. People talk and when you showed up in Jonesville with three Amish people along with you, tongues really started to wag."

"Well, I'm not Amish anymore—haven't been since I was a kid."

"But your brother and sisters are and you could go back to it, right?"

Levi looked at her incredulously. "Oh, yeah, sure. I could just say I took a little time off to build a fortune by doing circus shows around the country—a profession that would not exactly endear me to the clan. Oh, and I could tell them that by the way, I would be heading back to Florida in October for the next season of performances. Yeah, that would work."

Lily shrugged and sprang nimbly to her feet. "Just a thought. Got to run. Almost time for my entrance." She gave him a platonic peck on the cheek as she left. "Think about it," she whispered. "I think Hannah might be worth it."

* * *

It was hard not to share Pleasant's doubts about the idea of living with the other women. The matinee was still going on as they carried their few belongings from Levi's car to the women's sleeping car. Hannah led the way down the narrow and shadowy center aisle to the far end of the coach.

Along the way she could not help but take note of the berths they passed. Far more than a place to sleep, many of them seemed to be like a small house. There were makeshift shelves that held dog-eared novels, framed family photos and other memorabilia. There were curtains and coverlets of different fabrics and colors. There were canvas shoe bags, the pockets holding not shoes but personal items such as lotions and reading glasses and letters from home.

When they reached the far end of the car, Hannah pointed to two top berths across the aisle from one another. "These two," she said. "You choose."

Pleasant looked at the bunk hung just inches from the ceiling of the car and then back at Hannah. "But..."

"We're the new girls," Hannah explained, using the lingo Lily had used to explain things to her. "If someone leaves then we get to move down to the second tier of bunks."

"And that's so likely to happen over the next ten days," Pleasant grumbled as she ripped a threadbare blanket off one bunk and held it up with two fingers. "Where can I dispose of this?"

"I'll take care of it," Hannah said, laying it on top of her bunk before turning back to Pleasant. "Here, let me help you get settled."

But Pleasant had already climbed up the wooden ladder and started making up her bunk. Within minutes, she had transformed the space from dreary to cheery with the use of a quilt she'd made and her very pristine organization of her clothing on the shallow shelf at the foot of the bunk. Hannah watched as wordlessly her sister-in-law leaned back on the ladder to inspect her work, and then catapulted herself into the space. She lay flat on her back, her arms folded over her stomach, her legs straight.

And then Hannah noticed that the bunk had begun to shake and realized that Pleasant was laughing, tears running down her cheeks.

"What is it?" Hannah asked, fearing Pleasant might be having an attack of hysteria.

"It's…it's like…I can't…" The more she tried to speak, the harder she laughed until Hannah could no longer contain her own laughter. "You try it," Pleasant managed to get out before setting off on a fresh round of giggles.

Hannah quickly spread out her own quilt and climbed in. Just trying to maneuver so she could lie down she bumped her head twice and her knees and elbows several times. Finally, she plopped onto her back. "It's a little cramped," she said, which set the two of them off again laughing so hard that they were unaware that the matinee had ended and the women were slowly coming back to the sleeping car.

Moments later, they looked down to see several of the female performers gathered below them watching them. Both struck their heads as they tried to sit up, setting off a chorus of sympathetic murmurs from the women below.

"It gets easier," one said. "Took me a week but…"

"The trick is to…" another offered and was interrupted by two others with different advice.

Outside they heard the clang of the dinner bell. "Supper time," one woman bellowed as she turned and hurried back down the aisle. And like a herd of sheep the others followed.

"You coming?"

Pleasant glanced over and Hannah was relieved to see that she was still smiling. The two of them wrestled with the acrobatics of getting out of the bunks they had thought were so difficult to get into, and followed their dozens of roommates out into the late afternoon sun and on to the dining tent.

Time was so short between the matinee and evening performances that most of the company ate with their costumes and makeup on. So when Levi stopped by, telling himself that he just wanted to be sure things were running smoothly, he had some trouble locating Hannah among the throng of performers.

Then he saw the white prayer cap. She was sitting at a table with Pleasant, Lily and Fred and three other performers. He positioned himself next to one of the large tent poles, glad to have this opportunity to watch her without her being aware he was anywhere nearby.

He knew Fred well enough to know that the clown was in rare form, keeping Lily and Hannah so consumed with giggles at his antics and tricks that they had barely touched their food. Even Pleasant was smiling. He couldn't help but wonder if Hannah and her sister-in-law had insisted on saying grace before taking their supper, or had been intimidated by the throng of performers and stagehands and decided against it.

And then to his amazement, she said something to the others. Lily looked over at Fred, who had a fork filled with mashed potatoes halfway to his lips and he stared

back at her for an instant and then slowly lowered the
fork to his plate and took Lily's hand. One by one the oc-
cupants of the table completed the circle of linked hands
and bowed their heads. Like a wave, silence settled over
the tent as those at nearby tables observed the action and
grew still. And while no one else repeated the practice,
everyone waited respectfully for Hannah and Pleasant
to complete their prayer and raise their heads.

If he hadn't seen it with his own eyes, Levi would
have thought it impossible for two Amish women to quiet
a tent filled with rowdy circus people. Not that there
weren't some among the company who were religious.
Long ago, he'd hired a retired minister to travel with the
company and offer Sunday services. But those services
were poorly attended, his employees preferring to take
their day off and use it for much-needed sleep or to catch
up on chores such as laundry or letter writing.

And as suddenly as the silence had descended, it
was gone and the usual chatter and clang of utensils
against tin plates prevailed. *As if it had never been*, Levi
thought, and suddenly remembered the way the tornado
had roared across the plains, straight for his father's farm
and just as quickly been gone, leaving death and destruc-
tion in its wake and changing Levi's life forever.

"Hey there, boss man," Fred bellowed, spotting Levi
from across the room. "Come join us."

It wasn't unusual for Levi to take meals with the company. It got pretty lonely eating alone in his private car
and now that Hannah and Pleasant had moved out, Gunther had insisted on taking his meals with Hans and the
rest of Levi's personal staff.

Lily and Fred scooted closer together on the narrow wooden bench making room for him and he had

no choice but to sit across from Hannah. Someone set a plate of food in front of him and filled his glass with fresh milk that he knew had been bought from a local farm.

"You missed saying grace," Fred said.

"I was here," Levi replied, unfolding his napkin and laying it across his lap.

"What a lovely tradition," Lily said. "I was think-ing, Levi…"

"Always a danger sign," Levi teased, glad to be able to focus on his star rather than have to deal with the fact that keeping his knee from brushing Hannah's skirt under the table was becoming a problem.

"I'm serious. We should have a prayer circle before every performance—nothing too formal. Just all gather round and take a moment to pray for safety and a good performance."

"Then afterward we could do it again," Fred agreed. "Then it would be a prayer of thanksgiving that we all made it safely through another show."

"I don't know," Levi hedged. "Some folks…"

"Well, let's ask them," Fred said and before Levi could stop him, he had leaped onto the bench and was bang-ing his fork and knife against an empty metal tray that one of the waiters had been taking back to the kitchen. "Hey, everybody listen up," he bellowed.

And because this was Fred and because in many ways the employees saw him as their spokesperson, everyone stopped talking and turned to hear what the clown had to say. In less than three minutes Fred had laid out the idea, allowed time for people to object and called for a motion, a second and then a vote.

It was unanimous and the company chaplain stood

and volunteered to lead the first prayer circle that very evening before and after the performance.

Slowly, Levi got to his feet. He did not need to stand on the bench for he knew that every eye was riveted on him. He was, after all, the boss.

"One thing," he said. "This is a voluntary activity. Anyone who chooses not to participate has that right and anyone who shames or intimidates such a person will be reprimanded. Understood?"

There was a general murmur of agreement and Levi saw that a few of those assembled look relieved. It occurred to him that he should feel comforted by the idea that he was not the only one around who had long ago turned away from the faith of his father. Instead, he looked at those individuals and wondered what kind of pain had damaged their belief in a higher being, a loving God.

"Father will be so pleased," Levi heard Pleasant whisper excitedly to Hannah as he sat down again and everyone resumed eating, and the conversations they'd been enjoying before Fred made his announcement.

"Yes," Hannah replied, but she was watching Levi and the tiniest of frowns marred her perfect face. "If you'll all excuse me," she added, dabbing at the corners of her mouth with her napkin. "I want to finish those ledger entries," she said as if Levi had asked for some explanation.

"And I've got mending to complete before the next performance," Pleasant said, hurrying to add as she swallowed a bite of chocolate cake and finished her milk. It was clear that it was one thing to sit with the circus folks in the company of her sister-in-law, but Pleasant was not yet comfortable being alone with them.

Lily and Fred and the others followed the Goodloe

women's lead. Before he knew it, Levi was finishing his dinner alone after all as everyone left the long tables and headed off to prepare for their next show.

For the remainder of the week they followed the same routine. Arrive in town, unload the train, set up the circus, perform two shows and move on. All within twenty-four hours. Each night, Hannah wrote a long letter to Caleb and gave it to Hans to post the following morning.

She took great care not to talk too much about the circus and the friends she was making there. How could she deny her son this life if she admitted that she found the people and the adventure of the travel every bit as exciting as he must have? Instead, she wrote about Gunther and Pleasant and how much they were all missing the rest of the family back in Sarasota. She reminded him to say his prayers and to help with the chores and to be respectful of the people who had taken him in.

After a week, she had had no letter from her son. Instead, there had been daily wires from Miss Benson assuring her that Caleb continued to be well cared for and in good health and that he was anxious to see her. Hannah would carry the day's telegram in the pocket of her apron and take it out several times in the course of the day, hoping to find some turn of phrase that would give her more information.

To overcome her sadness and worry, she buried herself in work. Jake marveled at her ability to get through what to him seemed a full day's filing and correspondence before noon. "Ida had best watch out," he told Hannah. "You'll have her job."

"Oh, no," she protested. "I'm just doing this until we reach Baraboo. Then my son and I will return to Florida."

"And Miss Pleasant as well?" Jake asked, not looking up from his newspaper.

"Of course, Pleasant and my father-in-law—the four of us."

"And do you think the boy will try again?"

It was the single thought that haunted Hannah's dreams every night. "I don't know," she admitted. "I hope not, but then Levi…"

"You know his story then?"

"He told me that he ran away when he was only a few years older than Caleb."

"It's completely different," Jake assured her. "Levi had lost both his parents, not just the one, and he'd been farmed out to his grandparents and I take it he and his grandpa didn't see eye to eye on his future."

"So he ran away—and stayed away," Hannah said.

Jake folded his newspaper, uncrossed his legs and stood up. "Ah, now, don't go down that road. You can't know how things will go with your boy. My advice? Look for some way that you might offer him what he was looking for in the first place."

"He wanted to join the circus," she reminded him.

"Nope. He wanted a change—something out of the ordinary. The circus just happened to come to town about that same time."

"Our life is pretty…plain," she said, faltering for the right words.

"And yet from what you've told me, you and your husband and your father-in-law all left the farms of the Midwest and started over in Florida. I'd call that adventure. Maybe the boy doesn't know that whole story?"

Hannah felt a glimmer of hope. Jake was right. By the time Caleb was born, the family was settled in Florida.

He'd never known any other life. And then his father had died and there had been pressure on him to assume the role of man of the house.

"Show him his roots," Jake advised, "and the kid might just find his wings right there at home." As was his habit, he headed for the door citing some appointment that he was late for. "He'll be all right," he said as he left. "He's got a good mother who will see to that."

Hannah had gotten so caught up in the personal conversation with Jake that she had completely forgotten to show him some things she'd noticed while attending to the filings and bookkeeping assignments he left for her each day.

"Jake!" she shouted, but he just raised one hand and kept walking.

"Never mind," she mumbled to herself as she watched him go. "I'll take care of it."

She spotted the ledgers on Jake's desk. She could take care of it. She could look up the answers as easily as Jake could. She carried the heavy oversize ledger to her desk and set to work.

Chapter Eleven

On his way back to his private car after seeing the grand finale and congratulating the performers on yet another stellar performance, Levi noticed a single lamp still burning in the payroll car. He knew that Chester had left early that morning for the next town to make sure everything was ready for their arrival, and Jake had headed off to town as was his habit. His friend was quite the ladies' man and something of a legend within the company for his ability to balance multiple romantic relationships. Lily called him "The Juggler" and Jake smiled every time he heard her say it.

Truth was, Levi had been wary of having Hannah work in such close quarters with Jake, but he trusted his friend to know that trying to romance an Amish widow would be way out of line. Instead, it appeared that Hannah and Jake had become good friends. More than once he had heard Hannah laughing at something Jake said or inviting him to join the group she was sitting with in the dining tent.

Truth was, Levi was jealous of his friend's easy way with the ladies. No, he was jealous of Jake's friendship with Hannah. Jake had mentioned some things to Levi—things about the runaway boy and about the dead husband that Levi hadn't known. Things that Hannah must have felt comfortable confiding to Jake—but not to him.

He brushed the thought aside and headed for the payroll car. Most likely Chester had been in a rush to leave and left the lamp burning. Levi would have to speak to him about that—unnecessary lights cost money and these days the company could not afford waste.

Digging the keys from his pocket as he climbed the three steps to the platform outside the payroll door, Levi didn't see Hannah at first. But when he found the door unlocked, he peered in through the barred window and saw her, head down on her desk, a pencil in one hand. Not wanting to startle her, he turned the brass doorknob and stepped inside the car.

Her desk was at the far end of the car so he turned on the lamp on Jake's desk, then the one on Chester's as he made his way toward her. He didn't want her to wake up and see someone lurking in the shadows, and at the same time he realized he was making as little noise as possible, reluctant to disturb her sleep.

She slept with one cheek resting on a bent arm. Her breath came in even rhythmic sighs and her prayer cap had fallen a little to one side revealing the bun of hair that she kept hidden beneath it. Levi studied her hair for a long moment, recalling the Amish habit of a woman never cutting her hair—her crowning glory. And yet the only man who ever saw it down would have been her husband.

He imagined her sitting in her berth at night, releasing the golden strands from their bonds, shaking it free and then brushing the length of it until it shone. He reached out to touch it—just one touch to know the reality of its silkiness. But instead, he lowered his hand to her shoulder and shook her gently.

"Hannah?"

She stirred and blinked up at him and in the amber of the lamplight, he thought she had never been lovelier. Her lips were full and soft from the relaxation that came with sleep and he could not remember ever wanting to kiss a woman more. For one mad instant he thought of pulling Hannah Goodloe to her feet, wrapping his arms around her and kissing those sleep-heavy eyelids, the flushed cheeks and those lips that had haunted his dreams for days now.

Instead, he turned his attention to the ledger. "What's this?" he asked and was well aware that the desire he felt for her came out as gruffness in his tone.

Hannah sat up and righted her prayer cap in the same motion. "I was…I had some questions about some of the invoices and Jake had to leave and I thought that perhaps…"

"What questions?"

"It's nothing, really," she stammered, clearly unnerved by his irritable tone. "Have I done something wrong, Levi? I thought perhaps…"

He closed the ledger and placed it back on Jake's desk. "The ledgers are none of your concern," he said, his back to her as he tried to regain control of emotions that had, in a matter of minutes, gone from longing for her to annoyance that she had taken it upon herself to go snooping into his business affairs. "It's late," he said, still not looking at her. "The train will be pulling out soon. I'll see you back to your sleeping car."

Behind him, he heard her stacking papers and putting them away so that they would not scatter with the movement of the train. He heard the click of locks on the file cabinets and then she was beside him holding out the ring of keys he'd given her when she first started to work in the office.

"What's this?" he asked, automatically holding out his hand as she dropped the keys into his palm.

"I do not wish you to question my trustworthiness," she said. "I will work here only when either Jake or Chester are also here and they can unlock the files and such as I need them." Without another word she started for the door. "I can see myself out," she said. "Good night, Levi."

Warring with his frustration that she'd made too much of this and his admiration of her spunk, he allowed her to make it past Chester's desk before he overtook her. He spun her around and cupped her face in his palm. She met his gaze defiantly but did not pull away.

"You're angry with me," he said softly, his eyes roving over her features, memorizing each tiny frown line. He felt a smile pull at his lips.

"Was that your purpose then? To provoke me?"

"No," he admitted. "My purpose was to avoid what I can no longer avoid, Hannah." And he lowered his face to her, allowing his lips to rest lightly against her forehead and then move across to her temple, her now-closed eyes, her cheek and finally...

"No," she whispered and the sweetness of her breath against his lips was like a warm spring breeze.

He hesitated, not moving. Waiting.

"Yes." She raised onto her toes to meet his kiss.

Hannah fought against the guilt she felt in taking such joy in being in Levi's arms.

But when he lifted his lips from hers but did not release her from his embrace all she could think was, *How can such feelings shared be wrong?*

And yet she knew they were and she pulled away. "I must go," she said, her voice trembling as she made her way past Jake's desk to reach the door. To her relief, Levi did not try to stop her.

What could I have been thinking to allow such a thing? To invite such a thing? she thought as she ran alongside the unmoving train on her way to the sleeping car. Up and down the track she could hear men's voices calling out directions as they hooked the cars together and loaded the wagons and animals.

"Help me make this right," she prayed. "Show me Your way and guide my steps, my words and my actions until I can reunite with my son and both of us can return safely home again."

"Late date?" one of the women teased good-naturedly as Hannah boarded the car and climbed into her upper berth. She glanced over and saw Pleasant watching her curiously. "I was working and fell asleep," she offered and was relieved when Pleasant nodded and went back to reading her Bible.

Hannah hated the half truth of her statement. Surely this could only lead to more trouble for her. She had allowed herself to believe that she could befriend these people and maintain her Amish decorum. She had believed that she could look upon Levi as a man who had done a good deed for her family, a kind man in spite of his brooding and sometimes cantankerous exterior. She had believed that what she felt for him was gratitude.

She had been fooling herself.

She had fallen in love with Levi Harmon, and in his

arms she had permitted herself to forget everything and everyone else and surrender to what she had wanted for so many days now. Not his kindness or his polite hospitality, but his tenderness and affection. She had wanted what she'd seen in his eyes as he bent to kiss her—attraction that comes only between a man and a woman who believe they are destined to be together.

And yet the very idea was impossible. Levi was an outsider—a man of the world in ways that she couldn't begin to understand. He had wealth and power. His life was complex, wrapped up in the kingdom he had built and chosen to inhabit. His faith was shaky at best, maybe even nonexistent other than on the level of a polite respect for the faith of others.

No, she thought as she went through the necessary contortions to undress and get into her nightgown. She had lost her way just as Caleb had. She had permitted herself to be enticed by the colorful and exciting culture of life in the circus—just as Caleb had. But she was the adult here. Caleb could be forgiven for such transgressions against the ways of his people. Hannah would surely be shunned if anyone learned of this indiscretion.

"Only three days more," Pleasant said. She stretched and yawned then carefully lay the ribbon bookmark on the parchment pages of her Bible and turned out the little light she used for reading.

Three days until they reach Baraboo. Three days until Hannah was reunited with Caleb. Three days to be gotten through and then they would take Caleb and go home. And by the time Levi Harmon returned to his fine mansion in Sarasota, Hannah would have found her bearings and there would be no reason for them to have contact ever again.

"Hannah," Pleasant whispered leaning out her berth to tap Hannah's shoulder.

Hannah thought of pretending to be asleep but she had told enough half truths for one day. "Yes?"

"Do you think there's any possibility that Noah will live near Baraboo? That I might see him?"

Hannah was well aware that Noah was the young man who had come to Florida during the winter to visit his uncle and aunt. The man who had also developed the habit of stopping at the bakery every day that he was in town.

"I don't know, Pleasant. What if you do see him?"

There was a long silence punctuated by snores and coughs and grumblings up and down the car. "I might stay," Pleasant said softly, and Hannah sat up so suddenly that she cracked her head against the ceiling as the train car jolted into place and started to move.

The train had just started to move when Levi heard Lily shouting his name. "Levi, come quick! Hannah's been hurt!"

His heart skipped several beats but somehow his brain remained active and he followed his star through several cars on their way to the women's sleeping car.

"She cracked her head pretty hard," Lily was explaining as they moved from one car to the next, the rush of air catching her words and flinging them back at him. "There's quite a bump on top and she's dizzy and…"

"Did somebody send for Doc?"

Doc Jones was the veterinarian on staff but he knew enough human medicine to keep the company rolling. If one of the cast or crew needed something more, then Levi would call for the doctor in the next town.

"He's with her now along with her father-in-law," Lily said. "I also saw Hans and he's wiring Chester to make sure the town doctor is available in case we need him. I'm afraid she might have a concussion," Lily said, wringing her hands nervously.

The scene inside the women's sleeping car might have been comical under other circumstances. Pleasant was standing guard over Hannah laid out on Lily's private bunk in the front of the car. Doc was peering in over Gunther's shoulder as several of the other women pressed in for a better look. But Gunther was barring the entrance and wore an expression that dared anyone to try to get past him.

"I can't examine her, Gunther, unless you let me in there," Doc protested.

"It's not proper," Gunther argued. "Tell my daughter what to do and look for and she'll report."

Doc rolled his eyes and then saw Levi. "Maybe you can talk some sense into him," he muttered as he made way for Levi and Lily.

"Is she conscious?" Levi asked the vet.

"Far as I can tell."

"Gunther, we need to be sure she's all right. Doc doesn't need to touch her other than on her face and head."

Lily pulled a blanket from a nearby berth. "Maybe cover her with this," she suggested. "It's plain," she said, meeting Gunther's eyes.

"We should not have…I should never have agreed…" Gunther muttered to himself as he took the blanket.

"Here, Papa," Pleasant said and Levi thought he had never heard the woman speak with such gentleness. "Let me." She took the blanket from her father and covered

Hannah from her chin to her toes, then stood aside to make room for Doc.

"How did this happen?" Doc asked as he peered into Hannah's eyes and cradled her head in both hands.

"Oh, come now, Doc," Lily protested. "You know what those third berths are like. There's barely enough room to turn over much less sit up."

"I sat up," Hannah replied in answer to the vet's question. "I forgot," she added with a smile at Lily.

Levi could not help noticing that Pleasant seemed inordinately distressed, near tears. "Will she be all right?" she demanded, in what was her more usual no-nonsense voice.

"She will have a headache and a lump," Doc announced as he instructed Hannah to follow his finger without turning her head. "But I would say she'll live."

Several of the women tittered with nervous relief at this news and started to wander back toward their own berths. Lily leaned in to Hannah. "You sleep here tonight, honey," she said. "I'll take your berth."

"I couldn't," Hannah protested, attempting to get up, but clearly a wave of dizziness prevented her from making it any farther than to a half sitting position before Pleasant eased her back down to the pile of pillows covered in satins and silks at the head of Lily's berth.

"I'll stay with you," Pleasant assured her. "Thank you, Lily."

"Hans has made arrangements for her to be seen by the town doctor as soon as we arrive tomorrow," Levi assured Gunther, although he had no idea whether or not Hans had been able to make such arrangements. "Until then…"

"Until then," Lily said as she corralled the three males

toward the exit, "we've got things under control. Good night, gentlemen."

Levi had had every intention of taking up a position in the seat across from Lily's private berth for the night. It was separated from the rest of the sleeping car by the small toilet and galley and Pleasant would be right there. "I…" he protested.

"You get some sleep," Lily ordered. "If anything changes, we'll come get you, right, ladies?"

A bevy of female faces, some of them coated in cold cream like clown faces stared back at Levi and nodded. The sideshow fat lady practically filled the aisle with her bulk as she took her position outside Lily's berth.

Levi tried looking past her. He just wanted to see Hannah, see her eyes meet his, and reassure himself that she was not only all right but that they were all right, as well. But Pleasant was blocking his view, standing over Hannah and murmuring something to her.

"Go," the fat lady ordered and pointed one pudgy finger toward the exit. Levi saw the command mirrored in the eyes of the other women.

"Doc, you sleep here," he said pointing to the seat he'd intended to occupy. "That way," he added firmly, "no one has to go running through a moving train for help."

"I'm staying, as well," Gunther said and sat down next to the window.

"Really," Lily huffed, but neither she nor any of the other women rejected the compromise. "Could we just all get a little sleep? We've got two shows to do today." She nodded toward a wall clock in the galley that showed it was past midnight.

"Take care of her," Levi murmured to Lily as he reluctantly stepped onto the platform connecting the women's sleeping car to that of the men. "And if anything…"

"I'll send for you," Lily promised. She stroked his cheek with her palm. "She'll be all right, Levi."

"It's just…"

"I know," she replied. "I can see."

"See what?" he asked brusquely, but his heartbeat quickened like a kid caught sneaking under the circus tent without paying.

"You love her." She gave his cheek one final gentle pat and returned to the sleeping car, letting the door to the platform shut behind her.

Chapter Twelve

Love? Impossible.

Infatuation maybe. But love? What did he know of love? Vague memories of his parents' deep affection for each other flashed across his mind. He had never really understood how a man and woman could risk such intense feelings. What if one of them died?

What if they both did?

Levi had not been able to get Lily's comment out of his head ever since returning to his car and trying to concentrate on work instead of Hannah. She would be fine. She was being well cared for and tomorrow, as soon as the train rolled into the last town on the tour, he would make sure she was seen by the local doctor. In the meantime, he had to try to make sense of the bank statement before him.

I am not in love with her.

And even if I were...

As dawn approached, he pushed himself away from his desk and walked out to the observation platform—the very last piece of the long train chugging its way through the night. He caught the scent of freshly plowed fields after a May rain. He saw cows heading out to pasture and farmers driving their tractors along narrow country roads.

The sun wouldn't be up for hours yet but these men had fields to be planted and cows to be milked. The train entered a tunnel and the blackness engulfed Levi, the cold dampness of the rock walls sending a shiver through him. And when the train emerged at the far end of the tunnel, he saw in the distance the signature silhouette of an Amish buggy leaving a large white farm house surrounded by large willow trees. So many years had passed, but a memory jolted him, the memory of riding just such a buggy on just such a morning as this, and his father passing him the reins. "Take over, son."

He watched that buggy until it disappeared from sight. And only when he tasted the salt of his tears did Levi realize that he was crying.

Hannah's head hurt but the very idea of spending the day in bed was so foreign to her that it made her feel anxious. "Surely I could work," she told the doctor who had arrived shortly after the train pulled into their last stop before reaching Baraboo. "All I do is sit at a desk and post numbers in a ledger and file…"

The doctor frowned as he put away his stethoscope. "I suppose you could go in for an hour or so. But I am warning you, young lady, this injury is not to be trifled with. At the first sign of dizziness or blurred vision I want you back in bed and someone sent to get me."

"Yes, sir." Hannah thought she would have agreed to just about anything he asked so thrilled was she to think that soon she could be out of the close quarters of the sleeping car. And most of all she wanted to see Levi.

"I'll help you get dressed," Pleasant said when the doctor had left, giving Gunther a prescription for headache powders and promising to stop by later to see that she was doing all right.

"I'm fine, really." Pleasant had been hovering over her ever since she'd cracked her head. "It wasn't your fault," Hannah added.

Pleasant burst into tears. "Please don't say anything to Father about what I said that made you sit up so suddenly and…"

So that was it. Pleasant was afraid that Hannah might mention her comment about possibly staying in Wisconsin. "Oh, Pleasant," she said, wrapping her arms around her sister-in-law. "Why didn't you say that you were worried about that? Of course I won't mention it."

Pleasant sniffed back tears and studied Hannah's face seeking assurance that she could be trusted. "You do understand," she said softly, and then as if a match had suddenly flamed to life, she smiled. "You understand because of Levi."

Hannah stiffened. "I don't get your meaning."

Pleasant picked up Hannah's hairbrush from the pile of belongings Lily had brought and began brushing her sister-in-law's hair. "Yes, you do. Everyone is talking about it—the way he watches you and looks at you when you're together. In the costume shop, there's even speculation that he might propose, but I told them such a thing could never happen. We are Amish. I reminded them that he is not and besides, he is engaged in a profession that…"

Pleasant continued to chatter on while Hannah's mind

froze on the words "might propose." Of course, such a thing was unthinkable on every possible level. They barely knew one another for starters.

And yet you kissed him.

She could not deny the facts. Theirs was no stolen peck on the lips that he had trapped her into giving. Theirs was a shared kiss laden with all of the questions and curiosities that two adults who are attracted to each other can not resist exploring.

"…And so the point is…" Pleasant rambled on as she wound Hannah's hair into a tight bun and anchored it firmly with hairpins she pulled one by one from her mouth even as she continued talking.

The point is, Hannah thought, *that this must stop… today.* And she made up her mind to go and find Levi as soon as she was free to leave the sleeping car. On the other hand, if anyone saw them talking…

I'll write him a letter.

Chester Tuck was at his desk when Hannah got to the payroll car. She had met him only once before when Jake had introduced them as Chester was on his way to the next stop on the tour. The man was thin and stooped and nervous, always fidgeting with his hat and always seeming to be about to run away.

"It's what makes him a good twenty-four-hour man," Jake told her. "He likes to keep things moving."

And true to his nature, the minute he saw Hannah, Chester started moving papers around on his desk, shoveling them into a top drawer as he stood and grabbed his hat from the brass hat rack on the wall. "Morning, Mrs. Goodloe," he muttered without looking at her directly.

"Good morning. I hope I won't disturb you if I take care of some filing?"

"No, ma'am. Just on my way out." He edged toward the door and then stopped. "No need to file those things there," he said with an offhanded wave toward the wire basket on his desk. "I'll take care of those when I get back later."

"I'd be more than happy to…"

"No." The single word carried a hint of panic, but then he smiled. "I need to clear something up with one of the suppliers before we file those," he explained. "I'll take care of it. You have a good day now."

Hannah finished the day's filing—minus the papers on Chester's desk—within the hour. In that time she had heard Levi's laughter and the low rumble of his voice giving instructions, or engaged in conversation, but he had not come to the payroll car. Jake had been in and out several times, muttering something about suppliers not living up to their end of things and asking if she'd seen the invoice for the feed store delivery.

"No. It might be there," she said, pointing to the stack of papers on Chester's desk. "I offered to file them, but Chester said something about a supplier…"

Jake grabbed the stack of papers and scanned them, his usually easygoing nature tense and confused. "I don't get it," he muttered. "Okay," he said, putting the papers down, "if Chester comes back, tell him I need to see him right away."

He started out the door, then turned and smiled apologetically. "Sorry, Hannah. How are you feeling? You aren't overdoing, are you?"

"I'm fine," she assured him.

"Good. I'll let Levi know. The man's been jumpy as a frog all morning."

And with a wave he was gone, leaving Hannah standing at the door and thinking, *If Levi is so concerned then why not stop by to see for himself that I'm better?*

But that would indicate that he had feelings for her and she didn't want that…did she? She couldn't want that.

"This has to end now," she muttered aloud as she sat down at her desk—Ida's desk—and pulled out a piece of paper.

Levi was not having a good day. He was worried about Hannah but had determined not to try to see her, and instead had relied on others to provide information. Lily had taken it upon herself to give him a running commentary of how Hannah had done overnight.

"Slept some but restless, you know? I expect she was in considerable pain and she has quite a bruise on her forehead. I offered to cover the worst of it with makeup but then I was forgetting myself. She and Pleasant have become so much a part of the company that sometimes…"

"She's fine then? The doctor saw her?"

Lily eyed him curiously. "You know he did. I saw you grilling the man not two minutes after he left from examining her."

Levi had ended the conversation by insisting the need to find Jake. It was in the course of that conversation that he learned that Hannah was at work. He had taken three strides toward the payroll car before he caught himself. "Make sure she doesn't overdo," he told Jake and turned his attention to a new employee who was mishandling the unloading of a wagon.

He kept himself occupied through the matinee and the evening performance and only headed back to his car when he saw that the payroll car was dark. That's

when he found the envelope with his name on it propped
against the inkwell on his desk.

Her handwriting, like the woman herself, was simple
yet elegant. Block printing with each letter evenly spaced
and every word perfectly aligned on the single sheet of
unlined paper.

> *Levi,*
> *As we near the end of our journey, I wanted
> to take this opportunity to say how very grate-
> ful I am for the generosity and kindness you
> have shown to my son, our family and to me.
> We could not have been more blessed. Thanks
> to you we are soon to be reunited with Caleb
> and whatever comes next for our family, we will
> never forget the compassion you have shown us
> these past weeks. May God bless you.*
> *Hannah*

It was a letter of farewell.

He read it again to be sure, then crumpled it into a
ball, but could not bring himself to throw it away. Instead, he did what Levi always did when faced with a
situation he could not control—he acted on instinct and
headed for the women's sleeping car.

But on the way he found himself surrounded by the
sounds of the traveling community he had built. A lone
elephant trumpeted a late night howl, horses whinnied
and stamped their feet as they jostled one another for
more space. Several members of the company had gathered outside the dining tent where Fred was strumming
a ukulele, and others were singing along as they sat by
a campfire.

They had performed their last show of the tour and for once there was no rush to move on to the next town. The next stop would be Baraboo where they would set up for the summer, offering shows eight times a week. Some of the cast and crew would leave the show there to take other jobs. Others would supplement their incomes by offering training in acrobatics or clowning. Levi and Jake would stay for a month or so and then set out to audition new acts they might add to the show the coming season. He had always liked this last night on the road. The company of performers and crew never felt more like family than they did on this particular night.

He glanced over at the sleeping car and saw that most of the windows were open and he could hear laughter and conversation drifting out.

It would do no good to cause a scene, he decided. He and Hannah were already the subject of gossip throughout the company. He would talk to her tomorrow. He would send Hans for her and meet with her in the privacy of his sitting room. And he would tell her...

What?

It occurred to Hannah that neither she nor Pleasant were immune to the nostalgia that had spread through the company like a terrible cold. Emotions seemed to run the gamut from lethargy to relief and back again to outright depression. And the onset had been so sudden. Almost in concert with the sounding of the band's final notes, the performers and crew had slumped into their malaise. The women's sleeping car that was usually noisy and even boisterous as the women came back after a show was strangely subdued. And outside, instead of the usual rumble of wagons being loaded onto flatcars that had become the lullaby by which she'd learned to fall asleep, she heard the soft music of Fred's ukulele in tandem with a chorus of male voices as they gathered round a campfire.

Tomorrow.

The word had become her constant thought. Tomorrow they would leave this last town on the tour. Tomorrow they would arrive in Baraboo. Tomorrow she would see Caleb.

And the day after that she would say goodbye to Levi.

Sleep was impossible even after everyone had settled down for the night. Hannah had finally been able to persuade Pleasant that there was no need to keep watch and she had gone to sleep in her own berth. Fortunately, she had not been able to persuade Lily to return to her private room and so no one was around to see Hannah leave.

The night air was crisp and the skies were laden with stars. Under other circumstances Hannah might simply have gone for a walk, but she saw a light in the payroll car and that brought back the memory of something she had noticed the night she and Levi had kissed. It had nothing to do with the kiss. In fact, it was the kiss that had completely put the worrisome thing out of her mind.

Hoping that it was Levi working late, she headed across the compound. But when she opened the door she came face-to-face with Jake who was clearly taken aback to see her.

"Hannah? Something wrong?"

She thought about telling Jake exactly what had brought her there at such an hour, but decided to wait. After all, it might be nothing. "I couldn't sleep and the other day I didn't finish the filing. When we reach

Baraboo I don't want Ida to have to do work I should already have done."

Jake frowned briefly. "Well, I suppose. But lock the door while you're in there, okay? And don't stay too long."

"I will," she said. "Lock the door," she added, "and I won't be long."

"Because Levi would have my head if anything happened to you and you just never know. Seems like a nice enough town but you just never know."

Hannah was touched by Jake's concern. "I'll be fine," she assured him.

As soon as Jake left—she waited to hear the click of the lock—Hannah hurried to the filing cabinet that held the paid bills. She pulled out the most recent folder and spread the contents on her desk. She took the invoice she recalled questioning and studied it. It was from a dry goods store and the total amount of the bill was for several hundred dollars. It was stamped "Paid in Cash" and when she retrieved the ledger from Jake's desk and checked the entry, she saw that the two documents matched. But she remembered that earlier on that day, Pleasant had gone to town with the head seamstress to find fabric that might match a ripped costume. Her sister-in-law had talked at supper about the proprietress at Danvers Dry Goods. The two of them had become fast friends, sharing stories of serving customers and handling a business. Pleasant had been fairly glowing with the experience.

The problem was that this was a bill paid to General Dry Goods—not Danvers—and the order was for the same date. And had Danvers been paid? And if so, then what was this other store?

She paced the office and as she passed Chester's desk

a sliver of white paper peeped out from his desk drawer. She recalled how he'd shoved the papers insideearlier that day. What was he hiding?

She pulled open the drawer but found only blank paper. The papers he'd put away were gone. She tried closing the drawer but it stuck. Not wanting to have Chester know she'd been snooping, she bent to clear the path for the drawer and found that a rumpled invoice was the cause of the problem. She pulled it free and closed the drawer. Then she flattened the paper out and read, "Danvers Dry Goods." The date was the same. As was the list of items purchased. But the amount was half what had been paid to the other store.

Why would Chester pass up the opportunity to buy goods at half the cost? Perhaps it was because Danvers was owned by a woman. A widow like Hannah. Yes, she could see Chester not liking doing business with a woman. But to spend twice as much? There had to be some explanation.

Unaware of the passing of time, Hannah pulled out one file and then another as the trail that might lead to some logical explanation became more convoluted. She found a stream of invoices going back ten years or more paid to a "General Dry Goods" in a variety of towns up and down the East Coast and across mid-America. She found similar invoices paid to a feed company with the name "American Feed & Grain," again in a variety of towns and states.

Perhaps these were chain stores, she thought. She had heard of such businesses opening in small towns, but was the chain giving Levi the best price or was this just a convenience for Chester? He didn't seem the lazy type, but on the other hand, he did often seem harried and rushed so perhaps saving time was more important to him than saving money.

She stretched her aching back and rubbed her temples as she tried to make sense of the piles of papers she had pulled and reorganized by vendor—papers she would now need to refile. This was really none of her business after all. She had been given the task of filing but she could not help but recall comments Levi had made to Gunther when the two men sat discussing business at dinner. There had been no doubt that Levi was worried about the drop in attendance and the rising costs of goods to keep the circus on tour.

I should tell someone about this, she thought.

She could ask Chester. He probably had a perfectly logical explanation. But Jake had told her that Chester had gone on ahead to Baraboo and that she should file whatever was left on his desk.

Then she would show her findings to Jake. After all, he was the accountant and business manager for the company. Jake would know what to do.

She laid her head on her forearm, intending to give herself just enough time to rest her eyes before tackling the job of putting everything back in its place, and fell fast asleep.

Chapter Thirteen

Levi woke before sunrise, surprising Hans and the cook in the kitchen. He had just spent his last night on the train—another restless night.

"Breakfast?" the cook asked, already taking down a skillet and reaching for a bowl of eggs.

"Just coffee now," Levi replied. "I'm just going to walk the lot."

Hans nodded as the cook handed Levi a mug of black coffee. It was a long-standing tradition that on the morning after the last show of a tour, Levi would walk through the now deserted big top and sideshow tents. He would sit in the top row of seats staring down at the center ring, replaying the season's lineup of acts and already thinking about changes he would make for the coming season.

"Shall I come along and take notes?" Hans asked.

"Not today. Thanks." He saluted them with his coffee mug and swung down off the rear platform to the dusty ground below.

The truth was that Levi needed time to think—about the future of the show, but also about Hannah's future.

Not that he had any say in that, of course, and yet somehow her future seemed improbably tied to his own.

Impossible.

She would never leave her faith for him and that's what he would be asking of her. The very idea that she could marry a circus owner and travel around the country with a bunch of acrobats and clowns and not be shunned by her Amish community was ludicrous. And if he loved her—and that was still an undetermined quantity in his mind—would he ask such a thing? Wouldn't the greater love be to let her go? Take her son and return home to Florida where she might find an Amish widower or bachelor waiting to marry her?

After all, she'd already made her decision. The note she'd written—the one he'd crumpled into a wad and then smoothed out and now carried with him—could not have been more clear. He'd avoided any contact or conversation with her since receiving that note. Maybe now was the time to respond.

He reversed his path and headed for the payroll car. He would take out the cash Hannah and the others would need for the train back to Florida, put that in an envelope for Gunther with a note. Then he would write a note to Pleasant thanking her for her service in the costume shop. And finally a note to Hannah—a businesslike note, similar to the one he wrote to Pleasant that would leave no doubt that they had come to the end of their relationship.

So engrossed was he in his plan that he was inside the car and opening the safe before he saw Hannah slumped over her desk surrounded by piles of papers. His first thought was that she had come in to work and been overcome by the aftereffects of her head injury. But when he knelt next to her and gently touched her shoulder, she sighed, turned her face to the other cheek and slept on. Her breathing was normal and she certainly did not look as if she were in any distress.

Levi stood up and looked around trying to decide his next move. What had the woman been thinking to drag all of this out on the day they were scheduled to leave? Everything was out of order. Neat stacks sorted by vendor rather than his preferred system of filing by date covered not only the top of her desk, but also Chester's. This would take hours to set to rights.

And yet in his heart, he knew that Hannah had to have had her reasons. He studied the arrangement of files, trying to find some sense in what she had done. And slowly he began to grasp what Hannah's digging had uncovered.

Someone he knew and trusted was stealing from him—had been stealing from him for at least a year if these documents were correct. And the first name that came to mind was his old friend and business manager's. Only Jake had full access to whatever cash reserves they kept in the safe. Only Jake could sign checks in Levi's absence.

Not Jake, he thought. *Please.*

And that was the closest Levi had come to truly praying since the day his parents had been crushed in the tornado.

He picked up the stack of invoices from Danvers Dry Goods. He had traded with Travis Danvers and his wife, Ginny, for years. He'd come to Travis's funeral and made it clear to Chester that whenever the circus came to town, all possible supplies that could be bought from Ginny should be. Yet mixed in with the Danvers invoices were others from a vendor he didn't know. He studied an invoice for that other dry goods store dated three days earlier.

"Hannah, wake up."

The urgency in his voice jolted her upright. "What's happened? Oh, Levi, I can explain."

"No time," he said. "You need to get this stuff back in the files as quickly as possible. Don't worry about getting it right, just get it put away before Jake comes in. I have to go into town."

"I don't understand."

"I hope I don't either—I hope I'm dead wrong about this but…" He spotted the rumpled invoice she'd been lying on and picked it up. He compared it to the one in his hand. "I'll be back," he said tersely. "Do not mention this to anyone—not your family, not Lily and certainly not Jake, do you understand?"

She looked at him with those huge blue eyes of hers and he saw that her lip was trembling. So he retraced his steps and pulled her into his arms. "It's all right," he crooned. "You did nothing wrong, Hannah. In fact, you might have done me a huge favor. Now please get this stuff put away. I'll explain later, all right?"

She nodded and he kissed her forehead before letting her go. "If anyone asks, tell them I had to go into town—nothing more."

Again, she nodded and he was relieved to see that before he was out the door, she was already starting to gather the piles of papers and put them back into the open file drawers.

Hannah's head throbbed but she suspected it was not due to the bump she'd gotten reacting to Pleasant's announcement that she might stay in Wisconsin. No, nothing was making any sense at all right now. Clearly, Levi had seen something in the papers she'd spent hours sorting through that she had missed and he had instantly known what it meant.

He did not seem upset with her. In fact, he'd shown her a kind of tenderness that had tested her will to stand firm behind the note she had sent him. Any kindness from him made her question whether or not there might be any possibility that she and he could…

"Hannah?"

She had not heard Jake come in. "Good morning," she said brightly, even as she scanned the room for any documents she might have missed.

"You work late and come in early. I'm going to have to talk to Levi about giving you a raise." He tossed his hat across the narrow train car and it caught the brass hat rack and stayed. "Have you seen the boss?"

"He said something about going into town." Her breath quickened. She did not like lying but she would have to watch every word if she were to avoid that particular sin now.

To her relief, Jake grinned. "Figured as much. Levi has his traditions—last town on the tour is always special to him—a place where he's connected with some of the townsfolk over the years. He always goes downtown to thank them and say goodbye."

Outside they could hear the normal cadence of tents being dismantled while animals and wagons were loaded onto railway cars. The scent of bacon and sausage and strong black coffee wafted in through the open window and Hannah's stomach growled.

"I think I'll go get some breakfast," she said, thankful for any excuse to get away from Jake and the payroll car. "Can I bring you anything?"

Jake rubbed his stomach. "Nope. Already ate. You go on. Looks like you've got everything in order here, and I imagine you've got other things on your mind right now."

Hannah tried hard not to show surprise. "No. What things?"

"Your son—you'll be seeing him by supper time, Hannah," Jake said.

And suddenly, everything but the thought of reuniting with Caleb flew from Hannah's mind. She smiled at Jake. "That's right. It's always seemed as if it were so far in the future—weeks and then days away but now..."

"It's here. Today's the day."

Hannah could have hugged the man for setting her mind to rights, bringing her focus back to what was really important here. Caleb was all that mattered from this moment forward. "Yes," she said and she laughed. "Today is indeed the day." And when she entered the dining tent she was humming to herself.

"You're in a good mood," Pleasant observed, scowling up at her from her place at one of the long tables.

"Today we see Caleb," Hannah replied happily. She completely missed the unusually quiet reception she was receiving, not only from her sister-in-law but from Lily, as well.

"I have to pack," Lily muttered, picking up her dishes and leaving just as a waiter brought Hannah a plate filled with scrambled eggs, link sausages and fried potatoes.

"Milk?" he asked, holding up a pitcher from a nearby stand and Hannah nodded as she scooted onto the bench across from Pleasant.

"I'm famished," Hannah said. "Surely that means I'm

on the mend." She had assumed that Pleasant's sour mood had to do with the guilt she refused to relinquish for having caused Hannah's head injury.

Pleasant worked her lips into a disapproving pout. "I suppose staying out all night doing who knows what with who knows whom can lead a person to an appetite," she said primly, refusing to look at Hannah directly.

Hannah put down her fork. "I was working," she said, but could not help but glance around to see if anyone else might have heard Pleasant's statement.

This time Pleasant pinned her with a steely cold stare. "Do not add lying to your shame, Hannah," she ordered through clenched teeth. "I awoke after midnight and came to bring you a glass of water and see if you needed any of the headache powders. Your bed was empty and it remained so."

Hannah struggled with her sister-in-law's accusation and with the unspoken promise she had given Levi not to talk about what she'd been doing and had obviously discovered. "I was working," she repeated. "And I was alone."

"Oh, really. Then Lily must have been mistaken when she saw Levi rush out of the payroll car just after dawn and then saw you through the window."

"It's not what you think—either of you," Hannah said, and tried to concentrate on her breakfast, her appetite gone. She tried a sip of her milk. "Who else is talking about this?"

Hannah knew how quickly news spread in the traveling community. Most of the time she found it charming the way each of them seemed to care so much about everyone else, but there had been times when the gossip had been vicious—and untrue.

"I haven't spoken to Father if that's what you're worried about. As for Lily, I couldn't say. She did try to make excuses for both of you but then Lily has a soft spot when it comes to Levi—and to you."

Hannah wrestled with her options and decided that truth had always been her guiding principle. "Pleasant, you know me and I am telling you that I was working and that yes, Levi came to the office this morning. But it is business—all of it. I don't fully understand it and Levi has asked that I not mention anything to anyone— a promise I have just broken in talking to you. But I would rather break a promise to him than have you believe something that simply is not true."

She watched as Pleasant's expression softened from condemnation to confusion. "But what could you possibly...how much filing could there be that..."

Hannah reached across the table and took her sister-in-law's hand. "I saw something a few days ago that raised a question in my mind. I thought perhaps I might have made a mistake and I wanted to be sure that everything was in order before turning the files over to Ida again. That's why I went there last night."

"And did you find what you were looking for?" Pleasant was leaning closer now, her eyes bright with interest and curiosity.

Oh, I found so much more, Hannah thought. "I'm not certain, but whatever has to do with that is now in Levi's hands. All I plan to concentrate on for the rest of this day is what to say to Caleb when I see him. I am going to need your strength for that, Pleasant, and Gunther's as well, if we are to be successful in reuniting our family."

Pleasant picked at the fried potatoes on Hannah's plate. "How do you think the reunion will go? I mean, how do you expect Caleb to react to seeing you—and us—again?"

"I don't know. I have written him every day and have had only one short note back. The one I showed you."

Pleasant nodded. "The wire. 'I am fine. I miss you. And Auntie. And Gramps,'" she said in a singsong voice. "That one."

"Not exactly what I had hoped for and I suspect Ida was behind it being sent at all. Oh, Pleasant, what if he refuses to come home?"

"Father will make him."

"And then what? He'll run away again and this time things may not turn out so well." Her lighthearted mood of just moments earlier had completely disappeared. She was exhausted and confused and very, very afraid for what the day might bring.

Levi waited for Ginny Danvers to finish ringing up a sale for a customer and see her out.

"Well, Levi Harmon," she said when she spotted him. She came forward wiping her hands on her apron before offering him a businesslike handshake. "To what do I owe this honor?"

Levi grinned sheepishly. When Ginny's husband had been alive, Levi had made a habit of stopping by the store whenever he was in the area and spending an hour or so catching up. "It's been a while," he said.

Ginny nodded. "How about a cup of coffee? Black, right?"

"You wouldn't happen to have any of those ginger cookies back there, would you?"

Ginny laughed and minutes later the two of them were leaning across the counter, drinking coffee and nibbling ginger cookies while Ginny told him about her kids and grandkids. "You still not married?"

"Haven't found the right girl," he said, giving her the stock answer he'd always used. *Oh, but you have*, he thought.

"Clock's ticking," Ginny said with a jerk of her head toward the old grandfather clock that had stood in the corner of the store for as long as Levi could remember. "But you didn't come in here to look at pictures of my family, and you didn't come to talk about your love life." She refilled his cup. "What's going on?"

"It's nothing, really. I was wondering if you might have copies of the bills you submitted for say the past couple of years?"

Ginny lifted one eyebrow. "Sure."

"Could I see them?"

She went through a curtain where he could hear the slide of a metal file drawer opening and a moment later closing. Just then the front doorbell jangled as two customers entered the store.

"Here," Ginny said, sliding the file folder marked with his name across the counter. "Good morning, folks. How can I be of help?"

While Ginny served her customers, Levi studied the invoices. Three years earlier there had been a bill for one hundred dollars marked "paid in cash." It matched an invoice that he'd picked up from the stacks on Hannah's desk, except on his copy the amount paid was for four hundred dollars. By the time Ginny had come back to the counter to ring up her sales, he'd found three similar discrepancies.

Could Chester have pulled this off? Levi studied the changed figures closely. The four was smudged but he knew Jake's handwriting as well as he knew his own, and this wasn't his. Could they be in this thing together?

"You can take that file along if you like," she said. "I've got a duplicate."

"Thanks," Levi replied as he gathered the contents into the file and tipped his hat to the two customers. "Oh, Ginny, do you know of a dry goods business in the area called 'General Dry Goods'?"

"Never heard of 'em," Ginny replied. "Don't be such a stranger next time, okay?"

Outside the dry goods store, Levi stood for a long moment on the sidewalk trying to decide his next move. Down the block he saw a stone building that he knew held the town hall and the police department. There was enough Amish still in Levi that he hated the idea of involving outside law enforcement. He'd always prided himself on being able to manage his own security and business without having to rely on outsiders.

But someone was stealing from him—had been stealing from him for some time. And what that person had failed to understand was that stealing from Levi meant stealing from his hard-working performers and crew, as well. Fury welled up in Levi's chest until he thought he would choke. He had given every employee his trust and his loyalty, but one of them had betrayed him.

There could be only two suspects, he told the police chief. Chester was responsible for making all purchases and submitting the bills, but it was Jake who was responsible for writing the check or issuing the cash to pay those bills.

Please let there be some other explanation, Levi prayed, even as he watched the police chief fill out the warrant necessary to arrest his oldest and dearest friend.

Chapter Fourteen

As the train approached Milwaukee, Hannah and Pleasant decided to spend some time in the club car. It was a gathering place for the cast and more often than not, Fred could be found there strumming his ukulele while others read or talked quietly in small groups. Hannah liked the countryside she was seeing. Rolling fields, freshly plowed and planted, flashed by the wide windows like the patches of a quilt. The day was sunny and fruit trees were in peak blossom. It was late May but spring was just reaching its peak in this part of the country.

She imagined Caleb helping with chores on a farm like those they passed. Pristine, white clapboard farmhouses accented by bright red barns and tall silos and neatly fenced yards. *Please let him have found joy in this life*, she prayed, squeezing her eyes closed and clenching her fingers together.

She felt the train slow and opened her eyes. In the distance, she could see the blue waters of Lake Michigan as they approached the city. As they reached the station, she was aware that the general buzz of conversation had grown more animated. Everyone seemed intrigued as a man in a dark suit and derby hat boarded the train. He entered their car and walked the length of it, his hands behind his back as he studied each of them.

"Where would I find Mr. Harmon?" he asked of no one and at the same time everyone.

Fred jerked his head toward the rear of the train. "Private car three cars back," he said. Then he waited for the man to leave and signaled two other male performers to follow him. The three of them gave the stranger a head start and then trailed him back through the train.

It had already been an unsettling day. Levi had returned from his walk into town accompanied by the local police chief. They had gone into the payroll office and closed the door. Minutes later Jake had emerged, slammed his hat onto his head and strode off toward town even as the last of the railway cars snapped into place and the conductor signaled that it was time to be on board.

The women who had been watching the loading of the last wagon and speculating about Jake's sudden departure, had no choice but to get on board. Now yet another law enforcement officer had arrived.

"Federal agent," Lily whispered to Hannah. "Something's up."

Hannah thought about the invoices and the discrepancies in amounts paid. *Was Levi in trouble?* "Where are Fred and the others going?"

"To protect Levi and make sure there's no trouble, I expect."

Moments later, Levi and the agent walked back through the car, followed closely by Fred and his two friends. All of the men seemed intent on the same mission as they looked neither left nor right but headed straight into the next car forward…the payroll car. The women all crowded onto the platform connecting the two cars jostling each other for the best position to see what was happening.

Hannah had once gone into a movie theater to search for Caleb and his friends, and had been struck by the lack of sound while actors clearly in distress poured out their stories through gesture and expression. Watching what unfolded in the next few minutes behind the closed glass door of the payroll car was a little like that.

She saw the agent approach Chester who was sitting at his desk. Chester stood and began shouting and gesturing wildly. He started toward the door but Fred and his men blocked the way. The agent took out a pair of handcuffs and put them on Chester, who crumpled back into his desk chair and began to cry. Then he raised his head and began pleading with Levi.

And all the while Hannah watched as Levi stood stone still, arms folded across his body, with no discernible expression on his face. Then he turned, saw the women crowded outside the door and abruptly turned the other way then exited at the far end of the payroll car. Hannah saw his shoulders slump just before he went through the far door and realized that what she and the others had taken for indifference was in fact an emotion so strong that he'd barely been able to hold himself together.

She pushed her way through the gaggle of women returning to their seats and entered the payroll car.

"Got it covered," she heard Fred tell the law officer. "We'll be in Baraboo by supper time. The three of us can take turns keeping watch on him until then."

Chester raised his head and spotted Hannah. "Why don't you question her?" he sneered. "Ask her what she was doing here late at night—with the boss."

Hannah felt the heat of embarrassment rise up her neck until it flamed bright pink in her cheeks.

"You are?" the agent asked not yet looking up from the small notebook where he was fanning through pages, apparently searching for some piece of information he needed.

"Hannah Goodloe," she murmured.

He glanced her way and then his eyes widened. "You're Amish?"

"Yes."

He whipped off his hat. "On a circus train?"

"Yes."

"She worked here same as me," Chester said. "Had keys same as me."

"But was not here stealing from us for the past year— same as you," Fred said sarcastically. "My understanding is that it was Mrs. Goodloe who uncovered the evidence," he added, speaking to the agent but smiling at Hannah.

"That was good detective work, ma'am," the agent said.

"And what about Jake? Anybody think to look at him?" Chester continued to rant.

"Looked at him and cleared him," the agent flung over his shoulder. "Now shut up." He gave Hannah an apologetic smile. "Was there something you needed to tell me, ma'am?"

"No. I just…" She peered past him to the platform outside the rear door where she could see Levi leaning heavily against the railing, his eyes closed as he raised his face to the wind. "Mr. Harmon seems to be in some distress. I thought perhaps a glass of water?"

The federal agent nodded and Hannah rushed to the

water cooler. It burped and gurgled as she filled a cup and then balancing it carefully, headed for the door.

"Allow me," Fred said and pulled it open for her, giving Levi the sign that all was under control before allowing the door to close behind her.

Hannah handed Levi the water and it sloshed over his fingers a little as he drank it down. "Thanks," he mouthed, the sound of his voice carried away on the rush of wind that snatched at her skirts and prayer cap.

Hannah nodded but did not go back inside the payroll car. Instead, she stood by waiting to see what Levi might do. He had returned to the position of holding on to the guardrail, his head bent, his shoulders slumped. And then she was certain that she saw a tear fly from his cheek on the wind.

"I accused Jake," he said, as if he couldn't quite believe it. "My oldest and dearest friend and I accused him of stealing from me."

She opened her mouth but words would not come.

"I ruined a friendship and for what? Some missing money?"

"How did you find out it was Chester?"

"I didn't want to think it was either man, but after the way Jake looked at me and then just walked away, I knew I'd made a terrible mistake. I just couldn't figure out how Chester had pulled it off."

"And how did he?" Instinctively, she knew that it was best to let him talk, to let him relive the whole story.

"He created a couple of front companies. It's not hard to do—pick a name and file some paperwork. And then if there was a vendor he knew dealt only in cash, those were the ones he targeted. He would rewrite the order for his dummy company charging twice what the vendor charged, then he would submit the invoice to Jake who would give him the cash to pay the vendor—himself. Chester would pay the true vendor and pocket the rest."

"But you told Jake that you wanted supplies to be ordered from Danvers regardless of the cost."

"Because Jake was the only one who could hand out the cash," Levi said. "What was I supposed to think? How could Chester pull this off—especially for so long—without his help? I thought that they were in this together."

"But Jake didn't know?"

"Chester explained the orders from his dummy company by telling Jake that Danvers couldn't supply in the amounts we needed. Earlier, he stole the cash by changing the numbers on the invoices—a one turned into a four…like that. But that became too risky so he set up the companies and once he did that, stealing got a whole lot easier."

He still wasn't looking at her, just flinging his story out to the wind as if in doing so he might be rid of his shame.

"Did Jake say anything before he walked away?" She was suddenly afraid that the man Levi depended on the most had left for good.

"He said that I had changed and it wasn't for the better." Levi dropped his chin to his chest and his knuckles faded to white as he gripped the railing and a shudder ran the length of his body. "He won't be back and the truth is, I don't blame him."

Hannah stepped forward and placed her palm on his back as much to steady herself as to comfort him. But when she felt his shoulders heave she left it there and moved so that she was blocking him from view of the others. "It'll all work out," she crooned, moving close enough so that her mouth was close to his ear. "Everything will work out."

And silently she prayed that it might be so.

Dusk was settling in by the time they arrived in Baraboo, but Hannah was determined to see Caleb as soon as possible. Levi was occupied with the business of Chester's arrest and she hadn't wanted to trouble him with her problems. But as always, he had made all the necessary arrangements.

"Mrs. Goodloe?"

A gray-haired woman dressed in a lavender business suit was waiting on the platform. She stepped forward and offered Hannah a firm handshake. "I am Ida Benson. Levi asked that I arrange to take you and your in-laws out to the farm as soon as you arrived. I do hope this mode of transportation suits?"

She pointed to a black hack hitched to a gray horse. Standing next to it was a man dressed in plain clothes who nodded at her but did not come forward.

"This will do just fine," Hannah assured her then turned to introduce her to Pleasant and Gunther.

"Come and meet Matthew Harnisher," Ida said. "Caleb has been staying with Matthew and his wife, Mae, and their four children."

"You are Amish?" Gunther asked, eyeing the buggy and then Ida's lavender suit.

"No," she explained. "But Matthew and Mae are Old Order Amish—like your family." She made the introductions and then while Matthew supervised the loading of their luggage, the three of them crowded into the buggy—Pleasant and Hannah in back and Gunther sharing the driver's seat with Matthew.

"Your boy is well," Ida told Hannah, grasping her hand and commanding her attention.

"But?"

Ida nodded, clearly relieved that Hannah had understood that physical wellness was not the entire story. "He is…anxious about seeing you again. He knows he did wrong and yet…" She searched for the right words. "It may take some time, Hannah."

"I understand," Hannah assured her. But as she stared at her father-in-law's straight unyielding back on the ride from the station to the Harnisher farm, she couldn't help but wonder if understanding would be enough.

It hardly mattered in the end for as they drove into the yard of the farm, Matthew's wife, Mae, came running down the steps to meet them.

"He's gone," she called. "The boys and I searched everywhere, but he's not here."

Levi had meant to go with the Goodloes when they went to collect Caleb. He had thought to ease the way for the boy. Gunther was old school and would not take kindly to the trouble the boy had put them through. He was given to lecturing—as Levi's stable help had complained more than once over the past several days. And Levi well remembered that at young Caleb's age, the very last thing a boy would heed was a lecture.

But he would have to leave that to Ida and Matthew. His first concern had to be his business. The local police had met the train and taken Chester into custody. He would spend time in jail until a trial could be arranged. In the meantime, Levi would meet with his lawyer and build the case. The more he thought about what Chester had done, the angrier he got. And when he realized that Chester's betrayal had resulted in Levi accusing Jake, fury turned to rage and he was bent on seeking his revenge.

When it had been only money he had lost, he had thought he might be able to handle the whole thing himself. But when the policeman had questioned Jake, and Levi had seen the look of utter disbelief and disappointment on his friend's face, he had known that Chester had stolen something far more precious.

At least in the midst of all this trauma he could take some comfort in knowing that Hannah was being reunited with her son. Although that reunion also had a dark side in that it meant that far too soon the Goodloe family would take the first possible train back to Florida.

A wave of loneliness washed over Levi like the surf breaking on the beach on a stormy day. The feeling was so overpowering that it took his breath away. He was a man who many would say had everything anyone could hope for—money, power, friends. But he had destroyed his best friend's trust and after his parents had died he had willingly—and foolishly—walked away from the family he had left. Over the years, he had stayed in contact with his brother, Matt, but his letters to his grandparents and his sisters had all been returned unopened. Many times Matt had urged him to come home to Wisconsin and start a family of his own, but what kind of life could he offer a wife and children? What kind of stability?

And so the circus people had become his family. Ida and Lily, like sisters to him. Hans, Jake and Chester, like brothers. But now Jake was gone. Chester had betrayed him, and truth be told, he knew none of the others thought of him as "family." He was their employer—a benevolent one to be sure—but hardly their brother. If he were gone tomorrow, what would he have left as his legacy? A circus? A mansion in Florida?

Levi had dismissed his driver outside the police station, saying he needed to walk, and for the past two hours he'd been wandering aimlessly, trying to bring some order to the chaotic thoughts that raced through his mind. It was dark now and he found himself on a country road far from the railway station and far from the compound that served as the summer quarters for the circus. He heard the wail of a train whistle moving east and recalled how, as a boy, a similar whistle had been like a siren's song for him.

He realized that he had wandered all the way out to where his grandfather's farm—Matthew's farm now—bordered the road. It had started to rain so he shoved his hands into the pockets of his trousers and hunched his shoulders against a north wind as he recognized that the person he most needed to see was at that farm. Hannah.

Turning a corner, he made out another solitary figure limping badly along the road ahead of him. "Wait up," he shouted, and the person started to run, then stumbled and fell.

"I'm not going to hurt you," Levi said as he caught up and knelt down. He saw that this was a boy, hatless and dirty. "What happened?" he asked.

"Nothing. I fell."

"Falling isn't nothing," Levi said. "Did you twist your ankle?"

The boy nodded.

"Where were you headed?"

"Train." He choked on the word and Levi realized the

boy was crying. "But I just heard the whistle and now it's gone and…"

"My name's Levi," he said calmly as he gently probed the kid's ankle for the possibility of a broken bone. "And you are?"

"Caleb."

Levi put it together then. The plain clothes, muddy now from the two falls, the hair that hung straight and limp covering the boy's ears. The proximity to Matthew Harnisher's farm. He could take him back there but what was to keep the boy from trying to run again? From making the same mistake that he had made all those years ago? "Well, Caleb, tell you what. How about I help you get to my compound so we can have my doctor take a look at that ankle?"

"I don't think I can walk."

"Good point. Well, then let's just wait here. Somebody's bound to come along." Levi scooted his back up against the lower boughs of a sheltering evergreen tree, plopped his hat on the boy's head and then wrapped his arms around his knees. "Amish, are you?"

Caught off guard, the boy nodded.

"Me, too. Wanna hear a story while we wait?"

Again the nod.

It was quickly decided that Gunther and Pleasant would stay at the farm with Mae and the boys while Hannah went with Matthew to search for Caleb. There was little doubt which way he'd headed. Matthew's son, Lars, admitted that Caleb had told him of his plan and even tried to get Lars to join him.

"He'll have cut across that pasture and the cornfields

beyond and eventually come to the road back toward town," Matthew said. "We'll find him along the road."

Hannah nodded, no longer sure of anything. She wished Levi were with them. He would know what to do, what to say to Caleb to convince him to come home with her. As the horse trotted along the narrow road, Hannah did the only thing she knew to do in such circumstances—she prayed for the wisdom to know what words would change Caleb's mind about a life better than theirs in Florida once they found him. If they found him. If he would listen.

"Are you warm enough?" Matthew asked, jarring her from her meditation and back to the reality of their journey. It had started to rain again.

"Yes. Thank you for doing this. I hope that Caleb has not been thoughtless or unkind."

Matthew laughed. "On the contrary. The boy was so good-natured and helpful with chores and all, that we found him a good addition to our family." He let the horse amble along, reins slack.

Hannah fought against the urge to ask him to go faster.

"It was only as the time got closer that he changed," Matthew said.

"What time?"

"Your arrival. He got quieter then, nothing much to say, although he continued to tend to the chores and help Mae out around the house. Just went inside himself some and seemed to spend a good deal of his time following me around."

"He misses his father."

"*Ja.* That's what I told Levi." He tightened the reins and clucked softly to the horse as he peered ahead.

"How do you know Levi?" she asked more to keep the conversation alive than anything else.

Matthew glanced at her, his features shadowed by the dark and the wide brim of his hat. "He's my brother."

Hannah was certain she had heard him wrong. "You mean that you are friends—that..."

"Blood brothers," he said. "I see he did not tell you this."

"No." Her mind raced with myriad thoughts—Levi was Amish? But the last names were...

"He changed his name after he left the farm." He chuckled. "I tease him that he showed little imagination. Harmon and Harnisher. For a circus man, I thought he might have done better."

"How old were you when he left?"

"Just twelve. Levi was fourteen. He would have been baptized that year."

"You must have been very sad when he left."

Again the chuckle. "I was very angry to be sure. He was supposed to be the man of the family and now that would fall to me. Your boy and I talked about that some. About that responsibility coming on so suddenly and all."

"It seems that you met the responsibility," she ventured.

"*Ja.* And so will Caleb in time. He does not wish to leave his faith, Hannah. He just wishes to try his wings a bit, find his own way rather than the way of his father or grandfather."

"But isn't that what Levi did?"

Matthew shifted on the seat. "The difference is that my brother is still out there. He is still running away. Your Caleb is not Levi. Your Caleb runs because he knows he has a place to come home to. Levi never had that until it was too late."

"His grandfather?"

"Levi blamed him for sending Pa out that night and for not stopping Ma from following him. Our grandfather was the head of our household and in Levi's mind, the responsibility for the animals was his—not our father's. Levi couldn't forgive that."

"But you did forgive Levi for leaving?"

"He is my only brother. God showed me that I had a choice—I could hold on to my anger and disappointment or I could let it go. I chose to let it go and in time after the death of our grandparents, Levi came back to us."

Hannah thought suddenly of Jake. What if Jake never forgave Levi?

"Somebody's up there," Matthew muttered and urged the horse forward.

Hannah followed his gaze and saw a man standing on the side of the road waving to them. "It's Levi," she murmured, and knew in that moment that he had become such a part of her that she would know him anywhere even on the blackest of nights.

"Levi!" Matthew called out and drew the wagon closer then hopped down. "Are you all right?"

"Fine." The two men greeted each other with the traditional Amish handshake—one pump of their clasped hands. Then Levi looked past Matthew to Hannah. "He's all right," he said, and stood aside to reveal Caleb sound asleep against a tree. "Took a couple of tumbles and might have broken his ankle."

While Hannah climbed into the back of the buggy, Matthew helped Levi hoist Caleb into the buggy next to her. "Thank you," she whispered as she cradled her son in her arms. He stirred for only a minute before falling into a deeper sleep, his head resting on her shoulder. He seemed to have grown some in the short time he'd been gone, and yet he fit perfectly into the curve of her shoulder. "Thank you both."

"Let's take him into town and get that ankle looked at," Levi told Matthew as the two men climbed into the buggy. "Then you can all go back to the farm and get some rest."

"He was running away again," Hannah said as Matthew snapped the reins and they started toward town. "I heard the train whistle and I thought…" She could not find the words to go on.

Levi reached back and touched her cheek. "He's safe," he told her.

But for how long?

Chapter Fifteen

By the time they saw the doctor and got back to the farm, it was past midnight. Hannah really did not want to question Levi about his past with Matthew there, and so they did not speak of it.

"Are you all right?" he asked as Matthew carried Caleb across the yard and up the front porch steps.

"Yes. Thank you for finding him and for staying with him."

Mae was making a fuss over the boy, insisting that he get into dry clothes and have something to eat before he went to bed. Gunther waited until Matthew had gotten Caleb into the house and then turned and walked away.

"I should go," Hannah told Levi, although what she wanted most of all was to ask him why—why he had left the farm. Why he had changed his name. Why he had never told her that he was Amish. It made perfect sense now in hindsight. The way he seemed to know of their ways.

"May I stop by tomorrow?"

"Yes. Caleb would like that," she said, and ran across

the lawn and into the house before he could say anything more.

But that night she lay awake trying to imagine Levi living in this house. She heard the rumble of a freight train in the distance and wondered if Levi had lain awake planning his escape—if Caleb were even now lying awake planning to run away again.

Levi did not come the next day nor the day after that. Lily stopped by with Fred, who had Caleb laughing at his antics within five minutes of meeting him. It was so good to hear her son's laughter and she realized how very frightened she had been that she might never see him again.

"Levi had said he might come to visit Caleb," Hannah ventured later when she and Lily were sitting on the porch watching Fred and Caleb toss a baseball back and forth. Caleb had begged to get outside and Matthew had brought down an old wheelchair that his grandfather had used and set it up in the yard.

"He went to Milwaukee for a few days. Someone sent word that Jake had been there. He's been like a caged tiger waiting for any news at all so when he heard this, he drove all night to get there."

"I hope he finds him," Hannah said.

"Jake is a hothead," Lily said. "Hopefully he's cooled down enough to realize that if he'd been in Levi's shoes he would have thought the same thing. Those two can be oil and water, but in a good way. Without them, I doubt the company would have made it. These are hard times," she added almost as an afterthought, as she stared off into the distance. But then she shook off her melancholy and focused her attention on Caleb. "But you have your boy back and that's wonderful."

They sipped lemonade and watched the game of catch for a few minutes. Hannah couldn't help noticing that Lily seemed wistful as she watched Caleb.

"Lily? You once mentioned that you're a mother like me, but…"

"My son drowned accidentally when he was four," Lily said. "He would have been sixteen now. Sometimes when I see a boy—even a younger one like Caleb—I think about my Lonnie and wonder what he would have been like. He was such a happy kid—never a tear, never a frown. It made you smile just to look at him—like looking up at the sun."

"I'm sorry for your loss, Lily."

"After that, his father left and I just stayed on with the circus. It was Brody's Circus then—a ragtag bunch of acts with a couple of exotic animals. Then Levi took over and he brought Jake in to work with him and within a year, we were playing bigger towns and bringing in enough to buy more animals and so it grew."

Hannah fought against the question she had longed to ask Lily for weeks and lost. "Were you and Levi—I mean, did the two of you…"

Lily laughed. "Oh, honey, he was always so out of my league. I won't deny that I was interested—more than interested. I mean, the man is gorgeous and smart and kind in the bargain. We shared a couple of dinners but a girl knows when the guy's heart just isn't in it. His wasn't and I realized that having him for a friend was going to do me a lot more good. Now Jake…" she said and rolled her eyes. "That is a whole different can of worms."

"You love Jake?"

"I understand Jake," she corrected. "Love?" She frowned as if she'd just uttered a foreign word. "Yeah, maybe so." She stood up and drank the last of her lemonade. "Hey, Fred, you ready to go?"

As Hannah walked with Lily and Fred to their car, Lily linked arms with Hannah. "We miss you," she said. "You were good for us—you and Miss Pleasant and Gunther. You were good for Levi."

"You're embarrassing her," Fred said. "It is not her way to accept compliments." He grinned as they all recalled how many times one of the Goodloe family had had to explain that something was or was not "their way."

"Let us know when you're heading for Florida," Lily said, kissing Hannah on the cheek before climbing into the flashy yellow roadster that they had arrived in. "We'll have a big send-off waiting for you at the station—brass band—the works."

"No brass band," Hannah begged and then realized her friend was teasing her.

Fred gunned the motor and it split the idyllic quiet of the countryside. "Farewell, Hannah," he called as he spun the wheels and drove away with Lily waving wildly.

Hannah turned back to the house and saw Caleb still sitting in his wheelchair, idly tossing the ball in the air and catching it. When she came close enough, he lofted the ball in her direction and smiled when she caught it.

"Not bad, Ma."

She tossed it back to him. "You should rest."

"Ah, Ma, I broke a bone. It's not like I got pneumonia or something."

If Caleb had any intention of trying to run again, he was going to be hampered by the heavy plaster cast the doctor had applied after determining that indeed the boy had broken his ankle. Hannah had never imagined she would be thanking God for breaking her child's bone, but at the moment it did seem a blessing.

He glanced toward the stables. "When do you think I might be able to help Grandpa down there?"

Since their arrival at the farm, Gunther had taken charge of the horses and spent much of the day in the barn. Hannah suspected that it was at least in part due to his indecision about what to say to Caleb. She took hold of the handles for steering Caleb's wheelchair and started rolling him down to the barn. "Let's go see. Surely there's something you can do to help."

Gunther was sitting at a carpenter's bench mending a piece of harness when they entered the barn. He did not acknowledge either of them, and Hannah could practically feel Caleb's nervousness as she wheeled him toward his grandfather.

Before Caleb had run away, his relationship with Gunther had been a good one. The difference in generations had made Gunther less strict with Caleb than he had been with his own son. The two of them had gone fishing together in Sarasota Bay and returned with large live conch shells for her to figure out how best to clean and cook.

How they had laughed the first time they had handed her one of the beautiful shells so large that she had to hold it in two hands. But then the animal inhabiting the shell had begun to move and extend its strange foot and Hannah had yelped and dropped the shell on the ground. Gunther had nudged Caleb and winked and the two of them had collapsed into guffaws of laughter.

But ever since they had arrived in Wisconsin, Gunther had kept his distance from the boy. He did not come to visit him as he lay in bed recuperating. He did not ask about him at the supper table, although Hannah had seen his eyes brighten with interest when she and Mae discussed Caleb's progress.

Well, it's time to put a stop to this, Hannah thought and opened her mouth to address her father-in-law.

"Caleb," he said before she could get a word out. "Hand me that awl there on that haystack."

Hannah let go of the wheelchair handles and nodded to Caleb. He rolled himself over to the haystack to retrieve the awl and then transported it to Gunther.

"Now hold this like so," Gunther said, demonstrating how Caleb should anchor the harness strap for him.

As their heads bent toward one another and Gunther's litany of instruction continued, Hannah knew that everything was going to be all right between them. She slipped out of the barn without either of them noticing and did not see them again until Mae rang the bell calling everyone in for supper.

That night Caleb sat next to Gunther, regaling him with his ideas for how he had been thinking of offering his services for caring for horses once they got back to Florida. "If you'll help me," he added, looking shyly up at his grandfather.

"*Ja.* I can help," Gunther replied, and turned his attention back to his supper.

Caleb glanced over at Hannah and grinned, and in that moment she knew that her son was home to stay—or would be as soon as they could get a train back.

Levi was troubled. And he should have been relieved. He had caught the thief and Chester was safely behind bars. Hannah had been reunited with her son and, after his misadventures that had led to a broken ankle, the boy seemed content to return to Florida. The company had arrived safely back in Baraboo and as always, Ida had everything under control. In short, he had nothing to worry about for a change.

And yet…

He sat at his desk and studied the list of potential new acts that Jake had given him. In a week or so he would head east to audition the best of the lot. It was a trip he had always enjoyed, but it was a trip he and Jake had always made together. He had spent three days searching for Jake in Milwaukee and on down to Chicago with no success.

In spite of that, his life was about to get back to its normal routine so why was he so jumpy? So out of sorts?

Outside, the rain came in a steady downpour. It had rained for days now and there was talk of flooding to the west. Perhaps the train to Florida would be delayed.

And then what?

He had no future with Hannah so the wisest course had to be to let her go. But he wasn't yet ready to do that. Oh, he was well aware that the day had to come. He just wasn't ready for that day to come so soon.

Mae had settled Caleb back into the room he'd shared with Lars, the oldest of her four boys, but now he shared it with his grandfather as well as Lars. She and Matthew made up bunks in the barn for the other children so that Pleasant and Hannah could have their room. It was a tight fit but one that Caleb seemed to revel in.

"It's a real family, Ma," he said one day as she sat with him shelling spring peas and listening to the rain that continued to fall steadily.

"We're a real family, as well," she replied.

Caleb grew quiet and stared out the window to the

corn field that he'd helped Matthew and his sons plow and plant. "Not like this," he said softly.

Hannah set the bowl of shelled peas aside and sat down on the edge of Caleb's bed. "You miss your father," she said, combing his silky straight hair with her fingers. "So do I."

"I don't remember him so much," he admitted, "but I guess I miss the idea of a father—and brothers. Even sisters might be okay," he said miserably.

Hannah couldn't help it. She laughed and rumpled his hair, messing up the grooming she'd been doing. "I thought you didn't like girls."

Caleb grinned sheepishly. "Some of 'em are all right, I guess."

"Really? Anyone in particular?"

"Ah, Ma," he protested, and ducked away from her.

"You've got a visitor," Mae announced as she climbed the wooden stairs.

Hannah and Caleb looked toward the door. "Levi!" Caleb shouted.

"Mr. Harmon," Hannah corrected her son firmly.

Levi handed Caleb a package wrapped in brown paper and string, which the boy tore into immediately. It was a book on horses. "Thanks, Le…Mr. Harmon. Thanks a lot," Caleb said, and started turning the pages of the book.

"You didn't have to bring a gift," Hannah said shyly.

Levi shrugged. "The boy and I had some time to get to know each other the other night. I discovered that he likes hanging around horses. Must have picked that up from his grandfather." He shot Caleb a look. "I thought maybe you might like to share that with your grandfather," Levi added. "Word has it the two of you might be going into the horse business."

Caleb grinned and Hannah could have hugged the man for validating her son's idea. "Thank you," she said.

"Well, those peas are not going to cook themselves," Mae announced from her position in the doorway. "If you'll excuse me I need to start supper." She reached for the peas.

"I'll help," Hannah said.

"No, you've been cooped up in this house all day. It looks like we've finally a break in the showers so Levi, take the woman for a walk so she can get a little fresh air. It's a lovely spring day for all its dampness and we aren't always so blessed here in Wisconsin with such balmy breezes."

"Sounds like a fine idea," Levi said.

Hannah was torn, reluctant to let Caleb out of her sight. In spite of his plans to care for the horses of neighbors back in Sarasota, Hannah could not help but wonder if that would be enough excitement for the boy.

"He's not going anywhere," Mae said. "Are you, Caleb?"

Caleb blushed. "No, ma'am."

"I won't be long," Hannah promised, leaning in to kiss his forehead.

"Ah, Ma," he fussed and turned his attention back to his book.

Outside, she and Levi strolled toward the orchard, taking care to avoid the soggier parts of the lawn. All around them, cherry blossoms past their peak showered down like snow, their sweetness perfuming the warm spring air. Levi walked with his hands clenched behind his back while Hannah kept hers folded piously in front of her.

"It was kind of you to think of Caleb," she said, unable to bear the silence that stretched between them like a tightwire.

"He's a good boy. A bright boy," he added.

"Things between Caleb and his grandfather have not been easy, but with time I think perhaps…"

"I gathered as much. I ran into Gunther in town. He was making arrangements for your trip back to Florida and told me about the boy's idea. He seemed hopeful—but cautious, like you."

Hannah had known the day would come when they had to leave, but so soon? Caleb was still in the cast and…

"I can't let you go quite yet," Levi said, not looking at her but focusing instead on the horizon.

"I don't understand." But, oh, how she hoped. Was he going to ask her to stay? And what if he did?

Levi stopped walking and turned to face her. "I need you to testify in court in the case against Chester."

For an instant, it felt as if she had been doused with a bucket of cold water. Her mind had been so full of what if's and maybes but not in her wildest imaginings would she have expected such a statement.

"I couldn't possibly," she said, the words no more than a whisper around her shock that he would even ask such a thing. "We are Amish," she added as if he hadn't known that. "We do not take part in the English legal system. It is our way. You, of all people, know that we cannot swear an oath and we cannot…"

"Stop telling me what you can and cannot do," he snapped impatiently. "Without your testimony we may not have enough evidence to…"

"I cannot do this and you must not ask it of me," she interrupted and turned to head back to the house.

"You would let a thief go free—someone who stole not only from me but from people who have befriended you these past few weeks?"

She stopped and turned to face him. "It is…"

"…not your way. I get that." He removed his hat and ran his fingers through his thick hair in frustration.

"It is not *your* way." She covered the distance between them, wanting to shout the words at him. Instead, she pressed her fists to her skirt to stem the tide of her anger. "You are Amish."

"Was," he corrected. "I made my choice long ago. I am as much an outsider now as anyone in my company."

His bitterness surprised her.

"And at the moment," he continued, "it is my company I must think of. Chester has taken more than money. He has stolen the trust I worked so hard to build with these people. They look at each other now with suspicion and doubt. They look at me differently."

His pain was so obvious in his haggard features that Hannah had to resist touching his face. As if touching him would do anything to smooth away the exhaustion and distress she saw there.

"Levi, think of it. Chester has been your good friend and a valued employee. He was not always a thief. Why did he steal? Have you asked him that?"

"I don't know—greed, selfishness, because it was easy. What do the reasons matter? He did it and kept doing it. And I didn't see it. Nor did Jake. That's the point."

"And so he must go to jail? That is the only possible recourse? That will make things right with you?"

"What would you have me do, Hannah? Forgive and forget? This is not just about my selfish interests. These people work for me—if they see that nothing is done about a man who steals, then what?"

"It is not for me to say what you should do—only God can tell you that. But you must be willing to listen." She took half a step closer and stood her ground. "And I must ask that you respect that I cannot and will not break with my traditions to do what you think must be done."

He stared down at her for a long moment and then carefully picked an errant blossom petal from her hair. "I would walk through fire for you, Hannah," he said and had Mae not chosen that moment to sound the dinner bell, she realized that he would have kissed her.

Levi had thought that he could keep her close by insisting that she testify. He didn't really need her to do that. Chester had confessed to opening accounts for dummy companies that he'd established, as well as confessed to forging by changing the amounts on certain invoices.

When Levi realized the extent of Chester's deceit, he was furious. But just then in the orchard he had seen in Hannah's eyes and heard in her question, the truth of the situation. This was not about justice. It was about revenge. Chester had betrayed him, and Levi had the need to make an example of the man lest anyone else think they could hoodwink him in the future. His anger and hurt carried over to Jake who he felt should have questioned the bills, the higher prices.

But he'd seen the bills as well, noticed the higher costs. Had Levi questioned anything? No, he had trusted a man who had worked for him for over ten years. And yet throwing the man in jail did not feel right. Chester behind bars did not make Levi feel any sense of peace.

Only God can tell you what to do, Hannah had said.

Later that night Levi wandered into the kitchen of his modest Wisconsin home—a home far less elegant than the mansion in Sarasota. Hans sat at the kitchen table reading.

"Sir?" He was immediately on his feet ready to serve.

"Just came for some water," Levi said. "What are you reading there?"

"Scripture from the book of Matthew," Hans answered.

"I didn't realize you were a religious man, Hans."

"It was a habit I developed on the trip here. Gunther—Mr. Goodloe—read some every night. I found that it was a good way to set aside the worries of the day. We also started each morning with a reading," he added.

"So read me a passage," Levi said, as he leaned against the sink and drank his water.

Hans cleared his throat. "Blessed are the poor in spirit, for theirs is the kingdom of heaven. Blessed are they who mourn, for they shall be comforted. Blessed are the meek, for they shall inherit the earth. Blessed are they who hunger and thirst for righteousness, for they shall be satisfied. Blessed are the merciful, for they shall obtain mercy. Blessed are the pure of heart, for they shall see God. Blessed are the peacemakers, for they shall be called children of God. Blessed are they who are persecuted for the sake of righteousness, for theirs is the kingdom of heaven."

Levi stood for a long time staring out the kitchen window at the rain sluicing down the glass. "Thank you, Hans. Sleep well," he said softly.

"And you," Hans replied, and left Levi alone.

Chapter Sixteen

On Sunday, families came from all around the area to crowd into the Harnisher home for services. It was their turn to host the services and Mae had been cleaning for days. As the others arrived, Lars and his brothers took charge of unhitching the horses and getting them out of the rain into the barn. Men unloaded the backless benches from the bench wagon that moved with the services from house to house. Mae had insisted on leaving some of the more comfortable chairs in place for older members of the congregation.

The benches replaced the large table where the family normally gathered for meals. Men sat together at the front and women at the back. This was a small group and so everyone was able to crowd into the one room.

Three chairs had been placed at the very front of the room for the ministers and the bishop to occupy. While the first hymn was sung, the two ministers, bishop and deacon retired to another room to decide who would preach that day and in what order. During the hymn, people continued to arrive and find their place in the crowded room.

Caleb leaned on his crutches and took his place next to his grandfather. As the first hymn began, Hannah watched Caleb carefully, worried that it might be too soon for him to be up and around, when she heard Pleasant gasp.

"It's him," her sister-in-law whispered, her eyes darting quickly toward the door and then back again to her hands folded tightly in her lap. The hint of a smile tugged at the corners of her normally tight-lipped mouth.

Hannah watched a jovial young man greet several of his peers and elders gathered in the outer hallway. He was at least two inches shorter than Pleasant was. He had a ruddy round face and an easy smile, and Hannah could understand how a woman as reserved as Pleasant might be taken by such an easygoing and gregarious young man.

She nudged her sister-in-law with her shoulder and smiled her approval. Pleasant covered a girlish giggle of delight by pretending to cough. But then her eyes darkened, her face reddened and she went as still as a stone.

"What?" Hannah whispered, thinking Pleasant might have choked. She glanced toward the door ready to cry out for help when she saw the reason for Pleasant's distress. Or rather the reasons.

For following the young man into the room was a woman, small and heavy with child and three additional children who could not have looked any more like their father.

Pleasant threw off Hannah's hand of comfort and as the pregnant woman and her two youngest children slid on to the bench next to her, Pleasant sat up even straighter. Her jaw was firm, her eyes pinning the man with accusation. He glanced their way then, and clearly recognized Pleasant. To Hannah's shock, he smiled and nodded as he might in greeting someone he hadn't seen in some time but was pleased to see now.

All through the services Hannah tried to concentrate but she went through the rituals by rote. All the while next to her, Pleasant simmered with indignation and fury.

As the main sermon was being delivered in a singsong style and in the High German preferred by this group, Hannah could think only of what Pleasant had told her of the man. He had come to Florida to visit a sick uncle and offer help with the crops that winter. He had talked of looking at some land to buy, of possibly coming to Florida to live. She knew that he had come to the bakery every morning that he was in the area and that he and Pleasant had talked of the weather and the crops and his uncle's improving health. She knew that he had compli-mented Pleasant on her cake donuts, claiming they were lighter than air.

But there had been no more to it than that. He had not walked with Pleasant or taken her for a ride in his un-cle's buggy. Pleasant had admitted as much, hoping that perhaps if they could see each other again in Wisconsin, things might move to that next level of official courting. In the days that they had spent traveling north, Hannah could see now that Pleasant had built an entire picture in her mind of how things might develop between her and the boyish-looking farmer.

The hope that romance awaited her had been behind her announcement that night that she might just stay in Wisconsin. She stole a look at her sister-in-law as the sec-ond minister droned on. Pleasant's face was composed, her eyes seemingly riveted on the preacher while her hands writhed as she twisted a lace handkerchief into a coiled rope of her misery.

Hannah's heart went out to this woman who, over the duration of their journey, had become her friend. And then she had a thought that made all other thoughts fly away like the sound of the minister's words through the open windows in the close little room.

What if she had also misjudged Levi's feelings for her? What if she, like Pleasant, had taken his attentions for something more than was intended? What a fool she must appear to someone so worldly. She thought back to those moments when she had been most susceptible to his kindness, his gentle touch, his kiss...

In every case it could be said that he had wanted something from her, needed something. Like in the orchard the day before when he had told her he needed her to testify in court. Mortified, she closed her eyes tightly as she recalled how her heart had soared at the touch of his lips on hers that night in the payroll car that now seemed a thousand years ago. Why would a man like Levi have the slightest interest in a plain woman like her? He had his pick of the women in his company and of the women in the towns they traveled through. And there were the wealthy society women Hannah had seen on the streets of Sarasota riding through town in their fancy cars, the tops down and their laughter trailing behind them like expensive perfume.

As he had said, he had made his choice. It had been years since he had run away to the outside world and he had never come back.

Fool.

She felt Pleasant's eyes on her and realized that she, like her sister-in-law, had suddenly sat up a bit straighter and clenched her fingers into fists. Pleasant reached over and covered one of Hannah's fists with her open palm. Clearly, she thought that Hannah's anger was an expression of solidarity and perhaps in a way it was, for they had both been foolish and naive.

When the services finally ended, the room was transformed once again in preparation for the noon meal to be shared before everyone started for home. Because converting some benches to tables took more room and left less seating, the congregation would be served in shifts. While some stood talking on the covered side porch that ran the length of the house, others had their meal and then the order reversed until all were fed. Again, everyone squeezed onto the long benches set next to tables laden with a variety of dishes that would serve as a light lunch. Mae's best jam, apple butter and pickled beets filled dishes up and down the length of the table. There was homemade bread and cheese. Knowing that in just two days she and her family would be on a train back to Florida, Hannah stood a little to one side of the gathering taking it all in. Their gatherings in Florida were not so different from this one and she could not help wishing that Levi could somehow realize that this was where he belonged.

While everyone else was at church or sleeping in for the morning, Levi entered the small cell where his front man was being held. Chester's face was lined with exhaustion and remorse. "I'm so sorry, boss," he muttered without looking directly at Levi.

"Then you are done with trying to throw the blame onto others?" Levi asked.

Chester nodded. "I'm so ashamed of what I did. I

just..." He lifted his shoulders and let them drop as if words could not be found to explain what he had done.

Levi bowed his head for a moment and then certain that he was doing the right thing, he reached for Chester's hand. "Then I forgive you. I am dropping the charges against you."

This time Chester looked at him, his eyes wide with disbelief. "Why would you do that?"

"Because someone recently reminded me that the Bible teaches mercy and forgiveness. For a long time I had forgotten that and when I realized how you had betrayed my trust, all I wanted was justice. But that kind of justice is no more than revenge and makes me no better a man than you were when you decided to steal from me."

"But...thank you, Levi. Oh, thank you. I promise you that..."

Levi held up his hand. "I don't want your promises," he said, "but you can do something for me."

"Anything."

As Hannah helped serve the light lunch, she saw Pleasant's lost love approach her in-laws and make the introductions to his wife and children. It was obvious that he was none the wiser for the heartache he had left in his wake as he ushered his little family back inside to the table they shared with another family. But Hannah saw Pleasant make some excuse to her father and hurry off into the kitchen.

She thought of going after her, to comfort her, but she saw Caleb leaning on his crutches surrounded by a circle of girls and younger children at the far end of the porch. He appeared to be telling them a story and Hannah could not help but be curious. She moved closer.

"…And then the tornado came," he said as every child leaned closer. "It smashed across his father's farm sounding like the roar of a hundred freight trains. It destroyed livestock and the house and then it hit the barn…"

"…Where his parents had gone," one girl murmured.

Caleb nodded. "And when the storm had done its worst the boy crawled out from the cellar with his brother and sisters and saw that nothing was left."

Hannah inched closer. Where on earth had the boy come up with such a tale?

"What did he do then?" a child asked.

"For a while he lived with his grandparents but he was very very sad and lonely for his father and mother and so he ran away."

"What happened then?"

Caleb's face went blank, but he recovered quickly. "Oh, he had many adventures and became a very rich man. He had his own car," Caleb said in an awed tone and several of the young boys in his audience gasped with appreciation. "And a big house—two big houses," he added.

"But he was not happy," a girl prompted and Hannah saw Caleb glance at her and smile.

"No. He was not happy for he had gone into the outside world—and no matter what he did, he did not belong. He had no family there."

"And what happened then?"

Caleb faltered again and Hannah realized that he had no grand ending to his tale. "Nothing. He was trapped in that world. He wanted to go back but he couldn't."

The children started to grumble. "That's a terrible story," one boy groused as he got up and brushed the dust off his good Sunday trousers. "I'm going to see if there's pie." One by one the other boys followed him and the girls wandered away. Hannah stepped forward.

"Where did you hear that story, Caleb?"

"From Levi—Mr. Harmon. He told it to me the other night while we were waiting on the side of the road but I fell asleep and never heard the true end of it."

He eased himself to a sitting position and Hannah sat next to him. "What if that was the end of it? What if Mr. Harmon was telling you that story to teach a lesson?"

"Like in church?"

"Something like that. Maybe he wanted you to think about the true cost of running away—at least for that boy."

"That boy was him," Caleb said. "He turned out okay."

"How do you know the story was about Mr. Harmon?"

"Because he told me so. He told me that he used to be Amish, too, and when he ran away he didn't think about how he would never be able to go back. He was older than me and said he should have known better because once a plain man chooses the English world, that's it."

Hannah felt as if her breath could not find its way through her lungs. "And what do you think of that?"

Caleb shrugged. "I don't know, Ma. I like being who I am. It's just that sometimes I wish there was some adventure. But then it was sometimes pretty scary being out there by myself. When I came here, it was like coming home again, like a real family and I liked that better."

"Did you not miss your grandfather…or me?"

"Oh, Ma, I missed you a lot and I just kept thinking how perfect it would be if you could come live here with the Harnishers, too. Then maybe you wouldn't be so sad and we could be a family with them and…"

"We have our family," she reminded him.

"I know but I think about how Pa used to teach me stuff like Lars's dad does. Grandpa is always so busy. And there are only a few boys my age back home. Most guys my age live somewhere else and just come to Florida for visits."

It was true. Caleb's cousins lived in Ohio and the community in Florida was so new that it was either older couples who had raised their families and come south to farm in a warmer climate, or single men or young marrieds who saw Celery Fields as their future as Caleb's father had.

"It is the life God has chosen for us, son," Hannah said.

"I suppose," he said glumly.

Hannah looked around, trying to think of some distraction that would bring back Caleb's smile and saw the girl who'd been listening to his story coming from the kitchen.

"I brought you snitz and ice cream," the girl said, offering him the plate. "I made the snitz myself."

Caleb took a bite of the dried apple concoction and grinned. "Not as good as my Ma's," he said with a wink at Hannah.

"Oh, Mrs. Goodloe, I should have thought… I didn't bring you…"

"It's all right. If you'll sit with Caleb and make sure he doesn't overdo, I'll get some for myself. It looks delicious."

When she looked back, Caleb was teasing the girl by offering her a bite of the ice cream and then pulling the spoon away at the last minute. It was something his father would have done and Hannah smiled at the memory. And then she turned back to the house and saw Levi talking to her father-in-law and the bishop. But the most astonishing sight was that standing with them was Chester Tuck.

Levi seemed uncommonly nervous and kept wiping the palms of his hands against the sides of his suit trousers as Hannah approached. She was aware that her expression was one of confusion but she could not hide her curiosity at the strange assembly of men standing on the Harnisher's porch.

"Ah, Hannah," Gunther said when she reached the foot of the steps leading up to the porch. "Levi has been waiting for you."

In another time, the words might have been music to her ears. "Levi has been waiting for you…" would have been enough to launch her heart into flight. But that morning during services she had seen plainly the reasons for his interest in her. She wondered what it was that he wanted from her now.

"Chester," she acknowledged as she climbed the steps without looking at Levi.

"Ma'am," he murmured and started to say more but Levi placed a restraining hand on his sleeve.

"Shall we go inside?" the bishop suggested.

Hannah was perplexed by the seriousness of the mood and the unexpected presence of Chester, but when the four men turned and entered the house, she had little choice but to follow them.

Inside, Gunther led the way to a bedroom where benches had been added for the bishop, deacon and ministers to congregate before the services. Gunther indicated that Hannah should sit on one low bench while Chester and the bishop sat on the side of the bed facing her. Levi and Gunther remained standing.

"Mr. Tuck has something he wishes to say to you, Hannah," the bishop told her as he placed his hand on Chester's shoulder.

"Ma'am," Chester began, then cleared his throat and started again. "I've come to ask you to forgive me for accusing you the other day. I was the thief and I tried to throw suspicion onto others."

Hannah's heart went out to the man who looked so small and miserable sitting there. "Chester, I…"

"I thought I had good reason for the stealing," he said, "but the very idea that I could try to accuse someone like you—someone so pure and honest. I was just lashing out because you were the one who found me out."

Hannah looked to the bishop and Gunther and finally Levi, trying to understand this strange confession.

"Chester has asked to face those he accused and try to make amends," Gunther explained.

"It was his idea to come here," Levi added. "All I asked him to do was write letters to you and the others. He already met with the rest of the company earlier this morning."

"Was Jake there?"

Levi's eyes darkened with sadness and he shook his head. "No one has heard from him."

The bishop cleared his throat. "Do you forgive this man, Hannah?"

"Of course. He did me no real harm, but Levi, I still cannot testify in court."

"There will be no trial," Levi said. "I have dropped all charges. Chester was desperate. His mother needed an operation and medicine. His father was out of work.

The doctor insisted on payment up front. He meant to pay it all back but then it just got ahead of him."

Levi turned his attention to Chester. "You have been my friend for many long years," he said so softly that Hannah found herself leaning forward to catch the words. "We have seen many things together and had many adventures."

Chester nodded, his head bent low, his folded hands dangling between his knees.

"You stole from me and in taking from me you also stole from others who had been your friends. You could have come to me. I would have helped."

Chester sniffed back a choked sob and cleared his throat but he did not look up. "I was too proud."

"Pride goeth before a fall," the bishop said in German.

"And I meant to pay it back. I thought I could." He buried his face in his hands and burst into racking sobs.

Levi knelt next to Chester. "I forgive you," he murmured rubbing his friend's back. "It's over, Chester. I forgive you. It will do no one any good for you to go to jail. I won't recover my money. Your parents will be even more destitute. And I will have lost the best twenty-four-hour man working the circuit today."

"You mean it. It's over?"

"You can keep your job," Levi said as he reached into his pocket and handed Chester a check. "This should cover the medicine and expenses your parents might have for the next six months. During that time, I expect you to work on setting up some kind of budget and payment plan that you can live with."

Levi stood and offered Chester his handshake. Chester stood and accepted it. Levi delivered the traditional Amish handshake but then Chester embraced Levi, thanking him profusely. Then Chester turned to Gunther and Hannah and blubbered out his promise to mend his ways and make it all up to Levi and anyone he might have harmed through his actions. Unable to go on, he collapsed back onto the chair and broke down completely.

While Gunther and the bishop calmed Chester, Hannah found herself alone with Levi for the moment.

"Why?" she asked as the two of them moved out onto the porch.

He smiled and spoke to her in the language of her ancestors. "Because it is your way," he replied, "and as you now know it used to be my way, as well."

Hannah thought of the story he had told Caleb, recalling Caleb's words. "He was older…"

"It's hard to explain my reasoning, Hannah," he said in English. "This…" He waved a hand over the land. "This was my father's and grandfather's land but after my parents died…"

"I know the story, Levi. Matthew told me." She stared at the barn for a long moment.

"It was rebuilt," he said softly. "There was a barn-raising not long after…"

"Oh, Levi, how very painful this must all be for you—coming back to such memories."

"Not so much anymore. I made my peace with it years ago. It's partly the reason I decided to settle the circus here in Baraboo. I wanted to be close to what family I had left. Matthew and I worked it all out after our grandfather died. At least here I could see them from time to time."

It had started to rain again as a deputy escorted Chester down the porch steps to a car that had been parked around the side of the barn out of respect for the Amish.

All around them people were clearing the tables, loading the benches and preparing to leave.

Levi touched Hannah's arm. "I have to take care of some things—since I pressed charges in the English court, that all has to be legalized before Chester will be truly free," he said, "and I need to find Jake."

"You haven't seen or heard from him?"

"I doubted him, Hannah. My best friend—the one person who has been with me through all of this and I questioned that loyalty and friendship."

"He just needs time," she said, but wasn't sure that she was right. Jake was a proud man, especially when it came to all that he and Levi—"two dumb stowaways" as he liked to refer to them—had accomplished together. "He'll come around. The two of you are like brothers. In time…"

Levi clearly doubted that. "Perhaps. The first step is to find him."

"No one has seen him?"

"Lily says he left as we all boarded the train and she hasn't seen him since."

"You said he once worked in Chicago. Perhaps he went back there."

"That was a long time ago. No, he could be anywhere by now."

She rested her hand on his arm. "Give him some time," she advised.

He covered her hand with his, the warmth of his touch seeping through her like the balm of the first true spring day. "Hannah, could I come back later?"

"Oh, Levi, perhaps it would be best if…"

"I want to say a proper goodbye to the boy," he said, interrupting her and once again she realized that what she had taken for his feelings for her were really just a good man's concern.

Hannah thought her heart would surely break at the reminder that soon she would leave him—for good. She looked around at the others climbing back into their buggies and heading down the lane in a single line of identical black-topped, horse-drawn carriages toward home. She looked beyond the parade of vehicles to the surrounding countryside, green and verdant after the rain. And she looked up at the sky where a break in the clouds had freed the afternoon sun. *Maybe if we stayed... in time...*

She turned to face him, the words on her lips. But then over his shoulder she saw Pleasant, her shawl covering her head and shoulders as she stood beneath a weeping willow and watched as the young man and his family drove away. Two naive women—she and Pleasant—taken in by men who had meant no harm—only kindness.

"Yes," she told Levi. "Come and say goodbye." And she gathered her skirts and ran back inside the house before he could witness her tears.

Chapter Seventeen

When Levi returned later that evening it was evident that he would have no time alone with Hannah. She had made sure of that. Almost as soon as he arrived, Matthew called for him to come help with the evening milking. Once that was done and they returned to the house, Mae had supper prepared, a supper that Hannah and Pleasant helped to serve. After supper Hannah insisted that Caleb needed his rest and she had packing to do.

She thanked him profusely for all of his kindness and his help in finding Caleb and seeing that he was so well cared for. She prompted Caleb to do the same and that, in turn, prompted Gunther to add to the chorus of appreciation. They left him with little choice but to wish them all safe travels and ask that they write and let him know of their return.

And then she was gone. She followed Caleb down the dark narrow hallway to his room and closed the door. It was as if she could not get away from Levi fast enough. Her actions confused him. He had thought that once she knew that he was Amish, that once he publicly forgave

Chester, then she would see that he could change, that they could have a future together.

He had come to his brother's farm, not to say good-bye, but to ask her to stay and marry him. He loved her and he had been certain that she returned those feelings. *Had been...*

He glanced up to see pity in the eyes of his brother and his sister-in-law. "Tell me what to do," he pleaded, but Mae simply shrugged and Matthew wrapped his arm around Levi's shoulder and walked him out to the porch.

"Let her go," Matthew murmured. "In time you will both understand that it's for the best. We cannot go back, my brother." He gave Levi two sharp claps on the back and went inside the house.

Levi stood there for a long moment. The words his brother had just uttered went against everything Levi believed. Wrongs could be made right. Had he not just seen that with Chester? And how was it for the best for two people who loved each other to be torn apart? He glanced toward the barn—the ground where his parents had died. They had been together because they could not be apart and they had paid a terrible price, but sometimes love demanded such a price. No. Perhaps in taking them both, God had actually given the two of them the bless-ing of not having to go on alone.

He stepped off the porch and instead of heading down the lane toward town, he walked across the yard to the small cemetery where his parents, grandparents and five other generations of Harnishers were buried. He had lost almost everyone he'd ever cared about—his par-ents, his best friend and now Hannah. He found his par-ents' graves and knelt between them. And for the first

time in all the years since he'd run away, Levi prayed
for God's guidance.

And when he left the little graveyard and headed back
to his compound, he knew beyond a shadow of a doubt
what he must do to make everything right again. It would
take some time, but all he had was time. The first step
was to find Jake.

Hannah finished packing Caleb's things and tucked
him in for the night. Back in the room she shared with
Pleasant, she packed her own clothing and then stood
at the window looking out at the dark. She watched as
Levi crossed the lawn and stopped near two headstones
in the little cemetery she had noticed on her first walk
with Caleb to try out his crutches.

She saw him kneel and bow his head and every fiber
of her being tugged her to go to him. The roar of her need
was so loud in her head that she failed to hear Pleasant
enter the room until her sister-in-law was standing behind
her with her hands resting lightly on Hannah's shoulders.

"You love him," Pleasant said.

"Yes."

"And he loves you?"

"No." She had never been more certain of anything.
"He was only being kind like the young man who came
to the bakery."

"But he's free to love you and in time…"

"But I am not free to love him," Hannah said and
turned away from the window. "I can't live in the world
he has chosen, Pleasant, without abandoning everything
I believe in." She saw her misery reflected in Pleasant's
eyes. "If God wills it, you will find love, Pleasant." *And
perhaps, so shall I.*

"I've been such a fool," Pleasant said. Her eyes welling with tears.

"You were naive," Hannah corrected.

"I thought that Noah's attentions were…something more. All he meant was friendliness—a man who enjoys making people smile. He never intended…it was all in my head."

Hannah embraced her sister-in-law. "I know. We've both learned hard lessons on this journey. And yet, had you not persuaded Levi to convince Gunther that we should all come, I would still be waiting to see Caleb. You did that, Pleasant, and I am so very grateful."

Pleasant snorted derisively. "I didn't do it for you. I thought…"

"Whatever your reasons, it got me here. Oh, think of it, Pleasant. Think of the friends we have both made and the adventures we have shared. Think of what might have happened had Caleb not ended up here with Levi's brother or had Levi not told Caleb his story. I might have lost my son forever."

"I guess," Pleasant said, sniffing back her tears. "Do you think they will write to us? Lily and the others?"

"Of course. And next season when they are in Florida, we will have a reunion," she assured her.

"And will you invite Levi to that reunion?"

"Levi will always hold a special place in my heart," Hannah admitted. "I think that for some reason, God led me to his house that day. I think there is some purpose we can't begin to know in this journey we have made with Levi's circus, Pleasant."

"But will you see him when he comes back to Florida?"

"Oh, that's the future, Pleasant," Hannah replied,

knowing that she was avoiding a question that she couldn't begin to answer. "Tomorrow we head home to Florida where we will both start again all the wiser for the experiences we've shared." She hugged her sister-in-law. "This I am certain of—we are sisters as we have never been before and that in tandem with bringing Caleb home, makes everything worth whatever price we may have paid."

Levi had not made it in time. Torn between word that Jake had been seen in town and that Hannah's train was leaving, he had thought he could settle things with Jake and still make it to the station in time.

In time for what?

To beg her to stay.

Jake had been at the barbershop for a shave and haircut. Rather than try to approach him in front of others, Levi had waited outside, sitting on a park bench in the square and keeping an eye on the barbershop door. Finally, he saw Jake emerge.

"Jake?"

His friend hesitated, squinted into the sun and then turned and kept walking away.

"Give me a chance to explain," Levi said as he caught up to him and fell into step.

"This oughta be good, because from where I'm standing you have no explanation. How could you think I would ever…" Jake bit down on his lip and kept walking, his hands thrust into the pockets of his suit trousers.

"You're right," Levi admitted. "I couldn't figure out how Chester could pull it off since he had no direct access to the money."

"And I did," Jake said bitterly, then he wheeled around, stopping Levi in his tracks. "Do you know how it felt being questioned by the police? How it felt that other people—people I know and care about—knew?"

His face was almost purple with his suppressed fury.

"Would it help if you punched me?" Levi asked quietly.

Jake looked startled at the suggestion, then shrugged. "Naw. That'd be no fun because you'd never punch me back. You've got that much Amish in you."

They walked along for several blocks in silence.

"I can see only one way to make this right," Levi said after a while.

"Yeah? What's that?"

Levi pulled a document from his pocket and handed it to Jake. "I'm giving you my shares in the business. It's yours—all of it. I work for you now."

Jake thrust the paper back at him. "I don't want your business, Levi. I want your friendship and your trust."

This time it was Levi who put his hands in his pockets. "You have both right there in your hand. It's the only evidence I can offer—that and my apology. Think about it," he said. "I have to go to the train station, but when I get back…"

"I'll be there," Jake replied. "You never could run this thing by yourself."

Levi started off down the street at a trot.

"Hey," Jake shouted and Levi looked back but did not stop running toward the station. "Good luck."

But as Levi ran through the streets and into the station and then out the door to the platform, he saw that he had come too late.

"She's gone," Lily said, touching his arm as she and

the others headed back to their cars. "Maybe it's for the best."

Levi walked to the edge of the platform and stared after the train. He saw a lone figure—a woman in a plain gray-blue dress and white prayer covering—standing at the very back of the train. She did not wave, but she was watching and he knew that she knew that he had come.

The summer had flown by and at the same time it had seemed a lifetime since she had last seen Levi. On the day they had left Baraboo, Lily and Fred had organized a little impromptu parade to see them off. Fred had shown up at the station in full clown makeup and costume while Lily had presented them with a basket loaded with cheeses and sausages and breads.

Hans had been there and Chester, as well. But there had been no sign of Levi. He had offered Gunther the use of his private car to transport the family, but Gunther had turned him down. Still, she had hoped that he might...

"All aboard!" the conductor had shouted, and Gunther had hustled them onto the crowded car, anxious to get the seats that faced each other in the center of the car.

The train had chugged to life and slowly started to pull away from the platform when Hannah saw Levi.

He emerged from the train station, glancing up and down the track until he realized that he had arrived too late. As the others turned to go, he remained—a lone figure staring after the departing train.

"I'll be back," Hannah had told her father-in-law as she climbed over Pleasant and practically ran to the rear of the train. There she stepped out onto the little metal platform and craned to see him. She did not wave or try to catch his attention. It was enough to know that he had come.

"Goodbye," she had whispered as he grew smaller and smaller and finally disappeared from view altogether as the train rounded a curve.

Since then she had had letters from Lily filled with gossip and news—except about Levi. These two performers had eloped. This one had left the circus to become a nurse. Someone else had developed a new act. She chattered on excitedly about returning to Florida and seeing them again, but she said not one word about Levi.

And Hannah was reluctant to ask. After all, she knew what the gossip had been and now that it had calmed, why stir things up again by showing interest or curiosity? On the other hand, wasn't it odd that she didn't inquire about him?

In the end, she had decided against raising any question. After all this time, to do so surely would be cause for gossip. But oh, how she longed to know if he was well, if he and Jake had reunited, if he ever thought of her.

She forced her thoughts aside and went through her day's routine—washing, cooking, cleaning, ironing, tending the kitchen garden she had planted and taking care of the bookkeeping for the bakery.

Hannah could not recall a hotter, more humid September. Every morning she washed out the clothes the family had worn the day before, hung them on the line and then went inside the small house they all shared to start breakfast. Pleasant and Gunther left for the bakery at four and Hannah packed them a breakfast that Pleasant's half sister, Lydia, delivered on her way to her new job as the community's schoolteacher. At the same time,

Hannah packed a lunch for Caleb who spent his days going to school and then working the celery fields and carefully putting away what little money he could to buy a horse of his own.

Horses had healed the breach between Caleb and his grandfather. Their common love for the animals had brought them closer and Gunther had encouraged Caleb's dream of one day owning his own breeding stable by giving him sole responsibility for the care and feeding of the family's mare, as well as the team of Belgians that Gunther used for business.

That afternoon, Hannah was making the month's ledger entries when she heard the bell over the bakery door clang. She waited for Pleasant's usual, "We're closed," then remembered that her sister-in-law had left early that afternoon to deliver a cake for the birth of a neighbor's first child. Caleb and Gunther had gone to a horse auction.

"I'm sorry," Hannah said as she stepped from behind the curtained area that served as the bakery's office. "We're…" The words froze on her tongue.

For standing in front of the counter was Levi. Or was it only that her eyes and mind were playing tricks on her? Too much sun, she thought. The oppressive heat, she assured herself.

For this man who had Levi's face and Levi's smile was dressed plain. His dark, loose-fitting trousers were held up by black suspenders. His collarless shirt a deep shade of navy. His face clean-shaven as always but his copper highlighted hair hung straight and smooth covering his ears under a wide-brimmed Amish straw hat.

"*Guten Tag*, Hannah Goodloe," he said softly.

She grasped the countertop, her only defense against

giving in to the overwhelming urge to race around the counter and into his arms. "What is this?" she asked, unable to find the words as she nodded toward his unusual attire.

He removed his hat and spoke to her in the familiar Swiss-German dialect of the Amish. "*Ich bin* Levi Harnisher," he said and his eyes pleaded with her to understand something she could not begin to fathom.

Her uncertainty made her irritable. "You should not make light of…"

"I am not making light of anything, Hannah," he said, reverting to English. "I have come to ask you a very important question. I have come back."

"To what?"

"To my faith, my family and with God's blessing— to you."

"I don't understand."

"It's simple, really. I…" The doorbell jangled and together he and Hannah snapped, "We're closed."

"Well, I know that," Pleasant said and then she saw Levi and her mouth fell open.

"'Tis I," he said with a nervous laugh and a slight bow.

Pleasant considered him for a long moment. "I know that you are not a cruel man, Levi, and therefore I must assume that you have not come costumed like this to make fun of our ways."

"It is no costume," Levi said. "These are my clothes, made for me by my sister-in-law, Mae."

"And your fine suits?"

"Gone."

"And your private rail car?"

"Under new ownership."

"And the circus?"

"It all belongs to Jake now."

Pleasant studied him carefully while Hannah forced herself to breathe.

"And what about your mansion here on the bay?"

"I have donated that to the state as well as my other land holdings here, with the exception of one small parcel that I have kept for myself and another that I gave to Hans."

And after quizzing him, Pleasant came away with the same conclusion Hannah had voiced earlier. "I don't understand."

"Would it be presumptuous of me to ask myself to supper where I can explain everything?"

"Yes, it would be presumptuous," Pleasant said, "but you'll do as you please. You always have."

"That is the past," Levi said. "Hannah?"

"I will set another place," she said.

Levi smiled at them as if they had just handed him the moon and stars. He replaced his hat and moved to the door. *"Danke,"* he said and there could be no doubt that relief colored the breath he released as he opened the door and stepped outside.

Chapter Eighteen

For the rest of the afternoon, Hannah pondered this strange turn of events. While she scrubbed the bakery floor, Pleasant prattled on about Levi's changed appearance and short answers to her questions.

"Why would he abandon everything he's worked his entire life to build?" she asked repeatedly.

"Perhaps it was because he wanted to reunite with his family," Hannah guessed.

"He already has a relationship with Matthew and Mae," Pleasant argued.

"But not his sisters."

"But they all live in Iowa or Wisconsin. What's he doing here in Florida?"

Hannah saw the light then. He had come to take care of his business holdings—the mansion and other properties he owned. He had come to put all of that to rest. But he had mentioned keeping one plot of land for himself and another for Hans. Amish men were not given to establishing second homes the way some in the outside world did.

"I should go," she said, putting away the ledger and

files she had been working on. "Someone needs to tell Gunther that we will have a guest."

Gunther Goodloe was sitting at the kitchen table playing a game of dominoes with Caleb when Hannah entered the small house.

"Levi has come back," she said without preamble. On the walk from the bakery to the house she had practiced half a dozen ways of delivering this news, but in the end she had stated it plain and Gunther simply nodded.

"*Ja.* He was here." He placed his final tile, winning the game. "Time for chores, Caleb," he said.

"Levi looked plain," Caleb said as he put away the dominoes and picked up his hat. "Do you think that means that…"

"I don't know what it means," Hannah replied. "Now go."

She put on her apron and began assembling the evening meal.

"He's come back for you," Gunther said softly.

"He said that?"

"Didn't need to. Why else would a man like that change his entire life?"

"Then he has made a mistake," she said as she set the table, counting the places as if the addition of one were monumental.

"You do not care for him?"

"I…" She had almost said that she loved Levi but then she had realized she was talking to Gunther—her late husband's father.

"My son has been dead many years, Hannah. His memory lives on in Caleb. You are still young—young enough to start a new family. If Levi is the one…"

"He cannot think that it is enough to simply change

his clothes and grow his hair to cover his ears," she said, rubbing her palms over her apron. "Anyone can dress up on the outside. It is what is here that counts." She patted her heart.

"He…"

"Besides," she continued more to herself than to Gunther, "he ran away from his family and his faith." Everyone knew that in the Amish faith, choosing the outside world over the faith and community of one's birth could not be forgiven.

Gunther pushed himself to his feet. "Do not be too hard on him, Hannah. There may be more to his change than you know." He said no more as he walked slowly down the hall to his bedroom.

Supper was a quiet affair. Caleb and Gunther generated what limited conversation there was, while the women—Hannah, Pleasant and Pleasant's half sisters, Lydia and Greta, remained silent.

"How is Lars?" Caleb asked.

"He has grown another two inches," Levi reported. "He's taller than his mother now."

"I'm almost as tall as Ma," Caleb said, grinning at Hannah. "And taller than Lydia or Greta."

Gunther asked after the men he had worked with in the horse tent and after Levi assured him that they missed his help and expertise with the horses, silence fell over the table. Even Caleb seemed at a loss for words. Hannah felt as if every bite she took clogged her throat, leaving her unable to speak at all. She had made sure that Levi was not sitting next to her for the very idea of his taking her hand during grace was more than she thought she could bear.

Instead, she had taken her place at the far end of the

table next to Pleasant and across from Caleb. But that position had its problems as well for she could watch him—watch him watching her.

Finally, Gunther signaled the end of the meal with a loud belch—a compliment to Hannah for another good meal.

"Ma," Caleb said, his voice cracking. "I was wondering. Some boys from town are playing baseball this evening with our guys—just until dark and…"

"Have you done all your chores?" Hannah asked, relieved to be able to concentrate on something other than the overwhelming presence of Levi.

Caleb nodded, then ducked his head a moment. "Could I take the buggy?"

Hannah's emotions warred between knowing her son was growing up and needed some independence and the fact that once the game ended it would be dark and Gunther's buggy had only two dim side lanterns.

"I wouldn't mind watching the game," Levi said. "Perhaps your mother and I could come with you."

Caleb's eyes pleaded with Hannah to agree to this plan.

"All right," she said. "As soon as the dishes are finished."

"I can do the dishes," Pleasant's half sister Lydia volunteered. It had been clear from the moment she'd heard that Levi had returned that every romantic ideal she'd ever entertained had fully blossomed.

"Can I come to the game, too?" Greta asked. Greta found the games and activities—even the chores—usually assigned to boys far more interesting than those activities reserved for girls. "I can catch," she announced.

Levi chuckled while Caleb made a face.

"Yes," Hannah decided. "You can come as well, Greta." She couldn't help but take some small pleasure in the look that Caleb and Levi exchanged. Taking Greta along had clearly not been in either one's mind.

The baseball field was a makeshift affair on the edge of the celery fields. Several boys from Sarasota had already gathered and were tossing a ball around from player to player. Another smaller cluster of Amish boys stood on the sidelines talking and knocking sand off their shoes with handmade bats.

Caleb was out of the buggy and off to join his friends almost before the horse had come to a full stop. Levi helped Greta and then Hannah out and together they walked over to the edge of the playing field. Hannah saw several of the boys talking to Caleb and looking their way. After a while, Caleb broke away from the group and started toward them.

"We're a player short," he said to Levi without really looking at him. "The others were thinking maybe you might…"

"Sure," Levi said. "What position?"

"First base?"

"Okay," Levi agreed. "You ladies will be all right?" he asked.

Hannah nodded as Caleb and Levi trotted off toward the other players.

"He's cute," Greta said.

"Handsome," Hannah corrected her without thinking. "A man of Mr. Harmon's age…"

Greta looked up at her and laughed. "I didn't mean Mr. Harmon. I meant Caleb." The girl considered Levi for a moment. "I suppose for someone that old, Mr. Harmon is nice-looking. Better than some, anyway," she said.

Then she studied Hannah for a long moment. "You two would make a good match."

"Really? I didn't know that you had decided to serve as the community matchmaker," Hannah teased. Anything to turn Greta's interest to some other topic. "I thought you planned on raising horses."

"Well, just until I marry Joshua Troyer," she announced with such certainty that Hannah thought it just might come true.

Hannah sat on the grass and Greta did the same, each of them pulling their skirts down to cover the tops of their shoes and wrapping their arms around their knees as they watched the game in progress.

"And once Joshua and I marry, then our children will help out, as well," Greta continued as if the match with the bishop's grandson were already decided. "The boys can work in the stables and cut the hay in fall and the girls can help me in the house and with the little ones."

"You seem to have this all planned out," Hannah said, trying hard not to let her amusement show. "Does Joshua agree with these plans?"

"Oh, he hardly knows I'm alive," she said, resting her chin on her knees. "But he will. Someday."

Hannah watched the girl watching the game and thought back to when she and Caleb's father had shared dreams of a large family and a lifetime together. But they had not been blessed with many children—only Caleb. And she understood how that had put undue pressure on her son. There ought to have been siblings for him, but she had miscarried many times and then Caleb's father had died.

Greta nudged her as Levi came up to bat and before

facing the pitcher, he glanced back at her and pointed to the far right side of the field.

"Oh, that's so romantic," Greta squealed. "He's going to hit a home run just for you, Hannah."

The pitch came low and fast and Levi swung. There was a crack as ball met bat and then the ball was sailing in a high arc between first and second base. The fielder backed up but the ball stayed aloft until it landed several yards behind the fielder.

"Home run," several players on both teams crowed as Levi trotted around the bases, grinning like a schoolboy. They did not care about scores. They only cared about the sport of playing and when Levi crossed home plate both teams gathered to congratulate him.

Moments later he and Caleb walked back toward Hannah and Greta. They were rosy-cheeked and Levi was still breathing hard but he had his arm around Caleb's shoulders and Hannah could not help but think that he would make a good father.

And it hit her suddenly that Levi *should* be a father and if he insisted on pursuing her, he never would be. She had proven that she was barren save for Caleb. Any idea that she might entertain his attempts at courtship was sheer selfishness and she would have none of it.

They let Caleb drive the buggy home and once there, he and Greta set about unhitching and stabling the horse for the night.

"I have something to tell you," Levi said as he walked Hannah back to the house. "I have been taking instruction to be baptized."

Hannah stared at him, thinking this must be some sort of joke. He had run away and abandoned his family and his faith. Surely he understood that he could not simply go back…

"When I ran away I had not yet been baptized," he explained. "In fact, it was my grandfather's insistence that I prepare to join the church that was part of my reason for leaving. Once Bishop Troyer realized that, he reminded me that never having been baptized or never having accepted the responsibilities of living in the Amish faith, I was never shunned. It was he who suggested that it is never too late to join the church and accept the obligations that come with such an act."

"But how could you ever…"

"I have divested myself of anything connected with the outside world—the English world, Hannah. Jake owns the circus and the state has the mansion here and most of the land holdings I once owned. I have been preparing myself for this moment ever since that day when I watched your train leaving Baraboo. I…"

She placed her fingers over his lips unable to hear more. "You cannot come into the faith for false reasons, Levi. Being baptized and joining the church is not a means to an end—it is a commitment to live your life a certain way no matter what. Do not do this because of me."

"There was a time when I would have done anything if it meant that we could be together," he said. "When I first realized that I was in love with you…"

"No," she cried. "This is wrong and I will not allow it." She gathered her skirts and ran back to the house, closing the door behind her.

"Hannah?" Gunther glanced up from reading his bible. "Are you unwell?"

"I am…" She had meant to assure him that everything

was all right, that she was simply tired, that she would see him in the morning. But instead she started to weep and could not seem to stop.

Between her sobs she told him what Levi had told her, adding that she was certain he was doing this only because he thought he was in love with her. "And even if he were to return to the faith for the proper reasons, any idea that he and I might..."

"Why not?"

"He is a man catching up to the life he left behind. He wants marriage and a family." She broke down completely.

Gunther remained silent and slowly she regained control. "It's impossible," she finished on the hiccup of a sob.

"And yet, it seems to me that there is another way to look at this," Gunther suggested, stroking his gray beard. "Think of it, Hannah. Think of how Levi came into our lives. Think of how many times along the way he should have simply disappeared from our lives but did not. What if God has led the two of you to one another? What if God has used you, and Levi's love for you to bring him back to his faith? Where is the harm in that?"

Her head was spinning. "But surely if his only reason for..."

"And do you know for certain that you are his only reason, Hannah? That speaks of arrogance that you could have such influence."

Hannah bowed her head. Of course, Gunther was right. How immodest of her to set herself on such a high pedestal. She should have rejoiced in Levi's decision, not degraded it with her own conceit. "I can see your point. I should apologize," she said. "Thank you, Gunther."

Outside, she could hear Levi's laughter as he talked

with Caleb and Greta in the barn. She followed the golden light of the lantern the children had taken with them when they went to stable the horse. They were talking about the baseball game and when she stepped into the open door of the barn, she saw Levi showing Greta how to grip a bat properly.

"Children, it's late," she said when they looked up at her and the two of them nodded and headed for the house.

"I should go," Levi said as he put on his straw hat and rolled down his sleeves. He did not look at her as he passed her on his way out.

"I'm sorry to have doubted you," she said, and he stopped but did not turn around. "It is good that you have heard God's call for you to return to the faith of your ancestors. I am happy for you."

He picked up the lantern and used it to light her face. "You've been crying."

"Yes, but my tears were tears of pride and arrogance."

He stroked her cheek with the backs of his fingers. "Hannah, there are two things you must believe about me. I am serious about returning to my faith. For some time now I have been unsettled. In spite of everything I bought or acquired—success, power, material things— I was never able to find the one thing that makes life worth living. Contentment with who I am and how I pass my days."

She closed her eyes and leaned into his touch. "And the second thing?"

"I love you, Hannah. I think I fell in love with you the day I saw you coming up the drive of my mansion. I think I knew that somehow you were going to change my life in ways I could not begin to fathom—and you have."

He kissed her then, his lips warm on hers as he cradled her cheek and angled her face to receive his kiss and return it.

"Marry me, Hannah," he murmured.

Reality hit her like a slap and she drew back from him. "I cannot," she whispered. But this time she did not run from him. After everything they had shared, everything he had done to bring Caleb back to her, she owed him an explanation. "I love you," she began and realized that was not the best choice of a beginning to her explanation.

"But?" He ground the word out through gritted teeth.

Levi Harnisher might be plain on the outside but there was still some of the proud and powerful Levi Harmon that lived within. Hannah heard impatience and resistance in that single word.

"Hear me out," she pleaded.

He left one hand resting on her shoulder but gazed beyond her for a moment. Then he looked down at her. "All right. I'm listening."

"The Ordnung teaches us that marriage is meant for a clear purpose—the purpose of bringing children into the world."

"Seems to me for some it's also for the purpose of companionship," he argued.

"That's true—for someone like Gunther, for example. But you are not old, Levi."

"Neither are you." He ran one hand through his hair, a habit she'd found endearing when she'd first met him.

"I cannot have more children." There, she had said it but she should have taken into consideration that Levi never accepted easy answers.

"Because? What did the doctor tell you, Hannah?"

His question exasperated her because, of course, no doctor had told her anything. She had simply gathered the facts of her many miscarriages and drawn her own conclusion.

Levi hooked his forefinger under her chin and lifted her face so that the light from the lantern shone on her.

"My late husband and I tried to have more children," she said softly. "Except for Caleb, we lost them all."

Levi frowned and she thought perhaps she had convinced him and wondered why instead of relief, she felt only sadness.

"I am not your late husband," he said. "We will follow God's plan for us and if that brings children, so be it."

"And if not?"

"So be it," he said, biting each word off precisely so that there could be no doubt of his commitment. "Now, do you have any other reasons not to let me court you properly over the coming weeks?"

"Oh, Levi, you can't want…"

To her surprise he set down the lantern and cupped her face with both hands. "This is me you are speaking to, Hannah. Pleasant was partly correct when I asked to come for supper and she said I would do as I please anyway."

Hannah leaned into him. "Only partly correct?" she teased.

"In this particular circumstance, I cannot do as I please unless you are also doing as you please. So I will ask once more, Hannah. Will you marry me?"

And because her heart took flight on wings of pure joy and because she was more certain than she had been of anything she had ever done in her life, she wrapped her arms around him and whispered, "Yes, Levi Harnisher, I will marry you."

Chapter Nineteen

During the years he had owned the circus, Levi had prided himself on doing whatever manual labor might be necessary to keep things running smoothly. Often when they were short a man to unload the wagons, Levi had stepped in to help. He had worked with the animals, especially the elephants and horses that the company depended on to do the heavy work of setting up and tearing down the huge tents. But all of that had been child's play compared to the unending work of farming. From well before sunup until well after dusk it seemed there was work to be done—work that could not be postponed.

He had forgotten how great a factor a change in weather could be. A deluge of rain could ruin a day's work if the soil and seeds got washed away. In the aftermath of such a storm the plow could get mired in deep pockets of sandy mud left behind. It was a little like stepping into wet concrete. And no rain at all was even worse. He had set out to plant his fields with celery because that was a proven crop in these parts. But celery thrived in this part of the country because of the boggy, mucky, semiwet fields. Days of no rain dried those fields and left the tender young plants struggling to survive.

Levi was plowing the last rows of the field closest to the modest house he'd completed and thinking about his grandfather as he often did these days. As a boy, Levi had thought his grandfather was far too serious, too stern, too joyless. But now he was beginning to understand that along with the responsibility of a family came an enormous weight. The weight of "what if." What if there were a hurricane that wiped out everything? What if there were a fire in these dry days? What if the crop prices dropped? What if he failed?

Of course that was only half the worry. The other half came with fitting into a culture he had abandoned long ago. It was more than simply putting on different clothes or reverting to the language of his youth. There were times when he had found himself thinking about assigning some task to Hans or about a new marketing ploy that might help fill seats at the next performance. There were times when he missed the life he had so willingly handed over to others. Life among the Amish was so...plain.

As he pushed the plow through the muck, the muscles in his arms and legs screaming with overuse and exhaustion, he wondered if he and Hannah could be truly happy or if he—like his grandfather—would one day turn into a beaten down and bitter old man.

No, he thought as he pulled back on the reins looped around his shoulders and the team of horses paused. He took off his hat and wiped sweat from his brow with the back of his hand and gazed up at the sky—a cloudy gray sky that held the promise of rain before evening. *Show me the way,* he prayed. *The rest of the way on this jour-*

*ney You have set me on. Show me how to be a good hus-
band to Hannah and father to Caleb.*

The heat and humidity of the midday sun distorted his
view of the horizon as he stared at the house. It wavered
as if it were no more than a mirage. But then he saw Hannah coming across the fields toward him. She was carrying a bucket and stepping carefully over the furrows he'd
plowed. The hot west wind carried snatches of the hymn
she was humming, soothing away his worries as if they—
not the house or the fields or the life he had chosen—were
the mirage.

"I brought you some water," she said, filling the dipper and handing it to him. "You're not used to being out
in the hot sun, Levi. Perhaps you should—"

"I'm almost finished," he assured her. He drank down
the water and handed her the dipper, which she refilled
and handed back to him. "And if I can finish the plowing
today, then tomorrow I can start the planting and then—"

"Caleb could help you," she said. "He's only waiting
for you to ask."

He knew that she was asking another question entirely. The question of why he hadn't asked the boy to
help. She shaded her eyes with one hand and stared up
at him, waiting.

"I don't want Caleb to feel that I'm trying to take the
place of his father."

"His father died, Levi, as did yours. I had thought—
hoped—that you might understand what that means for
him. He misses—"

"It's because I understand, Hannah, that I'm taking
it slow."

She wrinkled her brow into a quizzical frown.

Levi touched her cheek. "After my father died, my

grandfather treated me as if nothing had changed. He was my father now and that's all I needed to understand as far as he was concerned. I had his assurance that he would protect and provide. That was supposed to be enough."

"But it wasn't."

"No. I missed my father's patience, his humor, his assumption that I would grow up to be a good man. And from what Caleb told me about his father that night we sat in the rain along the side of the road, he misses those same things."

"Then give him those things," Hannah said. "His father is gone, Levi, but you are here and if we are to truly be a family, then Caleb needs your love and guidance."

"I've never been a husband or a father," Levi said. "It's a lot of responsibility and I'm—"

Her eyes widened with fear. "Do you regret leaving that other life, Levi? Because if you're not sure…"

He cupped her jaw and forced her eyes to meet his. "I have never been more certain of anything as I am that I love you and that my life without you would be unendurable."

"Then, what is it?"

"I'm afraid I might fail you—and Caleb. What if…?"

She laid her fingers on his lips and shushed him. "Our love for one another and God's love for us will see us through whatever lies ahead, Levi. We are starting from a good place. We have a home and this land and an entire community to help us through whatever may come. We're going to be all right."

The horses snorted and stamped, and Hannah laughed. "See? Even the horses agree. Now come in out of this heat and rest for a bit. You and Caleb can finish plowing this evening after the rain."

Together they unhitched the horses and led them back to the yard. "Caleb?" Levi called when he spotted the boy sitting alone near the barn, working on a piece of harness. He looked up, an eager smile on his face, and Levi wondered why he hadn't recognized that look. It was the same look he had given his grandfather in the days following his parents' death. It was a smile filled with hope. *Let me in*, that smile said. *Let me be part of your life.*

Hannah breathed a sigh of relief as she went to washing the windows of the home they would share and watched Levi and Caleb tend the horses. They would be all right. And even if God decided not to bless them with more children, it would be enough. They would be a family. And with Gunther and his daughters and her cousins and aunts and uncles back in Ohio and Levi's family in Wisconsin...

She polished a pane of glass and thought about Levi's family—his sisters who had joined their grandparents in shunning a boy who had never been baptized into the faith in the first place. As she and Levi had set about planning their wedding, she had noticed how he carefully avoided any mention of his sisters.

"Matthew and Mae and the kids could make the trip," he'd told her, "and then maybe we could travel back with them and visit your people in Ohio as we work our way back here." Tradition called for them to leave the day after their wedding and spend several weeks traveling around visiting family and friends. Jake had insisted that they allow him to provide transportation on what was now his private railway car for the journey. "I'll even make it plain for you," he assured Hannah.

But there had been no mention of Levi's sisters and

their families. "Well, this won't do," Hannah muttered
as she polished the glass panes. "If we are to truly be a
family, then we need to mend these fences."

That night, after Levi had taken her and Caleb back to
Gunther's house and everyone was asleep, Hannah wrote
a letter to Mae Harnisher and enclosed separate letters
for each of Levi's sisters that she asked Mae to deliver.
She introduced herself to them and invited them to come
for the wedding, making sure to note that she realized
it was a long trip and certainly she and Levi would understand if they could not get away. Then she asked if
she and Levi might call upon them when they came to
Wisconsin after the wedding. She was about to end the
letters there when she decided that she had perhaps been
too circumspect. And before she could change her mind
she added the following note to each letter.

> *The one thing that our families share is the pain
> of great loss. And had it not been for Levi's kind-
> ness, I might have lost my only child as well to a
> life that would have taken him away from me as
> Levi's choice took him from you. I cannot know
> what your thoughts may be, but I do know that
> Levi thinks of you often and misses you. I am
> asking you to open your hearts to us as we begin
> this new chapter in our lives and join us in cel-
> ebrating the great joy that God has given us.*

She sealed the envelopes before she could rethink
a word of the letters. As soon as Yoder's Dry Goods
opened, she would post the letter to Mae and then pray
that Mae would take it from there.

* * *

In his career with the circus, Levi had stood before
crowds of hundreds—even thousands—of spectators,
making speeches or acting as ringmaster for the show.
But never had he been more nervous than he was on this
Sunday morning sitting in the front row of the small
Amish congregation that had gathered for services in
Gunther's house. And yet, he had never in his life felt
more certain about the path he had chosen.

When he had run away from his grandfather's farm,
he hadn't been certain of anything except the strong need
to get away from the memories and the pain of loss. From
that day to this he had lived his life on the move, making decisions based more on expediency than what the
long-term consequences might be. For years it had all
seemed to work in his favor.

He had met Jake, and the two of them had eventually
become a formidable business team. He had acquired
assets beyond anything he might have dreamed. He had
become a respected figure in the communities where
he had established bases for his business. But through it
all he realized now that he had never stopped running,
never stopped searching for whatever it was that he had
left the farm to find.

And then Hannah had walked up that driveway and
into his life. It occurred to him now that on that day he
had felt something shift. He had not understood it, but
there had been no denying it. Now he felt more certain
than ever before in his life that God had sent Hannah to
him that day, not to find her lost son—but to find him
and bring him home to his roots.

After the last sermon and hymn, Bishop Troyer rose
and cleared his throat. "We have a special request to

consider," he said. "Levi Harnisher has asked to be accepted into this congregation. If you agree, he will join those applicants already accepted in being baptized at our next service."

Behind him, Levi was aware of a rustle of whispers as the men murmured comment in their Swiss-German dialect to their neighbors.

"Circus…"

"Wisconsin…"

"The widow Goodloe…"

He held his breath and closed his eyes, praying silently that they would accept that this was what he wanted for himself—whether or not he had won Hannah's love in the bargain.

"We will vote by show of hands," the bishop said, silencing the murmured discussion. "Those in favor?"

Levi did not dare turn around.

"Opposed?"

He squeezed his eyes more tightly shut and realized he was clenching his fists, as well.

"Then it is done," the bishop intoned.

Levi's eyes flew open and he glanced around, confused. What was done? Had he passed or not?

The bishop smiled and offered him the traditional one-pump Amish handshake. "Welcome, my brother."

Levi released the breath he'd been holding and pumped the bishop's hand up and down. *"Danke,"* he murmured. He looked around for Hannah and found her among a cluster of women, all dressed in dark, plain dresses with identical prayer coverings and yet, she alone was the woman he saw.

Their eyes met, hers sparkling blue with a tenderness and caring that he realized had been missing for far too long in his life. He saw the future then—the two of them and Caleb, of course, building a life together.

Two Sundays later at the next biweekly services, Levi joined a small group of teenaged boys and girls to receive baptism. As soon as the hymns and sermons were completed, the bishop asked the applicants to kneel, and reminded them that they were about to make their promise to God before this congregation. He moved down the row asking the four questions that signaled their commitment to the church. With the help of the deacon, Bishop Troyer poured water from a wooden bucket onto the head of each applicant. He did this three times in the name of the Father, the Son and the Holy Ghost.

Then Bishop Troyer helped each applicant to stand, uttering the traditional words in German. "In the name of the Lord and the Church, we extend to you the hand of fellowship. Rise up and be a faithful member of the church."

When the bishop leaned in to bestow the Holy Kiss on his cheek, Levi felt a rush of such utter contentment and peace pass through him that he could not hide the tears that filled his eyes. He had come home at last.

On her wedding day, Hannah went about her chores in the usual way. She was up before sunrise, gathering eggs from the hen house and scattering feed for the chickens before starting breakfast for the family. Only her memories accompanied her through this daily routine.

Hannah's marriage to Caleb's father had taken place in Ohio in early December. There had been a heavy frost that morning in contrast to the heavy dew of humidity that clung to everything on this wedding day. Two years later, after Hannah had already suffered two miscarriages, the bakery had burned to the ground and Gunther's second wife was not fitting into the community. So the entire family had migrated to Florida for what Gunther had assured them would be a fresh start.

A year after that, Caleb had been born and eight years and no other children later, her husband had died when a reckless driver ran his buggy off the road one dark night. She had thought of taking Caleb and moving back to Ohio—back to where her sisters and brothers still lived. But Caleb had balked at moving from the only home he'd ever known and on top of that, Gunther's second wife had died a year earlier and in spite of her ability as a baker, Pleasant was not much of a housekeeper or cook. Gunther had needed Hannah to mother Lydia and Greta, his children with his second wife, even though Lydia had then been fifteen and Greta was Caleb's age. And so she had stayed.

She could not help but think how wondrous were the ways that God led his children in directions they could not imagine and often fought against. Take Levi...

"Good morning," he said, coming alongside her and relieving her of the basket she'd used to gather the eggs.

"Levi Harnisher, you startled me," she chastised him, but she was smiling and she reached up and caressed his cheek with her fingers.

Levi set the basket down and wrapped his arms around her, "Hello, wife," he murmured.

"Not yet," she said, "but before this day's over."

Their kiss spoke of all the promise and hope they both held for their years together. Hannah even dared to hope that there might be children and she knew that Levi wanted that, as well. He would not speak of it because he knew that it upset her to think she might not be able to give him the family every Amish man hopes for.

The rumble of metal wheels and clop of horse hooves on the shell-packed path that led to Gunther's house announced the arrival of their first guests—the wedding party come to help set up and welcome the others. Because this was her second marriage, theirs would be a quieter ceremony with far less of the usual fuss that came with a first wedding.

Hannah had made herself a new dress, apron and covering—items she would wear on Sundays for the coming years. Levi had bought a new suit barren of the lapels and buttons that had decorated the suits he'd worn as a businessman.

"Wife," he whispered against her temple as he released her and gave her back the egg basket. He greeted the men and helped unload the benches that would need to be set up for the ceremony, and later would convert to tables for the two meals to be served in the daylong celebration.

Behind the church bench wagon, women were spilling out of a small parade of buggies. They talked softly but excitedly as they started toward the house bearing covered dishes of food, and carrying the good Sunday clothing they would change into once the work of setting up was done.

An hour later, the members of the wedding party had all had their breakfast and changed into their finer clothes. They took up their posts, waiting to greet the guests as they arrived. And arrive they did—on foot, by buggy and by three-wheeled bicycle—all anxious to witness the marriage of the widow to the reformed circus baron. To Levi's surprise, his sisters and their families had arrived along with Matthew and Mae a few days earlier. They had quietly embraced the brother they had not seen in decades, and Levi had welcomed them back into his life with open arms.

Now Hannah and Levi waited with the bishop in Gunther's small bedroom. While Bishop Troyer spoke to them of the duties and obligations of marriage and family, Hannah could hear the guests singing hymns. She found herself thinking of the times she had sat in the business car of Levi's circus train, the strains of the circus band's brass fanfares surrounding her. But the sound of voices raised in song without benefit of instrumental accompaniment seemed twice as sweet.

"Shall we?" Bishop Troyer rose and indicated that they should follow him into the larger room where their guests waited. Hannah's smile widened as she saw Hans, Fred and Jake seated together in the back row of the men's section. Then spotted Lily and three of the other women she had befriended seated in the very center of the women's section, their floral hats standing out like parrots among the more somber coverings of the Amish women. She squeezed Levi's hand and nodded and he grinned down at her.

"Surprise," he mouthed. "I got special permission."

To either side of the room sat the attendants or *newehockers* for each of them. Pleasant, Lydia and Hannah's soon-to-be sister-in-law, Mae, sat opposite Caleb, Gunther and Matthew. Hannah smoothed the skirt of her new deep blue dress and straightened her cape and apron before taking her place on the bench reserved for Levi and her.

The ceremony began with prayer followed by one of the ministers reading a passage of scripture. Levi had requested the Beatitudes for he reminded them all that it was this passage that had turned his life around and brought him home to his faith and to Hannah.

The sermon seemed to go on forever and Hannah could not help but smile as she recalled how Levi had admitted that the lengthy sermons was one part of being Amish that was going to take some getting used to. She couldn't help but wonder how their friends from the circus were surviving the closeness of the room and the droning of the minister's words when she heard a distinct snore coming from somewhere behind her, and then Jake's startled yelp when Fred obviously nudged him.

The minister paused for a second to allow the titters of laughter to die and then droned on. Finally, he called Hannah and Levi forward, administered the required questioning that was akin to an English couple stating their vows and then blessed them. As soon as the bishop stepped forward to offer the final prayer, Hannah felt an aura of excitement permeate the room. And the moment the prayer ended, the room exploded into action.

Women hurried off to the kitchen while men transformed the benches into tables set in a u-shape in the yard. As soon as the tables were in place, the women filled them with a feast of roasted chicken, mashed potatoes, gravy, creamed celery, coleslaw, fruit salad, tapioca rice pudding, applesauce, and bread, butter and jam. For dessert there was Pleasant's cherry pie and hand-cranked ice cream.

"Who gets married at the crack of dawn on a Tuesday?" Jake asked as he made a show of stretching and yawning and then grabbed Levi in a bearhug.

"Eight o'clock is hardly the crack of dawn," Levi told him. "And Tuesday's a day as good as any other day."

"Hello, Hannah," Jake said. "I've missed you—Ida's okay but not nearly so pretty."

Hannah blushed and Levi leaned in to explain Jake's mistake to him. "It is not our way…"

"…to pass out compliments," Jake finished. "Just stating the facts, my friend. Nothing more."

"We're so pleased you came," Hannah said, noticing the other guests hanging back and whispering among themselves, reluctant to approach the newlyweds with the outsiders around. "We…"

"…need to attend to your other guests," Lily said, taking Jake firmly by the arm. "Go talk horses with Gunther," she instructed, and winked at Hannah as she and the other women from the circus headed off to see if they could help in the kitchen.

Once the tables were set up and the food had been brought out, Hannah and Levi took their places at one corner of the "u" with the women sitting down the side of the table next to Hannah and the men next to Levi. Hannah sat on Levi's left as she would now whenever they went anywhere in the buggy. As tradition dictated, Hannah's family from Ohio and Matthew and Levi's sisters and their families ate in the kitchen.

At first, Hannah had worried that Lily and the other circus women might be uncomfortable. Jake, Fred and Hans could easily take part in the male conversation about baseball, livestock and such, but the women were a different matter.

"They'll be all right," Levi whispered, reading her mind as usual.

And then she heard Lily say, "The one thing I have never been able to understand is how you get all that stuffing inside the chicken." That led to a sharing of recipes for stuffing a chicken, which led to a discussion of the variety of recipes for stuffing which led to Lily's memories of her mother's Thanksgiving turkey and so on, until Hannah knew she had nothing to worry about. She could not remember a time when she had been happier in her life. And she could not imagine that the future might hold any more joy than she was experiencing at that very moment.

As soon as everyone had eaten, the crowd broke off into small groups. The younger guests played games or flocked to the shade of a tree to talk, while single men and women paired off or gathered in small clusters. Hannah and Levi made the rounds visiting with each guest until it was time for yet another meal, then more visiting, and finally around ten o'clock, the guests took their leave.

As Hannah stood with Levi saying their goodbyes, she could not help but marvel at the fact that on this day she had become Mrs. Levi Harnisher. Her life had changed so much in just a few short months and yet she had never felt more certain of her path than she did on this night standing side by side with Levi.

"You must be exhausted," Levi said, wrapping his arm around her waist as she waved to the last of the buggies making its way down the lane.

"Oh, no," she protested. "I want this day to go on and on." But she could not stifle the yawn that forced its way through her lips, and Levi laughed.

"Walk with me," he invited, holding out his hand to her.

From this day forward, I will always walk with you, she thought as she took his hand and walked with him down the now-deserted lane.

"Looks like we'll have good weather to begin our

journey north tomorrow," he mused, glancing up at the clear, starlit sky and crescent moon.

"Not a cloud in the sky," she replied. But although the heavens were filled with stars, there was only one cloud hanging over the perfect day. Regardless of what Levi might say, she wanted so much to give him children. At Levi's insistence, she had been examined by a doctor and told that there was no physical reason she could not conceive. But the problem had never been conceiving. The problem had been bringing the child to term, and the doctor had admitted to her in private that he could not predict such a thing.

Levi felt the tension that had gripped her as they walked. He let go of her hand and wrapped his arm around her shoulders. "Let's sit awhile," he said, leading her to the tangled roots of a large banyan tree where they sat side by side on one of the giant tendrils running out from the tree's base, their arms around each other.

They were both nervous, he realized—a product of the fact that they did not yet know each other's habits. "Are you happy?" he asked.

She shifted until she could look up at him. "Yes. And you?" She traced the shape of his mouth with her finger, and he smiled.

"I cannot recall a time when I felt more at peace, more content with what the future might bring as I do at this moment, Hannah. Whatever challenges life may present to us, I know that with you at my side we can meet them."

"And God's blessing," she reminded him gently.

"For me, you are that blessing," he said. "My wife— my love," he murmured as he kissed her.

Her prayer covering scratched his chin as she laid her cheek against his chest and sighed happily.

"Hannah?"

"Mmm?"

"Now that I'm a married man, I'll have to grow out my beard," he reminded her.

She laughed, the sound muffled against his shirt until she raised her face to his and stroked his smooth cheek. "Perhaps you can give your razor and shaving brush to Caleb. I saw him running his hand over his jaw the other day the way you sometimes do."

"Peach fuzz," Levi said and laughed. "But then, he is growing up."

"It will be another bond between you," she reminded him.

"*Ja.* I'll give them to him before we leave tomorrow." He pulled her close again, but after a moment she sat up and faced him.

"I have a gift for you, my husband," she said softly. Then she reached up to remove her prayer covering and his breath caught as he realized that for the first time he would see her hair undone.

"Let me," he said.

She dropped her hands to her sides and waited while he removed the long hairpins that held the weight of her hair in place. He took his time, laying each pin in a cup of her hands so none would be lost.

He pulled the last pin free and watched as her hair tumbled to her waist, thick and heavy against her back in waves made permanent by years of the same twists and turns. He looked forward to the morning when he would watch her tame it all into the precise bun that he had come to love. And for all the days and nights of their lives this would be their special moment—that moment of release when he and he alone would know the full blossom of her beauty. And then in the morning she would tuck it all away again. They were man and wife and for as long as God gave them, neither of them would ever be alone—or lonely—again.

They sat together in silence, him stroking his fingers through her hair as she rested her head against his shoulder. He kissed her temple.

"We should go in," she murmured. "It's been a long and wonderful day."

"With more to come tomorrow and the day after that and the day…"

She sat up and pulled the weight of her hair over one shoulder. Then she took his hand in hers. "Pray with me," she said softly. She fit her fingers between each of his and turned so that her forehead and his were touching as they bowed their heads and silently thanked God for the blessings He had given them.

Chapter Twenty

They returned from their wedding trip two days before Christmas and as far as Hannah was concerned the best gift she could possibly receive was seeing Caleb again.

"Look at you," she kept saying as Caleb rolled his eyes and Levi gave him a sympathetic smile. "Why, you've grown and filled out so much."

"Ma, it's only been six weeks," he reminded her.

"Still, look at you," she repeated and hugged him.

"How's the horse business?" Levi asked.

"I've got eleven customers," Caleb reported.

"Twelve," Levi corrected and nodded toward their newly built barn. "I bought a pair of Belgians from Jake to help with the planting, and there's a mare in there you could ride from farm to farm. Might save you some time and make it possible to add new customers."

Caleb's eyes grew huge with delight. "Really?"

Levi shrugged. "Go see for yourself." He wrapped his arm around Hannah's shoulder as they watched the boy take off for the barn at a run. A moment after he entered the barn, they heard a loud cheer and a moment after that, he came out leading the gray dappled mare by a lead rope.

"You'll spoil him," Hannah said.

"We'll consider it an early Christmas present. Besides, all I'm doing is encouraging his work ethic," Levi protested. Then with a wink, he added, "The only person I'm interested in spoiling is you." He pulled her close and kissed her forehead.

His soft beard brushed her skin and she looked up at him. In the six weeks since their wedding he had grown the beard that all married Amish men had. But Levi's beard was a rich shade of copper and she would not have believed it possible, but he was even more handsome with it than he had been clean-shaven.

"How are you feeling?" he asked, the wide brim of his straw hat shading his worried expression.

"Better," she assured him. She was well aware of what her problem was but Levi had not yet caught on and she was not yet ready to tell him.

She was pregnant. By her count, she was entering her second month and as had always been her pattern, she was suffering from morning sickness. She knew she should explain it to Levi but then what if she lost this baby as she had all the others? He would be devastated. Watching him with his nieces and nephews and then hers as they traveled around during their wedding trip, she had seen how very much he enjoyed being around children. He would be such a wonderful father—already was one to Caleb. How could she disappoint him? She almost wished she weren't pregnant.

The thought shocked her and she silently begged God's forgiveness. *Thy will be done...* she reminded herself firmly. Whether or not she carried this child to term was not in her hands or Levi's—it was God's will and there was a reason for whatever way things went. But she could not help praying nightly for their child's health and well-being.

"Are you sure you're up to having everyone come here?" Levi was asking her as they watched Caleb mount the horse bareback and ride around the farmyard.

They had insisted on hosting the celebration known as "second Christmas" held on the twenty-sixth. "Of course. Everyone is bringing something to share so there's not much work to do."

"And you're sure having Lily and the others is all right?"

"They are our friends," she said firmly. "And they have no place to go for the day. If that is upsetting to anyone, well, then…" Actually, she wasn't sure. She knew there were some in the small Amish community who did not care for their ongoing association with these outsiders.

"Too worldly," she had heard one matron hiss to her neighbor as she passed the two women after last Sunday's services.

And Pleasant had told her outright that there were those in the community who were less than convinced that Levi's baptism had been legitimate. "Merle says that several of the men think he came back to the church because of you. Merle also says that if Levi were sincere, he would have no further association with his former employees."

Hannah had learned that "Merle says" had become a staple in Pleasant's conversation over the weeks that she and Levi had been gone. Merle Obermeier was a widower who had made no secret of his decision to pursue

Pleasant as his second wife and the mother of his four children. He was a decade older than Pleasant, a dour and suspicious man who always seemed to look for the dark side of things.

"Do you love him?" Hannah had asked Pleasant after becoming aware of the relationship.

Pleasant had shrugged and Hannah's heart had gone out to her. Did Pleasant not deserve the same happiness that Hannah had found with Levi? Surely there was a man out there somewhere who could give her sister-in-law that kind of happiness.

"Don't just settle because you think…"

"I don't just think," Pleasant had replied bitterly. "I know. Merle Obermeier may be my last chance. He's a good man, Hannah."

And Hannah had understood that the discussion of Pleasant's future was closed. Well, Merle Obermeier might think otherwise but she knew that Levi had genuinely found his faith. He seemed almost relieved to be back living the plain life of his youth. As for Lily and the others, Merle could disapprove but Hannah and Levi would not turn their backs on their English friends. People would just have to understand. And if they didn't? Well, she had no doubt that Levi would deal with that if the time ever came.

Levi was aware that Hannah might be pregnant. The signs were all there, and yet she said nothing. In the mornings when she fought against waves of nausea, she mumbled something about a virus and sipped ginger tea to settle her stomach. He knew why she was keeping the news to herself. She was afraid of miscarrying and nothing he could do or say could quell that fear.

He had talked to the doctor privately, seeking the man's assurance that there was no medical reason why Hannah could not give birth. The doctor had advised patience. "The one thing you don't want to be doing is adding to her fears."

But Levi felt such a compulsion to care for his wife and unborn child that it was all he could do not to tell Hannah what he suspected and demand that she allow him to worry with her. *Demand*, he thought as he watched her hanging laundry on the clothesline he had stretched like a tightrope between two large palm trees outside their back door. Demanding was the way of Levi Harmon, a man used to having his way. A man used to others giving him his way as if that were somehow his right.

But Levi Harnisher understood that such thoughts were a part of the outside world. In the Amish world it was not his will, but God's will that mattered. "Well, then," he prayed quietly, "if it be Your will, give us this baby, this child that we share, and let us raise him or her in the way of our ancestors."

He pushed himself out of the rocker on the porch and went to help Hannah. The wind had caught a sheet she was trying to hang and it whipped away from her like a sail broken free of its mast.

"Got it," he called as he rescued the damp sheet from its landing place in her herb garden and carried it back to her.

"It will have to be washed again," she fussed as she wadded it into a ball.

He picked it up and spread it over the clothesline, pulling clothespins from where she had clipped them to her apron and anchoring it there. "It's fine," he told her and then he placed his hands on her shoulders until she looked up at him. "Everything will be fine."

The tears welled in her blue eyes and he pulled her into his embrace and rocked her side to side.

"How long have you known?" Her voice was muffled against his chest.

"A while now."

"And yet you said nothing."

"Nor did you," he reminded her. "But now we know—the three of us and…"

She pulled back. "You told Caleb?"

He chuckled. "No."

"Then who are the three of us?"

"You. Me." He placed one palm gently over her midsection. "And this child of ours."

She covered his hand with hers. "Tell me again," she said softly.

"Everything will be fine," he repeated then added, "whatever happens. We have already been blessed beyond all measure just by finding each other, Hannah. If God sees fit to give us a child, then I would have to say that our cup would runneth over."

The sheer relief Hannah felt at being able to share the worries and joys of her pregnancy with Levi had the surprising effect of making her feel much better. On Christmas morning she hardly had any nausea at all, but she was glad that the routine called for prayer, fasting and quiet reflection on the true meaning of the day.

With Gunther and his three daughters, Hannah, Levi and Caleb attended services at Merle Obermeier's farm. He had the largest house so that everyone could be in the same room. The yard was already filled with buggies, unhitched and parked in a circle when they arrived, and more buggies had followed them up the lane. Caleb joined his friends to help lead the horses away either to the barn or to pasture. Hannah was relieved that Caleb had made new friends. New families had come to Florida in the last year—young families with children. The settlement growing up around the celery fields was becoming its own little community.

Inside the house the air was warm because of so many people crowded into one room and also because Merle refused to open any windows, assuring everyone that the house would stay far cooler if they would simply come in quickly and close the door behind them. He stood sentry at the front door to see that his instructions were followed.

"All that fanning of the door—opening and then closing it only to immediately open it again. That's the cause of all this hot air—that and Obermeier's lecturing," Gunther grumbled.

"Papa, please." Pleasant squeezed her father's forearm. "It's his house."

Hannah could not help looking around and trying to imagine Pleasant living here. Merle had been a widower for less than a year. There had been a time when rumor had it that he had cast his eye on Hannah as a possible second wife. But then she had boarded the circus train to go and find Caleb and Merle had made it plain to Pleasant that he could not tolerate such open trafficking with outsiders.

Of course, Hannah pointed out the fact that Pleasant had made that same journey, but she explained that Merle saw her participation as unavoidable. After all, Gunther could hardly expect Hannah to travel alone. In his view,

Gunther had gone along to keep an eye on Levi, and Pleasant's role was to watch over Hannah.

Hannah noticed that Merle's two youngest children were running in and out of the house and up and down the stairs without one word from their father. Would Pleasant be able to teach them some manners and discipline them? Would Merle allow such a thing? For although he regularly reprimanded his eldest son and only daughter and cast sour looks in the direction of any mother whose baby was crying or whose toddler was making faces at another child, he turned a blind eye to the shenanigans of his own toddlers. Lydia had reported that the older two often missed school. The older boy was often ill, and Lydia worried that Merle's daughter was being expected to take on far too much responsibility at home.

Surely, Pleasant could do better than this, Hannah thought, and then she immediately sought God's forgiveness. It was not for her to say whether or not Pleasant and Merle should wed. No more than it was for her to say if she and Levi would be blessed with the birth of their own child.

Levi and Caleb sat shoulder to shoulder on the bench in front of her. Levi glanced back, his deep chocolate eyes inquiring as to her health.

"I'm fine," she mouthed and motioned for him—and Caleb—to turn their faces forward. But the truth was that the oppressive heat that was building in the room with each new arrival was getting to her. She felt flushed and lightheaded. The women were seated so close together on the bench that there was barely any room for what little air there was to circulate.

She heard others singing the opening hymn and tried to follow along. Then Bishop Troyer said, "Shall we pray?" And suddenly the room began to undulate as if she had been pushed underwater and was trying to fight her way back to the surface. A thud and then nothing until she felt blessed fresh air and smelled the scent of newly mown grass.

"Hannah?"

Levi was on his knees cradling her in his arms. Pleasant arrived on the run, spilling half of the glass of water she carried. Caleb was fanning her with his broadbrimmed Sunday black hat.

"Ma?"

"I'm all right," she told him. "Just overcome by the heat is all."

Caleb heaved a sigh of relief and grinned. "You weren't the only one." He pointed across the yard where others were attending to three other people—a woman, a girl and an older man.

Levi chuckled. "When the fourth person went down, the bishop told Merle to open the windows or he was moving the services outside."

Hannah glanced toward the house and saw that every window had been opened wide. From inside she could hear the drone of the sermon the first minister was delivering. He was quoting the story of Jesus's birth as recorded in the book of Matthew.

"Hannah?" Levi leaned near. "The baby?"

"We're fine," she assured him. "Now shush. I want to hear the story." She clasped hands with Levi and leaned against him as the familiar words rolled out through the open windows and across the yard. She couldn't help thinking that even though most people thought of snow and cold weather when they thought of Christmas, Jesus had been born in the tropics—a place not so very dif-

ferent from this place. Somehow that gave her a measure of comfort.

When the services ended, Hannah insisted that she
help the other women lay out a light lunch for everyone
to enjoy before they headed for home. The meal was plain
and sparse and the talk was of the feasts they would all
enjoy the following day after the children presented their
Christmas pageant at the school.

"Let's go home. You need to rest," Levi told her when
he came looking for her after the meal and found her
scrubbing pans in Merle's kitchen—pans that she suspected had nothing to do with the meal just served.

"Yes, go," Pleasant urged. "I can finish this."

"Where's Caleb?" Hannah asked as Levi helped her
into their buggy.

"He's walking home with a couple of his friends."

On the ride home, Hannah was overcome with exhaustion and within minutes of leaving Merle's farm, her
head rested on Levi's shoulder and she was fast asleep.
When they reached their farm, she roused enough to realize that Levi was carrying her into the house and up
to their bedroom.

"I have to…" she protested sleepily.

"You have to rest," he said. "We have a full day tomorrow." He laid her gently on their bed, removed her
shoes and then her prayer covering and pulled the pins
from her hair, fanning it over the pillow. "Merry Christmas, my Hannah," he whispered as he kissed her lightly
on the lips and then tiptoed from the room.

Hannah woke the following morning and realized that
she had slept through most of the afternoon and all of the
night. The first thing she noticed was that Levi was not in

the room, although it was obvious that he had slept next to her as always. Then she heard muffled laughter and whispers in the hallway outside the closed bedroom door.

Something clunked against the wall and then she heard Levi announce, "Special delivery!" followed by Caleb's giggle.

Hannah got up and put on her robe as she padded barefoot to the door and opened it. Caleb and Levi were standing there, both grinning broadly and each holding one end of the most beautiful cradle Hannah had ever seen.

Her first instinct was to protest that it was too soon, that they could not be sure, that there might be no baby to fill such a wonderful cradle. But then she looked at Caleb and saw his pride in what he had obviously helped Levi build. "Do you like it, Ma?"

"It's wonderful," she said.

"It's also heavy," Levi added.

Hannah swung the bedroom door open and stood aside while they carried the cradle into the room.

"Where do you want it?" Caleb asked, glancing around the sparsely furnished room.

"I think there," Hannah said, pointing to her side of the bed. "That way I can rock the baby and go back to sleep."

"Ah, then I suppose the other piece will be on my side of the bed," Levi said as he and Caleb set the cradle in place.

"What other piece?" Hannah asked.

Caleb was already back out in the hall and came through the door carrying a bentwood rocker. "This one." He set it down in the corner. "Go ahead, Ma, give it a trial run—or rock, I guess."

Hannah sat in the beautifully crafted chair, running her palms over the smooth wood of the arms and pushing the chair into motion with one foot. "I love it," she said huskily. Then she looked over at the cradle. "I love them both. But how…"

"We worked on them down at the circus shop," Caleb said. "Levi said we weren't ready to let folks know about the baby yet and Jake—Mr. Jenkins—and the others promised to keep it secret so it all worked out just fine."

He was beaming. Hannah had not seen her son so happy since they had returned to Florida. "Thank you," she said and held out her arms to him.

"Ah, Ma," he protested but he came to her and accepted the kiss she gave him on each cheek.

Levi had stepped out into the hall again and returned with packages wrapped in brown paper and string. "I found these in the closet where you keep your sewing," he said. He turned one package over, eyeing it curiously. "I thought just maybe…"

"Yes, there's one for each of you," Hannah said, laughing. "That one's Caleb's."

Levi tossed the boy his package and Caleb sat on the side of the bed tearing off the string and paper. Inside were three new shirts and two pair of trousers.

"You're growing so fast," Hannah said.

"Thanks, Ma. Can I wear one outfit today for the pageant?"

Hannah nodded.

"There's one more thing," Levi said, handing Caleb a small package.

Caleb unwrapped it to reveal a pocketknife. "It was my father's," Levi told him, and Hannah thought her heart would burst with joy at this sign that Levi had come to think of Caleb as his son.

Caleb studied the knife for a long moment, turning it over in his hand. Then he looked from Hannah to Levi. "You know I was thinking," he began, his voice cracking, "I mean with a new baby coming and all…"

"What is it, Caleb?" Hannah felt her throat close with fear that maybe Caleb would not welcome a new child—another child.

"It might be confusing for the kid if I'm calling you 'Levi' and he's calling you 'Pa,' so I was thinking maybe—I mean if you wouldn't care, I was thinking I could call you Pa?"

Levi wrapped the boy in a bear hug and Hannah heard her husband's voice crack as her son's had when he said, "I think that would be a fine idea, son."

Hannah sniffed back tears of joy and rose from the rocker to complete the circle, wrapping her arms around the two of them and laying her cheek against Levi's back.

"Hey," Caleb said as he wriggled his way free, his cheeks flushed with embarrassment at having caused such a scene, "you didn't open your present from Ma yet."

"So I didn't," Levi said as he picked up the last package and turned it slowly over in his hands. "What could this be?" He squeezed the thick soft package.

"Open it," Caleb urged.

Levi grinned and tore off the paper, revealing a large cotton quilt. He spread it over the bed and examined it. The background was a patchwork of solid dark blues, greens, browns and purples—the fabrics commonly used to make Amish clothing. But the center was a feast of brilliant reds, yellows and oranges.

"It looks just like one of the wheels on the circus wagons," Caleb said.

And when Levi realized that the boy was right, he looked at Hannah, his eyes full of questions.

"I wanted you to have something to remind you of how we came together—of how we became a family," she said shyly. "I can change it and make it all plain," she added, suddenly afraid that he didn't want to be reminded of those days.

"Don't change it," he said huskily. "I was just thinking that maybe you could make a smaller one for the baby."

"And one for my bed," Caleb added.

"We're going to raise some eyebrows when that quilt is washed and hanging on the line," Hannah warned them.

Both Caleb and Levi shrugged.

"I'm not one to live by what others may think of me, Hannah."

"Neither am I," Caleb chorused.

Hannah smiled. "Neither am I."

Epilogue

❧

June, 1929

Hannah awoke with a start, her gown soaked through in the oppressive heat that even at daybreak was overwhelming. Her hair clung to her cheeks and sometime during the night, she and Levi had both kicked off the covers.

She rolled onto her side and saw that Levi was already up. There had been no rain for weeks now and Levi and the other Amish farmers worried constantly about their crops. It was odd to think of the parched fields when it felt as if she were swimming in dampness.

She sat up and was gripped by a pain so sharp that she bit down on her lip to keep from crying out. She could hear Caleb passing her bedroom door on his way downstairs and she did not want to alarm him.

But oh, the pain came in waves that threatened to pull her under like the heavy undertow in the Gulf. She clutched the edge of the bed and rode out the pain. Then when it seemed to have passed, she pushed herself to her feet. But she was only able to make it as far as the foot of the bed where she was reaching to retrieve the circus quilt when the next wave hit.

Her knees buckled and this time she cried out.

"Ma!" She heard the pound of Caleb's footsteps coming back up the stairs. He flung open the door and froze.

"Get your father," she managed.

Caleb stood there, his eyes focused not on her but on the bed. Hannah followed his gaze and saw the dark stain of blood. "Go," she said. "Now!"

She eased herself onto the floor and clutched the quilt against her as she heard Caleb's cries for help echoing across the farmyard.

"Please," she prayed, "please not when we've come so far. Please."

But they had not come far enough. The baby was not due for another six weeks, at least. It was too soon and there was blood and…

Hannah wept.

Levi's boots hit each stair in rhythm with Caleb's horse galloping off.

"I sent Caleb for the doctor," Levi said, kneeling next to her.

"It's too soon," she said.

"Maybe not," he replied and held her close.

They stayed that way, him tightening his hold on her as together they rode out every labor pain, her collapsing against him once the pain had passed, until they heard voices in the yard, then in the house.

"Up here," Levi bellowed, and Hannah heard for the first time in his voice the fear and panic that he had spent the past several minutes swallowing down as he tried to convince her that everything would be all right.

"Let's get her on the bed," the doctor said, taking charge as Pleasant followed him into the room.

They both looked at the soiled sheets.

"Caleb's room," Pleasant said and led the way as Levi carried Hannah, and the doctor followed. In the hall Caleb hung back, his eyes wide with fear.

"Go get your grandfather now," the doctor ordered, and Caleb raced down the stairs. "It'll occupy the boy," the doctor explained when Levi seemed about to question why Gunther should be called. "He can keep the boy calm."

Levi lay Hannah on Caleb's bed and sat next to her, gripping her hand as yet another pain hit.

"You should wait outside," the doctor said as he prepared to examine her, and Pleasant rushed about gathering towels and a basin.

"Not leaving," Levi said and refused to look at the doctor.

"Stubborn," Hannah managed when the doctor met her eyes, his bushy white eyebrows questioning what she would prefer. "Let him stay. He'll just worry."

"Very well. Pleasant, I'll need your help. Are you up to this?"

"I've participated in deliveries before, but…" Pleasant huffed. "Not human babies perhaps but…"

"Fine. Do exactly as I ask and don't hesitate, all right?"

Hannah saw Pleasant's lips narrow into the familiar line of determination that was her trademark and felt comforted by that until the pain came again and threatened to rip her in half.

"I'm here," Levi said, his eyes filled with tears as he witnessed her pain. "Doc, do something," he growled.

"All right, Hannah, now the next time you feel the pain I need for you to push hard. Ready?"

Hannah nodded and waited as she might wait for the next wave to crash onto the beach in a tropical storm.

"Now!" the doctor coached.

Hannah fought with everything she had to push past the pain and when it passed, she felt exhausted. And then she heard a sound she had thought would never be hers to hear again. She heard the cry of her baby.

"Not done yet," the doctor said when she raised herself half onto her side to see her child. A fresh wave of pain hit her, knocking her flat.

"Push!" the doctor bellowed.

Hannah had little choice but to follow his command. But this time the effort was more than she could take and she felt the pain pulling her under and then everything went dark.

Slowly, Hannah became aware of movement in the room and yet everything seemed quieter, less chaotic. She opened her eyes and saw Levi talking quietly with the doctor. She glanced around Caleb's room.

There was no sign of the baby.

Tears leaked from the corners of her eyes as she understood that they had almost made it this time. The baby had lived at least for a moment for she had heard the cry, but then...

"She's awake," Pleasant said as she dipped a cloth in water and used it to wipe Hannah's brow.

Levi was next to her in an instant and the doctor stood at the foot of the bed. "Well, young lady, you gave us a bit of a fright there," he said. "We thought we'd lost you."

Hannah ignored him and turned to Levi. "The baby?"

Levi smiled. "Looks like Caleb and I are going to have to build another cradle."

"I…" Hannah was confused. Levi was smiling. So was the doctor. So—miracle of miracles—was Pleasant.

"It's twins," Pleasant told her. "A boy and a girl."

"Twins?" Hannah fought past all the fears and anxieties of the past several months as she tried to accept what they were telling her. "And they are all right?"

As if on cue, she heard the wail of two different babies coming from across the hall. And then Greta and Lydia were standing in the doorway, each of them holding a bundle that looked for all the world like a sack of flour.

"They are hungry," Levi said as he stood and took the bundle that Greta held and placed the child in Hannah's arms. "And they would like to know their names," he added.

Hannah had put off Levi's attempts to choose names for their child in advance. Now there were two of them.

"What was your father's name?" Hannah asked as she examined her son, counting his fingers and toes to be sure he was as perfect as he appeared.

"Reuben," Levi whispered.

Hannah held out her free arm for the baby that Lydia held. "And your mother?"

"Emma."

"Then hello, Reuben and Emma Harnisher," she said softly, kissing each. She looked up at Levi then. "All right?"

Unable to speak, Levi nodded and then sat on the edge of the bed and took his daughter in his arms and rocked her slowly from side to side.

Out in the yard they heard a commotion, as several buggies seemed to arrive at the same moment. Pleasant went to see what was happening and the doctor chose that moment to take his leave as well, leaving Levi and Hannah alone with their babies.

Levi cupped Hannah's cheek with his free hand. "Are you truly all right?"

"A little sore and tired," she said, "but I have never been happier, and I have never loved you more."

As Levi leaned in to kiss Hannah, Emma started to squirm and fuss and Levi looked so utterly lost that Hannah couldn't help but laugh. "Here," she said, exchanging son for daughter. "She favors you," she said, stroking Emma's tuft of copper-colored hair as her daughter settled into the curve of her arm.

Downstairs they heard voices.

"Truly, I don't think…" Pleasant was protesting as they heard footsteps in the lower hallway.

"Let them come," Levi called out.

There was quiet for one long moment. Then one by one they shyly entered the small room.

First Caleb and then Gunther followed by the bishop and a parade of their neighbors.

"Come meet your brother and sister," Hannah said, coaxing Caleb forward after Levi had introduced the twins to everyone.

"Do you want to hold him?" Levi offered, holding Reuben out to Caleb.

Caleb looked panicked and then swallowed hard. "Maybe later," he muttered as he leaned in for a closer look. "They're really tiny."

"They'll grow," one of the women said and the other women all giggled.

From outside, came the unmistakable sound of a motorcar approaching the house.

"It's Jake and Lily and Fred and Ida," Caleb announced from his position by the window.

Hannah did not even bother to remind her son that he was being too familiar using their first names like that. She saw one or two of the neighbor women raise their eyebrows and scoot a little closer to each other.

"They are family," she said quietly. "Levi's family—and mine."

Their circus family crowded into the room explaining that they had come as soon as Jake had returned from seeing the doctor and reported that his appointment had been cut short when Caleb had burst into the doc's office and announced that his Ma was having the baby. The way they told it—interrupting one another to supply every detail—it was impossible not to be charmed. And when Lily produced two rattles—one pink and one blue—for the babies, the neighbors crowded in closer.

"Not much of a present but it'll do until we have time to shop," Lily said as Fred gently shook the rattle in front of Reuben and the baby seemed to actually smile.

"Ah," chorused the neighbors and they smiled at Lily.

After that, conversation seemed to flow naturally among the gathering as Pleasant announced that Hannah needed her rest and herded everyone from the room. For several moments after they left, Levi and Hannah could hear voices outside their window. Gunther asking Fred about someone he had worked with in the horse tent. Lily telling Pleasant about one of the women from the costume department who had left the circus to marry a Chicago banker. And the buzz of the neighbors—talking among themselves, but no doubt taking in the easy exchange between the Goodloes and the circus people.

Hannah held out her hand to Levi, who stood at the

window cradling Reuben as he watched the departure of their guests. "Come sit with me," she said.

Levi nodded but then leaned out the window. "Caleb? Come up here, okay?"

A moment later Caleb stood at the door.

"Bring that rocking chair over here," Levi said, and the boy did as he was asked.

"Now have a seat," Levi said with a wink at Hannah.

Caleb eyed him suspiciously but sat.

Levi placed Reuben in his brother's arms. Then he crossed the hall and carried the cradle into the small room. He placed Emma in the cradle, then sat on the bed with Hannah. Gathering Hannah into his arms, he rocked the cradle with the toe of his boot.

Hannah cuddled into his shoulder. "Our little family," she murmured happily.

"It's a good start," Levi answered, and then he grinned and to Caleb's obvious embarrassment, Levi kissed his wife.

* * * * *

Ruby Plank comes to Seven Poplars to find a husband and soon literally stumbles into the arms of Joseph Brenneman. But will a secret threaten to keep them apart?

Read on for a sneak preview of
A GROOM FOR RUBY *by* **Emma Miller,**
available August 2017 from Love Inspired!

A young woman lay stretched out on a blanket, apparently lost in a book. But the most startling thing to Joseph was her hair. The woman's hair wasn't pinned up under a *kapp* or covered with a scarf. It rippled in a thick, shimmering mane down the back of her neck and over her shoulders nearly to her waist.

Joseph's mouth gaped. He clutched the bouquet of flowers so tightly between his hands that he distinctly heard several stems snap. He swallowed, unable to stop staring at her beautiful hair. It was brown, but brown in so many shades…tawny and russet, the color of shiny acorns in winter and the hue of ripe wheat. He'd intruded on a private moment, seen what he shouldn't. He should turn and walk away. But he couldn't.

"Hello," he stammered. "I'm sorry, I was looking for—"

"Ach!" The young woman rose on one elbow and twisted to face him. It was Ruby. Her eyes widened in surprise. "Joseph?"

"*Ya.* It's me."

Ruby sat up, dropping her paperback onto the blanket, pulling her knees up and tucking her feet under her skirt. "I was drying my hair," she said. "I washed it. I still had mud in it from last night."

Joseph grimaced. "Sorry."

"Everyone else went to Byler's store." She blushed. "But I stayed home. To wash my hair. What must you think of me without my *kapp*?"

She had a merry laugh, Joseph thought, a laugh as beautiful as she was. She was regarding him with definite interest. Her eyes were the shade of cinnamon splashed with swirls of chocolate. His mouth went dry.

She smiled encouragingly.

A dozen thoughts tumbled in his mind, but nothing seemed like the right thing to say. "I…I never know what to say to pretty girls," he admitted as he tore his gaze away from hers. "You must think I'm thickheaded." He shuffled his feet. "I'll come back another time when—"

"Who are those flowers for?" Ruby asked. "Did you bring them for Sara?"

"*Ne*, not Sara." Joseph's face grew hot. He tried to say, "I brought them for you," but again the words stuck in his throat. Dumbly, he held them out to her. It took every ounce of his courage not to turn and run.

Don't miss
A GROOM FOR RUBY
by Emma Miller, available August 2017 wherever
Love Inspired® books and ebooks are sold.

www.LoveInspired.com

Love Inspired®

Inspirational Romance to Warm Your Heart and Soul

Join our social communities to connect with other readers who share your love!

Sign up for the Love Inspired newsletter at **www.LoveInspired.com** to be the first to find out about upcoming titles, special promotions and exclusive content.

CONNECT WITH US AT:

Harlequin.com/Community

 Facebook.com/LoveInspiredBooks

 Twitter.com/LoveInspiredBks

LISOCIAL2017